FROMMER'S
WHERE TO STAY USA

COUNCIL ON INTERNATIONAL
EDUCATIONAL EXCHANGE

Written by Marjorie A. Cohen
Edited by Donna Morin

KAY WHITSON   (Camp NYDA USA 1987)

1986-87 Edition

Published by the Council on International Educational Exchange
205 East 42nd Street
New York, NY 10017
and
Frommer/Pasmantier Publishers
A Division of Simon & Schuster, Inc.
1230 Avenue of the Americas
New York, NY 10020

ISBN: 0-671-55632-0

Manufactured in the United States of America

*Although every effort was made to ensure the accuracy of price information appearing in this book,
it should be kept in mind that prices can and do fluctuate in the course of time.*

Contents

About This Book

When we first sat down to write *Where to Stay USA* 13 years ago, our purpose was simple enough: We wanted as many people as possible to enjoy an American experience, and we wanted them to be able to do it even on a limited budget. We've done what we set out to do, judging from the letters of praise and encouragement that we've received from readers. Many of these readers have sent us suggestions for additions, and we've followed up on all of them. You'll notice italicized quotes all the way through the book—these are from our readers.

We now have sections on 15 of the most visited U.S. cities. We cover New York, Washington, D.C., Denver, Houston, Phoenix, Los Angeles, San Francisco, San Diego, Chicago, Boston, St. Louis, Seattle, Miami, New Orleans, and Atlanta. In these sections we've tried to put enough information to give travelers a good start in a new, sometimes overwhelming city. We've included information on how to get around, where to stay, where to eat, what to see and do, and where to go for help and information.

The philosophy behind the book *Where to Stay* is uncomplicated—the book is primarily for use on the road, and it's meant to be carried with you. Although some of the introductory sections should be read before you begin your trip, the bulk of the book is meant to serve you as you travel. See page 19 for an explanation of how the listings are set up—and be sure to read Chapter 2 so that you know what to expect from some of the accommodation facilities.

We should probably explain how we at the Council on International Educational Exchange (CIEE) first came to write this book on low-cost travel in the U.S. CIEE was founded in 1947 as the Council on Student Travel (it became CIEE in 1967), and since then it has been actively involved in helping thousands of students plan their trips both abroad and in the U.S. It is a membership organization made up of nearly 200 colleges, universities, secondary schools, national organizations, and youth-serving agencies. Since its founding, CIEE has been arranging transportation and providing information and advisory services for both educational groups and individual students. Any U.S. student planning to travel abroad or in North America will want to get a free copy of CIEE's *Student Travel Catalog,* which describes the services offered by CIEE to both students and nonstudents. These services include the international Student Identity Card (ISIC), which entitles eligible U.S. students to a number of discounts and services in the U.S. and abroad; flight information and services to Europe, Asia, and the Middle East; scheduled transportation from the U.S. to all parts of the world and within the U.S.; student / budget flights connecting European cities with points in the Middle East, Africa, and Asia; international student tours; information and publications on international study, travel, and work opportunities—including *Work, Study, Travel Abroad: The Whole World Handbook, Volunteer! The Comprehensive Guide to Voluntary Service in the*

U.S. and Abroad, and the 80-page *Student Travel Catalog;* year-round jobs in Britain, France, and Ireland, and summer jobs in Germany, New Zealand, and Costa Rica—a service that provides U.S. students with work permits and information on how to find jobs; a student center and student hotel at William Sloane House, 356 West 34th St., New York, NY 10001.

If you have anything to tell us about low-cost travel in the U.S., we'd love to hear from you. Write to us at 205 East 42nd St., New York, NY 10017, and if we are able to use what you tell us in the next edition of *Where to Stay USA,* we'll send you a complimentary copy.

Council Travel Offices

New York: 205 East 42nd St., New York, NY 10017
New York: 356 West 34th St., New York, NY 10001
San Francisco: 312 Sutter St., San Francisco, CA 94108
San Francisco: 919 Irving St., San Francisco, CA 94122
Los Angeles: 1093 Broxton Ave., Los Angeles, CA 90024
Berkeley: 2511 Channing Way, Berkeley, CA 94704
San Diego: UCSD Student Center, B-123, La Jolla, CA 92093
Pacific Beach: 4429 Cass St., San Diego, CA 92109
Long Beach: 5500 Atherton, Long Beach, CA 90815
Austin: 1904 Guadalupe, Suite 6, Austin, TX 78705
Seattle: 1314 N.E. 43rd St., Seattle, WA 98105
Portland: 715 S.W. Morrison St., Suite 1020, Portland, OR 97205
Boston: 729 Boylston St., Boston, MA 02116
Amherst: 79 South Pleasant St., 2nd Fl. (near rear), Amherst, MA 01002
Providence: 171 Angell St., Suite 212, Providence, RI 02906

Acknowledgments

There are lots of people who need to be thanked for helping to put together this eighth edition of *Where to Stay USA*—some on CIEE's staff and some from other organizations too.

We want to thank Mindy Naiman for her help and encouragement from the beginning to the end of the project, and Donna Morin, who helped organize and compile absolutely everything that's here.

Special thanks to the following people who helped us put the city sections together: Cindy Lake, Margo Robbins, Jadwiga Lopez, Doris Regulski, Jennifer Rodes, Gerdine Joseph, Mindy Goodman, Mary Lohre, Mara Abolins, Debbie Shore, Kai Lynch, Steve R. Beaver, Tomiesenia S. Wiles, and Marilyn B. Bouma.

This is also the best place to thank the people who answered the letters and questionnaires that we sent all over the U.S. in order to collect firsthand information on each area. Some of the people to whom we wrote filled in the questionnaires and returned them, and we are grateful for that. But others who went even further and offered encouragement and additional information deserve our collective and special thanks.

Finally, to everyone who helped in the process of putting together *Where to Stay USA,* our thanks.

MARJORIE A. COHEN

The International Student Identity Card

What Is the ISIC?

As soon as American students decide to make a trip abroad, they go out and buy an ISIC. For more than 16 years, American young people have been setting out on their travels with the ISIC tucked carefully into their wallets. High school and university students have found the ISIC to be their passport to low-cost travel—it is proof to anyone who needs to know, anywhere in the world, that the holder is a student and is eligible for special student privileges, discounts, and travel bargains. In more than 50 countries, ISIC holders can obtain lower air fares, tours and accommodations, and reduced or free admission to many museums, theaters, cultural and historical sites. With an ISIC, students are eligible, too, for discounts of up to 50% on a special network of student flights that criss-crosses Europe and connects it with several cities in Africa, Asia, and the Middle East, and now ISIC holders are eligible for savings of up to 50% on regular transatlantic and transpacific fares. Holders of the ISIC also receive $2000 of accident and medical insurance. The card is valid for 16 months and costs $10.

The idea of the ISIC was initiated and is administered by the International Student Travel Conference (ISTC), a federation of national student travel bureaus representing more than 50 countries. The U.S. sponsor of the ISIC is the Council on International Educational Exchange (CIEE). For information on the ISIC and its discounts, contact any Council Travel Office.

Please send me an application for the International Student Identity Card.

Name _____

Address _____

_____

Return to: **CIEE - WTS**
I.D. Department
205 East 42nd St.
New York, NY 10017

Where to Get the ISIC

Students may obtain their International Student Identity Card at one of the almost 400 college campuses across the U.S. (check to see whether your campus issues the ISIC—try the international studies office, student travel office, or modern languages department, for example). Or students may obtain the ISIC directly from Council Travel offices. We've included a reply coupon for you above in case you would like to order the ISIC directly from the Council.

Who Is Eligible

You are eligible to receive the ISIC if you are (1) at least 12 years of age or older; (2) a high school / vocational school / college or university student; and (3) able to provide documentation as to your current student status.

Explanation of Symbols

Ⓢ   ISIC discount
V   Senior Citizens discount
★   *Where to Stay* book discount
♿   Access facilities

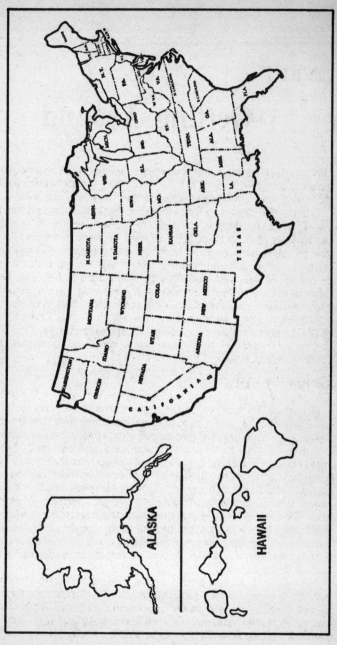

CHAPTER 1

Getting Around

How are you going to get from one place to another in this enormous and fascinating country? Will you fly? Drive? Hitchhike? What's best for you? What's the least expensive way to go? What kinds of "deals" are available?

In this first chapter we'll consider all of the possibilities, and then it's up to you. To make your decision you'll have to consider a number of variables. How much money you have to spend is important, of course, but so is understanding your own style. Some people wouldn't consider going any other way than hitchhiking; others would never be comfortable trying to thumb a ride from a stranger. A little old-fashioned know-thyself is what's called for first of all. Because so many of our readers are from abroad, it's important, too, to emphasize the enormous size of this country. The distance from New York to California is over 3000 miles, or 5100 kilometers; from New York to Florida it's over 1000 miles, or 1700 kilometers. Many people forget about the expanse that is the U.S. when they set out to plan their visit, so they plan an unrealistic itinerary that has them covering too much, too quickly.

Going by Air

Except on very short trips, the quickest way to travel between two points in the U.S. is by air. There are ways of saving money on air fares, but the airlines are making it a bit difficult for us to tell you about them since they are constantly thinking up, instituting, and then canceling their own promotional fares. In addition, new airlines have recently appeared on the scene, causing even more rapid and dramatic change as established airlines alter their fares to compete. These new carriers generally offer low-cost service on short-haul routes. It's not realistic for us to say anything very specific about prices since they are bound to change from the time we go to press to the time you read them. What we can tell you—and it's important—is that there are lots and lots of bargain fares around and finding out about them can be a bit tricky. For the very latest in air-fare bargains, we suggest contacting your nearest Council Travel office (see page 2 for a listing). The people there keep up with the subject and can advise you and book your flights, too.

To illustrate the variety of fares that are available on any given route and how much money it's possible to save over the regular economy fare, we summoned the following information from one of the Council Travel office's computers: A regular economy flight on Eastern Airlines from New York to Houston is $330 one way; a night flight is $248; a 14-day advance purchase plan is $119; a standby fare is $144; a special coach fare is $160 (on some off-peak flights) and the cheapest of all, "a moonlight" or "red eye special" (which leaves between midnight and 6 a.m.) is $69 one way.

The moral of the story: Be merciless in questioning the airline's reservation clerk or your travel agent in order to uncover the best fare for you.

One airline that has earned a reputation for low-cost fares is People Express, but by now the other airlines have taken up the challenge and often offer fares that are as low as People's. Comparison shop.

At press time, Eastern Airlines had instituted a youth pass available to people between 17 and 24. It costs $399.95 for 30 days of summer travel. It may or may not exist when you read this—check on it.

"Night flights are cheap, it's true, but you arrive in a strange city at an ungodly hour in the morning."

Shuttles: Some well-traveled routes (e.g., New York–Boston, New York–Washington) have shuttle service—a no-frills arrangement where you just board, pay for your ticket on the plane, and get off without having any food or drinks. Shuttles generally run every hour during weekdays. Although shuttles offer the convenience of travel without reservations, they don't save you any money over the regular fares, except on weekends when there are special excursion fares available. The New York–Boston shuttle is $65 (weekends, $45), New York–Washington is $75, and the Saturday-Sunday round-trip excursion special is $45. But, People Express beats them with a $33 one-way fare on each route several days a week.

Foreign visitors are entitled to some special discounts on domestic air-fare arrangements. See Chapter 3 for details.

So you see, it's going to be a bit complicated sorting out the air-fare part of your trip, but the effort should result in a fairly substantial saving for you. For help, go to a Council Travel office, travel agent, or the airline itself. Ask lots of questions and don't settle for anything less than the best possible deal.

The Aviation Consumer Action Project, a nonprofit consumer group founded by Ralph Nader, puts out a pamphlet that's meant to inform air travelers of their rights, how to handle a complaint, precautions to take when checking baggage, etc. A copy of *Facts and Advice for Airline Passengers* can be obtained by sending $2 to ACAP, P.O. Box 19029, Washington, D.C. 20036.

"Hitchhiking by small plane can be a quick, cheap way to get around the U.S. To do this, go to a small airport or the private hangar section of the larger airports. You may find a pilot who is willing to give you a lift in the direction you're going."

In a letter from a reader, we got some more interesting advice on how to save on air fare.

"I have found that great travel savings are possible on trips to some of the smaller U.S. cities if I fly to a major city nearby and then rent a car for the rest of the trip. For example, I had to go from Lubbock, Texas to Longview. My wife and I flew to Dallas and then rented a car for three days. The total cost of the car rental, including maximum insurance coverage, was less than the cost of one Dallas–Longview fare. We saved over $100 on air fare and we would have had to rent a car in Longview anyway."

Going by Bus

"The bus is a terrific way to explore the U.S.A., especially for the first time. The bus goes everywhere and is on time. But you shouldn't spend too much time at the terminals, especially overnight. They're often not located in the best neighborhoods."

"Bus travel is usually a good thing, but sometimes you miss the small cities, which is a real pity."

Bus travel has always been inexpensive so it's no wonder that the bus is such a popular way (especially for young people) to travel around the U.S. Buses are almost always air-conditioned in the summer, well heated in the winter. Service is efficient, connecting most cities and towns of the U.S. no matter how small, and if you break your trip into several short trips, you won't be too uncomfortable.

For years, the best bargains in bus travel have been the unlimited travel plans—Greyhound's Ameripass and Trailways' Eaglepass. This is how they work: As of press time, you pay $189 for 7 days, $249 for 15 days, and $349 for one month of practically unlimited travel in the continental U.S. and Canada. The Ameripass and Eaglepass are actually booklets of coupons which must be presented to an agent at each bus station. As long as the pass is valid you can use as many coupons as you need, i.e., you may cover as much territory as possible in the time allotted. The passes can be extended for a $10-per-day charge; but the extensions must be made before the pass expires. There are some side trips, usually to specific attractions or national parks, which are not covered by the passes.

"One disadvantage of the pass is that it cannot be used in the national parks, although there are discounts on national park tours to pass holders."

We've talked to lots of people who have traveled with the Ameripass or Eaglepass, and they're generally pretty enthusiastic about it. One friend from Minnesota told us:

"In two months I made four separate round trips lasting 9 to 12 days each. During that time I covered thousands of miles, 39 states, three Canadian provinces, and one Mexican city. In general, bus travel is best if you're not in a hurry and you've never been that route before. It's an excellent way to see the country and to meet people along the way. Most of the bus drivers are friendly and helpful."

"Bus trips are such an easy way to meet people—for me that advantage outweighs any of the discomforts I felt."

Senior citizens are entitled to discounts of 11% on bus fares. Check with Greyhound and Trailways for details.

Don't overlook the fact that traveling by bus can also save you money on accommodations. If you travel at night, you can sleep on the bus and avoid paying for a place to stay. Ameripasses are available from Council Travel offices, both Ameripasses and Eaglepasses may be purchased from travel agents or from the bus lines directly.

"For greater comfort on the bus, bring an AM-FM transistor radio (with ear- or headphones), a Thermos bottle, a pillow, and earplugs for sound sleep."

An "alternative bus company," the Green Tortoise, calls itself a vacation/ transportation service for budget travelers. "We use sleep-aboard, fuel-efficient diesel coaches and have frequent stops for hot springs, swimming, hiking, rafting, and sailing. We do a lot of cooking out, which helps to keep food costs low. . . ." The Green Tortoise connects San Francisco, Los Angeles, Seattle, Boston, and New York City. It goes to New Orleans every year from the East and West Coasts, and during Mardi Gras the buses remain in the French Quarter for two weeks in order to provide accommodations. The Green Tortoise also travels from the West Coast to Alaska and Mexico. At press time, a one-way, cross-country trip of seven to ten days was $199; the four-week Alaska trip was $650; and the trip between Seattle and Los Angeles was $79. For information, write to the Green Tortoise, P.O. Box 4459, San Francisco, CA 94124; or call: in Boston, 617/265-8533; in New York, 212/431-3348; and in San Francisco, 415/ 821-0803.

Going by Train

"If a person wants to have a relaxed—though long—trip and still see the country, he or she should take the train. I was on Amtrak from New York to New Mexico and from Kansas to Boston. I was able to do what I wanted to do. I saw the country without feeling cramped and met many people and I didn't have to pay for overnight accommodations since the coaches had comfortable seats. I found it more economical to bring fruits, biscuits, etc., on board rather than to have meals on the train."

Amtrak—the National Railroad Passenger Corporation, which has control of the nation's passenger railroads—is trying to entice people away from planes and buses and onto trains.

A spokesman for Amtrak's public relations department said: "We have made a special effort to attract young people back to the trains and have succeeded in many parts of the country. If you ride our *Montrealer,* for instance, between New York and Montreal, you see many college students enjoying themselves hugely. Our *Coast Starlight,* which operates between Los Angeles and San Francisco and on to Seattle, is also heavily patronized by young people, who obviously are having a fine time. Our San Francisco *Zephyr* also attracts a lively crowd."

Unfortunately, Amtrak has stopped selling its unlimited-travel USA Rail Pass to Americans—it is available now only to foreign visitors. But there is, at least at press time, something called the "All Aboard America" fare, which offers maximum coach fares for trips taken within a certain period of time. Under the plan, tickets must be purchased and reservations made at least five days before the beginning of the trip. The plan divides the country into three regions— Eastern, Central, and Western. Travel in one region is $150; in two, $250 and in three, $325. Passengers have 30 days to make their "All Aboard America" trips. There are also some family plans available whereby the head of household pays full fare and the spouse and children ages 12 to 21 pay only half fare; children 2 to 11 pay one-quarter fare, and children under 2 travel free. To qualify for family fares, travel can begin any day of the week.

You can save money if you take advantage of round-trip excursion fares on certain routes between major cities, e.g., Boston–Washington, New York–Miami or New York–Orlando, Chicago–Denver, or Los Angeles–San Francisco. There are usually some restrictions on dates when the fares are valid and the return trip must be made within a certain period of time. For example, along the Northeast Corridor between Boston and Washington the round-trip excursion fares are good for travel anytime except between 11 a.m. and midnight on Friday and Sunday and some holiday dates. At press time, the excursion fare between New York and Washington was $38 one way; $57 round trip; the normal round-trip coach fare was $78 and the round-trip Metroliner was $98. Excursion travel must be completed within 30 days of the purchase of the ticket. Amtrak also offers a 25 percent discount on fares to people 65 and over and to those who are handicapped. (Amtrak recently renovated many of its passenger cars and stations to conform to the needs of the handicapped.)

From time to time, Amtrak offers special promotional deals, too. For instance, at press time, it was offering a round-trip Chicago/New York fare for $99. Call 800/USA-RAIL for current information.

"Traveling by train was an easy way to meet people and it was also comfortable. The only problem is that we were never on time."

If train is your choice, you may want to get a copy of *Train Trips: Exploring America by Rail* ($9.95), by William Scheller, published by East Woods Press, 429 East Blvd., Charlotte, NC 28203. The book is a guide to American passenger service and includes Canadian routes as well.

Going by Car

It's not cheap to maintain a car, and all sorts of things can go wrong with a car en route. But if you want to be able to travel at your own pace and come and go as you please, travel by car is probably best for you. If you don't have your own car you can either rent one, buy a used one, take advantage of the driveaway system, or find someone to ride with—all possibilities that are discussed below. (Special information for foreign visitors who intend to drive in the U.S. can be found in Chapter 3.)

If you're going to be driving in the U.S., you'll need a good map, which you can sometimes get at a gas station. If you don't mind waiting a while, Exxon Touring Service, P.O. Box 3633, Houston, TX 77001, will send you one.

DRIVEAWAYS: There are several agencies throughout the U.S. that arrange the transport of cars from one part of the country to another. This provides an excellent opportunity for students over 21 years of age—or sometimes over 25—to go long distances at minimal cost. The car owner usually pays for the tolls and occasionally for the gas. A direct route must be followed, since the agencies usually contract to get the car to its destination by a certain time. The time allotted is reasonable, though; no one expects you to drive day and night. It's typical for a company to require that you cover about 400 miles per day. Most large cities have driveaway companies, which are listed in the classified section of the telephone book—the Yellow Pages—usually under the heading "Automobile Transport and Driveaway Companies." Probably the most popular routes for driveaways are between New York, Philadelphia, or Boston and Florida and California. The classified sections of the daily newspapers are also a source of current driveaway possibilities.

The process of contracting with a driveaway company involves making a deposit of between $50 and $100 and being fingerprinted. If you get a choice of cars, take the smaller one so you can save on gasoline. Most cars are late models, privately owned, and are given to the driver with a full tank of gas.

If you're a foreign student interested in a driveaway, your English must be fluent before most companies will let you have a car and you must have an International Driving Permit as well.

As with all things, before you sign on the dotted line for a driveaway you should be confident of the firm's reliability. One student who traveled across country via a driveaway said this:

"I strongly recommend checking into driveaway cars. My experience was with A A ACON, a large agency with offices in over 80 cities. I walked in, filled out a detailed application, gave them four passport photos, my fingerprints, and a $50 deposit. I paid gas and oil and had my deposit refunded when I delivered the car. The advantages are many. It's cheap (the only cheaper way is hitchhiking); it's convenient—we were given six days to travel 2000 miles so we had time to sightsee along the way—and it's comfortable, especially compared to a bus. You may have difficulty getting a car to the exact city you're headed for. If so, get a car going to another city close by and hop a bus—you're still ahead moneywise. The cars are not always in tip-top shape, but the owner is responsible for any repair costs that are incurred."

Other companies with offices throughout the U.S. are Driveaway Service, Inc., Auto Driveaway Company, Dependable Car Service, Inc., and Nationwide Auto Transporters, Inc.

CAR RENTALS: In some cities of the U.S., car-rental companies require that you be 25 or over in order to rent one of their cars. Others will rent to anyone 21 or over. New York is one place that requires you to be 25, but if a friend who is over 25 actually rents the car you may go along as a driver even if you are younger. Also, if you have a major credit card, companies will often adjust the minimum age requirement. Having a major credit card will make car rental easier—some companies won't rent to you without one, or if they do, they will charge an enormous deposit. (The situation for foreign visitors is a bit different. The minimum age is 18 as long as you have a valid International Driver's Permit and can show a return ticket and a passport.)

Most of you have heard of the major car-rental companies—National, Hertz, and Avis—but when you're thinking of renting a car, consider some of the smaller companies as well. Although the larger companies, with offices all over the world, offer such advantages as allowing you to pick up a car in one city and leave it in another, the smaller companies often charge less and may have more economy cars available than the larger ones.

The cost of car rental varies considerably from city to city. For instance, one week of unlimited mileage in Miami will cost much less than a car rented for the same period in New York. The difference can easily be $100.

To give you a general idea of how much it will cost to rent a car, consider that most of the companies have special one-week rates that provide unlimited mileage for approximately $100. This rate does not include the cost of gasoline. You can also get special weekday, weekend, and monthly rates that can make car rental an economical way to travel—especially if you have some friends along to share costs. Be sure to investigate all the possibilities.

"I don't know if two people can live cheaper than one but they sure can travel cheaper. Three is even better when you're splitting the gas, motel bills, and driving. We found a fellow traveler on our way home and the added savings and companionship were most welcome."

USED CARS: If you're the kind who enjoys taking chances, you can buy yourself a used car and hope for the best. An American car that is only a few years old may sell for half its original price; a car five to ten years old may sell for under $800 and can usually be resold at a small loss, as long as you can keep it in one piece. It's best to buy used cars through ads in the newspapers rather than from used-car dealers. Here's one good suggestion we got from someone who has bought several used cars: check the tires since their condition is a good measure of the care that the previous owner gave the car.

"We bought an old car in Boston to take cross-country to California. We paid $200 for it. On our way to see the Grand Canyon, a woman who wasn't paying attention to what she was doing ran into us. Not wanting to jeopardize her insurance renewal, she gave us $200 on the spot for repairs. When we got to California we sold the car for $200. Our trip was free!"

Exercise great caution, though, in buying a used car. We received a letter from a man in Switzerland telling us that, in response to an advertisement in a Swiss newspaper, he made arrangements to buy a used car in Florida for $1200. He sent a deposit of $400 and paid the balance when he got to the States. The car turned out to be a mess and he was able to get only half his money back. Buying anything, especially a used car, sight unseen, is foolish.

Once you've bought a car, there are registration and insurance formalities that must be completed. Contact the nearest office of the American Automobile Association, the definitive source of information on anything auto-related.

Going by Bicycle

A lot of people are deciding that two wheels are better than four. There's been an incredible boom in bicycling in recent years, and that's a good thing both for the people who are doing the bicycling and for the ones who aren't, since they're being spared the pollution of another car.

There are lots of bicycle clubs and organizations in the U.S. One of the best-known organizations associated with bicycle travel is American Youth Hostels, Inc., which has been around since 1934. AYH was operating hostels throughout the U.S. and organizing bicycle tours for its members for years before the present bicycle boom began. Membership cards, available from the AYH National Administrative Office, 1332 I St. NW, Suite 800, Washington, D.C. 20005, or from any of AYH's 31 councils or 250 pass-selling agents, cost $10 for anyone under 18, $20 for anyone 18 to 59, and $10 for anyone over 60. See Chapter 2 for more about AYH and its hostels.

Because of the recent bicycle boom, many communities are agitating for more bikeways. The word "bikeway" is a bit misleading—it is used to refer to a signposted route on streets and roads that are considered suitable for bicycling; it does not mean a roadway set aside only for bicyclists. According to the International Bicycle Touring Society (2115 Paseo Dorado, La Jolla, CA 92037), "Bikeways exist in hundreds of towns and cities, but they are of questionable value because they don't go anywhere." The average length of a bikeway in America is four miles. Only Wisconsin has a longer one. It stretches from Kenosha to La Crosse, a distance of 300 miles. For a copy of a newly revised set of bike maps showing 10,000 miles of routes in 72 counties, send $2.25 to Wisconsin Department of Transportation, Documents and Map Sales, 3617 Pierstorff Street, Madison, WI 53707.

One of the newer groups of bicycle people is called Bikecentennial, an organization that celebrated America's birthday by inaugurating a 4500-mile Trans America Bicycle Trail. Besides running organized trips for bicyclists during the summer, Bikecentennial has 12,000 miles of researched bicycle routes. The newest is the Iowa-to-Maine route from Muscatine, Iowa, to Bar Harbor, Maine—1,725 miles in all. The group's catalog, *Cyclosource,* which includes its trips program, accessories, order forms for map routes, and books on cycling in the U.S. and abroad, is free from Bikecentennial, P.O. Box 8308, Missoula, MT 59807. Telephone: 406/721-1776.

The League of American Wheelmen (L.A.W.) is a membership organization of, by, and for bicyclists in all 50 states with 20,000 individual members and about 500 affiliated bicycle clubs. L.A.W., P.O. Box 988, Baltimore, MD 21203, actively works to protect bicyclists' rights to the road, and it provides safety and touring information. *American Wheelmen,* a monthly magazine, contains an extensive and timely listing of bicycle events in the U.S. Included in the group's yearly directory are a list of "Hospitality Homes," people willing to accommodate touring League cyclists for the night, and a list of touring information directors, people willing to help members plan a bicycle trip to their state.

In general, bike books can be divided into two different categories: the ones that tell you how to buy, maintain, and repair your bike; and the ones that tell you where you can go with your bike. One of the first type that is most often recommended is *The New Complete Book of Bicycling,* by Eugene A. Sloane, Simon and Schuster, 1981 ($12.95 softcover, $19.95 hardcover).

Going by Thumb
"Hitching is living by the seat of one's pants. It's surviving on guts and instinct."

This is a tricky subject. A lot of people are completely and absolutely turned off by the whole idea of hitchhiking. Many consider it too dangerous, too risky, to ever attempt. Others wouldn't think of traveling any other way. In an article in the *New York Times* a few years ago, hitchhiking was called "an accepted mode of travel, well on its way to respectability." One French student who hitched from coast to coast told us: "Hitching was very easy. We never had to wait long in one place. We traveled 600 miles or more each day." We suspect that this had a lot to do with the fact that he is not American. Drivers respond more positively to hitchhikers from other countries.

"Foreigners may find it helpful to wave their national flag around when trying to thumb a ride. This I feel would apply especially to the British and was, in fact, recommended to me by an English chap who went from New York to Atlanta on one hop like this."

Since there is no cheaper way to travel, we discuss the subject of hitchhiking here. We sent a questionnaire to the state police of each of the 50 states; the responses, when helpful, are included in each state chapter. We've also included information on the attitude toward hitchhiking in each state—a more subjective view from readers and friends.

From what people told us, we sense a growing feeling of paranoia about hitchhiking-related crimes. Nowadays, it seems people are convinced that the potential danger is greater for the hitchhiker than for the driver. In the past it was the driver who felt threatened.

For help in understanding the legal situation regarding hitchhiking in this country, we went to Tom Grimm, author of *Hitchhiker's Handbook* (published by New American Library, but unfortunately now out of print). Here's what we learned from him: Many people think that hitchhiking is illegal in the U.S., but this is not true. There are no nationwide laws regarding hitchhiking, and individual cities and states are able to make their own laws and regulations on the subject. And there's another wrinkle. Whether a law exists or not, the attitude of the police toward hitchhikers is something that can't be regulated and varies from area to area. Some police are cordial, even helpful, to hitchhikers, and others treat thumbers like escaped criminals. Perhaps the only way to know ahead of time what the prevailing attitudes are in any particular area is to ask someone who has hitched there. Law books can't tell you anything about attitudes, and we haven't room to tell you much in our state-by-state listings.

Most of the states prohibit hitchhiking on the "roadway," and usually "roadway" is defined as the traveled portion—the paved part—of the road. This means that soliciting a ride from the shoulder is permissible in most states. Since pedestrians are generally prohibited from walking on limited-access highways, like large Interstates, hitchhiking on these highways is, of course, prohibited too. However, it is still possible to thumb rides at the entrance roads to these highways.

If, after weighing the pros and cons, you decide to hitchhike, here's some general advice: If you are going to hitchhike, you will have to travel light. *"Travel light and smile."* It is best to carry your gear in a knapsack, since it leaves your hands free to hold a sign—clearly lettered—telling where you're headed. If you're in an area where people feel threatened by less conventional hairstyles, tuck your hair into a hat. Carry maps, clothing suited to the climate you're going to be traveling through, and a supply of water for hot, dusty, rideless days. How safe is hitchhiking? That depends on luck and your judgment. Follow your instincts—if you think for any reason that the ride you are being offered may lead to trouble, don't take it. Women should never hitch alone. A boy-girl combination is probably the most likely to get rides. Hitchhiking at night is not a good idea for anyone—drivers just can't see you. A sensible pamphlet on hitchhiking put out by Travelers Aid Society of Detroit lists six suggestions for successful hitchhiking:

1. Be visible, wear bright clothing, and stand where you can be seen.
2. Carry as little as possible.
3. Choose morning and late afternoon for soliciting long rides—lunchtime is almost impossible.
4. Hitch on highways rather than expressways.
5. Try to find people who are already traveling—people at rest stops and gas

stations. It's better for you to pick your driver than for your driver to pick you.
6. A little paranoia is fine.

One reader disagrees with this last one: *"No. No. No. Fear shows. An invitation to trouble. Paranoia is not fine. It is pointless, can keep one from enjoying the experience of a lifetime, and can be dangerously distracting. A little caution and common sense will do nicely."*

"Out of 29 different rides, all were good. Most people went out of their way to let us off at a convenient point. We were never stopped by officials. People who picked us up usually wanted company, wanted to hear about our travels, and had a lot of interesting things to tell, themselves."

"I usually tried to find a ride at a truck stop by asking the drivers at the entrance of a restaurant or coffeeshop. . . . Even though I was a little scared at the beginning, after listening to all the tales of mugging, I had a wonderful time talking with great Americans."

Going on Foot

If you like to walk with a group, you might want to find out about the many clubs throughout the U.S. that promote hiking and sponsor organized outdoor trips —generally in the parks and wilderness areas. Most of these organizations are regional or statewide.

A listing of more than 25 key hiking clubs along the East Coast can be obtained by writing to the Appalachian Trail Conference, P.O. Box 807, Harpers Ferry, WV 25425. This conference of trail clubs manages the 2000-mile Maine-to-Georgia Appalachian Trail, in conjunction with the National Park Service. For 50¢, they'll send you an information packet about the trail, membership, etc. Be sure to ask specifically for the list of clubs, or you can ask for the names of clubs in a particular area.

One of the hiking clubs on the East Coast is the Adirondack Mountain Club, 172 Ridge St., Glens Falls, NY 12801 (telephone: 518/793-7737). The club sponsors hiking outings, does conservation work, operates year-round Adirondack High Peaks lodges for hikers, and publishes trail guides, natural history books, and a magazine.

On the West Coast, there's the well-known Sierra Club, which has chapters in all 50 states throughout the U.S. If you write to their headquarters at 530 Bush St., San Francisco, CA 94108, they can direct you to the nearest chapter. They can provide information about the Pacific Crest Trail, which stretches for 2400 miles along the Pacific Coast from Canada to Mexico.

A book especially for walkers is called *Walking: A Guide to Beautiful Walks and Trails in America,* by Jean Calder, published by William Morrow ($3.95). The book lists walks in every state and rates the walks from easy to hard.

Going by Boat

Had you thought of this one? Paddlers can get all the information they need on canoes, kayaks, rafts, accessories, rentals, books, maps, and where to use them, from the Chicagoland Canoe Base, Inc., 4019 North Narragansett Ave., Chicago, IL 60634. Send a stamped, self-addressed envelope for a copy of their book list, or visit if you're in the area.

The Appalachian Mountain Club publishes seven books that would interest canoeists and kayakers: *AMC River Guide: Maine* ($7.95); *AMC River Guide: New Hampshire and Vermont* ($8.95); *The Wildest Country: A Guide to Thoreau's Maine* ($11.95); *AMC River Guide: Massachusetts, Connecticut, Rhode Island* ($8.95); *New England White Water River Guide,* by Ray Gabler ($8.95); *Whitewater Handbook,* by John Urban and T. Walley Williams ($5.95); and *River Rescue,* by Les Bechdel and Slim Ray ($9.95). All are available by mail (add $1.50 shipping on orders for one book, 25¢ for each additional title) from AMC Books, 5 Joy St., Boston, MA 02108.

Some Books to Read

Here are some books that we can recommend to help you get some background on the places you're going to visit. To really get yourself in the mood for your trip, you should read novels about the areas you're going to be visiting and see movies set in the places you'll eventually see. But for information on how to actually get around the various cities, where to eat cheaply and well, and for other practical advice, consult some of the following guidebooks:

There are three series of guides, all published by Frommer/Pasmantier Publishers, that might interest you.

Books on Hawaii, New York, and Washington, D.C., started out as part of Frommer's well-known $5-a-Day series, but with things the way they are, they are now entitled *Hawaii on $35 a Day, New York on $45 a Day,* and *Washington, D.C., on $40 a Day.* They are available at $10.95 each for Hawaii and D.C., $9.95 for New York.

Another Frommer production is the Arthur Frommer City Guide series, which includes guides to Washington, D.C., Boston, New York, New Orleans, Philadelphia, Atlantic City/Cape May, Las Vegas, Los Angeles, San Francisco, Orlando/Disney World/EPCOT, and Hawaii. They cost $4.95 each. Recently Frommer has added six guides to its Dollarwise series: *Florida*; *California and Las Vegas*; *New England*; *The Southeast and New Orleans*; *The Northwest*; and *The Southwest. California* is $9.95; *New England* and *The Southeast* are $11.95, and the others are $10.95. Frommer's *How to Beat the High Cost of Travel* tells how to save money on absolutely all travel-related items. It costs $4.95. Other Frommer offerings are: *Bed and Breakfast—North America* ($7.95) and *Marilyn Wood's Wonderful Weekends* ($9.95), which covers Connecticut, Massachusetts, Rhode Island, New York, Pennsylvania, New Jersey, and Vermont ($9.95).

All Frommer Guides are available at bookstores or from Frommer/Pasmantier Publishers, 1230 Avenue of the Americas, New York, NY 10020.

Another well-known series is the one by Fodor. The following regional titles are available in bookstores or from David McKay Company, 2 Park Ave., New York, NY 10016, all in paperback. Some choices: *Fodor's American Cities on a Budget* ($12.50); *Fodor's Far West* ($11.95); *Fodor's New England* ($10.95); *Fodor's Pacific Northwest Coast* ($9.95); *Fodor's South* ($12.95). The same people do guides to individual cities and states, e.g., California, New Orleans, New York, Texas, and on and on.

The *Mobil Travel Guides,* published by Rand McNally, are also popular with travelers. There are seven regional guides: *California and the West, Great Lakes Area, Middle Atlantic States, Northwest and Great Plains States, Southeastern States, Southwest and South Central States,* and *Northeastern States.* Each guide has about 300 pages and includes hotels, restaurants, and sightseeing information; the 1986 editions cost $8.95 each. Another Mobil guide is *The Mobil Travel Guide: Major Cities*, which concentrates on the 48 most-visited U.S. cities; the 1986 edition costs $8.95.

For budget travel advice, we recommend *Let's Go: USA*, one of the excellent Harvard Student Agencies' travel series published by St. Martin's Press ($8.95).

Farm, Ranch & Country Vacations, by Pat Dickerman, is a 240-page listing of ranches, farms, and lodges in the U.S. and Canada where city people can go to enjoy some country living. Some of these places are working farms, but don't be alarmed: "At a working farm or ranch, guests don't do the work—they *watch* it—unless, of course, they have a special hankering for pitching hay or moving cattle." The 1986 edition costs $12.95 postpaid in the U.S. and $16 by check drawn on a U.S. bank for airmail delivery abroad; it is available from Farm and Ranch Vacations, 36 East 57th St., New York, NY 10022.

One of the newer entries in the field of travel books is *United States 1985*, a "Get'em and Go Travel Guide" to the "finest in 40 cities," edited by Stephen Birnbaum, published by Houghton Mifflin ($11.95). It is revised and updated annually.

And there are more:

A Literary Tour Guide to the United States: West and Midwest, by Rita Stein, published by William Morrow, 1979 ($9.95).

A Literary Tour Guide to the United States: South and Southwest, by Rita Stein, published by William Morrow, 1979 ($9.95).

Adventure Travel North America, by Pat Dickerman, published by Adventure Guides, Inc., 1986 ($12.95). Who, what, where, when and how much for outdoor vacations—scaling rock, backpacking, riding horseback into the wilderness, river rafting and more. Send orders to Adventure Guides, Inc., 36 East 57th St., New York, NY 10022.

Guide to the Recommended Country Inns of New England, by Elizabeth Squier, published by The Globe Pequot Press, Old Chester Rd., Chester, CT 06412 ($9.95). A delightful book with the personal touch. Descriptions of menus at each inn will make your mouth water.

Budget Dining and Lodging in New England, another Globe Pequot Press offering; this one is a guide to 400 places to eat and to spend a night or two. The authors must have had great fun researching this one—the result is a well-organized, homey kind of guide.

Bed and Breakfast American Style, by Norman T. Simpson, published by The Berkshire Traveller Press ($9.95), is another in the fast-growing number of books that list guest house–type accommodations. Simpson's is one of the better ones—with full-page descriptions of 325 bed-and-breakfast places throughout North America.

More on New England can be found in *Day Trips and Budget Vacations in New England*, by Patricia and Robert Foulke, published by Globe Pequot Press ($8.95). Based on six recommended itineraries that go from the coast to the mountains, from busy cities to quiet colonial-style villages.

There's a series of guides describing inns in various parts of the country published by Burt Franklin and Co., Inc., 235 East 44th St., New York, NY 10017. The titles in the series are *Country New England Inns*, *Country Inns of the Mid Atlantic States*, *Country Inns of the Midwest/Rocky Mountains*, and *Country Inns of the West/Southwest*. The 1983–84 editions of these books cost $5.95 each and are available from the publisher.

Made in America: A Guide to Tours of Workshops, Farms, Mines and Industries, by Susan Farlow, Hastings House, 1979 ($7.95). Some American companies that invite you in to see how they work.

For any of you who are serious about shopping, you might want a copy of a book called *Save on Shopping Directory*, "the only national Directory of factory outlet and retail clearance stores," by Iris Ellis. For a copy, send $7.95 plus $1 for postage to SOS, Box 10482, Jacksonville, FL 32207.

Michelin has recently released a *Green Guide to New England*, which we recommend, particularly for foreign visitors. Published by the Michelin Tire people, P.O. Box 3305, Spartanburg, SC 29304 ($9.95), it's crammed with interesting facts and includes an excellent tourist map.

The New England Bed and Breakfast Book and *The Southern Bed and Breakfast Book* are being written at the time we went to press for publication by the East Woods Press, 429 East Blvd., Charlotte, NC 28203. They should be in bookstores by the time you read this.

Favorite Daytrips in New England, by Michael Schuman, published by Yankee Books, Dublin, NH 03444 ($8.95). Forty ways to get to know New England a little better; in its third edition.

The National Art Museum and Gallery Guide, published by Art Now/Inc., 320 Bonnie Burn Road, Scotch Plains, NJ 07076. A monthly magazine which lists exhibits in over 1100 galleries and museums from coast to coast. $3 per copy; $22 for 11 issues.

And for those of you who want to keep informed, on a regular basis, of what's happening in the world of value travel—in the U.S. and everywhere else as well—you may want to consider a subscription to *Travel Smart*, a newsletter published monthly. Filled with news on the latest fares, hotel bargains, etc., it costs $29 for a one-year subscription, $55 for two years. Write to Communications House, Dobbs Ferry, NY 10522 to order.

The Sierra Club has a series of guides to natural areas of Colorado and Utah, California and Oregon, and Washington; they plan soon to have similar guides to Arizona, Nevada, New Mexico, Idaho, Montana, and Wyoming. For details, write to Sierra Club Catalog, 1142 West Indian School Rd., Phoenix, AZ 85013.

CHAPTER 2

Staying Awhile

When we first began searching out inexpensive places to stay in the U.S., we got mostly encouragement from the people we talked to. But one of our favorite responses was a letter that said: "You must be kidding or out of your minds. For that amount of money you can't even get accommodations in a tent—you are wasting your time."

We are delighted to say that the person who wrote that was completely and absolutely wrong. We have uncovered hundreds of places to stay that are $30 and under per person per night. Some of the accommodations listed are spartan —room for a sleeping bag on a gymnasium floor for a few dollars a night—but we've also found luxurious rooms in a modern resort with just about every recreation facility imaginable for $30 a night. We've been able to list places suitable for people of all ages, although we do have some "students only" information. In general, we have listed any and every place we could find that offers a place to stay for $30 or less for a single per night, our limit. (At times, in some of the larger cities, we've listed hotels where singles are more than $30 but doubles work out to $30 or less per person.) Needless to say, we haven't found everything that exists in this category. So if you come across a good place to stay that's within our range, let us know; we'll contact the people who run it and maybe list it in our next edition. Many of the additions to this year's listings have come via our readers and we're pleased about their willingness to help.

Accommodations are listed here by state and then by city. In order to make it easier for you to know where the cities listed are in relation to where you are, we have provided a map at the beginning of each state section and have put on that map the cities where we have listings. Fifteen of the largest U.S. cities have expanded sections incorporated into the state-by-state listings. These sections include information not only on accommodations but also on places to eat, things to do, how to get around, etc.

In each accommodation listing we have included the name of the facility, the address, the telephone number, and, when helpful, the name of the person to ask for when calling for information. Whenever a facility has agreed to offer a special discount rate to holders of the International Student Identity Card (ISIC), readers of *Where to Stay,* senior citizens, or has access facilities for the disabled, we have indicated this with the following symbols:

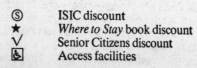

    Ⓢ   ISIC discount
    ★   *Where to Stay* book discount
    √   Senior Citizens discount
    ♿   Access facilities

We have listed the rates (per room unless otherwise indicated) and have noted whether accommodations are for men or women only and whether children can be accommodated. If the facility is open only at a certain time of the year, the dates are given, and if reservations are necessary this is also indicated. Any other information that we thought was either interesting or helpful or both, we put into the listings. To help you understand the types of accommodations in this book, we've described below the different kinds of places we have listed, what to expect from them, and, in some cases, what they expect from you.

"Where did I stay? In motels, campgrounds, youth hostels, with friends and relatives, in a barn, a school bus, on a picnic table, in a cave, and in a university dorm."

American Youth Hostels

". . . Youth hostels were my salvation. Without fail, the houseparents were friendly and helpful, accommodation was good if sometimes basic, and prices were rock-bottom. I almost always found someone to travel with for a few days and saw none of the school parties and strictly enforced rules that so often mar English and European hostels. Altogether, a really good deal."

There are about 300 youth hostels scattered throughout the U.S. that are operated by the American Youth Hostels, Inc., a member of the International Youth Hostel Federation. AYH hostels are sometimes in private homes, and because they are meant for people who travel under their own steam—hikers, bicyclists, canoeists, skiers, or horseback riders—are often located in rural areas near parks, forests, or preserves. They are often in particularly beautiful settings, off the beaten path. There are now many AYH facilities in the larger cities as well—cities like Washington, D.C., Phoenix, Philadelphia, Boston, San Francisco, Los Angeles, San Diego, etc.

In order to use the hostel facilities of AYH, you must be a member of the organization. One year's membership costs $10 for anyone under 18 or over 59 years of age and $20 for anyone else. Membership passes are available from American Youth Hostels, 1332 I St., NW, Suite 800, Washington, D.C. 20005 (tel. 202/783-8161) and from AYH councils and agencies in certain metropolitan areas. Check the telephone directory for listings or ask a travel agent. Visiting foreign students should have a membership card from their own national youth hostel association; in emergencies they may obtain an International Guest Pass from AYH National Headquarters (see above address).

"A youth hostel card, bought either in the U.S. or in a foreign visitor's home country, is strongly recommended. For example, in one place, if you don't have a card, the cost of an overnight will be $30; with the card it is $7.50."

Not all AYH facilities are the same; there are, in fact, three categories of hostels. By definition, a full hostel is a low-cost, supervised, overnight accommodation for people traveling. It has maximum fees established by AYH, Inc., resident houseparents, separate dormitories and washing/toilet facilities, a kitchen, and a dining room and common room. A "home hostel" is someone's private residence and usually has all the basic elements of a hostel. The difference is size. A hostel usually has between 10 and 100 beds; a home hostel usually has only one to eight beds. Often the kitchen is the homeowner's private kitchen and, while meals may be provided, the hostelers cannot always expect to prepare their own meals. Home hostels always require advance reservations. Overnight rates vary from hostel to hostel and sometimes change with the seasons. Rates are usually from $3 to $8 per night; exact rates that were in effect at press time are given in the individual listings. Some hostels set a limit to the number of nights you may stay—anywhere from three to seven days.

And finally, there are "supplemental accommodations" (indicated in our book by "AYH-SA" in parentheses after the name), which provide most of the facilities of a regular hostel but are lacking one or more of the basic elements of a hostel—usually this is a kitchen or a houseparent, since the supplemental accommodations are often YMCAs, camps, etc. Rates at supplemental facilities are higher than standard hostel rates, and AYH membership is not usually required. Unless otherwise stated, the AYH-SA rates given in *Where to Stay*'s listings are for AYH members; nonmembers can expect a higher rate.

Reservations are generally recommended for overnight stays in hostels and should be made as far in advance as possible. To make a reservation, send the hostel a deposit equal to one night's accommodation. If reservations are absolutely required, the listings will indicate it.

A new International Advanced Booking Voucher scheme, whereby hostelers can make reservations at hostels all over the world before they set off on their trip, is now in operation. Write to the AYH National Headquarters for details.

All hostels share a common set of what *Hosteling USA* calls "customs": cooking, cleaning, and general hostel duties must be shared by hostelers; drinking, smoking, and illegal drugs are not allowed; check-out time is 9:30 a.m., and hostels are usually closed between 10 a.m. and 4 p.m.

A manual called the *AYH Guide and Handbook* comes free with every AYH membership; copies of *Hosteling USA*, a more elaborate version of the handbook, are available for $7.95 in bookstores or from AYH, Inc., at the above address. When ordering the book directly from AYH, add $1.50 for postage and handling.

Other Hostels

As you read through the accommodation listings in *Where to Stay USA*, you will find some facilities that call themselves hostels but are not affiliated with American Youth Hostels and do not have AYH written after their name. These are independent accommodation facilities set up by a variety of people and groups but all with one goal in common: to provide a cheap, relatively comfortable, and friendly place for people on the road to spend a night or two. Many of these hostels are in urban areas; often they have cooking facilities and sometimes even free kitchens. These independent hostels are operated by churches, community groups, and sometimes even by YMCAs.

Many of the hostels described above are open only a few hours a day for registration, since they are often short-staffed, so we suggest that you call ahead to find out the best time to arrive. All of these places are adamant about some basic rules which always include the prohibition of alcohol, drugs, or weapons on the premises. It is also common for the facilities to have a minimum age requirement. This is because in some states sheltering anyone under 16, or even 18, may be defined legally as "housing a runaway." If you are under 18 and traveling, it may be wise to carry a letter from your parents stating that they know you are traveling and that you have their permission to do so.

Most of these independent hostels also limit the length of your stay to two or three nights. They are, after all, for people passing through, and you must leave room for others who need what is usually rather limited space.

YMCAs and YWCAs

Young Men's Christian Associations (YMCAs) and Young Women's Christian Associations (YWCAs) are well known all over the world as organizations that will often provide inexpensive housing to transients. Ys are completely non-denominational in spite of their name and provide, besides accommodations, many recreational facilities such as swimming pools, gymnasiums, ball courts, and various programmed activities.

Not all Ys have accommodation facilities, but we contacted the ones that do and have listed the ones that responded. There are certain generalizations that we can make about staying in Y facilities. Usually rooms in Ys do not have private baths or showers, and you must share these facilities with others on your floor. Some YMCAs can accommodate both men and women, but most YWCAs can accommodate only women. This is indicated in the listings. Usually you may use the Y's recreational facilities at no extra cost when you spend the night there; sometimes if you are not a member of the YMCA or YWCA you will be required to pay a small membership fee along with the overnight rate. In well-traveled areas Ys are popular places to stay, so it is usually wise to call ahead to see if there is room for you. Some Ys require reservations; our listing will indicate if this is the case. Reservations at YMCAs in the larger metropolitan areas may be made by contacting "Y's Way International" at 356 West 34th Street, New York, NY 10001; telephone: 212/760-5856. "The Y's Way International" is a central reservation service for over 130 YMCAs and accommodation centers located in 80 North American cities and 24 countries overseas. Particularly when you want accommodations in the more popular cities—New York, Montreal, Seattle, New Orleans, San Francisco, or Los Angeles—it's best to contact the "Y's Way International" as far in advance of your trip as possible.

Dormitories and Residence Halls

There are many dormitories and residence halls at both large and small schools that are willing and able to put up travelers. We received a positive response from the housing offices of many U.S. colleges and universities and would certainly recommend that whenever you are in the neighborhood of a campus you check out its accommodation facilities. Even if a campus is not listed here, we would suggest your calling the housing office or asking at the student union about a place where you can spend the night. You will rarely be turned away.

Besides the dormitories and residence halls that are operated by colleges, there are residence halls that are operated privately to serve the local student population. Most of these residence halls are only a few years old and are quite luxurious. Usually they are divided into apartment-type areas with four single bedrooms, one kitchen, and one bathroom to each area. The buildings are often equipped with swimming pools, tennis courts, etc.

Although we don't have any to list, try sorority and fraternity houses too when you're on a campus. They may have room for you.

"I traveled with another guy for most of my trip. We found the easiest places to crash were fraternity houses. We stayed in them at Northwestern, Washington University (St. Louis, Mo.), and at the University of Utah in Salt Lake City. The best thing about frats is they usually have kitchens. Bring a sleeping bag to use on the floor."

Low-Cost Motel Chains

Something exciting has happened in the motel management field, and that's the development of the low-cost motel chain. Based on the reasonable premise that travelers were getting tired of paying exorbitant prices for motel rooms, a few U.S. capitalists decided to build no-frills facilities that would not have to charge high rates to stay in business. This meant cutting out some of the extras such as restaurants on the property (they built their buildings across the street from the existing restaurants instead), wall-to-wall carpeting, etc. The first low-cost motel chain did so well that others have followed the lead, and now there are quite a few motels all over the U.S. where you can spend the night comfortably and cheaply. We've included the following low-cost motel chains in our listings:

Best Value Inn/Superior Motels/Magic Key Inns, Budget Host Inns, Allstar Inns, Days Inns of America, E-Z 8 Motels, Econo Lodges, Exel Inns, Friendship Inns, Imperial 400 Motor Inns, Motel 6, Red Roof Inns, TraveLodge/Viscount Inns, Regal 8 Inns, Hospitality International, Sixpence Inns, Susse Chalet Motor Lodges and Inns, Thrifty Scot Motels, Select Inns, and Quality International Inns.

The rates of the various low-cost motels vary from chain to chain, and often even within the chain, but, in general, the more people you can fit into one room the more money you will save. It is always advisable to make reservations in advance at these motels, since they have become extremely popular with travelers.

"The budget motels are very heavily booked especially during the summer and the chance of getting a room after 2 p.m. is slim indeed."

Remember that in order to stay at any of these motels, you will probably need to have a car—very, very few are accessible by public transportation.

For free directories of all the facilities in any of the low-cost chains, you can write to the following addresses. If a chain has a toll-free telephone reservation number, it's included below:

International Motel Group
Best Value Inns/Superior Motels/Magic Key Inns
P.O. Box 729
Goodlettsville, TN 37072
Toll-free reservations number: 800/872-4667

Budget Host Inns
P.O. Box 10656
Fort Worth, TX 76114

Allstar Inns, Inc.
P.O. Box 3070
Santa Barbara, CA 93130

Days Inns of America, Inc.
2751 Buford Hwy. NE
Atlanta, GA 30324
Toll-free reservations numbers for each state are given in free directory.

E-Z 8 Motels, Inc.
2484 Hotel Circle Pl.
San Diego, CA 92108

Econo Lodges of America, Inc.
6135 Park Rd., Suite 200
Charlotte, NC 28210
Toll-free reservations numbers: 800/368-7283
(In North Carolina, 704/554-0088)

Exel Inns of America
4706 East Washington Ave.
Madison, WI 53704
Toll-free reservations numbers: 800/356-8013
(In Wisconsin, 800/362-5478)

Friendship Inns International
739 South 400 West
Salt Lake City, UT 84101
Toll-free reservations numbers: 800/453-4511
(In Utah, 800/438-5400)

Imperial 400 National, Inc.
1000 Wilson Blvd., Suite 820
Arlington, VA 22209
Toll-free reservations numbers: 800/368-4400
(In Virginia, 800/572-2200)

Motel 6, Inc.
51 Hitchcock Way
Santa Barbara, CA 93105

Red Roof Inns, Inc.
4355 Davidson Rd.
Hilliard, OH 43026
Toll-free reservations number: 800/848-7878

TraveLodge/Viscount Hotels
Corporate Headquarters
1973 Friendship Dr.
El Cajon, CA 92090
Toll-free reservations number: 800/255-3050

Regal 8 Inns
P.O. Box 1268
Mt. Vernon, IL 62864
Toll-free reservations number: 800/851-8888

Hospitality International (Scottish, Red Carpet, and Master Hosts Inns)
1152 Spring St., Suite A
Atlanta, GA 30309
Toll-free reservations number: 800/251-1962

Sixpence Inns of America, Inc.
1751 East Garry Ave.
Santa Ana, CA 92705

Chalet Susse International, Inc.
Chalet Dr.
Wilton, NH 03086
Toll-free reservations numbers: 800/258-1980
(In New Hampshire, 800/572-1880)

Thrifty Scot Motels, Inc.
One Sunwood Dr.
P.O. Box 399
St. Cloud, MN 56302
Toll-free reservations number: 800/228-3222
(In Nebraska and Canada, call collect: 402/493-0333)

Select Inns
Box 2603
Fargo, ND 58108

Quality International
10750 Columbia Pike
Silver Spring, MD 20901
Toll-free reservations number: 800/638-6714

Pilot Books, 103 Cooper St., Babylon, NY 11702, publishes a *National Directory of Budget Motels*. The 1985–86 edition is available for $4.95 postpaid.

"Motels can be a great value. Particularly at touristy places out of season, it really pays to bargain. For example, when we were in Fort Lauderdale, Fla., the first two places told us it would be $26 for a double everywhere. Next door we got it down to $24 and next door to that, to $22. We checked next to this last place and

then returned to say the bloke next door was charging $18. We ended up with a magnificent room for $15."

Bed-and-Breakfast Accommodations

A relatively new and extremely welcome phenomenon is the development of bed-and-breakfast facilities throughout the U.S. Taking the cue from other countries where bed-and-breakfast establishments have been an institution for a long, long time, many men and women are opening their homes to travelers— providing a room and breakfast in pleasant surroundings for a rate much lower than that offered in many commercial hotels and motels.

Many of these people who want to host travelers in their homes have joined organizations that serve to publicize their facilities and help them simplify their reservations process.

One of the organizations that is involved in this movement is The International Spareroom, 839 Second St., Encinitas, CA 92024, which keeps a list of people in many U.S. locations who have a room to rent in their homes for a minimum stay of two nights. Rates vary from home to home, and some provide access facilities. Write for details.

Anyone traveling in Washington, Oregon, Idaho, or California who wants to stay in a private home can contact Northwest Bed and Breakfast, 7707 Southwest Locust St., Tigard, OR 97227. Telephone: 503/246-8366. The annual membership fee is $15 for one person, $20 for a family. Overnight rates vary from $14 to $25 for a single, $18 to $40 for a double; family rates are also available. A descriptive listing of approximately 300 homes in the Northwest network is available for $5 plus $1 postage; this amount will be credited to your membership fee.

Bed & Breakfast International, 151 Ardmore Rd., Kensington, CA 94707, is another organization that places people in private homes in San Francisco, Los Angeles, San Diego, and other locations in California, as well as in Hawaii, New York City, Washington, D.C., Seattle, and Las Vegas. It is the oldest organization of its kind—it was set up in 1978. The cost is $30 to $85 for two people, $6 less for the single traveler. Special rates are available to students. For an application, write to the address above and enclose a stamped, self-addressed envelope or call 415/525-4569 during business hours.

Another bed-and-breakfast scheme is Bed and Breakfast Registry, P.O. Box 80174, St. Paul, MN 55108. With listings in 39 states, the registry lists accommodations that cost from $20 to $55 for a single and from $25 to $90 for a double. There's no registration fee; call 612/646-4238 for information. They have a detailed directory available for $9.25.

And the latest we've come across is Pineapple Hospitality, Inc., 384 Rodney French Blvd., New Bedford, MA 02744, telephone 617/990-1696, which acts as a reservation service for Maine, Vermont, New Hampshire, Massachusetts, Connecticut, and Rhode Island in the cities and way out in the country as well. The directory costs $3.98.

Throughout this book we refer to statewide bed-and-breakfast networks— check the introductory section of the state you're going to visit for any such organizations.

A book that lists guest houses, tourist homes, and bed-and-breakfasts throughout the U.S. and one that we've seen grow from brochure size to a full-fledged paperback in only a few years, is *Bed and Breakfast USA: A Guide to Guest Houses and Tourist Homes*, by Betty Rundback and Nancy Kramer. The book, published by E.P. Dutton, is available in bookstores or from Tourist House Associates, Inc., RD 2, Box 355A, Greentown, PA 18426, for $8.95. Besides the listing of 500 facilities in all 50 states and Canada, the authors also include over 100 reservations services—the kind we mentioned above—which give readers access to 10,000 homes. The average rate for two is $40. According to the authors: "You are always made to feel more like a welcome guest than a paying customer."

Two other books on the subject are *The New England Guest House Book*, by Corinne Madden Ross, published by East Woods Press, 429 East Blvd., Charlotte, NC 28203 ($7.95), and *The Southern Guest House Book*, by the same author and publisher ($6.95). Ms. Ross defines her subject matter as a place "that provides only lodging and is, on the average, smaller than an inn, with fewer rooms." Many of the places she lists are in popular resort areas where hotels and motels tend to be expensive and a guest house makes a terrific alternative. And finally, there's *Bed & Breakfast in the Northeast*, by Bernice Chesler, published by Globe/Pequot Press, Old Chester Rd., Chester, CT 06412 ($9.95). It covers Connecticut, Maine, Massachusetts, New Hampshire, New Jersey, New York, Pennsylvania, Rhode Island, Vermont, and Washington, D.C., plus a long list of Bed & Breakfast registration services that can lead to accommodations all over the U.S. and eastern Canada as well.

America Bed and Breakfast, Box 23486, Washington, D.C. 20024 (telephone: 202/379-4242), issues a list of facilities twice a year—their Hostlist is $7.95 per copy and contains bare-bones entries for 1300 cities and towns across the U.S., and "A Treasury of Bed and Breakfast" lists 2700 bed-and-breakfasts from Hawaii to Nova Scotia described more fully than in the smaller Hostlist. Copies of the Treasury cost $14.95 with postage included.

Another organization of bed-and-breakfast places, the National Bed and Breakfast Association, publishes yet another guide to the subject: *Bed and Breakfast Guide for the U.S. and Canada*, by Phyllis Featherstone and Barbara Ostler, lists 459 bed-and-breakfast homes and small family-owned and operated inns. The explanation and the "How to Use the Guide" sections are written in English, French, and Spanish. The book is sold in many U.S. bookstores or can be ordered from the Association directly for $9.95 plus $1.25 for postage and handling. The Association is at 148 East Rocks Rd., P.O. Box 332, Norwalk, CT 06852.

And finally, there's a country-wide network of bed-and-breakfast services which at last count had 20 members. For a brochure listing the various members, write to the National Network, P.O. Box 4616, Springfield, MA or P.O. Box 162, Oreland, PA 19075.

Camping

Camping in the U.S. can be a fabulous experience. The facilities are widespread and generally excellent, and it shouldn't be too difficult for you to avoid the trailer set and enjoy the great outdoors. Our favorites are the state and national parks, which are much more beautiful than most private campgrounds. Be warned, though, that state and national parks are extremely popular with campers, and it's possible that some will be filled to capacity when you decide to go.

In our state listings we have room to list only national parks, with a few exceptions. For complete information on state parks, just write or call the state tourist office listed for each state. Most publish lists and accompanying maps describing facilities, and will send them to you—all free of charge, of course.

Anyone who intends to use the national park system extensively should purchase a *Golden Eagle Passport*, which is sold at all parks. The passport costs $10 and provides free entry to all areas of the national park system that charge entrance fees. The free entry applies to the permit holder and everyone accompanying him or her in a private, noncommercial vehicle; it is valid for the calendar year. Normally the entrance fees to the parks range from $1 to $3 per passenger vehicle.

The *Golden Age Passport* is issued to any U.S. citizen age 62 or older upon presentation of proof of age at any park, and a *Golden Access Passport* is issued free to blind and disabled people who are eligible for federal disability benefits. Both permit free admission to all areas of the national park system and a 50% discount on recreation fees. Applicants must apply in person.

Most campsites in the national park system are available on a first-come first-served basis only. However, reservations can be obtained for campsites at Dinosaur National Monument, and campgrounds at Acadia and Grand Canyon National Parks, Chickasaw National Recreation Area, and Cumberland Island and Point Reyes National Seashores. For reservations, write to the addresses given in the listings for these campgrounds, to the attention of the superintendent. Reservations may be made through Ticketron for Acadia National Park, Joshua Tree National Monument, Mammoth Cave National Park, Cape Hatteras National Seashore, Great Smoky Mountains National Park, Shenandoah National Park, Grand Canyon National Park, Rocky Mountain National Park, Sequoia–Kings Canyon National Park, and Yosemite National Park. Reservation forms are available at Ticketron outlets and the Ticketron Reservations Office, P.O. Box 2715, San Francisco, CA 94126.

Since campsites in the national parks are so much in demand, it has been necessary for the park service to limit the number of days a person may occupy a site at some of the parks during the peak season. This time limit, and all other information about the park, is available from the address listed in each state section. Remember that the address we list here for the park is not necessarily the location of the campground—it is a mailing address only. In some cases, campgrounds may be many, many miles from the town listed as the mailing address.

For a list of the 104 areas maintained by the National Park Service, and information on their facilities, send $1.50 to the Superintendent of Documents, U.S. Government Printing Office, Washington, D.C. 20402, and ask for *Camping in the National Park System*.

One other useful publication available from the same source is *Lesser-Known Areas of the National Park System* ($1.50).

For a comprehensive listing of all campgrounds in the U.S., both public and private, we recommend the *Rand McNally Campground and Trailer Park Guide*; the 1985 edition costs $13.95 and is available in most bookstores. The Rand McNally guide is especially useful, since it contains maps of each state with every campground listed marked on them. This makes it easy to plan your travel route according to available campgrounds. Rand McNally also publishes its guide in East and West editions; the 1985 editions are $8.95 each.

If the idea of camping on Indian lands interests you, write to the U.S. Department of the Interior, Bureau of Indian Affairs, Washington, D.C. 20242, and ask for its map of Indian Areas. On the back of the map are listed the addresses of area and agency offices of BIA where you can write for specific information on existing sites.

Not everyone knows that many of the state and national parks have cabins and lodges that are available to the public. To find out what's where and how to arrange a cabin stay, see *The Complete Guide to Cabins and Lodges in America's State and National Parks*, by George Zimmerman; published by Little, Brown and Co. ($12.95).

Crashing

There's not much one can say about this kind of accommodations. You find it where you can, and whether you do or not depends on your own resourcefulness. More and more areas of the country have gotten used to the idea of crashing, and if you carry a sleeping bag along you'll find crashing a lot easier. College towns are the most likely places to find crashing space; stop at some of the on-campus addresses given in the state listings to ask about the chances for crashing in the neighborhood. Or check out a local underground paper or a flourishing health food store—the people there will probably know where to send you. Many of the hotlines listed in *Where to Stay USA* will also be able to tell you whether there's any crashing space around.

Names of people who are willing to share their home with travelers who may someday make space for them can be found in the *Traveler's Directory*. The Directory is available only to people who are willing to be listed in it themselves. It is published by Tom Linn, 6224 Baynton St., Philadelphia, PA 19144. Write to ask for a questionnaire, and he'll send you what you need in order to be listed. Listings cost $15 each and the fee includes back issues of the Directory when available. Traveler's Directory members receive free copies of *The Vagabonds' Shoes*, the organization's semi-annual newsletter, which includes travel features, transportation bargains, mutual-aid columns, and travel book reviews. Nonmembers may order a year's subscription for $3.50.

None of the Above

An interesting organization that we discovered and one that doesn't really fit under any other heading is one called Innter Lodging Co-op. The Co-op is a group of families who agree to make their homes available to travelers for at least three months a year. In return, when they travel they can stay at other members' homes for $4 or $5 per night (no meals included). To find out more about the Co-op, write to Innter Lodging Co-op, P.O. Box 7044, Tacoma, WA 98407. The telephone number is 206/756-0343.

Last Resorts

"I met two guys who had had their packs ripped off in Colorado Springs and had nothing to their names. I went with them to the Salvation Army, where they were able to get $4 worth of groceries and $6 worth of clothes—they also told them about churches, etc., that gave out free food. I'd advise anyone in trouble to check out a Salvation Army."

People Who Can Help

The idea of community switchboards, hotlines, free clinics, and help lines has caught on all over the country, and there isn't any place that you'll be where help is farther than a telephone call away. If you have a problem, need a place to stay or some medical care, or just want to hear a friendly voice, you can call the help lines listed in each state section.

In researching *Where to Stay USA*, we asked friends all over the country about the help lines and crisis centers that were located in their areas so that we could include them in our book. Hotlines seem to come and go with great rapidity; the telephone numbers that we have here were in service when we went to press and hopefully still are.

In the "Help" section of each state listing, besides the telephone numbers of hotlines and crisis centers you'll often find the addresses and telephone numbers of Travelers Aid offices. Travelers Aid (its full name is Travelers Aid Association of America) is a social work agency with branches in airports, bus stations, and railroad stations that has been set up to assist people on the move by providing emergency assistance, protective care, and professional counseling service. Feel free to call on them if you need help.

Two other organizations that should be mentioned here are CONTACT Teleministries and the National Runaway Switchboard. CONTACT is a network of crisis intervention, information, and referral help lines. There are 100 centers in operation in 150 different calling areas. Forty-one of these centers provide "Deaf CONTACT/TTY Services"—teletypewriter programs to serve the deaf. You can get a complete list of these services and their phone numbers by writing to CONTACT Teleministries USA, Inc., Room 125, 900 South Arlington Ave., Harrisburg, PA 17109, or by calling 717/652-3410.

The National Runaway Switchboard is operated by Metro-Help, Inc., in Chicago. It takes calls from around the country on a toll-free line. "Kids can call us from anywhere in the continental U.S. and get information on over 3000 runaway centers, central community switchboards, and counseling agencies around the country. In addition, we can also use a conferencing device on the phone to allow kids to talk directly with any of these agencies or their parents. If a runaway wants to let his or her parents know that he or she is all right, we'll also deliver the message. . . ." The toll-free number is 800/621-4000 and is available 24 hours a day. All services are confidential.

For the Handicapped

For far too long, handicapped travelers were ignored; there was very, very little information for them and facilities that could make their travel at least possible, and at most pleasurable, were minimal. That has changed and much has been done to develop facilities for these people and many new publications are available to them.

A travel guide for the handicapped is the *Wheelchair Traveler*, by Douglas Annand. The book lists 6000 hotels, motels, restaurants, and sightseeing attractions that are accessible to the handicapped. For information about the book, write to Douglas Annand, Ball Hill Rd., Milford, NH 03055.

Another valuable travel book is the *Guide for the Disabled Traveler*, by author and wheelchair traveler Frances Barish. This guide is helpful for anyone who has a problem with mobility (including people who are blind or deaf). It also gives invaluable information about trip preparation, telephone numbers of organizations that will help in an emergency, and specifics about entrances, ramps, elevators, restrooms, etc., in individual airports, bus and train stations in major cities in the U.S. This guide is available at bookstores or directly from the publisher—Frommer/Pasmantier Publishers, 1230 Avenue of the Americas, New York, NY 10020 ($10.95).

An excellent source of information for the handicapped is Mobility International USA, an organization dedicated to integrating disabled people into travel and educational programs in the U.S. and other countries as well. *A World of Options: A Guide to International Educational Exchange, Community Service and Travel for Persons with Disabilities* offers firsthand information on successful wheelchair travel and a resource section on books and agencies that will help the disabled traveler. Contact MIUSA at P.O. Box 3551, Eugene, OR 97403, or call 503/343-1284.

And something new for "people with travel limitations" is *LTD Travel*, a newsletter published in California. The founder, who has traveled in a wheelchair for 30 years, has designed the newsletter to serve travelers with limitations and especially families "with one limited member who hates being a burden but also hates being left home." Recent issues have included articles on wheelchair camping, and touring northern California wine country. Sample copies are $2; subscriptions are $15 for four issues per year. Write to LTD Travel, 116 Harbor Seal Court, San Mateo, CA 94404. Telephone: 415/573-7998.

For Senior Citizens

The American Association of Retired Persons (AARP), with national headquarters at 1909 K St. NW, Washington, D.C. 20049, offers members a Purchase Privilege Program which includes discounts for major hotels and motels, car rentals and bus service, the AARP Motoring Plan with emergency and other road services for an annual fee, and AARP travel services with group travel programs all over the U.S. and the world. For information on membership and these programs, write to Member Communications at the above address.

Another organization that serves senior citizens and has become extremely popular in the past few years is Elderhostel, a Boston-based group that sponsors study vacations on college campuses all over the U.S. Friends of ours who have participated in Elderhostel said that it was the best vacation they'd had in over 40 years of vacationing. For a catalog of Elderhostel programs, write to the organization at 810 Boylston St., Suite 400, Boston, MA 02116.

Also of interest to senior citizens is *The Discount Guide for Travelers Over 55*, by Caroline and Walter Weintz; published by E.P. Dutton ($5.75).

Many budget motel chains offer special discounts to senior citizens—check with the head offices of the individual chains (addresses on pages 23 to 25) for information.

Paying Your Way

As you travel, it may be possible to pick up jobs here and there to give you enough money to keep you going. This is probably going to be a difficult year for finding jobs, though, since unemployment is a serious problem in many areas.

State employment offices can usually offer good advice on the current work situation in any particular area—feel free to call on them for advice.

If you run out of money and need a job immediately in order to keep you going, you can try calling the help-line numbers. Sometimes they can refer you to a temporary job that will give you enough money to move on.

There are some sweeping generalizations that can be made about job-finding in the U.S. One is, don't count on finding work in California or Michigan, where too many others are job-seeking. If you're going cross-country and think you're going to need some more money to see you through, try Texas instead—the economy there is booming and jobs should not be too difficult to find. Big cities are good places to look for jobs—especially in the service industries—as waiters, waitresses, sales help, etc.

Note: Foreign visitors with B (visitors) visas may not seek paid employment during their stay in the U.S. To work without the proper visa is illegal.

Volunteering

The National Park Service recruits volunteers for the national parks who are asked to perform a variety of tasks at the parks in the areas of interpretation (helping visitors understand the natural and human history of the area); arts and crafts; history; archeology; natural science; environmental study; and resource management. You can get a brochure, *Volunteers in Parks*, and an application from the National Park Service, U.S. Department of the Interior, Washington, D.C. 20240.

Eating

It's going to be tempting, as you travel, to do most of your eating at the fast-food chain restaurants that are springing up all over America. That's why we decided to list a few of our friends' favorite eating places in the state listings and have resisted mentioning any of the chains; we hope to prove that you can still find good, filling, low-cost meals without having to resort to the chains.

If you're trying to economize, why not forget eating in restaurants altogether; buy your food in supermarkets, and have yourself a picnic.

Many of the accommodations listed in *Where to Stay USA* have cooking facilities available; whenever this is true, be sure to take advantage of them. We have one friend who used to cook hamburgers in his hotel room on a travel iron that he carried around with him—there are all sorts of ways to save money if you put your mind to it.

If food is important and you want some help deciding where to eat wherever you are, you might be interested in the book called *Where to Eat in America*, edited by William Rice and Benton Wolf and published by Random House ($7.95). This book covers 50 cities and, according to the editors, is "intended for anyone away from home who is hungry or about to be hungry."

We can recommend one more book for those who care about what they eat. It is *Goodfood*, by Jane and Michael Stern, published by Random House ($8.95). According to the Sterns, "It is possible to escape the homogenized cuisine that lines the highways and makes eating in Arizona indistinguishable from eating in Maine." They point the way, listing what they consider America's best regional restaurants.

CHAPTER 3

Especially for Foreign Visitors

The U.S., often judged so harshly by natives, usually gets rave reviews from foreign visitors. If you're anything like the people from abroad who stopped by to see us after their trips around the U.S., you're going to have a wonderful time here. One of the reasons for this, and probably the most important, is that Americans really are a friendly bunch, especially the ones who live beyond the large cities and have more time for everything, including enjoying a visitor from another country. One young Frenchman put it neatly: "Everywhere we are welcome."

In this section we've organized a few things that you should know before you start out on your trip in the U.S. Some are related to special discounts available to you because you are an international visitor. (Remember that all special discounts are, unfortunately, subject to change or cancellation without warning.) Others are more practical, everyday bits of information designed to save you the common traumas of travel, e.g., your first phone call from a pay telephone or your first taxi ride.

Don't forget to read the introductory chapters, too, since they contain information that everyone—American or foreign—needs when traveling in this country.

Transportation Discounts

To know what discounts exist at any given time, you have to be an expert in the field. For help in finding what bargains exist once you are in the U.S., consult a Council Travel Office (addresses on page 2).

BY AIR: Air travel is extremely popular in the U.S. There are planes flying in and out of 1000 different airports across the country, and with the help of air-taxi services it's possible to fly to many of the smaller cities and towns too. For long distance travel, it is often as inexpensive or even less expensive to go by air than by train (and even by bus in some cases) for the same distance. And discounting airport delays and traffic jams getting to the airport, it's the fastest way to get from one place to another.

You will probably find that travel in the U.S. is less expensive mile-for-mile than it is at home, and if you take advantage of the following special discounts, you can travel by air and still keep to a modest budget:

As a foreign visitor, you can take advantage of deals that are unavailable to U.S. citizens. These deals vary from airline to airline but, to give you an example of some possibilities, we contacted Republic Airlines. Republic offers three possibilities:

The first is the Travel America Air Pass, which must be purchased before you leave home. It costs $370 for 30 days of unlimited travel on a standby basis—a terrific price. If standby is too "iffy" for you, you can get a "See America Fare" good for 60 days of confirmed flights for 4 trips ($370-$400); 8 trips ($475-$525); or 12 trips ($575-$625). (The higher prices are for peak-season travel, July 1 to September 10.)

The third possibility is called the Visit U.S.A. fare but, be warned, it is often more expensive than special fares you can get once you're in the U.S. For example, the Visit USA fare from New York to Houston is $229, and as you can see on page 6, you can do much better than that. On some flights though, the Visit USA fare really may be a bargain. You'll have to research it carefully.

BY BUS: Bus travel is inexpensive and a favorite with young people, both because of the cost and because you get to see a lot of the U.S. from a seat in a bus—everything that you'd miss if you went by plane. See "Going by Bus" in Chapter 1 for information on the Ameripass and Eaglepass and other bargains to which both foreign visitors and Americans are entitled.

BY TRAIN: People who live outside the U.S. are entitled to two kinds of passes —a national and a regional rail pass. The National Pass is good for periods of 14, 21 or 30 days and costs $375, $450, and $525 respectively (half price for children under 12). The Regional Pass covers 14 days of travel in four sections of the country—West ($225); Far West ($125); Eastern ($215); and Northeastern ($125).

It will be necessary to present your pass at an Amtrak ticket office, where you will receive tickets for the particular trips you want to take.

The U.S.A. Rail Pass is good for travel on any part of the Amtrak system, except the Metroliner and the Auto Train. According to the people in the public relations department of Amtrak, "a pass holder could simply ride a train to enjoy a reasonably priced meal on an Amtrak diner." Details and passes should be available in your country from most travel agents. Remember that on the more popular long-distance runs in the U.S. it is necessary to have reservations in advance of your train trip. U.S.A. Rail Pass holders should be sure to make reservations; there is no charge for them.

BY CAR: To drive in the U.S. all you'll need is a valid driver's license from your own country, as long as it's one of the 161 countries that have agreed to the Geneva Road Traffic Convention of 1949. (If you are not from one of these countries, you'll have to obtain a U.S. driver's license at your point of entry into the U.S.) It is advisable to carry an International Driving Permit, which is printed in the official languages of the United Nations. It is especially helpful to local police speaking only English, and may be essential in case of an emergency.

Anyone from abroad who drives in the U.S. should have a copy of *U.S.A. Travel Information*. This 71-page booklet contains all the information you need on traffic regulations, insurance requirements, highways, mileage, etc.; it also lists the 161 countries mentioned above. It's available from offices of the U.S. Travel and Tourism Administration in Frankfurt, London, Paris, Mexico City, and Tokyo.

Most car-rental companies require that Americans be at least 21 years of age to rent a car (it's 25 in New York), but foreign visitors only have to be 18. When you rent a car, you'll have to make a fairly large deposit—the exact amount depends on the place where you pick up the car. Americans *must* pay the deposit with a credit card but foreign visitors may pay in cash. Don't forget the possibility of finding a "drive-away" car (see Chapter 1) or of buying a used car and then selling it when your trip is over.

Other Possibilities

Although there is no set nationwide policy, there are many hotels, motels, and tourist attractions that will give foreign visitors special rates. Always ask whether such a special rate exists—you have nothing to lose by trying.

Meeting Americans in Their Homes

Since there's no better way to get to understand the U.S. and Americans than to spend some time with them at home, you'll probably want to explore some of the following possibilities for arranging a visit to an American home. Chances are that if you do not prearrange such a visit through one of these organizations you will still get to meet Americans in their homes, since Americans are free with their invitations. When an American invites you to be his guest, don't feel he is just being polite—he wouldn't ask you to come if he didn't really want you to.

If you are interested in joining a summer or long-term program in the U.S. involving a family homestay, a partial listing of exchange programs is available on request from the Institute of International Education. Write for the *International Home Hospitality Programs List* to: Communications Division, IIE, 809 United Nations Plaza, New York, NY 10017.

SERVAS: One organization that sponsors a worldwide program of exchange hospitality for travelers in 80 countries including the U.S. is Servas. Its goal: to help build peace, goodwill, and understanding through home visits and other contact between people. Here's how Servas works: you apply and are interviewed; if accepted, you receive a personal briefing, written instructions, a list of Servas hosts in the area you are going to visit, and an introductory letter. You arrange your visits in advance by writing or calling the hosts. The usual stay with a Servas host is two nights. For information on Servas, contact the Servas office in your home country, or if you don't know where it is, write to the U.S. Servas Committee, Inc., 11 John St., Room 706, New York, NY 10038. Servas asks for a donation of $30 for its services.

CHRISTMAS INTERNATIONAL HOUSE: This organization, based in Atlanta, places international college and graduate school students in American homes from mid-December to after New Year's Day, to share the holidays with an American family. For details, write to the organization, 341 Ponce de Leon Ave. NE, Atlanta, GA 30365 (telephone: 404/873-1531).

Community Organizations

There are also several community-based organizations around the country that have been set up specifically to cater to the needs of foreign visitors. These organizations are located all over the U.S., and most of them belong to a central organization, the National Council for International Visitors (NCIV), located in Washington, D.C.

Some of these organizations are equipped to place foreign students or visitors with families in their area for two- or three-day stays, although this is not necessarily their major function. These organizations should not be confused with accommodations bureaus; they are simply groups of people who wish to further international understanding and feel that one way to do this is to offer hospitality and program assistance to visitors from abroad. They are usually staffed by volunteers who give their time because they believe in what they are doing, and their help and hospitality should never be abused. Some community organizations can arrange home hospitality only for people who are visiting the U.S. as part of a prearranged program. Most of the ones we list below are willing to offer their sponsored services to unsponsored visitors. Understandably, all these organizations require advance notice of one week to one month to allow time to contact the host family and make arrangements.

In order to arrange a home visit with one of these groups in a specific state, write to the address listed here giving basic information about yourself, your interests, and your background. Even if you are not planning a home visit, you can feel free to consult these organizations for general information on the area. Most are anxious to help you and many have 24-hour answering services so they can provide assistance in emergencies.

You may want to write to the NCIV and ask for a copy of its pamphlet *Where to Phone*, which provides a complete listing of the phone numbers of NCIV members who are willing to assist international visitors, whether or not they are sent by a national programming agency. NCIV's address: Meridian House, 1630 Crescent Place NW, Washington, D.C. 20009.

ALABAMA: Birmingham Council for International Visitors, Suite 300, Commerce Center, 2027 First Ave. N., Birmingham, AL 35203. Telephone: 205/252-9825. Will provide homestay and home hospitality for sponsored visitors with ten-day advance notice. Open 8:30 a.m. to 5 p.m., Monday to Friday.

ARIZONA: World Affairs Council of Phoenix, Inc., 401 North 1st St., Ramada Inn Downtown, Room 233, Phoenix, AZ 85004. Telephone: 602/254-3345. Does professional and social programming for international visitors; provides home visits and overnight stays for visitors and hosts with common interests Open 9:30 a.m. to 12:30 p.m. during the week.

CALIFORNIA: International Visitor's Center, 312 Sutter St., Room 402, San Francisco, CA 94108. Telephone: 415/986-1388. Open 9 a.m. to 5 p.m., Monday to Friday. Provides home hospitality in the form of dinner invitations on four-day notice.

COLORADO: International Hospitality Center of the Colorado Division, UNA, USA-UNESCO, 980 Grant St., Denver, CO 80203. Telephone: 303/832-4234. Open 10 a.m. to 4 p.m., Monday to Friday. Arranges home visits and homestays with one month's notice. Drop-in visitors can pick up tourist information.

Institute of International Education, 700 Broadway, Suite 112, Denver, CO 80203. Telephone: 303/837-0788. Open 8:30 a.m. to 4:30 p.m., Monday to Friday. Brochures, maps, and general information about Denver for drop-ins.

With one month's notice and an adequate description of the students, will arrange a two- or three-day homestay. Student must also give exact date and time of arrival and departure.

CONNECTICUT: World Affairs Center, Inc., 1380 Asylum Ave., Hartford, CT 06105. Telephone: 203/236-4331. Office open or answering service Monday to Friday, 9:30 a.m. to 4 p.m. With adequate notice, home hospitality is available in addition to professional contacts and reservations for low-cost lodging.

DISTRICT OF COLUMBIA: Foreign Student Service Council, 1623 Belmont St. NW, Washington, D.C. 20009. Telephone: 202/232-4979. Open 9 a.m. to 5 p.m., Monday to Friday. Homestays of up to three nights may be arranged for international university students with host families or individuals in the area. At least two weeks' advance notice must be given. Send name, age, school, studies, nationality, date, time, and means of arrival in Washington, and address where you can be reached prior to your visit there. A $2-per-person registration fee, payable by check or money order, is required for this service. International Student Identity Cards are available, as well as advice on low-cost accommodation and sightseeing tours. Similar homestays can be arranged for national graduate students pursuing specific and advanced research. Three weeks' advance notice is necessary.

International Visitors Information Service, 801 19th St. NW, Washington, D.C. 20006. Telephone: 202/872-8747. Open 9 a.m. to 5 p.m., Monday to Friday. Provides bilingual tourist information and 24-hour telephone language assistance.

FLORIDA: Council for International Visitors of Greater Miami, Inc., 607 Olympia Building, 174 East Flagler St., Miami, FL 33131. Telephone: 305/379-4610 or 305/379-4615. Open Monday to Friday, 9 a.m. to 5 p.m. No homestays for unsponsored visitors, but "we never deny a welcome to foreign visitors. We welcome their inquiries, will assist by giving local orientation and in general make these students comfortable in our community."

INDIANA: Council for International Visitors, 8753 Washington Blvd. East Dr., Indianapolis, IN 46240. Telephone: 317/846-6806. If enough advance notice is given, a three-day homestay is possible. Overnight stays, sightseeing, and information would be more easily available. Some documentation would be required from the visitor.

MICHIGAN: International Visitors Council, 100 Renaissance Center, Suite 1405, Detroit, MI 48243. Telephone: 313/259-2680. Open 9 a.m. to 5 p.m. weekdays. Help with sightseeing information, maps, etc. No home hospitality for unsponsored visitors.

World Affairs Council of Western Michigan, 143 Bostwick NE, Grand Rapids, MI 49503. Telephone: 616/458-9535. Open Monday to Friday, 9 a.m. to 5 p.m. "Some of our members have expressed an interest in acting as host families for short-term visits by foreign guests. We could also arrange visits to local colleges and places of business."

NEW MEXICO: Council on International Relations, 100 East San Francisco,

P.O. Box 1223 La Fonda Hotel, Sante Fe, NM 87504. Telephone: 505/982-4931. Open 9 a.m. to noon weekdays; in summer, hours vary. Many members are willing to serve as host families for foreign travelers. "We ask for a donation of $9 per person per night, part of which goes to the host family, part to our office." Plenty of advance notice is requested.

NEW YORK STATE: The International Center of Syracuse, 500 South Warren St., Hotel Syracuse, Syracuse, NY 13202. Telephone: 315/471-0252 or 471-1222. Open 9 a.m. to 3 p.m., Monday to Friday; you may leave a message at other times. They can no longer provide home visits but will gladly give information.

OHIO: International Visitors Center, 600 Vine St., Suite 630, Cincinnati, OH 45202. Telephone: 513/241-7384. Open 9 a.m. to 3:30 p.m. weekdays. Although no home hospitality is available for unsponsored visitors, they'll help students with sightseeing information, maps, etc.

OKLAHOMA: International Visitors Council, Oklahoma Chamber of Commerce, No. 1 Santa Fe Plaza, Oklahoma City, OK 73102. Telephone: 405/278-8900. Open 9 a.m. to 4:30 p.m. Will provide bed and breakfast and some sightseeing help, but they need advance notice.

OREGON: World Affairs Council of Oregon, 1912 Southwest Sixth Ave., Room 252, Portland, OR 97201. Telephone: 503/229-3049. Will recommend places to stay. Open 9 a.m. to 5 p.m. weekdays.

PENNSYLVANIA: Pittsburgh Council for International Visitors, 139 University Pl., 263 Thackery Hall, Pittsburgh, PA 15260. Telephone: 412/682-7929. Open 9 a.m. to 5 p.m., Monday to Friday. They are able to provide information about the city and make reservations for visiting foreign students.

International Visitors of Philadelphia, Civic Center Museum, 34th St. and Civic Center Blvd., Philadelphia, PA 19104. Telephone: 215/823-7261. Open weekdays from 9 a.m. to 5 p.m. Offers 24-hour language assistance in an emergency (call 215/879-5248).

RHODE ISLAND: Council for International Visitors, 40 Dearborn St., Newport, RI 02840. Telephone: 401/846-0222. Open Monday through Friday, 9 a.m. to 5 p.m. Provides general information and maps.

TENNESSEE: Center for International Education, University of Tennessee at Knoxville, 201 Alumni Hall, Knoxville, TN 37996. Telephone: 615/974-3177. Basic information and general assistance.

Tennessee Valley Authority, 400 West Summit Hill Dr., East Tower Plaza, EPB-24, Knoxville, TN 37902. Telephone: 615/632-3974. Open 8 a.m. to 4:45 p.m. "General orientation to include visit to a project."

TEXAS: El Paso Tourist Information Center, 5 Civic Center Plaza, El Paso, TX 79987. Telephone: 915/534-0500 (ext. 32). "We have a volunteer on duty Monday to Friday from 9 a.m. to 4 p.m. to provide tourist information for foreign visitors, particularly students, and are also able to provide occasional home hospitality of varying types dependent on the amount of prior notification, i.e., after-dinner hospitality, supper, and sometimes an overnight stay" (at a cost of $6 per night for unsponsored visitors).

UTAH: International Visitors—Utah Council West in Hotel Utah, Salt Lake City, UT 84111. Telephone: 801/532-4747. Open 8 a.m. to 4 p.m., Monday to Friday. Usually able to provide a meal in a member's home and someone to take a visitor sightseeing; always happy to provide information on the area and make suggestions about what to do and see.

Study in the U.S.

The Institute of International Education (IIE), 809 United Nations Plaza, New York, NY 10017, publishes a book that can help you plan your study in the U.S. *English Language and Orientation Programs in the United States* ($15.95) is a directory of intensive and nonintensive English-language and orientation programs offered to foreign students admitted to U.S. postsecondary institutions. A new edition is planned for 1986.

The College Board, 888 Seventh Ave., New York, NY 10106 publishes two useful booklets: *Financial Planning for Study in the United States* and *Entering Higher Education in the U.S.*

Basic Survival Tips

This is the section that is meant to prepare you for some of the basic facts of life in the U.S.

THE TELEPHONE: Telephone numbers all over the U.S. have ten digits, e.g., 212/661-1414. The first three digits are called the "area code," and the last seven digits are the number of the home or office you are calling.

A *local* call is one placed to a number within the same town as the telephone from which you are calling. The cost ranges from 10¢ to 30¢ and will be posted at the top of the telephone. Generally, the procedure when dialing a local call is to insert the money and dial the last seven digits of the number. On some phones, you may be instructed to dial first and pay when someone answers.

When dialing a *long-distance* call, have plenty of change on hand. To call someone in another town within the same area code, dial "1" and the seven-digit number. To call someone in another state or another area code, dial "1" first and the area code and then the seven-digit number. The operator will answer first and tell you how much money to insert before she/he connects you. This amount will allow you to talk for three minutes and then the operator will interrupt you for more money. If you are using a private telephone, keep in mind that long-distance calls are discounted 35% from 5 p.m. to 11 p.m. and 60% from 11 p.m. to 8 a.m. weekdays, all day on Saturday, and until 5 p.m. on Sunday.

You may place a *person-to-person* call if you are not sure whether the person you are calling will be there. You will be charged only if the person you ask for is there, but the rates for these calls are higher. If the person you are calling is willing to pay for the call, you can place a *collect* call. When placing a person-to-person or collect call, dial "0" and the area code and then the seven-digit number and tell the operator what call you are making.

If you need assistance, you can dial the operator or "0" (zero, not the letter "oh") and when the operator answers you will get your money back.

There are two types of telephone directories: the general directory or white pages, which lists alphabetically the telephone numbers and addresses for individuals and businesses, and the Yellow Pages, which classifies businesses alphabetically by type, listing together all bookstores, all cleaners, etc. In smaller cities or towns, the white and Yellow Pages will be combined into one book, with the Yellow Pages at the back.

If you do not have access to telephone books, you can get a telephone number from the operator. For a number in the local area, dial 411. For a number within the same area code, dial 555-1212, and for one in another area code, dial "1" and the area code and then 555-1212. The operator will first ask "what city" and then the person's name.

TELEGRAMS: Telegrams are usually sent via Western Union, a privately owned company. The number of Western Union offices has diminished tremendously in the past few years. Telegrams are generally sent by telephone—check the telephone book under Western Union for the number to call. The price of a telegram depends on the number of words and where it is going. On telegrams sent overseas you are charged for the number of words in the address and for your signature, but not on telegrams sent within the U.S. A night letter, which is transmitted at night when the telegraph lines are less busy, is usually cheaper than a regular telegram; ask the Western Union operator for details.

You can also telegraph money to a stranded friend if necessary. Bring cash or a money order (they won't take checks), and for a fee—depending on where it is going—the money will be transferred to your needy friend.

MAIL: You can mail packages or letters at any of the post offices located throughout the cities and towns of the U.S. or, if you prefer, you can drop your stamped letters into a mailbox (they're located on many street corners and say "U.S. Mail" on them). Post offices are generally open from 8 a.m. to 5 p.m., Monday through Friday, and from 8 a.m. to noon on Saturday. Stamps may be purchased from a post office or a vending machine in stationery, drug, or variety stores. If possible, avoid using the machines since stamps cost more that way.

Aerograms are the cheapest and most efficient way to send letters abroad. You can buy them at any post office.

The following postage rates are in effect at press time:

U.S.A., Canada, Mexico

postcard (first class and airmail)	14¢
letter (first class and airmail)	22¢ per ounce

Overseas

aerogram	36¢
airmail letter	44¢ per half ounce
airmail postcard	33¢
surface postcard	25¢

When mailing a heavy letter or package, you must have it weighed at the post office. It's wise, too, to insure anything of value that you mail.

If you don't have a friend who can hold mail for you while you are traveling in the U.S., you can have mail addressed to you in care of General Delivery in any city of the U.S. The mail will be held at the main post office of that city for 30 days and will be returned to the sender if unclaimed by that time. To pick up mail sent to General Delivery, you will need to show official identification—your passport will do. Or if you'd like, you can have your friend write to you (as long as it's marked clearly) in care of CIEE Student Mail Service, New York Student Center, William Sloane House, 356 West 34th St., New York, NY 10001.

MONEY AND BANKS: Ours is a decimal system based on the dollar, which contains 100 cents. There are six coins; a penny or 1¢, a nickel or 5¢, a dime or 10¢, a quarter or 25¢, a half dollar or 50¢, and a dollar coin. As for paper money, the dollar bill is the most common denomination. There also are $2 bills (rare), and $5, $10, $20, $50, $100, $500, and higher bills.

You can check the exchange rate between your own currency and U.S. currency in any commercial U.S. bank or American Express office.

To protect yourself against loss or theft of money, you would be wise to buy travelers checks, which can be used just like cash. They usually cost one cent for every dollar's worth purchased.

Banks are usually open from 9 a.m. to 3 p.m., Monday through Friday. Some have evening hours on certain weeknights, but these vary from bank to bank. Banks are always closed on the following national holidays, many of which fall on Monday as a result of legislation:

New Year's Day	January 1
Washington's Birthday	Monday closest to February 22
Memorial Day	Monday closest to May 30
Fourth of July	July 4 (How could it be any other date?)
Labor Day	First Monday in September
Columbus Day	Monday closest to October 12
Veterans Day	Fourth Monday in October or November 11
Thanksgiving Day	Fourth Thursday in November
Christmas Day	December 25

TIPPING: You are generally expected to tip waiters and waitresses, taxi drivers, porters, hairdressers, and sometimes doormen. You do not have to tip the usher at the theater. Porters should get 50¢ per bag if they carry your bags to your room, waiters and waitresses 20% of the bill, hairdressers approximately 20% of the bill, and taxi drivers the same.

A good way to save money is to avoid situations where you are expected to tip; carry your own bags, have a friend cut your hair, and eat in a self-service cafeteria.

DRINKING: More and more states are passing legislation requiring that you be 21 years old to be served in a bar or buy liquor from a liquor store; in others you may be 18 or 19. If you look as if you are under the drinking age, you should carry proof of your age if you intend to drink. There are all kinds of bars in the larger U.S. cities—bars for single people, bars for literary people, bars for gay people, bars for businessmen. Bars are good places to meet people, but puritan ethics die hard, and a girl alone just won't feel comfortable in many U.S. bars.

DRUGS: If you are going to get involved with the youth culture of the U.S. at all, you will probably come into contact with drugs. However, the whole drug thing is nowhere near as evident now as it was several years ago. At some point in your travels you may be offered marijuana or whatever happens to be in fashion and in supply at the time. In some places people will approach you right out in the street and you will be surprised at how open drug dealing seems to be. Remember that possession of any narcotic—and marijuana is included—is against the law, and penalties can be severe. Besides the legal problems involved in narcotics usage, it is possible that drugs sold on the streets may be impure and may very well contain lethal ingredients.

MEDICAL ADVICE: Medical care in the U.S. is incredibly expensive. You must be aware of the fact that a visit to a doctor for a physical examination can cost $100 and that having a tooth extracted can cost as much. Hospitals charge as much as $300 per day per room—and that doesn't even include the doctor's fee, the high cost of medication, etc. *All this makes medical insurance a must.* Be sure to arrange for this in advance of your trip.

In case of emergency, you can get medical help, an ambulance, or the police by dialing "0" (zero) for Operator or 911. In some communities there are free clinics that will attend to your needs as best they can, but they are usually limited by lack of funds and lack of staff so you can't count on them as a substitute for adequate insurance. To find out about free medical services, check the local underground papers or call the help lines listed in each state section.

CHAPTER 4

State by State

This chapter is divided alphabetically into states and further into cities within each state. Each state section begins with a map of the state, indicating the locations of cities listed in the section. It would be of no help to you to know that there is a place to spend the night somewhere if you have no idea how close or far away from it you are. Each state section begins with some general, totally subjective commentary on the state, a list of some special events in the state that might be fun to see, a comment on the laws and attitudes about hitchhiking in the state, and the address of the state tourist office.

After the introductory material, the state is divided alphabetically into cities. We have further divided the city listings into the following subheadings: Tourist Information, Help, On Campus, Accommodations, and Camping. Not all cities have all subheadings; although we put in all the information we were able to uncover, for some cities we have prepared special, more detailed sections. In general, the city listings will include: places to stay, places to eat, things to do and see, how to get around, where to shop, etc. For the other cities and towns listed, you will find some or all of the following information:

● **Tourist Information:** Indicates the address of the city tourist office; this is given only for large cities that can send you lots of glossy, slick brochures on their own territories. Use these information offices freely; beneath the public-relations exterior you'll usually find some helpful information and useful maps.

● **Help:** Here we list the telephone numbers of hotlines and crisis centers that can assist you in an emergency. Some are phone services; others are drop-in centers. Travelers Aid offices are also listed. See Chapter 2 for a description of how they can help you.

● **On Campus:** This section tells you where to go on a particular campus to meet students, get information, find a good, cheap meal, or just enjoy yourself. We had the cooperation of a lot of people on a lot of campuses throughout the U.S. in getting information for the on-campus sections and are grateful for it all.

● **Accommodations:** These are the places to stay in each city or town. A variety of accommodations facilities are included, many of which offer various kinds of discounts and/or have access (for the handicapped) facilities. They are all described in Chapter 2.

● **Camping:** This heading is self-explanatory; it indicates the National Park Service campgrounds that are open to individual travelers.

Every once in a while you'll see a listing called "camping and accommodations"—this refers to campgrounds that have cabins to rent as well as tent space.

Now you are ready to use this book in the way it is meant to be used—to help you have fun, stay relatively comfortable, and get the most out of your travels in the U.S.

Alabama

Things are definitely looking up. In the first edition we complained that Alabama, with very few low-cost accommodations, made a discouraging beginning to a basically optimistic book. Since then, the Alabama listings have grown considerably. We're also delighted to pass on some good news about traveling in Alabama, and in the South in general. "No more *Easy Rider* image, please," said a friend at the University of Alabama. "Things have changed a great deal since the early '60s, and although we are stereotyped as intolerant and conservative . . . people are very tolerant and congenial to outsiders, and especially those who come to our area to visit and learn more about us."

One of the cities that you will want to visit is Birmingham, with its mansions and landmarks reminiscent of the Old South, including the Arlington Antebellum Home and Gardens. In Montgomery, the first capital of the Confederacy, you can visit the Capitol building and the W.A. Gayle Space Transit Planetarium. For space and rocket buffs we recommend a visit to Huntsville, the home of the Alabama Space and Rocket Center, where you can take a simulated ride to the moon. South Alabama is the closest to the image of the Deep South as it's been portrayed in movies, books, and songs. Here the Spanish moss hangs heavy and azaleas bloom. In Bayou LaBatre the city hall is a shrimp boat; Mobile has its own Mardi Gras, in fact, the original Mardi Gras; and near Mobile, in Theodore, is the quintessential reminder of the Deep South—Bellingrath Gardens and Home. A good introduction to Alabama is the booklet, simply titled *Alabama,* available free from the Alabama Bureau of Tourism and Travel (address below).

For those who enjoy bed-and-breakfast accommodations, the Brunton House Bed and Breakfast of Alabama is the first to appear in the state. The cost is $24 single, $29 double. Write to the Brunton House B&B of Alabama, 112 College Ave., Scottsboro, AL 35768, for details, or call 205/259-1298.

Some Special Events: Mardi Gras in Mobile (March); Mobile Azalea Festival (March-April); Birmingham Arts Festival (April-May); Eufaula Pilgrimage in Eufaula (April); Spirit of America Festival (July); Alabama Shakespeare Festival in Montgomery (December-August); National Shrimp Festival in Gulf Shores, and National Peanut Festival in Dothan (October); and Christmas on the River in Demopolis (December).

Hitching: Officially, according to the Alabama Department of Public Safety, hitchhiking is permissible except on Interstate routes; "on other streets and highways people may not stand in the roadway for the purpose of soliciting a ride." "Roadway," in Alabama, means the paved portion of the highway. Our campus sources seem to agree that hitching "is acceptable, but not really recommended." A sergeant of the Highway Patrol says: "There are no good roads for hitchhiking. Don't hitchhike!"

Tourist Information: Alabama Bureau of Tourism and Travel, 532 South Perry St., Montgomery, AL 36104. Telephone: toll free 800/252-2262 out of state; or 800/392-8096 in Alabama.

Attalla

Accommodation: Red Carpet Inn, √, 507 Cherry St., 35954. Telephone: 205/538-9925. $28 to $35 for one; $34 to $41 for two in one bed; $38 to $45 for two in two beds.

Bessemer

Accommodation: Motel 6, 1000 Shiloh Lane, 35020. Telephone: 205/424-8939. $17.95 for one; $21.95 for two; $2 for each additional person.

Birmingham

Tourist Information: Greater Birmingham Convention and Visitors Bureau, 2027 First Ave. N., 300 Commerce Ctr., 35203. Telephone: 205/252-9825.

Help: Travelers Aid, 3600 Eighth Ave. S., Room 110-E, 35222. Telephone: 205/322-5426.

● Crisis Center, 205/323-7777.

Accommodations: YWCA, Ⓢ, 309 North 23rd St., 35203. Telephone: 205/322-9922. Women only. $10 per night transient. $5 linen charge and $2 key deposit required. Weekly rates vary. Only 2½ blocks from bus station. Advance reservations suggested.

● Ranch House Motel, 2127 Seventh Ave. S., 35233. Telephone: 205/322-0691. $22 for one; $24 for two in one bed; $26 for two in two beds.

● Days Inn, 1011 9th Ave. SW, 35023. Telephone: 205/424-9690. $25 for one; $30 for two.

● Econo Lodge, √, 103 Green Springs Hwy., 35209. Telephone: 205/942-1263. $24.50 for one; $29.50 for two in one bed; $33.50 for two in two beds.

● Econo Lodge, √, 2224 Fifth Ave. N., 35203. Telephone: 205/324-6688. $28.95 for one; $36.95 for two in one bed; $39.95 for two in two beds.

● Scottish Inn, ♿, 624 Decatur Hwy., 35068. Telephone: 205/849-7431. $18.88 for one; $20.88 for two in one bed; $22.88 for two in two beds.

● Red Roof Inn, ♿, I-65 & Oxmore Rd., 35209. Telephone: 205/942-

9414. $25.95 for one; $30.95 for two in one bed; $32.95 for two in two beds; $34.95 for three or four in two beds.

Cullman

Accommodation: Days Inn, 🖔, I-65 & U.S. 278, 1841 4th St. SW, 35055. Telephone: 205/739-3800. $27 for one; $32 for two.

Dothan

Accommodations: Days Inn, 🖔, 2841 Ross Clark Circle SW, P.O. Drawer 1890, 36301. Telephone: 205/793-2550. $28.88 for one; $32.88 for two.
● Econo Lodge, V 🖔, 2901 Ross Clark Circle SW, 36301. Telephone: 205/793-5200. $29 for one; $33 for two in one or two beds.
● Quality Inn, V 🖔, 3591 Ross Clark Circle, 36303. Telephone: 205/793-9090. $29 to $30 for one; $33 to $34 for two.

Florence

Accommodations: Master Hosts Inn, V, 1241 Florence Blvd., 35630. Telephone: 205/764-5421. $25 to $29 single; $35 to $39 double.
● TraveLodge, 🖔, 402 East Tennessee, 35630. Telephone: 205/766-5350. $20 for one; $24 for two in one bed; $28 for two in two beds.

Mobile

Tourist Information: Convention and Visitors Department, Mobile Area Chamber of Commerce, 451 Government St., P.O. Box 2187, 36652. Telephone: 205/433-6951.
Help: Travelers Aid, Family Counseling Center, 6 South Florida St., 36606. Telephone: 205/471-3466.
● Helpline, 205/342-3333.
Accommodations: Motel 6, 1520 Matzenger Dr., 36605. Telephone: 205/471-3088. See Bessemer listing for rates.
● Regal 8 Inn, 400 South Beltline Hwy. 36608. Telephone: 205/343-8448. $23.88 for one; $28.88 for two in one bed; $33.88 for two in two beds.
● Red Carpet Inn, V, 1061 Government St., 36604. Telephone: 205/438-4653. $22.95 for one; $25.95 for two in one bed; $28.95 for two in two beds. Higher rates apply during special events.
● Red Roof Inn, 🖔, I-65 & Dauphin St. Telephone: 205/476-2004. $23.95 for one; $28.95 for two in one bed; $30.95 for two in two beds; $32.95 for three or four in two beds.
● Red Roof Inn, 🖔, I-10 & U.S. 90, Exit 15B. Telephone: 205/666-1044. See above listing for rates.

Montgomery

Help: Travelers Aid, Family Guidance Center, 925 Forest Ave., 36106. Telephone: 205/265-0568 or 262-6669.

Accommodations: Motel 6, 1051 Eastern Bypass, 36117. Telephone: 205/277-0600. See Bessemer listing for rates.
- Scottish Inn, Rte. 1, Box 264, U.S. 231 S., 36064. Telephone: 205/288-1501. $25 for one; $27 for two in one bed; $32 for two in two beds.
- Days Inn, I-65 & 1150 West South Blvd., 36105. Telephone: 205/281-8000. $29.88 to $33.88 for one; $33.88 to $38.88 for two.
- Days Inn, Hope Hull Exit, I-65 & U.S. 31, 36043. Telephone: 205/281-7151. Airport courtesy van. $24 to $28 for one; $28 to $31 for two.
- Econo Lodge, √, 2625 Zelda Rd., 36107. Telephone: 205/269-9611. $30 for one; $34 for two in one bed; $36 for two in two beds.
- TraveLodge, √ ⓑ, 1550 Federal Dr., 36109. Telephone: 205/265-0586. $24 for one; $31 for two in one bed; $33 for two in two beds.

Northport

Accommodation: Budget Host—Travel Inn Motel, √ ⓑ, 3020 Hwy. 82 W., 35476. Telephone: 205/339-3900. $21 to $24 for one; $24 to $28 for two in one bed; $28 to $30 for two in two beds; $3 for each additional person.

Opelika

Accommodations: Motel 6, 1015 Columbus Pkwy., 36801. Telephone: 205/749-0850. See Bessemer listing for rates.
- Red Carpet Inn, I-85 & U.S. 280 & U.S. 431, Exit 62, 36801. Telephone: 205/749-6154. $17.95 to $19.95 for one; $20.95 to $22.95 for two.

Oxford/Anniston

Accommodation: Days Inn, I-20 & Alabama 21, P.O. Drawer F, 36203. Telephone: 205/831-5463. $27 for one; $31 for two.

Phenix City

Accommodation: Econo Lodge, ⓑ, 1506 Phenix City Bypass, 36867. Telephone: 205/298-5255. $23.95 for one; $26.95 for two in one bed; $30.95 for two in two beds. Higher rates apply on weekends and during special events.

Scottsboro

Accommodations: Brunton House, 112 College Ave., 35768. Telephone: 205/259-1298. $19 single; $24 double. "Bed and breakfast in a 60-year-old late Victorian home."
- Econo Lodge, √ ⓑ, 1106 John T. Reid Pkwy. Telephone: 205/574-1212. $29 for one; $33 for two in one bed; $35 for two in two beds.

Selma

Accommodation: Cahawba Inn, ⑤∨★, 2006 Highland Ave. W., 36701. Telephone: 205/875-9231. $22.88 single; $24.88 double; $28.88 triple; $35 quad.

Troy

Help: Help-a-Crisis, Emergency Telephone Counseling, c/o East Central Mental Health/Mental Retardation, Inc. Telephone: 205/566-6022.

Accommodation: Econo Lodge, ∨♿, 1031 U.S. Hwy. #231, 36081. Telephone: 205/566-4960. $29 for one; $33 for two in one bed; $35 for two in two beds.

Tuscaloosa (See University, below)

Help: University Switchboard, 205/566-3000.

Accommodations: Days Inn, ♿, 3600 McFarland Blvd., 35405. Telephone: 205/556-2010. $27 to $32 for one; $32 to $37 for two.

● Motel 6, 4700 McFarland Blvd., 35405. Telephone: 205/349-4896. See Bessemer listing for rates.

University

On Campus: According to a friend at the University of Alabama, which is (appropriately enough) in University (University is a Zip Code; the main campus is actually in Tuscaloosa), the school is "lovely and has a vibrant history." She told us that the Continuing Education Center on campus is open day and night and "offers housing for those on quasi-university business—that is, looking at the campus." If you're feeling lonely, go to the Side Track, Solomon's, or Time Out. Three good restaurants are Ruby Tuesday's and the Landing, a steakhouse, both on McFarland Blvd., and Storyville, right off campus. You'll easily find someone to talk to at any of these.

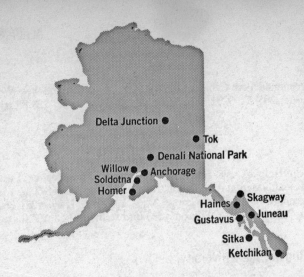

Delta Junction
Tok
Denali National Park
Willow
Soldotna Anchorage
Homer
Haines Skagway
Gustavus Juneau
Sitka
Ketchikan

Alaska

Alaska is huge. Superimposed on a map of the U.S. it stretches from Seattle to Miami. And in all this space there are only 403,000 Alaskans.

Not many Americans get as far as Alaska, but one adventurous New York student told us about her two months in the town of Homer. "From Seattle I took a ferry that takes three days. I traveled fifth class and brought my own food. I got off at Haines and hitchhiked to Homer on the Alaskan Highway. There are quite a few kids in Homer and if you settle down for more than a week you're no longer considered a stranger. Alaska is a rather expensive place—food especially."

The Alaska Division of Tourism gave us some good news and some bad news about low-cost accommodation in their state. The good news: The U.S. Forest Service rents 135 cabins in the Tongass National Forest for $5 a night. The bad news: Most of the cabins can be reached only after a plane ride in a single-engine De Havilland Beaver.

For all the tourist information you could want on Alaska, we recommend three publications:

One is *The Milepost*, published by the people who publish *Alaska Magazine*, Box 4EEE, Anchorage, AK 99509. The book is a mile-by-mile log of the northern highways, including the Alaskan Highway, with maps and specifics for everyone from fishermen to rock hounds. Copies are $12.95 plus $1 postage and handling. Another is *Alaska Travel Guide*, published by Alaska Travel Guide, P.O. Box 15889, Salt Lake City, UT 84115. It costs $9.95 plus $2 postage and contains information on hotels, motels, history, national parks, etc. It is released annually in April and includes a free copy of the Rand McNally map of the Alaska-Yukon. The third recommended guide is *The Inside Passage Traveler*, by Ellen Searby, Windham Bay Press, P.O. Box 1332, Juneau, AK 99802. It costs $7.95; add $1.50 for airmail postage. Written by a one time member of a ferry crew, this book tells you how to make the most of the ferry system and how to find your way from the dock around the town. It includes information on air, rail, and road connections, hotels, sights to see, etc.

Adventuring in Alaska, by Peggy Wayburn is a Sierra Club book which explores wild and urban Alaska. Copies are $10.95 and are available from Sierra Club Books, 530 Bash St., San Francisco, CA 94108.

Another book about Alaska, not a travel guide but a wonderful introduction nonetheless, is John McPhee's *Coming into the Country.*

Some Special Events: World championships including dog-sled races and snowmobile races (February); Fairbanks Winter Carnival (March); Break-Up Drama Festival in Dawson City, Yukon-Canada (May); Gold Rush Days in Valdez, an annual festival which celebrates the good old days of gold discovery in Alaska (August); Alaska Festival of Music in Anchorage (September); and Alaska Day in Sitka (October).

"Originally I was hitching from Houston to San Francisco to New York but then found a job with the U.S. Forest Service as a technician in Ketchikan and I'm still here."

Hitching: Hitchhiking is not legal here. To quote the law (from a large book of highway regulations), "a person may not stand on a roadway in a manner that will distract a driver's attention for the purpose of soliciting a ride, employment, business, or contributions from the occupant of a vehicle."

A German student who hitched in Alaska told us: "Hitchhiking in Alaska between Anchorage and Fairbanks is good. Hitchhiking into Alaska is a question of luck. On my way back my driver went straight from Delta Junction, Alaska, to Montana."

Tourist Information: Alaska Division of Tourism, Pouch E, Juneau, AK 99811. Ask for *Alaska and Canada's Yukon Vacation Planner,* the official State of Alaska vacation booklet.

N.B. If you're going to Alaska, it might be wise to contact Stay with a Friend, Box 173-3605 Arctic Blvd., Anchorage (telephone: 907/274-6445). A member of the American Bed and Breakfast Association, this service has homes for you to stay in in Palmer, Hatcher Pass, Kenai, Homer, Seldovia, and Nome. According to the owner of the service, this is a chance to "get your information over a cup of coffee when you need it and enjoy privacy when you want it." Stay With a Friend also publishes a guide to Alaska called the *Cheechako Guide*—it costs $3.

Anchorage

Help: Youth & Family Crisis Line, 907/279-0552.

Accommodation: Anchorage Youth Hostel (AYH), P.O. Box 4-1226, 99509. Telephone: 907/276-3635. $8 for AYH members.

On Campus: The bulletin board in the student center of Anchorage Community College is a good source of information on rides and accommodations. For an inexpensive meal, go to Lucy Cuddy Center at the college; for conversation, go to the Cauldron Restaurant.

Delta Junction

Accommodation: Delta Youth Hostel (AYH), Box 971, 99737. Telephone: 907/895-4627. Open Memorial Day to Labor Day. $4.25 for AYH members. Camping is available for $2 per night. Sleeping bags required.

Denali National Park

Camping: Denali National Park and Preserve, P.O. Box 9, 99755. Telephone: 907/683-2294. Walking distance from bus and train station. Seven campgrounds with 225 sites. $8 per campsite per night at Riley Creek, Savage River, Teklanika River, and Wonder Lake. There is no fee at Morino, Sanctuary River, and Igloo Creek.

Gustavus

Camping: Glacier Bay National Park, 99826. Telephone: 907/697-2232. Wilderness camping from June 1 to August 31. Access by plane or boat only from Juneau.

Haines

Accommodation: Bear Creek Camp and Hostel (AYH-SA), P.O. Box 334, Lot 36A, Small Tract Rd., 99827. Telephone: 907/766-2259. Open year-round except for month of January. $6.75 summer, $7.75 winter for AYH members. Advance reservations suggested May 1 through October 1. "Our hostel has small rustic cabins sleeping 4 to 6 people. No electricity. Wood stoves supply heat (wood costs $2.50 a bundle, which is enough for one night). The hostel is open during the day for rest and relaxation."

Homer

Accommodation: Homer Youth Hostel (AYH), 243 West Pioneer Ave., 99603. Telephone: 907/235-6711. $7.50 for AYH members. Advance reservations suggested.

Juneau

Accommodation: Juneau Youth Hostel (AYH-SA), 614 Harris St., 99802. Telephone: 907/586-9559. Open year-round. $6.50 for AYH members.

Ketchikan

Accommodation: Ketchikan Youth Hostel (AYH-SA), 400 Main St., P.O. Box 8515, 99901. Telephone: 907/225-3319. Access to Ketchikan is by Alaska State Ferry or Alaska Airlines. Open Memorial Day to Labor Day. $4 for AYH members. Sleeping bags required.

Sitka

Accommodation: Sitka Youth Hostel (AYH-SA), Sitka United Methodist Church, 303 Kimsham St., 99835. Telephone: 907/747-6332. Sitka can be reached by Alaska Ferry or Alaska Airlines. Open June 1 to September 1. $3 for AYH members. Sleeping bags required.

Skagway

Camping: Klondike Gold Rush National Historical Park, P.O. Box 517, 99840. Telephone: 907/983-2921. Camping from May through September at primitive campsites.

Soldotna

Accommodation: Soldotna International Youth Hostel (AYH), 444 Riverview Ave., 99669. Telephone: 907/262-4369. $7.50 for AYH members. Advance reservations necessary November to March.

Tok

Accommodation: Tok Youth Hostel (AYH-SA), c/o General Delivery, 99780. Open May 15 to September 15. $5 for AYH members.

Willow

Accommodation: Susitna Youth Hostel (AYH), Star Rte. A, Box 650, 99688. Telephone: 907/733-2775. Closed May to October. $2 for cabin; $5 for dorm bed for AYH members.

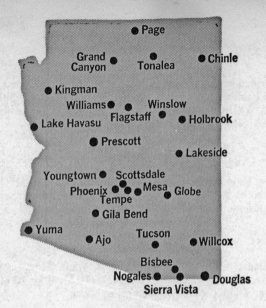

Arizona

Lots of the people who go to Arizona are there to see the Grand Canyon, a multicolored fissure 217 miles long, 3 to 17 miles wide, about a mile deep, and very probably one of the most spectacular natural sights you will ever see. Since the largest crowds come during the summer, visit if you can in the spring or fall when you can enjoy the relative solitude.

The state's southern half—with its largest cities, Tucson and Phoenix—has the kind of warm, dry air that makes people feel good, so many go to the area's resorts to do just that. Arizona may well be one of the most beautiful of our states. Besides the Grand Canyon, the attractions of the state include Hoover Dam, Lake Mead, 15 national monuments, several Indian villages and reservations, the Painted Desert, and the Petrified Forest.

Some Special Events: Cinco de Mayo Celebrations in Prescott, Phoenix, Tucson, Scottsdale, Winslow, Willcox, and Mesa (May); Shakespeare Under the Stars in Tucson, and Annual Old Timers' Picnic in Casa Grande (June); Navajo Pow Wow and Rodeo in Window Rock, and Homemakers' Ice Cream Social in Pine (July); Turkey Creek Rodeo in White River, and Navajo County Fair in Holbrook (August); Annual Gold Camp Days in Oatman, and Cochise County Fair in Douglas (September).

Hitching: The Arizona Department of Public Safety wrote to say that "Frankly, while it is not strictly illegal, we attempt to discourage hitchhiking on our highways. Also, while it is legal for the hitchhiker to solicit a ride if he is not standing on the roadway, a motorist who stops to pick up a hitchhiker is often in violation of the law, blocking traffic behind him." Pedestrians are not allowed on the Interstate highway system.

Tourist Information: Office of Tourism, 1480 East Bethany Home Rd., Phoenix, AZ 85012. Telephone: 602/255-3618.

Ajo

Camping: Organ Pipe Cactus National Monument, Rte. 1, P.O. Box 100, 85321. Telephone: 602/387-6849. Open year round. $6 per campsite per night; 32' RV limit.

Bisbee

Accommodation: YWCA, ♿ (limited), 26 Howell Ave., 85603. Telephone: 602/432-3542. $12 single; $18 double. "In the middle of a picturesque mining town with European buildings and charm."

Chinle

Camping: Canyon de Chelly National Monument, P.O. Box 588, 86503. Camping at Cottonwood, one mile south of entrance, year-round.

Douglas

Accommodations: Motel 6, 111 16th St., 85607. Telephone: 602/364-5461. $17.95 for one; $21.95 for two; $2 for each additional person.
● TraveLodge, √ ♿, 1030 19th St., 85607. Telephone: 602/364-8434. $27 for one; $29 for two in one bed; $35 for two in two beds.

Flagstaff

Help: Crisis Intervention, 519 North Leroux St., 86001. Telephone: 602/774-2727.

Accommodations: Weatherford Hotel (AYH), 23 North Leroux St., 86001. Telephone: 602/774-2731. Open year-round. Near bus and train station. Restaurant on premises. Dormitory-style: $7.60 for AYH members; $3 charge for introductory pass for members. $15 to $18 for hotel rooms. Call and check on availability of rooms. Recommended by a reader who told us that "the Weatherford is named in Zane Grey's book *Call of the Canyon* and is very special."
● Motel 6, 2010 East Butler Ave., 86001. Telephone: 602/774-3533. See Douglas listing for rates.
● TraveLodge, √, 1030 19th St., 85607. Telephone: 602/364-8434. $28 for one; $30 for two in one bed; $35 for two in two beds.
● Friendship Autolodge Inn, 1313 South Milton, 86001. Telephone: 602/774-6621. $28 to $30 for one or two in one bed; $34 to $36 for two in two beds.
● Regal 8 Inn, 2440 East Lucky Lane, 86001. Telephone: 602/774-8756. $26.88 for one; $31.88 for two in one bed; $36.88 for two in two beds.
● Budget Host—Frontier Motel, 1700 East Santa Fe Ave., 86001. Telephone: 602/774-8993. $20 to $25 for one; $28 to $48 for two and three.

● Allstar Inn, 🅰, 2500 Lucky Lane, 86001. Telephone: 602/779-6184. $25.95 single; $28.95 double; $31.95 triple; $34.95 quad.

Camping: Sunset Crater National Monument, Rte. 3, Box 149, 86001. Telephone: 602/527-7042. Camping at Bonito Campground (opposite Visitor Center). Open April 15 to November 15. $5 per campsite per night.

Gila Bend

Accommodation: Friendship Sea Shell Inn, 515 Pima St., 85337. Telephone: 602/683-2294. $17 for one; $23 for two in one bed; $26 for two in two beds.

Globe

Accommodation: Friendship Ember Inn, 1105 North Broad St., 85501. Telephone: 602/425-5736. $18 to $20 for one; $24 to $28 for two in one bed; $28 to $32 for two in two beds.

Grand Canyon

Accommodation: Grand Canyon International Hostel (AYH-SA), 76 Tonto St., P.O. Box 270, 86023. Telephone: 602/638-9018. $7.25 per person. Advance reservations of one month necessary. "Built in 1925, this was the first ranger dormitory in the Park."

Camping: Grand Canyon National Park, P.O. Box 129, 86023. Telephone: 602/638-7888. Three tenting campgrounds; one open year-round, two closed during winter months. $6. Reservations for three hike-in campgrounds available at above address, c/o Superintendent.

Holbrook

Accommodations: Motel 6, 2514 Navajo Blvd., 86025. Telephone: 602/524-2666. See Douglas listing for rates.

● Arizona Rancho Motor Lodge (AYH-SA), corner of Apache Dr. and 57 Tovar St., P.O. Box 698, 86025. Telephone: 602/524-6770. Near bus station. $6 summer, $7 winter for AYH members.

Kingman

Accommodations: Motel 6, 3270 East Andy Devine Ave., 86401. Telephone: 602/757-4777. See Douglas listing for rates.

● Pony Soldier Motel, 2939 East Andy Devine Ave., 86401. Telephone: 602/753-5586. $17 to $26 for one; $21 to $28 for two in one bed; $24 to $30 for two in two beds.

● Friendship Space Age Inn, 1967 East Andy Devine Ave., 86401. Telephone: 602/753-5511. $18 to $24 for one; $22 to $26 for two in one bed; $28 to $32 for two in two beds.

● TraveLodge, √ 🅰, 1001 Andy Devine Ave., 86401. Telephone: 602/753-5541. $29 for one; $37 for two in one bed; $39 for two in two beds.

- Allstar Inn, 3351 West Andy Devine Ave., 86401. Telephone: 602/757-7151. $23.95 to $25.95 for one; $3 for each additional person.
- Econo Lodge, √, 3100 East Andy Devine Ave., 86401. Telephone: 602/753-6262. $16.99 for one; $20.99 for two in one or two beds.

Lake Havasu

Accommodations: E-Z 8 Motel, 41 Acoma Blvd., 86403. Telephone: 602/855-4023. $17.88 for one; $20.88 for two in one bed; $25.88 for three or four in two beds.
- Shakespeare Inn, 2190 McCulloch Blvd., 86403. Telephone: 602/855-4157. $22.95 for one; $25.95 for two in one bed; $27.95 for two in two beds.

Lakeside

Accommodation: White Mountain Youth Hostel (AYH), Rte. 1, Box 210K, 85929. Telephone: 602/367-4036. $4.25 for AYH members. Advance reservations necessary.

Mesa

Accommodations: Allstar Inn, ♿, 630 West Main St., 85201. Telephone: 602/969-8111. See Kingman listing for rates.
- Motel 6, 336 West Hampton Ave., 85202. Telephone: 602/898-9467. See Douglas listing for rates.
- TraveLodge, √ ♿, 22 South Country Club Dr., 85202. Telephone: 602/964-5694. $27 for one; $30 for two in one bed; $34 for two in two beds.
- Sixpence Inn, 1511 South Country Club Dr., 85201. Telephone: 602/834-0066. $20 to $28 for up to four.

Nogales

Accommodation: Motel 6, 2210 Tucson Hwy., 85621. Telephone: 602/281-0703. See Douglas listing for rates.

Page

Camping: Glen Canyon National Recreation Area, P.O. Box 1507, 86040. Open year-round. $5 per campsite per night.

Phoenix

Wherever you go in Phoenix, you will be aware of the influence that Indian culture has had on its evolution.

The city that is now the capital of Arizona, which began as a small settlement on the banks of the Salt River, has become quite a popular tourist stop. One of the biggest attractions is the weather—one Phoenician promises "absolutely sunny skies more than 300 days of the year." The Phoenix and Valley of the Sun Convention and Visitors Bureau, 4455 East Camelback, Suite 146D,

Phoenix, AZ 85018 (tel. 602/952-8687), will be glad to send you information on their favorite city, including their *Valley of the Sun Visitors' Guide.* If you'd like more, you can get copies of the *Insiders' Guide,* by Boye de Mente (Phoenix Book Publishers, 6505 North 43rd Pl., Paradise Valley, AZ 85253; $3). Once you're in Phoenix, you'll want to check the *Phoenix Republic* and the *Gazette,* the local newspapers, and *New Times,* the "alternative" weekly publication.

Tempe, the location of Arizona State University, is not far from Phoenix and it has its own listing. There are some restaurants located in Tempe, though, that are listed here.

Getting There: From the airport, a taxi will cost about $5.50 to the downtown area. Airport limousine service costs $2.50 to downtown or $3 to Tempe, as long as there are other passengers; if not, it will cost $6. There's no airport bus service. The Continental Trailways terminal is at 433 East Washington (tel. 257-0257) and Greyhound's is nearby at 525 East Washington (tel. 248-4040). Amtrak is at 401 West Harrison (tel. 253-0121).

Getting Around: Once you're in the city, you can take a taxi for $2.05 for the first mile, $1.20 for each additional mile. Dial Yellow Cab Company (tel. 252-5071), and a taxi will come and get you. Since local bus service is very poor (no service after 7 p.m. or on Sunday), you may want to rent a car. To do this, check Budget Rent-a-Car, 219 South 24th St. (tel. 249-6124). To rent a Ford Escort or similar car costs $17.95 per day, with 100 miles included, 17¢ per mile after that, and $134 for the week with 1000 free miles. At Ajax Rental (tel. 244-9889), a Ford Escort costs $26.90 per day with unlimited mileage and $139 per week with 1050 free miles. If you insist on using the bus, you can get a printed schedule and route map from the Phoenix Transit Corporation's information booth, First St. and Adams.

Help: Valley of the Sun Convention Bureau, 602/952-8687.
- Doctors' Referral Service, 602/252-6094.
- Visitor Hot Line (what's happening in Phoenix), 602/840-4636.

Accommodations: Valley of the Sun International Hostel (AYH), 1026 North 9th St., 85006. Telephone: 602/262-9439. $7 for AYH members; $10 for nonmembers.
- YMCA, 🏷, 350 North First Ave., 85003. Telephone: 602/253-6181. Near the Civic Plaza. Men and women. This hotel is well kept and centrally located. $11 single; $32 per person double. Weekly rate: $55 single. $5 refundable key deposit.
- Sand's Hotel, 3320 East Van Buren St., 85008. Telephone: 602/275-7848. Call for limousine service from the bus station or airport. Near the Phoenix Zoo. $26 to $30 single; $30 to $36 double.
- Motel 6, 2323 East Van Buren St., 85006. Telephone: 602/267-1397. See Douglas listing for rates.
- Motel 6, 5315 East Van Buren St., 85008. Telephone: 602/267-8553. See Douglas listing for rates.
- Motel 6, 2330 West Bell Rd., 85023. Telephone: 602/863-1666. See Douglas listing for rates.
- Friendship Inn 6 Motel, 201 North Seventh Ave., 85007. Telephone: 602/254-6521. $18 to $25 for one; $20 to $34 for two in one bed; $25 to $42 for two in two beds.
- Allstar Inn, 🏷, 214 South 24th St., 85034. Telephone: 602/244-1155. See Flagstaff listing for rates.

- Allstar Inn, ♿, 4130 North Black Canyon Hwy., 85017. Telephone: 602/277-5501. See Flagstaff listing for rates.
- Budget Host—Del Ward's Motor Hotel, 3037 East Van Buren St., 85008. Telephone: 602/273-1601. Courtesy car available upon request. $20 to $26 for one; $20 to $28 for two in one bed; $24 to $30 for two in two beds. Two heated pools, spa.
- Days Inn, I-17 and 2735 West Sweetwater, 85029. Telephone: 602/993-7200. $25 to $32 for one; $29 to $36 for two.
- Sixpence Inn, 1624 North Black Canyon Hwy., 85009. Telephone: 602/269-6281. $20 to $28 for up to four.
- Regal 8 Inn, 2548 West Indian School Rd., 85017. Telephone: 602/248-8881. $22.88 to $23.88 for one; $28.88 to $29.88 for two in one bed; $32.88 to $33.88 for two in two beds.
- Regal 8 Inn, 8152 North Black Canyon Hwy., 85021. Telephone: 602/995-7892. $23.88 to $24.88 for one; $27.88 to $28.88 for two in one bed; $33.88 to $34.88 for two in two beds.
- Econo Lodge, √, 2247 East Van Buren St., 85006. Telephone: 602/244-9341. $26 for one; $28 for two in one bed; $30 for two in two beds.
- Chalet Motor Inn, 938 East Van Buren St., 85006. Telephone: 602/252-3447. $24 to $28 single; $26 to $30 double; $32 to $36 triple; $35 to $40 quad.
- TraveLodge, √, 2900 East Van Buren St., 85008. Telephone: 602/275-7651. Airport transportation available. $28 for one; $30 for two in one bed; $34 for two in two beds.
- TraveLodge, √ ♿, 965 East Van Buren St., 85006. Telephone: 602/252-6823. $29 for one; $32 for two in one bed; $36 for two in two beds.

Where to Eat: Earthen Joy, 36 East 5th St., Tempe. Telephone: 968-4710. Open 11:30 a.m. to 10 p.m. From fresh carrot juice to delicious cheesecake, sandwiches on 14-grain bread, and salads. Every evening there's a special entree. The setting is informal and eating is done surrounded by bright colored pillows, an aquarium, and lots of plants.

- Monti's Casa Vieja, 3 West 1st St., Tempe. Telephone: 967-7594. Open 11:30 a.m. to midnight. "One of the best Western steakhouses. The atmosphere is rustic; prices are reasonable."
- La Casita Café, 1021 South Central Ave. Telephone: 262-9322. Open from 11 a.m. daily except Tuesday. This Mexican cafe serves all the dishes you'd expect and has been a landmark for decades.
- Willy and Guillermo's, 1120 East Apache Blvd., Tempe and 5600 North Central Ave. Mexican food in a comfortable setting.
- China Doll, 3336 North Seventh Ave. Telephone: 264-0538. Good and reasonably priced Chinese food with dim sum on weekends.
- Café Casino, 4824 North 24th St. Telephone: 955-3430. Near the Arizona Biltmore Hotel, a marvelous example of Frank Lloyd Wright's architecture. This French-style cafeteria-boulangerie is modestly priced.
- Thai Lahna, 3738 East Indian School Rd. Telephone: 955-4658. A small, comfortable place for good Thai food.
- Lucille's Soul Food, 1202 East Washington. Telephone: 262-9835. Not far from Heritage Square, downtown. Reasonably priced chicken, ribs, and other Southern goodies.
- Pinnacle Peak Patio, 10426 East Pinnacle Peak Rd., Scottsdale. This is about 12 miles north of Phoenix and is a popular tourist attraction. Steak and

beans in a Western atmosphere; entertainment includes a melodrama where it's perfectly acceptable—in fact encouraged—to hiss and boo the players.

• Mr. Lucky's, 3660 North Grand. Telephone: 246-0686. Located at the State Fair Grounds, this large nightclub offers buffet-style ribs, ham, pot roast—$2.99 for all you can eat!

• Melany's Pizza, 1135 East Glendale. Telephone: 277-5322. This family-run restaurant serves spaghetti, gyros, dolmades, and pizza. No atmosphere but the food is fine.

• Ham's, 3302 North 24th St. Telephone: 956-9911. Homestyle cooking—dishes like pork chops and meat loaf at low, low prices in this neighborhood tavern. Two people can eat for about $10 and that includes a couple of beers besides.

• Po' Folks, 3301 West Indian School Rd. Telephone: 263-0910. Country cooking—things like chicken and dumplings, red beans and rice for less than $5. Popular so expect a crowd.

• Pa Clark's, 3317 West Van Buren. Telephone: 272-0851. "The best Philly-style steak sandwiches in Phoenix. Nothing to look at, but a real bargain."

What to See: Heard Museum of Anthropology and Primitive Art, 22 East Monte Vista Rd. Telephone: 252-8848. Open Monday to Saturday from 10 a.m. to 5 p.m.; Sunday from 1 to 5 p.m. One of the West's finest collections of Indian arts and crafts, prehistoric and modern, from all over the world. Every year, during the first week in March, the museum sponsors an Indian arts-and-crafts fair with dancing, food, and craft demonstrations. It's a very popular fair, indeed.

• Pueblo Grande Museum and Ruins, 4619 East Washington. Telephone: 275-3452. Open 9 a.m. to 5 p.m. weekdays, 1 to 5 p.m. Sunday; closed Saturday. Where the Hohokam Indians, the earliest inhabitants of Phoenix lived. There's a museum with artifacts to visit, too.

• Japanese Flower Gardens. Along Baseline Rd. there's a two-mile stretch of flower farms. The peak of their beauty is from February to April. Citrus fruits and dates are sold at roadside stands along the way.

• South Mountain Park. The entrance to this municipal park is at the end of South Central Ave. Within the park's boundaries are petroglyphs, picnic areas, and superb views of the city.

• Desert Botanical Gardens, 5800 East Van Buren St. 3000 acres of Papago Park devoted to desert plants from all over the world.

• Phoenix Zoo, 5800 East Van Buren St. Telephone: 273-7771.

• Taliesin West, East Shea Blvd. Telephone: 948-6670. Once the winter home and school of Frank Lloyd Wright, located in an area of virgin desert. Now open for visitors October to May, 10 a.m. to 4 p.m. daily; noon to 4 p.m. Sunday.

• Paolo Soleri Cosanti Foundation, 6433 Doubletree Rd. Telephone: 948-6145. Workshop for innovative architectural designers where you can see models of future city projects.

• Gila River Indian Arts and Crafts Center. Approximately 20 miles southeast of Phoenix, just off the Phoenix-Tucson Freeway. Museum and a crafts shop that features pottery, baskets, and jewelry made by various Arizona tribes. Open 9 a.m. to 5:30 p.m.

• For the sports-minded, check on the sporting events while you're in town. The possibilities include the Phoenix Suns (basketball), PGA golf tournaments, horse and dog racing, Indy and stock car races, major league baseball spring training, the Phoenix Giants (AAA minor league baseball), Phoenix Outlaws (USFL football team).

At Night: Boojum Tree Restaurant, Second Ave. and Osborn. Telephone: 248-0222. Open until 1 a.m. A place to go to hear well-known jazz recording stars.

● El Bandido, 1617 East Thomas Rd. Open until 1 a.m. Good dancing and very good Mexican food.

● Timothy's, 6335 North 16th St. Jazz gets started at 8 or 9 p.m. "The best local jazz in the valley."

● Phoenix Little Theater, 25 East Coronado. Telephone: 254-2151. Curtain rises at 8:30 p.m. at this, the oldest continuously operated community theater in the U.S.

● Valley Art Theater, 509 Mill Ave., Tempe. Telephone: 967-6664. If you're in the mood for a film, you'll find either a classic, a foreign film, an underground movie, or a current new feature at this theater near the university.

● Phoenix Symphony, Symphony Hall, 225 East Adams. Telephone: 264-4754. The season runs from October through May at Symphony Hall in the new Civic Plaza.

● Arizona Ballet Theater, Symphony Hall, or Scottsdale Center for the Arts. Telephone: 258-2354. This resident professional dance company performs classical and modern ballet world premieres and classic revivals.

● Mr. Lucky's, 3660 Grand Ave. Upstairs you can dance to country and western, downstairs to rock bands.

Shopping: Changing Hands, 9 East 5th St., Tempe. The emphasis here is on "humanistic self-growth books"—everything from solar energy to vegetarian cooking.

● Al's Family Bookstore, 1454 East Van Buren St. For a wide range of books, new and secondhand.

● Pushoff Books, Ltd., 3106 East Camelback Rd. A good general bookstore.

● Guidon Books, 7117 East Main, Scottsdale. Specializing in Arizona lore and Western Americana.

● Circles, 800 North Central Ave. An impressive variety of records.

● Odyssey Records and Tapes, 1127 East Camelback Rd. Jazz, rock, and classical music for sale.

● Holubar, 232 West Southern, Tempe, and 3925 East Indian School Rd. Good for camping equipment and outdoor gear.

● Arizona Hiking Shack, 11645 North Cave Creek Rd. Another source of camping equipment.

Prescott

Accommodations: Motel 6, 1111 East Sheldon St., 86301. Telephone: 602/778-0200. See Douglas listing for rates.

● Country Manor Motel, 420 East Hwy. 70, 85546. Telephone: 602/428-2451. $26 for one; $28 for two in one bed; $31 for two in two beds.

Scottsdale

Accommodations: Motel 6, 6848 East Camelback Rd., 85251. Telephone: 602/947-7321. Pool and Jacuzzi. See Douglas listing for rates.

● Allstar Inn, 🖰, 1612 North Scottsdale Rd., 85281. Telephone: 602/945-9506. See Kingman listing for rates.

Sierra Vista

Accommodation: Motel 6, 1551 East Fry Blvd., 85635. Telephone: 602/459-0666. See Douglas listing for rates.

Tempe

On Campus: Arizona State University is in Tempe and on the ASU campus is an auditorium designed by Frank Lloyd Wright; nearby is Wright's Taliesin West. To meet ASU students, go to Minderbinder's Restaurant, 715 South Hayden Rd., where you can get a huge hamburger "with fixings" for a moderate price. For inexpensive Mexican food, try the Dash Inn, 731 East Apache, and for good food in a crowded atmosphere, Monti's La Casa Vieja, 3 West 1st St.

Note: See Phoenix listing for restaurants, etc., in Tempe, which is a suburb of that city.

Accommodations: Allstar Inn, 🖰, 513 West Broadway, 85282. Telephone: 602/967-8696. See Kingman listing for rates.

● Regal 8 Inn, 1720 South Priest Dr., 85281. Telephone: 602/968-4401. $21.88 to $24.88 for one; $26.88 to $29.88 for two in one bed; $31.88 to $34.88 for two in two beds.

● TraveLodge, √, 902 Mill Ave., 85281. Telephone: 602/966-7221. $23 for one; $25 for two in one bed; $27 for two in two beds.

Tonalea

Camping: Navajo National Monument, 86044. Telephone: 602/672-2366. Open May 15 to October 15. Reservations must be made with the superintendent for trips to Keet Steel Ruin. No charge.

Tucson

Help: Tucson Travelers Aid Society, 40 West Veterans Blvd., 85713. Telephone: 602/622-8900.

● Information and Referral, 602/881-1794.

● Free Clinic Switchboard, 602/573-0096.

Accommodations: YMCA, 516 North Fifth Ave., 85705. Telephone: 602/624-7471. Men only. $12 per night plus $5 refundable key and towel deposit. Weekly rate: $70.

● Hotel Congress, 311 East Congress St., 85702. Telephone: 602/622-8848. Near bus and train station. $18 single; $20 double; $23 triple. Advance reservations suggested in winter.

● Days Inn, 🖰, I-10 at Palo Verde and Irvington (Exit 264), 3700 East Irvington, 85714. Telephone: 602/571-1400. June 1 to September 30: $29.50 to $33.50 for one; $33.50 to $37.50 for two. October 1 to November 30: $33 to $37 for one; $37 to $41 for two.

● Regal 8 Inn, 1222 South Freeway, 85713. Telephone: 602/624-2516. $21.88

to $24.88 for one; $26.88 to $29.88 for two in one bed; $31.88 to $34.88 for two in two beds.

● Budget Host—Sunny 6 Motel, √ (July to September), 1248 North Stone, 85705. Telephone: 602/622-6446. $22 for one; $24 for two in one bed; $28 for two in two beds; $35 to $45 for three. Higher rates apply during special events.

● Motel 6, 960 South Freeway, 85745. Telephone: 602/624-6345. See Douglas listing for rates.

● Motel 6, 1031 East Benson Hwy., 85714. Telephone: 602/884-8107. See Douglas listing for rates.

● Lamp Post Motel, Ⓢ ★, 5451 East 30th St. at Craycroft, 85711. Telephone: 602/795-0483. $27 single; $29 double; $32 family.

● E-Z 8 Motel, 720 West 29th St., 85713. Telephone: 602/624-8291. $16.88 for one; $19.88 for two in one bed; $23.88 for three or four in two beds.

● E-Z 8 Motel, 1007 South Freeway, 85745. Telephone: 602/624-9843. See above listing for rates.

● Allstar Inn, 🚻, 1388 West Grant Rd., 85745. Telephone: 602/622-4784. See Kingman listing for rates.

● Allstar Inn, 🚻, 755 East Benson Hwy., 85713. Telephone: 602/622-4614. See Kingman listing for rates.

● TraveLodge, √ 🚻, 1136 North Stone Ave., 85705. Telephone: 602/622-6714. $21 for one; $25 for two in one bed; $29 for two in two beds.

● TraveLodge, √, 222 South Freeway, 85705. Telephone: 602/791-7511. $21 for one; $23 for two in one bed; $28 for two in two beds.

● Friendship Franciscan Inn, 1165 North Stone Ave., 85705. Telephone: 602/622-7763. $28 to $33 for one or two in one bed; $33 to $38 for two in two beds.

● Imperial 400 Motor Inn, 1248 North Stone Ave., 85705. Telephone: 602/622-6446. $21 to $24 for one; $26 to $30 for two in one bed; $28 to $32 for two in two beds.

● Old Pueblo Youth Hostel (AYH), 411 East 9th St., 85705. Telephone: 602/791-0583. Near bus station. $6 summer, $7 winter for AYH members. Sleeping bag required.

Willcox

Accommodations: Motel 6, 921 North Bisbee, 85643. Telephone: 602/384-2168. See Douglas listing for rates.

● Budget Host—Sunny 6 Motel, √ (July and August only), 340 South Haskell Ave., 85643. Telephone: 602/384-2237. $15.95 for one; $19.95 for two in one bed; $24 for two in two beds. Higher rates apply during special events.

● TraveLodge, √, 590 South Haskell Ave., 85643. Telephone: 602/384-2266. $21 for one; $25 for two in one bed; $28 for two in two beds.

Williams

Accommodations: Budget Host-Patio Motel, 128 East Bill Williams Ave., 86046. Telephone: 602/635-4791. $14 to $26 for one; $18 to $28 for two in one bed; $20 to $30 for two in two beds. Gateway to Grand Canyon. Higher rates apply April 15 to September 15.

● Friendship Belaire Inn, 620 West Bill Williams Ave. on Hwy. 66, 86046.

Telephone: 602/635-4415. May 1 to September 30: $28 for one; $32 for two in one bed; $34 for two in two beds. October 1 to April 3: $18 for one; $22 for two in one bed; $28 for two in two beds.

● Williams International Youth Hostel (AYH), Grand Canyon Hotel Annex, 134 West Bill Williams Ave., 86046. Telephone: 602/635-9908. Near bus station. $6.75 summer, $7.25 winter for AYH members.

Winslow

Accommodations: Royal Motel, √ (10%), 1221 East 3rd St., 86047. Telephone: 602/289-4631. $16 for one; $18 for two in one bed; $22 for two in two beds.

● Motel 6, 725 West 3rd St., 86047. Telephone: 602/289-3903. See Douglas listings for rates.

● Friendship Inn of Winslow, Hwy. I-40 at Northpark Dr., 86047. Telephone: 602/289-4687. $18 to $28 for one; $22 to $32 for two in one bed; $26 to $36 for two in two beds.

● Budget Host—Mayfair Motel, √ ($1, off season only), 1925 West Hwy. 66, 86047. Telephone: 602/289-5445. Courtesy car available. $16 to $22 for one; $18 to $25 for two in one bed; $21 to $30 for two in two beds.

Youngtown

Accommodation: Motel 6, 11133 Grand Ave., 85363. Telephone: 602/933-0541. See Douglas listing for rates.

Yuma

Accommodations: Motel 6, 2730 Fourth Ave., 85364. Telephone: 602/344-3550. See Douglas listing for rates.

● Motel 6, 1640 Arizona Ave., 85634. Telephone: 602/782-2873. See Douglas listing for rates.

● TraveLodge, √, 2050 Fourth Ave., Box 4608, 85364. Telephone: 602/782-3831. $27 for one; $30 for two in one bed; $35 for two in two beds.

● Friendship Torch Lite Lodge, 2501 Fourth Ave., 85364. Telephone: 602/344-1600. $19 to $55 for one; $20 to $55 for two in one bed; $25 to $59 for two in two beds. Lower rates apply from April 10 to December 25.

● Friendship Pikes Motel, 200 Fourth Ave., 85364. Telephone: 602/783-3391. $22 to $30 for one; $24 to $36 for two in one bed; $26 to $39 for two in two beds.

● Sixpence Inn, 1445 East 16th St., 85365. Telephone: 602/782-9521. $20 to $28 for up to four.

Arkansas

Here's one of the strangest stories ever told—how Arkansas got its name. It started with the name of a tribe called Quapaw which the Algonquins pronounced Oo-ka-na-sa. Marquette wrote it as Arkansoa, La Salle as Arkensa, De Tonti as Arkancas, and La Harpe as Arkansas. In 1881 the legislature had to appoint a committee to decide on the right pronunciation of the last syllable. May we suggest a similar committee, preferably of Algonquins, to decide how Quanaw could possibly have been pronounced Oo-ka-na-sa?

Probably the biggest tourist attraction in Arkansas is the world-famous Hot Springs National Park, with 47 thermal springs that are collected and distributed to bathhouses throughout the park and the city of Hot Springs. Fifty-four miles from Hot Springs is Little Rock, the capital of Arkansas, where you can visit the Arkansas Art Center, Arkansas Territorial Restoration, and the first State Capitol, the Old State House. In Arkansas there are a number of state parks that offer housekeeping cottages for rent within the boundaries of each park. The overnight rental for two people is well within this book's budget and the settings are quite beautiful. For information, write to the Arkansas Department of Parks and Tourism at the address below.

A guide to the area that we can recommend is *The Greatest Ozarks Guidebook,* available from Greatest Graphics, Inc., P.O. Box 4467 G.S., Springfield, MO 65804 ($7.95 postpaid).

If you're going to spend any time at all in Arkansas, you'll want a set of the Arkansas Department of Parks and Tourism's Special Rate Coupons. They include reductions in the admission prices to the Eureka Springs Passion Play and other tourist attractions and discounts at some hotels and restaurants throughout the state. Just write to the address below for your set.

Some Special Events: Annual Jonquil Festival in Old Washington State Park, and the Annual Pioneer Craft Festival in Rison (March); Annual Arkansas Folk Festival in Mountain View (April); Arkansas Heritage Week held statewide, Annual Historic Helena Tour in Helena, and Riverfest in Little Rock (May); Annual Hope Watermelon Festival in Hope (August); Annual Prairie Grove Battlefield Clothesline Arts and Crafts Fair in Prairie Grove (Labor Day weekend); Ozarks Art and Craft Festival on War Eagle Mills Farm, Arkansas Oktoberfest in Hot Springs, and Annual Family Harvest Festival at Ozark Folk Center (October); and the Annual Ozark Christmas at Ozark Folk Center (December).

Hitching: Hitching is prohibited on the roadways, and Arkansas law interprets roadway as including the shoulder, so if you hitch, stay off the road and the shoulder. A few words on the subject from friends in Arkansas: "Hitchhiking is difficult on the smaller country roads" and "much depends on the prevailing mood of any police officer you may meet." The assistant commander of the Highway Patrol advises any hitchhiker to be sure to carry "adequate and proper identification."

Tourist Information: Arkansas Department of Parks and Tourism, One Capitol Mall, Little Rock, AR 72201. Telephone: toll free 800/643-8383 out of state; 800/482-8999 in state.

Bald Knob

Accommodation: Scottish Inn, 703 Hwy. Blvd., P.O. Box 126, 72101. Telephone: 501/724-3204. July 1 to September 2: $25 for one; $28 for two in one bed; $31 for two in two beds. September 3 to December 31: $22.95 for one; $26 for two in one bed; $29 for two in two beds.

Benton

Accommodation: Budget Host—Troutt Motel, √ ($1), I-30 West (Exit 116), 72015. Telephone: 501/778-3633. $17 to $20 for one; $20 to $25 for two in one bed; $23 to $28 for two in two beds.

Blytheville

Accommodation: Days Inn, 🔣, I-55 & Ark. 18E, P.O. Box 1342, 72315. Telephone: 501/763-1241. $28.88 to $29.88 for one; $33.88 to $34.88 for two.

Clarksville

Accommodation: Econo Lodge, √, I-40, Exit 58, P.O. Box 755, 72830. Telephone: 501/754-2990. $23.95 for one; $25.95 for two in one bed; $27.95 for two in two beds.

Conway

Accommodations: Town House Motel, √, Hwy. 65B, 1200 Harkrider,

72032. Telephone: 501/329-3846. $25 for one; $31 for two in one bed; $35 for two in two beds.

- Motel 6, Hwy. 65B & I-40, 72032. Telephone: 501/327-6571. $17.95 for one; $21.95 for two; $2 for each additional person.

Dardanelle

Accommodation and Camping: Mt. Nebo State Park, Rte. 3, P.O. Box 374, 72834. Telephone: 501/229-3655. Besides camping in the park ($4 to $5 per campsite), there are 14 natural stone cabins "with breathtaking views of the valley 1800 feet below," with all-electric kitchens, full baths, a bedroom, living room, and fireplace. Cabins rent for $35 to $40 per night for two persons; $3 extra for each additional person up to six. You must be 18 or over to rent a cabin. Reservations are recommended two to three months in advance for cabins.

Eureka Springs

Tourist Information: Eureka Springs Chamber of Commerce, P.O. Box 551, 72632. Telephone: 501/253-8737.

Eureka Springs has been described as "the most unique and beautiful small town in the country and the center of an Ozark back-to-the-land movement." There are lots of young people passing through the Ozarks and many staying and homesteading. While you're in the area, "see the mountains, trees, lakes, rivers, Victorian architecture, and native crafts. Listen to the bluegrass, canoe, bicycle, or hike." Be sure to stop at Bon Appetit, 63 Spring St., in the New Orleans Hotel. The food is natural and reasonable.

Accommodation: Budget Host—Country Holiday Motel, √ (March, April, September), 102 Kingshighway, 72632. Open February 25 to November 30. Telephone: 501/253-8863. $24 to $36 for one or two in one bed; $28 to $38 for two in two beds.

Fayetteville

Help: Information Desk, 401 Arkansas Union, University of Arkansas. Telephone: 501/575-2304.

On Campus: We get lots of good information from the people who work on the school newspaper at the University of Arkansas. From what we can tell, if you're going to be in Arkansas at all you should be sure to get to Fayetteville. The counterculture seems to be alive and well there. There's a Union building on Garland St. right in front of the library. In the Union you'll find the On-Campus Activities Office and the Information Center—the two best sources of information on what's going on in the community. The Student Government Office has a small job list and an off-campus housing directory that they might let you share.

When you get hungry, go to the Restaurant on the Corner, 248 West Dickson; King Pizza, 203 West Dickson; Bogey's Restaurant, 9 South School; or Hugo's, 25½ North Block. Check the local newspaper, *The Grapevine*, for information on what's happening.

"The Ozark food co-op in the Green Warehouse on Watson and West Sts. has a Community Bulletin Board as well as a wide variety of patrons who would be good sources of information for folks traveling through."

Accommodation: Town House and Sands Motel, 215-229 North College, Bus. 62 & 71, 72701. Telephone: 501/442-2313. Six blocks from University of Arkansas. Swimming pool. $18 for one; $20 for two in one bed; $22 for two in two beds. Higher rates apply during the three big football weekends in the fall.

Fort Smith

Accommodations: Continental Inn, 1421 North 11th St., 72901. Telephone: 501/785-1471. $18 for one; $20 for two in one bed; $28 for two in two beds.
● Regal 8 Inn, 1021 Garrison Ave., 72901. Telephone: 501/785-2611. $21.88 for one; $26.88 for two in one bed; $31.88 for two in two beds.
● Motel 6, 6001 Rogers Ave., 72901. Telephone: 501/452-1924. See Conway listing for rates.

Harrison

Camping: Buffalo National River, P.O. Box 1173, 72601. Telephone: 501/741-5443. Buffalo Point is open year-round. Canoe rentals. $7 per campsite per night for drive-ins; $4 for walk-ins.

Hope

Accommodations: Friendship Dean's Motor Lodge, Hwy. 29 & I-30, P.O. Box 930, 71801. Telephone: 501/777-4665. $19 to $22 for one; $24 to $26 for two in one bed; $26 to $28 for two in two beds.
● Red Carpet Inn, √, I-30 & Hwy. 4, 71801. Telephone: 501/777-9222. Airport courtesy car available. $30 for one; $34 for two in one bed; $36 for two in two beds.

Hot Springs

Tourist Information: Hot Springs Chamber of Commerce, P.O. Box 1500, 71901. Telephone: toll free 800/643-1570 out of state; 800/272-2081 in state.
Camping: Hot Springs National Park, P.O. Box 1860, 71902. Campsites at Gulpha Gorge, two miles east of Hot Springs. Open year round. $5 per campsite per night.

Jonesboro

Accommodation: Motel 6, 2300 South Caraway Rd., 72401. Telephone: 501/972-6000. See Conway listing for rates.

Little Rock

Tourist Information: Little Rock Bureau for Conventions and Visitors, Markham and Broadway, 72201. Telephone: 501/376-4781.

Accommodations: YMCA, 6th and Broadway, 72201. Telephone: 501/372-5421. Men only. Weekly rate: $40.

● Motel 6, 9525 Interstate 30, 72209. Telephone: 501/562-1914. See Conway listing for rates.

● Regal 8 Inn, 9709 Interstate 30, 72209. Telephone: 501/568-1200. See Fort Smith listing for rates.

● Acme Motel, 3301 West Roosevelt Rd., 72204. Telephone: 501/663-6361. $18.25 for one or two in one bed; $25 for two in two beds.

● Red Roof Inn, ♿, I-30 at Scott Hamilton Dr. Exit 134. Telephone: 501/562-2694. $23.95 for one; $28.95 for two in one bed; $30.95 for two in two beds; $32.95 for three or four in two beds.

● Hampton Inn, 500 West 29th St., 72114. Telephone: 501/771-2090. $27 to $32 single; $30 to $35 double; $32 to $37 triple; $34 to $39 quad.

● Imperial 400 Motor Inn, 322 East Capital Ave., 72202. Telephone: 501/376-3661. $23 to $27 for one; $27 to $31 for two in one bed; $30 to $34 for two in two beds.

Marion

Accommodation: Scottish Inn, I-55, Exit 10, 72364. Telephone: 501/732-1640 or 734-3186. $30 for one; $26.88 to $38 for two in one bed; $31.98 to $40 for two in two beds.

Morrilton

Accommodation: Friendship Pacesetter Inn, State Road, Box 9, 72110. $23 to $27 for one; $25 to $29 for two in one bed; $28 to $34 for two in two beds.

Mountain Home

Accommodation: Town & Country Motor Inn, 145 South Main St., 72653. Telephone: 501/425-9525. $26 for one; $28 for two in one bed; $30 for two in two beds.

North Little Rock

Accommodations: Days Inn, I-40 & Protho Jct. (Exit 157), 2508 Jacksonville Hwy., 72117. Telephone: 501/945-4167. $27 to $34 for one; $32 to $39 for two.

● Days Inn, I-40 & Ark. 107, 3100 North Main, 72114. Telephone: 501/758-8110. $27 to $34 for one; $32 to $39 for two.

Paragould

Accommodation: Sunset Motel, Ⓢ ★ √ ♿, 1509 West Kingshighway, 72450. Telephone: 501/236-7631. $16 single; $19 double; $22 triple; $25 quads. Advance reservations of one week necessary.

Pine Bluff

Accommodation: Comfort Inn, √ ♿, 210 North Blake St., 71601. Telephone: 501/534-7222. $30 for one; $34 to $38 for two.

Russellville

Accommodations: Merrick Motel, √, Hwy. 64 E., 1320 East Main St., 72801. Telephone: 501/968-6332. $24.95 for one or two in one bed; $27.95 for two in two beds.
● Motel 6, I-40 & County Rd., Rte. 6, Box 306, 72801. Telephone: 501/968-3666. See Conway listing for rates.
● Friendship Inn, Hwy. 64 E., 72807. Telephone: 501/968-7774. $21 to $24 for one; $25 to $30 for two in one bed; $28 to $36 for two in two beds.

Springdale

Accommodation: Scottish Inn, Hwy. 71 S., 72734. Telephone: 501/751-4874. $21 for one; $25 for two in one bed; $28 for two in two beds; $32 for three in three beds; $35 to $55 during special events.

Texarkana

Accommodation: Motel 6, 900 Realtor Ave., 75502. Telephone: 501/772-5490. See Conway listing for rates.

West Memphis

Accommodation: Scottish Inn, 2315 Hwy. I-55 & I-40, P.O. Box 1208, 72301. $28 to $34 for one or two in one bed; $34 to $38 for two in two beds.

California

Everyone wants to visit California. Ask any Easterner, or anyone from abroad, and they'll tell you their dreams about California. California is now as much myth as reality, but no one is making a mistake when they decide to go there. It's a complex, vibrant, and interesting piece of the U.S. and has a lot to offer any traveler. Because California is so beautifully situated between the Pacific Ocean and the mountains, visitors can sail, surf, swim, ski, or hike. Of course, there are Disneyland, Sea World, lots of zoos, and historical missions up and down the state, not to mention Hollywood and all that the glamour capital has to offer. California has television studios, some of the best shopping areas in the world, and a major university, the University of California, with nine campuses covering the entire state. California is the number one producer of agricultural products in the world and supplies most of the U.S. with its harvests. Of course, California is a leading wine-producing state, and some of the finest wines in the country—some might even say the world—come from the northern part of the state.

San Francisco is a jewel city, not to be missed. Los Angeles is another "must visit" place. The Huntington Library in San Marino, near Los Angeles, has a famous collection of paintings and illuminated manuscripts of great interest to anyone who's interested in art history.

Then there's the Getty Museum near Santa Monica and the Hearst Castle in San Simeon. The Carmel Valley, home of many fine artists and craftsmen, is a fascinating place to visit, and finally, Monterey, with its Cannery Row made famous by John Steinbeck, is a lovely city that should be on every visitor's itinerary.

While you're in California, stop at the offices of CIEE at 2511 Channing Way, Berkeley, CA 94704 (tel. 415/848-8604); 1093 Broxton Ave., Los Angeles 94108 (tel. 213/208-3551) and 312 Sutter St., San Diego, CA 94108 (tel. 415/421-3473). In addition to helping you find your way around California, they are a good source of information on low-cost travel all over the U.S. and the world.

"In California, I slept under the stars lots of times, on beaches or in the woods. On the coast there are lots of state parks where you can stay for almost nothing."

Some Special Events: Tournament of Roses Parade and Football Game in Pasadena, and the Winter Carnival in South Lake Tahoe (January); Chinese New Year Celebration in San Francisco (February); Steinbeck Birthday Celebration in Salinas, and San Luis Obispo Mardi Gras and Fiesta de la Golondrias (Return of the Swallows) in San Juan Capistrano (March); Renaissance Pleasure Faire in Agoura (April weekends); Dixieland Jazz Jubilee in Sacramento (May); Strawberry Festival in Los Gatos, and San Francisco Birthday Celebration (June); World's Biggest Salmon Barbecue in Fort Bragg, and County Fair in Sonoma (July); County Fairs in Stockton, Napa, Woodland, Ferndale, and San Jose (August); and Marin County (Blackpoint Forest) Renaissance Faire (weekends in August and September).

Hitching: Someone who returned from a trip cross-country had something to say about hitching in California, where it seems that hitching is a popular way to get around. He says that "hitching from San Francisco to Los Angeles can be done quickly if you use Interstate 5. Since there's nothing on the Interstate from Los Angeles to Oakland, you're pretty much assured of a ride all the way. But be prepared for a dull ride. If you aren't in a big hurry take U.S. 101, the coast road, instead. It may mean slow hitching, but it also means beautiful scenery and friendly rides. Going north from San Francisco you can choose Route 1, slow and beautiful; U.S. 101, which goes through wine and redwood country but is slow in summer because of all the other hitchhikers; or Interstate 5, for a fast ride north to Oregon or Washington."

A lieutenant of the California Highway Patrol, although anxious to point out the risks of hitching, did say that the best highways for hitching are Interstate 5 and U.S. 99 and 101 for north-south travel and Interstate 8, 10, 15, 40, and 80 for east-west routes. No hitchhiking is permitted on or along freeways, but it is allowed if you stay off the roadway, e.g., on the curb.

Tourist Information: California Office of Tourism, 1121 L St., Sacramento, CA 95814. Telephone: 916/322-1396. Offers an excellent visitor's map and other travel information.

N.B. A group that places people in private homes in San Francisco, Los Angeles, San Diego, and other locations in California on the West Coast, is Bed and Breakfast International, 151 Ardmore Rd., Kensington, CA 94707 (Kensington borders Berkeley). The cost of a double, with breakfast included, is $30 to $85 (students may request lower rates); the minimum stay is two nights. To obtain an application, write to the address above and enclose a stamped, self-addressed envelope.

Anaheim

Accommodations: Motel 6, 921 South Beach Blvd., 92804. Telephone: 714/827-9450. $17.95 for one; $21.95 for two; $2 for each additional person.
● Sixpence Inn, 2020 Via Burton, 92806. Telephone: 714/956-9690. $20 to $28 for up to four.
● Akua Motor Hotel, 1018 East Orangethorpe, 92801. Telephone: 714/871-2830. $30 to $36 for one; $32 to $38 for two in one bed; $34 to $42 for two in two beds.
● Friendship Sahara Inn, 845 South Beach Blvd., 92804. Telephone: 714/828-1030. $18 to $30 for one; $20 to $32 for two in one bed; $24 to $36 for two in two beds.
● Friendship Tropicana Inn, 1540 South Harbor Blvd., 92802. Telephone: 714/635-4082, toll free: 800/453-4511. $26 to $40 for one; $32 to $44 for two in one bed; $34 to $46 for two in two beds.

Arcadia

Accommodation: Motel 6, 225 Colorado Pl., 91006. Telephone: 818/445-2801. See Anaheim listing for rates.

Arcata

Help: Humboldt Open Door Clinic, 770 10th St., 95521. Telephone: 707/822-2957.
Accommodations: Jolly Giant Conference Center, Jolly Giant Commons, Humboldt State University, 95521. Telephone: 707/826-3451. Must be on specific HSU business or there for educational purposes. Summer only. $13 single; $18 double.
● Arcata Crew House Hostel, Ⓢ★, 1390 I St., 95521. Telephone: 707/822-9995. Open June 20 to September 20. $5.50 for AYH members and ISIC holders; $7.75 for nonmembers. "The hostel is an old Victorian house with some excellent redwood burlwork. It is homey and quiet." Bring your own linen.
● Motel 6, 4755 Valley West Blvd., 95521. Telephone: 707/822-1745. See Anaheim listing for rates.

Atascadero

Accommodation: Motel 6, 9400 El Camino Real, 93422. Telephone: 805/466-6606. See Anaheim listing for rates.

Bakersfield

Accommodations: Motel 6, 350 Oak St., 93304. Telephone: 805/327-5913. See Anaheim listing for rates.
● Motel 6, 5241 Olive Tree Ct., 93308. Telephone: 805/392-1028. See Anaheim listing for rates.

- Motel 6, 2727 White Lane, 93304. Telephone: 805/834-6411. See Anaheim listing for rates.
- Sixpence Inn, 8223 East Brundage Lane, 93307. Telephone: 805/366-7231. $20 to $28 for up to four.
- TraveLodge, √ 🕭, 525 Union Ave., 93307. Telephone: 805/324-4593. $23 for one; $28 for two in one bed; $34 for two in two beds.
- Allstar Inn, 1350 Easton Dr., 93309. Telephone: 805/327-1686. $23.95 to $25.95 for one; $3 for each additional person.
- Friendship Downtowner, 1301 Chester Ave., 93301. Telephone: 805/327-7122. $29 to $33 for one; $34 to $38 for two in one bed; $39 to $41 for two in two beds.
- E-Z 8 Motel, 2604 Pierce Rd., 93308. Telephone: 805/322-1901. $21.88 for one; $24.88 for two in one bed; $29.88 for three or four in two beds.
- E-Z 8 Motel, 5200 Olive Tree Ct., 93308. Telephone: 805/392-1511. See above listing for rates.

Baldwin Park

Accommodation: Sixpence Inn, 14510 Garvey Ave., 91706. Telephone: 818/960-5011. $20 to $28 for up to four.

Barstow

Accommodations: Motel 6, 31951 East Main St., 92311. Telephone: 619/256-8778. See Anaheim listing for rates.
- Imperial 400 Motor Inn, 1281 East Main St., 92311. Telephone: 619/256-6836. $30 to $32 for one; $30 to $34 for two in one bed; $34 to $38 for two in two beds.
- Allstar Inn, 150 Yucca Ave., 92311. Telephone: 619/256-1752. See Bakersfield listing for rates.

Beaumont

Accommodation: Budget Host—Golden West Motel, √, 625 East 5th St., 92223. Telephone: 714/845-2185. $26 to $30 for one; $29 to $33 for two in one bed; $33 to $37 for two in two beds.

Berkeley

On Campus: A branch of the University of California is here in this lively, diverse college town. "Everything passes by without comment in Berkeley—everything 'goes'". To meet students in the area, stop at Sufficient Grounds, Café Roma, Henry's, Manuela's, or The Hermosa.

Accommodations: International House, 🕭 (limited), University of California, 94720. Telephone: 415/642-9470. To stay you "must have affiliation with the University of California as registered students, guests of residents, scholars visiting the campus, etc." Open to temporary visitors in summer only. Minimum one-week stay. $206 single; $162 per person double. Includes 19 meals per week.

- YMCA, 2001 Allston Way, 94704. Telephone: 415/848-6800. Men only. $14 to $16 single.

Big Bear

Accommodations: Motel 6, 1200 Big Bear Blvd., P.O. Box M28-6, 92315. Telephone: 714/585-3996. Near Big Bear Lake. See Anaheim listing for rates.
- Singing Pines Lodge Hostel (AYH), 657 Modoc, P.O. Box 1082, 92315. Telephone: 714/866-2532. $6 summer, $7 winter for AYH members. Advance reservations suggested during the week, essential for weekends and during major holiday periods.

Bishop

Accommodation: Friendship Thunderbird, 190 West Pine St., 93514. Telephone: 619/873-4215. $26 to $30 for one; $30 to $34 for two in one bed; $34 to $40 for two in two beds.

Blythe

Accommodations: Motel 6, 500 West Donlon St., 92225. Telephone: 619/922-6661. See Anaheim listing for rates.
- E-Z 8 Motel, 900 West Rice St., 92225. Telephone: 619/922-9191. $18.88 for one; $21.88 for two in one bed; $26.88 for three or four in two beds.
- Friendship Desert Inn, 850 West Hobson Way, 92225. Telephone: 619/922-5145. $24 to $30 for one; $27 to $34 for two in one bed; $34 to $40 for two in two beds.
- Friendship Dunes Inn, 9820 East Hobson Way, 92225. Telephone: 619/922-4216. $22 to $28 for one; $24 to $30 for two in one bed; $26 to $32 for two in two beds.

Buellton

Accommodations: Motel 6, 333 McMurray Rd., P.O. Box 1670, 93427. Telephone: 805/688-3293. See Anaheim listing for rates.
- Allstar Inn, Second St. & Zaca Creek, 93427. Telephone: 805/688-0336. See Bakersfield listing for rates.

Buena Park

Accommodation: Friendship Gaslite, 7777 Beach Blvd., 90620. Telephone: 714/522-8444. $24 to $34 for one or two in one bed; $28 to $36 for two in two beds.

Buttonwillow

Accommodations: Motel 6, 3810 Tracy Ave., 93206. Telephone: 805/764-5166. See Anaheim listing for rates.

● Allstar Inn, 20638 Tracy Ave., 93206. Telephone: 805/764-5153. See Bakersfield listing for rates.

Camarillo

Accommodation: Motel 6, 1641 East Daily Dr., 93010. Telephone: 805/482-5611. See Anaheim listing for rates.

Campbell

Accommodation: Allstar Inn, 1240 Camden Ave., 95008. Telephone: 408/371-8870. See Bakersfield listing for rates.

Carlsbad

Accommodations: Sixpence Inn, 1006 East Elm Ave., 92008. Telephone: 619/434-7135. $20 to $28 for up to four.
● Allstar Inn, 6117 Paseo del Norte, 92008. Telephone: 619/438-1242. See Bakersfield listing for rates.

Carpenteria

Accommodations: Motel 6, U.S. Hwy. 101 & Santa Monica Rd., 93013. Telephone: 805/684-4616. See Anaheim listing for rates.
● Friendship Reef Motel, 4160 Via Real, 93013. Telephone: 805/684-4176. $30 to $36 for one; $32 to $42 for two in one bed; $34 to $40 for two in two beds.

Carson

Accommodation: Allstar Inn, 213121 Avalon Blvd., 90745. Telephone: 213/835-0333. See Bakersfield listing for rates.

Chico

Accommodations: Motel 6, 665 Manzanita Ct., 95926. Telephone: 916/343-5806. See Anaheim listing for rates.
● Imperial 400 Motor Inn, 630 Main St., 95926. Telephone: 916/895-1323. $27 to $30 for one; $32 to $34 for two in one bed; $35 to $38 for two in two beds.

Chino

Accommodation: Sixpence Inn, 12266 Central Ave., 91710. Telephone: 714/591-3877. $20 to $28 for up to four.

Claremont

On Campus: There are five colleges in Claremont, "a small town in the old-fashioned sense—everyone knows each other in this town of beautiful old houses and lots of trees." The colleges are Pomona, Scripps, Pitzer, Claremont-McKenna, and Harvey Mudd. At Pomona, the hub of student activity is the Edmunds Union. To meet students, go to Edmunds or the Coop at Pomona, the Motley Coffeehouse at Scripps, Red Baron Pizza or the McConnell Center at Pitzer College. The general information number for the five colleges is 714/621-8000; the paper for the five colleges is called *Collage*.

Coalinga

Accommodations: Motel 6, 25278 West Dorris Ave., 93210. Telephone: 209/935-2866. See Anaheim listing for rates.
- Allstar Inn, 25008 West Dorris Ave., 93210. Telephone: 209/935-1536. See Bakersfield listing for rates.

Corning

Accommodation: Friendship Corning Inn, 2165 Solano St., 96021. Telephone: 916/824-2468. $23 to $27 for one; $27 to $31 for two in one bed; $29 to $33 for two in two beds.

Costa Mesa

Accommodation: Allstar Inn, 1441 Gisler Ave., 92626. Telephone: 714/957-3063. See Bakersfield listing for rates.

Crescent City

Accommodation: Rustic Inn, 220 M St., 95531. Telephone: 707/464-9553. Winter: $16 for one; $18 for two in one bed; $24 for two in two beds. Summer: $25 for one; $28 to $32 for two in one bed; $34 to $36 for two in two beds.

Davis

On Campus: There is a branch of the University of California in Davis, and you can get campus information by calling 916/752-2222. You'll find a ride board in the Memorial Union and housing possibilities in the Housing Office. There are two spots on campus where students tend to meet: The Housing Office, and the Pub. You can also find students off campus at the Brewster House in the evening.

Accommodation: Motel 6, 4835 Chiles Rd., 95616. Telephone: 916/756-6662. See Anaheim for rates.

Death Valley

Camping: Death Valley National Monument, Furnace Creek, 92328. Telephone: 619/786-2331. Nine campgrounds with a total of approximately 1600 campsites. Furnace Creek, Mesquite Springs, and Wildrose are open year round; Texas Spring Sunset and Stove Pipe Wells are open November through April; Emigrant is open May through October, Thorndike, Pinyon Mesa, and Mahogany Flat are open March through November. No entrance fee; $5 per vehicle.

● Friendship Cedar Lodge, 4201 Dunsmuir Ave., 96025. Telephone: 916/235-2836. $17 to $21 for one; $19 to $26 for two in one bed; $21 to $28 for two in two beds.

● Friendship El Rancho Motel, V, 400 Dunsmuir Ave., 96025. Telephone: 916/235-2884. $24 for one; $28 for two in one bed; $32 for two in two beds.

El Centro

Accommodations: Motel 6, 330 North Imperial Ave., 92243. Telephone: 619/352-8400. See Anaheim listing for rates.

● Motel 6, 395 Smoketree Dr., 92243. Telephone: 619/352-1780. See Anaheim listing for rates.

● E-Z 8 Motel, 455 Wake Ave., 92243. Telephone: 619/352-6620. $17.88 for one; $20.88 for two in one bed; $25.88 for two in two beds.

El Monte

Accommodations: Motel 6, 3429 Peck Rd., 91731. Telephone: 818/442-7380. See Anaheim listing for rates.

● TraveLodge, V &, 12031 Garvey Ave., 91732. Telephone: 818/443-4111. $30 for one; $35 for two in one bed; $40 for two in two beds.

Escondido

Accommodation: Motel 6, 509 West Washington Ave., 92025. Telephone: 619/743-1331. See Anaheim listing for rates.

Eureka

Accommodations: Allstar Inn, 1934 Broadway, 95501. Telephone: 707/445-9631. See Bakersfield listing for rates.

● Safari Budget Motel, 7th & Broadway, 95501. Telephone: 707/443-4891. $22 to $36 for one; $24 to $40 for two in one bed; $28 to $45 for two in two beds.

● Friendship Flamingo Inn, 4255 South Broadway. Telephone: 707/443-4556 or 443-4557. October 1 to May 26: $18 to $22 for one; $20 to $24 for two in one bed; $22 to $28 for two in two beds. May 27 to September 30: $24 to $32 for one; $26 to $32 for two in one bed; $28 to $36 for two in two beds.

- Friendship Town House Motel, ∨, corner of 4th & K Sts., 95501. Telephone: 707/443-4536. October 1 to May 23: $22 to $28 for one; $26 to $30 for two in one bed; $28 to $32 for two in two beds.
- Imperial 400 Motor Inn, 1630 4th St., 95501. Telephone: 707/443-8041. $26 to $36 for one; $28 to $36 for two in one bed; $30 to $40 for two in two beds.

Fairfield

Accommodation: Motel 6, 2353 Magellan Rd., 94533. Telephone: 707/422-4060. See Anaheim listing for rates.

Fontana

Accommodation: Motel 6, 10195 Sierra Ave., 92335. Telephone: 714/822-0541. See Anaheim listing for rates.

Fort Bragg

Accommodation: Friendship Driftwood Inn, 820 North Main St., 95437. Telephone: 707/964-4061. $20 to $34 for one; $24 to $38 for two in one bed; $30 to $44 for two in two beds.

Fresno

Accommodations: YWCA (AYH), 1660 M St., 93721. Telephone: 209/237-4704. Women only. Eight blocks from bus station. $5.25 for AYH members.
- Motel 6, 949 North Parkway Dr. at Hwy. 99, 93728. Telephone: 209/268-1936. See Anaheim listing for rates.
- Motel 6, 4245 North Blackstone Ave., Hwy. 41 N., 93726. Telephone: 209/227-3523. See Anaheim listing for rates.
- Friendship Vagabond Motor Inn, 1807 Broadway, 93721. Telephone: 209/268-0916. $21 to $24 for one; $24 to $26 for two in one bed; $26 to $30 for two in two beds.
- Allstar Inn, 4080 North Blackstone Ave., 93726. Telephone: 209/222-2431. Gateway to Sequoia and Yosemite National Parks. See Bakersfield listing for rates.
- Allstar Inn, 1240 North Crystal Ave., 93728. Telephone: 209/237-0855. Gateway to Sequoia and Yosemite National Parks. See Bakersfield listing for rates.
- Sixpence Inn, 445 North Parkway Dr., 93706. Telephone: 209/485-5011. $20 to $28 for up to four.

Fullerton

Accommodation: Allstar Inn, 1415 South Euclid Ave., 92632. Telephone: 714/992-0660. See Bakersfield listing for rates.

Gilroy

Accommodation: Motel 6, 6110 Monterey Hwy. (Hwy. 101), 95020. Telephone: 408/842-9306. See Anaheim listing for rates.

Glendale

Accommodation: YMCA, 140 North Louise St., 91206. Telephone: 818/240-4130. Ten blocks from bus station. Men only. $14.45 single; $3 key deposit.

Hacienda Heights

Accommodation: Allstar Inn, 1154 South Seventh Ave., 91745. Telephone: 818/968-9462. See Bakersfield listing for rates.

Harbor City

Accommodation: Sixpence Inn, 820 West Sepulveda Blvd., 90710. Telephone: 213/549-9560. $20 to $28 for up to four.

Hayward

Accommodation: Allstar Inn, 30155 Industrial Pkwy. SW, 94544. Telephone: 415/489-8333. See Bakersfield listing for rates.

Hollywood

Accommodations: Hollywood YMCA, 1553 North Hudson Ave., 90028. Telephone: 213/467-4161. Men and women. $20.50 single; $29.50 double.
● Friendship Hollywood Premier, 5333 Hollywood Blvd., 90027. Telephone: 213/466-1691. $28 to $36 for one; $30 to $38 for two in one bed; $32 to $40 for two in two beds.
● Howard's Weekly Apartments, 1738 North Whitley, 90038. Telephone: 213/466-6943. Near bus station. Weekly only: $109.95 to $114.95 per person; $124.95 to $144.95 for two people. Advance reservations of one month are required along with a $50 deposit, which is refundable at end of stay. No small children.
● Cherokee Motor Hotel, 1620 North Cherokee Ave., 90028. Telephone: 213/467-8913. $18 single; $28 double. "Located in the center of Hollywood, the facility is clean, safe, and quiet, with all facilities included in price."
● Hollywood Inn, ⑤∨ ★ (all $2 off), 2011 North Highlands Ave., 90068. Telephone: 213/851-1800. $28 for one; $34 double; $38 triple; $40 quad.

Huntington Beach

Accommodation: Colonial Inn Hostel (AYH), 421 8th St., 92648. Telephone: 714/536-3315. $7.50 for AYH members; $9 for nonmembers. "In the heart of Orange County recreation area."

Imperial Beach

Accommodation: Imperial Beach Hostel (AYH), 170 Palm Ave., 92032. Telephone: 619/423-8039. Near bus station. $7 for AYH members; $10 for non-members. Advance reservations of one week necessary during summer months.

Indio

Accommodations: Motel 6, 82195 Indio Blvd., 92201. Telephone: 619/347-6582. See Anaheim listing for rates.
● Motel 6, 78100 Varner Rd., 92201. Telephone: 619/345-2242. See Anaheim listing for rates.

Inglewood

Accommodation: Northrop University Residence Hall, ♿ (limited), 733 South Hindry Ave., 90307. Telephone: 213/641-3470. Near city bus. $10 per person. Must be a student or his/her guest. Housing for married couples also; no small children.

King City

Accommodations: Motel 6, 6 Broadway Circle, 93930. Telephone: 408/385-6666. See Anaheim listing for rates.
● Friendship Crown DD Lodge, 1130 Broadway, 93930. Telephone: 408/385-5921. $26 to $40 for one; $32 to $55 for two in one bed; $34 to $55 for two in two beds.

La Habra

Accommodation: Allstar Inn, 870 North Beach Blvd., 90631. Telephone: 213/694-2158. See Bakersfield listing for rates.

La Mesa

Accommodations: Allstar Inn, 7621 Alvarado Rd., 92041. Telephone: 619/464-7151. See Bakersfield listing for rates.
● San Diego East County YMCA Youth Hostel (AYH), 8881 Dallas St., 92041. Telephone: 619/464-1323. Call if hostel is not staffed upon arrival. $5.75 for AYH members. Advance reservations necessary.

Lancaster

Accommodations: Allstar Inn, 43540 17th St. W., 93534. Telephone: 805/948-0435. See Bakersfield listing for rates.

- E-Z 8 Motel, 43530 North 17th St. NW, 93534. Telephone: 805/945-9477. $24.88 for one; $26.88 for two in one bed; $31.88 for three or four in two beds.

Lemon Grove

Accommodation: Friendship Oak Motor Inn, 8429 Broadway, 92045. Telephone: 619/463-9353. $30 to $38 for one; $32 to $40 for two in one bed; $35 to $45 for two in two beds.

Lemoore

Accommodation: Lemoore Home Hostel (AYH), 525 Lombardy Lane, 93245. Telephone: 209/924-2835. $5 for AYH members. Advance reservations necessary.

Livermore

Accommodation: Allstar Inn, 4673 Lassen Rd., 94550. Telephone: 415/449-0900. See Bakersfield listing for rates.

Lompoc

Accommodations: Motel 6, 1415 East Ocean Ave., 93436. Telephone: 805/736-4053. See Anaheim listing for rates.
- Allstar Inn, 1425 North "H" St., 93436. Telephone: 805/735-7631. See Bakersfield listing for rates.

Long Beach

Help: Travelers Aid, 947 East 4th St., 90802. Telephone: 213/432-4743.
Accommodation: Allstar Inn, 5665 East 7th St., 90804. Telephone: 213/597-1311. See Bakersfield listing for rates.

Los Alamos

Accommodation: Budget Host—Skyview Motel, 9150 U.S. Hwy. 101, Box 126, 93440. Telephone: 805/344-3770. Transportation available. $25 to $35 for one; $29 to $42 for two in one bed; $34 to $52 for two in two beds. Rates may vary on weekends.

Los Altos

Accommodation: Hidden Villa Ranch (AYH), 26870 Moody Rd., 94022. Telephone: 415/941-6407. Closed June 1 to September 1. Located on 2000 acres of farm and ranch. $5 for AYH members. Advance reservations necessary for weekends.

Los Angeles

Los Angeles is a legend. Here's the movie kingdom, the home of the leisure suit, 20th-century America at its extreme. L.A. can be a confusing city for a visitor—its sprawl is mind-boggling, its freeways are restless, and its beaches are endless. In order to avoid culture shock when you arrive, consult any of these books: Arthur Frommer's *Guide to Los Angeles* ($4.95), an excellent guide to the city's sights and restaurants; *LA Access,* by Richard S. Wurman, Access Press ($9.95), not a budget guide but still good, which subdivides Los Angeles into sections and lists lots of interesting places to see; the *Moneywise Guide to California,* by Vicki Leon, published by Presidio Press ($9.95) with a good chapter on Los Angeles. *The Hip Pocket Guide to Los Angeles,* by Vanessa Weeks Page ($8.95), Colophon/Harper and Row, is a compilation of what's what in L.A. according to some people who live there; *The City Observed: Los Angeles,* by Charles Moore, Peter Becker and Regula Campbell ($11.95), Vintage Books, is a guide to the architecture and landscapes of the city.

Contact the Greater Los Angeles Visitors and Convention Bureau, 5051 South Flower St., 90071 (tel. 213/239-0204), for maps and information. "Extremely helpful." And once you're there, check the *Los Angeles Times* entertainment section; *Los Angeles* magazine; *Reader,* a free weekly that comes out every Thursday; and *L.A. Weekly,* another free guide that is out on Thursday and "from an Angelino's perspective, the best guide to what's happening." And you can always check in with the people at Council Travel, 1093 Broxton Ave. (tel. 213/208-3551).

We've included one Angelino's unabashedly subjective guide to the "neighborhoods" of Los Angeles—just because we liked it and because it will give you a feel for what's out there:

Chinatown: Not as exciting as San Francisco's Chinatown, but L.A.'s Chinatown still holds a certain charm and lots of good restaurants and shopping. Located downtown, its center is at the Mandarin Plaza Mall at 970 North Broadway.

Little Tokyo: Another small ethnic center that's fun for shopping or just running around. It's in downtown L.A., located between Alameda and Los Angeles St. and 1st and 3rd Sts.

Venice Beach: Venice was once the center for the hippie culture, then for artists, then for nudists. Now it has lots of stalls set up with food, handmade jewelry, posters, etc. . . . Sometimes there are street musicians too. "Last time I was there I saw a man with a boa constrictor, and another who likes just to stand in place and freeze." Watch the men and women at muscle beach (part of Venice), as they try to make their biceps as large as Arnold Schwarzenegger's—they love an audience!

Beverly Hills: Come to see how Los Angeles' rich live. If you're interested in seeing stars, this is the place you'd most likely see them. For the most exclusive shops, walk down Rodeo Drive—you may even find a sale!

Melrose Avenue: Between LaBrea and Santa Monica Blvd., Melrose Ave. is a very West Hollywood place to be. Very artsy area with lots of antique shops, little bars, restaurants, playhouses, etc. The clothing stores feature some of the vintage things—the first Hawaiian shirts, big jackets from the '40s, etc.

Hollywood: Once the Avenue of the Stars, now a twisted, perverse, and exciting place to be. So much history here! Walk on the huge stars planted in the sidewalk, each with a different star's name, as you browse through 100 huge shops. Today's Hollywood is still interesting but slightly sleazy; on any day you can usually see a couple of religious fanatics, a few punks, a drunk, and a few hookers.

Santa Monica Boulevard: Between Sunset Blvd. and Melrose Ave., stretching from Hollywood to the ocean, this is the heart of L.A.'s gay community. The area is well kept and has some interesting shops, restaurants, and buildings, e.g., the art deco bank on San Vicente.

Westwood Village: Located close to UCLA, Westwood still gives the appearance of a college town. Though a business area, with lots of interesting (if sometimes expensive) shops and restaurants, it is a very young area. Lots of movie houses are located here, and at night it becomes a massive "cruise" area.

Hancock Park: Located in the mid-Wilshire area, this park is lovely for a walk or a bike ride past wealthy houses on wide-laned, tree-lined streets.

The Valley: Otherwise known as the San Fernando Valley, made infamous by the song "Valley Girls." Not much to see or do here, hardly a cultural extravaganza. There are some nice clubs, though, and the Sherman Oaks Galleria is an excellent place to shop.

Sunset Boulevard: Another must, especially at night. Wall-to-wall cars cruising the flashy, well-lit street. Sunset is an odd mixture of the rich and sophisticated and the poor and dirty. On the same corner, one can expect to see limousines and streetwalkers. Lots of nice shops and clubs here too. The hills above Sunset are very lovely, with luxurious houses overlooking the lights of the city.

Koreatown: Centered on Olympic Blvd. between Crenshaw and Vermont, this ethnic community has sprung up quickly in the past couple of years. It has lots of interesting restaurants and markets.

Fairfax Boulevard: This old Jewish part of Los Angeles is a great place for delicatessen food—lots of great bakeries too.

Malibu: Located off the Pacific Coast Hwy. just north of L.A., this area was made famous by the '50s beach movies. It's still a lovely beach, and it's especially nice to drive down Sunset Blvd. all the way to Malibu, a lovely drive to a lovely place.

Olveras Street: In the heart of downtown, across from the train station. This is where Los Angeles began. Now it's a touristy Mexican area with lots of shops and restaurants. It's fun to spend the afternoon.

Getting There: From the Airport: Los Angeles International Airport is 17 miles southwest of downtown L.A. The least expensive way to get from there to downtown is via public bus, but it's inconvenient; try instead the Airport Bus Service (tel. 213/723-4636); the fare is $6 to downtown, Beverly Hills, Hollywood, and San Fernando Valley.

• From the Bus and Train Stations: The bus station is located at 208 East 6th St., and the train station, Union Station, is right off the Hollywood Freeway at 800 North Alameda. To call Continental Trailways, dial 742-1200; Greyhound, 620-1200; and Amtrak, 624-0171. RTD (Rapid Transit District) bus transportation is available from the bus and train stations to other parts of the city.

Getting Around: If you travel by taxi (Santa Monica Checker Cab can be summoned by dialing 394-1144), you'll pay $1.90 for the first one-eighth mile and $1.40 for each additional mile (that's why we recommend taxis only for emergencies). L.A. Rapid Transit operates buses every 10 to 15 minutes that cost 50¢ locally and 10¢ for a transfer, but very few people depend on buses in L.A. Most people get around the city by car (or on skates). If you don't have a car but want to rent, two of the least expensive places to try are Rent a Wreck (tel. 478-0676); $16.95 per day, first 100 miles free, and Bob Leech's Autorental, 4810 West Imperial Hwy., Inglewood (tel. 673-2727); $13.95 per day with first 100 miles free and then 10¢ per mile for a subcompact car.

Keep in mind, when planning your trip to L.A., that the car is king there; if you do not have access to a car, stay near Westwood where the public transportation is better than in other parts of the city.

Help: Los Angeles Free Clinic, 213/653-1990.
● Travelers Aid, 656 South Los Angeles St., 90014. Telephone: 213/625-2501.
● Southern California Visitor's Council, 213/239-0204.
● Community Access Line (for the handicapped), toll free 800/372-6641.
● Feminist Women's Health Center, 213/469-4844.
● Gay Community Hotline, 213/464-7400.

Accommodations: YMCA, 1006 East 28th St., 90011. Telephone: 213/232-7193. About 20 minutes by local bus from central bus station. Men only. $20. "We are located in a black and Hispanic neighborhood and our building is old but being renovated."
● Mary Andrews Clark Home, YWCA, 306 Loma Dr., 90017. Telephone: 213/483-5780. Women only. $30 single, including two meals, for members; $35 for nonmembers. The building was built in 1912, patterned after a French chateau.
● Bill Baker International Youth Hostel (AYH-SA), 8015 South Sepulveda Blvd., 90045. Telephone: 213/670-4316 or 776-0922. Open June 1 to September 15. Must be 18 or older. $6 for AYH members; $7 for nonmembers.
● Hollywood Inn, Ⓢ ($2), 2011 North Highland Ave., 90068. Telephone: 213/851-1800. $30 to $34 for one; $34 to $40 for two in one bed; $36 to $42 for up to four in two beds.
● Garden Grove Motel, Ⓢ($2), 7900 Garden Grove Blvd., Garden Grove, 92641. Telephone: 213/898-1306. $28 to $34 for one; $32 to $40 for two in one bed; $36 to $42 for two to four in two beds.
● Rainbow Hotel, Ⓢ★ (all 10%), 536 South Hope St., 90071. Telephone: 213/627-9941. $22 single, $28 double (without bath). $44 single, $50 double, $58 triple (with bath).
● Mira Hershey Hall, UCLA, ♿ (limited), 801 Hilgard Ave., 90024. Telephone: 213/825-3691. Open mid-May to mid-September. $28 single; $14 double. Maid service is included in price; $3 per day for parking.
● Friendship Motel De Ville, 1123 West 7th St., 90017. Telephone: 213/624-8474. $27 to $31 for one; $29 to $35 for two in one bed; $31 to $35 for two in two beds.
● Hollywood-Cherokee Motor-Hotel, Ⓢ√★, 1620 North Cherokee Ave., 90028. Telephone: 213/467-8913 or 462-0288. Discounted rates for above symbols: $18 single; $28 double; $38 triple; $48 quad. Regular rates: $38 single; $48 double; $58 triple; $68 quad. No small children.
● Carmel Hotel, Ⓢ★, 201 Broadway, Santa Monica, 90401. Telephone:

213/451-2469. Discounted rates for above symbols: $35 or $40 double. Regular rates: $40 to $45. The Airport Bus Service will take you right there. "The rooms are clean and it's a good place to start out your L.A. trip—a bit less mind-boggling than downtown L.A."

● The Crescent Hotel, 403 North Crescent Dr., Beverly Hills, 90210. Telephone: 213/274-7595. In the heart of Beverly Hills. Although singles are $30 to $40 and doubles are $35 to $45, this is really a low price considering the location.

● Friendship Manchester House, 901 West Manchester Blvd., Inglewood, 90301. Telephone: 213/649-0800. Limited airport service available. $30 to $38 for one; $34 to $42 for two in one bed; $40 to $48 for two in two beds.

● Friendship Garfield Inn, 2222 South Garfield Ave., 91754. Telephone: 213/728-6688. $29 to $35 for one; $34 to $39 for two in one bed; $40 to $45 for two in two beds.

● Los Angeles International Hostel (AYH), 🛆, 1502 Palos Verdes Dr. N., Harbor City, 90710. Telephone: 213/831-8109. $6.25 for AYH members; $8.25 for nonmembers. Advance reservations of one week with first night's payment suggested.

● Hollywood YMCA Youth Hostel (AYH-SA), 1553 North Hudson Ave., 90028. Telephone: 213/467-4161. $6 for AYH members. $18.50 single; $26 double. Must bring sleeping bag. Cafe on premises.

Where to Eat: Farmer's Market, West 3rd St. at Fairfax. Telephone: 933-9211. This popular tourist attraction is an open market with souvenirs for sale, restaurants, fresh produce stands, bakeries, candy stands, etc. You can have a Chinese platter at one of the stands—a main dish, tea, and a cookie for under $5. If Chinese food doesn't interest you, you can choose from Mexican, Italian, and American. Hours: Monday to Saturday, 9 a.m. to 6:30 p.m.; Sunday, 10 a.m. to 5 p.m.

● Side Walk Café, 1401 Ocean Front Walk, Venice. Telephone: 399-5547. American food and innovative omelets and sandwiches. Early in the day, enjoy brunch while you watch the skaters, or later on admire the Pacific sunset as you sip a sangria. A meal will cost about $5.

● Duke Tropicana Coffee Shop, 8585 Santa Monica Blvd. Telephone: 652-3100. A popular place with truck drivers, students, and artists in the heart of Hollywood's artist colony. There is a wait of at least a half an hour on a Saturday.

● King's Head, 116 Santa Monica Blvd., Santa Monica. Telephone: 394-9458. Fresh fish and chips, good beers, and delectable desserts in a British pub atmosphere complete with darts. Half an order of fish and chips at $2.50 should fill you up.

● Atomic Café, 422 East 1st St. Telephone: 628-6433. In Little Tokyo near Chinatown. American and Japanese food; new wave and Japanese music from 4 p.m. to 4 a.m. every day.

● Lares Mexican Café, 2909 Pico Blvd., Santa Monica. Telephone: 829-4559. Open 7:30 p.m. to 12:30 a.m. Mexican food for under $7. "The greatest margaritas and sunrises and a chance to practice your Spanish."

● Barney's Beanery, 8447 Santa Monica Blvd., Hollywood. Telephone: 654-2287. Open 10 a.m. to 2 a.m. every day. Sandwiches and a vast selection of imported beers. Good service too.

● El Coyotes Restaurant, 7312 Beverly Blvd. Telephone: 939-7766. In West

Hollywood, Mexican food—a margarita, burrito, and chips—will fill you up for $3.50. The decor is tacky—very West Hollywood—but it's an interesting place with good food served in large portions.

● The Pantry, 877 South Figueroa. Telephone: 972-9279. A typical American steak house that makes up in value for what it lacks in decor. Said to be the oldest restaurant in L.A., it has some employees who have worked there for over 40 years. Prime ribs with French bread, vegetables, and a potato are only $6.75.

● The Hard Rock Café, 8600 Beverly Blvd. Telephone: 276-7605. In the Beverly Center. The burgers are good, if a bit pricey, but the atmosphere is what you're paying for. This is a copy of the famous London spot and is the latest "place to be." The decor is, to say the least, unique, e.g., a Cadillac protruding from the ceiling. "Great place to sit back and watch L.A. people at their best and their worst."

● Chan Daras, 1511 North Cahuenga, Hollywood. Telephone: 464-8585. Very reasonable Thai food in the heart of Hollywood.

● Canter's Delicatessen, 1119 North Fairfax Ave. Telephone: 651-2030. A Jewish deli open 24 hours a day, whenever a craving for corned beef or pastrami strikes.

● Café Figaro, 9010 Melrose Ave. Telephone: 274-7664. Dinners from $6 to $8 in a friendly Hollywood atmosphere. A great place for coffee and dessert, open weekends till 3 a.m.

● Falafel King, 10940 Weyburn Ave., Westwood. Telephone: 208-5782. Take-out or eat-in Lebanese food. Complete meals from $2 to $5.

● La Barbaras, 11813 Wilshire Blvd. Pizza, pasta, and more. Very reasonable prices; open till 1:30 a.m.

● Casa Vallarta, 3360 Ocean Park Blvd., Santa Monica. Telephone: 450-8665. All-you-can eat Sunday brunch buffet for $5.50.

● Gorky's Russian Café, 536 East 8th St. Telephone: 627-4060. A haven in the less-populated part of downtown L.A.; an artists' hangout. Inexpensive Russian and American foods served buffet style. Meals from $4 to $7. Open 24 hours.

What to See and Do: NBC Studios, 3000 West Alameda, Burbank. Telephone: 840-4444. Take a look at the inside of a television studio, controls, wardrobes, departments, and sound stages. Tours run from 9 a.m. to 4 p.m., Monday through Sunday; $4.50 for adults; $3.25 for children.

● Universal Studios, 100 Universal City Plaza. Telephone: 877-2121. A two-hour guided tour aboard a tram winds through sound stages, the back lot, a star's dressing room. There are animal shows and special-effects demonstrations, including *Jaws*. Tours are available daily, 8 a.m. to 5 p.m. $12.50 for adults; $9.50 for children (under 3, free).

● Disneyland, junction of Santa Ana Freeway and Harbor Blvd. in Anaheim, 27 miles from downtown Los Angeles. The world according to Disney—a fantasyland of these parks, adventures, and rides. Call 999-4565 for hours and rates. "The happiest place on earth."

● Huntington Library, Art Gallery, and Botanical Gardens, 1151 Oxford Rd., San Marino. Telephone: 792-6141. The art gallery has 22 galleries of paintings, furniture, and tapestries; and the gardens cover over 200 acres. No admission fee; closed Monday.

● Farmer's Market. We mentioned it above under "Where to Eat," but it's a genuine tourist attraction too.

● J.P. Getty Museum, 17985 Pacific Coast Hwy., Malibu. Telephone: 459-2306. You may enter only by car and must make parking reservations in advance by calling 454-6541. Called "Pompeii by the Pacific," it has a beautiful colonnaded garden with Greek and Roman sculpture to admire.

● Mann's Chinese Theatre, 6925 Hollywood Blvd. Telephone: 464-8111. Used to be Grauman's Chinese Theatre, where the footsteps of the stars were immortalized in concrete. The name is changed but the footprints are still there to see.

● Griffith Observatory and Park, at the northern extremity of Vermont Blvd. above Hollywood. An excellent planetarium and laserium with shows every night. Call 664-1191 for the schedule. The park itself is a perfect spot for an outing or picnic, and there are horses to rent.

● Mulholland Drive. For a spectacular view of the city at night, drive up Mulholland Drive and park at one of the viewing spots.

● The *Queen Mary* and *Spruce Goose*, Long Beach Pier 7. Telephone: 432-6964. See the old cruise ship in all her glory and Howard Hughes's plane that was too large to fly. Admission is $10.95 for adults; $6.95 for children.

● Burbank Studios, 4000 Warner Blvd. Telephone: 954-1744. Many popular shows are filmed here, and the tour that you'll get is highly technical and educational. Advance reservations are required and the tour costs a hefty $18. No children under 12 allowed.

● George C. Page Laboratory Discovery Museum and the LaBrea Tar Pits, 5801 Wilshire Blvd. Telephone: 936-2230. Closed Monday; open 10 a.m. to 5 p.m. every other day. Many prehistoric animals were caught in the small tar pits located here. The museum offers many reconstructed animals and other things of interest found in the pits. Surrounded by a little park, it's a nice getaway in the middle of the city. Admission is $1.50 for adults; 75¢ for children and students.

● Waddles Park is a small park at the top of Curson Blvd. north of Hollywood. It's a good place for a picnic or short hike with some good views of L.A.

● Los Angeles Zoo, in Griffith Park. Telephone: 666-4090. Although it's not as spectacular as the one in San Diego, it's still worth seeing. Admission is $4 for ages 16 and over; $1.50 for ages 5 to 15; under 5 is free.

● The Beverly Center. Located on the corner of LaClenega and Beverly, the Beverly Center is a huge new shopping complex where they'll sell you anything from clothes and jewels to dinner and a movie. Interesting for its architecture and its outside stairway.

● Marineland, Palos Verdes. Telephone: 541-5663. An amusement park of the sea, or everything you always wanted to know about fish but were afraid to ask. Open 10 a.m. to 7 p.m. $9.95 for adults; $6.95 for children. Call for directions.

At Night: In summer there are concerts—classical, rock, and jazz—at the Hollywood Bowl, 2301 North Highland Ave., probably the world's most famous amphitheater. Admission varies with performance—from free to $15. Call 87-MUSIC for information.

● The Music Center for the Performing Arts, 1st St. and Grand Ave., includes the Dorothy Chandler Pavilion, home of the Los Angeles Philharmonic Orchestra, the Ahmanson Theater, and the Mark Taper Forum. To find out what's on while you're in town, call 626-7210.

● From June to September there are outdoor performances by big-name stars in the Greek Theater in a natural canyon in Griffith Park, 2700 North Vermont Ave. Call 660-8400 for up-to-the-minute information.

- If you like country and western music, go to the Palamino Club, 6907 Lankershim, North Hollywood. Telephone: 765-9256. "The best country and western music in L.A." Casual atmosphere, drinks, and dinner. Well-known stars like Linda Ronstadt appear. On Thursday nights there's a talent showcase. $2.50 and up cover.

- To hear jazz, go to the Come Back Inn, 1633 West Washington Blvd. in Venice. Telephone: 396-7255. A different group every night; Wednesday and Saturday are the liveliest. $3 to $5 cover. The atmosphere is relaxed and the music is good.

- To dance, try The Palace, 1735 North Vine, Hollywood. Telephone: 462-8135. Cover can be $8 to $12, but on ladies' night there's no cover. This once-famous theater that dates from the '30s has retained some of its past glories—a huge dance floor, high ceilings, and three floors.

- For that rarity—the $2 movie—try the Gordon Theater at 614 North LaBrea on weekends. Telephone: 934-2944.

- The Comedy Store, 8433 Sunset Blvd., Hollywood, is a place where lots of comedians got their start—some still stop by. Admission is $5. "A great place for a good time and lots of laughs." Telephone: 656-6225.

- Aero Theater, 1328 Montana Ave., Santa Monica. Telephone: 395-4990. First-rate double feature movies for $3.

    Shopping: B. Dalton Pickwick Books, 6743 Hollywood Blvd. Telephone: 469-8191. One of the largest bookstores in southern California.

- Papa Bach, 11317 Santa Monica Blvd. Telephone: 478-2374. If you can't find it in another bookstore, try this one—from L.A. underground magazines to how to cultivate your own garden.

- Crown Books, 10912 Lindbrook Dr., Westwood Village. Books all discounted 10 percent.

- Tower Records, 8801 West Sunset Blvd. Telephone: 657-7300. Large selection, low prices.

- Warehouse Records, 1093 Broxton Ave., Westwood Village. Good sales, a Westwood hangout.

- Aaron's Record Store, 7725 Melrose Ave. Telephone: 653-8170. New, used, promos, and international records and tapes. "The cheapest I've found yet."

- Pier One, 5711 Hollywood Blvd. Handicrafts of wicker, glass, pottery. A good place to find a gift to take back home with you.

- Millers Outpost, 1100 Westwood Blvd. Good buys on the very popular jeans and shirts.

- Army and Navy Surplus Store, 5649 Santa Monica Blvd. Telephone: 469-0488. Camping equipment—useful and cheap.

- Aahs, 1087 Broxton Ave., Westwood. Telephone: 824-1688. Everything and anything—our favorite is a toothbrush that plays "Strangers in the Night."

Los Baños

Accommodations: Motel 6, 12733 South Hwy. 33, Gustine, 95322. Telephone: 209/826-6664. See Anaheim listing for rates.

- Allstar Inn, 13090 South Hwy. 33, Santa Nella, 95322. Telephone: 209/826-0880. See Bakersfield listing for rates.

Lost Hills

Accommodation: Motel 6, 14685 Warren St., 93249. Telephone: 805/797-2524. See Anaheim listing for rates.

Madera

Accommodation: Friendship Gateway Inn, Hwy. 99 at Ave. 16, 93637. Telephone: 209/674-8817. $18 to $26 for one; $20 to $26 for two in one bed; $24 to $30 for two in two beds.

Mammoth Lakes

Camping: Devil's Postpile National Monument, Box 501, 93546. Telephone: 209/565-3341. Open August to October. $4 per campsite per night.
Accommodation: Motel 6, 473372 Main St., P.O. Box 1260, 93546. Telephone: 619/934-4959. See Anaheim listing for rates.

Manteca

Accommodation: Friendship Travelers Inn, 1160 West Yosemite Ave., 95336. Telephone: 209/823-3141. $23 to $25 for one; $28 to $33 for two in one bed; $33 for two in two beds.

Marina

Accommodation: Sixpence Inn, 100 Reservation Rd., 93933. Telephone: 408/384-1000. $20 to $28 for up to four.

Marysville

Accommodations: Imperial 400 Motor Inn, 721 10th St., 95901. Telephone: 916/742-8586. $26 to $28 for one; $32 to $36 for two in one bed; $34 to $38 for two in two beds.
● Holiday Lodge Motel, √ ($1), 530 10th St., 95901. Telephone: 916/742-7147. $24.44 for one; $26.52 for two in one bed; $30.68 for two in two beds; $34.32 for three or four in two beds.
● Capri Motel, 803 E St., Hwy. 70, 95901. Telephone: 916/743-5465. $22 single; $24 for two in one bed; $30 for two in two beds.
● TraveLodge, √, 9th & E St., 95901. Telephone: 916/743-1531. $29 for one; $33 for two in one bed; $37 for two in two beds.

Merced

Accommodations: Allstar Inn, 1215 "R" St., 95340. Telephone: 209/722-2737. Gateway to Sequoia and Yosemite National Parks. See Bakersfield listing for rates.

- Motel 6, 1983 East Childs Ave. & Hwy. 99 S., 95340. Telephone: 209/723-3271. See Anaheim listing for rates.
- Friendship Sierra Lodge Inn, 951 Motel Dr., 95340. Telephone: 209/722-3926. Limited airport service available. $24 to $28 for one; $28 to $32 for two in one bed; $32 to $40 for two in two beds.
- Sixpence Inn, 1410 "V" St., 95340. Telephone: 209/384-2181. $20 to $28 for up to four.

Midpines

Accommodation: Midpines Home Hostel (AYH), P.O. Box 173, 95345. Telephone: 209/742-6318. Call for exact directions. Open March 1 to November 30. $5.50 for AYH members. Advance reservations suggested for weekends.

Mineral

Camping: Lassen Volcanic National Park, 96063. Telephone: 916/595-4444. Six campgrounds open May or June to September or October. $3 to $6 per campsite per night.

Mission Valley

Accommodation: E-Z 8 Motel, 2484 Hotel Circle Pl., 92108. Telephone: 619/291-8252. $30.90 for one; $33.04 for two in one bed; $35.88 for two in two beds; $38.39 for up to four people.

Modesto

Accommodations: Allstar Inn, 1920 West Orangeburg Ave., 95350. Telephone: 209/522-7271. See Bakersfield listing for rates.
- Friendship Inn Apex Motel, ∨, 2225 Yosemite Blvd., 95351. Telephone: 209/529-4750. $26 for one; $30 for two in one bed; $32 for three in two beds.
- Motel 6, 722 Kansas Ave., 95351. Telephone: 209/521-6130. See Anaheim listing for rates.

Mojave

Accommodations: Best Inn, 15620 Sierra Hwy., 93501. Telephone: 805/824-4523. $24 to $28 for one or two in one bed; $30 for two in two beds.
- Motel 6, Calif. 58 & 14, 93501. Telephone: 805/824-2284. See Anaheim listing for rates.
- Imperial 400 Motor Inn, 2145 Hwy. 58, 93501. Telephone: 805/824-2463. $29 to $32 for one; $33 to $36 for two in one bed; $36 to $39 for two in two beds.

Montara

Accommodation: Montara Lighthouse Hostel (AYH), P.O. Box 737, 16th St. & Cabrillo Hwy., 94037. Telephone: 405/728-7177. Near bus stop and private beach; hostel is on a cliff overlooking the Pacific Ocean. Men, women, and children. $5.50 for AYH members. Advance reservations necessary during summer.

Monterey

Help: Mental Health Crisis Team, Community Hospital, 408/624-5311, extension 1623.

Accommodations: YMCA and Hostel of the Monterey Peninsula (AYH), 600 Camino El Estero, 93940. Telephone: 408/373-4166. Open June 17 to August 25. $5.50 for AYH members; $7.50 for nonmembers.

● Motel 6, 2124 Fremont St. (Old Hwy. 1), 93940. Telephone: 408/373-3500. See Anaheim listing for rates.

● Friendship Thunderbird Motel, 1933 Fremont Blvd., Seaside, 93955. Telephone: 408/394-6797. Winter: $24 to $34 for one; $30 to $40 for two in one bed; $35 to $45 for two in two beds. Summer: $35 to $44 for one; $40 to $45 for two in one bed; $40 to $50 for two in two beds.

Morro Bay

Accommodation: Motel 6, 298 Atascadero Rd., 93442. Telephone: 805/772-8881. Near a major beach resort area. See Anaheim listing for rates.

Mount Shasta

Accommodations: Swiss Holiday Lodge, ∨, near jct. 15 & Calif. 89. Telephone: 916/926-4587. $21.95 to $25.95 for one; $25.95 to $28.95 for two in one bed; $28.95 to $34.95 for two in two beds; $50 suite; $33.95 to $39.95 family suite. Community kitchen.

● Friendship Alpine Lodge Motel, 908 South Mt. Shasta Blvd., 96067. Telephone: 916/926-3145. $21.50 to $25.50 for one; $25.50 to $29.50 for two in one bed; $26.50 to $30.50 for two in two beds.

Mountain View

Accommodation: Cozy 8 Motel, 1984 El Camino Real, 94040. Telephone: 415/967-6901. $29.88 for one; $31.88 for two in one bed; $33.88 for two in two beds.

Napa

Accommodation: Motel 6, 3380 Solano Ave., 94558. Telephone: 707/226-1811. See Anaheim listing for rates.

National City

Accommodations: E-Z 8 Motel, 1700 Plaza Blvd., 92050. Telephone: 619/474-6491. $26.88 for one; $28.88 for two in one bed; $33.88 for two in two beds.

● E-Z 8 Motel, 607 Roosevelt Ave., 92050. Telephone: 619/474-7502. See above listing for rates.

Needles

Accommodations: Motel 6, 1420 J St., 92363. Telephone: 619/326-4411. See Anaheim listing for rates.

● Imperial 400 Motor Inn, 644 Broadway, 92363. Telephone: 619/326-2145. $25 to $29 for one; $28 to $33 for two in one bed; $32 to $37 for two in two beds.

● Allstar Inn, 1215 Hospitality Inn, 92363. Telephone: 619/326-5131. See Bakersfield listing for rates.

● Friendship Inn River Valley Lodge, 1707 West Broadway, 92363. Telephone: 619/326-3839. Limited airport service available. $20 to $28 for one; $26 to $30 for two in one bed; $28 to $33 for two in two beds.

Newark

Accommodations: Motel 6, 5600 Cedar Ct., 94560. Telephone: 415/791-1663. See Anaheim listing for rates.

● E-Z 8 Motel, 5553 Cedar Ct., 94560. Telephone: 415/794-7775. $28.88 for one; $30.88 for two in one bed; $35.88 for three or four in two beds.

Norden

Accommodation: Ski-Inn Lodge (AYH-SA), P.O. Box 7, 95724. Telephone: 916/426-3079. Open year-round. Ski lodge with ten rooms and two dorms. Winter: $7.75 for AYH members; $11.50 for nonmembers; $25 for room plus $5 per additional person. Summer: $6.25 for AYH members; $8.50 for nonmembers; $20 for room.

Norwalk

Accommodation: Allstar Inn, 10646 East Rosencrans, 90650. Telephone: 213/864-2567. See Bakersfield listing for rates.

Oakland

Help: Travelers Aid, 1515 Webster St., 94612. Telephone: 415/444-6834.

Accommodations: YMCA, 2101 Telegraph Ave., 94612. Telephone: 415/451-8033. One block from bus station. Men and women. $13.37 for AYH members.

● Motel 6, 4919 Coliseum Way, 94601. Telephone: 415/534-8185. See Anaheim listing for rates.

● Sixpence Inn, 8480 Edes Ave., 94621. Telephone: 415/638-1180. $20 to $28 for up to four.

● Budget Host-Civic Center Lodge, √ ($2), 50 6th St., 94607. Telephone: 415/444-4139. $26 to $30 one in one bed; $26 to $32 for two in one bed; $30 to $42 for two in two beds.

Oceanside

Accommodations: Motel 6, 1403 Mission Ave., 92054. Telephone: 619/757-3492. See Anaheim listing for rates.
● Motel 6, 1-5 & Poinsettia Lane, Carlsbad, 92008. See Anaheim listing for rates.

Ontario

Accommodations: Motel 6, 1515 North Mountain Ave., 91762. Telephone: 714/986-1915. See Anaheim listing for rates.
● Sixpence Inn, 1560 East 4th St., 91761. Telephone: 714/984-2424. $20 to $28 for up to four.

Orange

Accommodation: Sixpence Inn, 2920 West Chapman Ave., 92668. Telephone: 714/634-2441. $20 to $28 for up to four people.

Oroville

Accommodation: Motel 6, 505 Montgomery St., 95965. Telephone: 916/534-9666. See Anaheim listing for rates.

Paicines

Camping: Pinnacles National Monument, East District, 95043. Telephone: 408/389-4578 or 389-4579. Campgrounds open year-round at $5 per campsite per night. $1 entrance fee.

Palm Springs

Accommodations: Motel 6, 595 East Palm Canyon Dr., 92262. Telephone: 619/327-2044. See Anaheim listing for rates.
● Allstar Inn, 69-570 Hwy. 111, 92270. Telephone: 619/324-8475. See Bakersfield listing for rates.

Palmdale

Accommodation: Motel 6, 407 Palmdale Blvd., 93550. Telephone: 805/947-2866. See Anaheim listing for rates.

Paso Robles

Accommodation: Allstar Inn, 1134 Black Oak Dr., 93346. Telephone: 805/239-2114. See Bakersfield listing for rates.

Pescadero

Accommodation: Pigeon Point Lighthouse Hostel (AYH), 🚳, Pigeon Point Rd. (off Hwy. 1), 94060. Telephone: 415/879-0633. $5.50 for AYH members; $7.50 for nonmembers. Advance reservations necessary for weekends; always call ahead. "Three modern bungalows, once U.S. Coast Guard family quarters, nestled beside a 115-foot-tall lighthouse . . . beautiful coastline view."

Petaluma

Accommodations: Motel 6, 5135 Old Redwood Hwy., 94952. Telephone: 707/795-8000. See Anaheim listing for rates.
● Allstar Inn, 1368 North McDowell Blvd., 94952. Telephone: 707/792-1642. See Bakersfield listing for rates.

Pico Rivera

Accommodation: Budget Host—Rivera Motel, √, 9118 Slauson Ave., 90660. Telephone: 213/948-4044. $28 to $32 for one; $30 to $38 for two in one bed; $32 to $42 for two in two beds.

Pismo Beach

Accommodations: Motel 6, 860 4th St., 93449. Telephone: 805/773-4081. See Anaheim listing for rates.
● E-Z 8 Motel, 555 Camino Mercado, Arroyo Grande, 93420. Telephone: 805/481-4774. $26.88 for one; $28.88 for two in one bed; $33.88 for two in two beds.

Pittsburg

Accommodation: Motel 6, 2101 Loveridge Rd., 94565. Telephone: 415/4320-6699. See Anaheim listing for rates.

Pleasanton

Accommodation: Allstar Inn, 5102 Hopyard Rd., 94566. Telephone: 415/463-2626. See Bakersfield listing for rates.

Point Reyes

Help: Mental Health Emergencies, 415/663-8231.
Accommodation: Point Reyes Hostel (AYH), P.O. Box 247, 94956. Telephone: 415/669-7414. $6 for AYH members. Beach two miles from hostel. Advance reservations suggested for weekends.

Camping: Point Reyes National Seashore, 94956. Telephone: 415/663-1092. Four hike-in campgrounds with approximately 12 sites each; open year round. No fees. Advance reservations of two months suggested in summer.

Pomona

Accommodations: Pomona Valley YMCA, 350 North Garey Ave., 91767. Telephone: 714/623-6433. Men only. $10 single with $5 key deposit; $45 weekly.
● Allstar Inn, 2470 South Garey, 91766. Telephone: 714/591-1871. See Bakersfield listing for rates.

Porterville

Accommodation: Motel 6, 935 West Morton Ave., 93257. Telephone: 209/781-6662. See Anaheim listing for rates.

Rancho Cordova

Accommodation: Allstar Inn, 10694 Olson Dr., 95670. Telephone: 916/635-8784. See Bakersfield listing for rates.

Red Bluff

Accommodation: Motel 6, 20 Williams Ave., 96080. Telephone: 916/527-8107. See Anaheim listing for rates.

Redding

Accommodations: Budget Host—Shasta Lodge, √ ★ ♿, 1245 Pine St., 96001. Telephone: 916/243-6133. Call motel for courtesy car from train station. $22 to $24 for one; $28 to $30 double; $33 triple. Advance reservations of one week suggested for summer weekends.
● Motel 6, 1640 Hilltop Dr., 96001. Telephone: 916/221-6900. See Anaheim listing for rates.
● Friendship Bel Air Motel, 540 North Market St., 96003. Telephone: 916/243-5291. $25 to $28 for one; $28 to $34 for two in one bed; $31 to $35 for two in two beds.
● Imperial 400 Motor Inn, 2010 Pine St., 96001. Telephone: 916/243-3336. $20 to $24 for one or two in one bed; $25 to $29 for two in two beds.
● Allstar Inn, 2385 Bechelli Lane, 96001. Telephone: 916/221-0562. See Bakersfield listing for rates.

Redlands

Accommodations: Motel 6, 1160 Arizona St., 92373. Telephone: 714/793-3511. See Anaheim listing for rates.
● Redlands Inn, 1235 West Colton Ave., 92373. Telephone: 714/793-6648. $29.40 for one; $33 for two; $35 for three; $40 for four.

- TraveLodge, $\vee$, 511 East Redlands Blvd., 92373. Telephone: 714/793-2536. $27 for one; $32 for two in one bed; $36 for two in two beds.

Ridgecrest

Accommodation: Motel 6, 535 South China Lake Blvd., 93555. Telephone: 619/375-9666. See Anaheim listing for rates.

Riverside

"A desert community, well-populated, one hour from L.A. with a campus of the University of California."

Help: Helpline, 714/686-HELP (24 hours).
Accommodations: Motel 6, 4045 University Ave., 92501. Telephone: 714/682-2250. See Anaheim listing for rates.
- Motel 6, 23581 Alessandro Blvd., 92508. Telephone: 714/653-2131. See Anaheim listing for rates.
- Motel 6, 6830 Valley Way, Rubidoux, 92509. Telephone: 714/685-0691. See Anaheim listing for rates.
- Allstar Inn, 1260 University Ave., 92507. Telephone: 714/784-2131. See Bakersfield listing for rates.
- Sixpence Inn, 3663 La Sierra Ave., 92505. Telephone: 714/351-0764. $20 to $28 for up to four.

Rosemead

Accommodations: Motel 6, 1001 San Gabriel Blvd., 91770. Telephone: 818/288-5700. See Anaheim listing for rates.
- Friendship Flamingo Inn Motel, 8621 East Garvey Ave., 91770. Telephone: 818/571-0170. $28 to $30 for one; $30 to $32 for two in one bed; $32 to $35 for two in two beds.

Rowland Heights

Accommodation: Sixpence Inn, 18970 East Labin Ct., 91748. Telephone: 213/964-5333. $20 to $28 for up to four.

Sacramento

Help: Travelers Aid, 717 Kay St., Suite 501, 95814. Telephone: 916/443-1719.
On Campus: You'll be able to find helpful information on the bulletin board at the Off-Campus Housing Office at this branch of California State University. A friend there recommends the Big Yellow House, which has "lots of good food," and the Coffee House on campus.
Accommodations: Motel 6, 1415 30th St., 95816. Telephone: 916/452-5581. See Anaheim listing for rates.

- Motel 6, 10271 Folsom Blvd., Rancho Cordova, 95670. Telephone: 916/362-3262. See Anaheim listing for rates.
- Sixpence Inn, 4600 Watt Ave., 95660. Telephone: 916/973-8637. $20 to $28 for up to four people.
- Sixpence Inn, 7780 Stockton Blvd., 95823. Telephone: 916/689-9141. See rates above.
- Sixpence Inn, 7850 College Town Dr., 95826. Telephone: 916/383-8110. See rates above.
- Friendship Inn Sands Motel, 2160 Auburn Blvd., 95821. Telephone: 916/925-8584. $18 to $22 for one; $24 to $28 for two in one bed; $28 to $32 for two in two beds.
- Budget Host—Desert Sand Motel, √ ($1), 623 16th St., 95814. Telephone: 916/444-7530. $20 to $28 for one; $22 to $32 for two in one bed; $26 to $40 for two in two beds.
- Allstar Inn, 227 Jibboom St., 95814. Telephone: 916/441-0733. See Bakersfield listing for rates.
- Allstar Inn, 5110 Interstate St., 95842. Telephone: 916/331-8100. See Bakersfield listing for rates.
- Allstar Inn, 10694 Olson Dr., 95670. Telephone: 916/635-8784. See Bakersfield listing for rates.
- Allstar Inn, 1254 Halyard Dr., West Sacramento, 95691. Telephone: 916/372-3624. See Bakersfield listing for rates.
- Friendship Sky Ranch Motel, 1800 West Capital Ave., 95691. Telephone: 916/371-8707. $18 to $22 for one; $24 to $26 for two in one bed; $26 to $28 for two in two beds.
- Arden Motel, √, 1700 Del Paso Blvd., 95815. Telephone: 916/925-3556. $25 for one; $28 for two in one bed; $32 for two in two beds.
- Imperial 400 Motor Inn, 1319 30th St., 95816. Telephone: 916/454-4400. $32 to $34 for one; $37 to $39 for two in one bed; $39 to $42 for two in two beds.

Salinas

Accommodations: Sandstone Motel, Ⓢ √ ★ (all 10%), 214 John St., 93901. Telephone: 408/424-6468. $26 to $40 for one; $28 to $40 for double; $5 for each additional person. Discounts may not apply during certain times of year.

- Motel 6, 1010 Fairview Ave., 93901. Telephone: 408/758-2791. See Anaheim listing for rates.
- Allstar Inn, 140 Kern St., 93901. Telephone: 408/424-0123. See Bakersfield listing for rates.
- Friendship Barbary Coast Inn, 808 North Main St., 93906. Telephone: 408/424-8661. Limited airport service available. $29.50 for one; $36.50 for two in one bed; $39.50 for two in two beds.

San Bernardino

Accommodations: Motel 6, 111 Redlands Blvd., 92408. Telephone: 714/824-3535. See Anaheim listing for rates.

- Royal Motel, 755 West 5th St., 92410. Telephone: 714/889-0401. $21 for one; $25 to $28 for two in one bed; $28 to $32 for two in two beds.
- Motel 6, I-215 & State College Pkwy., 92407. See Anaheim listing for rates.
- E-Z 8 Motel, 1750 South Waterman Ave., 92408. Telephone: 714/888-4827. See Pismo Beach listing for rates.

San Clemente

Accommodation: San Clemente Hostel (AYH), 233 Avenida Granada, 92672. Telephone: 714/492-2848. $7 for AYH members.

San Diego

"We have the finest year-round climate in the world, but if you miss shoveling snow you'll find some just one hour away."

San Diego is the first and oldest city in California. For a glimpse of its beginnings, you can visit Old Town, a park that recreates the setting of life in California during its Mexican and early American periods. Two buildings here that have been restored are the Casa de Estudillo and the Machado/Stewart Adobe. For a view of the more modern San Diego, you can take a cruise in San Diego Harbor and see the impressive skyline of the city, which has grown to be the second-largest in the West. To read up on San Diego, we suggest the *Greater San Diego Metroguide,* San Diego Chamber of Commerce, 110 West C St., San Diego, 92101 ($4.50), designed for residents and prospective residents but includes tourist-type information as well. *The Student Survival Guide to San Diego,* by Barbara Peters and Phil Hopkins, Humbird Hopkins, Inc. ($2.50), includes all you'll need to know about the town from a student's point of view.

Getting There: From the airport: The airport is only three miles northwest of the city. To get from there to downtown, you simply board a no. 2 bus—the fare is 80¢.
- From the train and bus stations: Amtrak is located at 1050 Kettner Blvd.; the Greyhound bus station is at First Ave. and Broadway, and Trailways is at 310 West C St. All three stations are in the heart of downtown.

Getting Around: You can get a free copy of "Getting Around San Diego Without a Car" from UCSD Parking and Transit Systems, Q-040, La Jolla, 92093. Telephone: 619/452-0630. You can also request a regional transit guide. For a free map of San Diego, contact the San Diego Convention and Visitors Bureau, 1200 Third Ave., Suite 824, 92101. Telephone: 619/239-3101.
- City buses cost 80¢ and run every 15–20 minutes. For information, call San Diego Transit at 233-3004 or North County Transit at 438-2550 or 484-2550. To get information on the San Diego Trolley, which goes downtown to the U.S.-Mexico border, call 231-1466 or 231-8549. The trolley is the cheapest way to get to the border, it costs $1.50.
- The Molley Trolley, 739 5th Ave., Suite 20 (telephone: 233-9177), operates for 50¢ everyday but Monday connecting the airport, Seaport Village, the Embarcadero, Shelter Island, Harbor Island and the Zoo. A taxi costs $2.20 for the

first mile and $1.20 for each additional mile. To rent a car, call San Diego Rent-A-Wreck for a $16.95 daily deal.

Help: Help Center, 5059 College Ave. Telephone: 619/582-4357. Counseling.

● Crisis Center/Hotline, 619/236-3339.

● Travelers Aid, 1122 Fourth Ave. Telephone: 619/232-7991. At the airport: 231-7361.

● Free Clinic, 619/488-0644.

Tourist Information: Balboa Park Information Center House of Hospitality, Balboa Park. Telephone: 619/239-0512.

● Chula Vista Visitors Center, 99 Bonita Rd. (I-805 and E St.). Telephone: 619/425-2390.

● Escondido Visitors Information Bureau, 720 North Broadway. Telephone: 619/745-4741.

● Mexican Consulate, 1333 Front St. Telephone: 619/231-8414.

● Mission Bay Visitors Information Center, 2688 East Mission Bay Dr. Telephone: 619/276-8200.

● San Diego Visitors Information Center, 202 C St. Telephone: 619/231-3101.

● San Diego-North Coast Visitors Center, 640 Via de Valle. Telephone: 619/481-1811.

● State Parks Information for San Diego County, Old Town Visitors Center, 2645 San Diego Ave. Telephone: 619/237-6770.

Accommodations: Tenochia Hall, San Diego State University, ♿, 92182. Telephone: 619/265-5742. Open June 1 through August 15. $20 per night per room. A "reservations request" card should be requested from the Housing Office and returned two weeks prior to the first night of lodging.

● San Diego Armed Services YMCA (AYH-SA), 500 West Broadway, 92101. Telephone: 619/232-1133. Men and women. $5 for AYH members; $8 for nonmembers.

● Motel 6, 2424 Hotel Circle North, 92108. Telephone: 619/297-4871. See Anaheim listing for rates.

● Friendship Holiday Lodge Motel, 672 East San Ysidro Blvd., 92073. Telephone: 619/428-1105. $20 to $24 for one; $34 to $36 for two.

● Campus Hitching Post Motel, ♿, 6235 El Cajon Blvd., 92115. Telephone: 619/583-1456. Near the college districts and public transportation. $32 to $40 single; $35 to $45 double; $40 to $50 triple; $45 to $55 quad. Higher rates apply in summer.

● Point Loma Hostel (AYH), 3790 Udall St., 92107. Right off bus line #35. Near Mission Bay Park and Sea World. Telephone: 619/223-4778. $7 for AYH members; $9 for nonmembers. "Large two-story stucco structure with room for 60 people." Advance reservations recommended during summer months.

● Imperial Beach Hostel (AYH), 170 Palm Ave., 92032. Telephone: 619/423-8039. Five miles from the Mexican border and 14 miles south of downtown San Diego. One-quarter block to the beach. $7 for AYH members; $10 for nonmembers. Family room is $25. Advance reservations of one week necessary during summer months. "A converted fire station with bunk beds."

● Clarke's Lodge, ⓈV ♿ (all 10%), 1765 Union St., 92101. Telephone: 619/234-6787. Near downtown. $30 for one or two in one bed; $39 for up to four in two beds. Pool and color television.

● E-Z 8 Motel, 2484 Hotel Circle Place N., 92108. Telephone: 619/291-8252.

Mission Valley area. $28.88 for one; $30.88 for two in one bed; $35.88 for two in two beds.

- YWCA, 🔊, 1012 C St., 92101. Telephone: 619/239-0355. On bus lines #9 and #34. Women only. Community bathrooms and kitchen. $15 single; $25 double. Reservations required with deposit of $21.50 one month in advance. Indoor pool and other recreational facilities.

- Sixpence Inn, 5592 Clairemont Mesa Blvd., 92117. Telephone: 619/268-9758. $20 to $28 for up to four people.

- Old Town Budget Inn, 4444 Pacific Hwy., 92110. Telephone: 619/260-8024. $26 to $27 single; $29 double.

- Western Shores Motel, 🔊, 4345 Mission Bay Dr., 92109. Telephone: 619/273-1121. $29 to $38 single; $33 to $41 double. Advance reservations suggested during summer.

- Friendship Holiday, 672 East San Ysidro Blvd., 92073. Telephone: 619/428-1105. $20 to $24 for one or two in one bed; $34 to $35 for two in two beds.

- Friendship Town House, 810 Ash St., 92101. Telephone: 619/233-8826. $29 to $33 for one; $33 to $37 for two in one bed; $37 to $41 for two in two beds.

- TraveLodge, V, 6675 El Cajon Blvd., 92115. Telephone: 619/469-6106. $32 for one; $37 for two in one bed; $40 for two in two beds.

- E-Z 8 Motel, 7851 Fletcher Pkwy., 92041. Telephone: 619/698-9444. See Newark listing for rates.

- E-Z 8 Motel, 3333 Channel Way, 92110. Telephone: 619/223-9500. See Newark listing for rates.

- E-Z 8 Motel, 4747 Pacific Hwy., 92110. Telephone: 619/294-2512. See Newark listing for rates.

- E-Z 8 Motel, 7458 Broadway, 92045. Telephone: 619/462-7022. See Pismo Beach listing for rates.

- E-Z 8 Motel, 1700 Plaza Blvd., 92050. Telephone: 619/474-6491. See Pismo Beach listing for rates.

- E-Z 8 Motel, 1010 Outer Rd., 92154. Telephone: 619/575-8808. See Lancaster listing for rates.

Where to Eat: Being so close to the Mexican border, it's not surprising that some of the popular kinds of restaurants in San Diego feature cooking from south of the border. Here are some possibilities:

- El Indio Torita Shop, 3695 India St. Telephone: 299-0333. One of the most popular fast-food Mexican restaurants in San Diego. The food is so good here that it's always busy but worth the wait. Nice outside patio too.

- Casa de Pico, 2754 Calhoun Rd. Telephone: 296-3267. Traditional Mexican food with mariachi music every day from 1 p.m. Tables outside on patio.

- Old Town Mexican Café, 2489 San Diego Ave. Telephone: 297-4330. The best carnitas in town. From the sidewalk, you can watch Mexican women making the tortillas you are about to eat.

- Salazar's Taco Shop, 4101 Genesee Ave. Telephone: 571-9352. Other locations throughout the city. You can get two rolled tacos, a bean tostada, or a beef taco for just $1.69! "Excellent food, especially the machaca burritos."

- Alfonso's, 12151 Prospect Ave., La Jolla. Telephone: 454-2232. Mexican food in an appropriate setting. À la carte ranges from $2 to $4; complete dinners from $6 to $10. "Great nachos and margaritas." Popular with UC/San Diego students.

- Tug's, 4650 Mission Blvd., Mission Beach. Telephone: 483-8847. On Thursday, a special of three taquitos, salad, and tostada for $1.25!

When you tire of Mexican fare, you can try one of the following:

● Boll Weevil (9 locations, check telephone directory). A real hamburger for just $1.99.

● Doodle Burgers (various locations throughout San Diego). Hamburgers in all styles to fit all needs.

● Board and Brew, 1212 Camino del Mar, Del Mar. Telephone: 481-1021. A great place to grab deli sandwiches and then head over to the 15th St. Park on the ocean for a picnic. Prices for sandwiches range between $2.45 and $4.25. They also have wines, beers, desserts, and frozen yogurt.

● O'Hungrys, 2547 San Diego Ave., Old Town. Telephone: 298-0133. Soups, sandwiches, yards of beer, and music from 9 p.m. to 11 p.m.

● Chicken Pie Shop, 3801 5th Ave., Hillcrest. Telephone: 295-0156. Cafeteria-style. Open every day. Lots of food for not much money.

● Baltimore Bagel, 7523 Fay Ave., La Jolla. Telephone: 456-0716. Open from 8 a.m. to 6 p.m. from Monday through Saturday. If you're a bagel-lover, you must taste these. They come in all varieties and to decorate yours, try cream cheese, lox spread, walnut spread, or egg salad.

● Firehouse Deli, 722 Grand Ave., Pacific Beach. Telephone: 272-1999. A good place for Sunday brunch. All omelets come with a basket of freshly baked sweet rolls. Sit upstairs on a nice day and enjoy the ocean view.

● Clay's Texas Pit Bar-B-Q, 5752 La Jolla Blvd. Telephone: 452-2388. Delicious ribs, barbecued beef, and apple pie at the end. Prices start at $2.75.

● V.G.'s, 106 Aberdene, Cardiff-by-the-Sea. Telephone: 753-2400. People come for miles around for their doughnuts.

● Vieux Carré, 828 5th Ave. Telephone: 238-0863. A taste of New Orleans in downtown San Diego. Morning special is 3 baguettes and a cup of coffee for 99¢. "Dinners are Southern style and delicious."

● Sze-chuan Restaurant, 4951-A Clairemont Square Shopping Center. Telephone: 270-0251. The tastiest ethnic Szechuan in town. It's so good that a couple of friends come all the way from Denver just to eat here. Prices range from $5 to $8 for dishes. The more people, the more tastes.

● Phuong Nam, 426 University Ave., Hillcrest. Telephone: 298-0810. A second location at 1303 Fifth Ave., downtown (tel. 233-6090). Authentic Vietnamese cuisine at prices from $3.50 to $5.

● The Hong Kong Restaurant, 3871 4th Ave. Telephone: 299-9449. Good Chinese food in this "neighborhood place" that stays open to 4 a.m.

● Ichiban, 1449 University Ave. Telephone: 299-7203. A small place with good and inexpensive Japanese food.

● Pasta la Vista, 808 West Washington, Hillcrest. Telephone: 296-8010. Wine bar and fresh pasta—delicious and reasonable too.

● Carino's Italian Restaurant and Pizza, 7508 La Jolla Blvd. Telephone: 459-1400. If you like your pizza with thin crust and rich cheese, this is the place.

● The Chocolate Affair, 806 West Washington, Hillcrest. Telephone: 296-1311. Great for dessert. Heavenly cheesecake with harp accompaniment at night.

N.B. From 4 p.m. to 7 p.m. is usually happy hour in most San Diego restaurant bars. Food is free and drinks are reduced at many places around town. Some suggestions: Fat City, Mony Mony's, Shooters, Humphrey's, and Café Vid.

What to See and Do in and Around San Diego: Consult either the free *San Diego Reader*, or the *North County Entertainer*. Also check the *San Diego*

Union or the *Tribune*'s entertainment section for a guide to what's going on.

● Balboa Park. 1400 acres of park with the world-famous San Diego Zoo and from June to September the city's Shakespeare Festival in the Old Globe and live shows during summer evenings in the Starlight Theatre. The park includes the Aerospace Museum, which displays a replica of the Spirit of St. Louis, a Museum of Man, the Museum of Art, and the Natural History Museum. For information, call 239-0512.

● Old Town. This is where San Diego began. The first Spanish settlement on the California coast began here. A historical walking tour of the area leaves every day at 2 p.m. from Casa Machado y Silvas. Don't miss Presidio Park and Padre Junipero Serra Mission. For a free brochure on Old Town, write to: Old Town Brochure, 2723 San Diego Ave., San Diego, CA 92110 or call 619/298-9167.

● Harbor Excursion. You can choose from a one- or two-hour cruise that goes year-round and daily from the Broadway Pier at Harbor Drive. Adults pay $8 for the two-hour cruise, $5.50 for the one-hour cruise. Dinner cruise—dinner, dancing, and an open bar is $28.50. For information, call 234-4111.

● Sea World. Telephone: 224-3562. Everything aquatic plus a dolphin quiz show and the fabulous killer whale show starring "Shamu." Don't miss the penguins at the end of the park. Leave a whole day for this one! $12.95 for adults, $9.95 for children ages 4–12 and senior citizens.

● Maritime Museum, 1306 North Harbor Dr. Telephone: 234-9153. Three restored ships to visit.

● Mission Bay. Sailing, swimming, frisbee, jogging, picnicking, and lots of other things on all the time.

● Beaches (as rated by a native). Black's Beach for nude bathing; La Jolla Shores, Torrey Pines, and Del Mar, all recommended; Pacific Beach, Mission Beach, Ocean Beach for young crowds; and for great waves Mission Bay, Coronado Island, and Cardiff-by-the-Sea.

● Navy Ship Tours. San Diego has the largest naval base on the West Coast so you should probably take a look. On weekends the Navy puts one of its ships on exhibition—tours are free. To find out what's on view at the Broadway Pier at Embarcadero, call 232-3534.

● Cabrillo National Monument located at the tip of Point Loma. The view from here is spectacular! On a clear day you can see Mexico, Coronado Hotel del Coronado, the Bridge, North Island Naval Base, downtown, and Ballast Point (where the first Spanish landing occurred and now the home of the San Diego submarine base). You may even see as far as the Cleveland National Forest. During the migration of the California Gray Whale (January to March) this is an excellent lookout point, especially in the morning. This land is owned and operated by the National Park System and hours are 9 a.m. to sunset, daily. For more information call 293-5450.

● Scripps Institute of Oceanography and Aquarium Museum. Known worldwide for its research; admission to the aquarium is free.

● La Jolla Cove. A good place to watch the waves roll in and crash against the cliffs and a perfect place to scuba dive.

● Glider Port. The bluffs off the coast of La Jolla make this one of the best places for hang gliders and sail planes. To participate, you must be licensed or taking lessons. On a clear day the sky is filled with them.

● Mount Soledad. For a magnificent view of La Jolla, San Diego city, and the Pacific as far south as Mexico.

- Torrey Pines State Park. The Torrey pine tree grows in the park and it's the only place in the world where it grows. Rangers lead hikes which start at 1 p.m. daily.
- Palomar Mountain and Observatory. A good place to go to escape from the city and have a picnic. You can take a look at the inside of an observatory and see how it works.
- Coronado. San Diego's "Crown City" is reliving the Victorian era. The world-famous landmark, the Hotel del Coronado, has hosted many famous people from all over the world. It's worth a walk through the hotel just to see all the old photographs displayed on the walls. Coronado is situated at the end of a long peninsula, known as the Silver Strand, which forms the western land edge of San Diego Harbor; it is directly west of downtown San Diego.
- Bike Rides. Every Sunday morning at 9:30 a.m., American Youth Hostels sponsors a free bike ride around the city. The ride lasts about three hours and all you need is a bike. There's a slow, medium, and fast group, so you won't have to get left behind. Riders meet at the City Administration Building, downtown on Pacific Coast Hwy.
- Hamel's Action Sports Center, 704 Ventura Place, Mission Beach. Bicycles and roller skates for rent at $3 per day.
- Del Mar Fair/Del Mar Racetrack and Fairgrounds. Usually a fair takes place during the last 2 weeks of June and the first week of July. After that, the racetrack opens and operates through the summer.
- Gaslamp Quarter and Downtown. The newest tourist attraction is this recently renovated part of town. Horton Plaza, a brand new mall, features boutiques, restaurants, and department stores.

At Night: Call 452-EDNA to find out what's going on on the campus of UC/San Diego.

- Concerts: Often there are concerts at Balboa Park, or you can check with the UC/San Diego State (tel. 452-EDNA), which often presents a recital or a concert at its Amphitheater.
- Belly Up Tavern, 143 South Cedros, Solano Beach. Telephone: 481-9022. $2 to $10 cover charge from 9 p.m. to 1:30 a.m.; free swing concerts on Wednesday, Friday, and Sunday from 6 to 8 p.m. Music every night of the week—could be blues, rock, reggae, country, or swing on the night you're there. Dancing and good food too.
- Humphrey's Restaurant, 2241 Shelter Island Dr., Shelter Island. Jazz concerts and easy rock all summer long on the lawn. Tickets are $6 to $15. Humphrey's is on the bay and the piano bar is open nightly with no cover charge.
- Cafe Vid, 7353 El Cajon Blvd., La Mesa. Telephone: 460-7353. A restaurant with video night club featuring Cajun cooking.
- Confetti's, 5373 Mission Center Rd., Mission Bay. Telephone: 291-8635. Drinks and dancing and confetti too.

Shopping: Map Centre, 2611 University Ave. Travel books and maps of all kinds.

- Assorted Vinyl, UCSD, La Jolla. Co-op record store. New and used records at 30% to 50% off. Closed during the summer.
- Tower Records, 3601 Sports Arena Blvd. Super discount prices; open until midnight.
- Eagle Creek Pack Factory, 143 South Cedros, Solana Beach. Travel gear, equipment for outdoor sports. A 10% discount to ISIC holders.

- Marshall's, 3902 Clairmont Square Shopping Center. Brand names at discount.

- Seaport Village, on San Diego Bay, 849 West Harbor Dr. Boutiques for tourists, restaurants, and a carousel.

- Weekend Swap Meets. If you like the sport of bargain hunting, you might want to try one of the swap meets held on Saturday and Sunday—three are the Orange County Swap Meet, 88 Fair Drive, at the fairgrounds in Costa Mesa; the Spring Valley Swap Meet, 6377 Quarry Rd.; and the Sports Arena Swap Meet at the San Diego Sports Arena.

San Francisco

A lovely city, San Francisco. The Convention and Visitors Bureau boasts that it has two big advantages over other cities—it's so very scenic and it's so compact. San Francisco is an easy place to be a visitor—it seems smaller than it is because the excellent public transportation makes it so easy to get around. To read up on what Somerset Maugham called "the most civilized city in America," try:

The Native's Guidebook: San Francisco Free and Easy, edited by William Ristow, Bay Guardian Books, Downwind Publications, San Francisco ($5.95). The ultimate guide to the city's entertainment, restaurants, bars, and other interesting places.

The Dolphin Guide to San Francisco and the Bay Area, by Curt Gentry and Tom Horton, Dolphin Books, Doubleday ($6.95). A good, basic guide to the city.

Arthur Frommer's Guide to San Francisco, Frommer-Pasmantier Publishers ($4.95). Another dependable guide to the city. Includes excursions to favorite spots in the Bay area.

San Francisco at Your Feet, by Margot Patterson Doss, Grove Press ($5.95). An excellent walking guide to the city's neighborhoods. Doss publishes other walking guides to areas beyond the city.

The Access Guide to San Francisco, Access Press ($9.95). A complete guide to San Francisco and the Bay Area in the Michelin mode.

San Francisco by Cable Car, by George Young, published by Wingbow Press ($7.95). Touring the city, using the cable cars which the author insists are like the city itself—"romantic, sweet, comic, exciting, and full of mystery and assorted unexpected sidetracks."

San Francisco on a Shoestring, by Louis Madison ($4.95). An excellent guide for travelers who are on a limited budget—includes restaurant listing.

San Francisco Insider's Guide, John K. Bailey ($4.95), Non-Stop Books. Another guide to low-cost pleasures.

And finally, a good restaurant guide, *Best Restaurants of San Francisco,* 101 Publications ($4.95).

The weekly *Bay Guardian* (every Wednesday) lists coming events. A relatively new supplement to the *Guardian,* which is sold separately, is called *After Dark,* and it includes a full listing of what's happening where.

The pink section of the *Sunday Chronicle* is another all-inclusive list of the coming week's happenings. For information about art exhibits and performances at alternative spaces around town, call The Artline, 558-9222. The San Francisco Convention and Visitors Bureau, at the Powell St. BART Station (Powell at Market), has a Dial-an-Event phone line, 391-2000, with tapes in

French, Spanish, German, and Japanese. The staff there has helpful information and maps for drop-in visitors.

Getting There: From the Airport: The San Francisco International Airport is 15 miles south of the city. You can go by Airporter Express bus from the airport to a downtown terminal for $6. These buses run every 15 minutes during the day, every half hour after 10 p.m., and take about 30 minutes for the trip. The Airporter terminal is at 301 Ellis St.

From Oakland Airport, you can take the shuttle to Coliseum BART Station and proceed on the San Francisco/Daly City train to the city. The fare will be about $1.50, depending on where you get off in San Francisco.

The Greyhound Bus Station is located at 50 Seventh Street and from there local Muni buses connect to other points for 60¢. Call 433-1500 for information.

The Trailways station is located at the Transbay Terminal, 1st and Mission in downtown San Francisco. The train station for Cal Train to the South Bay is located at 4th and Townsend; more Muni buses there. The Amtrak station is at 4th and Townsend (tel. 982-8512 or 872-7245).

Getting Around: Muni is the name of the city transit system that covers almost every corner of town. The fare is 60¢. A transfer, good for two hours, is available for the buses and the Metro. Call 673-MUNI for information. A monthly Muni pass is $20. Muni Metro is the underground train that leads from downtown San Francisco to the outer boundaries of the city. L Taravel goes to the zoo, N Judah to the University of California Medical Center and the Sunset District, the K Line to San Francisco State. The cable cars are back in operation, running from Powell Street in downtown to the Wharf, under the auspices of Muni. The fare is $1 and you can use the Muni Monthly Pass on the cable cars as well. BART (Bay Area Rapid Transit) underground trains crisscross the Bay to reach main points in the East Bay, Berkeley, etc. The fare is charged according to the distance traveled—60¢ is the minimum. Call 788-7278 for information.

AC Transit buses leave from Transbay Terminal for almost any point in the East Bay; Golden Gate Transit buses take you to Marin County and points north. Call 332-6600 for details. A ferry to Sausalito from the San Francisco Ferry Terminal takes 30 minutes and costs $2.75 one-way on weekdays, $3 on weekends.

Taxis are difficult to flag down, unless you're in midtown.

To rent a car, try Reliable Rent-A-Car, 349 Mason, one block from Union Square. The cost is $19 per day. Most car rental places will offer you a special weekend deal.

Help: Haight-Ashbury Switchboard, 415/621-6211. Stop in at their office at 1539 Haight St. and ask for a copy of the excellent, free *San Francisco Survival Manual*. Also pick up a copy of the one-page information sheet on *Job Resources in San Francisco*.

● Woman's Switchboard, 3543 18th St. Telephone: 415/431-1414.

● Travelers Aid, 38 Mason St., 94102. Telephone: 415/781-6738.

● Gay Switchboard and Counseling Service. Telephone: 415/841-6224.

● Advocates for Women, 414 Mason St. Telephone: 415/391-4870. "Great job board for all to use."

Accommodations: Mary Ward Hall, San Francisco State University, 🦽, 800 Font Blvd., 94132. Off I-280. Telephone: 415/469-1067. Students, faculty, and educationally related visitors only. $40 for one or two people. Guest meals available in nearby University Dining Center.

● The University of California at San Francisco Residence Halls, 🦽, 510

Parnassus Ave., 94143. Telephone: 415/666-2231. Open July 1 to September 10. $42 for a room which accommodates two people; two rooms share one bath. Five minutes from Golden Gate Park and on main bus routes downtown. Swimming pool and cafeteria in building. Advance reservations suggested.

● Pensione San Francisco, 1668 Market St., 94102. Telephone: 415/864-1271. $29 to $32 single; $35 to $38 double; $38 triple; $50 quad. Hotel is convenient to BART, Muni Metro, and several bus lines. "Each room is individually designed by a designer who is one of the owners. Room themes focus on the American West, with photos, antiques, etc. that owners gathered while contemplating opening the hotel. Great breakfast at the cafe."

● Hotel Sequoia, ⑤⟨⟩ ★, 520 Jones St., 94102. Telephone: 415/673-0234. $25 single with private bath; $20 single with shared bath; $5 additional for two; $10 additional for three; $15 additional for four. Centrally located hotel (near Union Station); ". . . built in the 1920s with an art deco lobby and architecture . . . catering to the young student and international traveler . . . we try to keep an up-to-date, young, rock 'n' roll image."

● San Francisco International Hostel (AYH), ⟨⟩, Bldg. 240, Fort Mason, 94123. Telephone: 415/771-7277. Two blocks inside Franklin & Bay Sts. Park entrance, behind park headquarters building. $7 for all guests. Must show photo ID. Advance reservations of at least two weeks recommended. "A spacious, historical Civil War building with an inspiring view of the Golden Gate Bridge."

● Golden Gate Hostel (AYH), 941 Fort Barry, Sausalito, 94965. Telephone: 415/331-2777. Located within the Golden Gate National Recreation Area, so follow the signs from Alexander Ave. The hostel was previously Officers' Headquarters and is listed in the National Register of Historic Places. $6. Photo ID required to register. Advance reservations recommended. "Scenic country setting only eight miles from San Francisco."

● Obrero Hotel and Basque Restaurant, 1208 Stockton St., 94133. Telephone: 415/986-3960. $28 single; $39 double; $45 triple; $48 quad. Price includes breakfast. Inexpensive meals available daily. "European-style pension located in Chinatown."

● Ansonia Residence Club, 711 Post St., 94109. Two and one-half blocks from Union Square. Telephone: 415/673-2670. Daily rate: $20 to $25 single or double. Weekly rate: $130 to $145 single, $80 to $100 per person double, which includes breakfast and dinner six days a week; brunch on the seventh. "Great place to meet students from abroad."

● Golden Gate Hotel, ⑤★ with passport, 775 Bush St., 94108. Telephone: 415/392-3702. Walking distance from bus and train; one-half block from cable car. Located very centrally. $29 to $49 single; $35 to $55 double; $8 for each additional person. Advance reservations recommended during summer and holiday periods.

● Essex Hotel, ⑤ ★ √, 684 Ellis St., 94109. Telephone: 415/474-4664. Near bus and train station. $26 to $34 single; $30 to $44 double; $8 for each additional person; $68 quad. Advance reservations of one day necessary. "A very elegant corner hotel in the heart of San Francisco with a charming European atmosphere and friendly, multilingual staff."

● YWCA Hotel, 620 Sutter St., 94102. Telephone: 415/775-6500. $25 single; $30 single with private bath; $32 double; $38 double with private bath.

● European Guest House, 761 Minna St., 94103. Telephone: 415/861-6634.

$7 per night in dorm-style accommodations. No small children. "The place is run by hip Americans and caters primarily to foreign young people. "I've stayed there many times and it's the only place I stay in San Francisco. The atmosphere is friendly, laid-back and freewheeling."

● The Amsterdam Hotel, 749 Taylor St., 94108. Telephone: 415/441-9014. Close to the Airporter Downtown Terminal. $42 single with private bath; $47 double; $35 single sharing bath with one other room; $40 double; $30 for single with a sink and shared bath; $35 double. "A little bit of Europe in one of America's most European cities."

● The Olympic Hotel, √ ($2), 140 Mason St., 94102. Telephone: 415/982-5010. $17 single or double with detached bath; $35 single or double with shower and TV; parking is available.

● The Windsor Hotel, 238 Eddy St., 94102. Telephone: 415/885-0101. Doubles only. Rates start at $25 and go to $35.

● Union Square Plaza, 432 Geary St., 94102. Near Union Square. Telephone: 415/776-7585. $30 single without bath; $35 double with bath.

Where to Eat: Salmagundi's. There are several locations but probably the most convenient is the one at Civic Center, near Symphony Hall and the San Francisco Museum of Modern Art. Cafeteria-style dining in a hi-tech interior, where you can sip a cup of coffee for hours without being bothered. Different soups every day; soup, salad, and roll with a drink costs about $5 to $7.

● Hong Kong Café, 245 Church St., Castro area. Telephone: 621-3020. Chinese food that's good and very reasonable ($4 to $6 for a meal).

● United States Restaurant, 431 Columbus in North Beach. Telephone: 362-6251. Full Italian dinners for $5 to $7 in what looks like a greasy spoon but isn't. "Old-fashioned Italian; soggy vegetables but excellent calamari."

● La Mediterranee, 2210 Fillmore, with a new one on Market St. Telephone: 921-2956. Middle Eastern atmosphere, the food is good in this small place. A dinner costs from $6 to $8.

● Tomasso's Famous Pizzeria, 1042 Kearny St. Telephone: 398-9696. A great late-night hangout in North Beach. Often crowded but worth the wait. Large pizzas are $7 to $14.

● Pasand Madras, 1857 Union St. Telephone: 522-4498. Southern Indian food like masala dosas, large lentil pancakes filled with vegetarian curry, and biryianas, filling rice and curry dishes—about $8.50 for a full meal including an appetizer. (There's another Pasand in Berkeley on Shattuck.) One friend eats here twice a week and considers it to be one of the best buys in town—especially good value compared to other high-priced restaurants on Union St.

● La Taqueria, 2889 Mission St. Telephone: 285-7117. One block from the 24th St. BART station and open every day from 10 a.m. to 10 p.m. Their burritos are supposed to be the best in the city. Mexican frescoes on the wall; there are two tables outside if the weather cooperates. $3 will buy you a large burrito and a fresh fruit drink. After dinner, walk one block to La Bohème Coffee House for a cappuccino.

● Hang Ah Tearoom, One Hang Ah St. (an alley off Sacramento St. below Stockton). Telephone: 982-5686. A quiet dim sum place especially recommended for a Sunday brunch. "My favorite is pork bow, a doughy bun filled with barbequed pork and steamed." The interior is pleasant and two can eat here for $10."

● Le Bigamist, 1293 Haight. No telephone. A typical Vietnamese hangout, one of many in the city, located right in the heart of a popular tourist area.

- Pasta II, 381 South Van Ness. Telephone: 864-4116. A menu of nothing but pasta that's filling and usually good. The interior is black and white and funky with mismatched tables and chairs. Pasta II is not far from the Symphony and Ballet at Civic Center.
- Castro Gardens, 558 Castro. Telephone: 621-2566. Castro eggs with or without cheese, something like a souffle, or a Denver omelet—almost $12 for two.
- Mai's Vietnamese Restaurants on Union, Clement & Irving Streets. Telephone: 221-3046. A dependable selection of good Vietnamese food. Entrees average $5.
- Indonesian Java Restaurant, 417 Clement St. Telephone: 752-1541. $2.95 special Chinese/Indonesian lunches in a truck-stop atmosphere.
- Hong Kong Café, 387 Clement St. A small Chinese bakery with dim sum to eat in or take out. Consider carrying some over to Mountain Lake Park for a picnic.
- Acme Café, 3917 24th St. Telephone: 824-3555. A hangout with a casual feeling in the popular Noe Valley neighborhood. (Lots of transplanted New Yorkers live here.) Omelettes, soups, salads and sandwiches—if you choose carefully you can eat for under $6.
- Milano Pizza, 1330 Ninth St., between Irving and Judah. A good pizza place in what real estate people call, "an up-and-coming neighborhood."
- The Kublai Khan's Mongolian Barbecue, 1160 Polk at Fillmore. Telephone: 885-1378. All-you-can-eat Chinese buffet for $4.95 at lunchtime; $5.95 at dinner.

What to Do and See: Fisherman's Wharf. This is the home of the fishing fleet, with seafood restaurants, shops, boat tours, and sailing ships. In October, the fishing fleet is blessed and the Procession of Maria del Lume follows.

- Golden Gate Park. There's lots going on here in the world's largest artificial park. You'll find the De Young Museum, the Asian Art Museum with its Avery Brundage Collection, the Academy of Sciences Museum with the aquarium; a planetarium, and a laserium. Other attractions of the park include the Japanese Tea Garden, a meadow full of roaming buffalo, a series of man-made lakes, and the Chinese Pavilion at Stow Lake, a gift from the People's Republic of China to the people of San Francisco. For information about the park, call 558-3706.
- Chinatown. The largest Chinese settlement outside China. Grant Avenue is the heart of the area. Enjoy a dim sum lunch in a basement restaurant and shop for small gifts.
- The Cannery. Leavenworth and Beach Sts. Once a Del Monte fruitpacking plant, now restored with art galleries, restaurants, shops, etc.
- Ghirardelli Square, Northpoint and Larkin Sts. Once a chocolate and spice factory but now redone as a miscellany of shops, restaurants, and inviting plazas.
- North Beach. The city's Italian section, which started out as the fishing center. Chinatown is beginning to spill over into this part of town. Many artists live around Columbus Ave. Take a walk from Coit Tower. You'll get views of Alcatraz and find the quiet gardens of Telegraph Hill.
- St. Mary's Square is the center of the area; the large church dominates the plaza, just like a small European village.
- Haight-Ashbury. Not what it was in the 60s—in fact, it's become a chic area of shops for the affluent young. Full of old Victorian homes that are being lovingly restored, so it's still worth the visit.

● Fort Mason Center, Bay and Laguna. Three old piers that have been renovated into theaters, galleries, and small museums, including the Mexican Museum, and the Italian-American Museum. The Liberty Ship, a fighting ship from World War II, is docked at the end of the pier and is open to the public. From here, there are excellent views of the Golden Gate Bridge, and close to the marina is a nice, nice spot for a picnic.

● Stern Grove Concert Series. Held every summer in a lovely park surrounded by eucalyptus trees. Free. Call 558-3706 for information.

● Ferry Boat Ride. You can take a ferry from the San Francisco pier on the Embarcadero to Sausalito, across the bay in Marin County, Angel Island, and Alcatraz. Call 332-6600 for details.

● San Francisco Art Institute, 600 Chestnut St. Close to North Beach. Besides the art, the views from the cafeteria are remarkable. A lively place.

● The Mission District, 24th & Mission Sts., is the center of the Spanish-speaking part of the city. The food here is cheap and often Mexican. Visit the Café La Bohème at the crossing of 24th St. and Mission, and join the writers and artists of the city for an espresso.

● The Golden Gate National Recreation Area is a national park within the city's borders, extending from Fort Mason to Land's End, and it includes one of San Francisco's better beaches, Baker's Beach.

● The Zoo, Sloat Boulevard in the southern part of the city. The new primate center and a nineteenth-century carousel are two highlights.

● Palace of Fine Arts, Exploratorium Museum, Bay and Lyons Sts. The first hands-on science museum in the country housed in a building dating from the 1915 World's Fair. Lots of fun!

● Legion of Honor Museum, on a bluff overlooking the ocean in Lincoln Park. Devoted to French art; the view on a clear day rivals the art.

● Civic Center. Here you'll find the Museum of Modern Art, Davies Symphony Hall, City Hall complete with a Beaux-Arts rotunda and a public library that offers free walking tours of the city. Call 558-3981 for a schedule.

At Night: To hear jazz, go to the Keystone Corner, 750 Vallejo St. Telephone: 781-0697. "One of the country's best jazz clubs." Cover charge varies with the performer—can be quite expensive if it's someone famous. Call the KJAZ line (tel. 521-9336) for an update on concerts and jam sessions in the Bay Area.

● For disco dancing, try I-Beam, 1245 Haight. Telephone: 495-0185. $6 cover, but students enter free on Wednesdays and Thursdays.

● More disco at Trocadero Transfer, 520 4th St. Telephone: 495-6620. Cover charge varies; starts at $5.

● Studio West, Vallejo & Front St. Telephone: 781-6357. The cover is $6. "A good crowd of both gays and straights."

● Major Pond's, corner of California and Divisadero. Telephone: 567-5010. A good spot for a drink and music that may be jazz or folk or something in between.

● Rockin Robin's, 1840 Haight St. at Stanyan St. Telephone: 221-1960. Dancing to 50's and 60's music; $2 cover charge on weekends.

● For half-price theater tickets on the day of performance, try STUBS ticket outlet at Union Square facing Stockton St. Telephone: 433-7827.

● Besides the well established ACT Theater, there are lots of alternative, experimental plays being performed at places like the Magic Theater (tel. 421-

8822), the One Act Theatre Company, near Union Square (tel. 421-6162), and the Theatre Artaud (tel. 621-7797). All of the above will give special prices to students.

- Castro Theater, 420 Castro. Telephone: 621-6120. It's worth a trip just to see the architecture or hear the organist. Call for the schedule.
- York Theater, 24th St. at Portero Ave. Telephone: 282-0316. A neighborhood movie theater with a 30's decor. $3.50 for a movie.
- Ploughshares Coffeehouse, at Fort Mason. Telephone: 441-8910. About $3.50 cover. Good place for anyone serious about folk music.
- The Plough and The Star, 116 Clement St. Telephone: 751-1122. An authentic Irish pub with dancing and an open microphone.
- Davies Symphony Hall, Civic Center, Grove & Van Ness. Telephone: 431-5400. Where the San Francisco Symphony is located. Tours of the hall every day.
- Dance is an integral part of the life of the Bay Area. The San Francisco Ballet performs at the Opera House on Van Ness Ave. at Grove St. across from Davies Hall. Tickets go from $4 all the way up. There are lots of small dance companies in the area too, including the Margaret Jenkins Dance Studio, which performs at the Performance Gallery, 3153 17th St. (tel. 863-9834).

Shopping: City Lights, 261 Columbus Ave. Lawrence Ferlinghetti's gift to San Francisco. One of the first paperback bookstores in the world and a literary meeting place.

- Green Apple Books, 506 Clement St. Friendly staff sells used books. You can browse for hours.
- A Clean, Well-lighted Bookstore, in the Opera Plaza on Van Ness. A friendly, new place that's well stocked.
- Revolver Records, 520 Clement. Used records, all types of music. Many records as low as $2.
- Tower Records, Columbus Ave. & Bay St. Sells a large selection of records until midnight.
- Discount Records, 656 Market St. The name says it all.
- Union St. all the way from Steiner to Gough St. has all types of stores—selling antiques, gifts, art, clothing, and flowers. Try the Fillmore District between Fillmore and Bush, and California St. for a string of small boutiques with interesting art objects on display and some great used clothing places like Repeat Performance and Seconds to Go.
- California Surplus Sales, 966 Mission St. and on Market St. For a large selection of camping equipment at reasonable prices.
- Cost Plus, 2552 Taylor St. at Fisherman's Wharf. A huge warehouse full of imports from all over the world. Two blocks for browsing.
- Clement St. Best part of town for bargain shopping. Many used clothing stores, factory outlets, small boutiques, coffeeshops, and cafes away from the regular tourist haunts.
- Noe Valley. Lots of "new wave" boutiques on the direct Metro line downtown on the J Church.

San Jose

Accommodations: Joe West Hall, San Jose State University, 375 South 9th St., 95112. Telephone: 408/277-2114. Open June 1 to August 15 for students,

individuals, and groups affiliated with educational institutions only. $18 single; $14 per person double.
- Motel 6, 2560 Fontaine Rd., 95121. Telephone: 408/274-2900. See Anaheim listing for rates.
- E-Z 8 Motel, 1550 North 1st St., 95112. Telephone: 408/292-1830. $31.88 for one: $33.88 for two in one bed; $38.80 for three or four in two beds.
- E-Z 8 Motel, 2050 North 1st St., 95131. Telephone: 408/295-4606. See above listing for rates.
- Sixpence Inn, 2081 North 1st St., 95131. Telephone: 408/288-5880. $20 to $28 for up to four people.

San Leandro

Accommodation: Friendship Budget Inn, 16500 Foothill Blvd., 94578. Telephone: 415/276-6290. $24 to $34 for one; $24 to $36 for two in one bed; $35 to $45 for two in two beds.

San Luis Obispo

Accommodations: Motel 6, 1433 Calle Joaquin, 93401. Telephone: 805/544-8400. See Anaheim listing for rates.
- Allstar Inn, 1625 Calle Joaquin, 93401. Telephone: 805/541-6992. See Bakersfield listing for rates.

San Pedro

Accommodation: Imperial 400 Motor Inn, 411 South Pacific Ave., 90731. Telephone: 213/831-0195. $24 to $26 for one; $28 to $32 for two in one bed; $30 to $36 for two in two beds.

San Ysidro

Accommodation: Motel 6, 160 East Calle Primero, 92073. Telephone: 619/428-4491. See Anaheim listing for rates.

Santa Ana

Accommodation: YMCA, 205 West Civic Center Dr., 92701. Telephone: 714/542-3511. Three blocks from bus, half a mile from train. Men only. $14.20 single; $21 double. Weekly rate: $80.

Santa Barbara

On Campus: The University of California has a branch in this city—"one of the most beautiful cities on the West Coast right on the ocean." For organic food, try the Playa Azul, 902 South Santa Barbara.
Accommodations: Motel 6, 443 Corona Del Mar, 93103. Telephone: 805/965-0300. See Anaheim listing for rates.

- Motel 6, 5897 Calle Real, Goleta, 93117. Telephone: 805/964-1812. See Anaheim listing for rates.
- Motel 6, 3505 State St., 93105. Telephone: 805/687-5400. See Anaheim listing for rates.
- Allstar Inn, 5550 Carpinteria Ave., 93013. Telephone: 805/684-8602. See Bakersfield listing for rates.

Santa Clara

Accommodation: Motel 6, 3208 El Camino Real, 95051. Telephone: 408/248-2479. See Anaheim listing for rates.

Santa Cruz

Accommodation: Santa Cruz Hostel Project (AYH-SA), P.O. Box 1241, 95061. Telephone: 408/423-8304. Open mid-June to end of August.

Santa Fe Springs

Accommodation: Allstar Inn, 13412 Excelsior, 90670. Telephone: 213/921-0596. See Bakersfield listing for rates.

Santa Maria

Accommodation: Motel 6, 839 East Main St., 93454. Telephone: 805/922-6461. See Anaheim listing for rates.

Santa Rosa

Help: Helpline, 707/544-HELP.
Accommodations: Motel 6, 2760 Cleveland Ave., 95401. Telephone: 707/546-9563. See Anaheim listing for rates.
- Allstar Inn, 3145 Cleveland Ave., 95401. Telephone: 707/525-9010. See Bakersfield listing for rates.

Saratoga

Accommodation: Sanborn Park Hostel (AYH), 🚹, 15808 Sanborn Rd., 95070. Telephone: 408/741-9555. $5 for AYH/IYHF members; $7.50 for nonmembers. "Beautiful old building listed in National Register of Historic Places and set in a forest of redwoods, oak, and madrone trees."

Sepulveda

Accommodation: Friendship Tahiti Motel, 9151 Sepulveda Blvd., 91343. Telephone: 818/894-4051. $24 to $26 for one or two in one bed; $30 for two in two beds.

Simi Valley

Accommodation: Motel 6, 2566 North Erringer Rd., 93065. Telephone: 805/526-3666. See Anaheim listing for rates.

South Lake Tahoe

Accommodations: Motel 6, 2375 Lake Tahoe Rd., P.O. Box 7756, 95731. Telephone: 916/541-6272. See Anaheim listing for rates.
● South Lake Tahoe Hostel (AYH), 1043 Martin St., Box 7054, 95731. Telephone: 916/544-3834. Closed April 1 to May 15 and November 1 to December 20. $7 summer, $8 winter for AYH members. Advance reservations suggested June to September and Christmas. Sleeping bag required.

Stanford

Help: The Bridge, 415/497-3392.
Accommodation: Stanford University Residence Halls, 🛆, Stanford Conference Office, 123 Encina Commons, 94305. Telephone: 415/497-3126. Men, women, and children. Open mid-June to mid-September. $21.75 single; $16 per person in shared room.

Stanton

Accommodation: Motel 6, 7450 Katella Ave., 90680. Telephone: 714/898-1179. See Anaheim listing for rates.

Stockton

Accommodations: Motel 6, 4100 Waterloo Rd., 95205. Telephone: 209/931-1710. See Anaheim listing for rates.
● Motel 6, 1625 French Camp Turnpike Rd., 95206. Telephone: 209/943-0953. See Anaheim listing for rates.
● Allstar Inn, 817 Navy Dr., 95206. Telephone: 209/946-0923. See Bakersfield listing for rates.
● Allstar Inn, 6717 Plymouth Rd., 95207. Telephone: 209/951-8120. See Bakersfield listing for rates.
● Eden Park Inn, √, 1005 North El Dorado, 95202. Telephone: 209/466-2711. $29 for one; $31 for two in one bed; $32 to $36 for two in two beds.
● Sixpence Inn, 2717 West March Lane, 95207. Telephone: 209/477-5576. $20 to $28 for up to four people.

Sunnyvale

Accommodation: Motel 6, 806 Ahwanee Ave., 94086. Telephone: 408/739-4450. See Anaheim listing for rates.

Sylmar

Accommodation: Motel 6, 12775 Encinitas Ave., 91342. Telephone: 818/365-7954. See Anaheim listing for rates.

Thousand Oaks

"A beautiful city midway between Santa Barbara and Los Angeles, 30 minutes from Malibu."

Accommodations: Motel 6, 2850 Camino Dos Rios, Newbury Park, 91320. Telephone: 805/498-1669. See Anaheim listing for rates.
● Allstar Inn, 1510 Newbury Rd., 91360. Telephone: 805/499-5888. See Bakersfield listing for rates.

Three Rivers

Camping: Kings Canyon National Park, 93633. Telephone: 209/565-3341. Campgrounds at Azalea Canyon View, Crystal Springs, Sunset, and Cedar Grove. Azalea is open all year; the others are open from May to October. $6 per campsite per night.
● Sequoia National Park, 93271. Six campgrounds at Atwell Mill, Buckeye Flat, and Dorst, which are open during the summer season; and Lodgepole, South Fork, and Potwisha, which are open year round. $6 fee except for Atwell and South Fork, which have a $4 fee.

Tracy

Accommodation: Motel 6, 3810 Tracy Blvd., 95376. Telephone: 209/835-8666. See Anaheim listing for rates.

Truckee

Accommodation: Star Hotel (AYH), P.O. Box 1227, 10015 West River St., 95734. Telephone: 916/587-3007. $6 summer, $7 winter for AYH members; $9 summer, $10 winter for nonmembers.

Tulare

Accommodations: Motel 6, 1111 North Blackstone, 93274. Telephone: 209/688-8507. See Anaheim listing for rates.
● Tulare Inn, √, Hwy. 99 at East Paige Ave., 93274. Telephone: 209/686-8571. $25 for one; $27 to $30 for two in one bed; $29 for two in two beds; $35 for three in two beds; $42 for four in two beds.
● TraveLodge, √, 1050 East Rankin Ave., 200 & SR 99, 93274. Telephone:

209/688-6671. Airport transportation available. $29 for one; $33 for two in one bed; $37 for two in two beds.

Tulelake

Camping: Lava Beds National Monument, ⬧, P.O. Box 867, 96134. Telephone: 916/667-2282. Forty campsites open year round; water is shut off in winter. $5 per campsite per night.

Turlock

Accommodations: Motel 6, 250 South Walnut Rd., 95380. Telephone: 209/632-6668. Near Yosemite National Park. See Anaheim listing for rates.
• Accord Home Hostel (AYH), c/o Don and Lynn. Telephone: 209/634-2691. $5 for AYH members. Advance reservations necessary.

Tustin

Accommodation: Sixpence Inn, 1611 Laguna Rd., 92680. Telephone: 714/832-3220. See Anaheim listing for rates.

Twentynine Palms

Camping: Joshua Tree National Monument, 74458 National Monument Dr., 92277. Telephone: 619/367-7511. Eight campgrounds at Belle, Black Rock Canyon, Cottonwood Spring, Hidden Valley, Indian Cove, Jumbo Rocks, Ryan and White Tank are open from October 1 to June 1. Only Hidden Valley and A Loop at Cottonwood Spring are open during the summer. No entrance fee; $5 per campsite at Black Rock Canyon and Cottonwood Spring. (Black Rock Canyon may close in 1986 due to funding shortages. If open, it will be on the Ticketron Reservation System.)

Ukiah

Accommodation: Motel 6, 1208 South State St., 95482. Telephone: 707/462-8763. See Anaheim listing for rates.

Vacaville

Accommodation: Motel 6, 107 Lawrence Dr., 95688. Telephone: 707/448-6663. See Anaheim listing for rates.

Vallejo

Accommodations: Motel 6, 101 Maritime Academy Dr., 94590. Telephone: 707/552-3666. See Anaheim listing for rates.
• Allstar Inn, 1455 Sears Point Rd., 94590. Telephone: 707/643-7611. See Bakersfield listing for rates.

- Allstar Inn, 597 Sandy Beach Rd., 94590. Telephone: 707/552-2912. See Bakersfield listing for rates.
- E-Z 8 Motel, 4 Mariposa St., 94590. Telephone: 707/554-1840. See Pismo Beach listing for rates.

Van Nuys

Accommodation: Allstar Inn, 15711 Roscoe Blvd., 91343. Telephone: 818/894-9341. See Bakersfield listing for rates.

Ventura

Accommodation: Motel 6, 2145 East Harbor Blvd., 93003. Telephone: 805/648-3366. See Anaheim listing for rates.

Victorville

Accommodations: Motel 6, 16901 Stoddard Wells Rd., 92392. Telephone: 619/245-9548. See Anaheim listing for rates.
- E-Z 8 Motel, 15401 Park Ave. E., 92392. Telephone: 619/243-1227. $22.88 for one; $25.88 for two in one bed; $30.88 for three or four in two beds.
- E-Z 8 Motel, 15366 La Paz Ave., 92392. Telephone: 619/243-2220. See above listing for rates.

Walnut Creek

Accommodation: Motel 6, 2389 North Main St., 94596. Telephone: 415/939-8181. See Anaheim listing for rates.

Weed

Accommodation: Motel 6, 466 North Weed Blvd., 96094. Telephone: 916/938-3675. See Anaheim listing for rates.

Westminster

Accommodation: Motel 6, 6266 Westminster Ave., 92683. Telephone: 714/894-9811. See Anaheim listing for rates.

Whiskeytown

Camping: Whiskeytown National Recreation Area, √ &, P.O. Box 188, 96095. Telephone: 916/241-6584. Three campgrounds at Brandy Creek, Dry Creek, and Oak Bottom (walk-in only). Open all year. $5 per campsite per night at Oak Bottom. Fee varies at other areas depending upon size of group. "Two National Park Service Campgrounds; one for groups with reservations only. One self-contained with RVs only. Also one campground operated by National Park Service concessionaire with 105 tent sites and 50 RV sites."

Whittier

Accommodations: Motel 6, 8221 South Pioneer Blvd., 90606. Telephone: 213/695-0078. See Anaheim listing for rates.
● Friendship Blue Pacific Motel, 12702 East Whittier Blvd., 90602. Telephone: 213/698-0125. $24 to $28 for one; $26 to $30 for two in one bed; $30 to $38 for two in two beds.

Williams

Accommodation: Motel 6, 455 4th St., 95987. Telephone: 916/473-2995. See Anaheim listing for rates.

Woodland

Accommodation: Motel 6, 1564 East Main St., 95695. Telephone: 916/666-4611. See Anaheim listing for rates.

Yosemite

Accommodations: The Yosemite Park and Curry Company, √, Yosemite National Park, 95389, operates several accommodations within Yosemite National Park. Reservations are requested as far in advance as possible and may be made by phone. Telephone: 209/252-4848. Some of these accommodations are out of the price range of this book, but the following aren't:
● Yosemite Lodge Cabins. Without bath or water. $31 for one or two people; $5 for each additional person; $2.50 for each child under 12. Use central bathhouse. Linen supplied.
● Curry Village Tent Cabins. $19 for one or two people; $4 for each additional person; $2 for each child under 12. Use central bathhouse. Linen supplied.
● Housekeeping Camp. Units for one to four persons. $23.25 per day. Summer only. You supply your own linen and use central bathhouse.
● White Wolf Lodge Tents. $22.50 for one or two people; $5 for each additional person. Use central bathhouse. Linen supplied.
Camping: National Park Service, P.O. Box 577, 95389. Telephone: 209/372-1000. There are restrictions on the length of time you may camp in Yosemite, particularly during summer season. Check with National Park Service. Twenty-two campgrounds are available and most are open from May or June to September or October. Lower Pines and Sunnyside in Yosemite Valley, Wawona and Hodgdon Meadow in Oak Flat are open year round.
Reservations are required for campsites in Yosemite Valley's auto campground from early May through September. Campground reservations may be made up to, but no more than eight weeks in advance of, your visit, at any Ticketron outlet; by mail order; or in person at the National Park Service Campground Reservation office in Yosemite Valley (open May-September). All other campgrounds in the Park Service are operated on a first-come, first-served basis. $2 entrance fee plus $7 per campsite per night (plus $3.50 reservation system fee).
Note: In summer, Yosemite Valley is filled to capacity. It is suggested that

you try outlying and remote areas of the park if you want to experience wilderness.

Yreka

Accommodations: Budget Host-Thunderbird Lodge, ∨, 526 South Main St., 96097. Telephone: 916/842-4404. $26 for one; $32 to $36 for two in one bed; $34 to $40 for two in two beds.
- Motel 6, 1785 South Main St., 96097. Telephone: 916/842-1266. See Anaheim listing for rates.
- Friendship Klamath Motor Lodge, 1111 South Main St., 96097. $24 to $28 for one; $26 to $30 for two in one bed; $28 to $32 for two in two beds.
- TraveLodge, ∨ ♿, 136 Montague Rd., 96097. Telephone: 916/842-5781. $28 for one; $33 for two in one bed; $40 for two in two beds.

Yuba City

Accommodation: Motel 6, 700 North Polara, 95991. Telephone: 916/673-1893. See Anaheim listing for rates.

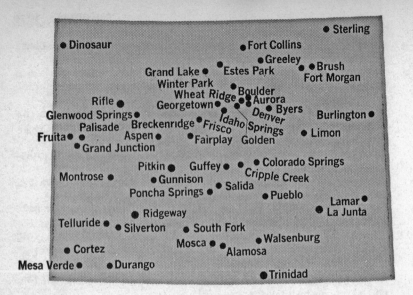

Colorado

Most of Colorado is located in the Rocky Mountains, and its natural beauty is extraordinary. Boulder is the student center of the state and Vail and Aspen are where everyone from the East Coast wants to go skiing.

The Colorado Tourism Board promises 300 days of sunshine and crisp, clean air in what they call their 104,000-square-mile outdoor amphitheater. About one-third of Colorado is under government jurisdiction so it cannot be spoiled. There are 11 national forests, national parks, national monuments, national recreation areas, and national grasslands. Whatever your outdoor fun is, you can probably do it in Colorado. Before the snow falls, backpacking is a favorite Colorado activity and you can do it to your heart's content in the wilderness areas of Rocky Mountain National Park; south of Pikes Peak, near Colorado Springs; west of Denver in the Mount Evans area; in the San Juan mountain range in the southwest; north of Glenwood Springs, in the Flattops and Rabbit Ears Pass Area near Steamboat Springs; and in the Ten Mile Range south of Vail.

When winter comes, everyone in Colorado talks "ski." The Rocky Mountains have a powder snow that skiers dream about. For a guide to Colorado ski areas, write to Colorado Ski Country USA, Brownleigh Court, Suite A201, 1410 Grant St., Denver, CO 80203, or phone 303/837-0793.

Another favorite Colorado activity is river tripping. The state tourist office (address below) will supply you with a list of 14 companies that operate river trips—trips that last from one hour to a week or more and can be booked with a guide who does all the paddling or without for a do-it-yourself experience!

Note: Colorado has an active and ever-growing number of youth hostels. At some you must be an AYH card holder; at others you may buy introductory passes. Call individual hostels to make sure.

Some Special Events: Ullrfest Winter Carnival in Breckenridge and National Western Stock Show in Denver (January); American Ski Classic in Vail (March); Subaru Freestyle Nationals in Winter Park (April); Annual Kinetic Sculpture Challenge in Boulder (May); Annual Bluegrass and Country Music Festival in Telluride (June); Jazz Festival in Central City (August); Scottish Highland Festival in Estes Park and Fall Rendezvous of Mountain Men in La Junta (September); Parade of Lights in Denver (December).

Hitching: A friend in Boulder says that people do hitchhike there, even though the police are against it. He recommends, however, that it be done with caution. Another, in Denver, says that hitching is accepted by most people and that if you stay on the curb while hitching and carry good identification with you, you shouldn't have difficulty with the police.

The Colorado State Police sent us a copy of the state law pertaining to hitchhiking, which states: "No person shall stand in a roadway for the purpose of soliciting a ride from the driver of any private vehicle." Added in 1975 was the sentence: "For the purposes of this subsection, 'roadway' means that portion of the road normally used by moving motor vehicle traffic."

Tourist Information: Colorado Tourism Board, 5500 South Syracuse St., Suite 267, Englewood, CO 80111. Telephone: 303/779-1067.

Alamosa

Accommodation: Walsh Hotel (AYH-SA) ♿ ★, 617 6th St., 81101. Telephone: 303/589-6641. $7 to $17 single; $9 to $19 double; $14 to $21 triple.

Aspen

Accommodation: Highlands Inn (AYH-SA), P.O. Box 4708, 1650 Maroon Creek Rd., 81612. Telephone: 303/925-5050. $9 summer, $13 winter for AYH members. The inn is open from November 1 through April; June through September. It is located at the base of Aspen Highlands ski area. "Here AYH'ers can enjoy all the facilities of a luxury hotel including pool, sauna, Jacuzzi, and free buses to town and to hiking areas—at what are probably the cheapest rates in all Aspen." Advance reservations suggested in July, August, and during winter season.

Aurora

Help: COMITIS Crisis Center, 9840 East 17th Ave., 80010. Telephone: 303/343-9890. 24-hour switchboard for information, referrals, and help.

Accommodations: Budget Host—Riviera Motel, 9100 East Colfax, 80010. Telephone: 303/366-2681. Six minutes from Denver airport. Courtesy car available. Summer: $27 for one; $32 for two in one bed; $35 for two in two beds.

Winter: $24 for one; $26 for two in one bed; $28 for two in two beds. Heated pool.
 • Friendship Dunes Motel, 13000 East Colfax Ave., 80010. Telephone: 303/344-3220. Airport transportation available. $23 to $27 for one; $28 to $30 for two in one bed; $30 to $32 for two in two beds.

Boulder

Help: Women's Line, 303/492-8910.

On Campus: A friend from the University of Colorado calls this "Mork-and-Mindy land, or East Coast/West Coast slick with a little hint of western laid-back for flavor." He goes on to explain that a few years ago Boulder was summer headquarters for the street people and the locals didn't like it at all. Some of the feelings persist, but in general young travelers are welcome—"if you're reasonably clean, sober at noon, and don't try to sleep in Central Park you won't be hassled."

When you're hungry in Boulder and want vegetarian food, try Hanna's New Age Foods (open at lunchtime only), located above the New Age Food Store at 10th and Pearl. For not-so-organic eating, try Don's Cheese and Sausage Mart, 28th and Baseline. Other possibilities: The Harvest, at 18th and Pearl, for healthful food; Marie's on North Broadway, for reasonable prices and an occasional Czech specialty; and the New York Deli at the Pearl St. Mall. Tulagi is a restaurant and nightclub located at 1129 13th, on "The Hill," near campus. They serve lunch and dinner from the same menu offering "stuffer" sandwiches for about $2.50. All drinks are $1.50. The best deal in town is probably the food service in the University Memorial Center on campus, at either the Tabor Inn or the Alfred E. Packer Memorial Grill, named after the U.S.'s only convicted cannibal.

If you're in Boulder during the warm weather you'll surely walk along the Mall with a Häagen-Dazs ice cream cone and enjoy the jugglers, magicians, tightrope walkers, belly dancers, musicians, and all the other people. And if you're around in the beginning of April, you'll get to enjoy the annual campus Trivia Bowl.

To know what's going on, check the *Colorado Daily,* the campus paper, or the *Grapevine.* For disco, the place to be seen is Anthony's Gardens in the Harvest House Hotel, and if your desires run to an English/Irish pub-type place, try the James, just off the Mall. When it's time to leave Boulder, you can check the rider board next to the Packer Grill in the University Memorial Center—it's divided into geographical areas and gets lots of use.

"If you're clean, tan, and play Frisbee, there's a place for you."

Accommodation: Boulder International Hostel (AYH-SA), √ ★, 1107 12th St., 80302. Telephone: 303/442-0522. Near bus station. $6.25 for AYH members in the dorm; an introductory pass available for nonmembers. $18 twin; $27 triple; $30 quad. Family and private rooms are often available too. Bring your own sleeping bag, sheet, sleeping sack, or linen, or rent linen for 50¢. There's a kitchen too, which can accommodate several cooks at once.

Breckenridge

Tourist Information: Breckenridge Resort Chamber of Commerce, 303/453-2918.

Accommodation: Fireside Inn (AYH-SA), 200 Wellington St., 80424. Telephone: 303/453-6456. Summer: $24 single; $29 double; $12 in dorm. Winter: $45 single or double; $16 in dorm. Continental breakfast included in summer prices. "A cozy, friendly place in an interesting refurbished Western mining town." Excellent summer and winter recreational facilities.

Brush

Accommodation: Budget Host—Empire Motel, 1408 West Edison, 80723. Telephone: 303/842-2876. $19 to $21 for one; $21.60 to $24 for two in one bed; $26.50 to $29 for two in two beds.

Burlington

Accommodations: Sloan's Motel, 1901 Rose Ave., 80807. Telephone: 303/346-5333. $24 for one; $28 for two in one bed; $32 for two in two beds.
 ● Budget Host—Western Motor Inn, 2222 Rose Ave., 80807. Telephone: 303/346-5371. Summer: $22 to $27 for one; $24 to $29 for two in one bed; $27 to $32 for two in two beds. Winter: $18 to $21 for one; $21 to $24 for two in one bed; $24 to $26 for two in two beds.
 ● Econo Lodge, √, 450 South Lincoln, P.O. Box 188, 80807. Telephone: 303/346-5555. $30 for one; $34 for two in one bed; $39 for two in two beds.

Byers

Accommodation: Longhorn Motel, jct. I-70 & Hwy. 36 at Exit 316, P.O. Box 196, 80103. Telephone: 303/822-5205. $26 to $30 for one; $28 to $33 for two in one bed; $32 to $40 for two in two beds.

Colorado Springs

Help: Terros, 303/471-4127. "We would be sympathetic to and interested in helping any travelers who should contact us." Terros can help you to find low-cost housing in this fast-growing town. They also mentioned that "the hitchhiker isn't really hassled but he isn't welcomed either."

Accommodations: Colorado Springs Hostel (AYH-SA), Farragut Hall, 17 Farragut Ave., 80909. Telephone: 303/634-9657 or 471-2938. $7.75 for AYH members.
 ● Motel 6, 3228 North Chestnut St., 80907. Telephone: 303/471-2340. $17.95 for one; $21.95 for two; $2 for each additional person.
 ● Friendship Dale Downtown Motel, 620 West Colorado Ave., 80905. Telephone: 303/636-3721. $21 to $31 for one; $23 to $31 for two in one bed; $25 to $35 for two in two beds.
 ● Budget Host—Frontier Motel, 4300 North Nevada Ave., 80907. Telephone: 303/598-1563. Airport transportation available. $26 to $34 for one; $28

to $36 for two in one bed; $31 to $38 for two in two beds. September 15 to May 15: $22 to $28 for one or two in one bed.

● Friendship Spruce Lodge Inn, 2724 North Nevada Ave., 80907. Telephone: 303/635-3523. $20 to $32 for one; $22 to $34 for two in one bed; $24 to $40 for two in two beds.

● Econo Lodge, ♿, I-25 & Garden of the Gods Rd., 80907. Telephone: 303/594-0964. April 1 to April 30: $26.95 for one; $30.95 for two in one bed; $38.95 for two in two beds. May 1 to September 15: $44.95 for one; $48.95 for two. September 16 to September 30: $28.95 for one; $32.95 for two.

● Econo Lodge, √♿, 6875 East Hwy., 80916. April 1 to May 14 and September 16 to September 30: $26.95 for one; $30.95 for two in one bed; $32.95 for two in two beds. May 15 to September 15: $30.95 for one; $34.95 for two in one bed; $38.95 for two in two beds.

● Imperial 400 Motor Inn, 714 North Nevada Ave., 80903. Telephone: 303/636-3385. $22 to $28 for one; $26 to $32 for two in one bed; $28 to $36 for two in two beds.

● Imperial 400 Motor Inn, 1231 South Nevada Ave., 80903. Telephone: 303/634-1545. $24 to $30 for one; $26 to $32 for two in one bed; $30 to $36 for two in two beds.

Cortez

Accommodation: Friendship Inn Aneith Lodge, 645 East Main St., 81321. Telephone: 303/565-3453. $24 to $32 for one; $26 to $32 for two in one bed; $38 for two in two beds.

Cripple Creek

Accommodation: Westward Ho Motel, 236 West Bennett, 80813. Telephone: 303/689-2374. Open June 1 to October 1. $22 single; $29 double; $34 triple; $37 quad. "A small motel with 'Old West' exterior and modern interior; located in an old gold-mining district."

Denver

Denver is the mile-high capital of Colorado, exactly 5280 feet above sea level. One native says that anyone visiting the city should first "see Red Rocks Park—an incredibly beautiful natural amphitheater right outside Denver—and then move on to the mountains." Before heading for the mountains, though, there are some things that one should see in the city: Larimer Square, between 13th and 15th Sts., is a rebuilt section of downtown reminiscent of the 1890s; the Denver Art Museum, adjacent to the City Center and housed in an ultramodern building, is worth a visit; and the Denver Museum of Natural History is well known for its collections, including dioramas of native birds and animals, meteorites, and Indian artifacts. For what's happening where, check the *Denver Post*'s weekend section that comes out on Friday and *Rocky Mountain News*.

Two recommended guidebooks to the city are *Denver Guidebook*, by Tami Abell, Johnson Publishing Co., 1880 South 57th Court, Boulder, CO 80301 ($3.95), a basic book on eating, drinking, dancing, etc. in Denver and *The Visi-*

tors' Sight Seeing Tour: Denver in a Day, by Dallas Boyd, Stonehenge Publishers, 2969 Baseline Rd., Boulder, CO 80303 ($4.95)—a self-guided driving tour of the city with lots of photos.

Getting There: Stapleton International Airport is seven miles from downtown and there's a no. 32 bus connecting the town with the airport that costs 70¢ from 6 to 9 a.m. and from 4 to 6 p.m.; 35¢ at other times. You can catch this bus on the lower level, between doors 1 and 5. A taxi ride on the same route would cost more than $8. The bus terminals are located at Broadway and Colfax and 16th and Market; the train station is at 17th and Wynkoop. For Amtrak information, call 800/421-8320; for Rio Grande, 303/629-5533.

Getting Around: By Bus: The city buses run frequently, seven days a week from 5 a.m. until midnight. At rush hour, from 6 to 9 a.m. and from 3 to 6 p.m., the fare is 70¢; half that any other time. Call 778-6000 for information. A free shuttle bus goes along 16th Street Mall from Broadway to Market Street.

● By Taxi: Yellow Cab (tel. 292-1212) and Ritz Cab (294-9199) charge $2.25 for the first mile and $1 for each mile after that. Each additional passenger is 40¢. Zone Cab (tel. 861-2323) charges $1 for the first one-fifth mile; $1 for each additional mile.

● By Car: To rent a car, try one of these: Budget Rent-a-Car, 2150 Broadway (tel. 861-4125; $25.95 per day with unlimited mileage for an economy car); American International Rent-a-Car, 4000 Quebec (tel. 399-5020); $17 per day with unlimited mileage; and Rex on Wheels, 4690 Pecos (tel. 477-1635); five- to ten-year-old cars rent for $9 per day, with the first 20 miles free and 10¢ per mile after that.

Help: Denver and Colorado Convention and Visitors Bureau, 225 West Colfax Ave., 80202 (one block west of Civic Center Park). Telephone: 303/892-1112. (Information booth at airport.)

● Travelers Aid, 504 East 14th Ave., 80204. Telephone: 303/832-3194.

● COMITIS, 9840 East 17th Ave., Aurora. Telephone: 303/343-9890. 24-hour switchboard for information, referrals, and help.

Accommodations: Denver Youth Hostel (AYH), 1452 Detroit, 80206. Telephone: 303/333-7672. $5.50 summer, $6.50 winter for AYH members. "Dormitory-style rooms, clean and friendly."

● YMCA, 25 East 16th Ave., 80202. Telephone: 303/861-8300. Men and women. $16.30 single without bath, $21.25 single with bath; $31.25 double with private bath, $27.50 double with shared bath. Convenient to downtown. Small cafeteria.

● Ranch Manor Motor Inn, 1490 South Sante Fe, 80223. Telephone: 303/733-5581. $19.88 for one; $24.88 for two; $29.88 for three. Two heated pools (summer only).

● Regal 8 Inn, 12033 East 38th Ave. at Peoria St., 80239. Telephone: 303/371-0740. $21.88 for one; $26.88 for two in one bed; $31.88 for two in two beds.

● Regal 8 Inn, 3050 West 49th Ave. at Federal, 80221. Telephone: 303/455-8888. See above listing for rates.

● Motel 6, 12020 East 39th Ave., 80239. Telephone: 303/371-7410. See Colorado Springs listing for rates.

● Motel 6, 6 West 83rd Place, 80221. Telephone: 303/650-0186. See Colorado Springs listing for rates.

● Motel 6, 480 Wadsworth Blvd., 80226. Telephone: 303/238-6471. See Colorado Springs listing for rates.

● Friendship Aristocrat Motor Hotel, 4855 West Colfax Ave., 80204. Telephone: 303/825-2755. $21 to $25 for one; $23 to $27 for two in one bed; $25 to $28 for two in two beds.

● Friendship Belcaro Motel, 1025 South Colorado Blvd., 80222. Telephone: 303/756-3631. $28 to $40 for one; $36 to $44 for two in one bed; $40 to $48 for two in two beds.

● Friendship Valli Hi Inn, 7320 Pecos, 80221. Telephone: 303/429-3551. $29 to $35 for one or two in one bed; $31 to $37 for two in two beds.

● Econo Lodge, √, 930 Valley Hwy., 80204. Telephone: 303/592-1555. $24.95 to $27.95 for one; $31.95 to $35.95 for two. Higher rates apply during special events.

Where to Eat: Beau Jo's, 2024 East Colfax. Telephone: 388-7600. Open 11:30 a.m. to 9:30 p.m., until 11:30 on weekends. A pizza big enough for three costs $5.75.

● Red Moon Pizzeria, 329 East Colfax. Telephone: 861-9930. Open 11 a.m. to 9 p.m. except on Sunday.

● Zach's Ltd., 1480 Humboldt St. Telephone: 831-0870. Open 11 a.m. to 2 a.m., Monday through Saturday; 4 p.m. to midnight Sunday. Features natural foods.

● Chada Thai, 408 East 20th Ave. (downtown). Telephone: 861-7246. Authentic Thai food in a crowded spot; on weekends you'd better have reservations.

● La Bola, 900 Jersey. Telephone: 333-3888. Mexican food dished out in generous portions. Busy neighborhood-type place. Margaritas are a specialty.

● Ohle's, 1520 East Colfax. Telephone: 832-5086. A German deli that shares space with a small food market. Open until 6 p.m., on Saturday to 4 p.m.

● Rich's Café, 80 South Madison. Telephone: 399-4488. Popular watering hole for lunch and after work. Lots of young professional types.

● Le Central, 8th and Lincoln. Telephone: 863-8094. For French cuisine that's not too, too expensive.

● Buckhorn Exchange, 1000 Osage (at 10th Ave.). Telephone: 534-9505. This is the oldest eatery and bar in Colorado. The building dates from 1886. The ambiance is strictly Old West—big game trophies, a gun collection, and a carved wooden bar. Buffalo, elk, and quail are on the menu; lunches from $3.95 to $6.95, dinners from $10.95 to $19.95.

● Le Peep, 915 17th St. (one block from 16th Street Mall at Curtis St.) Telephone: 298-7337. Open 6:30 a.m. to 2 p.m. for breakfast and brunches of eggs, pancakes, and sandwiches.

● Chili Pepper, 2150 Bryant. Telephone: 433-8406. Mexican food for less than $6 a meal. An outdoor patio and a lovely nighttime view.

● Goldie's Delicatessen, 511 16th St. Telephone: 623-6007. Right in the 16th Street Mall between Glenarm and Welton. A popular deli with an outdoor patio.

What to See and Do: Skiing: November through June is ski season in Colorado, and Denver is headquarters for skiers on their way to any one of the state's slopes. Colorado Ski Country, 1410 Grant St. (tel. 837-9907), has ski information and the latest snow reports.

● Cowboys: Every year Denver hosts a ten-day celebration of its cowboy heritage with a rodeo and a show and sale of the finest blue-blooded cattle in the world. Stockmen come from all over the country to look and to buy; the world champion bull is exhibited right in the plush lobby of the Brown Palace Hotel. For ten days, *everybody's* a cowboy.

- Larimer Square, between 13th and 15th Sts. on Larimer St. A re-creation of the area as it appeared in the 1890s with antiques, restaurants, galleries, movies, etc. Often there are street fairs and other celebrations in the square.
- Denver Art Museum, in the Civic Center. Interesting collection in a controversial building designed by Gio Ponti. Admission is $2.50; $1.50 for students and seniors. Closed Monday.
- Denver Botanic Gardens, 1005 York St. Outdoor gardens and a unique conservatory with lush native and exotic plants. Adults, $3; ages 7–15, $1; under 7, free. Open 9 a.m. to 4:45 p.m. every day.
- Colorado Heritage Center, 1300 Broadway. Dioramas, exhibits, and multimedia shows depicting the colorful history of the city and the state. $2.50 for adults; $1 for children and seniors.
- U.S. Mint, Colfax Ave. and Cherokee St. The largest depository of gold bullion outside Fort Knox, the mint makes over 1,000,000 coins per year. Free 20-minute tours every 30 minutes. There's a numismatic shop adjacent to the mint. Telephone: 844-3582 for information.
- Denver Museum of Natural History, in City Park on Colorado Blvd. Everything you'd expect in a natural history museum, plus daily shows in the Gates Planetarium and the IMAX Theater that are spectacular. "Definitely worth a visit." Telephone: 370-6363 for information.

At Night: Aspen City Limits, 4501 East Virginia Ave. Telephone: 377-2701. Open 1 p.m. to 2 a.m., Monday through Saturday; 7 p.m. to midnight Sunday. Live rock and roll. The cover charge is $3 on Friday and Saturday. This is the place to dance—it looks like a ski lodge and has a restaurant on the second floor. There's a free buffet if you get there by 7:30 p.m.

- Swallow Hill Music Association presents programs of folk and acoustic music in different locations around the city. Telephone: 393-6202.
- Jazz: Two possibilities are The Bay Wolf, 231 Milwaukee, in Cherry Creek Shopping Center and The Mall Exchange, corner of 16th and Lawrence.
- To dance: For big band dancing, go to the lobby-lounge of the Park Suite Hotel, 1881 Curtis.
- Theater: Denver Center Theater, at Denver Center for Performing Arts, 14th and Curtis, is headquarters for a repertory company; 20 original productions a year, many by local playwrights, are given at Changing Scene, 1527 ½ Champa (tel. 893-5775) on Thursdays, Fridays, Saturdays, and Sundays.
- Classical Music: The Denver Symphony Orchestra performs September to April at Boetchen Concert Hall, 14th and Curtis. Call 592-7777 for ticket information.
- Ballet: Denver has its own professional resident ballet company performing at the Center for Performing Arts. Call 298-0677 for information.

Shopping: 16th Street Mall, 16th St. from Broadway to Market St. A street devoted to shopping—no traffic and free buses from one end to the other.

- Together Books, 200 East 13th Ave. (13th and Sherman). Telephone: 832-5171. Books on philosophy, survival, women, yoga, the occult, etc.
- Eastern Mountain Sports, 1428 East 15th St. Telephone: 571-1160. Backpacking, camping, climbing, ski touring supplies, and jogging gear. Open until 9 p.m. on Monday, Thursday, and Friday.
- Gart Brothers, 1000 Broadway. Telephone: 861-1122. A large retail store specializing in sports and photographic equipment. (By now you've caught on to the fact that Denverites are very outdoorsy types.)
- Cherry Creek Shopping Center. This is a large complex in the middle of a

residential area bounded by University Ave., Third Ave., Steele St., and North Cherry Creek Dr. It includes a wide variety of stores, large and small—from Sears to exclusive specialty shops, restaurants, and cinemas. Music for All, 2908 East Third Ave. in the shopping center is the place for classical and international music. Some shops in the center are open on Sunday.

● The Tattered Cover, 2930 East Second Ave. A wonderful place to browse for books, maps, posters, and cards.

● Pickwick Discount Books, University Hills Shopping Center, 2553 South Colorado Blvd. Over 10,000 current titles discounted.

● Budget Tapes and Records, 250 Detroit Ave.

Dinosaur

Camping: Dinosaur National Monument, P.O. Box 210, 81610. Telephone: 303/374-2216. Backcountry river sites: many accessible by boat only. Some open year round, some just summer and fall. $5 fee for Green River and Split Mountain campgrounds; the Rainbow Park Campground is free.

Durango

Accommodations: Durango Hostel, P.O. Box 1445, 543 East Second Ave., 81301. Telephone: 303/247-5477 or 247-9905. $7 summer, $8 winter for AYH members. Advance reservations necessary October to March; other times advised. "In a Victorian lodging house originally meant to house railroaders and miners."

● Friendship Sunset Inn, 2855 Main St., 81301. Telephone: 303/247-2653. May to October: $30 to $39 for one; $32 to $42 for two in one bed; $44 to $50 for two in two beds. Winter: $25 to $29 for one; $28 to $32 for two in one bed; $36 to $39 for two in two beds.

Estes Park

Accommodations: H-Bar-Ranch Hostel (AYH), 3500 H-Bar-G Rd., 80517. Six miles northeast of Estes Park, near Rocky Mountain National Park. Telephone: 303/586-3688. Open May 25 to September 12. Six miles from bus station. Hostel owner will pick you up at the Chamber of Commerce Tourist Information Center at 5 p.m. $5.50 for AYH members; membership available at hostel. Advance reservations recommended July 10 to August 25. Bring food to cook because the nearest grocery store is six miles away. "Formerly a Dude Ranch, the hostel has a main building and several cabins with a superb view of the Rocky Mountains."

● Friendship Four Winds, 1120 Big Thompson Hwy., 80517. Telephone: 303/586-3313. Summer: $29 to $39 for one; $33 to $45 for two in one bed; $35 to $49 for two in two beds. Rest of year: $29 to $35 for one or two in one bed; $33 to $45 for two in two beds.

Camping: Rocky Mountain National Park, U.S. 36, two and one half miles west of Estes Park, 80517. Five campgrounds at Aspenglen, Glacier Basin, Longs Peak, Moraine Park, and Timber Creek. $6 per campsite per night; trail camps with no fee, permit required, however. During peak season, you may have to wait a few days for permit issuance.

"For family-style cooking, go to Mountain Man Restaurant, Estes Kountry Kitchen, the Mountaineer, or Crowley's Hi Country Restaurant."

Fairplay

Accommodation: The Historic Fairplay Hotel, 500 Main St., 80440. Telephone: 303/836-2565. $26 single, $30 double without bath; $30 single, $35 double with bath. "A Victorian resort hotel in the Rocky Mountains with a restaurant and bar."

Fort Collins

Help: Community Crisis Center, 303/493-3888.

On Campus: Fort Collins is the home of Colorado State University and the town has a good attitude toward young people. A student there told us that hitchhiking is common but that it is sometimes difficult to catch rides.

The United Campus Ministry at 629 South Howes might be able to help you find an inexpensive or free place to stay. You can call them at 303/482-8487. For outdoor recreational information, call the CSM Experimental Learning Program at 491-7226.

There are inexpensive movies at the Student Center throughout the weekends and a number of concerts and theater performances on and off campus throughout the year. Call 491-5402 for details.

The least expensive place to eat is Freebie's on College Ave., near the University. *The Collegian,* the student newspaper, can provide all kinds of useful information on entertainment, rides, accommodations, and the like.

Accommodations: Motel 6, 3900 East Mulberry, 80524. Telephone: 303/484-6662. See Colorado Springs listing for rates.

● Thrifty Scot Motel, 3625 East Mulberry, 80524. Telephone: 303/221-5490. $25.90 to $29.90 for one; $28.90 to $32.90 for two.

Fort Morgan

Accommodation: Friendship Old Fort Motor Inn, I-76 & Barlow Rd., 80701. Telephone: 303/867-9481. Airport transportation available. $23 to $25 for one; $27 to $29 for two in one bed; $28 to $32 for two in two beds.

Frisco

Accommodation: Woods Inn (AYH-SA), ★, 205 South 2nd Ave., 80443. Telephone: 303/668-3389. Daily, weekly, and monthly rates available (in winter, rates are higher and no weekly rates are offered). $15 to as high as $29 single (depending on type of room); $18 to $32 double; $27 to $39 triple; $32 to $44 quad. Breakfast and linens included in price. Advance reservations of two weeks necessary in winter.

Fruita

Camping: Colorado National Monument, 81521. Telephone: 303/858-3617. Camping at Saddle Horn, four miles south of the West Entrance. Open year round. $5 per campsite per night.

Glenwood Springs

Accommodations: Pinon Pines Apartments, 3210 County Rd., 81601. Telephone: 303/945-8102. One- or two-bedroom furnished apartments. Heated swimming pool and sauna on premises, surrounded by 300 acres of open mountain area. Forty minutes from Aspen. $30 for room with twin beds; $40 for room with four beds. Advance reservations of two to seven days necessary.
● Ponderosa Lodge, 51793 Hwy. 6 & 24, 81601. Telephone: 303/945-5058. $47.50 to $57.50 for two. Some rooms have kitchens, some have fireplaces.
● Friendship Inn Silver Spruce, 162 West Sixth St., 81601. Telephone: 303/945-5458. November 1 to February 28: $21.50 for one; $29.50 for two in one bed; $34.50 for two in two beds. March 1 to May 31: $26.50 for one; $34.50 for two in one bed; $39.50 for two in two beds.
● Friendship Homestead Inn Motel, 52039 Hwy. 6 & 24. Telephone: 303/945-8817. May 15 to September 15: $30 to $38 for two in one bed; $40 to $50 for two in two beds.

Golden

Accommodation: Budget Host—Mountain View Motel, 14825 West Colfax Ave., 80401. Telephone: 303/279-2526. $26 to $32 for one or two in one bed; $32 to $38 for two in two beds. Heated pool.

Grand Junction

Accommodation: Motel 6, 776 Horizon Dr., 81501. Telephone: 303/245-6668. See Colorado Springs listing for rates.

Grand Lake

Accommodations: Shadowcliff Lodge (AYH), P.O. Box 658, 80447. Telephone: 303/627-9966. Situated at the southwest entrance to the Rocky Mountain National Park. Sixteen miles from bus and train station in Granby. You can hitch a ride to Grand Lake with local residents. Open June 1 to October 10. $4.75 for AYH members.
● Dougal's Mountain Inn (AYH-SA), P.O. Box 1, 612 Grand Ave., 80447. Telephone: 303/627-3385. One mile from Rocky Mountain National Park. Open November 15 to April 15. $6.25 for AYH members. Advance reservations necessary. "Built entirely of logs and perched on a cliff overlooking Grand Lake Village and the Colorado 'Great Lakes' area, with a view up North Inlet Stream of Rocky Mountain National Park."

Greeley

On Campus: For general information about this college town, home of the University of Northern Colorado, stop at the Office of International Education, Carter Hall, Room 209. The University Center is the central spot on the UNC campus; it's there that you'll find a bulletin board with rides, and a cafeteria that's a popular meeting place on campus. During the summer, contact the director of housing at the university—there may be a place for you to stay on campus. For collectors of curious facts: Greeley is the home of the number-one cattle feed manufacturer in the world—Monfort of Colorado. You can visit one of their feedlots if you'd like.

Accommodations: Motel 6, 3015 Eighth Ave., Evans, 80620. Telephone: 303/353-6665. See Colorado Springs listing for rates.
● Friendship Inn—Greeley Lamplighter Motel, √ ($2), 2905 Eighth Ave., Evans, 80620. Telephone: 303/352-7070. $23 to $27 for one; $25 to $29 for two in one bed; $30 to $34 for two in two beds.

Guffey

Accommodation: Currant Creek Hostel (AYH-SA), 6121 Rte. 9, 80820. No phone. $2.50 for AYH members; $2.75 for nonmembers. Primarily tent camping. There are three 8' x 10' wall tents and an 18' tipi or use your own tent. On the trans-America bicycle route. Open year round unless winter is too severe. Advisable to contact ahead of time for winter weather conditions. No hookups for RV's.

Gunnison

Accommodations: Friendship Colorado West, 400 East Tomichi, 81230. Telephone: 303/641-1288. $28 to $32 for one; $28 to $34 for two in one bed; $32 to $38 for two in two beds.
● Budget Host—Western Motel, 403 East Tomichi Ave., 81230. Telephone: 303/641-1722. Complimentary airport transportation. $25 to $28 for one; $28 to $34 for two in one bed; $29 to $34 for two in two beds. Heated pool.
Camping: Curecanti National Recreational Area, P.O. Box 1040, 81230. Telephone: 303/641-2337. Camping at Elk Creek (open year-round), Lake Fork, Old Stevens Creek, and Cimarron (open April through November), all on Blue Mesa Lake or Hwy. 50. $5 per campsite per night, except for Stevens Creek, which is $4. Facility is operated by the National Park Service.

Idaho Springs

Accommodation: Best Value Six & Forty Motel, 2920 Colorado Blvd., 80415. Telephone: 303/567-2691. $18 to $30 for up to four people.

La Junta

Accommodation: TraveLodge, √, 110 East First St., 81050. Telephone: 303/384-2504. $24 for one; $30 for two in one bed; $34 for two in two beds.

Lamar

Accommodations: Plaza Motel/Restaurant and Lounge, 905 East Olive, 81052. Telephone: 303/336-7701. $18 to $22 for one; $22 to $27 for two in one bed; $24 to $30 for two in two beds.

● Budget Host—Stagecoach Motor Inn, 1201 North Main St., 81052. Telephone: 303/336-7471. Airport courtesy car. Winter: $20 to $28 for one; $24 to $34 for two in one bed; $26 to $34 for two in two beds. Summer: $24 to $36 for one; $26 to $38 for two in one bed; $28 to $38 for two in two beds. Heated pool.

Limon

Accommodation: Friendship Silver Spur Motel, 514 Main St., 80828. Telephone: 303/775-9561. $22 to $30 for one; $24 to $30 for two in one bed; $28 to $38 for two in two beds.

Mesa Verde

Camping: Mesa Verde National Park, 81330. Telephone: 303/529-4461. Campground at Morefield Canyon. Open May 1 to October 15. $5 per campsite per night.

Montrose

Accommodation: Friendship Black Canyon, one mile east on U.S. 50, P.O. Box 1325, 81402. Airport transportation service available. Telephone: 303/249-3495. $30 to $34 for one or two in one bed; $32 to $38 for two in two beds.

Mosca

Camping: Great Sand Dunes National Monument, 81146. Telephone: 303/378-2312. Campgrounds at Dunes open April 1 to October 31. $5 per campsite per night during summer season. Park is open year round. "Biggest sandbox in the state!"

Palisade

Accommodation: Superior Mesa View Motel, √, Hwys. 6 & 24, 81526. Telephone: 303/464-5618 or 464-5619. $16 for one; $24.10 for two in one bed; $26.25 for two in two beds.

Pitkin

Accommodation: Pitkin Hotel & Hostel (AYH-SA), Ⓢ √ ★, 400 Main St., 81237. Telephone: 303/641-2757. Call ahead to arrange ride from Gunnison bus station. Dorm: $5 summer, $7 winter for AYH members. Private rooms: $15 single; $17 double; $19 triple; $21 quad. Advance reservations of one week suggested; call first in winter.

Poncha Springs

Accommodation: Rocky Mountain Lodge, √, 446 East Hwy. 50, Box 172, 81242. Telephone: 303/539-6008. $22 for one; $24 for two in one bed; $28 for two in two beds.

Pueblo

Accommodations: Pueblo YWCA (AYH), 801 North Santa Fe Ave., 81003. Telephone: 303/542-6904. $5 for AYH members.
● University of Southern Colorado Hostel (AYH-SA), 2200 North Bonforte Blvd., 81007. Telephone: 303/549-2149. Open June 7 to August 20. $5.50 for AYH members. Advance reservations suggested. Cafeteria on premises.
● Regal 8 Inn, 960 Hwy. 50 W., 81008. Telephone: 303/543-8900. See Denver listing for rates.
● Motel 6, 4103 North Elizabeth, 81008. Telephone: 303/545-8429. See Colorado Springs listing for rates.
● Friendship Rambler Motel, 4400 North Elizabeth St., 81008. Telephone: 303/543-4173. $22 to $23 for one; $25 to $26 for two in one bed; $27 to $29 for two in two beds.

Ridgeway

Accommodation: The Pueblo Hostel & Cantina (AYH-SA), 251 Liddell Dr., 81432. Telephone: 303/626-5939. $2 per person in dorms. $16 single, $24 double in private rooms. Breakfast included. Advance reservations of two weeks suggested for July 4th and Labor Day.

Rifle

Accommodation: Econo Lodge, √ &, 717 Taghenbaugh Rd., 81650. Telephone: 303/625-4320. Airport courtesy car available. $29.95 for one; $34.95 for two in one bed; $39.95 for two in two beds. Complimentary continental breakfast.

Salida

Accommodation: Friendship Ranch House Motor Lodge, 7545 West Hwy. 50, 81201. Telephone: 303/539-6655. $24 to $38 for one; $26 to $36 for two in one bed; $32 to $44 for two in two beds.

Silverton

Accommodation: Teller House Hostel (AYH-SA), P.O. Box 457, 81433. Telephone: 303/387-5423. $6.75 for AYH members. "European-style hotel with breakfast included in price of room. In a small gold-mining town (population 800) in the San Juan Mountains."

South Fork

Accommodation: Spruce Lodge (AYH-SA), Ⓢ✔️♿, 29432 S.W. Hwy. 160, 81154. Telephone: 303/873-9980. Call for ride from bus station. $8 for AYH members. Families welcome. "Homelike atmosphere."

Sterling

Accommodations: Friendship El Patio Motel, 100 Logan St., 80751. Telephone: 303/522-5353. $25 for one; $28 for two in one bed; $32 to $35 for two in two beds.
● Budget Host—Blue Bird Motel, ✔️, Hwy. 6 at Iris Dr., 80751. Telephone: 303/522-5300. Courtesy car available upon request. $22 for one; $24 for two in one bed; $26 for two in two beds.

Telluride

Accommodation: Oak Street Inn (AYH-SA), Ⓢ✔️♿★, 134 North Oak St., 81435. Telephone: 303/728-3383. $12.50 summer, $14 winter for AYH members; $16 single, $27 double, $40 triple, $50 quad for nonmembers. Open year round. Transportation arrangements from bus ($15 one way) or train ($30 one way) station must be made 24 hours in advance with Telluride Transit (tel. 303/728-4105). "Inn built in 1893 as a church and is in National Historic Registry."

Trinidad

Accommodation: Friendship Inn Derrick, RR 1, Box 427B, 81082. Telephone: 303/846-3307. Airport transport service available. $20.95 for one; $24.95 for two in one bed; $28.95 for two in two beds. Higher rates apply during races and special events.

Walsenburg

Accommodations: Friendship Country Host, P.O. Box 190, 81089. Telephone: 303/738-3800. $24 to $30 for one or two in one bed; $28 to $38 for two in two beds.
● Budget Host—Crescent Motel, 802 Walsen Ave., 81089. Telephone: 303/738-2435. $20 to $28 for one or two in one bed; $32 to $39 for two in two beds.

Wheat Ridge

Accommodations: Motel 6, I-70 & Kipling St., 80033. See Colorado Springs listing for rates.

● Sixpence Inn, 9920 West 49th Ave., 80033. Telephone: 303/424-0658. $20 to $28 for up to four people.

Winter Park

Accommodations: Winter Park Hostel (AYH-SA), behind Conoco gas station, P.O. Box 3323, 80482. Telephone: 303/726-5356. $5 summer, $9 winter for AYH members; $6 summer, $11 winter for nonmembers. Equipped kitchen. Continental Trailways stops 100 yards from hostel door. Advance reservations necessary December 15 to April 15.

● Friendship Olympia, 78572 U.S. Hwy. 40, 80482. Telephone: 303/726-8843. April 26 to November 15: $20 to $24 for one; $26 to $30 for two in one bed; $28 to $34 for two in two beds. November 16 to April 25: $36 to $50 for one; $44 to $50 for two in one bed; $58 to $66 for two in two beds.

Connecticut

Connecticut is usually a lovely place to be. The southwestern part of the state has some of New York's bedroom communities, but the rest has its very own identity and is often very interesting. No point in the state is more than two hours from any other, so even if your time is limited, you can see quite a bit of Connecticut.

The capital city, Hartford, was enjoying a renaissance of its downtown area when the roof on its civic center caved in. The recently rebuilt Civic Center attests to the city's determination to revive its downtown. Hartford is as proud of its past as it is of its present and within the city are several interesting historical sites to visit: the Mark Twain House and, right next to it, the Harriet Beecher Stowe House are faithfully restored reminders of a gracious, literary 19th century; the Old State House on Main St., the oldest in the nation, has just recently become a tourist attraction with its restored Senate and House chambers; and the Wadsworth Atheneum, Hartford's art museum, has an appealing collection of paintings, sculpture, silver, textiles, etc.

New Haven is another Connecticut town worth a visit. The home of Yale University, it has two museums worth a stop—the Yale Center for British Art and the Yale University Art Gallery—and all of the cultural events you'd expect from a university town. The Long Wharf Theater, also in New Haven, in a former food terminal warehouse, can usually be counted on for top-rate performances of new and revived plays.

In summer, the place to go is the Connecticut shore—to Westbrook, Saybrook, Lyme, and to Mystic with its Seaport, which is the state's number-one tourist attraction, a living museum that recreates a 19th-century maritime village with ships, shops, homes, and the last of the wooden whalers, the *Charles W. Morgan*. Throughout the state there are wooded hillsides, lakes, streams, colonial villages, and historic homes.

For general information on Connecticut and its attractions, send for *Connecticut Vacation Guide* from the address given under tourist information below. For more specific books on Connecticut, consider the following:

Coastal Connecticut, Eastern Region, by Barry and Susan Hildebrandt, and *Coastal Connecticut, Western Region,* by March Beaubelle, Peregrine Press, Old Saybrook, CT 06475 ($4.95). Cover the Connecticut shore from Guilford to Stonington giving historical sketches, things to do, and restaurant recommendations.

Fifty Hikes in Connecticut, by Gerry and Sue Hardy, Backcountry Publications, P.O. Box 175, Woodstock, VT 05091. $8.95; add $1.50 postage and handling.

Connecticut Walk Book, Connecticut Forest and Park Association, Inc., P.O. Box 8537, East Hartford, CT 06108 ($11.60 by mail). Detailed description of trails with maps.

Globe Pequot Press, Old Chester Rd., Chester, CT 06412, publishes *Where to Eat in Connecticut, The Best and the Very Best Deals,* by Jane and Michael Stern, and *Short Bike Rides in Connecticut,* by Edwin Mullen and Jane Griffith.

Some Special Events: A Battle for Madison in Madison, and Dogwood Festival in Fairfield (May); Rose and Arts Festival in Norwich, and Barnum Festival (P.T. Barnum, founder of the Greatest Show on Earth was also the mayor of Bridgeport for a while) in Bridgeport (early June); Bluegrass Music Festival in Preston (early June); Audubon Festival in Sharon, and Railroad Days (July); the Oyster Festival in Milford, and Outdoor Arts Festival in Mystic (August); Chrysanthemum Festival in Bristol (late September to mid-October); and the Apple Harvest Festival in Southington (early October).

Hitching: In 1975, Public Act 75220 permitting hitchhiking in Connecticut came into effect. It states that soliciting a ride is permissible from the shoulder except on limited-access highways. A friend from the University of Hartford recommends hitching; a state trooper does not. "Hitchhiking is a practice which is not condoned by the Connecticut State Police Department."

Tourist Information: Connecticut Department of Economic Development, Vacation-Travel Promotion, 210 Washington St., Hartford, CT 06106. Telephone: toll free 800/842-7492 in Connecticut, and 800/243-1645 in Maine through Virginia. They have lots of good material, especially *Better Yet Connecticut,* a vacation guide.

N.B. An excellent reservation service for bed-and-breakfast facilities throughout Connecticut is Nutmeg Bed and Breakfast, 222 Girard Ave., West Hartford, CT 06105. Telephone: 203/236-6698. Accommodations range from modest homes to restored brownstones, historic farmhouses, and beachfront estates. The Nutmeg directory is available for $2.39.

Bolton

Accommodation: Bolton Home Hostel (AYH), Ⓢ★, 42 Clark Rd., 06040. Telephone: 203/649-3905. $6 for AYH members. Open April 15 to October 15. Must arrive on foot or by bicycle; no cars or motorcycles allowed. Hostel is two miles from bus station. Call hostel from station on arrival. Advance reservations suggested by calling after 5 p.m.

Branford

Accommodation: Econo Lodge, ✓ ♿, 309 East Main St., 06405. Telephone: 203/488-4035. $29.95 for one; $34.95 for two in one bed; $39.95 for two in two beds.

Bridgeport

Help: Infoline, 203/333-7555.
Accommodation: YMCA, 651 State St. by Park Ave., 06604. Five blocks from I-95. Telephone: 203/334-5551. Men only. $16, plus $5 key deposit. All buses stop at the Y; the train station is on the same street, three blocks away.

East Hartford

Accommodation: Imperial 400 Motor Inn, 927 Main St., 06108. Telephone: 203/289-7781. $30 to $34 for one; $35 to $39 for two in one bed; $39 to $44 for two in two beds.

Enfield

Accommodation: Red Roof Inn, 5 Hazard Ave., 06082. Telephone: 203/741-2571. $27.95 for one; $32.95 for two in one bed; $34.95 for two in two beds; $36.95 for three or four in two beds.

Hartford

Help: University of Hartford General Info, 203/243-4204.
● Info Line, 999 Asylum Ave., 06105. Telephone: 203/522-4636. "Information, referral, advocacy."
● Travelers Aid, 30 High St., Suite 4, 06103. Telephone: 203/522-2247.
On Campus: Trinity College is in Hartford. You can go to the movies at the Cine Studio there for $1.50 with a student ID card. Check the bulletin board at the Mather Campus Center for listings of apartments, rides, etc. To meet students go to Trinity's Cave in Mather Center, Trinity's Pub in the same place, and the Corner Tap Bar.
On the campus of the University of Hartford you can go to the Gengras Student Union to meet people—the campus is at 200 Bloomfield Ave. Or when you're hungry for a delicious, low-priced vegetarian meal, follow the advice of U of H students and head for Cheese and Stuff at 137 Sisson Ave. If you crave a hearty Italian meal, Pippie's at 682 Wethersfield Ave. is the place. Our U of H contact seems to think Hartford is "getting better and becoming more than just a stopover between New York and Boston." While in town, stop at the Congress Street Café at 7–9 Congress St. "Happy hour here could be rated as the best in the city!" Other suggested restaurants for the budget-minded—a substantial meal for under $7 and a nice atmosphere besides—are Timothy's, near Trinity on Zion Street; Readers Feast, 529 Farmington Ave; Jasper's, Capitol Ave.

Accommodations: YMCA, 160 Jewell St., 06103. Telephone: 203/522-4183. Men and women. $18.70 with private bath; $14.70 with shared bath. "One of the newest YMCAs in America. All rooms are carpeted and air-conditioned. Full-service YMCA with all facilities—health and fitness centers, pool and two gyms."

● YWCA, 🏷, 135 Broad St., 06105. Telephone: 203/525-1163. Women only. $13 with shared bath to $19 with private bath single; $8 for each additional person. This is a new building with a kitchen and a laundry on each of the seven floors. Reservations preferred one or two weeks in advance. Two blocks from bus and train stations.

● Susse Chalet Inn, I-91 (Exit 27) on Brainard Rd., 06114. Telephone: 203/525-9306. $30.70 for one; $34.70 for two; $37.70 for three; $40.70 for four.

Lakeside

Accommodation: Bantam Lake Youth Hostel (AYH), East Shore Rd., 06758. Telephone: 203/567-9258. $6 summer, $7 winter for AYH members. Advance reservations necessary. "Historic area of great national beauty offering a variety of outdoor activities in all seasons."

Meriden

Help: Info Line, 203/235-7974.

Accommodations: YMCA, 110 West Main St., 06450. Telephone: 203/235-6386. Men and women. $9 single. Weekly rate: $39. Near bus and train.

● Home & Travel Motor Hotel, √, 1102 East Main St., 06450. Telephone: 203/634-4700. $22 for one; $24.50 for two in one bed; $28 for two in two beds. Advance reservations preferred.

Milford

Accommodation: Best Value Mayflower Motel, √, 219 Woodmount Rd., 06460. Telephone: 203/878-6854. $36 for one; $40 for two in one bed; $46 for two in two beds.

New Britain

Accommodation: YMCA, 50 High St., 06051. Two miles from Exit 35 off Hwy. 84, via Rte. 72 to Columbus Avenue exit. Telephone: 203/229-3787. Men only. Single: $67.89 per week. Two blocks from bus station.

New Haven

Help: Travelers Aid, One State St., 06511. Telephone: 203/787-3959.

● Info Line: 203/624-4143.

● New Haven Convention and Visitors Bureau, 155 Church St. Telephone: 203/787-8367; with a branch office right off I-95 at Long Wharf.

On Campus: Yale University is here and students are everywhere. "This is a beautiful historic campus—surrounded by a depressed neighborhood, surrounded by scenic New England." Two favorite student restaurants are Clark's Dairy, 68 Whitney Ave., for sandwiches, salads, omelettes, etc., and the Educated Burger, 51 Broadway. Tours of Yale are available, and if you want to get out of the urban setting, you can go to Sleeping Giant State Park in nearby Hamden for hiking and picnicking. To meet someone in a comfortable atmosphere, try any pizza or ice-cream place around campus or Lourdes Cafeteria at the Commons. For rock, go to Toad's Place on York Street.

Accommodations: Hotel Duncan, Ⓢ√ ★, 1151 Chapel St., 06511. Telephone: 203/787-1273. Walking distance from bus and train. $25 without bath, $32 with bath single; $43 double; $50 triple; $55 quad. Advance reservations of one week suggested.

● International Center Residence, 442 Temple St., P.O. Box 94A, 06520. Telephone: 203/787-3531. Men and women. Summer only. Closed last two weeks in August. $10. (There may be room for one person to stay for a night or two during the academic year—call ahead to check.) "This was once a private home and is situated in an attractive residential area."

● YMCA, 52 Howe St., 06511. Telephone: 203/865-3161. Men and women. $17.20 single. Weekly rate: $70. Coffeeshop in building.

New London

Accommodation: Susse Chalet Motor Lodge, I-95 (Exit 74), 06357. Telephone: 203/739-6991. $27.70 for one; $31.70 for two; $34.70 for three; $37.70 for four.

Norwich

Accommodation: YMCA, 337 Main St., 06360. Telephone: 203/889-7349. Men only. $11.77 per night; $54.83 per week.

Southington

Accommodations: Sixpence Inn, 625 Queen St., 06489. Telephone: 203/621-7351. $20 to $28 for up to four people.

● Susse Chalet Motor Lodge, I-84 (Exit 32). Telephone: 203/621-0181. See New London listing for rates.

Stamford

Help: Info-Line, 203/324-1010.

Accommodation: YMCA, 909 Washington Blvd., 06901. Telephone: 203/357-7000. Men and women 18 and over. Although the single rate is $28.65 in this high-rise facility with private baths, color TV, phone, and maid service, a double is $39.32, and the weekly rate is within our budget at $123.20. Advance reservations necessary.

"Forget any story you may have heard before about other Ys—some facilities are suffering 'old age' symptoms but not here."

Wethersfield

Accommodation: Sixpence Inn, 1341 Silas Deane Hwy., 06109. Telephone: 203/563-5900. $20 to $28 for up to four people.

Windsor

Accommodation: Windsor Home Hostel (AYH), c/o Lois Macomber, 126 Giddings Ave., 06095. Telephone: 203/683-2847 or 726-8950. $6 for AYH members. Advance reservations necessary.

Woodstock

Accommodation: Woodstock Home Hostel, c/o Meryl and Henri Caldwell, Rte. 171, Box 278, South Woodstock, 06267. Telephone: 203/974-0490. Open April 16 to October 14. $6 for AYH members. Advance reservations necessary; call between 5 and 8 p.m.

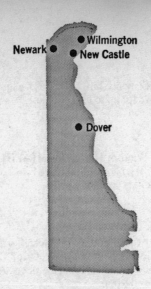

Newark ● ● Wilmington
● New Castle

● Dover

Delaware

It's a mini-state, and most of it either belongs or belonged to the du Ponts, one of the world's richest families. In 1802, Eleuthere du Pont built a powder mill on Brandywine Creek, and in the 150 years since, Delaware has, with the help of the du Ponts, become the chemical capital of the world. Other corporations have been lured by the state's attractive incorporation and tax laws.

One of the nicest things the du Ponts did for Delaware was to give it the Henry Francis du Pont 198-room pied-a-terre in Winterthur. Now the Winterthur Museum contains a collection of American decorative arts from 1640 to 1840 and is definitely worth seeing. Some day-long tours are available by reservation only; they vary in price with the season. Another tourist attraction in Delaware is also du Pont–related. It's the Hagley Museum, an 185-acre complex where visitors are told the story of American industry from the du Pont point of view. It should come, then, as no great surprise that the name of Delaware's governor is Pierre S. du Pont.

Some Special Events: Day in Old New Castle in Old New Castle, and Old Dover Days in Dover (May); Crafts Fair in Delaware Arts Museum in Wilmington (June); An Old Fashioned Fourth with fireworks on the boardwalk in Rehoboth (July); Arts Festival in Bethany (August); and Nanticoke Tribe Pow Wow, six miles east of Millsboro (September).

Hitching: Illegal on highways, and in Delaware "highway" means the road, the shoulders, and even beyond the shoulders. This terse advice comes from a captain in the Delaware State Police: "Don't come through Delaware."

Tourist Information: Delaware Tourism Office, 99 Kings Hwy., P.O. Box 1401, Dover, DE 19903.

N.B. Delaware has a bed-and-breakfast organization, a registration service that arranges accommodations for visitors in private homes throughout northern Delaware—in the Brandywine area around Wilmington and the university town of Newark. Rates range from $20 to $35 for a single; $40 to $60 for a double. To contact Bed and Breakfast of Delaware, write to 1804 Breen Lane, Wilmington, DE 19810, or if you're in a hurry, call 302/475-0340 from 3 to 6 p.m. Advance reservations of three days necessary.

Dover

Accommodation: Econo Lodge, √ &, 561 North du Pont Hwy., 19901. Telephone: 302/678-8900. $26.95 for one; $30.95 for two in one bed; $32.95 for two in two beds. Higher rates apply during special events.

New Castle

Accommodations: Tremont Motel, √, 196 North du Pont Hwy., 19720. Telephone: 302/328-6211 $25 single; $29 double.
● Motel 6, 1200 West Ave., State Hwy. 9, 19720. Telephone: 302/656-8440. $17.95 for one; $21.95 for two; $2 for each additional person.

Newark

On Campus: This is where you'll find the University of Delaware. To meet the students, go to the Student Center Scrounge or to the International Center at 52 West Delaware Ave. To get something inexpensive to eat, someone at the university suggests Jimmy's Diner or the Post House Restaurant, both on East Main St. A popular Sunday brunch spot is Klondike Kate's, also on East Main St. To meet students, try the Deer Park, or the Stone Balloon—all on (you guessed it) Main St. The Down Under is a new favorite of students. According to someone on the staff at the U of D, the school is "a commuter institution, and consequently loses most of its students over the weekends when they go home."

Wilmington

Help: Travelers Aid, 809 Washington St., 19801. Telephone: 302/658-9885.
Accommodations: YWCA, 908 King St., 19801. Telephone: 302/658-7161. Women only. $13 to $15 single. Weekly rate: $40 to $45. Advance reservations of two weeks necessary.
● YMCA, 10th & Walnut Sts., 19801. Telephone: 302/571-6935. Men only. $9.25 single. Weekly rate: $41.75. Advance reservations necessary.

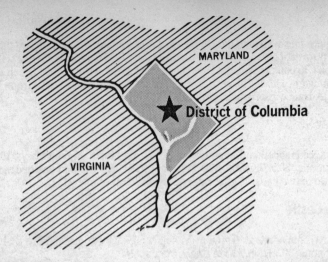

MARYLAND

★ District of Columbia

VIRGINIA

District of Columbia (Washington, D.C.)

Washington, D.C. is ready if you are. When you get there, you'll want to stop by one of the information centers that are available to assist visitors to the capitol district. They include the International Visitor Information Service, with an office at 804 19th St. NW (tel. 872-8747), which provides 24-hour language assistance in over 50 languages; Visitors Association, Suite 250, 1575 I St. NW (tel. 789-7000); and the Information Center for Handicapped Individuals, 605 G St. NW (tel. 347-4986, teletype 347-8320). The Visitor Information Center, operated by the Convention and Visitors Bureau, is located at 1400 Pennsylvania Ave. and is open seven days a week. The telephone number is 789-7000; for a recording of current events in the district, call 737-8866.

Two guidebooks to the city are *Washington, D.C., in Your Pocket,* published by Barron's ($1.95), a directory of stores, museums, landmarks, etc., and *Washington, D.C., on $40 a Day,* by Rena Bulkin, published by Frommer/ Pasmantier ($10.95). For maps of everything, get *Instant Guide to Washington,* by Tony Lasher, Flashmaps Publishing ($4.95).

Getting There: Washington's National Airport is about five miles south of town. The best way to get from there to downtown is to take the Metro, an elevated train. The fare is 80¢ during nonrush hours, and during rush hours it depends on the distance traveled. Taxi fare from the airport is about $11. The Greyhound station is at 1110 New York Ave. (tel. 565-2662), and Trailways is at 1st and L Sts. NE, one block from Union Station. The train Station, Union Station, is at 50 Massachusetts Ave. NE (tel. 484-7540).

Getting Around: The best way to get from place to place is the quiet and fast subway system, or Metro. There's a hitch, though: Metro runs only from 6 a.m. to midnight on weekdays, 8 a.m. to midnight on Saturday, and 10 a.m. to 6 p.m. on Sunday. Trains run every five minutes during rush hours (6 to 9:30 a.m. and 3 to 6:30 p.m.); every ten minutes during nonrush hours. Fare is 80¢ during nonrush hours; during rush hours the fare depends on distance traveled. Many of the buses connect with the Metro and are free. The fare on the regular bus is 75¢ for nonrush, 80¢ for rush hours. You can call 637-2437 for bus and Metro information.

● Taxis charge by the zone. One zone is $2.10 and each additional zone is about 75¢. One Washingtonian advises: "When taking a cab, always establish the fare before you get in—otherwise it may double or triple by the time you get to where you're going—especially at night." You can call Diamond Taxi (387-6200) or Yellow Taxi (544-1212).

● If you're going to tour within the city, avoid using a car. If you do bring your car, you'll just end up buying it back from the parking lot at the end of the day. The most popular sites are close together and the subway, bus, and tourmobiles are inexpensive and uncomplicated. The tourmobiles stop at 17 sites, and tourists are able to get on and off wherever they want, as often as they want. Fares are $6.50 for adults and $3.25 for children for a full-day ticket, 9 a.m. to 6:30 p.m. in summer; 9:30 a.m. to 4:30 p.m. in winter. For touring outside the center city area, you might consider renting a car from Hertz (tel. 659-8702), Budget Rent-a-Car (tel. 628-2750) or Avis (tel. toll free 800/467-6588).

● Help: Travelers Aid, 1015 12th St. NW, 20005. Telephone: 202/347-0101; Washington National Airport, 202/684-3472; and Union Station, 202/347-0101.

● International Visitors Information Services, 801 19th St. NW. Telephone: 202/872-8747. Language assistance in over 50 languages is available 24 hours a day.

● Foreign Service Lounge, State Department. Telephone: 632-3432. Foreign students can get information on how to reach any embassy at all.

On Campus: The American University is here. For information on rides, apartments, etc., check the bulletin board in the Mary Graydon Student Center or look at a copy of the campus newspaper, *The Eagle.* When you're hungry or thirsty, try the Pub or the Cafeteria on AU campus, or Quigley's, a favorite student hangout nearby.

Accommodations: Since so many people visit Washington and need a place to stay, there's an organization that specializes in helping them do just that; it's the Women's Information Center, 3918 West St. NW, 20007. Telephone: 202/338-8163. The staff there finds housing especially for women and foreign visitors. Their bed-and-breakfast network specializes in finding inexpensive, comfortable, and friendly accommodations for travelers. They also have information on long-term housing (group housing, apartments, etc.), jobs, rides, and local organizations.

● Washington International Hostel (AYH-SA), 1332 I St. NW, 20005. Telephone: 202/347-3125. One block west of bus stations. On Metro rail line from train station and airport, hostel is half a block east of 14th St. exit of the McPherson Square Station. Within walking distance of the White House, shopping, theater districts, and the Smithsonian Institution. Dormitory rooms have from four to eight beds per room (some bunk beds), $12. There are a dining room and cooking facilities too. Reservations must be made in advance with full payment and a stamped, self-addressed envelope. No refunds.

"One of the best hostels I've seen in the whole U.S.A."

- Franklin Park Hotel, 1332 I St. NW, 20005. Telephone: 202/347-3125. This is the same hotel that houses the Washington International Hostel above. $26 single; $36 double; $48 triple; $55 quad. All rooms are comfortable and air-conditioned. "Three blocks to White House; very convenient to all major attractions."
- International Student House, 1825 R St. NW, 20009. Telephone: 202/232-4007. Students only. Very few vacancies, but worth a try. $490 to $555 single per month; $455 to $510 (per person) double per month. All rates include breakfast and dinner seven days a week. Advance reservations required. This is a grand mansion built in 1912 with a dormitory wing built in 1969. It is primarily for long-term graduate students, but transients planning to stay at least a week are welcome. Weekly rates are $155 to $175 single; $145 to $160 per person double.
- Bed & Breakfast Ltd. of Washington, D.C., P.O. Box 12011, 20005. Telephone: 202/328-3510. A network of 80 homes, almost all located in the city's historic downtown areas, providing bed and breakfast. Advance reservations recommended. Prices range from $25 to $55 for a single; $40 to $75 for a double; $10 extra for each additional person in same room.
- The Connecticut-Woodly Guest House, 2647 Woodley Rd. NW, 20008. Telephone: 202/667-0218. Two blocks from Woodley Zoo metro. $24 to $37 single; $30 to $43 double; $36 to $48 triple; $40 to $52 quad. "Large, old house converted into a guest house."
- International Residence, 1516 U St. NW, 20009. Telephone: 202/745-5784. $35 for one; $40 for two. Weekly rate: $75.
- The "2005" Guest House, Ⓢ √, 2005 Columbia Rd. NW, 20009. Telephone: 202/265-4006. $15 to $20 single; $20 to $40 double; $30 to $42 triple; $27 to $52 quad.
- Meg's International Guest House, Ⓢ Ⓖ √, 1315 Euclid St. NW, 20009. Telephone: 202/232-5837, 387-9623 or toll free 800/824-7008. $20 to $25 single; $38 to $48 double; $45 to $50 triple. Complimentary breakfast included. Reserve space prior to arrival. The house is located in a diverse cosmopolitan area which is close to all the national monuments and the Capitol.
- Hawthorne Hotel, 2134 G St. NW, 20037. Telephone: 202/338-7810. Foggy Bottom stop on Metro three blocks from hotel. $23 single; $34 double. Near George Washington University and six blocks from the White House.
- 1440 Hotel Annex, 1440 Rhode Island Ave. NW, 20005. Telephone: 202/232-7800. Farragut Metro Station is three blocks from hotel. $23.70 single; $27.70 double.
- Columbia House, 800 E St. NE, 20002. Telephone: 202/543-8800. Within walking distance of the congressional offices, monuments, and galleries. $21.90 single; $29.05 double. Rooms are without private bath.
- International Guest House, 1441 Kennedy St. NW, 20011. Telephone: 202/726-5808. $13.46 per person. Internationals are preferred, but anyone, including children, can be accommodated. "A home away from home for traveling internationals." Advance reservations of one month necessary.
- Parkview Residence, 1855 Irving St. NW, 20010. Telephone: 202/265-6610. No small children. $40 per person includes dinner and breakfast the next morning. "Friendly international student house."
- Davis House, 1822 R St. NW, 20009. Telephone: 202/232-3196. Near Metro and bus lines. $16 per person. Advance reservations of one month necessary. "Small, non-profit guest house with priority given to international visitors."

- The Kalorama Guest House at Kalorama Park, $\vee$ ★, 1854 Mintwood Pl. NW, 20009. Telephone: 202/667-6369. Near Metro and bus. $35 to $50 single; $40 to $65 double; $45 to $70 triple. Prices include continental breakfast. Advance reservations necessary March to October. Higher rates apply March to October. "Large Victorian townhouse furnished with antiques."
- The Kalorama Guest House at Woodley Park, ⓈV, 2700 Cathedral Ave. NW, 20008. Telephone: 202/328-0860. $25 to $50 single; $30 to $60 double; $35 to $65 triple. Seventh night free if you stay the week. Complimentary continental breakfast included. Advance reservations necessary March to October. Rates slightly higher March 1 to October 31. "Turn-of-the-century townhouse near Metro and bus stop."
- Econo Lodge, $\vee$, 1600 New York Ave. NE, 20002. Telephone: 202/832-3200. $34.95 for one; $39.95 for two in one or two beds.
- Red Roof Inn, ♿, 497 Quince Orchard Rd., 20878. Telephone: 301/977-3311. $29.95 for one; $34.95 for two in one bed; $36.95 for two in two beds; $38.95 for three or four in two beds.
- Red Roof Inn, ♿, 7306 Parkway Dr., 21076. Telephone: 301/796-7700. See above listing for rates.
- Adams Inn Bed and Breakfast, 1744 Lanier Place NW, 20009. Telephone: 202/745-3600. On the Metro line. $25 to $60 single; $30 to $60 double. "The rooms are small but nice and clean. It's a friendly place in a good location."

Where to Eat: Holloway House Cafeteria, 14th St. and New York Ave. NW. The service is fast and pleasant and the food is inexpensive.

- Patent Pending, in courtyard between National Collection of Fine Arts (8th and G Sts. NW) and the National Portrait Gallery (7th and F Sts. NW). Perfectly located if you're sightseeing around the Mall. This cafeteria offers an interesting menu including courtyard salad, nitrite-free hot dogs made interesting, and big bowls of soup. You can eat outdoors or in. Open every day for lunch.
- Kramerbooks and Afterwards, 1517 Connecticut Ave. NW. Telephone: 387-1400. Just north of Dupont Circle. Popular indoor/outdoor café with an adjoining bookstore. Croissants for breakfast, quiches and salads for dinner.
- Tucson Cantina, 2605 Connecticut Ave. NW. Telephone: 462-6410. Near the National Zoo. The food is Mexican via the Southwest—tacos, burritos, enchiladas. Service is fast and entrees are $3.50 or under.
- The Dubliner, 4 F St. NW, directly across from Union Station. Telephone: 737-3773. Irish-American food; conveniently located near Capitol Hill. Irish traditional music live every night with no cover charged.
- The Booeymonger, 5250 Wisconsin Ave. NW. Telephone: 686-5805. Indoor and outdoor seating attracts a young crowd who like the salads and sandwiches like "The Exorcist," a roast beef "possessed" by bleu cheese with sprouts on French bread, $3.25. Open 24 hours.
- The Tune Inn, 331½ Pennsylvania Ave. SE. Telephone: 543-2725. On a popular strip; filled with people who work on Capitol Hill. Burgers and fries. A pitcher of beer is $3.25.
- The Omega, 1856–58 Columbia Rd. NW. Telephone: 462-1732. Spanish food very close to Dupont Circle. "Lots of food for your money."
- The Cold Duck, 1732 Connecticut Ave. NW. Telephone: 667-6211. Inexpensive and good food in one of the few authentically "neighborhood" bar/restaurants left in D.C. Best known for their chili, fried chicken, burgers, and pies. "There's a small bar with a friendly crowd that always welcomes a new face."

- The Newsroom Café, 1753 Connecticut Ave. Telephone: 332-1489. This spot, at a lively intersection near Dupont Circle, has newspapers and magazines from all over the U.S. and the world; the menu is on newsprint and features international food and drink possibilities. You can sit indoors or out until midnight on weekdays, 2 a.m. on weekends.

- Millie and Al's, 2440 18th St. NW. A favorite for cheap pizza and beer by the pitcher. Open every day.

- Geppetto, 2917 M St. NW. In Georgetown and winner of *The Washingtonian* magazine's best-tasting pizza competition.

- Trio's, 1537 17th St. NW. Telephone: 232-5611. This diner is popular because of its cheap, good food, and in spite of its nasty waitresses.

- New Orleans Café, 1790 Columbia Road (just north of Dupont Circle). Telephone: 234-5111. As you'd expect, New Orleans cooking—dishes like oyster loaf, ham and sausage gumbo, crayfish bisque. Long lines on weekends for brunch but worth the wait.

- Mi Riconcito, 1703 Connecticut Ave. NW. Telephone: 387-4515. A quaint Mexican restaurant with an outdoor cafe, bar, and international coffees.

- Florida Avenue Grill, 11th and Florida, NW. Telephone: 265-1586. Soul food—ham hocks, peanut pie, short ribs and breakfasts of eggs, grits, bacon, and toast in a crowded and noisy spot.

- Au Pied du Cochon, 1335 Wisconsin Ave. NW, Georgetown. Telephone: 333-5440. An old D.C. favorite for food and people-watching. Menu prices from $4.25 to $8.

What to See: For an up-to-the-minute guide to what's going on, check the Amusement Section of the *Sunday Washington Post*, a monthly, *Washingtonian* magazine, and radio station Q 107 FM.

- The Mall and its Museums: From the Capitol to the Washington Monument lies the National Mall, laid out in 1791. All along the Mall are buildings that you'll want to visit. Seven of these are Smithsonian Institution Museums, including the Freer Gallery of Art, Arts and Industries Building, the Hirshhorn Museum and Sculpture Garden (20th-century art indoors and sculpture outdoors), the National Museum of History and Technology, the National Museum of Natural History, the Smithsonian Institution Building (where the Visitors Information Center is located), the National Gallery of Art, and the extraordinarily popular National Air and Space Museum. At the National Air and Space Museum you can trace the history of flight as you look at the Wright Flyer, Lindbergh's *Spirit of St. Louis*, John Glenn's Mercury Capsule, Gemini 4, the Apollo 11 command module *Columbia*, and finally, a moon rock. The Albert Einstein Spacearium on the second floor presents sky and space spectaculars. For information on the Smithsonian Institution buildings, hours, exhibits, etc., call 381-6270.

- National Portrait Gallery, 7th and F Sts. NW. Life portraits of "men and women who have made significant contributions to the history, development, and culture of the people in the United States." Is yours there? This is a Smithsonian Institution, and although it's not in the Mall, it's not far away at all.

- National Collection of Fine Arts, 8th and G Sts. NW. Another Smithsonian Institution, right across from the Portrait Gallery, which contains a panorama of American painting, graphic art, and sculpture from the 18th century to now.

- The U.S. Capitol, Capitol Hill. Of all the buildings in Washington, this most symbolizes the federal government. You can visit the House and Senate galleries with passes that can be obtained from your representative or senator. There are tours every day starting from the Rotunda from 9 a.m. to 4:30 p.m. Call 224-3121 for information.

- U.S. Supreme Court, 1st and Maryland Ave. NE. Tours of the highest court in the land are conducted from 9:30 a.m. to 4 p.m. Call 252-3211.
- Washington Monument, Constitution Ave. at 15th St. NW. You can take an elevator up and enjoy the view from 8 a.m. to midnight in summer. Call 426-6841.
- The White House, 1600 Pennsylvania Ave. NW. Nancy and Ron would like you to come and see their home. Tours are conducted from 10 a.m. to noon, Tuesday to Saturday. If there's an official function on the day you want to go and you haven't received a personal invitation, you won't be able to take the tour.
- Lincoln Memorial, foot of 23rd St. NW. A very moving tribute to Lincoln and worth a quiet visit.
- Federal Buildings: Just about every government agency offers a tour of its premises. Some possibilities are: Bureau of Engraving and Printing (tel. 566-2000), Federal Bureau of Investigation (tel. 324-3447), Department of State (tel. 632-3241).
- Dumbarton Oaks and Gardens, 1703 32nd St. NW. Telephone: 342-3200. The house is headquarters for the Colonial Dames of America. Adjacent to it you can enjoy 16 acres of beautiful gardens with terraces and reflecting pools.
- Washington National Zoo, 3000 Connecticut Ave. Telephone: 673-4800. Easily reached by buses L-2, L-4, and L-6, and the Metro. The stars of the zoo are two giant pandas. The zoo is divided into six trails that are well marked and easy to follow. The grounds are open from 8 a.m. to 8 p.m., the animal houses from 10 a.m. to 6 p.m.
- Library of Congress, 10 First St. SE. Telephone: 287-6400. Over 80 million items in 470 languages. Free tours.
- Old Post Office Pavilion, 1100 Pennsylvania Ave. Telephone: 289-4224. No longer a post office but rather a courtyard surrounded by boutiques and restaurants where people-watching is the sport of choice.
- Vietnam Veterans Memorial, Constitution Ave. between Henry Bacon Dr. and 21st St. NW. Telephone: 426-6700. A very, very moving memorial inscribed with the names of the nearly 58,000 Americans who died in Vietnam.
- Arlington National Cemetery, Arlington, VA 22111. Telephone: 703/692-0931. The burial place for many of America's heroes. Every hour there's a changing of the guard at the Tomb of the Unknown Soldier.
- Beyond Washington: Two recommended day trips are to Annapolis (40 minutes away), a charming small town that's the home of the U.S. Naval Academy, and to Harpers Ferry in West Virginia (about 1½ hours away), a national historic park with a visitors' center that explains the history of the community and John Brown's raid and capture here in 1859. Visitors can explore the park grounds and even do a bit of mountain climbing. Baltimore is only 40 miles from D.C.

At Night: Kennedy Center, New Hampshire Ave. at F St. NW. This is where you can see a play, enjoy a concert, listen to opera, see a dance performance, or watch a film. For information on what is going on at the Eisenhower Theater, the Opera House, the Concert Hall, the American Film Institute, or the Terrace Theater, call 202/872-0466. Student discounts are available at times.

● Blue Alley, 1073 Wisconsin Ave. NW. Telephone: 337-4141. This restaurant/nightclub presents big-name and local jazz performers and serves New Orleans-style food. The cover is between $10 and $12.

● Pier 9, 1824 Half St. SW. Telephone: 488-1205. There's room for 700 people to dance to a disco beat. Minimum every night; closed Monday and Tuesday nights.

● Déjà Vu, 2119 M St. NW. Telephone: 452-1966. No cover or minimum. Enormous stained-glass windows, palm trees, and working fireplaces set the scene of this very colorful dance hall/bar that's always busy. Every night there's bopping (remember that?) to the tunes of the '50 and '60s. You can let loose on the dance floor or go to one of the quieter adjoining rooms. No food is served and the drinks are reasonable.

● Biograph Theater, 2819 M St. NW. Telephone: 333-2696. $3.50 will buy you a double feature of either a golden oldie or a more recent classic; film festivals, celebrity actors, directors, countries, etc., are featured periodically.

● One Step Down, 2517 Pennsylvania Ave. NW. Telephone: 331-8863. Big-name jazz bands in a small, smoky, and crowded atmosphere. Cover charge on weekends can go as high as $7; during the week it may be only $1.50 on some nights.

● Pier Street Annex, 1210 19th St. NW. Telephone: 466-4040. Enormous dance hall with disco and rock. Drinks served outdoors. "Attracts all kinds."

● Gallagher's Pub, 3319 Connecticut Ave. NW. Telephone: 686-9189. A large pub that serves great hamburgers and often features folk and country music.

● The 930 Club, 930 F St. NW. Telephone: 993-0930. The premier punk club of D.C. The average cover is $5.

● The Saba, 1214 18th St. below Dupont Circle. Telephone: 296-9292. Reggae and rock—new and very popular.

● The Kilimanjaro, 1724 California Ave. NW. Dancing to live music until 3:30 a.m. A favorite of many Africans.

● The Birchmere, 3901 Mt. Vernon Ave. Telephone: 703/549-5919. Bluegrass and acoustic music. Very big and *very* popular right now.

Shopping: Discount Records and Books, 1340 Connecticut Ave. NW. A popular place—the name tells you why.

● Crown Books, 1710 G St. NW, and 2020 K St. NW and other locations. General selection of books at a hefty discount.

● Second Story Books, 2000 P St. NW. Telephone: 659-8884. Rare, used, and out of print books.

● Common Concerns, 1347 Connecticut Ave. NW. Telephone: 463-6500. Books on political and international topics.

● Tower Records, 2000 Pennsylvania Ave. NW. Telephone: 331-2400. Biggest record store in the city.

● International Learning Center, 1715 Connecticut Ave. NW. The stock includes international cookbooks, travel guides to the U.S., and dictionaries in 100 languages.

● Record and Tape Limited, 19th and L Sts. NW, or 1239 Wisconsin Ave. NW. Everything at a discount.

● Serenade Record Shop, 1710 Pennsylvania Ave. NW, and 1800 M St. NW. Jazz, popular, classical, rock, and soul at a discount.

● Gary's Discount Records, 1445 K St. NW. All kinds of records and tapes discounted.

- Garfinkel's, 1401 F St. NW. Washington's best-known department store—with a nice selection of gifts if you don't have to worry too much about prices.
- Hudson Trail Outfitters, 4437 Wisconsin Ave. NW. Sleeping bags, clothing, and other outdoor gear.
- Georgetown. The whole area—an eight-square-block area with hub at Wisconsin Ave. and M St. NW—teems with galleries, specialty shops, boutiques, and eateries. The Georgetown Mall on M St. is a big neighborhood attraction.
- Second Hand Rose, 1516 Wisconsin Ave. NW. Telephone: 337-3378. In Georgetown, a popular source of resale clothes and accessories for women.

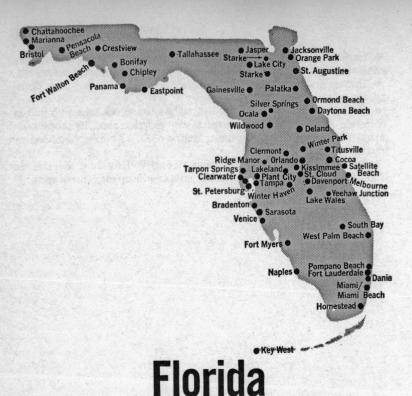

Florida

Florida means vacation for most people. When the winter winds blow up North, down they all come. The biggest tourist attraction in all of Florida is Disney World, about 20 miles south of Orlando. Everyone seems to agree that the place is a lot of fun. One friend's favorite Florida sight is the Stephen Foster Memorial on the Suwannee River (near White Springs), which is a sight in itself with its oak-lined banks and Spanish moss.

There are lots of sea attractions in Florida, like Sea World in central Florida, Marineland in St. Augustine, and the Seaquarium in Miami. A real must-see, if you can stand the traffic, is Miami Beach with its famous hotel row where each hotel vies with the next for splendor.

The farthest point south in the U.S. is Key West, with the Atlantic on one side and the Gulf of Mexico on the other. Here you can still see men practicing the old art of shelling conch.

If you're attracted by state capitals then you'll want to visit Tallahassee. But one city that you should really try to include in your plans is St. Augustine, just 50 miles south of the Georgia-Florida line. This was the first place in the U.S. settled by the Spaniards in the 1500s and its original fort still stands. Tampa still has an Hispanic flavor.

The southern portion of Florida, from the Keys to the Broward County area, has become home for many who have left Castro's Cuba. One section of Miami is called Little Havana, more than 20 years after the first exodus. Southern Florida is still home to many natives, but in the past 30 years many Northerners have relocated to take advantage of the climate. Central and northern Florida are still mostly "home-grown" people, but they too are being "colonized" by people who can't stand the Northern winters.

Some Special Events: Orange Bowl in Miami (January, on New Year's night); Seafood Festival in Grant (February); Old Island Days in Key West (February to March); Frontier Days in Orange City, and Ponce de Leon Festival in Port Charlotte (March); Rodeo in Palatka, and Catfish Festival in Crescent City (April); Billy Bowlegs Festival (Billy Bowlegs was a pirate) in Fort Walton Beach (May); Sea Turtle Watch in Jensen Beach (June); Everglades Outdoor Music Festival (the annual festival of the Miccosukee Tribe) in Miami (July); Fun Day and Possum Festival in Wausau (August); International Worm Fiddling Contest (who can create the best vibration on a wooden stake to bring up the most worms) in Caryville, and Seafood Festival in Pensacola (September); and Hispanic Heritage Week in Dade County (October).

Hitching: According to the Florida Highway Patrol, hitchhiking is legal in Florida, except on Interstates or turnpikes or when a specific prohibition is posted. In practice, it seems, from the reactions we got from people at several of the colleges in Florida, that the attitude toward hitchhiking in the state is conservative and that Floridians are hesitant to pick up hitchhikers. When we asked about the general attitude toward young people "on the road" in the Miami area, we got two opposite views. One person said it was good: "Miami is heavily populated with tourists so young people visiting Miami or surrounding areas are not considered unusual." The other person said that the attitude was discouraging: "This is a tourist-industry economy and flocks of students are considered disruptive." It must be all in the way you look at it.

Tourist Information: Division of Tourism, Florida Department of Commerce, Collins Bldg., Tallahassee, FL 32301. Telephone: 904/488-8230.

Bonifay

Accommodation: Econo Lodge, ∨, I-10 & S.R. 79, Rte. 1, Box 2021, 32425. Telephone: 904/547-9345. $30 single; $35 double.

Bradenton

Accommodation: Plaza Motel, 4410 14th St. West (U.S. 41), 33507. Telephone: 813/755-9032. $23 to $25 for one or two in one bed; $28 to $45 for two in two beds.

Bristol

Camping: Torreya State Park, Rt. #2, Box 70, 32321. Campground along the Apalachicola River with 35 sites open year round. $6 per campsite per night; $8 for electric site.

Chattahoochee

Accommodation: Morgan Motel, U.S. 90 E., 32324. Telephone: 904/663-4336. $21 for one; $24 for two in one bed; $25 for two in two beds.

Chipley

Camping: Falling Waters State Recreation Area, Rte. 5, Box 660, 32428. Campground with 24 sites open year round. $6 per campsite per night for inland areas; $7 for coastal areas; $8 for Florida Key areas.

Clearwater

Accommodations: Red Carpet Inn, ⮾ √, 2940 Gulf-to-Bay Blvd., 33519. Telephone: 813/799-0100. $24 to $52 for one; $28 to $56 for two. Courtesy car available.
- Days Inn, 1690 U.S. 19 N., 33575. Telephone: 813/799-2678. $28 to $32 for one; $32 to $36 for two.
- TraveLodge, √⮾, 711 Cleveland St., 33515. Telephone: 813/446-9183. $28 for one; $32 for two in one bed; $36 for two in two beds.
- Friendship Town House, 1471 Court St., 33516. Telephone: 813/446-8586. $15 to $48 for one; $16 to $50 for two in one or two beds.
- Friendship Clearwater Inn, 1744 North Ft. Harrison Ave., 33515. Telephone: 813/442-8067. Limited airport service available. $20 to $40 for one; $22 to $44 for two in one bed; $23 to $48 for two in two beds.

Clermont

Accommodation: Comfort Inn, √, U.S. 27 & Turnpike Exit 88, Rte. 2, Box 105K, 32711. Telephone: 904/429-2151. $16.95 to $18.95 single; $22.95 to $24.95 double.

Cocoa

Accommodation: Brevard Hotel, Ⓢ√, 112 Riverside Dr., 32922. Telephone: 305/636-1411. On the banks of the Indian River. Call hotel for ride from bus station. $20 single; $30 double; $35 triple; $40 quad. "We are the best and least expensive."

Cocoa Beach

Accommodations: Motel 6, 3701 North Atlantic Ave., 32931. Telephone: 805/783-0890. $17.95 for one; $21.95 for two; $2 for each additional person. Just minutes from the Kennedy Space Center.
- Days Inn, 5600 S.R. 524, 32922. Telephone: 305/636-2580. $27 for one; $32 for two.
- Scottish Inn, √, 4150 West King St., 32922. Telephone: 305/632-5721. $21 for one or two in one bed; $23 for two in two beds.

Crestview

Accommodations: Scottish Inn, √, U.S. 90 W., 32536. Telephone: 904/682-3832. July 1 to October 31: $19.95 for one; $22.95 for two in one bed; $25.95

for two in two beds. November 1 to December 31: $19 for one; $21 for two in one bed; $23 for two in two beds.

● Econo Lodge, 🚻, I-10 & Fla. 85, Exit 12, P.O. Box 1466, 82536. Telephone: 904/682-6255. $24.95 for one: $30.95 for two in one bed; $34.95 for two in two beds.

Dania

Accommodation: Motel 6, 825 East Dania Beach Blvd., 33004. Telephone: 305/922-0988. See Cocoa Beach listing for rates.

Davenport

Accommodations: Susse Motor Lodge, I-4 & U.S. 27, 33837. Telephone: 813/424-2521. $21.70 for one; $25.70 for two; $28.70 for three; $31.70 for four. Near Disney World.

● Scottish Inn, √ 🚻, Hwy. 27, Rte. 2, Box 373, 33837. Telephone: 813/424-2444. July 1 to August 30 and December 1 to December 31: $25 for one; $28 for two in one bed; $34 for two in two beds. September 1 to November 31: $20 for one; $24 for two in one bed; $28 for two in two beds.

Daytona Beach

Tourist Information: Convention and Tourism Department, The Area Chamber of Commerce, Daytona Beach & Halifax area, City Island, 32015. Telephone: 904/255-0981.

Help: Travelers Aid, 771 Briarwood Dr., 32017. Telephone: 904/252-4752.

Accommodations: Red Carpet Inn, I-95 & U.S. 1, 32074. Telephone: 904/672-7341. $25 for all rooms. Higher rates apply during special events.

● Days Inn, I-95 & U.S. 92, 2800 Volusia Ave., 32015. Telephone: 904/255-0541. $27 to $44 for one; $33 to $50 for two.

● Days Inn, 1909 South Atlantic Ave., 32018. Telephone: 904/255-4492. $29 to $73 for one or two in one bed; $35 to $79 for efficiency.

● Days Inn, 3209 South Atlantic Ave., 32018. Telephone: 904/761-2050. $27 to $70 for one; $33 to $74 for efficiency.

● Stardust Inn, Ⓢ√ ★, 1220 North Atlantic Ave., 32018. Telephone: 904/252-3681. $18 single; $23 double; $28 triple; $33 quad. Rates are higher and reservations are suggested during special events (February to April, June to August).

● Rip Van Winkle Motel, 1025 North Atlantic Ave., 32018. Telephone: 904/252-6213. $18 for one; $22 for two in one bed; $24 for two in two beds.

● Scottish Inn, √, 133 South Ocean Ave., 32018. Telephone: 904/253-0666. $33 to $42 for oceanfront efficiency; $30 to $44 for oceanfront room; $27 to $40 for side efficiency; $24 to $37 for side room. Heated pool.

● YWCA, 344 South Beach St., 32014. Telephone: 904/252-3253. Women only. $12 single; $10 per person double; $8 per person in dorm-style accommodations. Weekly rates: $65 single; $55 per person double; $45 per person in dorm. Advance reservations of three weeks necessary. "A comfortable, clean establishment with its own outdoor pool."

● Daytona Beach Youth Hostel (AYH-SA), 140 South Atlantic Ave., 32018. Telephone: 904/258-6937. $8.75 for AYH members.

● Econo Lodge, 2250 Volusia Ave., 32014. Telephone: 904/255-3661. $23.50 for one or two in one bed; $28.50 for two in two beds. Higher rates apply during special events.

DeLand

On Campus: At Stetson University, your first stop, if you want help finding your way around, is the Carlton Union. Stetson students should be easy to meet at the Commons.

Eastpoint

Camping: St. George Island State Park, ⑤ ∨, P.O. Box 62, 32328. Telephone: 904/670-2111. Cost per campsite: $1.05 per night, primitive; $7.35 per night, no electricity; $9.45 per night with electricity. Advance reservations of up to 60 days recommended. "A beautiful, quiet, secluded, clean, and pristine park about 80 miles from Tallahassee."

Fort Lauderdale

Accommodations: Motel 6, 1801 Fla. 84, 33315. Telephone: 305/525-1363. See Cocoa Beach listing for rates.

● Days Inn, I-95 & Fla. 84 (Exit 27), 2640 S.R. 84, 33312. Telephone: 305/792-4700. $32 to $36 for one; $37 to $41 for two.

● Lauderdale Biltmore, Ⓢ ∨ ★, 435 North Atlantic Blvd., 33304. Telephone: 305/462-0444. May 1 to November 30: $36 single or twin; $44 triple; $54 quad. December 1 to April 30: $35 single; $39 twin; $47 triple; $55 quad. "Newly renovated oceanfront property."

Fort Myers

Accommodations: Days Inn, ⑤, 1099 U.S. 41 N., Cleveland Ave., 33903. Telephone: 813/995-0535. $30 to $35 for one; $35 to $40 for two.

● Days Inn, ⑤, 11435 Cleveland Ave., 33907. Telephone: 813/936-1311. $29 to $44 for one; $34 to $49 for two.

● Red Carpet Inn, ⑤, 4811 Cleveland Ave., 33907. Telephone: 813/936-3229. $31 single; $35 double.

● Budget Host—Sea Chest Motel, 2571 First St., Rte. 80, 33901. Telephone: 813/332-1545. $20 for two in one bed; $25 for two in two beds. Higher rates apply December 15 to April 15.

● Econo Lodge, ∨, 1089 U.S. Hwy. 41, 33903. Telephone: 813/995-0571. April 1 to 10: $33.95 for one; $37.95 for two in one bed; $40.95 for two in two beds. April 11 to October 1: $24.95 for one or two in one bed; $26.95 for two in two beds.

- Green Wave Motel, √ ★, 4523 Palm Beach Blvd., 33905. Telephone: 813/694-0185. Call for ride from bus station. $28 single; $35 double. Advance reservations necessary.
- TraveLodge, √ ♿, 2038 West First St., 33901. Telephone: 813/334-2284. $28 for one; $32 for two in one bed; $36 for two in two beds.

Fort Walton Beach

Accommodation: Econo Lodge, √ ♿, 100 Miracle Strip Pkwy. SW, 32548. Telephone: 904/244-0121. April 1 to May 23 and September 3 to September 30: $25.95 to $26.95 for one; $29.95 to $30.95 for two in one bed; $31.95 to $32.95 for two in two beds. May 24 to September 2: $36.95 for one; $39.95 for two in one bed; $41.95 for two in two beds.

Gainesville

On Campus: The University of Florida is in Gainesville, and according to one student, "there are so many students in Gainesville that strangers will blend right in." For food, go to the Copper Monkey, Purple Porpoise II, or Knife and Fork. At night, try Richenbacher's for jazz and Spectrum Disco for dancing. The J. Wayne Reitz Union on the Univ. of Florida campus has a ride board on the ground floor and cheap movies are shown on the second floor. Buses in town are a bargain at 50¢. The student newspaper, *Independent Florida Alligator*, is distributed all over town free, and the Corner Drug Store has leads on places to stay.

Accommodations: Econo Lodge, √, 2649 S.W. 13th St., 32608. Telephone: 904/373-7816. $23.95 for one; $27.95 for two in one bed; $30.95 for two in two beds.
- Econo Lodge, √, 700 N.W. 75th St., 32601. Telephone: 904/378-2346. $24.95 for one; $27.95 for two in one bed; $31.95 for two in two beds.
- Days Inn, ♿, I-75 & Fla. 26, 6901 Eighth Ave., 32601. Telephone: 904/376-1601. June 1 to September 2: $32 to $49 single; $37 to $49 double. September 3 to November 30: $27 single; $32 double.
- Days Inn, I-75 & Fla. 234, Rte. 2, Box 804, 32667. Telephone: 904/466-3152. $20 single; $24 double.
- Motel 6, 4000 S.W. 40th Blvd., 32608. Telephone: 904/375-8244. See Cocoa Beach listing for rates.
- TraveLodge, √ (15%), 413 West University Ave., 32601. Telephone: 904/376-1224. $28 single; $32 for two in one bed; $36 for two in two beds.

Homestead

Camping: Everglades National Park, P.O. Box 279, 33030. Telephone: 305/247-6211. If you plan to visit the park, it is strongly recommended that you have a private vehicle to get there and around. There are 29 backcountry campsites and two regular campgrounds (Long Pine Key and Flamingo) with a total of over 300 sites. Backcountry campsites are accessible by boat only, and a permit is required for their use. $4 to $5 per campsite per night in regular campgrounds. $2 entrance fee for occupants with cars or motorcycles; 50¢ for all others.

● Biscayne National Park Campground, P.O. Box 1369, 33090. Telephone: 305/247-7275. Camping year round at Elliot Key. Access by boat only. No fee. "One of the largest marine preserves administered by the National Park Service. There is a self-guiding nature trail from Biscayne Bay to the Atlantic. Campers must bring their own tents."

Jacksonville

Tourist Information: Convention and Visitors Bureau of Jacksonville and Jacksonville Beaches, 206 Hogan St., 32202. Telephone: 904/353-9736.

Help: Travelers Aid, 33 South Hogan St., 32202. Telephone: 904/356-0249.
● Central Crisis Center, 904/384-2234.

Accommodations: YWCA, 325 East Duval St., 32202. Telephone: 904/354-6681. Women and up to two children (boys up to age 8). $30 to $37.75 single; $36.75 double. $5 key deposit.

● Econo Lodge, V, 5018 University Blvd. West, 32216. Telephone: 904/731-0800. $24 for one; $26 for two in one bed; $28 for two in two beds. Higher rates apply during special events.

● Econo Lodge, V, 6560 Ramona Blvd., 32205. Telephone: 904/786-2794. $30.95 for one; $34.95 for two in one bed; $36.95 for two in two beds. Higher rates apply during special events.

● Econo Lodge, V, 2300 Phillips Hwy., 32207. Telephone: 904/396-2301. $22.95 for one; $24.95 for two in one bed; $26.95 for two in two beds. Higher rates apply during special events.

● Days Inn, I-95 & Jax International Airport Exit, P.O. Box 18217, 32229. Telephone: 904/757-5000. $29 to $65 for one.

● Red Carpet Inn, 5331 University Blvd. West, 32216. Telephone: 904/733-8110. $26.95 for one to five people in one or two beds.

● Scottish Inn, 747 Arlington Rd., 32211. Telephone: 904/725-9600. $22.95 single; $25.95 double. Higher rates apply during special events.

● Red Roof Inn, 🅰, I-95 & Airport Rd., 14701 Duval Rd., 32218. Telephone: 904/751-4110. $24.95 for one; $29.95 for two in one bed; $31.95 for two in two beds; $33.95 for three or four in two beds.

● Red Roof Inn, 🅰, I-295 & Blanding Blvd., 6099 Youngerman Circle, 32244. Telephone: 904/777-1000. See above listing for rates.

● Motel 6, 10885 Harts Rd., 32218. Telephone: 904/751-2344. See Cocoa Beach listing for rates.

● Motel 6, 6107 Youngerman Circle, 32244. Telephone: 904/772-8228. See Cocoa Beach listing for rates.

● Econo Lodge, 1055 Golfair Blvd., 32209. Telephone: 904/764-2551. $25.95; $27.95 for two in one or two beds.

● Sunshine Inn, I-10 at Lane Ave. Exit, 460 South Lane Ave., 32205. Telephone: 904/786-7550. $24 to $26 single; $31 double.

● Scottish Inn, V 🅰, I-295 & Hwy. 17, 337 Park Ave., 32073. Telephone:

904/264-0511. $29 single; $33 double. Higher rates apply during special events.

- Friendship Gold Coast Motel, 731 North 1st St., 32250. Telephone: 904/249-5006. $28 to $48 single; $30 to $64 double.
- Red Carpet Inn, √, 881 Golfair Blvd., 32209. Telephone: 904/764-7511. $20.95 single; $32.95 double; $70 during special events.

Jasper

Accommodation: Scottish Inn, √, I-75 & S.R.6, Rte. 3, Box 136, 32052. Telephone: 904/792-1234. $20 to $24 single; $22 to $26 for two in one bed; $24 to $28 for two in two beds.

Key West

Accommodation: Key West Hostel and Sea Shell Motel, Ⓢ★, 718 South St., 33041. Telephone: 305/296-5719. Within walking distance of bus station. $25 to $35 single; $12.50 to $17.50 per person double; $10 to $13.50 per person triple; $7.50 to $9.50 per person quad. Rates vary according to season; highest in winter. Advance reservations are necessary.

Kissimmee

Accommodations: Days Inn, ♿, East Spacecoast Pkwy., 32741. Telephone: 305/396-7969, toll free: 800/327-9126 outside of Florida, 800/432-9103 in Florida. $30 to $50 single; $35 to $55 double.

- Days Inn, 5820 Spacecoast Pkwy., 32741. Telephone: 305/396-7900, toll free (same as above listing). These are 3-room suites with full kitchens, which accommodate up to 6 people per suite. $30 to $47 for one; $35 to $52 for two; $45 to $72 for a lodge; $6 for each additional person.

Lake City

Accommodations: Days Inn, I-75 & U.S. 90, Rte. 13, P.O. Box 1140, 32055. Telephone: 904/752-9350. $26 to $28 single; $31 to $32 double.

- Days Inn, I-4 & U.S. 98 (Exit 18 to U.S. 98S.), 3223 U.S. 98, 33805. Telephone: 813/688-6031. June 1 to August 31: $26 to $30 single; $31 to $35 double. September 1 to November 30: $22 to $26 single; $27 to $31 double.
- Scottish Inn, √, I-75 & Fla. 47, Rte. 10, Box 596, 32055. Telephone: 904/752-6450. $15.88 for one; $18.88 for two in one bed; $21.88 for two in two beds.
- Econo Lodge, I-75 at U.S. 90 W., P.O. Box 430, 32055. Telephone: 904/752-7550. $21.88 for one; $24.88 for two in one bed; $25.88 for two in two beds.
- Motel 6, U.S. 90 & Ross Allen Rd., 32055. Telephone: 904/755-2657. See Cocoa Beach listing for rates.
- TraveLodge, √ (15%), U.S. 90 W. & I-75 (P.O. Box 1238), 32055. Telephone: 904/752-7550. $21 single; $25 double.

Lake Wales

Accommodations: Econo Lodge, √, 501 South Hwy. 27, P.O. Box 1637, 33853. Telephone: 813/676-7963. $24.50 for one; $27.50 for two in one bed; $30.50 for two in two beds.
● Emerald Motel, 530 South Scenic Hwy., 33853. Telephone: 813/676-3310. $20 single; $22.50 double.

Lakeland

Accommodations: Scottish Inn, √, 244 North Florida Ave., 33801. Telephone: 813/687-2530. July 1 to December 31: $20 to $22 for one; $23 to $26 for two in one bed; $25 to $28 for two in two beds. February 1 to April 5: $25 to $35 for one; $28 to $38 for two in one bed; $32 to $42 for two in two beds.
● Red Carpet Inn, 3410 U.S. 98 N., 33805. Telephone: 813/858-3851. $25 single; $29.50 double.
● Econo Lodge, √ ⑤, 1115 West North Blvd., U.S. N. Hwy. 441, 32748. Telephone: 904/787-3131. $30 for one; $32 for two in one bed; $34 for two in two beds.

Marianna

Accommodations: Econo Lodge, √, 1119 West Lafayette St., 32446. Telephone: 904/526-3710. $24 for one; $27 for two in one bed; $30 for two in two beds.
Camping: Florida Caverns State Park, √, 2701 Caverns Rd., 32446. Telephone: 904/482-3632. Area surrounding Florida's only publicly accessible limestone caverns. Campground with 32 sites open year round. $6.30 per campsite per night for non-electric sites; $8.40 for electric.

Melbourne

Accommodations: Econo Lodge, √, 4505 West New Haven Ave., 32901. Telephone: 305/724-5450. $30.50 to $38.50 for one; $34.50 to $43.50 for two. Higher rates apply during special events.
● Red Carpet Inn, 1423 South Harbor City Blvd., 32901. Telephone: 305/727-2950. $22.88 single; $26.88 double.
● TraveLodge, √ ⑤, I-95 & U.S. 195, 32901. Telephone: toll free 800/255-3050. $30 for one; $35 for two in one bed; $40 for two in two beds.

Miami Beach/Miami

Sixty years ago this was swampland but now it's high-rise hotel land. People flock to Miami every winter for the sun and the ocean and many have decided to stay, so the Miami area is full of transplants from other, more northerly spots. Because Miami is such a popular resort area, prices can be high. If you want to keep your expenses down, keep in mind this advice from the Miami Beach Visitor and Convention Authority: "Hotels and restaurants in the southern end of Miami Beach are the least expensive—that is, from Lincoln Road south." A square mile of this area has recently been placed in the National Register of Historic Places—it's called the Art Deco District, a neighborhood with the world's largest collection of depression-era, whimsical architecture. When to visit? One friend writes: "In September the hotels are not as busy and the rates are still low; later on it's too crowded and earlier it's too hot."

One neighborhood you'll want to visit is Little Havana, in southwest Miami, which was established back in 1959 by Cubans and has been growing ever since. Now you'll find restaurants, shops, discos, and hotels all in the Cuban tradition—a lively place to visit and practice your Spanish. To know what's going on in Miami, check with *Miami/South Florida Magazine* or contact the Miami Beach Visitor and Convention Authority, 555 17th St., 33139 (tel. 305/673-7080).

Getting There: Miami International Airport is five miles northwest of the city. A taxi ride from the airport will cost about $10 to $12, but you can take a bus—the no. 20, no. 28 or no. 34—and it will cost only 75¢. The bus station is at 300 N.W. 32nd Ave. in Miami (tel. 638-6700), with another terminal in downtown Coral Gables.

Getting Around: Taxi fares start at $1, and $1.20 is added for each additional mile. The bus fare is 75¢, with a discount for senior citizens between 9 a.m. and 4 p.m. and after 6 p.m. Be sure to check the schedule, too, of the new rapid Metrorail System which services many areas of the city and costs $1. Information is available by calling 638-6700. To rent a car, you might try Way-Lo Rent-a-Car, at three locations in Miami Beach and one in downtown Miami. Rates are $99.50 per week for Ford Escorts and Toyotas.

Or take a self-guided bike tour through Coral Gables and around the University of Miami. You can rent a bike for approximately $10 per day at the Dade Cycle Shop, 3216 Grand Ave. (tel. 443-6075).

Help: United Way Information Referral, 955 S.W. 2nd Ave., 33130. Telephone: 805/854-8311. Will help travelers in need contact family or other helpful organizations.

Someone at Travelers Aid mentioned that the area around the bus terminals is hazardous, although the neighborhood improves within a few blocks.

Accommodations: Haddon Hall Hotel (AYH-SA), ⑤, 1500 Collins Ave., 33139. Telephone: 305/531-1251. In Miami's art deco area, one block from Greyhound station. Men, women, and children. May 1 to July 1 and from September 1 to November 15: $15 to $20 single or double. July 2 to August 31: $15 to $18 single; $18 to $25 double. Higher rates apply in winter. Rooms have refrigerators, sinks, and cooking facilities. "We have our own Olympic-size pool and are a block from the ocean. We're in the heart of Miami Beach." The above rates are special for *Where to Stay* readers. Ask about AYH rates.

● Hotel Netherland, ★, 1330 Ocean Dr., Miami Beach, 33139. Telephone: 305/534-4791. Summer: $18 single; $19 to $31 double; $25 to $45 triple. Winter: Add $2 to summer rates.

● Winterhaven Hotel, ⑤★, 1400 Ocean Dr., 33139. Telephone: 305/534-4791. $12 to $20 single. Rooms face the ocean and have kitchenettes. Recommended by a reader who said the management was "very friendly." Advance reservations suggested during winter.

● Willard Garden Hotel, ⑤★, 124 NE 14th St., 33132. Telephone: 305/374-9112. $15 single; $21 double; $29 triple. Advance reservations of one week necessary.

- Clay Hotel/Miami Beach Youth Hostel (AYH), ⓈV ★, 1438 Washington Ave., 33139. Telephone: 305/534-2988. $15 single; $20 double; $27 triple; $32 quad. Rates slightly higher December to March. Advance reservations suggested December to April.

Where to Eat: D'Pizza of U.M., 1118 South Dixie Hwy., Coral Gables, near University of Miami. Telephone: 666-5841. What you'd expect—pizza, lasagne, pasta, plus a popular Italian fish soup.

- Bagel Emporium, 1238 South Dixie Hwy., Coral Gables, across from University of Miami. Telephone: 666-9519. Nine varieties of the popular little roll with the hole in the middle.
- Uncle Tom's Cabin Barbecue, S.W. 8th St. and 40th Ave. Telephone: 446-9528. Relaxing, old-style Western setting. $4 to 6 for a meal consisting of barbecued chicken, ribs, or pork, with coleslaw and bread.
- Mr. Pizza, 18120 Collins Ave. Telephone: 932-6915. In the shopping center opposite the ocean. Pizza of course, with a do-it-yourself sundae bar.
- Granada Restaurant, 1446 Washington Ave. Telephone: 534-9922. Near the Miami Beach Theater of the Performing Arts and the Bass Art Museum. Good Spanish food—daily specials of meat or chicken with rice or beans, plantains, or french fries.
- La Carreta, four locations with the original at 3632 S.W. 8th St. Telephone: 444-7501. A good place to try typical Cuban food.
- Versailles Restaurant, 3555 S.W. 8th St. Telephone: 444-0240. Cuban too, and very popular for late-night dining.
- Monty Trainers, 2560 Bayshore Dr. Telephone: 858-1431. Dine outdoors by the water in a casual atmosphere.
- Sakura Japanese Restaurant, 440 South Dixie Hwy. Telephone: 665-7020. Authentic and good Japanese food.

What to See: You'll probably want to stay horizontal on the beach for most of your stay, but if the weather is bad or you get tired of sun and sand, there are lots of tourist attractions in the area. These include the Miami Seaquarium, a 60-acre aquatic park on Rickenbacker Causeway in Biscayne Bay complete with performing whales. Call 361-5703 for information.

- Monkey Jungle, 14805 S.W. 216th St. Telephone: 235-1611. Gorillas, orangutans, and chimpanzees doing what they do in the open while the visitors watch from enclosed walkways. Performing chimps, besides.
- Villa Vizcaya, 3251 South Miami Ave. Telephone: 579-2708. This 70-room Italian-style extravaganza was once the home of the industrialist James Deering and is now the property of the Dade County Art Museum. Inside the villa you'll see rugs, tapestries, and sculpture, and outside you can walk through formal gardens.
- Art Deco District. All-day tours begin each Saturday at 10:30 a.m.—docents are designers, architects, writers, and historians. Call 672-2014 for information.
- Six Flag Atlantis—The Water Kingdom, 2700 Stirling Rd., Hollywood. About a 15-minute ride from Miami Beach. Telephone: 926-1000. A water theme park, with a song-and-dance revue and a water-ski show.
- Museum of Science Planetarium, 3280 South Miami Ave. Call 854-2222 for information.
- Fairchild Tropical Gardens, 10901 Old Cutler Rd. Telephone: 667-1651. A paradise of tropical plants from around the world. Train rides or a self-guided walking tour.

• Jai-alai, 3500 N.W. 37th Ave. Telephone: 633-6400. From December to September. One of Miami's most exciting spectator sports.

At Night: The big hotels have shows at night—big-name stars and some not-so-big-name stars. Check *Miami/South Florida Magazine* to see who's where while you're in town. Some other possibilities:

• Flamenco, 991 N.E. 79th St. Telephone: 751-8631. Two shows every night and dancing. A $5 minimum cover charge. Spanish entertainment—two floor shows every night.

• Dade County Auditorium, 2901 West Flagler St. Telephone: 547-5414. This is the heart of Miami's cultural life—call to see whether there's a concert, a play, or a dance company booked into this popular theater and whether there are any tickets.

• Ronnie's, 2373 Le Jeune Rd., across from the airport. Open from 9:30 p.m. to 5 in the morning for dancing to big-band sounds, to disco and other kinds of music too.

Shopping: The Grove Book Worm, 3025 Fuller St. Telephone: 443-6411. All hard- and soft-cover books.

• Books and Books, Inc., 296 Aragon Ave., Coral Gables. A thoughtful selection of books; frequent guest appearances by well-known authors.

• Spec's Music Shop, Dadeland Mall, 7535 North Kendall Dr. and other locations. Telephone: 666-5941. Records galore.

• Shoe Villa, 17220 Collins Ave., Sunny Isles. Telephone: 949-9276. All kinds of shoes with a 25% discount to ISIC holders.

• Lincoln Road Mall on Miami Beach has 80 stores in an eight-block area, if you want to do some serious shopping.

• Southwest 8th St. (Calle Ocho to most) is for shopping with a Latin flavor—you can bargain with shopkeepers here. A must if you want to get a feel of what today's Miami is all about.

Naples

Accommodation: Days Inn, ♿, U.S. 41 & Fla. 84, Alligator Alley, 1925 Davis Blvd., 33942. Telephone: 813/774-3117. $28 to $31 for one; $39 for one or two in lodge.

Ocala

Accommodations: Days Inn, I-75 & Fla. 40, 4040 S.W. Broadway, 32671. Telephone: 904/629-8850. June 1 to August 25 and October 1 to November 30: $24 to $32 single; $29 to $37 double. August 25 to September 30: $22 to $27 single; $27 to $32 double.

• Budget Inn—Western Motel, 4013 N.W. Blichton Rd., 32675. Telephone: 904/732-6940. April 16 to January 14: $19 single; $24 double. Rest of year: $19 single; $27 double.

• Motor Inns Motel, 3601 West Silver Springs Dr., 32670. Telephone: 904/629-6902. $19 to $24 single; $25 to $28 double.

• Econo Lodge, √ ♿, 3951 N.W. Blichton Rd., 32675. Telephone: 904/629-7021. $18.95 for one; $21.95 for two in one bed; $26.95 for two in two beds.

- Red Carpet Inn, ★, 3960 N.W. Blichton Rd., Exit 70 on I-75, 32675. Telephone: 904/629-8681. $19.95 single; $26.95 double; $29.95 for three in two beds; $32.95 for four in two beds. Advance reservations of one month necessary.
- Quality Inn, Ⓢ√★, 3767 N.W. Blichton Rd., 32675. Telephone: 904/732-2300. $21.95 single; $30.95 double; $5 for each additional person.
- TraveLodge, √[♿], 1626 S.W. Pine Ave., 32670. Telephone: 904/622-4121. $28 for one; $32 for two in one bed; $36 for two in two beds.

Orlando

All of the budget motels in the Orlando area are here to accommodate all of the people who come to Disney World and to Sea World.

Help: We Care, Inc., 112 Pasadena Place, 32803. Telephone: 305/628-1227. 24-hour crisis/suicide prevention. Someone from We Care, Inc., told us that if you're really in a bind, a place called Daily Bread will serve you a free meal at noon. But for the most part, "people who are stranded find little help."

Accommodations: Young Women's Community Club (AYH-SA), [♿], 107 East Hillcrest St., 32801. Telephone: 305/425-2502. Women 16-37 only. $8.50 in dorm-style room. Breakfast and dinner served on the premises daily at no extra cost.

- Budget Host—Motel South, 1820 North Mills Ave., 32803. Telephone: 305/896-3611. $28 to $30 for one or two in one bed; $34 to $36 for two in two beds.
- Orlando International House (AYH), 420 Highland Ave., 32801. Telephone: 305/841-8867. Call first for transportation from airport. $6.50 summer; $5.25 winter for AYH members.
- Days Inn, I-4 & Fla. 46, Sanford, 32771. Telephone: 305/323-6500. $28 to $33 for one; $33 to $38 for two.
- Days Inn, I-4 & West 33rd St., 1600 West 33rd St., Days Park, 32805. Telephone: 305/423-7646. Recreational vehicle park. June 1 to November 30: $14 single; $2 for each additional person over 2 years old.
- Days Inn, I-4 & 33rd St., 2500 West 33rd St., 32809. Telephone: 305/841-3731. $29 to $41 for one; $34 to $46 for two.
- Days Airport Inn, 2333 McCoy Rd., 32809. Telephone: 305/859-6100. $29 to $40 for one; $34 to $45 for two.
- Days Inn—Landstreet Inn & Lodge, 1221 West Landstreet Rd., 32809. Telephone: 305/859-7700. $29 to $42 for one; $37 to $47 for two.
- Econo Lodge, √, 5870 Orange Blossom Trail S., 32809. Telephone: 305/851-5410. $28.50 for one or two in one bed; $33.50 for two in two beds.
- Friendship Inn Orlando Motor Lodge, 1825 North Mills Ave., 32803. Telephone: 305/896-4111. $25 to $28 for one or two in one bed; $29 to $38 for two in two beds.
- Motel 6, Interstate 4 & Hwy. 192, 32714. See Cocoa Beach listing for rates.
- Motel 6, 7455 West Space Coast Pkwy., 32741. Telephone: 305/396-1755. See Cocoa Beach listing for rates.

Orange Park

Accommodation: Scottish Inn, 337 Park Ave., 32073. Telephone: 904/264-0511. $29 single; $33 double; $45 during Gator Bowl.

Ormond Beach

Accommodations: Econo Lodge, 1634 North U.S. 1, 32074. Telephone: 904/672-6222. $21.50 for one or two in one bed; $26.50 for two in two beds. Higher rates apply during special events.

● Red Carpet Inn, √, I-95 & U.S. 1, 32704. Telephone: 904/672-7341. $24.88 for one; $26.88 for two in one bed; $28.88 for two in two beds.

● Quality Inn, √, I-95 & U.S. 1, Exit 89, 32074. Telephone: 904/672-8621. $21.95 to $35.95 single; $29.95 to $45.95 double. Rates vary with season.

Palatka

Accommodation: Budget Host—Town House Motel, √, 100 Moseley Ave., 32077. Telephone: 904/328-1533. $22 to $26 for one or two in one bed; $27 to $32 for two in two beds.

Panama City

Accommodations: Sangraal-by-the-Sea, (AYH-SA) #2 Myrtlewood Lodge (AYH-SA), 226 College Ave., 32401. Telephone: 904/785-6226. $5.50 summer, $6.50 winter for AYH members. Advance reservations suggested.

● Scottish Inn, √ ♿, 4907 West Hwy. 98, 32401. Telephone: 904/769-2432. September 3 to December 31: $25 to $28 single; $28 to $31 for two in one bed; $31 to $34 for two in two beds. Higher rates apply July 1 to September 2.

● Scottish Inn, √, 11000 West Alternate Hwy. 98, 32407. Telephone: 904/234-3351. September 3 to December 31: $18 to $24 for one; $24 to $30 for two in one bed; $30 to $35 for two in two beds. Higher rates apply July 1 to September 2.

● Friendship Inn of Panama City, 3910 West Hwy. 98, 30401. Telephone: 904/785-8559 or 785-9758. $20 to $35 for one; $25 to $45 for two in one bed; $28 to $50 for two in two beds.

Pensacola Beach

Camping: Gulf Islands National Seashore, 1400 Fort Pickens Rd., 32561. Telephone: 904/932-5018. Campground with 189 sites open year-round. $8 to $10 per campsite per night.

Pensacola

Help: Help Line, 904/438-1617.

● Information & Referral, 904/436-9777.

Accommodations: Econo Lodge, √, I-10 & Hwy. 291, Plantation Rd., 32504. Telephone: 904/474-1060. $28.95 for one; $32.95 for two in one bed; $32.95 for two in two beds.

● Regal 8 Inn, 7827 North Davis Hwy., 32514. Telephone: 904/476-5386. $23.88 for one; $28.88 for two in one bed; $33.88 for two in two beds.

- Motel 6, 5829 Pensacola Blvd., 32505. Telephone: 904/477-2152. See Cocoa Beach listing for rates.
- Days Inn, 6911 Pensacola Blvd., 32505. Telephone: 904/477-9000. $30 single; $34 double.
- Red Roof Inn, ⟨⟩, I-10 & Fla. 291, Exit 5, 7340 Plantation Rd., 32504. Telephone: 904/476-7960. $27.95 for one; $32.95 for two in one bed; $34.95 for two in two beds; $36.95 for three or four in two beds.
- Red Carpet Inn, √, 4448 Mobile Hwy., 32506. Telephone: 904/456-7411. July 1 to September 30: $22 for one or two in one bed; $25 for two in two beds. October 1 to December 31: $20 for one or two in one bed; $24 for two in two beds.
- Friendship Inn Maria Motel, 451 Mobile Hwy. 90 W., 32506. Telephone: 904/455-0303. $22 to $45 for one; $22 to $55 for two in one bed; $30 to $55 for two in two beds.

Plant City

Accommodation: Berkeley Inn, √⟨⟩, I-4 & Fla. 39, 301 South Frontage Rd., 33566. Telephone: 813/752-0570. $25.95 for one or two in one bed; $29.95 for two in two beds.

Pompano Beach

Accommodations: Days Inn, 1411 N.W. 31st Ave., 33060. Telephone: 305/972-3700. $26 to $32 for one; $32 to $38 for two.
- Motel 6, 1201 N.W. 31st Ave., 33069. Telephone: 305/972-6366. See Cocoa Beach listing for rates.

Ridge Manor

Accommodation: Budget Host-Ridge Manor Motel, 7555 Hwy. 301 N., 33525. Telephone: 904/583-2109. $18 to $24 for one; $24 to $28 for two in one bed; $26 to $33 for two in two beds.

St. Augustine

Accommodations: Econo Lodge, √, 3101 Ponce de Leon Blvd., 32084. Telephone: 904/829-3461. $22.50 to $27.50 for one; $24.50 to $29.50 for two in one bed; $26.50 to $32.50 for two in two beds. Higher rates apply during special events.
- Sunshine Inn, Ⓢ√ (10%), I-95 & S.R. 16, Rte. 2, Box 278, 32084. Telephone: 904/824-4436. $19.95 single; $23.95 for two in one bed; $25.95 for two in two beds.
- Scottish Inn, √⟨⟩, Rte. 2, Box 277X, 32084. Telephone: 904/829-5643. $18.95 to $24.95 for one; $22.95 to $28.95 for two in one bed; $24.95 to $32.95 for two in two beds. Higher rates apply during special events.
- Scottish Inn, √, 427 Anastasia Blvd., A1A South, 32084. Telephone: 904/824-5055. September 7 to December 31: $18 to $26 for one; $20 to $28 for two in

one bed; $22 to $30 for two in two beds. July 1 to September 6: $26 to $30 for one; $28 to $32 for two in one bed; $30 to $36 for two in two beds. Higher rates apply July 4 and Labor Day.

- Days Inn, I-95 & Fla. 16, Rte. 2, Box 277Y, 32084. Telephone: 904/824-4341. June 1 to September 1: $23.88 single; $28.88 double. September 2 to November 30: $21 single; $26 double.
- Days Inn, ♿, 2800 Ponce de Leon Blvd., 32084. Telephone: 904/829-6581. June 1 to September 1: $28 single; $33 double. September 2 to November 30: $23 to $28.
- Red Carpet Inn, ♿, I-95 & S.R. 16, P.O. Box D-1, 32084. Telephone: 904/824-4306. $18.95 to $24.95 for one; $22.95 to $28.95 for two in one bed; $24.95 to $32.95 for two in two beds. Higher rates apply during special events.
- Scottish Inn, 110 San Marco Ave., 32084. Telephone: 904/824-2871. $26 to $30 for one; $28 to $32 for two in one bed; $30 to $34 for two in two beds. Higher rates apply during special events.

St. Cloud

Accommodation: Polynesian Inn, √, 2900 13th St., 32769. Telephone: 305/892-5131. $30 to $40 double. April 20 to June 10 and September 1 to December 20: $20 to $30.

St. Petersburg

Tourist Information: Convention and Tourist Division, St. Petersburg Convention Bureau, St. Petersburg Area Chamber of Commerce, P.O. Box 1371, 33731. Telephone: 813/821-4069.

Accommodations: St. Petersburg Family YMCA, Ⓢ ★, 116 5th St. S., 33701. Telephone: 813/822-3911. Men only. $15. Weekly rate: $44.

- Friendship Inn Tops Motel, 7141 4th St. N., 33702. Telephone: 813/526-9071. Limited airport service available. $22 to $32 for one; $25 to $32 for two in one bed; $34 to $40 for two in two beds.
- Friendship Valley Forge, 6825 Central Ave., 33710. Telephone: 813/345-0135. Limited airport service available. $25 to $37 for one; $30 to $38 for two in one bed; $35 to $38 for two in two beds.
- Days Inn, 9359 U.S. 19 N., 33565. Telephone: 813/577-3838. $27 single; $32 double.

Sarasota

Accommodations: Friendship Inn-Imperial Motel, 4807 North Tamiami Trail, 33580. Telephone: 813/355-5247. $18 to $38 for one; $21 to $42 for two in one bed; $24 to $48 for two in two beds.

- Econo Lodge, √, 5340 North Tamiami Trail, 33580. Telephone: 813/355-8867. $29.95 for one; $32.95 for two in one bed; $36.95 for two in two beds. Higher rates apply during special events.
- Cadillac Motel, 4021 North Tamiami Trail, 33580. Telephone: 813/355-7108. $22 for one or two in one bed; $25 for two in two beds.

● TraveLodge, √ (15%), 270 North Tamiami Trail, 33577. Telephone: 813/ 366-0414. $26 for one; $29 for two in one bed; $32 for two in two beds.

Satellite Beach

Accommodation: Econo Lodge, √ &, 180 Hwy. A1A, 32937. $26.95 to $32.95 for one; $30.95 to $36.95 for two in one bed; $33.95 to $39.95 for two in two beds. Higher rates apply during special events.

Silver Springs

Accommodation: Scottish Inn, √, P.O. Box 277, 5331 N.E. Silver Springs Blvd., 32688. Telephone: 904/236-2383. July 1 to September 6: $24 for one; $26 for two in one bed; $28 for two in two beds. September 1 to December 31: $20 for one; $22 for two in one bed; $24 for two in two beds.

South Bay

Accommodation: Econo Lodge, √ &, 225 Hwy. 27 N., 33493. Telephone: 305/996-6517. $30 for one; $34 for two in one bed; $38 for two in two beds.

Starke

Accommodations: Dixie Motel, 744 North Temple Ave., 32091. Telephone: 904/964-5590. $22 to $26 for one; $24 to $28 for two in one bed; $28 to $32 for two in two beds.
● Econo Lodge, √ &, Hwy. 301 N., P.O. Box 1090, 32091. Telephone: 904/964-7600. $29 single; $35 double.

Tallahassee

On Campus: If you're in Tallahassee and want to meet some of Florida State University's students, stop at Poor Paul's Poorhouse, The Alley, The Phyrst, Radcliff's, or Bullwinkle's, all friendly local pubs with music.

Family-style meals at very inexpensive prices can be found at Tucker's Drive Inn Restaurant, 3520 Woodville Hwy. All-you-can-eat chicken dinners.

Accommodations: Econo Lodge, √ &, 2681 North Monroe St., 32303. Telephone: 904/385-6155. $28.95 for one; $32.95 for two in one bed; $35.95 for two in two beds. Higher rates apply during special events.
● Motel 6, 1481 Timberlane Dr., 32308. Telephone: 904/893-7587. See Cocoa Beach listing for rates.
● Master Hosts Inn—Tallahassee Motor Hotel, &, 1630 North Monroe St., 32303. Telephone: 904/224-6183. $24 to $30 for one; $29 to $34 for two in one bed; $31 to $36 for two in two beds.
● Red Roof Inn, &, 2930 Hospitality Rd., 32303. Telephone: 904/385-7884. $24.95 for one; $29.95 for two in one bed; $31.95 for two in two beds; $33.95 for three or four in two beds.

Tampa

On Campus: You can contact the Overseas Information Center, SOC 107, Room 301, at the University of South Florida (tel. 813/974-3104) for help in finding temporary accommodations "with someone from the University community." You might also find apartment listings in the *Oracle*, the University of South Florida's newspaper.

A good place to meet people is the Empty Keg, the student bar at the University Center. There are also several pubs along Fletcher Ave. where students burn the midnight oil. For good pizza, ask directions to the popular C.D.B. Pizza.

Tourist Information: Tampa/Hillsborough Convention and Visitors Association, P.O. Box 519, 33601. Telephone: 813/228-7777.

Accommodations: Econo Lodge, √, 11414 Central Ave., 33612. Telephone: 813/933-7831. $26.95 for one; $30.95 for two in one bed; $34.95 for two in two beds. Higher rates apply during special events.

● Econo Lodge, ⓰, 321 East Fletcher St., 33612. Telephone: 813/933-4545. $26.95 to $29.95 for one; $31.95 to $33.95 for two in one bed; $34.95 to $37.95 for two in two beds.

● Motel 6, 333 East Fowler Ave., 33612. Telephone: 813/932-2912. See Cocoa Beach listing for rates.

● Scottish Inn, ⓰, 1201 North New Hampshire Ave., 32778. Telephone: 904/343-4666. $25 to $26 for one; $28 to $29 for two in one bed; $29 to $30 for two in two beds.

● Days Inn, I-75 & Fla. 54 W., Zephyrhills, 33599. Telephone: 813/973-0155. $27 to $38 for one; $37 to $43 for two.

● Days Inn, 701 East Fletcher Ave., 33612. Telephone: 813/977-1550. $29 to $39 single; $34 to $44 double.

● Days Inn, 2901 East Busch Blvd., 33612. Telephone: 813/933-6471. $29 to $33 for one; $33 to $37 for two.

● Days Inn, 6010 Fla. 579 N., Seffner, 33584. Telephone: 813/621-4681. $29 to $40 single; $34 to $45 double.

● Red Carpet Inn, Ⓢ √ ⓰ ★, 4528 East Columbus Dr., 33605. Telephone: 813/621-4651. $22.95 single; $26.95 double; $30.95 triple.

● Red Roof Inn, 5001 North U.S. 301, 33610. Telephone: 813/623-5245. See Tallahassee listing for rates.

Tarpon Springs

Accommodation: Days Inn, ⓰, 816 U.S. 19 S., 33589. Telephone: 813/934-0859. $27 to $47 for one; $32 to $52 for two; $45 to $55 for lodge.

Titusville

Accommodations: Rodeway Inn, √ (10%), 3655 Chaney Hwy., 32780. Telephone: 305/269-7110. $28 to $40 single; $31 to $35 double. Complimentary breakfast. Higher rates apply during shuttle launches.

● Three Oaks Motel, ⓰ ★, 707 South Hopkins Ave., 32780. Telephone: 305/267-6272. $24 to $26 single; $26 to $28 double.

● Days Inn, ☐, 3480 Garden St., 32796. Telephone: 305/269-9310. $27 to $30 for one; $30 to $36 for two.

● Budget Host—Town Motel, 612 South Washington Ave., 32796. Telephone: 305/267-4211. $22 to $26 for one; $24 to $28 for two; $28 to $32 for three; $28 to $34 for four. Higher rates apply during special events.

Venice

Accommodation: Motel 6, 281 Venice Bypass N., 33595. Telephone: 813/488-7395. See Cocoa Beach listing for rates.

West Palm Beach

Help: The Center for Family Services (Travelers Aid), 2218 South Dr., 33401. Telephone: 305/655-4483.

● Crisis Line, 305/588-1121.

Accommodation: Days Inn, 2300 West 45th St., 33407. Telephone: 305/689-0450. $29 to $31 single; $34 to $36 double.

Wildwood

Accommodations: Days Inn, I-75 & Fla. 44, Rte. 2, Box 65E, 32785. Telephone: 904/748-2000. $20 to $25 for one; $25 to $30 for two; $35 to $40 for lodge.

● Econo Lodge, Rte. 2, Box 62, 32785. Telephone: 904/748-2005. $19.95 for one; $23.95 for two in one bed; $27.95 for two in two beds.

● Red Carpet Inn, ☐, I-75 & Fla. 44, Exit 66, P.O. Box 159, 32785. $17.99 for one; $20.99 for two in one bed; $23.99 for two in two beds.

● Red Carpet Inn, √, U.S. 301 & Fla. Turnpike, P.O. Box 88, 32785. Telephone: 904/748-3197. See above listing for rates.

Winter Haven

Accommodations: Budget Host—Banyan Beach Motel, 1630 6th St. NW, 33880. Telephone: 813/293-3658. April 15 to December 14: $26 for two in two beds; $30 efficiency with kitchen. December 15 to April 14: $34 for one; $40 for two in two beds; $44 to $50 for efficiency with kitchen. Pontoon boat trips to Cypress Gardens and the beach.

● Red Carpet Inn, √, 2000 Cypress Gardens Blvd., S.R. 540, 33880. Telephone: 813/324-6334. $22 to $30 for one; $22 to $30 for two in one bed; $24 to $38 for two in two beds.

● Scottish Inn, √, 3525 U.S. Hwy. 17 N., 33880. Telephone: 813/294-2804. July 1 to September 2: $24 to $38 for one or two in one bed; $40 to $50 for two in two beds. September 3 to December 31: $22 to $28 for one or two in one bed; $24 to $38 for two in two beds.

Winter Park

On Campus: In this "charming, small town next to Orlando in Central Florida," you'll find Rollins College, the oldest private institution of higher learning in Florida. The center of life on campus is in the Student Center and right outside the Center and the Rose Skillman Dining Hall, there's a bulletin board where rides, apartments and other available commodities are listed. To meet students, try Decades, Two Flights Up, East India Ice Cream Parlor and The Good Earth, all on Park Avenue. Right on campus you can visit the Cornell Art Gallery and the Beall-Maltbie Shell Museum.

Accommodation: Days Inn, ♿, I-4 & Lee Rd., 650 Lee Rd., 32810. Telephone: 305/628-2727. June 1 to September 2: $30 to $37 for one; $6 for each additional person.

Yeehaw Junction

Accommodation: Econo Lodge, √♿, Exit 60 Fla. Turnpike (441) & Fla. 60, 33472. Telephone: 305/436-1211. $27.95 single; $32.95 double.

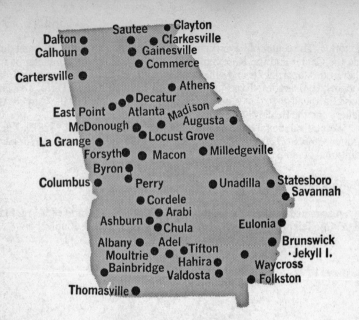

Georgia

Georgia is a bit confusing. Its image as part of the Deep South just doesn't jibe with what goes on in its most popular city, Atlanta.

The Tourist Office people have recently mounted a campaign to entice visitors their way and they've divided Georgia into seven travel regions: Pioneer Territory, in the northwest, which includes Chickamauga Battlefield, scene of one of the Civil War's bloodiest battles; the Northeast Georgia Mountains, where the attractions are out-of-doors; the Classic South, with hundreds of antebellum mansions, the Cotton Exchange Building and the Old Slave Market Column in Augusta, and the preserved home of Alexander H. Stephens, vice-president of the Confederacy, in Crawfordsville; the Colonial Coast, where you'll find the lovely city of Savannah and the vast and intriguing Okefenokee Swamp; the "Heart of Georgia," center of the state which includes the city of Macon with its restored Grand Opera House and 24-room Renaissance Hay House and Ocmulgee National Monument, the largest archeological restoration of ancient Indian civilization in the East; Plains Country, with Jimmy Carter's hometown and the national headquarters of the American Camellia Society; and finally, what the tourist people call the Big "A," with Atlanta at its hub.

For full descriptions of each area, write to the Georgia Department of Industry and Trade (address below) and ask for the 76-page *Georgia: This Way to Fun.* And, for a book with 400 vacation discounts, write to the Georgia Department of Industry and Trade Tourist Division, P.O. Box 1776, Atlanta, GA 30301.

Some Special Events: St. Patrick's Day in Savannah, Oktoberfest in Helen,

Arts Festival of Atlanta, Cherry Blossom Festival in Macon, Rose Festival in Thomasville, Praters Mill County Fair in Dalton, National Pecan Festival in Albany, and Dogwood Festival in Atlanta.

Hitching: Georgia law states: "No person shall stand in a roadway for the purpose of soliciting a ride."

Tourist Information: Tourist Division, Georgia Department of Industry and Trade, P.O. Box 1776, Atlanta, GA 30301. Telephone: 404/656-3590.

Adel

Accommodations: Econo Lodge, I-75 (Exit 10) & West 4th St., 31620. Telephone: 912/896-4574. $17.99 to $19.99 single; $21.99 to $23.99 double. Higher rates apply during special events.
● Comfort Inn, √ &, I-75 (Exit 10) & S.R. 37, 31620. Telephone: 912/896-4523. $17.99 to $21.99 single; $21.99 to $25.99 double.

Albany

Accommodations: Motel 6, 301 South Thornton Dr., 31705. Telephone: 912/439-8028. $17.95 for one; $21.95 for two; $2 for each additional person.
● Quality Inn, √ &, I-75 (Exit 10) & Ga. 37, 31620. Telephone: 912/896-2244. $19.99 to $23.99 single; $23.99 to $27.99 double.
● Motel 6, 301 South Thornton Dr., 31705. Telephone: 912/439-8028. $17.95 single; $21.95 double; $2 for each additional person.

Arabi

Accommodation: Red Carpet Inn, √, I-75 & Arabi Rd., Exit 30, 31712. Telephone: 912/273-8586. $17.95 single; $21.95 double.

Ashburn

Accommodations: Budget Host—Ashburn Motor Inn, I-75 at Exit 28, 31714. Telephone: 912/567-3346. Courtesy car available. $19.88 for all rooms.
● Quality Inn, √, I-75 & Ashburn-Amboy Exit 29, P.O. Box 806, 31714. Telephone: 912/567-3334. $22.88 to $24.88 single; $24.88 to $26.88 double.

Athens

On Campus: A friend at the University of Georgia describes Athens as a "serene and ruggedly beautiful Southern town with very hospitable people." Athens and the surrounding areas are rich in Civil War history, particularly Madison, "the town Sherman would not burn," and the many pre-Civil War plantations that still stand.

The university students can most often be found at O'Malley's, the Madhatter, Smokes, and the Speakeasy. You can find them eating at El Dorado

Natural Foods, 199 West Washington (quiche and salad for $2), or at Hunan, where you can get a complete lunch for $2.45.

Look into the welcome center in the middle of Athens for information about the area, and get a copy of the *Red & Black* student newspaper for information on student events, rides, etc. If you happen to be in Athens during the first weekend in May, you won't want to miss the annual downtown bed race.

Accommodations: Days Inn, 2741 Atlanta Hwy., 30606. Telephone: 404/546-9750. $25 to $30 single; $29 to $34 double.

● Scottish Inn, 410 Macon Hwy., 30606. Telephone: 404/546-8161. $20 for one; $22 to $24 for two in one bed; $24 to $28 for two in two beds.

● Red Carpet Inn, √, 2715 Atlanta Hwy., 30606. Telephone: 404/549-1530. $27 single; $30 double.

● Athens Home Hostel (AYH), c/o Joseph L. Fail, Jr., & Meta H. Thompson, 185 Virginia Ave., 30601. Telephone: 404/548-6293. Open January 2 to December 14. $5 for AYH members.

Atlanta

"This city is cosmopolitan, alive, friendly, slower-paced than many other big cities and less conservative than other areas of the South."

Atlanta started out as a railroad workers' camp right near today's Omni International Complex. The camp was called "The Terminus," and one civil engineer at the time noted that the place had little future. Atlanta is now home to 2.2 million people, a veritable boom town American style. The phoenix is the symbol of Atlanta, commemorating its amazing resurrection after General Sherman put the town to torch. That was in 1864, when eight out of every nine homes were burned. Who can ever forget the scene of a burning Atlanta in Margaret Mitchell's *Gone with the Wind*?

In the '80s Atlanta is thriving. The city celebrates itself several times a year: at the Piedmont Park Art Festival in early May, where hundreds of artisans display their works in the city's largest park; the Dogwood Festival, a nine-day celebration at the peak of dogwood season including parades, music, dance, and drama productions scheduled throughout the city; the July 4th Peachtree Parade and Peachtree Road Race; and the annual Atlanta Independent Film and Video Festival, the first week in April.

To find out what's happening and when, check the "Weekend" supplement to the Saturday *Atlanta Constitution and Journal*; *Creative Loafing*, an alternative newspaper; and the monthly *Atlanta Magazine*.

Getting There: From the Airport: The Atlanta airport, with the largest passenger terminal complex in the world, is about eight miles from the city. You can get from the airport to town on MARTA bus 72 to Lakewood rail stations to Five Points Station Downtown for 60¢. A taxi from the airport will cost about $14. The Atlanta Airport Shuttle has regular service to the downtown and metropolitan area from 5:30 a.m. to 2:00 a.m.; the ride costs $6. For shuttle information, call 525-2177.

● From the Bus Stations: The Greyhound Terminal is at 81 International Blvd., right behind the Peachtree Center area (522-6300); Trailways is at 200 Spring St. (524-2441).

Getting Around: Atlanta streets follow old rail rights-of-way and cow paths; no symmetrical grid-like pattern here. The city is divided into quadrants, which come together at the junction of Peachtree St., Edgewood Ave., and Marietta-Decatur Sts.

● MARTA is constructing a rapid rail system (see those "MARTA at work" signs). MARTA bus and train fares were, at the time of writing, 60¢ with no extra charge for a transfer, but were expected to go up. Call 522-4711 for MARTA information. Taxis cost $1 for the first one-fifth mile and 10¢ for each additional one-fifth mile, with 25¢ extra for each additional passenger.

Tourist Information: Atlanta Convention and Visitors Bureau, 233 Peachtree St. NW, Suite 200, 30343. Telephone: 404/521-6600.

Help: Travelers Aid, 110 Spring St. NW, 30303. Telephone: 404/523-0585.

● Emergency Mental Health Services, 404/522-9222.

Accommodations: Alamo Plaza Motel, 2370 Stewart Ave. SW, 30315. Telephone: 404/767-1521. On MARTA routes 19 & 41. $20 single; $27 double. An older building.

● Georgian Motel, √, 4300 Buford Hwy., 30329. Telephone: 404/636-4344. Accessible from downtown on MARTA bus no. 44, 65, or 130. $25 single; $29 double.

● Best Way Inn, √ (10%), 144 14th St. NW, 30318. Telephone: 404/873-4171. Six blocks from Georgia Tech to the southwest and Piedmont Park to the east. $30 single; $35 double; $41 triple; $47 quad.

● Sky Host Inn, √, 1360 Virginia Ave., 30344. Telephone: 404/761-5201. Take MARTA bus no. 72 from downtown. One mile from airport; free shuttle available. $25 to $28 single; $36 to $40 double.

● Bed & Breakfast Atlanta, 1801 Piedmont Ave., Suite 208, 30324. Telephone: 404/875-0525. "Each host home has been visited and selected to provide a comfortable, convenient, and more personal alternative to commercial lodging." $24 to $36 single; $28 to $40 double. Price includes continental breakfast. Advance reservations necessary.

● YMCA, 22 Butler St. NE, 30303. Telephone: 404/659-8085. Men only. $11.58 single without bath. Weekly rate: $56.72.

● Motel 6, 4427 Commerce Dr., 30344. Telephone: 404/762-1606. See Albany listing for rates.

● Motel 6, 4100 Wendell Dr. SW, 30336. Telephone: 404/696-4084. See Albany listing for rates.

● Scottish Inn, 1848 Howell Mill Rd., 30318. Telephone: 404/351-1220. $24.88 for one. $28.88 to $32.88 for two in one bed; $36.88 for two in two beds.

● Red Carpet Inn, √, 4552 Old Dixie Hwy., 30050. Telephone: 404/363-4290. $23.95 single; $26.95 double.

● Atlanta Motel, 277 Moreland Ave., 30316. Telephone: 404/659-2455. $30 single; $35 double.

● Scottish Inn/Six Flags, 4430 Frederick Dr. SW, 30336. Telephone: 404/691-6310. $19.88 for one; $22.88 to $32.88 for two in one bed; $38.88 for two in two beds.

● Flag View Motel, √ ★, Hwy. 6 & I-20, Exit 12, Austell, 30001. Telephone: 404/941-6600. $20 to $35 single; $35 to $45 double; $45 to $55 triple. Higher rates apply April to August. Advance reservations necessary April to August.

● Red Carpet Inn/Sky Host Inn, 1360 Virginia Ave., 30344. Telephone: 404/761-5201. $23 for one; $25 for two in one bed; $32 for two in two beds.

● Scottish Inn, 3118 Sylvan Ave., I-85 at Sylvan Rd., 30354. Telephone: 404/762-8801. $19.88 for one; $22.88 to $32.88 for two in one bed; $26.88 for two in two beds.

- Days Inn, I-75 Frontage Rd. & Farmer's Market, Forest Park, 30050. Telephone: 404/363-0800. $28 to $33 single; $33 to $38 double.
- Days Inn, 2788 Forest Hills Dr., 30315. Telephone: 404/768-7750. $29 to $37 single; $35 to $43 double.
- Dogwood Motel, 5140 Buford Hwy., 30340. Telephone: 404/457-7246. $30.99 for single or double.
- Red Roof Inn, &, I-75 & Windy Hill, Exit 110, 2200 Corporate Plaza, Smyrna, 30080. Telephone: 404/952-6966. $27.95 for one; $33.00 for two in one bed; $34.95 for two in two beds; $36.95 for three or four in two beds.
- Red Roof Inn, &, I-285, I-85 & Old National Hwy. (Exit 16, 2471), Old National Parkway, Collect Park, 30349. See above listing for rates.
- Red Roof Inn, &, I-85 & Druid Hills, 1960 North Druid Hills Rd., 30329. See above listing for rates.
- Red Roof Inn, &, I-20 & Fulton Industrial Blvd., Exit 11, 4265 Shirley Dr. SW, 30336. Telephone: 404/696-4391. $26.95 for one; $31.95 for two in one bed; $33.95 for two in two beds; $35.95 for three or four in two beds.
- Red Roof Inn, &, I-75 & S.R. 54, Exit 76, 1348 South Lake Plaza Dr., Morrow, 30260. Telephone: 404/968-1483. $24.95 for one; $29.95 for two in one bed; $31.95 for two in two beds; $33.95 for three or four in two beds.

Where to Eat: Café de la Paix, Atlanta Hilton Hotel, 255 Courtland and Harris Sts. Telephone: 659-2000. Eat as much as you'd like; choose from eight entrees, three vegetables, fruit, fresh baked breads, and desserts. $6.95 Monday to Saturday; $11.95 Sunday brunch.

- Snack Shack, 37 Pryor St. SW. Telephone: 523-5054. About two blocks from Woodruff Park in downtown. "Sandwiches are huge and excellent."
- Livingston's Library and Pub, 22 Ivy St. Telephone: 521-2584. Downtown, one block from Woodruff Park. Soups and burgers. "Great place for a literary lunch or after-work libation."
- Mary Mac's, 224 Ponce de Leon Ave. NE. Telephone: 876-6604. About ten minutes by car from Peachtree Plaza. Family-style down-home cooking in just the right atmosphere. Country-fried steak, two vegetables, and dessert costs $5 at dinnertime.
- Eat Your Vegetables Café, 438 Moreland Ave. Telephone: 523-2671. Healthy food like a mushroom melt, love burger, salads, a fruit plate, tempura, etc. A friendly and comfortable place where a full lunch costs under $4. Brunch on Sundays from 11 a.m. to 3 p.m.
- The Mansion, 179 Ponce de Leon Ave. NE. Telephone: 876-0727. An unusual and charming restaurant in an old Victorian house surrounded by trees. Lunch is about $5 to $10; dinner from $11.95 to $18.50.
- Grandma's Biscuits, 233 Peachtree, Peachtree Center. Telephone: 577-1500. Simple Southern cooking. Meat, two vegetables, and biscuit or cornbread is under $4.
- Thelma's Kitchen, 223 Marietta St. Telephone: 688-5855. Southern cooking in a corner restaurant frequented by lots of regulars. Thelma would like to talk to you; tell her how you find her place. Fried chicken, and two vegetables— maybe sweet potatoes and okra—for $3.25.
- Capo's Café, 992 Virginia Ave. NE. Telephone: 876-5655. Lovely menu includes chicken salad Nora (chunks of chicken, apples, walnuts, and raisins with a curry cream dressing), $5.25; scallops Parisienne, $7.95; fettuccine Alfredo, $4.95; and the house specialty, chicken diavolo, $8.75. "One of the least expensive good restaurants around."

- Cha Gio Vietnamese Restaurant, 998 Peachtree St. NE. Telephone: 876-1817. This unimposing downtown restaurant has a friendly atmosphere, good Oriental food, and lots of followers. A substantial dinner for two of spring rolls, soup, pork fried rice, garlic beef, and broccoli and chicken, flan, and tea is only $12.
- Dannon Yogurt Bar, 25 Exchange Place (near Woodruff Park). Popular at lunch hour, this spot serves hot and cold sandwiches on pita bread (try the avocado melt) and frozen yogurt for dessert.
- Little Five Points Community Pub, 1174 Euclid Ave. NE. Telephone: 577-7767. Right in the middle of the Little Five Points area, this is the place for nachos, burgers, deli sandwiches, and homemade ice cream.

What to See and Do: Stone Mountain Park. About 16 miles east of Atlanta. A 3200-acre park complete with museums, skylift, riverboat, scenic railroad, campground, and more. MARTA bus marked "120 Stone Mountain" from the Avondale rail station will get you there.

- Six Flags Atlanta. 15 minutes from downtown Atlanta. Telephone: 948-9290. A family entertainment park with 100 rides, shows, and attractions. Open weekends during the fall and spring, daily from May 20 to September 1. Accessible from downtown by MARTA rail and bus: take rail line to Hightower Station and from there take bus marked "201 Six Flags." The trip costs $1.25 plus 60¢ rail fare each way; a one-price ticket to Six Flags costs $14.50 and entitles you to all rides and most shows.
- Toy Museum of Atlanta, 2800 Peachtree St. Telephone: 266-8697. Antique toys and dolls dating from the 1850s. $2 adults; $1.50 children 6 to 12.
- Martin Luther King Historic District. This two-block area includes King's birthplace, the Ebenezer Baptist Church where he preached, and Dr. King's gravesite. Information center for the area is on the tour site; further information available by calling 524-1956.
- Grant Park and Atlanta Zoo, Boulevard Ave., SE. Telephone: 658-6374 or 658-7059. The largest reptile collection in the country. $2.50 adults; $1.25 for children 4 to 11.
- Fernbank Science Center, 156 Heaton Park Dr., Decatur. Telephone: 378-4311. Science exhibits, botanical gardens, 65-acre forest with two miles of walking trails, and the third-largest planetarium in the U.S. Museum admission is free; planetarium is $2 for adults, $1 for students.
- Wren's Nest, 1050 Gordon St. Telephone: 753-8535. Once the home of Joel Chandler Harris, creator of the Uncle Remus stories, with some of the original furniture on display. $2.50 adults; $1.25 teens; 75¢ children; $2 seniors.
- Omni International, Marietta St. at International Blvd. A commercial and recreation center with a hotel, restaurants, and lots of shops.
- Peachtree Center, bounded by Baker, Ellis, Williams, and Courtland Sts. A commercial and entertainment center, including the world's tallest hotel, the Peachtree Plaza.
- Atlanta Memorial Arts Center, 1280 Peachtree St. NE. Telephone: 892-3600. Home of the High Museum of Art, the Atlanta Symphony Orchestra, and the Alliance Theater.

At Night: For jazz: Carlos McGee's, 3035 Peachtree St., NE (tel. 231-7879); Harvest Moon Saloon, 2423 Piedmont (tel. 233-7821); E.J.'s, 128 East Andrews Dr. (tel. 262-1377); Clarence Foster's, 1915 Peachtree Rd. (tel. 351-0002).

- To dance: Limelight, 3330 Piedmont Rd. Telephone: 231-3520. An entertainment complex which includes disco and a screening room.
- For dinner or drinks and a film: Buckhead Cinema 'n' Drafthouse, 3110 Roswell Rd. NE. Telephone: 231-5811.
- For inexpensive films: Toco Hills, 298 North Druid Hills Rd. Telephone: 636-1858. 99¢ at all times.

Shopping: Atlantans love shopping centers and there are three enormous ones in town—Lenox Square at 3393 Peachtree Rd. NE, Peachtree Center Shopping Gallery at 225 Peachtree St., and Omni International at Marietta St. and International Blvd.

- Turtle's Records and Tapes, 3337 Buford Hwy. NE and other locations. Telephone: 663-2539. Records and tapes at discount.
- Blue Ridge Mountain Sports, Ltd., Lenox Square Shopping Center. Telephone: 266-8372. Sells all kinds of outdoor equipment, and rents backpacking and canoeing equipment.
- Old Sarge Army-Navy Surplus Store, 5316 Buford Hwy., Doraville and three other locations. All kinds of surplus outdoor gear.
- Marshall's, in the mall at Buford Hwy. and Clairmont Rd. Telephone: 329-0200. All kinds of name-brand clothing at substantial discounts.

Augusta

Accommodations: Days Inn, 3026 Washington Rd., 30907. Telephone: 404/738-0131. $29 single; $33 double.
- Econo Lodge, √, 906 Molly Pond Rd., 30901. Telephone: 404/722-6841. $23.95 for one; $27.95 for two in one bed; $30.95 for two in two beds. Higher rates apply during special events.
- Econo Lodge, ⑤, 3034 Washington Rd., 30907. Telephone: 404/860-8485. $23.95 for one; $25.95 for two in one bed; $27.95 for two in two beds. Higher rates apply during special events.
- Red Carpet Inn, ⑤, 444 Broad St., 30901. Telephone: 404/724-0993. $25 to $35 for one; $30 to $35 for two.
- Uptowner Inn, 801 Reynolds St., 30902. Telephone: 404/722-5361. $23 single; $28 double. Higher rates apply in April.
- Motel 6, 2560 Center West Pkwy., 30909. Telephone: 404/738-1410. See Albany listing for rates.

Bainbridge

Accommodation: Glen Oaks Motel and Campground, Hwy. 27 S., 31717. Telephone: 912/246-4343. $19 single; $21 for two in one bed; $26 for two in two beds.

Brunswick

Help: Crisis Line, 912/264-7311.
Accommodations: Hostel in the Forest (AYH), ⑤ √ ★, U.S. Hwy. 84, P.O. Box 1496, 31538. Telephone: 912/264-9783. Call for ride to hostel between 8 a.m. and 8 p.m. for $2. $5 for AYH members; $7 for nonmembers.

"Housing in two geodesic domes and two tree houses situated on 90 acres of Georgia forest."
● Days Inn, 409 New Jesup Hwy., 31520. Telephone: 912/264-4330. $30 to $36 single; $34 to $40 double.

Byron

Accommodations: Budget Host—Byron Inn, √ (10%), I-75 & Ga. 49, 31008. Telephone: 912/956-5100. Bus service to/from airport. $21.88 single; $26.88 double. Advance reservations suggested.
● Red Carpet Inn, √ &, I-75, Exit 45, Rte. 3, Box 114-X, 31008. Telephone: 912/956-5300. $20.88 for one; $23.88 for two in one bed; $26.88 for two in two beds.

Calhoun

Accommodations: Budget Host—Shepherd Motel, Jct. I-75 & Ga. 53, 30701. Telephone: 404/629-8644. $20.88 to $22.88 for one; $22.88 to $23.88 for two in one bed; $24.88 to $26.88 for two in two beds.
● Scottish Inn, √, I-75, Exit 130, 30701. Telephone: 404/629-8261. $19.95 to $22.95 for one; $21.95 to $25.95 for two in one bed; $26.95 to $29.95 for two in two beds.
● Red Carpet Inn, √ &, I-75, Exit 129, Rte. 5, Box 167, 30701. Telephone: 404/629-9501. $22.95 to $26.95 for one; $24.95 to $28.95 for two in one bed; $27.95 to $32.95 for two in two beds.
● Days Inn, I-75 & Ga. 53, Rte. 6, 30701. Telephone: 404/629-8271. $23 to $29 single; $27 to $34 double.

Cartersville

Accommodations: Days Inn, I-75 & Cassville-White Rd., 30120. Telephone: 404/386-0350. $25 to $30 single; $30 to $35 double; $34 to $38 single lodge; $34 to $43 double lodge.
● Pioneer Motel, √, I-75, Exit 127, 30120. Telephone: 404/386-0700. $27.88 single; $31.88 double.
● Quality Inn, √ &, U.S. 41 & Dixie Ave., P.O. Box 158, 30120. Telephone: 404/386-0510. $27 to $28 single; $30 to $34 double.

Chula

Accommodation: Red Carpet Inn, √, I-75 at Brookfield Rd. Exit 23, P.O. Box 40, 31733. Telephone: 912/382-2686. $18 to $20 for one; $20 to $24 for two in one bed; $22 to $25 for two in two beds. Higher rates apply during special events.

Clarkesville

Accommodation: LaPrade's Cabins, Restaurant, and Marina, Rte. 1, Hwy. 197, 30523. Telephone: 404/947-3312. Open April 1 to December 1. $24 per person. Rustic mountain fisherman cabins accommodate 1 to 12 people. Advance reservations of two weeks necessary.

Clayton

Accommodation: Red Carpet Inn, √, Hwy. 441 S., P.O. Box 1164, 30525. Telephone: 404/782-4258. July 1 to November 15: $25 to $35 single; $35 to $45 double. November 16 to December 31: $14.77 single; $25 double.

Columbus

Accommodations: YMCA, 118 East 11th St., 31901. Telephone: 404/322-8269. Men only. $8 single. Weekly rate: $25 plus $3 key deposit.
● Motel 6, 3050 Victory Dr., 31903. Telephone: 404/689-0020. See Albany listing for rates.

Commerce

Accommodations: Red Carpet Inn, √, I-85 & U.S. 441, 30529. Telephone: 404/335-5191. $19.95 to $23.95 single; $23.95 to $27.95 double.
● Quality Inn, √, I-85 & U.S. 441, 30529. Telephone: 404/335-5581. $24.95 to $32.95 single; $32.95 to $42.95 double.

Cordele

Accommodation: Days Inn, I-75 & Tremont Rd., 31015. Telephone: 912/273-6161. $24 single; $28 double.

Dalton

Accommodation: San Quinton Motel, 1407 Chattanooga Rd., 30720. Telephone: 404/278-3693. $17.68 single; $19.76 for two in one bed; $21.48 for two in two beds.

Decatur

On Campus: Agnes Scott College is in this small town about 15 minutes from Atlanta. When you get hungry in Decatur, go to Athens Pizza and Spaghetti House, 1369 Clairmont Rd., or the Freight Room, within walking distance from the college, 301 East Howard St. To know what's going on around campus, check the bulletin board outside the bookstore in the Letitia Pate Evans Dining Hall.

Accommodation: Heart of Decatur Motor Inn, 🖾, 245 East Trinity Place, 30032. Telephone: 404/378-2501. $27.99 per person per night.

East Point

Accommodation: Red Carpet Sky Host Inn, ★, 1360 Virginia Ave., 30344. Telephone: 404/761-5201. Van service from train station. $22 single; $32 double; $36 triple; $40 quad.

Eulonia/Townsend/North Brunswick

Accommodation: Days Inn, ♿, I-95 & Ga. 99, 31331. Telephone: 912/832-4411. $30 single; $34 double.

Folkston

Accommodation: Red Carpet Inn, √ ♿, 1201 South Second St., 31537. Telephone: 912/496-2514. $24 single; $28 double.

Forsyth

Accommodations: Days Inn, I-75 & Ga. 42, 31029. Telephone: 912/994-5168. $20.88 to $24.88 single; $24.88 to $28.88 double.
● Quality Inn, √ ♿, I-75 & S.R. 83, Exit 62, 55 North Dr., 31029. Telephone: 912/994-5161. $20.88 to $29.88 single; $26.88 to $34.88 double. Rates vary with season.

Gainesville

Accommodation: Days Inn, ♿, U.S. 129 & Ga. 365, P.O. Drawer CC, 30503. Telephone: 404/532-7531. $30 single; $34 double; $40 single lodge; $44 double lodge.

Hahira/North Valdosta

Accommodation: Days Inn, I-75 & Ga. 122, 31632. Telephone: 912/794-3000. $22 single; $26 double.

Jekyll Island

Accommodation: Days Inn, ♿, 60 Beachview Dr. S., 31520. Telephone: 912/635-3319. $30 to $40 single; $34 to $44 double.

Locust Grove

Accommodations: Scottish Inn, I-75, Exit 68, 30248. Telephone: 404/957-9001. $16.98 to $19.98 single; $18.98 to $22.98 for two in one bed; $20.98 to $25.98 for two in two beds.
● Red Carpet Inn, √, I-75, Exit 68, P.O. Box 615, 30248. Telephone: 404/

957-2936. $18.88 for one; $21.88 for two in one bed; $23.88 for two in two beds; $25.88 to $30.88 during special events.

Macon

Accommodations: Red Carpet Inn, √, I-475 at U.S. 80, 4606 Chambers Rd., 31206. Telephone: 912/781-2810. $21 to $24 single; $24 to $28 for two in one bed; $28 to $32 for two in two beds.

● Scottish Inn, √, I-475 at U.S. 80, 31206. Telephone: 912/474-1661. $20 to $21 single; $24 to $25 for two in one bed; $26 to $27 for two in two beds.

● Days Inn, 4295 Pio Nono Ave., 31206. Telephone: 912/788-8910. $25 to $30 single; $29 to $34 double.

● Motel 6, 4991 Harrison Rd., 31206. Telephone: 912/474-9212. See Albany listing for rates.

Madison

Accommodation: Quality Inn, √, I-20 & U.S. 441, 30650. Telephone: 404/342-1839. $25.95 to $29.95 single; $29.95 to $39.95 double.

McDonough

Accommodations: Red Carpet Inn, I-75 & Ga. 81, Exit 70, P.O. Box 477, 30253. Telephone: 404/957-5821. $16.88 for one; $18.88 for two in one bed; $20.88 for two in two beds.

● Days Inn, 1311 McDonough Rd., 30253. Telephone: 404/957-5818. $25 to $30 single; $29 to $34 double.

Milledgeville

Accommodation: Days Inn, ♿, 3001 Heritage Rd. NW, 31061. Telephone: 912/453-3551. $25.88 single; $29.88 double.

Moultrie

Accommodation: Red Carpet Inn, √♿, 600 South Main St., 31768. Telephone: 912/985-3980. $22 single; $26 double.

Perry

Accommodation: Red Carpet Inn, √♿, I-75 & Hwy. 41, Exit 42, P.O. Box 539, 31069. Telephone: 912/987-2200. $17.88 for one; $20.88 for two in one bed; $23.88 for two in two beds.

Sautee

Accommodation: The Stovall House, Ⓢ♿ ★, Hwy. 255, Rte. 1, Box 152, 30571. Telephone: 404/878-3355. Transport from bus station available with prior notice only. $25 single; $50 double; $67.50 triple; $80 quad. Includes continental breakfast. Advance reservations of two months in fall and one month any other time necessary. "Provide guests with a relaxing 'country experience' in the cozy surroundings of a historical house."

Savannah

Tourist Information: Savannah Visitors Convention Bureau, 301 West Broad St., 31499. Telephone: 912/233-6651. Free 12-minute slide show, literature, and tour information to give you an idea of what to see. Open every day except Christmas.

Help: Family Counseling Center of Savannah, Inc. (Travelers Aid), 428 Bull St., 31401. Telephone: 912/233-5729.

Accommodations: Bed & Breakfast Inn, c/o Robert McAlister, Ⓢ(10%), 117 Gordon St. W. at Chatham Square, 31402. Telephone: 912/238-0518. Walking distance to bus station and waterfront. "1853 town house in the historic district." $30 single; $38 double. Price includes a full breakfast.

● Budget Inn, Ⓢ(10%), 3702 Ogeechee Rd., 31405. Telephone: 912/233-3633. $28 single; $33 double. The Cherokee Restaurant is right next door.

● Econo Lodge, √ ⓑ, 7500 Atherton, 31406. $29.95 for one; $32.95 for two in one bed; $34.95 for two in two beds. Higher rates apply during special events.

● Econo Lodge, ⓑ, I-95 & U.S. 17, Richmond Hill, 31324. Telephone: 912/756-3312. $23.95 for one; $27.95 for two in one bed; $28.95 for two in two beds. Higher rates apply during special events.

● TraveLodge, √ ⓑ, 512 West Oglethorpe Ave., 31401. Telephone: 912/233-9251. $29 for one; $35 for two in one bed; $38 for two in two beds.

● Motel 6, I-95 & U.S. Hwy. 17, Exit 14, Richmond Hill, 31324. Telephone: 912/756-3555. See Albany listing for rates.

Statesboro

Accommodation: Bryant's Master Hosts Inn, √ ⓑ, 461 South Main St., 30458. Telephone: 912/764-5666. $28 to $32 single; $30 to $34 for two in one bed; $34 to $38 for two in two beds.

Thomasville

Accommodation: Days Inn, U.S. 19 Bypass & U.S. 319, 31792. Telephone: 912/226-6025. $26 to $27 single; $30 to $31 double.

Tifton

Accommodations: Days Inn, I-75 & U.S. 82, Exit 18, Virginia Ave., 31793. Telephone: 912/382-8100. $19 to $30 single; $23 to $34 double.

● Scottish Inn, √, P.O. Box 1087, I-75 & U.S. 82 W., 31794. Telephone: 912/386-2350. $17 for one; $20 for two in one bed; $23 for two in two beds.

● Quality Inn, √ ⓑ, I-75 (Exit 19) & Second St., 31794. Telephone: 912/386-2100. $24.99 to $27.99 for single or double.

• Carson Motel, √ ($1), 309 West 7th St., 31794. Telephone: 912/382-3111. $14 to $16 single; $17 to $19 for two in one bed; $19 to $22 for two in two beds.
• Red Carpet Inn, √ 🅰, 1025 West 2nd St., 31794. Telephone: 912/382-0280. $17.88 for one; $20.88 for two in one bed; $23.88 for two in two beds.

Unadilla

Accommodation: Days Inn, I-75 & U.S. 41, Exit 39, P.O. Box 405, 31091. Telephone: 912/627-3211. $25.28 single; $29.32 double.

Valdosta/Lake Park

Accommodations: Days Inn, I-75 & Exit 1, 31636. Telephone: 912/559-7902. $23 to $27 single; $27 to $31 double.
• Budget Host—Azalea City Motel, √ (10%), 2015 West Hill Ave., Box 644, 31601. Telephone: 912/244-4350 or 244-4647. $13 to $16 single; $17 to $25 double. In-room saunas.
• Motel 6, 2003 West Hill Ave., 31601. Telephone: 912/244-6123. See Albany above listing for rates.
• Scottish Inn, 2525 North Ashley St., Hwy. 41 N., 31602. Telephone: 912/242-7676. $20 to $24 for one; $22 to $28 for two in one bed; $24 to $34 for two in two beds.
• Quality Inn, √, I-75 & S.R. 94, Exit 5, 31601. Telephone: 912/244-8510. $26.95 to $29.95 single; $29.95 to $35.95 double.
• Quality Inn, √ 🅰, 1902 West Hill Ave., 31601. Telephone: 912/244-4520. $27 to $28 single; $32 to $34 double.
• Comfort Inn, √, I-75 (Exit 6) & North Valdosta Rd., 31601. Telephone: 912/244-4460. $19.99 to $23.99 single; $23.99 to $27.99 double.

Waycross

Accommodation: Red Carpet Inn, √, 2016 Memorial Dr., 31501. Telephone: 912/285-4700. $26.88 single; $30.88 double.

Hawaii

James Michener calls the islands of Hawaii "unbelievably beautiful. They rise from the sea like a strand of pearls, each one with its own peculiar beauty, yet all suffused with the same grace and charm." Mark Twain called them "the loveliest fleet of islands that lies anchored in any sea." The state of Hawaii, 2000 miles west of California, is actually a cluster of islands and Hawaii is only one of these islands. The other largest ones are Kauai, Oahu (where Honolulu is), Molokai, Lanai, and Maui. Downtown Honolulu is a busy city with typical urban problems, but beyond it the islands are not heavily populated and are characterized by mountains, volcanoes, tropical foliage, sandy beaches, and rocky coast.

Because Hawaii is so far away from the mainland, air fares to and from it are high.

One friend suggests that you do what she did for six months: "Get a camping permit at Oahu's Department of Parks and Recreation, 650 South King St., rent camping equipment if you don't have your own (the Visitors Bureau will supply names and addresses), and camp around the island. The weather is always good, between 69 and 90 degrees . . . and as long as you renew your permit every two weeks you can go on like this forever."

"Hawaii's a great place, but don't be fooled into expecting a paradise or utopia."

A good guide to the islands is *Hawaii on $35 a Day,* by Faye Hammel and Sylvan Levey, Frommer/Pasmantier Publishers ($10.95).

More recommended reading on Hawaii is *Hidden Hawaii: The Adventurer's Guide* by Ray Riegert, published by Ulysses Press, Sathers Gate Station, Box 4000H, 94704. ($10.95). The book, which includes history as well as travel information, is special because it takes the reader behind the flashy facade of Hawaii back to the parks, trails, campsites, beaches, and volcanoes.

Some Special Events: Orchid Society Flower Show in Hilo, and Fiesta Filipina in Honolulu (July); Queen Kaahumanu Festival in Hana Bay, and Hula Festival in Waikiki (August); and Aloha Week Festivals on all islands (September and October).

Hitching: Hitchhiking is prohibited by state law unless permitted by county ordinance. In Honolulu, it is permitted at any official bus stop or in open areas where there are no official bus stops within a reasonable distance. "We don't encourage people to hitchhike, but if they do, we recommend that they use 'common sense.'"

Tourist Information: Hawaii Visitors Bureau, Waikiki Business Plaza, 2270 Kalakaua Ave., Honolulu, HI 96815. Telephone: 808/923-1811. (On the mainland, there are branch offices in Chicago, Los Angeles, New York, and San Francisco.) The Visitors Bureau has a free hotel list with rates, which includes some inexpensive accommodations as well as the more luxurious.

N.B.: Since accommodations are generally so expensive in Hawaii, you might find Bed & Breakfast International, an organization that places people in private homes, an appealing alternative to standard accommodations. A double, breakfast included, is $26 to $85; the minimum stay is two nights. For an application, write to the organization at 151 Ardmore Rd., Kensington, CA 94707, and enclose a stamped, self-addressed envelope, or phone 415/527-8836 or 525-4569.

Hawaii Volcanoes National Park, Hawaii

Camping and Accommodation: Hawaii Volcanoes National Park, 96718. Telephone: 808/967-7321. Besides three campgrounds that are available on a first-come, first-serve basis, are free and are open year-round, the park has camper cabins available. The Namakani Paio Cabins are unfurnished except for mattresses. You can rent linen, pillows, blankets, and towels, but must bring your own cooking utensils, wood, etc. The A-frame cabins are $14 per person and accommodate up to four people, with a $10 key deposit. Reservations are recommended as far in advance as possible. Write or call (808/967-7321) for reservations to: Volcano House, Hawaii National Park, HI 96718.

Honolulu, Oahu

Ray Reigert, the author of *Hidden Hawaii* (see first page of the Hawaii section) has written a book on Honolulu called, not surprisingly, *Hidden Honolulu.* A pocket-size guide, the book covers everything from the good life to the great outdoors—both of which exist in abundance in Honolulu, according to the author.

Tourist Information: Hawaii Visitors Bureau, 2270 Kalakaua Ave., 96815. Telephone: 808/923-1811.

Help: Information and Referral, 808/521-4566.
- Suicide and Crisis Center, 808/521-4555.

"Try to get out of the city and into the rural areas—great scenery!"

Accommodations: YWCA, 1566 Wilder Ave., 96822. Telephone: 808/941-2231. Women only. $9.50 plus $5 refundable key deposit for a room shared with one other person and bath shared with four others (dorm style). Rate includes breakfast and dinner. City bus stop nearby goes to the beach and the U. of Hawaii.
- YMCA, 401 Atkinson Dr., 96814. Telephone: 808/941-3344. Men only. $15 single without bath; $17.50 with bath. $27 to $31 per person double. Call

from airport to see if there is a room. Coffeeshop in building; restaurants in Ala Moana Shopping Center across the street.

● Honolulu International Youth Hostel (AYH), 2323A Seaview Ave., 96822. Telephone: 808/946-0591. Open year-round. Open 7 a.m. to 9 a.m. and from 4:30 p.m. to 9 p.m. $7 per night for AYH members; $9 for nonmembers. Advance reservations necessary; send stamped, self-addressed envelope and one night's deposit (money order or bank draft) for reservation. Near bus stop. "City bus system is an excellent way to sightsee."

"Don't expect to live on the beach or in any free housing. Jobs are difficult to find. Living expenses are very high. Don't carry expensive jewelry or large amounts of cash."

Keanae, Maui

Accommodation: Camp Keanae Maui YMCA (AYH), Box 820, Wailuku, 96793. Telephone: 808/244-3253. $5 for AYH members. Advance reservations of at least two weeks suggested. "We're 32 miles from the airport so we suggest you rent a car. Also buy food before arriving."

Makawao, Maui

Camping: Haleakala National Park, P.O. Box 369, 96768. Telephone: 808/572-9306. No entrance fee. Limit of three-night stay. Four undeveloped campgrounds and three primitive cabins. $5 per person per night. Advance reservations of three months necessary for cabins. Accessible by horseback or on foot only; located in Haleakala Crater. "Haleakala weather can change rapidly, sometimes going through the entire temperature range within one day. January to late May or early June is generally considered the wet season; July to October the dry. Be prepared at any time of year for rain and cold wind."

Waimea, Kauai

Accommodation: Kokee Lodge, P.O. Box 819, 96796. Telephone: 808/335-6061. Cabins that sleep three to seven and come equipped with linens and kitchen supplies, hot showers, and fireplaces. $25 per cabin per night. Breakfast and lunch available in restaurant on premises. Advance reservations necessary with $25 deposit (refundable if cancellation is made at least two weeks prior to reservation date); send a stamped, self-addressed envelope for confirmation. "Located high in Hawaii's 4345-acre Kokee State Park."

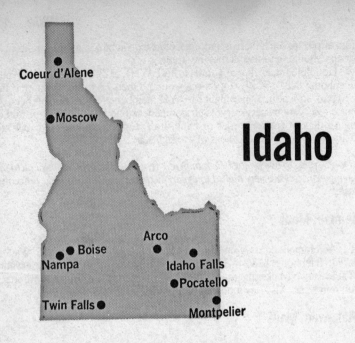

Idaho

We're convinced, having read through so many tourist office brochures, that there's one public relations man or woman who puts out the materials for all 50 states and just changes the name of the state to suit the latest client. All the brochures say that *blah* has it all, *blah* has something for everyone, *blah* is a year-round playground, and Lewis and Clark passed through *blah*. But in the case of Idaho it's all really true. There may not be many people in Idaho, but there certainly is a variety of landscape. The brochures don't fib. In central Idaho there's the Primitive Area where there are no roads, the Salmon River, and the Craters of the Moon National Monument. (This is a weird and wild landscape where the astronauts trained for their moon walk.) Northern Idaho has beautiful rivers, lakes, and mountains. In southeastern Idaho there are more mountains and rivers, plus an incredible combination of dry desert plains and rich farmland. Try to forgive Idaho's obsession with potatoes (Spud Cellar Lounge, the potato-processing capital of the world, Ski the Big Potato) and enjoy some of its extraordinary variety.

Some Special Events: Salmon River Rodeo in Riggins (May); Old Timers' Celebration in Harrison, featuring a theater revue, dance, and parade, and Idaho State Square and Round Dance Festival (July); a Roundup in Lewiston, including a cowboy breakfast and a rodeo, and Labor Day Festival in Bellevue, which includes a parade, a shootout, oldtime fiddlers, and a barbecue (September).

Hitching: It should be okay to hitchhike in Idaho—just be sure to stay on the shoulder. In some of the less populated areas you may have to wait a while for a ride to come along. One Idaho resident told us that hitchhikers he picks up while traveling around the state say that rides come quite easily there.

Tourist Information: Idaho Travel Council, State Capitol Building, Room 108, Boise, ID 83720.

Arco

Camping: Craters of the Moon National Monument, P.O. Box 29, 83213. Telephone: 208/527-3257. At Lava Flow Campground you can camp from April 15 to October 15. $5 per campsite per night.

Boise

Help: Hotline, 208/345-7888 (7 to 11 p.m., Sunday to Thursday; till 3 a.m. on Saturdays).
* Information and Referral, 208/378-0111 (during business hours).

Accommodation: Motel 6, 2323 Airport Way, 83705. Telephone: 208/342-7733. $17.95 single; $21.95 double; $2 for each additional person.
* TraveLodge, √ ⓑ, 1314 Grove St., 83702. Telephone: 208/342-9351. Airport transportation available. $29 for one; $33 for two in one bed; $37 for two in two beds.
* Econo Lodge, √, 1618 Main St., 83702. Telephone: 208/342-6503. $23.95 to $28.95 for one; $27.95 to $33.95 for two in one bed; $31.95 to $36.95 for two in two beds.
* Allstar Inn, 2275 Airport Way, 83705. Telephone: 208/336-7788. $23.95 to $25.95 single; $3 for each additional person.

Coeur D'Alene

Accommodations: Motel 6, 416 Appleway, 83814. Telephone: 208/765-6006. See Boise listing for rates.
* Friendship Pines Resort Motel, 1422 Northwest Blvd., 83814. Telephone: 208/664-8244. $20 to $40 for one; $34 to $42 for two.

Idaho Falls

Help: Information Referral Agency, 208/524-2433.
Accommodation: Motel 6, 1448 West Broadway, 83401. Telephone: 208/523-9265. See Boise listing for rates.

Montpelier

Accommodation: Sunset Motel and Café, 453 South 4th, 83254. Telephone: 208/847-1551. $18 to $22 single; $24 for two in one bed; $26 for two in two beds.

Moscow

Accommodation: Motel 6, 101 Baker St., 83843. Telephone: 208/882-6639. See Boise listing for rates.

Nampa

Accommodation: Pepper Mill Inn, 908 3rd St. S., 83651. Telephone: 208/466-3594. $28 for one; $32 for two in one bed; $34 for two in two beds.

Pocatello

Accommodations: Motel 6, 291 West Burnside Ave., 83201. Telephone: 208/237-6667. See Boise listing for rates.
● Imperial 400 Motor Inn, 1055 South Fifth Ave., 83201. Telephone: 208/233-5120. $20 to $23 for one; $22 to $24 for two in one bed; $24 to $28 for two in two beds.
● TraveLodge, √ &, 538 North Main St., 83201. Telephone: 208/232-8140. $26 for one; $31 for two in one bed; $36 for two in two beds.

Twin Falls

Accommodations: Motel 6, 1472 Blue Lakes Blvd. N., 83301. Telephone: 208/733-6663. See Boise listing for rates.
● Imperial 400 Motor Inn, 320 Main Ave. S., 83301. Telephone: 208/733-8770. $24 to $26 for one; $28 to $32 for two in one bed; $34 to $38 for two in two beds.
● TraveLodge, √ (15%), 248 Second Ave., 83301. Telephone: 208/733-5630. Airport transportation available. $28 for one; $31 for two in one bed; $35 for two in two beds.

Illinois

Chicago is the pulse of Illinois, and, in many ways, of the Midwest. It's where many of the young people from Midwestern states head when they leave school and it's most definitely worth a visit. See the special section on Chicago to help plan your days there.

If you have more time to explore the state, go beyond Chicago to the area around Springfield where Abraham Lincoln spent many years of his life. Lincoln's New Salem State Historic Site is a restoration of the village where Lincoln lived from 1831 to 1837. At New Salem, visit the building where he pored over his law books, the store where he clerked, and the post office he tended. Lincoln memorabilia are exhibited in an indoor museum within this village and tourists can visit 23 buildings that are meant to conjure up Lincoln's past. During the summer months, the Talisman Riverboat runs daily and the Great American People Show, a Lincoln presentation, is presented in an open-air theater.

Although it is the state of Utah that is most often thought of when Brigham Young is mentioned, it was in Illinois, on the banks of the Mississippi, where Joseph Smith founded the headquarters of the Church of Latter-Day Saints. The group was persecuted there, and after Smith was murdered Brigham Young led the exodus to Utah. Left behind in the town of Nauvoo are Smith's first log homestead, the restored Joseph Smith Mansion House, and the Brigham Young Home, Jonathan Browning Home, and the Temple Lot.

Anyone planning to visit Illinois should send for a free copy of the *Illinois* book, which is an overview of Illinois including information on attractions/historic sites; festivals and annual events; camping, biking, skiing, etc. Copies are available from the Illinois Department of Commerce and Community Affairs, address listed below.

Some Special Events: Rock Cut Winter Festival in Loves Park and Central Illinois Jazz Festival in Decatur (January); Maple Syrup Time in Springfield (February); Annual Orchid Display in Naperville (March); Old Settlers Day in Sumner (April); Dogwood Festival in Quincy, Lilac Festival in Lombard, and

Old Capitol Art Fair in Springfield (May); Fort de Chartres Rendezvous at Prairie du Rocher, Vermilion County Civil War Days in Danville, Grand Levee in Vandalia, and Old English Faire in Brimfield (June); Ravinia Festival in Highland Park (all summer); Taste of Chicago in Chicago, Petunia Festival in Dixon, Lincolnfest in Springfield, and Catfish Days in Wilmington (July); Illinois State Fair in Springfield, Indian Pow Wow in Arcola, and National Sweetcorn Festival in Mendota (August); Grape Festival in Nauvoo, Henry County Hog Festival in Kewanee, Apple Festival in Murphysboro, and Jordbruksdagarna in Bishop Hill (September); Spoon River Scenic Tour in Fulton County, Knox County Scenic Drive in Knox County, Fall Crafts Festival in Clayville, Fort Massac Encampment at Metropolis, and Burgoo Festival at Utica (October); Pope County Deer Festival in Golconda, Way of Lights in Belleville; Julmarknad at Bishop Hill and Country Christmas in Galena (November); Way of Lights in Belleville, Christmas at New Salem State Historic Site, Old Fashioned Christmas Walk at Galena, and Lucia Pageant and Festival in Chicago (December).

Hitching: The attitude toward hitching in Illinois seems lukewarm. It is legal except on Interstate highways. No one we talked to refused to recommend it, but no one seemed very enthusiastic about the possibilities. The official word from the Illinois State Police is that hitchhiking is "not recommended" and "fraught with danger."

Tourist Information: Illinois Department of Commerce and Community Affairs, Office of Tourism, 222 South College St., Springfield, IL 62706. Telephone: 217/782-7139.

Alton

Accommodation: TraveLodge, √ ⑤, 717 East Broadway, 62002. Telephone: 618/462-1011. $29 for one; $31 for two in one bed; $34 for two in two beds.

Aurora

Accommodation: Regal 8 Inn, 2380 North Farnsworth Ave. & East West Tollway #5, 60507. Telephone: 312/851-3600. $21.88 for one; $26.88 for two in one bed; $29.88 for two in two beds.

Belleville

Accommodation: Imperial 400 Motor Inn, 600 East Main St., 62220. Telephone: 618/234-9670. $22 to $24 for one; $24 to $30 for two in one bed; $30 to $40 for two in two beds.

Bloomington

Accommodations: Coachman Motel, 408 East Washington St., 61701. Telephone: 309/827-6186. $25 single; $29 double.

- Regal 8 Inn, 2304 Washington, 61701. Telephone: 309/662-4381. See Aurora listing for rates.
- Best Inns of America, I-74, I-57, & Market St., 61701. Telephone: 309/827-5333. $25.88 to $29.88 for one; $29.88 to $33.88 for two in one bed; $31.88 for two in two beds; $35 for three or four in two beds.

Champaign-Urbana

On Campus: The University of Illinois is in this fair-size town on the Illinois prairie. You may be able to stay at the Student Union for $30 single; $36 double, per night—contact Guest Room Reservations (tel. 217/333-1241). For a true "taste" of Champaign-Urbana, you have to visit Murphy's Pub for a steak sandwich or the Deluxe Lunch for a fish sandwich on Friday or Saturday. To meet students, you can also go to Cochrane's, R&R Sports Grill, or Garcia's Pizza. The Deluxe Lunch & Billiards, Inc. has a delicious fish sandwich and is open Friday and Saturday.

The *Daili Illini* newspaper can help you find out about rides and accommodations.

"Champaign-Urbana is an oasis of culture, fun, and entertainment on an otherwise barren prairie. It's a good stopover for anyone going cross country since it's at the intersection of Interstates 74 and 57."

Accommodations: Best Inns of America, 914 West Bloomington Rd., 61820. Telephone: 217/356-6000. $22.88 single; $26.88 double.
- Regal 8 Inn, 1701 South Neil St., 61820. Telephone: 217/359-8888. $22.88 for one; $27.88 for two in one bed; $32.88 for two in two beds.

Chicago

Chicago's most striking feature is its lakefront. Because of Lake Michigan, Chicago has beaches, parks, and marinas that give lots of pleasure to Chicagoans and visitors as well. While you're in Chicago, be sure to walk, bicycle, or jog along the lakefront, admiring the skyline on one side and the lake on the other. For example, you can walk through Grant Park's Rose Garden, watch the boats on the lake, Buckingham Fountain in the center, the skyline of the city beyond, and end up at the Field Museum, the Shedd Aquarium, and the Adler Planetarium. Another way to enjoy the lakeshore is to take a picnic to the Grant Park band shell (Columbus Drive at Jackson, across from the back door of the Art Institute), listen to a concert, then watch the evening color display at Buckingham Fountain. If you walk up Michigan Ave. to the Chicago River, you can find where the first Fort Dearborn has been outlined on the street, pick up a snack, and picnic along either side of the river.

For anyone with an interest in architecture, Chicago is a dream—you'll find the works of Louis Sullivan, Frank Lloyd Wright, and Mies van der Rohe, and two outstanding examples of the architecture of the '70s—the Sears Tower and the John Hancock Building. You can go to the Chicago Architecture Foundation's ArchiCenter, 330 South Dearborn, for information on Chicago's treasures. The Center also conducts walking tours that cost $4—the most popular is the Loop tour, which visits several downtown buildings. To see some outstanding outdoor sculpture, walk from the ArchiCenter north on Dearborn to see Calder's *Flamingo* on the Federal Center Plaza; Chagall's *Four Seasons* on the First National Bank Plaza (in summer, be there at lunch time so that you can catch the free entertainment); Miro's *Chicago* and Picasso's *Lady* facing each other on Daley Plaza across from City Hall; and, Dubuffet's *Monument with Standing Beast* in front of the brand-new State of Illinois building designed by Helmut Jahn. There are no formal tours of the new building, but visitors can wander in, explore the atrium, and ride the glass elevators.

Chicago starts to celebrate every year as soon as the weather gets nice. From June to August, there arc concerts by the Chicago Symphony Orchestra at the Ravinia Festival in Highland Park (can be reached by special train during concert season). During the summer, there are also free concerts in Grant Park. Just bring a picnic supper along and make yourself comfortable on the lawn.

For exploring the neighborhoods of Chicago, *Chicago Magazine's Guide to Chicago* ($8.95) is especially helpful; for an excellent pocket-size guide to the city, buy a copy of Marilyn Appleberg's *I Love Chicago Guide* ($4.95).

To know what's going on in Chicago while you're visiting, check the *Sun Times*, the *Tribune*, or the alternative paper called *The Reader*, which can be picked up free in many stores, especially on the North Side. *Chicago Magazine* ($2.25) is another good source of information—it comes out monthly and includes articles, restaurant listings, etc.

In May, you can enjoy the Chicago International Art Expo, Navy Pier. This is an impressive assemblage of art from all over the world. The Chicago Jazz Festival in late August is another very special event. Foreign college students visiting Chicago may want to contact the International Visitors Center, 520 North Michigan Ave., 60611, (tel. 312/645-1836) and ask about some of the special programs they organize.

Getting There: From the Airport: O'Hare is about 17 miles from the city and Midway is about 10 miles away. Continental Air Transport services both airports and the fare is $6.75 from O'Hare and $6 from Midway to the Loop.

Or you can go by public transport from O'Hare to the Loop. The El goes all the way to O'Hare and operates 24 hours a day (90¢ plus 10¢ for transfer). From Midway take bus no. 99A (90¢) or ride bus 54B to the Douglas El (90¢ plus 10¢ transfer).

● From the Train and Bus Stations: The Greyhound station is at Clark and Randolph and the Trailways station is at Randolph and State, in the heart of downtown. From these terminals you can catch a bus, an El, or a subway. Union Station, the train terminal, is located at Canal and Adams, the Northwestern Station is at Canal and Madison, and Illinois Central is at Randolph and Michigan. There are many bus routes that go to and from the train stations.

Getting Around: Taxis are expensive; it will cost you $1 to get in, then 90¢ per mile, plus 20¢ for every three-quarters of a minute of waiting time and 50¢ for each additional passenger.

● The Chicago Transit Authority operates trains and buses that arrive from north, south, and west of the city and circle the central business and shopping district—hence the name "Loop." The fare is 90¢ plus 10¢ for a transfer. Exact change is necessary on buses.

- The bus fare is the same and buses run every 5 to 15 minutes, usually. Look for rectangular signs that say CTA, with the number and route of the bus, at each bus stop. Exact change is required.
- The Chicago Transit Authority (CTA) distributes a Downtown Transit Map, which explains its routes in both English and Spanish. Their travel information number is 836-7000.
- CTA Culture Buses run June to September on north, south, and west routes starting at the Art Institute. The fare of $2 entitles riders to unlimited travel along the route from 10:35 a.m. to 4:45 p.m.

Tourist Information: Chicago Convention and Tourism Bureau's Water Tower Information Center, Michigan and Chicago Aves. Telephone: 312/225-5000, extension 276. All you need to know in this new center for tourists. Open seven days a week.

Help: Travelers Aid, O'Hare Airport, Concourse G between Air Canada and U.S. Air (tel: 312/686-7562); Greyhound Station, 74 West Randolph (tel. 435-4537); Union Station, 210 South Canal (tel. 435-4543).

Accommodations: For a brochure describing *Chicago Holidays* (two-in-a-room weekend specials), write to the Chicago Convention and Tourism Bureau, McCormick Place and the Lake, 60616.

"Some of the most elegant Chicago hotels offer special weekend rates that are not very widely publicized. A few phone calls might get you an elegant double for about $30 per person for two nights."

- Parkway Eleanor Club, 1550 North Dearborn Pkwy., 60610. Telephone: 312/664-8245. Women only. $20 single with breakfast and shared bath. Membership fee of $2.50 required. Advance reservations necessary.
- Budget Host—Dunham Inn, √, 1600 East Main St., Box 64, 60174. Telephone: 312/584-5300. Airport bus transportation available. $27 single; $35 for two in one or two beds. Heated pool.
- International House at the University of Chicago, 1414 East 59th St., 60613. Telephone: 312/753-2270 or 753-2280. Open June 1 to August 31. $19.50 per person per night. Advance reservations of three to seven days necessary. "A neo-Gothic limestone building with 507 single rooms and a full-service cafeteria. During the school year, it's a dormitory for University of Chicago students."
- YMCA, 501 North Central Ave., 60644. Telephone: 312/287-9120. Men only. $23.46 single includes $5 key deposit. Weekly rate: $48.60 to $53. Bus stops at the door.
- Lincoln Belmont YMCA, 3333 North Marshfield Ave., 60657. Telephone: 312/248-3333. Men over 18 only. $10.50 plus $3 key deposit per night in private room with shared washroom and shower. Weekly rate: $38 to $45. Advance reservations of one month necessary.
- Lawson YMCA, Ⓢ √ ⚿ ★, 30 West Chicago Ave., 60610. Telephone: 312/944-6211. Men and women. $20 single; $34 double.
- The Blackstone Hotel, Ⓢ √ ★, 636 South Michigan Ave. at Balbo, 60605. Telephone: 312/427-4300. $49 single; $59 double; $69 triple; $79 quad. Student and summer rates: $32 single; $37 double. "A small, intimate hotel

with European charm designed in French Renaissance style." Higher rates apply during special events.

- Friendship Edgebrook Motel, 6401 West Touhy Ave., 60648. Telephone: 312/774-4200. $24 to $27 for one; $27 to $33 for two in one bed; $29 to $35 for two in two beds.
- Regal 8 Inn, 2448 North Mannheim, Franklin Park, 60131. Telephone: 312/455-6500. See Aurora listing for rates.
- Admiral Oasis Motel, 9353 Waukegan Rd., Morton Grove, 60053. Telephone: 312/965-4000. $17.71 to $19.25 single; $19.71 to $21.40 double.
- Red Roof Inn, ⌖, 17301 South Halsted Rd., South Holland, 60473. Telephone: 312/331-1621. $24.95 for one; $29.95 for two in one bed; $31.95 for two in two beds; $33.95 for three or four in two beds.
- Red Roof Inn, ⌖, Ill. 5 & Highland Ave., 1113 Butterfield Rd., Downers Grove, 60515. Telephone: 312/963-4205. $28.95 for one; $33.95 for two in one bed; $35.95 for two in two beds; $37.95 for three or four in two beds.
- Red Roof Inn, ⌖, I-90 & Arlington Hts. Rd., 22 West Algonquin Rd., Arlington Hts., 60005. Telephone: 312/228-6650. See above listing for rates.
- Red Roof Inn, ⌖, 2450 East 173rd St., Lansing, 60438. Telephone: 312/895-9570. $24.95 for one; $29.95 for two in one bed; $31.95 for two in two beds; $33.95 for three or four in two beds.
- Days Inn, ⌖, I-80 & 294, East Hazelcrest, 60429. Telephone: 312/957-5900. $27 to $29 single; $33 to $35 double.
- Sixpence Inn, 9408 West Lawrence Ave., Schiller Park, 60176. Telephone: 312/671-4282. $20 to $28 for up to four people.
- Sixpence Inn, 1601 Oakton St., Elk Grove Village, 60007. Telephone: 312/981-9677. See above listing for rates.
- Econo Lodge, ∨, 510 East End Ave., 60409. Telephone: 312/862-2500. $25.95 for one; $28.95 for two in one bed; $30.95 for two in two beds.

Where to Eat: There are lots of chains that can be recommended because of both the quality of their food and their low prices. These include the Original Pancake House (at 2020 North Lincoln Park West and 30 other Chicago locations), McDonald's, Burger King, and other standbys. The Original Pancake House serves an apple pancake that's more like a souffle with apple slices and a cinnamon glaze on top. There's usually a long wait on weekends and the Pancake House is a popular restaurant for people with children.

- The Sears, IBM, and Standard Oil Building Cafeterias are open Monday through Friday for breakfast and lunch. Most museums have cafeterias that are open daily for lunch and for dinner on the night they stay open late. Marshall Field's, the huge department store on State Street, has nine restaurants—the least expensive are the Bowl and Basket and the Buffet on the seventh floor, the Dinette in the basement, and the Punch Bowl on the third floor. Use the *I Love Chicago Guide* or the *Chicago Magazine Guide* for restaurant suggestions. Here are a few of ours:

- The Berghoff, 17 West Adams. Telephone: 427-3170. Open Monday to Saturday, 11 a.m. to 9:30 p.m. In this German restaurant right in the heart of the Loop, you'll find one of the best food bargains in the city. Portions are generous and the price is reasonable. The restaurant is huge, one of the oldest in the city, and extremely busy at lunchtime.

"To try stuffed pizza, which is a layered deep-dish pie, go to one of the branches of

Giordano's (North Rush St., North Clark, West Irving Park, and South Black-stone), which Chicago Magazine *voted the best in the city."*

- French Baker, 26 West Madison. Telephone: 346-3532. Good, light food right in the center of town.
- Greek Islands, 766 West Madison. Telephone: 782-9855. One of several good restaurants in the Halsted St. Greek area.
- Acorn on Oak, 116 East Oak. Telephone: 944-6835. For burgers and late-night piano.
- Belden Corned Beef Center, 2315 North Clark. Telephone: 935-2752. Never closes.
- Carson's, 612 North Wells. Telephone: 280-9200. The place in town for ribs (and Chicago loves ribs).
- Pizzeria Uno, 29 East Ohio (tel. 321-1000), and Due, 619 North Wabash (tel. 943-2400). Famous Chicago-style deep-dish pizza.
- Tenkatsu, 3365 North Clark. Telephone: 549-8697. Good tempura and teriyaki in a no-frills atmosphere.
- Water Tower Place, 845 North Michigan. Telephone: 440-3165. Twelve eating places all together—try Vie de France, a bakery on the mezzanine; Theatre Café, a coffeeshop and chocolatier on two; or D.B. Kaplan's, a delicatessen on seven.
- Morry's Deli, 5500 South Cornell Ave. Telephone: 363-3800. Good sandwiches; a branch in the University of Chicago bookstore.
- Chances R, 5225 South Harper. Telephone: 363-1550. A mellow combination of burgers and Saturday night jazz.

What to See: A CTA elevated train ride to the end of the line and back gives visitors a unique view of the city skyline and Saul Bellow bits of neighborhood. The American (tel. 427-3100), Gray Line (tel. 346-9506), and Keeshin (tel. 427-9400) companies offer bus tours. To see the city by boat from the Chicago River and Lake Michigan from May to September, call Mercury (tel. 332-1353), Wendella (tel. 337-1446), or Shoreline Marine (tel. 427-2900). Many places will give guided tours with advance reservations, e.g., the Merchandise Mart, the Police Department, the *Chicago Sun-Times,* and the Quaker Oats Test Kitchens. For a good introduction to Chicago, see the dual-theater shows at the Water Tower Pumping Station, Michigan at Pearson Street. *Heartbeat Chicago* is a 63-projector, quadraphonic sound show, and *City of Dreams* is a 70mm film with aerial and special effects. Open every day from 10 a.m. to 10:30 p.m.; $3.75 admission.

- Art Institute of Chicago, Michigan Ave. at Adams. Telephone: 443-3500. The well known institute houses one of the best collections of French Impressionist paintings in the world and the renowned Thorne miniature replicas of rooms from the 16th to mid-20th centuries. Admission is $4.50 for adults; $2.25 for students, children, and senior citizens; and Tuesday it's free for all.
- Field Museum of Natural History. Telephone: 922-9410. In Grant Park, Roosevelt Rd. at Lake Shore Dr., this museum features animal dioramas, Indian art and archaeology collections, and exhibits tracing the history of man. On Thursday, admission is free; otherwise it's $2 for adults; $1 for students with ID. Right near the Field Museum are the Adler Planetarium (tel. 322-0300) and the John G. Shedd Aquarium (tel. 939-2426). Both are worth a side trip.
- Sears Tower. Telephone: 875-9696. You'll find this 110-story building at the

intersection of Wacker Dr. and Adams. For $1.50 you can enjoy a view from the top, seeing not only Chicago but also the suburbs, and parts of Indiana, Michigan, and Wisconsin too. Open from 9 a.m. to midnight.

● John Hancock Center, 875 North Michigan. Telephone: 751-3681. The world's fourth-tallest building. $2.50 for a view—for $3 more you can get a drink plus a view from the windows of Images, the bar on the 96th floor.

● Museum of Science and Industry, East 57th St. and South Shore Dr. Telephone: MU4-1414. The admission is free and the exhibits include an enormous model of the human heart and the Apollo 8 lunar module. Fun for anyone who likes to know how things work.

● Chicago Public Library Cultural Center, Washington at Michigan. Telephone: 269-2837. Stunning Tiffany mosaics and windows in halls and central room of 1897 landmark. Art and photo exhibits, concerts, and films. Free.

● Chicago Historical Society, Clark at North Ave. Telephone: 642-4600. The history of Chicago and Illinois on exhibit. $1 on Tuesday to Sunday; Monday is free.

● Expressway Children's Museum, 75 East Washington Street. Telephone: 269-3222. Hands-on exhibits designed for children 3 to 12.

● Peace Museum, 430 West Erie St. Telephone: 440-1860. Dedicated to peace education through the arts, it is the first and only such institution in the U.S. It's open Tuesday through Sunday, noon to 5 p.m., Thursday until 8:00 p.m. An interesting gift shop has posters, books, and crafts from various countries.

● Lincoln Park Conservatory and Zoo. Three acres of gardens under glass and 35 acres of natural habitat for 2000 animals. Free seven days a week.

At Night: Try sampling the scene at the intersection of Rush and State Sts. going north on State to Division; the bars, shops, and restaurants along Halsted from Armitage to Webster, west on Webster to Racine, south on Racine, and east on Armitage; or on the stretch along Lincoln Ave. from Armitage to Webster. Some telephone numbers that will come in handy as you plan your nights in Chicago are:

● Jazz Hotline, 666-1881.

● Jam's Rock Concert Hotline, 666-6667.

● Eventline, 225-2323.

● Fine Art Line, 346-3278.

● Sportsline, 976-1313.

● Rick's Café American, in the Holiday Inn, 644 North Lake Shore Dr. Telephone: 943-9200. In this re-creation of Rick's from the film *Casablanca*, the jazz is good, whether there are big names featured or local talent.

● Andy's, 11 East Hubbard St. Telephone: 642-6805. *The* place for jazz these days.

● Orphan's, 2462 North Lincoln. Telephone: 929-2677. More jazz.

● The Bulls Jazz Club, 1916 North Lincoln Park West. Telephone: 337-3000. Outstanding contemporary jazz groups, good food, and pleasant service give this spot, long popular with Chicago jazz lovers, an increasingly widespread reputation in the rest of the country and even abroad. On weekends, you'd better make reservations.

● B.L.U.E.S., 2519 North Halsted St. Telephone: 327-3331. It's near to Lincoln Park's nightlife area and features blues seven nights a week.

- The League of Chicago offers half-price tickets for over 40 Chicago theaters on the day of the performance. Go to the Hot Tix booth at 24 South State. Open Tuesday to Friday, 11 a.m. to 5:15 p.m.; Saturday, 10 a.m. to 5 p.m. Call 977-1755 for information.

"Chicago theaters should not be underrated even if they still operate from store-front locations. Steppenwolf, Wisdom Bridge, Victory Gardens, The Remains Theater, The Court Theater, and Body Politic—all deserve a try."

- Orchestra Hall, 220 South Michigan. Telephone: 435-8111. This is the home of the Chicago Symphony Orchestra, whose principal conductor is Georg Solti. Guest artists perform during the symphony's season, which runs from fall through spring.
- Civic Opera House, 20 North Wacker. Telephone: 346-0270. The Lyric Opera, a first-rate company, attracts top operatic talent during its fall season. Chicago is also visited each year by many famous dance companies, e.g., the Joffrey, Alvin Ailey, American Ballet Theater, etc.
- Second City, 1616 North Wells St. Telephone: 337-3992. This improvisational comedy theater was the starting place for most of "Saturday Night Live's" original cast, as well as Alan Alda. Call for details.
- Music Box Theater, 3733 North Southport. Telephone: 871-6604. Popular film revival house.

Shopping: Barbara's Book Store, 1434 North Wells, 2907 North Broadway, and 121 North Marion, Oak Park. Telephone: 642-5044. A fine selection of hard- and softcover books, specializing in small press literature and poetry, mysteries, fiction, and children's books.
- Joseph O'Gara, 1311 East 57th St. and a warehouse on Wabash. For used paperbacks and hardcovers.
- Rizzoli's, Water Tower Place, 835 North Michigan Ave. Books, records, foreign and domestic newspapers and magazines.
- Rose Records, 214 South Wabash. Huge selection of records and tapes, especially well stocked in the classics, opera, and jazz departments. The second floor has budget and out-of-print records. Other branches are at 1122 North State Parkway, 3155 North Broadway, 3529 North Ashland, and 4821 West Irving Park.
- Marshall Field, 111 North State. One reader insists that all visitors take a look at this, the city's most famous department store—a full city block with luxuries and bargains in a building with Tiffany mosaic domes.
- Eddie Bauer, Inc. 123 North Wabash Ave., across from Marshall Field. Specializes in high-quality down gear, ski wear, and backpacking equipment.
- Crate and Barrel, 850 North Michigan Ave., and 101 North Wabash. Here you'll find anything and everything you need to equip a kitchen—glassware, dishes, good gift possibilities. Most things are reasonably priced and the basement at the Michigan Ave. store and the Outlet Store at 1510 North Wells carry basics, closeouts, and discontinued merchandise—all worth checking out.
- Water Tower Place. North of Old Water Tower and Pumping Station is this shopping mall, a great place to meet friends and spend a day shopping, eating (McDonald's is the favorite), and seeing a film.

Dale

Accommodation: Budget Host—Stones Motel, √ ⑤, 410 South Washington St., 47523. Telephone: 812/937-4448. $23 for one; $25 two in one bed; $29 two in two beds.

Danville

Accommodation: YWCA, 201 North Hazel St., 61832. Telephone: 217/446-1217. Women only. $10 single with shared bath. Weekly rate: $25.

Davenport

Accommodation: Budget Host—Town House Budget Host, √, 7222 Northwest Blvd., 52806. Telephone: 319/391-8222. $22.95 for one; $25.95 for two in one bed; $27.95 for two in two beds.

Decatur

Accommodation: Lakeview Motel, √ (5%), 16 South Country Club Rd., 62521. Telephone: 217/428-4677. $21.88 single; $26.88 double.

De Kalb

Help: Crisis Line, 815/758-6655.

On Campus: Northern Illinois University is in De Kalb, and for $24.38 for a single or $29.68 for a double, you can stay in one of the hotel-like rooms in the Holmes Student Center there (call 815/753-1444 for information). Also in the Holmes Center is the Pow Wow Room where a full meal—meat, potatoes, vegetables, roll, and beverage—will be inexpensive. There are two other restaurants in the Student Center to choose from. Off campus, try Rosita's at 642 East Lincoln Hwy., where Mexican food is featured.

Accommodation: Motel 6, 1116 West Lincoln Hwy., 60115. Telephone: 815/756-6605. $17.95 single; $21.95 double.

Effingham

Accommodations: Days Inn, West Fayette Rd. & I-57 & I-70, 62401. Telephone: 217/342-9271. $26 to $32 single; $28 to $38 double.

• Friendship Lincoln Lodge, Exit 162 on I-70 & I-57, 62401. Telephone: 217/342-4133. $23.95 to $26.95 for one; $27.95 to $30.95 for two in one bed; $29.95 to $32.95 for two in two beds.

Elgin

Accommodation: Friendship Inn Colonial Lodge Motel, 788 Villa St., 60120. Telephone: 312/742-2790. $23.50 to $27.50 for one; $26.95 to $27.50 for two in one bed; $29 to $35 for two in two beds.

Evanston

Help: Crisis Intervention Referral Services, 312/492-6500.

On Campus: In Evanston, the suburban area adjacent to Chicago, you'll find the campus of Northwestern University. Northwestern students gather at The Spot, Fritz's, Jay's, Yesterday's, and The Main. There's a bulletin board you might want to check at Norris Center; pick up a copy of the *Daily Northwestern* to see what's going on when you arrive.

Accommodations: YMCA, 1000 Grove St., 60201. Telephone: 312/475-7400. In downtown Evanston, one block south of Davis St. Men only, age 18 and over. $19 single.

- Margarita Inn, 1566 Oak Ave., 60201. Telephone: 312/869-2273. $28 single; $34 double; $39 triple. "The inn is European-style . . . there are very few rooms with private baths but there are ample facilities on each floor."

Galesburg

Accommodations: Regal 8 Inn, 1487 North Henderson, 61401. Telephone: 309/344-2401. See Aurora listing for rates.

- TraveLodge, ∨ ⓓ, 565 West Main St., 61401. Telephone: 309/343-3191. $25 for one; $28 for two in one bed; $32 for two in two beds.

Granite City

Accommodation: TraveLodge, ∨ (15%), 1200 19th St., 62040. Telephone: 618/876-2600. $27 for one; $30 for two in one bed; $34 for two in two beds.

Jacksonville

Accommodation: Motel 6, 1716 West Morton Dr., 62650. Telephone: 217/243-5322. See De Kalb listing for rates.

Joliet

Accommodations: Kings Inn, ∨, 2219½ West Jefferson, 60435. Telephone: 815/744-1220. $22.88 single; $24.88 for two in one bed; $27.88 for two in two beds.

- Red Roof Inn, ⓓ, 1750 McDonough, 60436. Telephone: 815/741-2304. $23.95 for one; $28.95 for two in one bed; $30.95 for two in two beds; $32.95 for three or four in two beds.

Kankakee

Accommodations: Regal 8 Inn, Ill. 50 & Armour Rd., Bourbonnais, 60914. Telephone: 815/933-2300. See Aurora listing for rates.

- Scottish Inn, ⓓ, Rte. 45 S., RR 7, Box 336, 60901. Telephone: 815/939-4551. $25 for one; $28 for two in one bed; $31 for two in two beds.

La Grange

Accommodation: Richport YMCA, 31 East Ogden Ave., 60525. Telephone: 312/352-7600. Men and women. $17 single; $22 double. Cafeteria on the premises.

LaSalle

Accommodation: Motel 6, 1900 May St., Peru, 61354. Telephone: 815/224-2734. See De Kalb listing for rates.

Libertyville

Accommodation: Doe's Motel, Rtes. 45 & Ill. 137, 60048. Telephone: 312/362-0800. $31.55 for one; $34.45 for two in one bed; $36.55 for two in two beds.

Lombard

Accommodation: Highland Manor Motel, √ (10%), 19 West 545 Roosevelt Rd., 60418. Telephone: 312/627-5700. $26.50 for one or two in one bed; $28.65 for two in two beds.

Macomb

Accommodation: Olson Conference Center, Western Illinois University, West Adams St., 61455. Telephone: 309/298-2461. $15.50 single; $18 double. Rooms have two single beds, which are used as couches during the day. Each floor of the guest area has a lounge and a community bathroom. Meals in adjacent building. On Western Illinois University campus, one-half mile from bus and train stations.

Marion

Accommodation: Regal 8 Inn, I-57 & Rte. 13, 62959. Telephone: 618/993-2631. See Aurora listing for rates.

Moline

Accommodations: Regal 8 Inn, Quad City Airport Rd., 61265. Telephone: 309/764-8711. See Aurora listing for rates.
 ● Exel Inn, 2501 52nd Ave., 61265. Telephone: 309/797-5580. $25.95 for one; $30.95 for two in one bed; $32.95 for two in two beds.

Monmouth

Accommodation: Fulton Hall, North 7th St., 61462. Telephone: 309/457-2345. $9 per person dormitory style. Advance reservations necessary.

Mount Vernon

Accommodations: Regal 8 Inn, I-57 & Ill. 15, 62864. Telephone: 618/244-2383. See Aurora listing for rates.
- Best Inns of America, √ (10%), Rte. 15 & I-57, 62864. Telephone: 618/244-4343. $26.88 for one; $30.88 for two in one bed; $32.88 for two in two beds.

Morton Grove

Accommodation: Admiral Oasis Motel, 9353 Waukegan Rd., 60053. Telephone: 312/965-4000. $19.25 single; $21.40 double. Lower rates apply in winter.

Normal

On Campus: Illinois State University is in this town. Activities there center around the Bone Student center and sometimes move to one of the local bars— the Cellar, Hooter's, Garcia's, The Gallery, Benningan's, or Rocky's II. For information on campus events check *Vidette*, the student newspaper.
Accommodation: Motel 6, 1600 North Main St., 61761. Telephone: 309/452-9481. See De Kalb listing for rates.

Palos Park

Accommodation: Community Center Foundation (AYH-SA), 12700 Southwest Hwy., 60464. Telephone: 312/361-3650. $10 for AYH members. Advance reservations suggested.

Peoria

Accommodations: YWCA, 301 N.E. Jefferson St., 61602. Telephone: 309/674-1167. Women only. $13 single. Weekly rate of $60 includes linens. Centrally located. "1928 building with front parlors, tearoom, swimming pool, and a sauna."
- Motel 6, 104 West Camp St., 61611. Telephone: 309/694-3294. See De Kalb listing for rates.
- Imperial 400 Motor Inn, 202 N.E. Washington, 61602. Telephone: 309/676-8961. $23 to $27 for one; $27 to $31 for two in one bed; $29 to $33 for two in two beds.
- Red Roof Inn, &, 4031 North War Memorial Dr., 61614. Telephone: 309/685-3911. $24.95 for one; $29.95 for two in one bed; $31.95 for two in two beds; $33.95 for three or four in two beds.
- Days Inn, &, 2726 West Lake Ave., 61615. Telephone: 309/688-7000. $27 single; $31 double.
- Townehouse Motel, 1519 North Knoxville Ave., 61603. Telephone: 309/688-8646. $26.50 for one or two people in one bed; $29.50 for two in two beds.

Pocahontas

Accommodation: Wikiup Motel, Inc., Johnson & Plant Sts., 62275. Telephone: 618/669-2293. $20 to $25 for one; $22 to $27 for two in one bed; $24 to $30 for two in two beds.

Rockford

Help: Contact Rockford, 815/964-4044.

Accommodations: Motel 6, 4205 11th St., 61109. Telephone: 815/399-6266. See De Kalb listing for rates.

● Regal 8 Inn, 3851 11th St., 61109. Telephone: 815/398-6080. See Aurora listing for rates.

● Exel Inn, 220 South Lyford Rd., 61108. Telephone: 815/332-4915. $23.95 for one; $28.95 for two in one bed; $30.95 for two in two beds.

● Red Roof Inn, 🚹, I-90 at East State St. Bus. Rte. 20, 7434 East State St., 61108. Telephone: 815/398-9750. $22.95 for one; $26.95 for two in one bed; $27.95 for two in two beds; $29.95 for three or four in two beds.

● Econo Lodge, √, 733 East State St., 61104. Telephone: 815/964-3361. $22.95 for one; $24.95 for two in one bed; $26.95 for two in two beds.

Springfield

"An historical, amusing, clean, and educational town."

On Campus: Sangamon State University is here. For accommodations in the University area, stop at the Office of Student Life/Housing on Sheppard Rd. Telephone: 217/786-6190.

Accommodations: Capitol City Motel, √, 1620 North 9th St., 62702. Telephone: 217/528-0462. $22 to $26 for one; $26 to $30 for two in one bed; $26 to $35 for two in two beds.

● Red Roof Inn, 🚹, I-55 at South Grand Ave., Exit 96B. Telephone: 217/753-4302. See Joliet listing for rates.

● Regal 8 Inn, I-55 & Toronto Rd., 62703. Telephone: 217/529-1633. See Aurora listing for rates.

● Motel 6, 3125 Wide Track Dr., 62703. Telephone: 217/789-0520. See De Kalb listing for rates.

● Days Inn, 🚹, 3000 Stevenson Dr., 62703. Telephone: 217/529-0171. $29 single; $34 double.

● TraveLodge, √ (15%), 500 South Ninth St., 62701. Telephone: 217/528-4341. $28 for one; $31 for two in one bed; $36 for two in two beds.

Urbana (see also Champaign-Urbana)

Accommodations: Motel 6, 1906 North Cunningham Ave., 61801. Telephone: 217/344-8660. See De Kalb listing for rates.

● Hendrick House, 904 West Green St., 61801. Telephone: 217/344-4957. Open May 1 to August 15. $10.50 single; $8.50 per person double. Advance reservations of two months necessary.

Vandalia

Accommodation: TraveLodge, √ ♿, 1500 North 6th St., 62471. Telephone: 618/283-2363. May 15 to June 15: $24 for one; $29 for two in one bed; $31 for two in two beds. June 16 to September 10: $25 single; $31 for two in one bed; $34 for two in two beds.

Indiana

Most people think of the Indianapolis 500 when they think of Indiana; the race is probably Indiana's biggest claim to fame. It's held on Memorial Day and has attracted huge crowds since 1911 (with time off for the two World Wars). Other things to see in Indiana are Indiana Dunes National Lakeshore; Wayandotte Cave, a five-level cavern; the Indianapolis Motor Speedway, once a testing ground for vehicle performance and now the scene of the 500 and a museum of the racing art; Lincoln Boyhood National Memorial, the cabin and the grave of Lincoln's mother with a visitor center that features a film on the family's four years in Indiana; and New Harmony, the remains of what was once a utopian village.

Indiana Off the Beaten Path, by Bill and Phyllis Thomas ($16.95) is recommended if you're going to explore this state. "When the mood strikes, you can visit the world's largest underground mountain, a singular circus town, a one-of-a-kind jail, a walking sand dune, a small town with the most concentrated collection of contemporary architecture in the country, America's biggest navigable lost river, an extraordinary children's museum, the graves of James Dean and John Dillinger, the birthplace of Michael Jackson, and many other wacky, wonderful attractions." The book is published by The East Woods Press, 429 East Blvd., Charlotte, NC 28203.

Some Special Events: Parke County Maple Fair in Rockville (February); Dogwood Festival in Orleans, Indianapolis 500 Festival, and Civil War Weekend in Fort Wayne (all in May); Victoria Lockerbie Square Summer A'Fair in Indianapolis, and Rose Festival in Richmond (June); Circus City Festival in Peru (once winter headquarters for many great circuses), and Three Rivers Festival in Fort Wayne (July); War of 1812 Weekend in Fort Wayne, and State Fair in Indianapolis (August); James Whitcomb Riley Festival (a three-day celebration in honor of the Hoosier poet) in Greenfield, Village Tour of Homes in Zionville, and the Parke County Covered Bridge Festival in Rockville (all in October).

Hitching: It is illegal to hitchhike or walk on any interstate highway. On other roads, it is illegal to stand on the roadway for the purpose of soliciting a ride.

Tourist Information: Tourism Development Division, Department of Commerce, 440 North Meridian St., Indianapolis, IN 46204. Telephone: 317/232-8860. Ask for their *SceniCircle Drives* booklet, which lists the state's major historical, recreational, and scenic attractions organized in a series of 17 mini-tours.

Anderson

Accommodation: Motel 6, 5810 Scatterfield Rd., 46013. Telephone: 317/642-3333. $17.95 for one; $21.95 for two; $2 for each additional person.

Angola

Accommodation: Red Carpet Inn, √ &, Rte. 1, Box 405B, 46703. Telephone: 219/665-9561. $30 for one; $34 for two in one bed; $36 for two in two beds.

Bedford

Accommodation: Rosemount Motel, 1923 M St., 47421. Telephone: 812/275-5953. $23.10 single; $28.35 double; $3 for each additional person.

Bloomington

On Campus: Have you seen the film *Breaking Away?* That's Bloomington, scene of the Little 500 bicycle race and home of the University of Indiana, one of the "Big Ten."

Two places on campus where you may be able to spend a night are the Indiana Memorial Union and the Poplar's Research and Conference Center. If you're hungry, try The Commons, the IMO Cafeteria, or the Garden Patch—all in the Memorial Union on 7th and Park. Off-campus, try Rudi's and The Two on 10th and Indiana (deli and vegetarian food); Runcible Spoon, 6th and Grant (great coffee, teas, and brunches); and Daily Grind, Dunn and 5th (good for lunch). For great pasta, shop at Mamma Girisanti's, 850 Auto Mall Rd. For things to do, the IU Music School presents operas and concerts that are of very high quality, and student tickets are usually discounted. IU has its own art museum and it and the Nather's Museum of History, Anthropology, and Folklore have year-round exhibits and are open to the public. For an outdoor experience, you can go to nearby Lake Monroe, Hoosier National Forest, Brown Company, and McCormick's Creek State Park.

Accommodations: Motel 6, 126 South Franklin Rd., 47401. Telephone: 812/336-0689. See Anderson listing for rates.

● Down Town Motel, 509 North College Ave., 47401. Telephone: 812/336-6881. $16.95 single; $19.95 double; $28.95 triple; $30.95 quad. Advance reservations of three days necessary; a check or credit card number must be given with reservations.

Clarksville

Accommodation: Econo Lodge, √, 460 Auburn Ave., 47130. Telephone: 812/288-6661. $22.95 for one; $27.95 for two in one bed; $32.95 for two in two beds. Higher rates apply during special events.

Columbus

Accommodation: Imperial 400 Motor Inn, 101 3rd St., 47201. Telephone: 812/372-2835. $28 to $30 for one; $32 to $36 for two in one bed; $36 to $40 for two in two beds.

Dale

Accommodation: Budget Host—Stones Motel, √, 410 South Washington St., 47523. Telephone: 812/937-4448. $23 for one; $25 for two in one bed; $29 for two in two beds.

Elkhart

Help: Switchboard Concern, 219/293-8671.

Accommodations: Red Roof Inn, 2909 Cassopolis St., 46514. Telephone: 219/262-3691. $24.95 for one; $29.95 for two in one bed; $34.95 for two in two beds; $33.95 for three or four in two beds.

● Days Inn, 2820 Cassopolis St., 46514. Telephone: 219/262-3541. $24.88 for one; $28.88 for two.

Evansville

Accommodation: Regal 8 Inn, 4201 Hwy. 41 N. & Yokel Rd., 47711. Telephone: 812/424-6431. $22.88 for one; $27.88 for two in one bed; $32.88 for two in two beds.

Fort Wayne

Tourist Information: Greater Fort Wayne Chamber of Commerce, 826 Ewing, 46802. Telephone: 219/424-1435.

Help: Switchboard, Inc., 316 West Creighton Ave. Telephone: 219/456-4561. 24-hour crisis and information line.

Accommodations: Hallmark Inn, U.S. 24 & City Rte. 30 at jct. with U.S. 30, 46803. Telephone: 219/424-1980. $21.70 to $25.70 for one; $28.70 to $32.70 for two; $3 for each additional person.

- Motel 6, 1020 Coliseum Blvd. N., 46820. Telephone: 219/422-3840. See Anderson listing for rates.
- Motel 6, 3003 Coliseum Blvd. W., 46805. Telephone: 219/483-9225. See Anderson listing for rates.
- Courtesy Inn, √, 1401 West Washington Center Rd., 46825. Telephone: 219/489-3588. $22.95 single; $25.95 double; $27.95 for three or four in two beds.
- Red Roof Inn, 2920 Goshen Rd., 46808. Telephone: 219/484-8641. $22.95 for one; $27.95 for two in one bed; $29.95 for two in two beds; $31.95 for three or four in two beds.
- Days Inn, 3527 Coliseum Blvd., 46808. Telephone: 219/482-4511. $26.50 for one; $31.50 for two.
- Friendship Inn of Fort Wayne, 1011 East California Rd., 46825. Telephone: 219/483-6421. $20 to $24 for one; $23 to $27 for two in one bed; $26 to $35 for two in two beds.
- Red Carpet Inn, √, 4606 Lincoln Hwy. E., 46803. Telephone: 219/422-9511. $21.95 to $25.95 for one; $25.95 to $29.95 for two in one bed; $27.95 to $31.95 for two in two beds.
- Hallmark Inn, 3737 East Washington, 46805. Telephone: 219/424-1980. $19.70 for one; $23.70 two in one bed; $26.70 for two in two beds; $29.70 for three in two beds; $32.70 for four in two beds.

Goshen

On Campus: If you find yourself in need of conversation, the Oasis, a popular watering hole, is the place to go in Goshen. The Student Union of Goshen College has a bulletin board which might provide helpful information about rides, accommodations, and so forth. Goshen has been described by a friend at the college as "the town that voted for George Wallace when he ran in the presidential primary—need I say more?"

- Goshen Motor Inn, 65522 U.S. 33 East, 46526. Telephone: 219/642-4388, $24.68 for one bed; $27.83 for two beds.

Indianapolis

Tourist Information: Indianapolis Convention and Visitors Association, 100 South Capital Ave., 46225. Telephone: 317/635-9567.

Accommodations: YMCA, 860 West 10th St., 46202. Telephone: 317/634-2478. Men and women. $13.20 single; $24.40 double; $31.44 quad. Weekly rate: $46 single. "The people there were very friendly. Don't walk from the bus station—you have to go through a pretty raunchy neighborhood." Higher rates apply during race week.

- Clover West Motel, Ⓢ★, 9745 West Washington St., 46231. Telephone: 317/839-2324. $17 single; $24 double; $28 triple.
- Motel 6, 2851 Shadeland, 46219. Telephone: 317/546-1501. See Anderson listing for rates.

● USA Inn, 6990 Pendleton Pike, 46226. Telephone: 317/546-4971. $20.70 single; $25.70 double.

● Regal 8 Inn, 5241 West Broadway at Lynhurst, 46226. Telephone: 317/248-1231. $21.88 for one; $26.88 for two in one bed; $31.88 for two in two beds.

● Red Roof Inn, 🚹, 6415 Debonair Lane, 46224. Telephone: 317/293-6881. $21.95 for one; $26.95 for two in one bed; $28.95 for two in two beds; $30.95 for three or four in two beds.

● Red Roof Inn, 🚹, 9520 Valparaiso Ct., 46268. Telephone: 317/872-3030. See above listing for rates.

● Red Roof Inn, 5221 Victory Dr., 46203. Telephone: 317/788-9551. See above listing for rates.

● Days Inn, 🚹, 7314 East 21st St., 46219. Telephone: 317/359-5500. $26 to $28 for one; $32 to $34 for two.

● Days Inn, 5151 Elmwood Dr., 46203. Telephone: 317/785-5471. $24 for one; $29 for two.

● Days Inn, 🚹, 450 Bixler Rd., 46227. Telephone: 317/788-0811. $26.88 for one; $31.88 for two.

● Econo Lodge, ∨, 1501 East 38th St., 46205. Telephone: 317/926-4401. $21.95 for one; $24.95 for two in one or two beds. Higher rates apply during special events.

Kokomo

Accommodations: World Inn, ∨, 268 U.S. 31 S., 46902. Telephone: 317/453-7100. $24.95 for one; $28.95 for two.

● Econo Lodge, ∨, 2040 South Reed Rd., 46402. Telephone: 317/457-7561. $20.95 for one; $24.95 for two in one bed; $26.95 for two in two beds. Higher rates apply during special events.

Lafayette

Accommodations: Red Roof Inn, 🚹, 4201 State Road 26 E., 47905. Telephone: 317/448-4671. $23.95 for one; $28.95 for two in one bed; $30.95 for two in two beds; $32.95 for three or four in two beds.

● Prestige Inn, ∨, 1217 Sagamore Pkwy., 47906. Telephone: 317/463-1531. $21.55 for one; $26.55 for two in one bed; $31.55 for two in two beds.

Merrillville

Accommodation: Red Roof Inn, 8290 Georgia St., 46410. Telephone: 219/738-2430. See Indianapolis listing for rates.

Michigan City

Accommodations: Red Roof Inn, 110 West Kieffer Rd., 46360. Telephone: 219/874-5251. See Elkhart listing for rates.

- ABC Motel, √, 3948 Franklin St., 46360. Telephone: 219/879-0335. April through August: $30 single; $35 to $45 double. September to March: $20 to $25 single; $26 to $32 double.
- TraveLodge, √ ♿, 3944 South Franklin St., 46360. Telephone: 219/872-9441. $26 for one; $30 for two in one bed; $34 for two in two beds.

New Albany

On Campus: Indiana University Southeast is located in New Albany. According to one friend there, the place to eat is Lancaster's, one-half mile from campus on Grant Line Rd. Also recommended is the Cellar at 13th and Floodwall.

New Castle

Accommodation: Friendship New Castle Inn, 2005 South Memorial Dr., 47362. Telephone: 317/529-1670. $19 to $28 for one; $22 to $32 for two in one bed; $29 to $32 for two in two beds.

Plymouth

Accommodation: Motel 6, 2535 North Michigan, 46563. Telephone: 219/936-3106. See Anderson listing for rates.

Portage

Accommodation: Motel 6, 6101 Melton Rd., Rte. 20, 46368. Telephone: 219/762-3129. See Anderson listing for rates.

Remington

Accommodation: Days Inn, ♿, I-65 & U.S. 24, Rte. 2, Box 240B, 47977. Telephone: 219/261-2178. $23.88 for one; $28.88 for two.

Richmond

Accommodation: Susse Chalet Inn, I-70 at junction U.S. 40, 47374. Telephone: 317/966-7511. $30.70 for one; $34.70 for two; $37.70 for three; $40.70 for four.

San Pierre

Accommodation: River Bend Campground (AYH-SA), 46374. Telephone: 219/896-3339. Open May 1 to September 30. $2.75 for AYH members.

"This is a private campground with dorm. It is family run and on some weekends we have hog roasts and corn roasts. I have two families in the area I have promised to call in case anyone comes by from either Switzerland or Norway."

Schererville

Accommodation: Underwood Motel, V, 1108 Lincoln Hwy., Rte. 30, 46375. Telephone: 219/865-2451. $19.80 to $30 for up to five people.

Seymour

Accommodation: Days Inn, 302 Frontage Rd., 47274. Telephone: 812/522-3678. $25 to $30; $30 to $35 for two.

South Bend

"We have beautiful parks, two Frank Lloyd Wright houses, the Notre Dame and Indiana University campuses, and an auto museum."

Help: Hotline-Crisis Intervention, 219/232-3344.
● Information and Referral, 219/232-2522.
On Campus: Indiana University and Notre Dame are here, and you can meet some of their students at the bars along Eddy St., south of the Notre Dame campus, or at the Huddle, right on campus.

In addition to eating at the school cafeterias, you can find an excellent Chinese lunch at China Garden, 910 East Ireland Rd. for $2.95, or a Hungarian dinner at the Budapest Night for $4 to $6.

Indiana University has a good film series which costs $1.50 per film; a similar series exists at Notre Dame.

Accommodations: YWCA, ♿, 802 North Lafayette Blvd., 46601. Telephone: 219/233-9491. Women only. $15 plus $2.50 key deposit single. Weekly rate: $32 to $53 plus a deposit of one week's rent. Advance reservations of one week necessary. Cooking facilities available.
● Motel 6, 52624 U.S. Hwy. 31 N., 46637. Telephone: 219/277-1661. See Anderson listing for rates.

Spencer

Accommodation: McCormick's Creek State Park, ♿, RR1, P.O. Box 72, 47460. Telephone: 812/829-2235. Eighteen miles from Bloomington. Accommodations at the Canyon Inn (tel. 812/829-4881) for $31 to $33 and at cabins in the park for a full week only for $90 per week, April to October. These cabins accommodate six people and have two sleeping rooms, a kitchen, a lavatory, and showers. Advance reservations suggested.

Terre Haute

Accommodations: Regal 8 Inn, I-70 & U.S. 41, 47802. Telephone: 812/238-1586. See Evansville listing for rates.

Wabash

Accommodation: Scottish Inn, Jct. U.S. 24 & S.R. 13, Rte. 2, Box 35, 46992. Telephone: 219/563-2195. $23 for one; $26 for two in one bed; $29 for two in two beds.

Warsaw

Accommodation: Royal 6 Motel, U.S. 30 E., 46580. Telephone: 219/269-2601. $25 for one; $31.37 for two in one bed; $35.57 for two in two beds; $48.82 for three or four in two beds.

Spirit Lake
Mason City
Le Mars
Sioux City
Fort Dodge
Williams
Cedar Falls
Waterloo
Dubuque
Ames
Cedar Rapids
Mount Vernon
Clinton
Walnut
Des Moines
Newton
Iowa City
Davenport
Muscatine
Council Bluffs
Oskaloosa
Albia
Ottumwa
Villisca
Lamoni
Keokuk

Iowa

You probably never thought about it before, but wherever you are in the U.S. you're no more than 2½ driving days from Iowa. Lots of people pass through Iowa on their way cross-country on Interstate 80 and some, who like farmland and open spaces, decide to stay.

It was, in fact, Iowa's rich prairie soil that attracted people from all over Europe from the mid-1800s on. The farmer is king in Iowa—the state is patterned with farms that grow corn and soybeans and raise hogs and cattle. The major attractions in Iowa are the Amana Colonies, not far from Cedar Rapids, which represent an experiment in communal utopianism; the Herbert Hoover National Historic Site in West Branch, which includes the two-room cottage where the one-time president was born, a replica of his father's blacksmith shop, the Quaker meeting house where the family worshipped, and the Hoover Presidential Library Museum; Fort Dodge Historical Museum, Fort, and Stockade, reproduction of a fort where pioneers withstood hostile Indians; and Vesterheim in Decorah, a folk museum honoring the Norwegian pioneers of the area.

The Iowa Development Commission has seven information centers located on Interstate highways throughout the state which are open from mid-May to mid-September; check with them for maps and travel advice.

Some Special Events: Tulip Time in Pella (May); Grant Wood Arts Festival in Stone City, International Folk Festival in Bettendorf, and Steamboat Days in Burlington (June); Ragbrai Bike Race (different starting point each year), Riverboat Days in Clinton, and Bix Beiderbecke Memorial Jazz Festival in Davenport (July); National Hobo Convention in Britt, National Hot Air Balloon

Championships in Indianola, and Iowa State Fair in Des Moines (August); Tri-State Rodeo in Fort Madison (September); and Covered Bridge Festival in Winterset (October).

Hitching: Hitching is legal as long as you stay off the traveled portion of the road. Local cities and towns can prohibit hitchhiking within city limits. In Des Moines, for instance, hitching is illegal on I-235 within Des Moines and West Des Moines. Hitchhiking seems to be accepted in Iowa, and the attitude toward people on the road is good, more so in the larger cities than in the smaller towns. A friend from Iowa City writes that hitchhiking, especially in the Iowa City area, is good: "Most people are willing to pick you up—everyone from farmers to truckers—if you look clean and you smile. . . . The highway patrol may stop but usually just to talk with you and give you some good tips."

Tourist Information: Iowa Development Commission, Tourism and Travel Division, 600 East Court Ave., Des Moines, IA 50309. Telephone: 515/281-3251.

Albia

Accommodation: Holiday Motel, Hwy. 34 E., 52531. Telephone: 515/932-7181. $24 for one; $28 for two in one bed; $30 for two in two beds.

Ames

Help: Open Line, 515/292-7000. "We are a free confidential listing and info-referral service."
- University Switchboard, 515/294-4111.
- Campus Information, 515/294-4357.

On Campus: The campus of Iowa State University is in Ames. A place for the night on campus may be found at the Memorial Union ($28 for a single, $34 for a double); or by contacting the Office of International Educational Services, whose personnel will assist you in finding accommodations (tel. 515/294-1120). For rides, etc., check the bulletin board in the Memorial Union. To meet students, go to That Place, 205 Main St.; Grand Daddy's, 202 Market; or the Memorial Union's Commons. For good food, all in the university area and all in a $2-to-$5 price range, try Grubstake Barbecue, 2512 Lincoln Way (ribs, sandwiches, beer); Thumbs Up, 113 Welch Ave. (pizza, salad bar, beer); Dugan's Deli, 2900 West St. (deli sandwiches and salads); or Quarter-stove Café, in the basement of Alumni Hall on ISU campus, open at lunchtime (you can get a huge vegetarian meal here for $1.75 or even work for your meal).

Cedar Falls

Accommodations: Motel 6, 4117 University Ave., 50613. Telephone: 319/277-6900. $17.95 for one; $21.95 for two; $2 for each additional person.
- Exel Inn, 616 33rd Ave. SW, 52404. Telephone: 319/366-2475. $23.95 for one; $28.95 for two in one bed; $30.95 for two in two beds.

Cedar Rapids

Accommodations: Red Roof Inn, 🛇, 3325 Southgate Ct. SW, 52404. Telephone: 319/366-7523. $22.95 for one; $27.95 for two in one bed; $29.95 for two in two beds; $31.95 for three or four in two beds.

● Exel Inn, 616 33rd Ave. SW, 52404. Telephone: 319/366-2475. $23.95 for one; $28.95 for two in one bed; $30.95 for two in two beds.

Clinton

Accommodations: Imperial 400 Motor Inn, 1111 Camanche Ave., 52732. Telephone: 319/243-4621. $25 for one; $24 to $30 for two in one bed; $27 to $32 for two in two beds.

● TraveLodge, √ 🛇, 302 6th Ave., S., 52732. Telephone: 319/243-4730. $27 for one; $30 for two in one bed; $33 for two in two beds.

Council Bluffs

Accommodation: Motel 6, 1846 North 16th St., 51501. Telephone: 712/328-3851. See Cedar Falls listing for rates.

Davenport

Help: Information, Referral, and Assistance Services of Rock Island, Illinois, and Davenport, Iowa, 311 Ripley, 52801. Telephone: 319/324-0625.

Accommodations: Friendship Bronze Lantern Inn, 1661 West Kimberly Rd., 52806. Telephone: 319/391-5570. $19.95 to $23 for one; $21.95 to $27 for two in one bed; $24.95 to $30 for two in two beds.

● Motel 6, 6111 North Brady St., 52806. Telephone: 319/391-1300. See Cedar Falls listing for rates.

● Exel Inn, 6310 North Brady St., 52804. Telephone: 319/386-6350. $24.95 for one; $29.95 for two in one bed; $31.95 for two in two beds.

● Budget Host—Town House, 7222 Northwest Blvd., 52806. Telephone: 319/391-8222. $22.95 for one; $25.95 for two in one bed; $27.95 for two in two beds.

Des Moines

Tourist Information: Greater Des Moines Convention and Visitors Bureau, 800 High St., 50307. Telephone: 515/286-4971.

Help: First Call for Help (Travelers Aid), 700 Sixth Ave., 50309. Telephone: 515/244-8646.

Accommodations: YMCA, 🛇, 101 Locust St., 50309. Telephone: 515/288-0131. Men only. $19.03 single; $47.78 per week (available after a three-day stay at the regular rate). Advance reservations suggested.

● YWCA Residence, 717 Grand Ave., 50309. Telephone: 515/244-8961.

Women only. Eight blocks from bus station. $7.50 single. Weekly rate: $59 in shared room. Eight-year-old building with pool and gym.

- Kirkwood Civic Center Hotel, Ⓢ √ ★, 400 Walnut St., 50309. Telephone: 515/244-9191. $30 to $48 single; $36 to $48 double; $48 triple or quad.
- Motel 6, 4817 Fleur Dr., 50321. Telephone: 515/285-4720. See Cedar Falls listing for rates.
- Econo Lodge, √, 5626 Douglas Ave., 50310. Telephone: 515/278-1601. $25.50 for one; $28.50 for two in one bed; $31.50 for two in two beds. Higher rates apply during special events.
- Beacon Motel, Ⓢ √ ★, 4144 Hubbell Ave., 50317. Telephone: 515/266-1166. $20 single; $22.50 double; $28.50 triple; $35 quad. Newly decorated.
- Friendship Plaza Inn, 5626 Douglas Ave., 50310. Telephone: 515/278-1601. $22.50 for one; $25.50 for two in one bed; $28.50 for two in two beds.
- TraveLodge, √ ♿, 2021 Grand Ave., 50312. Telephone: 515/283-1600. Airport transportation available. $27 for one; $30 for two in one bed; $33 for two in two beds.

Dubuque

Accommodation: Regal 8 Inn, 2670 Dodge St., 52001. Telephone: 319/556-0880. $21.88 for one; $26.88 for two in one bed; $31.88 for two in two beds.

Fort Dodge

Accommodations: Towers Motel, Hwys. 169 & 20, 50501. Telephone: 515/955-8575. $20 to $22 for one; $22 to $24 for two in one bed; $27 to $29 for two in two beds.

- YWCA, 826 First Ave. N., 50501. Telephone: 515/573-2911. Women only. $9 single. Weekly rate: $28.

Iowa City

Help: Crisis Center, 26 East Market. Telephone: 319/351-0140.

On Campus: The University of Iowa has a ride board outside the Wheel Room of the Iowa Memorial Union. One eating place recommended by an Iowa City native is Bushnell's Turtle, on the Mall on East College (for large subs, homemade soup, and hot apple cider). The Bijou, the movie theater at the Iowa Memorial Union, shows old and new films for only $2.

Accommodations: Wesley House Youth Hostel (AYH), 120 North Dubuque St., 52240. Telephone: 319/338-1179. Two miles south of I-80. Closed November 23 to 26 and December 21 to January 3. Students only. $6 for AYH members.

- Friendship MarKee, 707 First Ave., P.O. Box 5426, 52241. Telephone: 319/351-6131. $24 to $27 for one; $27 to $30 for two in one bed; $30.50 to $33.50 for two in two beds.
- Friendship Alamo Inn, Hwys. 6 & 218 West, I-80 Exit 242, Coralville, 52241. Telephone: 319/354-4000. $22.85 to $26.85 for one; $25.85 to $28.85 for two in one bed; $28.85 to $32.85 for two in two beds.

● Motel 6, 810 First Ave., Coralville, 52241. Telephone: 319/351-0586. See Cedar Falls listing for rates.

Keokuk

Accommodation: Globe Motel, Main St. Rd. on Hwy. 218 N., 52632. Telephone: 319/524-4312. $15.95 for one; $18.95 to $23 double; $27 triple; $31 quad.

Lamoni

On Campus: According to a friend from Graceland College, people are generally friendly toward strangers. When it's time to eat, all of the restaurants are "good and inexpensive compared with big-city prices." If you're in Lamoni on a Thursday night, visit the cattle auction at the Sale Barn. The café attached to the barn serves "a very country, very wholesome, filling meal for about $3.50." To meet students, stop in at the K Bar C, T/D Corral, the Pizza Shack, the Out Post, the Swarm Inn or Pizza Hut. Contact the director of housing for temporary on-campus housing.

Le Mars

On Campus: Westmar College is here and you can spend a night or two at the College Residence Hall—contact the dean of students for information. "We're just corn fields—Sioux City is 25 miles south." Three good eating spots are the Pantry Café, Central Ave. and 1st St. NE; the Club Café, 20 Plymouth St. SW; or Munro's, south on Hwy. 75. For a bit of culture, ask someone about the "excellent collection of exotic musical instruments" in the city. There's a museum on 4th St. SW and Second Ave.

Accommodation: TraveLodge, √ (15%), 3rd Ave. & Main St., 50158. Telephone: 515/753-6681. Airport transportation available. $30 for one; $34 for two in one bed; $38 for two in two beds.

Mason City

Accommodations: Thrifty Scot Motel, 2301 4th St. SW, 50401. Telephone: 515/424-0210. $22.90 for one; $26.90 for two in one bed; $29.90 for two in two beds.

● YMCA, 15 North Pennsylvania Ave., 50401. Telephone: 515/423-5526. Men only. $9.36 per night. Weekly rate: $26.

● TraveLodge, √ 🚻, 24 5th St., 50401. Telephone: 515/424-2910. $30 for one; $34 for two in one bed; $38 for two in two beds.

Mount Vernon

On Campus: Cornell College (the oldest coed college west of the Mississippi) is in this town, which is, according to one student, "friendly, small, picturesque, safe, and typical of Middle America. We welcome travelers into our homes as well as into the community." The college has guest rooms for $24 to $27 per night and, if they're full, there are rooming houses and hotels nearby.

Free tours of the campus and some of its more than 30 buildings are available for those with a historic bent.

Muscatine

Accommodation: YMCA, 312 Iowa Ave., 52761. Telephone: 319/263-4813. Men only. $11.75 single plus $5 key deposit. Weekly rate: $44. Meals available in several places within a six-block radius; the Mississippi River is close by.

Newton

Accommodation: Thrifty Scot Motel, 1605 West 19th St. S., P.O. Box 1031, 50208. Telephone: 515/792-2330. $22.90 to $29.90 for one; $26.90 to $34.90 for two.

Oskaloosa

Accommodation: Friendship Mahaska Motel, 1315 A Ave. E., 52577. Telephone: 515/673-8351. $25 for one; $30 for two in one bed; $35 for two in two beds.

Ottumwa

Accommodation: Comfort Inn, √ &, 125 West Joseph Ave., 52501. Telephone: 515/682-8526. $26 to $28 for one; $30 to $32 for two.

Sioux City

Help: AID Center, YMCA Building, 206 6th St., 51101. Telephone: 712/252-1861.

Accommodations: Sioux City YMCA (AYH-SA), 722 Nebraska St., 51101. Telephone: 712/252-3276. Men only. $4.50 for AYH members; $11 single for nonmembers.

● Motel 6, 6166 Harbor Dr., c/o General Delivery, Sergeant Bluff, 51054. Telephone: 712/277-2620. See Cedar Falls listing for rates.

Spirit Lake

Accommodation: Friendship Shamrock Inn, Hwys. 9 & 71 W., 51360. Telephone: 712/336-2668. $21 to $27 for one; $28 to $31 for two in one bed; $35 to $40 for two in two beds.

Villisca

Help: Villisca Emergency, 712/826-2222.

Accommodation: Camp Aldersgate, &, Rte. 1, 50864. Telephone: 712/826-8121. Men, women and children. $6 first night, $5 each succeeding night for multi-bedded rooms in a lodge or lodge annex. Bring a sleeping bag. Cooking facilities available. There's a state-owned lake across the road.

Walnut

Accommodation: Colonial Motor Inn, Exit 46 S. off I-80, 51577. Telephone: 712/784-2233. $21 to $23 for one; $23 for two in one bed; $30 for two in two beds.

Waterloo

Accommodations: YWCA, 425 Lafayette, 50703. Telephone: 319/234-7589. Women only. Weekly rate: $22.50. Advance reservations of two weeks necessary.
● Exel Inn, 3350 University Ave., 50701. Telephone: 319/235-2165. $24.95 for one; $29.95 for two in one bed; $31.95 for two in two beds.

Williams

Accommodation: Boondocks USA Motel, I-35 & U.S. 20, Exit 144, 50271. Telephone: 515/854-2201. $19.95 for one; $24.95 for two.

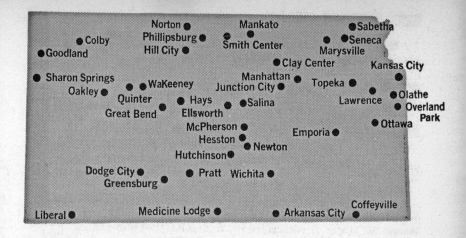

Kansas

Capitalizing on the ever-popular movie *The Wizard of Oz,* in which the heroine, Dorothy, comes from Kansas, Kansas calls itself the "Land of Ah's." There's even a replica of Dorothy's house, the yellow brick road, and all in the town of Liberal.

Kansas is the geographic center of the U.S. and the breadbasket of the world. When Dwight Eisenhower told a European audience "I come from the heart of America," he was referring to Abilene, Kansas, the town where he grew up. The Eisenhower family home is preserved and the Eisenhower library and museum were opened in 1962.

Many historic trails crossed through early Kansas—you can almost hear the wagonmaster's cry of "Wagons Ho!" in parts of the Chisholm Trail, along which Indian trader Jesse Chisholm drove his cattle on the way from Texas to Abilene; Lewis and Clark's route, which follows the Missouri River along the northeastern boundary of the state; the Oregon Trail, which was so heavily traveled in the years after 1848 by people heading for California gold; the Santa Fe Trail, which was used as a trade route with Mexico; and the Smoky Hill Trail, which was the quickest way to the Denver goldfields, discovered in 1859. There's an organization that operates one-day covered-wagon trips through the Scenic Flint Hills. Write to Flint Hills Overland Wagon Train Trips, P.O. Box 1076, El Dorado, KS 67042.

Some Special Events: Messiah Festival in Lindberg (during Easter Week); After Harvest Czech Festival in Wilson, and Mexican Fiesta in Topeka (July); Walnut Valley Bluegrass Festival, Flat-Picking Championship Contest in Winfield, and Renaissance Festival in Bonner Springs (September); Neewollah Celebration in Independence, Svensk Hyllnings Fest in Lindsborg, the Bibliesta in Humboldt, and Maple Leaf Festival in Baldwin City (all in October). Write to the Department of Economic Development for a *Calendar of Events.*

Hitching: The State Police say that it is legal to hitchhike on any road in Kansas except the Interstate system and the Kansas Turnpike. They advise that you "carry plenty of identification and enough money to sustain yourself." It seems to be an accepted means of transportation, for students especially. The Highway Patrol says that the federal and state highways are well traveled and should provide opportunities for rides. Someone from Kansas State University says to go ahead and hitchhike but "be wary of police and weird people." Sound enough advice.

Tourist Information: Travel and Tourism Division, Kansas Department of Economic Development, 503 Kansas, 6th Floor, Topeka, KS 66603. Telephone: 913/296-2009. The Department operates information centers in Topeka and on I-70 in Kansas City.

N.B. Kansas City Bed and Breakfast is a reservations service, with accommodations in Kansas City, Leawood, Lenexa, Merriam, Overland Park, Prairie Village, and Modoc. For details, write to them at P.O. Box 14781, Lenexa, KS 66215 or call 913/268-4214.

Arkansas City

Accommodation: Econo Lodge, √, 3232 North Summit, 67005. Telephone: 316/442-7700. $28.95 for one; $32.95 for two in one bed; $36.95 for two in two beds.

Clay Center

Accommodation: Budget Host—Cedar Court Motel, √ ($1), 9th & Hwy. 24, 67432. Telephone: 913/632-2148. $18 to $24 for one; $22 to $28 for two in one bed; $26 to $32 for two in two beds.

Coffeyville

Accommodation: Budget Host—Townsman Motel, 600 Northeast St., 67337. Telephone: 316/251-2010. Courtesy car available. $24 for one; $27 for two in one bed; $31 for two in two beds.

Colby

Accommodation: Budget Host—Country Club Motel, 460 Country Club, 66701. Telephone: 913/462-7568. Transportation to airport available. $17.88 for one; $19.88 to $22.88 for two in one bed; $22.88 to $24.88 for two in two beds.

Dodge City

Accommodation: Budget Host—Thunderbird Motel, 2300 West Wyatt Earp Blvd., 62801. Telephone: 316/225-4143. $21 for one; $22 to $28 for two in one bed; $28 to $34 for two in two beds. Heated pool.

Ellsworth

Accommodation: Budget Inn—Garden Motel, √ ($2), Jct. Hwys. 156 & 140, Box 44, 67439. Telephone: 913/472-3116. $24 to $27 for one; $27 to $30 for two in one bed; $31 to $34 for two in two beds.

Emporia

Accommodations: TraveLodge, √ (15%), 3021 West Hwy. 50, 66801. Telephone: 316/342-3770. Airport transportation available. $30 for one; $34 for two in one bed; $37 for two in two beds.
- Econo Lodge, √ &, 2630 West 18th Ave., 66801. Telephone: 316/343-1240. $24.95 for one; $28.95 for two in one bed; $30.95 for two in two beds.

Goodland

Accommodation: Motel 6, I-70 & Hwy. 27, Rte. 1, Box 96E, 67735. Telephone: 913/899-6466. $17.95 for one; $21.95 for two; $2 for each additional person.

Great Bend

Accommodations: Budget Host—Highland Lodge, & √ (10%), 5220 West 10th, 67530. Telephone: 316/792-1731. $27 for one; $31 for two in one bed; $35 for two in two beds.
- Econo Lodge, √ &, 4701 10th St., 67530. Telephone: 316/792-8235. $22.95 for one; $26.95 for two in one bed; $29.95 for two in two beds. Higher rates apply during special events.

Greensburg

Accommodation: Kansan Inn, √, 800 East Kansas Ave., 67054. Telephone: 316/723-2141. $19.75 to $23.75 for one; $27.75 for two in one bed; $29.95 for two in two beds.

Hays

Accommodations: Friendship Inn Fort Hays Motel, 527 East 8th St., 67601. Telephone: 913/625-2581. Limited airport service available. $18 to $22 for one; $22 to $26 for two in one bed; $26 to $30 for two in two beds.
- Motel 6, 3404 Vine St., 67601. Telephone: 913/628-1037. See Goodland listing for rates.
- Budget Host—Villa Budget Inn, 810 East 8th at Vine, 67601. Telephone: 913/625-2563. Part-time airport transportation available. $19 to $27 for one; $22 to $32 for two in one bed; $25 to $37 for two in two beds.

- Econo Lodge, √ &, Vine & I-70. $26.95 for one; $29.95 for two in one bed; $32.95 for two in two beds.
- Hampton Inn, 3801 Vine St., 67601. Telephone: 913/625-8103. $27 to $32 single.
- Frontier City Best Value Inn, I-70 & U.S. 183 Alt., 67601. Telephone: 913/628-1076. $13.59 for one; $18.45 for two in one bed; $21 for two in two beds.

Hesston

Accommodation: Budget Host—Hesston Heritage Inn, 606 Lincoln Blvd., Box 446, 67062. Telephone: 316/327-4231. $24 to $26 for one; $26 for two in one bed; $28 to $30 for two in two beds. Heated pool.

Hill City

Accommodation: Budget Host—Western Hills Motel, √, 800 West Hwy. 24 (Box 389), 67642. Telephone: 913/674-2141. Courtesy car on request. $22 to $32 for one; $28 to $38 for two in one bed; $38 to $50 for two in two beds.

Hutchinson

Accommodation: Budget Host—Sunset Motel, &, 2605 East 4th St., 67501. Telephone: 316/662-4429. $16 to $18 for one; $18 to $22 for two in one bed; $22 to $28 for two in two beds.

Junction City

Accommodation: Budget Host—Great Western Inn, √ &, 101 Continental (Box 287), 66441. Telephone: 913/238-5147. Limited courtesy car. $19 for one; $26 for two in one bed; $28 for two in two beds.

Kansas City

Accommodations: YMCA, 900 North 8th St., 66101. Telephone: 913/371-4400. Men only. $29.40 single.
- Days Inn, &, 9630 Rosehill Rd., Lenexa, 66215. Telephone: 913/492-7200. $27.88 for one; $31.88 for two.
- Red Roof Inn, &, 6800 West 108th St., Shawnee Mission, 66211. Telephone: 913/341-0100. $24.95 for one; $29.95 for two in one bed; $31.95 for two in two beds; $33.95 for three or four in two beds.
- Motel 6, 9725 Lenexa Dr., Lenexa, 66215. Telephone: 913/541-1266. See Goodland listing for rates.

Lawrence

On Campus: The University of Kansas is in Lawrence and the Union is a good place to meet U of K students. At night the scene switches to the minibars and restaurants on Massachusetts, the town's main street. You'll find Bogart's Rock Chalk Cafe, Harry Bear's, Boshombers, and The Wheel, among others. However, Kansas is "a dry state except for 3.2 beer. The real bars have to be private clubs." When hunger strikes, there's the Tin Pan Alley, where you can get sandwiches and salads, or La Tropicana, serving Mexican food. There is also an American Indian Junior College in Lawrence-Haskell.

Help: KU Information Center, 403 Kansas Union, 66045. Telephone: 913/864-3506. Open 24 hours. "We'll help with questions about directions, where to eat, what to do, etc. . . . The country around Lawrence is beautiful with a number of small and large lakes for swimming and fishing. The Information Center is here to tell you what is happening."

Help and Emergency Accommodation: Headquarters, Inc., 1419 Massachusetts, 66044. Telephone: 913/841-2345. Headquarters is a crisis-intervention center with volunteers who can help if you're going through a bad time and will tell you who else can help. Open 24 hours daily. In emergencies there's a bedroom that accommodates five people per night. There is a one-night limit and one hour's worth of housework is required as payment.

Accommodation: Econo Lodge, 2907 West 6th St., 66044. Telephone: 913/843-6611. $25.95 for one; $26.95 to $28.95 for two in one bed; $29.95 to $31.95 for two in two beds. Higher rates apply during special events.

Liberal

Accommodations: Spur Motel, √, 101 East Pancake Blvd., 67901. Telephone: 316/624-6231. $19.95 single; $24 double.

● Western-Ho Motel, √, U.S. 54 E., P.O. Box W, 67901. Telephone: 316/624-1921. $20 to $23 for one; $23 to $25 for two in one bed; $25 to $27 for two in two beds.

● Friendship Inn Ranch Motel, 304 U.S. 54 E., 67901. Telephone: 316/624-3897. Limited airport service available. $16 to $18 for one; $19 to $20 for two in one bed; $23 to $24 for two in two beds.

● Budget Host—Thunderbird Inn, 21 West 21st St. (Box 1511), 67901. Telephone: 316/624-7271. Courtesy car available. $20.88 for one; $23.88 for two in one bed; $26.88 for two in two beds.

● TraveLodge, √ (15%), 564 East Pancake Blvd., 67901. Telephone: 316/624-6203. $26 for one; $29 for two in one bed; $35 for two in two beds.

Manhattan

Tourist Information: Chamber of Commerce, 505 Poyntz, 66502. Telephone: 913/776-8829.

On Campus: A friend at Kansas State University says that Manhattan has a lot to offer, for being "stuck out in the middle of Kansas." Since it's the home of the Kansas State University Wildcats, the students have one of the biggest and best student unions around, the K-State Union. KSU also has an International Student Center to accommodate foreign visitors. The main hangout is Aggieville, a section right off campus. It's been said that if you put a roof over Aggieville, you'd have the biggest bar in the country. Since Kansas State is a state institution there are restrictions on alcoholic beverages allowed on campus, so you'll find the action either in Aggieville or at Tuttle Creek Reservoir when the weather's nice (there's camping there, too). The University Master Calendar, located in the Reservations Office, second floor of the K-State Union, is the place to find out what's going on—call 532-6591.

Manhattan has all the typical hamburger, taco, and fried-chicken places you'd expect, but for good down-home cooking try the Chef at 111 South 4th or Last Chance Restaurant and Saloon at 1215 Moro in Aggieville.

For rides out of town, there's a ride board on the second-floor concourse in the K-State Union that really works.

Accommodation: Motel 6, 510 Tuttle Creek Blvd., 66502. Telephone: 913/776-4033. See Goodland listing for rates.

Mankato

Accommodation: Dreamliner Motel, Rte. 1, Box 95, 66956. Telephone: 913/378-3107. $22 for one; $24 for two in one bed; $28 for two in two beds.

Marysville

Accommodation: Friendship Inn Thunderbird Motel, U.S. 36 W., 66508. Telephone: 913/562-2373. $25.75 for one; $32.70 for two in one bed; $33.75 for two in two beds.

McPherson

Accommodation: Budget Host—Wheat State Motel, ✓, 111 Roosevelt (Box 374), 67460. Telephone: 316/241-4230. $18 to $20 for one; $20 to $22 for two in one bed; $25 to $28 for two in two beds.

Medicine Lodge

Accommodation: Budget Host—Rancho Motel, ✓ &, 500 Black Gold, 67104. Telephone: 313/886-3453. $18 to $24 for one; $20 to $27 for two in one bed; $22 to $30 for two in two beds.

Newton

Accommodation: Econo Inn, ✓, 105 Manchester, 67114. Telephone: 316/283-6500. $20 for one; $25 for two in one bed; $30 for two in two beds.

Norton

Accommodation: Budget Host—Hillcrest Motel, West Hwy. 36 (Box 249), 67654. Telephone: 913/877-3343. Transportation to airport and bus station. $21 to $22 for one; $26 to $27 for two in one bed; $29 for two in two beds.

Oakley

Accommodations: Budget Inn—Country Club Motel, 709 Center, 67748. Telephone: 913/672-8894. Transport to airport available. $17.88 for one; $19.88 to $22.88 for two in one bed; $22.88 to $24.88 for two in two beds.
• TraveLodge, √ (15%), 708 North Center Ave., 67748. Telephone: 913/672-3226. $30 for one; $36 for two in one bed; $40 for two in two beds.

Olathe

Accommodation: Econo Lodge, √, 209 Flaming Rd., 66061. Telephone: 913/829-1312. $27.95 for one; $31.95 for two in one bed; $33.95 for two in two beds.

Ottawa

Accommodation: Friendship Inn Royal Manor, 1641 South Main St., 66067. Telephone: 913/242-4842. $17 to $21 for one; $20 to $24 for two in one bed; $22 to $26 for two in two beds.

Overland Park

Accommodation: Budget Host—Mission Inn Motel, √ &, 7508 West 63rd (Box 33), Mission, 66202. Telephone: 913/262-9600. $26 for one; $29.50 to $30.50 for two in one bed; $31.50 for two in two beds. Heated pool. Free use of washer and dryer.

Phillipsburg

Accommodation: Friendship Inn Silver Saddle Motel, Hwys. 36 & 183 E., 67661. Telephone: 913/543-2125. $18 to $25 for one; $22 to $30 for two in one bed; $26 to $36 for two in two beds.

Pratt

Accommodation: Friendship Catalina Motel, 1401 East 1st St., 67124. Telephone: 316/672-5588. $18 to $21 for one; $21 to $25 for two in one bed; $25 to $29 for two in two beds.

Quinter

Accommodation: Budget Host—Q Motel, I-70 Hwy. 212, 67752. Telephone: 913/754-3337. $23 for one; $27 for two in one bed; $30 for two in two beds.

Sabetha

Accommodation: Budget Host—Koch Motel, U.S. Hwy. 75 (Box 235), 66534. Telephone: 913/284-2145. $17 to $24 for one; $22 to $32 for two in one bed; $28 to $35 for two in two beds.

Salina

Accommodations: Budget Host—Vagabond Inn, 217 South Broadway, 67401. Telephone: 913/825-7265. $18 to $28 for one; $22 to $34 for two in one bed; $30 to $36 for two in two beds.
● TraveLodge, √ (15%), 245 South Broadway, 67401. Telephone: 913/827-9351. $27 for one; $34 for two in one bed; $36 for two in two beds.
● Tradewinds Motel, 1646 North 9th St., 67401. Telephone: 913/827-0371. $26 for one; $28 for two in one bed; $31 for three; $34 for four.

Seneca

Accommodations: Friendship Starlite Motel, Hwy. 36, between 4th & 5th Sts., 66538. Telephone: 913/336-2191. $17 to $18.50 for one; $18.50 for two in one bed; $24 to $28 for two in two beds.
● Budget Host—Seneca Motel, √, 1106 North St., 66538. Telephone: 913/336-2197. $18 for one; $20 for two in one bed; $23 for two in two beds.

Sharon Springs

Accommodation: Friendship Inn Traveler Motel, intersection of U.S. 40 & Kans. 27, 67758. Telephone: 913/852-4293. $16.48 for one; $18.54 for two in one bed; $20.60 for two in two beds.

Smith Center

Accommodations: Friendship Inn U.S. Center Motel, 116 East Hwy. 36, 66967. Telephone: 913/282-6611. Limited airport service available. $18 to $21 for one; $21 to $23 for two in one bed; $24 to $27 for two in two beds.
● Budget Host—Modern Aire Motel, √, 117 West Hwy. 36, Rte. 2 (Box 34B), 66967. Telephone: 913/282-6644. $20 to $24 for one; $22 to $26 for two in one bed; $26 to $30 for two in two beds.

Topeka

Accommodations: Motel 6, 3846 South Topeka Ave., 66609. Telephone: 913/267-3800. See Goodland listing for rates.

● Motel 6, 709 Fairlawn Rd., 66606. Telephone: 913/273-6582. See Goodland listing for rates.

WaKeeney

Accommodation: Friendship Inn Sundowner Lodge, I-70 & Hwy. 283, 67672. Telephone: 913/743-2129. $20 to $25 for one; $25 to $30 for two in one bed; $35 to $40 for two in two beds.

Wichita

Tourist Information: Wichita Convention and Visitors Bureau, 111 West Douglas, Suite 804, 67202. Telephone: 316/265-2800.

Accommodations: Motel 6, 5736 West Kellogg, 67209. Telephone: 316/945-9452. See Goodland listing for rates.

● Budget Host—English Village Motor Lodge, 🦽, 6727 East Kellogg, 67207. Telephone: 316/683-5613. $28 to $34 for one; $31 to $38 for two in one bed; $33 to $38 for two in two beds.

Kentucky

The theme is horses. They take them very seriously in Kentucky, from the breeding to the racing. If you're planning to go to the Kentucky Derby in May this year, be sure to check to see if there's room at the Derby Hostel at the University of Louisville.

Some of the major attractions in Kentucky are: in the north-central part of the state, the Abraham Lincoln Birthplace, Stephen Foster's "Old Kentucky Home" in Bardstown, Churchill Downs, and several famous horse farms; in eastern Kentucky, Cumberland Gap, Daniel Boone National Forest, and Black Mountain; in western Kentucky, Kentucky Lake, Lake Barkley, and 170,000-acre Land Between the Lakes; and in the south-central part of the state, Mammoth Cave National Park and Lake Cumberland—which lead the list of things to see.

Kentucky's State Park system includes 15 resort parks with both lodge and camping facilities. Some also have cottages and houseboat rentals. Information on the parks and their facilities is available in a brochure distributed by *Travel*, Frankfort, KY 40601. Rate information is available by calling toll free 800/255-PARK, or by writing to the Kentucky Department of Parks, Capital Plaza Tower, Frankfort, KY 40601.

For more about the state and its outdoors, consider the following publications:

A Guide to Kentucky Outdoors, by Arthur B. Lander, Jr., Menasha Ridge Press, Route 3, Box 450, Hillsboro, NC 27278 ($9.95).

A Guide to Backpacking and Day-Hiking Trails of Kentucky, by Arthur B. Lander, Jr., Menasha Ridge Press ($10.95).

A Canoeing and Kayaking Guide to the Streams of Kentucky, by Bob Sehlinger, Menasha Ridge Press ($12.95).

A free booklet, *The Kentucky Travel Guide,* is available from the Department of Travel Development (address below), and the *Guide to Trails and Natural Areas,* which lists trails and areas for backpacking, day hiking, bikeways, equestrian trails, and canoe routes, is available from the State Naturalist, Kentucky Department of Parks (address above).

According to the Kentucky Department of Travel Development, "Natural Bridge State Resort Park and the Red River Gorge are a fantastic draw among young people. They flock there for the beauty and solitude, camping and canoeing."

Some Special Events: Kentucky Derby Festival in Louisville (end of April and beginning of May); Capital Expo in Frankfort, and Heritage Weekend in Louisville (June); Shaker Festival in South Union (July); International Banana Festival (featuring a one-ton banana pudding) in Fulton (August); McClain Family Band Festival in Berea, Great American Dulcimer Convention in Pineville (September).

Hitching: Officially, no one may hitchhike from the roadway.

Tourist Information: Department of Travel Development, Capital Plaza Tower, Frankfort, KY 40601.

Bardstown

Accommodation: Scottish Inn, 523 North 3rd St., 40004. Telephone: 502/348-3073. July 1 to September 9: $26 for one or two in one bed; $30 to $35 for two in two beds. September 3 to December 31: $22 for one or two in one bed; $26 to $28 for two in two beds.

Benton

Accommodation: Friendship Inn Shamrock Motel, 806 Main, 42025. Telephone: 502/527-1341. $20 for one; $24 for two in one bed; $26 for two in two beds.

Berea

Accommodation: Econo Lodge, I-75 & Ky. 21, P.O. Box 183, 40403. Telephone: 606/986-9323. $28 for one; $28 for two in one or two beds; $30 for two in two beds. Higher rates apply during special events and holidays.

Bowling Green

On Campus: A friend at Western Kentucky University told us that his campus is not really used to transients, but that if you want to help them get more used to them you should probably head for the Downing Center on campus. He says there are good camping areas—it costs only $7.50 to get a campsite at Beech Bend Park. For good eating he recommends a popular truck stop on the Bypass called Mary's Restaurant. Two popular local bars are the Brass A and the General Store.

Accommodations: Motel 6, 3139 Scottsville Rd., 42101. Telephone: 502/781-6010. $17.95 for one; $21.95 for two; $2 for each additional person.

● Days Inn, 181 Cumberland Trail, 42101. Telephone: 502/781-6330. $26.88 to $28.88 for one; $31.88 to $35.88 for two.

● Econo Lodge, √, I-65 & Hwy. 31 W., Rte. 14, Box 61, 42101. Telephone: 502/781-6181. $22.95 for one; $26.95 for two in one bed; $30.95 for two in two beds.

- Scottish Inn, 3140 Scottsville Rd., 42101. Telephone: 502/781-6550. $25 for one; $28 for two in one or two beds.
- Friendship New's Inn, U.S. 231 & I-65, Exit 22, 42101. Telephone: 502/781-3460. $24 to $26 for one; $26 to $32 for two.
- TraveLodge, 🚹, 409 U.S. 31 West Bypass, 42101. Telephone: 502/843-3264. Airport transportation available. $27 for one; $31 for two in one bed; $36 for two in two beds.

Cave City

Accommodation: Quality Inn, √, I-65 at Exit 53, 42127. $19 to $26 for one; $27 to $39 for two. Rates vary with season.

Central City

Accommodation: Rambler Rose Motel, Hwys. 62 & 431 & West Kentucky Pkwy., 42330. Telephone: 502/754-2441. $18.95 for one; $20.95 for two in one bed; $24.95 for two in two beds.

Corbin

Accommodations: Days Inn, Cumberland Falls Rd., 40701. Telephone: 606/528-8150. $25.88 to $27.88 for one; $29.88 to $31.88 for two.
- Scottish Inn/Town House, 804 South Main St., 40701. Telephone: 606/528-3434. $15.95 for one; $20.95 for two in one bed; $24.95 for two in two beds.

Elizabethtown

Accommodations: Days Inn, 🚹, I-65 & U.S. 62 (Exit 94), P.O. Box 903, 42701. Telephone: 502/769-5522. $25.88 to $27.88 for one; $29.88 to $32.88 for two.
- Friendship Cloverleaf Inn, jct. I-65 & 31 W., 42701. Telephone: 502/765-2194. $17 to $20 for one; $20 to $28 for two in one bed; $22 to $32 for two in two beds.
- Motel 6, U.S. Hwy. 62 & I-65, 42701. Telephone: 502/769-3376. See Bowling Green listing for rates.

Florence

Accommodation: Scottish Inn, √, 7470 Woodspoint Dr., 41042. Telephone: 606/371-4860. $25 for one; $30 to $35 for two.

Frankfort

Accommodations: Days Inn, I-64 & U.S. 127 S., 40601. Telephone: 502/875-2200. $29 for one; $34 for two.
- TraveLodge, √🚹, 711 East Main St., 40601. Telephone: 502/223-2041. $29 for one; $31 for two in one bed; $36 for two in two beds.

Georgetown

Accommodations: Flag Inn, I-75 & U.S. 460, 40324. Telephone: 502/863-0713. $19.95 for one; $24.95 for two in one bed; $26.95 for two in two beds.
- Days Inn, I-75 & Delaplain Rd. (Exit 129), 40324. Telephone: 502/863-5000. $27 to $32.88 for one; $30 to $37 for two.

Horse Cave

Accommodation: Scottish Inn, √, I-65 Exit 58, S.R. 218, 42749. Telephone: 502/786-2165. July 1 to September 2: $19 to $28 for one; $25 to $35 for two in one bed; $28 to $40 for two in two beds. September 3 to December 31: $14 to $22 for one; $19 to $28 for two in one bed; $25 to $35 for two in two beds.

Lexington

"The place to visit if you are interested in horses or bluegrass."

On Campus: Visiting students can call Student Housing (tel. 257-3721) to rent a room for $20 a night. Favorite eating places near campus are High on Rose, a crowded bar with beer and Mexican food; Alfalfa, a mostly vegetarian restaurant; Joe Bologna, for pizza and Italian food; Jefferson Davis Inn, corner of Limestone and High St., Two Keys Tavern, Limestone St., and Charlie Brown's on Euclid Ave.
Accommodations: YMCA, 239 East High St., 40507. Telephone: 606/255-5651. Men only. $11 per night. Weekly rate: $60.
- Red Roof Inn, ♿, 483 Haggard Lane, 40505. Telephone: 606/293-2626. $25.95 for one; $30.95 for two in one bed; $32.95 for two in two beds; $34.95 for three or four in two beds.
- Days Inn, ♿, 1675 North Broadway, 40505. Telephone: 606/293-1421. $30.88 to $33.88 for one; $32.88 to $36.88 for two.

Louisville

Tourist Information: Louisville Visitors Bureau, Founders Square, 40202. Telephone: 502/582-3732. The people here told us that bus fares in Louisville go up from 35¢ to 60¢ during rush hours, so plan accordingly.
Help: Family and Children's Agency, Travelers Aid Service, P.O. Box 3775, 40201. Telephone: 502/584-8186.
- Crisis and Information Center, 502/589-4313.
On Campus: The University of Louisville's International Center can help foreign visitors find their way around. Telephone: 502/588-6602 to find out how to get to the center. To meet students, stop at the Butchertown Pub, 1335 Story Ave.; Bristol Bar and Grill, 1321 Bardstown Rd.; City Lights, 117 West Main; or Cardinal's Nest, and Red Barn restaurants in the student center. The people at the university's Red Barn run a hostel during Derby Weekend. For information, call 502/588-6691. For discounts in the area, contact the Student Government Association (tel. 588-6695).

Accommodations: Kentucky Derby Student Hostel, 2011 South Brook St., 40292. Telephone: 502/588-6691. "A tent city located in a secure area of campus offering indoor showers, continental breakfasts, and parking areas." Open Thursday through Sunday afternoon of Derby Weekend. Advance reservations suggested. $6 per night.
- Days Inn, ✓, I-65 & N. Hamburg Exit 7, Sellersburg, IN 47172. Telephone: 812/246-4451. $27 for one; $35 for two.
- Days Inn, 350 Eastern Blvd., Jeffersonville, 47130. Telephone: 502/288-9331. $26 to $28 for one; $32 to $34 for two.
- Days Inn, I-71 & Ky. 53, LaGrange, 40031. Telephone: 502/222-7192. $28 to $30 for one; $33 to $35 for two.
- Days Inn, I-65 & Ky. 44, 40165. Telephone: 502/543-3011. $27 to $29 for one; $32 to $34 for two.
- Motel 6, 3304 Bardstown Rd., 40218. Telephone: 502/458-3201. See Bowling Green listing for rates.
- Red Roof Inn, &, 9330 Blairwood Rd., 40222. Telephone: 502/426-7621. See Lexington listing for rates.
- Continental Inns of America, &, 1620 Arthur St., 40217. Telephone: 502/636-3781. $22 to $24 for one; $25 to $27 for two in one bed; $35 for two in two beds.
- Red Carpet Inn, ✓, 9512 Hurstbourne Lane, 40220. Telephone: 502/491-7320. $23.88 to $27.88 for one; $26.88 to $30.88 for two in one bed; $34.88 to $36.88 for two in two beds.

Madisonville

Accommodations: Econo Lodge, ✓, 1117 East Center St., P.O. Box 187, 42431. Telephone: 502/821-0364. $21.95 for one; $24.95 for two in one bed; $27.95 for two in two beds.
- Red Carpet Inn, ✓ &, U.S. Hwy. 41 N., P.O. Box 470, 42431. Telephone: 502/821-7677. $21.95 for one; $24.95 for two in one bed; $28.95 for two in two beds.

Mammoth Cave

Camping and Accommodation: Mammoth Cave National Park, 42259. There's camping at headquarters ($6 per campsite per night) and at Houchin's Ferry (no fee) all year.
- Mammoth Cave Hotel, &, Mammoth Cave National Park, 42259. Telephone: 502/758-2225. $28 to $35 single; $34 to $42 double; $40 to $49 triple; $45 to $55 quad. Hotel and cottages available. Advance reservations of two weeks necessary.

Middlesboro

Camping: Cumberland Gap National Historical Park, ✓, P.O. Box 1848, 40965. Telephone: 606/248-2817. 160 developed campsites; four backcountry campsites accessible by hiking. $5 per campsite per night.

Mount Sterling

Accommodation: Days Inn, √ &, I-64 & U.S. 460, Ragland Ave., 40353. Telephone: 606/498-4680. $24 to $26 for one; $28 to $30 for two.

Owensboro

Accommodations: Motel 6, 4585 Frederica St., 42301. Telephone: 502/684-9636. See Bowling Green listing for rates.
● Days Inn, &, U.S. 231 & 60 Bypass, P.O. Box 1707, 42301. Telephone: 502/684-9621. $26 for one; $30 for two.

Paducah

Accommodations: Regal 8 Inn, 2150 South Beltline, 42001. Telephone: 502/442-6171. $21.88 for one; $26.88 for two in one bed; $31.88 for two to four in two beds.
● Days Inn, &, I-24 & U.S. 60 W., 42001. Telephone: 502/442-7501. $28.88 for one; $34.88 for two.

Pippa Passes

Accommodation: Pippa Passes Home Hostel (AYH), c/o Ed and Charlotte Madden, P.O. Box 15, 41844. Telephone: 606/368-2753. $4.25 for AYH members.

Richmond

Accommodation: Days Inn, I-75 & U.S. 421, Exit South 90-A, North 90, 40475. Telephone: 606/623-0880. $30 for one; $35 for two.

Russell

Accommodation: YMCA, Mulberry St., 41169. Telephone: 606/836-6344. Men only. $10. Weekly rate: $38.

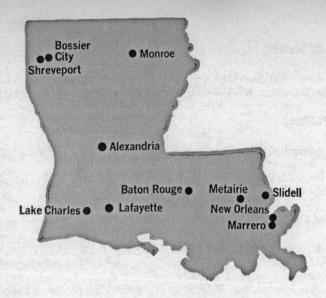

Louisiana

The big attraction is New Orleans with its Vieux Carré, Preservation Hall Jazz, and two weeks of Mardi Gras celebration that fall 47 days before Easter. It's a shame that most travelers making the typical cross-country trips never make it as far south as Louisiana—a detour might be worth considering.

Although New Orleans is probably the reason you'll be coming to Louisiana, there is more to see if you have the time. (See the New Orleans section, page 239.) To get a feeling for the state's past there are two historical sites, each about three hours from New Orleans, that deserve a visit. The first, the Acadian House Museum in St. Martinville, in the very heart of Cajun country, displays artifacts of the early French period of the area. Some say that this home may have once belonged to Louis Arcenaux, the model for Longfellow's Gabriel in his poem "Evangeline." The Acadians, or Cajuns, still keep their distinct subculture alive and well in the 20th century. The second is the Rosedown Plantation and Gardens, a restoration of an 1835 mansion that is lavishly furnished and surrounded by fabulous formal gardens designed in the 17th-century French manner; a tour of the house is available.

On the River Roads, on both sides of the Mississippi River between New Orleans and Baton Rouge, are several other plantations that also capture the flavor of Louisiana's past. They are San Francisco, Destrehan, and Houmas House on the east bank, and Oak Alley and Nottoway on the west. All are open to the public for a fee of from $3 to $4 and some have restaurant facilities.

Two books recommended by the Office of Tourism for those interested in Louisiana are *Louisiana,* by Joe Gray Taylor, W.W. Norton ($8.95) for a history of the state, and *The Pelican Guide to Plantation Homes of Louisiana,* by Nancy Harris Calhoun and James Calhoun, Pelican ($3.95). The Louisiana Office of Tourism (address below) offers a guidebook and highway map free of charge to travelers.

Some Special Events: New Orleans Jazz and Heritage Festival, and the Tomato Festival in Chalmette (May); Jumbalga Festival in Gonzales, and Louisiana Peach Festival in Ruston (June); New Orleans Food Festival, and Cajun Festival in Montegut (July); Seafood Festival in Lafitte (August); and the North Louisiana Cotton Festival and Fair in Bastrop (September).

Hitchhiking: Officially, as in most states, Louisiana law prohibits standing on the "roadway" for the purpose of soliciting a ride. The attitude toward hitching is improving, according to one friend, and students traveling near a campus are the most likely to get rides. It may mean a long wait in some areas, though. The Department of Public Safety adds that if you do hitchhike you should carry proper identification, but it warns of the dangers of hitching.

Tourist Information: Louisiana Office of Tourism, P.O. Box 44291, Baton Rouge, LA, 70804. Telephone: 504/925-3860; out of state, toll free: 800/231-4730.

N.B. New Orleans Bed & Breakfast is a reservations service listing homes in all areas of New Orleans and through Louisiana and Mississippi and can accommodate "one or a bunch." Rates run from $20 to $100 single. For information, write to them at P.O. Box 8163, New Orleans, LA 70182.

Alexandria

Tourist Information: Alexandria-Pineville Tourist Center, 110 Bolton Ave., 71309. Telephone: 318/442-6671.

Accommodation: Friendship Alexandria Inn, 1212 MacArthur Dr., 71301. Telephone: 318/473-2302. $25 to $30 for one or two in one bed; $29 to $32 for two in two beds.

Baton Rouge

Tourist Information: Baton Rouge Area Convention and Visitors Bureau, 275 South River Rd., 70801. Telephone: 504/383-1825.

On Campus: You may be able to spend a night or two on campus in Pleasant Hall, but first you must obtain special permission from the International Student Office at Louisiana State University.

If you go to Murphy's or the Bengal you'll be able to meet LSU students. They suggest Dragon Hall Cafeteria, 161 West State St., for inexpensive Chinese food, and Round-the-Corner, 3347 Highland.

There is a bulletin board located in the Union near "Tiger Lair" cafeteria, and you might be able to find helpful information in the Student Government Office, 327 Union.

Accommodations: Friendship Shades Inn, 8282 Airline Hwy., 70815. Telephone: 504/925-2401. $21.60 to $22.68 for one; $23.76 to $24.84 for two in one bed; $25.92 to $27 for two in two beds.

● Motel 6, 2800 I-10 Frontage Rd., Port Allen, 70767. $17.95 for one; $21.95 for two in one bed; $2 for each additional person.

● Regal 8 Inn, 9901 Gwen Adele, 70816. Telephone: 504/924-2130. $23.88 for one; $28.88 for two in one bed; $33.88 for two in two beds.

- Days Inn, 215 Lobdell Hwy., Port Allen, 70767. Telephone: 504/387-0671. $30 to $35 for one; $32 to $38 for two.
- Days Inn, 10245 Airline Hwy., 70815. Telephone: 504/293-9680. $30 to $35 for one; $32 to $38 for two.
- Red Carpet Inn, √, 2445 South Acadian Thruway, 70808. Telephone: 504/925-8141. $28 for one; $32 for two to four in two beds.
- Scottish Inn, √, 2142 West Hwy. 30, 70737. Telephone: 504/647-8787. $26 for one; $30 for two in one bed; $36 for two in two beds.

Bossier City

Accommodation: Motel 6, 210 John Wesley Blvd., 71112. Telephone: 318/742-6023. See Baton Rouge listing for rates.

Lafayette

Tourist Information: Lafayette Parish Convention and Visitors Commission, P.O. Box 52066, 70505. Telephone: 318/232-3737.

On Campus: Lafayette, the capital of Acadiana and the home of the University of Southwestern Louisiana, is one of the fastest-growing cities in the South. The multiple festivals in Acadiana—Music Festival, Crawfish Festival, Boudin Festival, La Grande Boucherie, Mardi Gras, Bayou Food Festival— depict the joie de vivre of the French-speaking Cajun people expressed in music and food. The joy and gentleness of the people are captivating.

For inexpensive seafood, there's Pat's in Henderson or Don's in Lafayette. To be with the young people of the area, you can go to The Key, Bonnie and Clyde's, Poet's, or Esprit.

Accommodations: Imperial 400 Motor Inn, 410 West Vermilion, 70501. Telephone: 318/235-9051. $23 to $27 for one; $26 to $30 for two in one bed; $28 to $32 for two in two beds.

- Motel 6, U.S. Hwy. 167 & Pont de Mouton, Lafayette, 70507. Telephone: 318/233-5222. See Baton Rouge listing for rates.
- Friendship Lafayette, √ (10%), 707 Frontage Rd., 70501. Telephone: 318/235-4591. $25 to $28 for one; $28 to $32 for two in one bed; $32 to $34 for two in two beds.
- Starlite Motor Inn, 711 Frontage Rd., 70501. Telephone: 318/232-0070. $26.98 for one or two people; $32.43 for three.
- Econo Lodge, √ &, I-10 & North University, P.O. Box 3783, 70502. Telephone: 318/232-6131. $28.95 for one; $33.95 for two in one bed; $37.95 for two in two beds.

Lake Charles

Accommodations: Friendship Lakeview Inn, 1000 North Shore Pkwy., 70601. Telephone: 318/436-3336. $25 to $26 for one; $26 to $30 for two in one bed; $30 to $36 for two in two beds.

- Motel 6, 335 Hwy. 71, 70601. Telephone: 318/491-9464. See Baton Rouge listing for rates.

● Imperial 400 Motor Inn, 825 Broad St., 70601. Telephone: 318/436-4311. $22 to $26 for one; $26 to $30 for two in one bed; $28 to $32 for two in two beds.

● Econo Lodge, ✓ ♿, 1301 West Prien Lake Rd., 70605. $29 for one; $33 for two in one bed; $35 for two in two beds.

Marrero

Accommodation: Regency Inn, ✓, 6613 West Bank Expressway, 70072. Telephone: 504/347-1502. $16.95 for one; $19.95 for two.

Metairie

Accommodation: Friendship Metairie Inn Motor Lodge, 5733 Airline Hwy., 70003. Limited airport service available. $25 to $35 for one; $30 to $40 for two in one bed; $35 to $45 for two in two beds.

Monroe

Accommodations: Motel 6, 1501 U.S. I-65 Bypass, 71203. See Baton Rouge listing for rates.

● TraveLodge, ✓ ♿, 401 Grammont St., 71201. Telephone: 318/325-0621. $29 for one; $31 for two in one bed; $36 for two in two beds.

● Red Carpet Inn, ✓ ♿, I-20 & Hwy. 137, Box 29, 71269. Telephone: 318/728-7269. $24.95 for one; $29.95 for two in one bed; $33.50 for two in two beds.

New Orleans

Two hundred fifty years of French, Spanish, Italian, West Indian, and finally American influence have made New Orleans the appealing place it is today, probably the most European city in all of North America. Narrow streets, antebellum mansions, oldtime jazz, Créole culture, and the busy Mississippi are all reminiscent of another time, one recalled so well in the books of Mark Twain, William Faulkner, and Tennessee Williams. In spite of the ultracontemporary hotels and the space-age Superdome, much of New Orleans is not new at all. Many old ways are alive and well in this city. Mardi Gras is, of course, New Orleans's big, big event. It always falls on the Tuesday 47 days before Easter. New Orlean's Carnival Parades begin many days before the actual Mardi Gras, on Fat Tuesday.

"During Mardi Gras, the French Quarter is just one long party."

Getting There: New Orleans (Moisant) International Airport is 12 miles west of the central business district and the French Quarter. Cab fares vary: the fare for one person to downtown is $18. Cheaper still is the Orleans Transportation Service's limousine service between the airport and the downtown hotels, which costs $6 per person. Call 464-0611 for reservations. And least expensive of all is the Louisiana Transit Company's express bus service, which will get you from the airport to a terminal on Tulane Ave. (near the Civic Center, downtown) for only 90¢. Call 737-9611 for information. Trailways' bus terminal is at 1314 Tulane Ave. (tel. 525-4201, near downtown), and Greyhound's terminal is at 1001 Loyola Ave. (tel. 525-9371, downtown, same as the train station).

Getting Around: If you need a map of the city, get a free one at the Tourist Commission, 334 rue Royal, in the French Quarter. The city bus system (called RTA) also has an information desk in the French Quarter, at 317 Baronne (tel. 529-4545), where you can pick up a map of bus routes. Bus service is inexpensive (60¢ for regular service) and generally efficient. The trolley line that links the French Quarter with the uptown district of the city is more than just a relic— it's a popular source of public transportation, day and night; at 60¢ there is no better self-guided tour of the city. Several bus companies provide transportation to the outlying parishes. St. Bernard Bus Lines, Inc. (tel. 279-5556) goes to Arabi, Chalmette, and places nearby. Gretna, Harvey, and various suburbs across the river are served by Westside Transit Lines, Inc. (tel. 366-3258). The airport and the surrounding East Jefferson Parish are served by the Louisiana Transit Company (tel. 737-9611). Algiers and communities on the West Bank are connected by a free ferry which leaves from the Canal and Jackson St. docks; the trip takes ten minutes and is especially beautiful at night.

Tourist Information: Greater New Orleans Tourist and Convention Commission, Inc., 334 Royal St., 70130. Telephone: 504/566-5011. Maps, hotel information, and a calendar of events are all here and are free.

Help: Volunteer and Information Agency, 504/524-HELP. "During Mardi Gras, a Mardi Gras coalition is formed to help visitors."

● Travelers Aid, 211 Camp St., Suite 400, 70130. Telephone: 504/525-7131. A United Way agency that can help travelers with almost any kind of problem.

Accommodations in the French Quarter: St. Peter Guest House, ⑤ ★, 1005 St. Peter, 70116. Telephone: 504/524-9232. $30 to $45 for one or two people. "A historic building in the center of the French Quarter with antique and period-furnished rooms, balcony, and courtyard."

● Old World Inn, 1330 Prytania St., 70130. Telephone: 504/566-1330. $27.50 to $37.50 single; $37.50 to $42.50 double. Price includes continental breakfast. "Atmosphere combines European warmth with Southern hospitality." Highly recommended.

● St. Charles Guest House, ⑤ ∨ ★, 1748 Prytania St., 70130. Telephone: 504/523-6556. $20 to $40 single; $25 to $45 double; $40 to $55 triple; $45 to $70 quad. Advance reservations suggested. "A simple, cozy, affordable bed-and-breakfast near French Quarter with patio and pool." Another hotel that gets high marks from a native of the city.

● Econo Lodge, ∨ ⓰, 4861 Chef Menteur Hwy., 70126. Telephone: 504/283-1531. $27 for one; $29 for two in one bed; $34 for two in two beds. Higher rates apply during special events.

● Friendship Park Plaza Inn, 4460 Chef Menteur Hwy., 70126. Telephone: 504/949-8301. $26 to $28 for one; $28 to $30 for two in one bed; $30 to $32 for two in two beds.

Accommodations near the French Quarter within easy access via trolley: Columns Hotel, 3811 St. Charles, 70115. Telephone: 504/899-9308. Rates begin at $35 for a double room. Rooms with balconies in a nice neighborhood. Continental breakfast included.

● YMCA, ⓰, 936 St. Charles, 70130. Telephone: 504/568-9622. Men, women, and children. $15.40 single; $22 double. "More than a room, with safety, comfort, convenience, cleanliness."

- India Hotel, 124 South Lopez, 70119. Telephone: 504/822-7833. $10 single; $12 double; $5 for dormitory room. Special discount rates for foreign visitors. Complimentary breakfast. "A bit like a European hostel."

- La Salle Hotel, ⑤∨★, 1113 Canal St., 70112. Telephone: 504/523-5831. Toll free in Louisiana 800/643-4955; out of state: 800/521-9450. $25 to $36 single; $30 to $42 double; $33 to $45 triple; $36 to $48 quad. *I stayed at the La Salle and liked it; they gave me a discount for being an Ameripass holder.*" Discounts do not apply during Mardi Gras when rates are slightly higher. Advance reservations suggested.

- Hummingbird Hotel and Grill, 804 St. Charles, 70130. Telephone: 504/561-9229 or 523-9165. $16 for one or two people; $18 to $22 for three or four. Breakfast, lunch, and dinner served in the grill, which is open 24 hours every day of the year. "Family-run historical landmark hotel . . . in a rundown neighborhood, but in a convenient location."

- Parkview Guest House, ⑤ ∨ ★ (10%), 7004 St. Charles, 70118. Telephone: 504/861-7564. $40 to $55 single; $50 to $65 double; $62 to $75 triple; $70 to $85 quad. Advance reservations preferred. "A Victorian guest house listed in the National Register of Historic Landmarks."

- Days Inn, 🏂, 1300 Veterans Blvd., 70062. Telephone: 504/469-2531. Free airport transportation. $28 to $32 for one; $33 to $37 for two; $40 to $44 single lodge; $45 to $49 double lodge.

- Days Inn, 🏂, 5801 Read Blvd., 70127. Telephone: 504/241-2500. $29 to $53 for one; $34 to $58 for two. "Twenty-five rooms furnished with antiques, many with balconies, overlooking Audubon Park and historic St. Charles Avenue."

- Canal Guest House, ⑤∨★, 2743 Canal St., 70119. Telephone: 504/821-9473. $25 single; $30 double; $35 triple. Advance reservations of two to three weeks suggested. "A renovated old house with quaint rooms . . . clean, safe, friendly, and in a convenient location."

- Marquette House (AYH), ⑤★ (10% to nonmembers), 2253 Carondelet St., 70130. Telephone: 504/523-3014. $7 per night for AYH members, $9 for nonmembers in winter. $7.75 for AYH members, $9.75 for nonmembers in summer; $21 for two nonmembers in private room; add $7 for each additional person. Advance reservations of one month necessary during Mardi Gras, and suggested during summer. "Housed in a 100-year-old home reminiscent of antebellum New Orleans."

Where to Eat: New Orleans is known for its food and its restaurants. Here's a list of some of the more popular, but not too expensive, restaurants. Keep in mind the fact that many of the city's restaurants are closed on Monday. For more on eating in New Orleans, see a copy of *The New Orleans Restaurant Guide,* by Richard and Rima Collin, Strether and Swann Publishers ($3.95).

In the French Quarter and Downtown: Buster Holmes, 721 Burgundy St. Telephone: 561-9375. Average meal $1.50 to $4.

- Café du Monde Coffee Stand, in the French Market, by the river. Try the beignets.

- Central Grocery, 923 Decatur St. Telephone: 523-1620. Sandwiches are $3.50; try the muffulettas.

- Chez Hélène, 1540 North Robertson St. Telephone: 947-9155. A good soul-food restaurant where a meal costs anywhere from $8 to $14.

- Felix, 739 Iberville St. Telephone: 522-4440. Have oysters on the half shell, at the bar, and be prepared to splurge.

- Gumbo Shop, 630 St. Peter St. Telephone: 525-1486. The gumbo is among the best in town; a meal costs from $8 to $10; a sandwich is about $4.
- Mother's, 401 Poydras St. Telephone: 523-9656. Taste the roast beef poor boy, dressed. $2.75 to $3.50. *"Probably the most famous and best poor boys in town."*
- The Coffee Pot, 714 St. Peter St. Telephone: 523-8215. For a breakfast served in a courtyard. A meal is about $5. Open all night. "The food is delicious."
- Café Maspero's, 601 Decatur St. Telephone: 523-8414. Nice setting with lots of dark varnished wood. A small menu but huge sandwiches that are excellent.
- Houlihan's, 315 Bourbon St. Telephone: 523-7412. A Créole bistro featuring French onion soup, spinach salad, and quiche Lorraine.
- Flamingo's Café, 1625 St. Charles Ave. Telephone: 523-6121. A gay restaurant that serves soups, salads, sandwiches, quiche, and great appetizers.
- Vera Cruz, 1141 Decatur (another one uptown at 7537 Maple St.). Telephone: 523-9377. The food is Texican, the portions are huge, and the quality is somewhere between good and excellent.
- Mama Rosa's Slice of Italy, 616 N. Rampart. Telephone: 523-5546. Wonderful pizza and home-baked bread. A small pizza, which is really large enough for 3 or 4 people, costs $8.

Uptown: Camellia Grill, 626 South Carrollton Ave. Telephone: 861-9311. Located on the trolley line. The cheeseburger is always a winner, but if you're feeling more adventurous try a "Cannibal Special." The freezes and the pecan pie are excellent. Omelettes for $4 are great.

- Casamento's, 4330 Magazine St. Telephone: 895-9761. Many people think that their oyster loaf is the best in town. Closed in summer.
- Tyler's Beer Garden, 5234 Magazine. Telephone: 891-4989. Oysters on the half shell at $2 per dozen are one of the best bargains in town. The atmosphere at Tyler's is relaxed and there's live music every night; cover charge.
- Parasol's, 2533 Constance. Telephone: 899-2054. Po' boy sandwiches. Neighborhood bar and restaurant in the Irish part of town.
- Bud's, 3137 Calhoun and Claiborne Sts. Telephone: 866-9294. A typical New Orleans-style seafood restaurant with tile floors and Formica tables. Meals are about $7. Near Tulane University.
- Café Savannah, 8324 Oak St. Telephone: 866-3223. A nice place with an open patio, ceiling fans, and other accessories. Meals are $7 to $9; sandwiches and omelets about $4.
- Mais Oui, 5908 Magazine St. Telephone: 897-1540. Cajun/Créole-soul-food kinds of meals for $7 to $12. Near Tulane.

What to Do: "The best things to do in New Orleans are walk and eat and drink. Other activities include antique shopping on Magazine St. and plantation tours outside the city."

For listings of what's going on in New Orleans, check the *Times Picayune/State Item, The Gambit,* the uptown weekly, and *New Orleans Magazine,* a monthly publication. *Wavelength* is another monthly with good information on the wheres and whens of local bands. It's free in record stores and bars.

- In the French Quarter, begin by walking; stroll around Jackson Square, see the Cabildo and the Presbytère. Ride the New Orleans Steamboats for a fascinating journey on the Mississippi or into bayou country. Boats dock at Toulouse St. and Canal St. wharves. Phone the tourist office for information (tel. 568-

5661). Be sure, too, to walk along the Moonwalk in the evening. It's along the river, just opposite Jackson Square. Some places that we recommend visiting are:

● New Orleans Museum of Art, Lelong Ave., City Park, 70179. Telephone: 488-2631. Open Tuesday through Sunday from 10 a.m. to 5 p.m. Free admission to ISIC-holders.

● Casa Hove, 723 Toulouse St., one of the oldest buildings in the Mississippi Valley, furnished in period pieces and open Monday to Saturday, 10 a.m. to 4:30 p.m. A tour costs $1.50.

● Gallier House, 1118-1132 Royal St. To tour this fine example of 19th-century architecture and furnishings costs $2.50. The house is open Monday to Saturday, 10 a.m. to 4:30 p.m.; Sunday, 1 to 4:30 p.m.

● Musée Conti Wax Museum, 917 Conti St. Telephone: 525-2605. Here you'll see the history of New Orleans unfold from 1682 to the 20th century. Open Monday to Friday, 9:30 a.m. to 5:30 p.m.; Saturday and Sunday, 10 a.m. to 9 p.m. Admission is $3.

● Voodoo Museum, 739 Bourbon St. Telephone: 523-2906. Exactly what its name says it is.

● At the corner of Canal and Carondelet Sts. you can step onto the St. Charles streetcar for a journey along broad St. Charles Ave. into uptown New Orleans and its magnificent Garden District. Between 1st and 7th Sts., from St. Charles to Magazine, the area has some of the finest antebellum architecture in the South. See the Old Cemetery in the Garden District, bounded by 6th, Coliseum, Prytania, and Washington Sts.; Audubon Park and Zoo, farther uptown than the Garden District, near the trolley line; and Audubon Place, across from the park, a palm tree-lined boulevard which is literally out of another century.

● Jazz and Heritage Festival. At the end of April, beginning of May, two weekends are crammed full of music—jazz, blues, gospel, and rock. There are food, crafts, and unbeatable people-watching possibilities.

● The Audubon Zoo. You can take a "zoo cruise"—a riverboat from downtown to the zoo where the animals live in a "natural" setting. A nice afternoon activity.

At Night: Jazz. As with our restaurant suggestions, the following listing is meant only as an appetizer. After all, jazz was born in New Orleans and it can be heard all over the French Quarter. Some favorites: Preservation Hall, 726 St. Peter, the classic place to hear oldtime jazz; Al Hirt's, 501 Bourbon St.; Pete Fountain's Place, Hilton Hotel, Poydras St. and the river; or Crazy Shirley's, 640 Bourbon St.

● You'll find jazz outside the Quarter too, as well as blues, rock, Cajun, reggae, and just about any other type of music you can name. Some popular music spots beyond the Quarter are Jed's, 8301 Oak, for country music and sometimes punk rock; the Dream Palace, 534 Frenchmen, a popular nightclub near the French Quarter; the Maple Leaf Bar, 8316 Oak, featuring a relaxed atmosphere and music anywhere from ragtime to blues; Jimmy's, around the corner from Jed's at 8200 Willow, where you'll hear mostly rock, country, and new wave and across the street from Jimmy's, Carrollton Station for jazz—in a neighborhood bar.

● Dancing. La Boucherie, 339 Chartres. Lives up to its name—a loud, disco-type place or Maple Leaf Bar, 8316 Oak, a down-to-earth dance spot.

● Films. The Prytania, 5339 Prytania, has $4 double features.

● Classical Music. The New Orleans Symphony's season runs from fall to spring; tickets run from $5 to $15. The symphony's home is the beautifully re-stored Orpheum Theater, 129 University Pl.

● Neighborhood bars. Two we like are the Mayfair, 1505 Amelia (corner of Prytania), and Charity's, 1005 Lowerline (uptown off Broadway).

● Cooter Brown's, 5095 Carrollton. Telephone: 865-9166. A good bar with darts, videos, a large selection of imported beers and pool tables, too. Oysters on the half shell, 15¢ apiece.

● Napoleon House, 500 Chartres. A very old bar in the French Quarter with lots of character—French doors open onto patio and street. Nice place for a drink.

Shopping: Maple Street Bookshop, 7529 Maple. All kinds of books.

● Leisure Landing Records, 5500 Magazine. Best in the city for whatever kind of music you like.

● Canoe and Trail Shop, 624 Moss. For all types of camping equipment.

● Uptown Square Shopping Center, 200 Broadway. Lots of boutiques with tempting things inside.

Shreveport

Tourist Information: Shreveport-Bossier Convention and Tourist Bureau, P.O. Box 1761, 629 Spring St., 71166. Telephone: 318/222-9391.

Accommodations: Motel 6, 4915 Monkhouse Dr., 71109. Telephone: 318/636-6452. See Baton Rouge listing for rates.

● Econo Lodge, √ 🔲, 4911 Monkhouse Dr., 71109. $28.95 for one; $31.95 for two in one bed; $35.95 for two in two beds. Higher rates apply during special events.

Slidell

Accommodations: Scottish Inn, √, I-10 & Gause Blvd., P.O. Box 9, 70459. Telephone: 504/641-0576. $23.95 for one; $29.95 for two.

● Econo Lodge, √, I-70 & Gause Blvd., P.O. Box 1358, 70459. Telephone: 504/641-2153. $26.95 for one; $28.95 for two in one bed; $30.95 for two in two beds. Higher rates apply during special events.

● Days Inn, 1645 Gause Blvd., 70458. Telephone: 504/641-3450. $33 for one; $37 for two.

● Motel 6, 136 Taos St., 70458. Telephone: 504/643-6040. See Baton Rouge listing for rates.

Maine

Maine is a beautiful state—its coastline attracts lots of visitors in the summer months, and Acadia National Park on Mount Desert Island is a mecca for campers, hikers, fishermen, and nature lovers. In this park you'll find mountains, lakes, seashore, and more than 75 carriage trails that are a hiker's dream. If you can get to Acadia in the spring or early fall you'll be able to appreciate it all the more. If the summer crowds get to you, head north of Bar Harbor to the miles of unspoiled wilderness and wooded area that stretch to the Canadian border.

Many tourists favor the southern coast of Maine from York to Bath, which includes Ogunquit, home of a well known summer playhouse. And those who have even the mildest interest in camping and things out-of-doors really should treat themselves to a visit to the headquarters of L.L. Bean, a store that campers and sportsmen dream about. Located in Freeport, L.L. Bean is open every single day of the year, 24 hours a day.

"We stopped at L.L. Bean at midnight on a summer Tuesday night and you might have thought, by the size of the crowd, that it was the day before Christmas!"

More attractions in Maine are Mt. Katahdin, the state's highest peak and the beginning of the Appalachian Trail, and Lily Bay State Park on Moosehead Lake, the largest natural lake within one state in the U.S.

When you get hungry in Maine, take advantage of the bean suppers, barbecues, and seafood festivals that are held in small towns all over the state, especially during the summer. The food is inexpensive, plentiful, and, best of all, homemade with love. Check for posters outside supermarkets and along the road.

The Appalachian Mountain Club publishes two very good outdoor guides to Maine, which are available from AMC, 5 Joy St., Boston, MA 02108. They are *AMC Maine Mountain Guide* ($9.95), and *AMC Guide to Mount Desert and Acadia National Park* ($3.50). Another recommended guidebook is *Maine —An Explorer's Guide,* by Christina Tree, The Countrymen Press, Woodstock, VT 05091 ($9.95).

Some Special Events: Annual Chicken Barbecue and Fiddlers Contest in Bowdoinham, Clam Festival in Yarmouth, and Seacoast Festival in Kennebunkport (July); Blueberry Festival in Union, and Downeast Jazz Festival in Camden (August); Common Ground Country Fair in Windsor (September); and Fair in Fryeburg (October).

Hitching: The law states: "It shall be unlawful for any person to hitchhike on the traveled portion of any public highway, including but not limited to the Maine Turnpike or any portion of any public highway during the nighttime . . ." The act goes on to say that it is still possible for municipalities to post signs prohibiting hitching in their own areas.

Tourist Information: Maine Publicity Bureau, 97 Winthrop St., Hollowel, ME 04347. Telephone: 207/289-2423.

Augusta

Help: Crisis Counseling, 207/623-4511.

Accommodation: Susse Chalet Motor Lodge, Maine Turnpike, I-95, Winthrop Exit, on Whitten Rd., 04330. Telephone: 207/622-3776. $27.70 for one; $31.70 for two; $35.70 for three; $37.70 for four.

Bangor

Accommodation: Susse Chalet Lodge, I-95 Exit 45B, Rte. 2 (Hermon Exit) on Hammond St., 04401. Telephone: 207/947-6921. $27.70 single; $31.70 double; $34.70 triple; $37.70 quad.

Bar Harbor

Camping: Acadia National Park, Rte. 1, P.O. Box 177, 04609. Blackwoods and Seawall are the two campgrounds with over 500 sites altogether. Blackwoods, five miles south of Bar Harbor, is open year-round. Seawall is open May to late September. $7 per campsite per night.

Accommodation: YWCA, 36 Mount Desert St., 04609. Telephone: 207/288-5008. Women only. $18 single; $15 per person double. A bed in the Solarium, a dorm which is open from June to September, costs $12. Reservations essential from June to Labor Day.

Blanchard Corner

Accommodation: Crossroads Inn (AYH), RFD 1, Box 54, 04406. Telephone: 207/997-3920. Open May 15 to October 15 and February 1 to 28. $4.25 summer, $6.25 winter for AYH members. Sleeping bags required. Reservations strongly advised. AYH members receive preference.

"Appalachian Trail passes the door; canoeing the Piscataquis River even closer."

Brewer

Accommodation: Twin City Motel, √ (10%), 453 Wilson St., 04412. Telephone: 207/989-5450. $28 for one; $30 for two in one bed; $38 for two in two beds. During July and August the rates are almost double.

Caribou

Accommodation: Red Brick Motel, RFD 3, Presque Isle Rd., 04736. Telephone: 207/492-7001. $23 for one; $27 for two in one bed; $29 for two in two beds.

Carmel

Accommodation: Ring Hill Hostel (AYH), Rte. 2, Box 235, 04419. Telephone: 207/848-2262. Open June 1 to September 30 and February 1 to 28. Transportation from Bangor International Airport available. $4.25 summer, $6.25 winter for AYH members. Advance reservations necessary.

Fort Kent

Accommodation: Residence Hall, 🏛, University of Maine at Fort Kent, 04743. Telephone: 207/834-3162. Open May 1 to September 1. Shuttle service from bus station (43 miles away) available at certain times of the year. Near Allagash Waterways. $10 per person; $2 deduction if guest provides own linen or sleeping bag. Advance reservations of one week necessary. Cafeteria on premises.

Georgetown

Camping: Knubble Bay Camp & Beal Island (mailing address: Robert and Carol Rehn, 75 Wilshire Park, Needham, MA 02192). Telephone: 617/449-0723. At least one person must be a member of the Appalachian Mountain Club and register at above address. Camping and self-service cottage available. Advance reservations of three months in summer and one to two weeks off-peak. Cottages: $15 per night for three people plus $5 for each additional person (AMC members) or $6 (nonmembers). Camping: $2 per night (AMC members); $3 (nonmembers); children under 12 are $1 per night. Canoes are $8 per day. Parking $1 per day.

Harrington

Accommodation: S.E.A.D.S., Inc. Hostel (AYH), Georgetown Rd., P.O. Box 262A, 04643. Telephone: 207/483-9763. $3.25 for AYH members.

Jonesboro

Accommodation: Blueberry Patch Motel and Cabins, √ ★, Rte. 1, 04648. Telephone: 207/434-5411. $22 single; $24 double. July and August: $26 single; $30 double. Cabins: $22 or $30 with cooking facilities. Open May 1 through October.

Monson

Accommodation: The Old Church, Ⓢ ★, 04464. Telephone: 207/997-3691. Open June 15 to October 15. $6 for AYH members; $7 for nonmembers.

Ogunquit

Accommodation: Admiral's Loft Guest House, 97 Main St., 03907. Telephone: 207/646-5496. Fifteen minutes from a three-mile-long sandy beach. Open May 15 to mid-October. $20 to $40 for one or two people; $7 for third person. A three-story Victorian sea captain's home that's over 150 years old. "Newly done and very clean."

Orono

On Campus: The University of Maine is in Orono and the Memorial Union Building is the hub of life there. For good food and entertainment, go to Barstans on Mill St.; to meet students, just stop at the Bear's Den in the Union. You might be able to pay a reasonable price for a dorm room in the summer—just check with the Student Affairs Office on the Main Floor of Memorial Union.

"I'm from Tennessee and I think this place is great—the people are friendly and there's lots and lots of snow for winter fun."

Portland

Help: Hotline, 207/774-4357.

Accommodations: YWCA, 87 Spring St., 04101. Telephone: 207/772-1906. Women only, at least 18 years of age. $15 to $18 single; $11 to $15 per person double. Higher rates apply in summer. Advance reservations of one week necessary.

● YMCA, 70 Forest Ave., 04101. Telephone: 207/773-1736. Men only. $16.75 single. Weekly rates: $46.

● Susse Chalet Motor Lodge, Maine Turnpike I-95 (Exit 8), on Brighton Ave., 04102. Telephone: 207/774-6101. See Bangor listing for rates.

Rangeley

Accommodation: The Farmhouse Inn (AYH), Rte. 4, Box 173, 04970. Telephone: 207/864-3446. $14 for first night's stay; $12 for two or more nights for AYH members dormitory-style; $35 double; $80 quad. Advance reservations necessary in winter. "A beautifully restored large farmhouse with acres of fields, woods, and a lake."

Rumford

Accommodation: Friendship Linnell Inn, U.S. 2 West on Prospect Ave., 04276. Telephone: 207/364-4511. $28 for one; $32 for two in one bed; $36 for two in two beds.

Southwest Harbor

Accommodation: Harbor Light, Main St., 04679. Telephone: 207/244-3835. $25 to $32 for room in high season (July 1 to Labor Day); $20 to $25 at other times. A large, old Victorian home with a very thoughtful family in charge. An excellent place to stay if you plan to explore the fabulous Acadia National Park. Call the owners about the possibility of arranging transportation (Harbor Light is 20 miles from the bus).

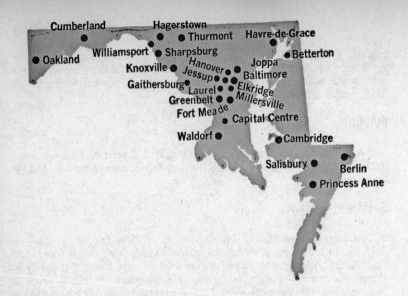

Maryland

Although many people limit their travel in Maryland to the suburban belt around Washington, D.C., there's lots of breathtaking farmland beyond. One of the most interesting features about Maryland is the Eastern Shore, named after the three states of Delaware, Maryland, and Virginia—the Delmarva Peninsula. On "The Shore" is a mixture of farmland, fishing villages, colonial towns, large estates, and a seaside resort. To set the mood for a visit, read James Michener's *Chesapeake.*

Annapolis, Maryland's historic capital, was the country's first peacetime capital and since 1845 it has been the home of the U.S. Naval Academy. The U.S. Department of the Interior has designated one square mile of downtown Annapolis as a historic district—and many landmarks still stand. A walking tour of Annapolis should include a look at the City Dock area with its restored City Market, shops, and seafood restaurants.

Baltimore is a city with a maritime atmosphere and a reputation for excellent seafood. Also well known for its association with the national anthem (Francis Scott Key wrote "The Star-Spangled Banner" there), it has many landmarks worth visiting: Fort McHenry, U.S.S. *Constellation,* B & O Railroad Museum, Harborplace, and the new National Aquarium.

Two books that concentrate on travel from Baltimore are *Day Trips from Baltimore,* by Gwyn Willis, East Woods Press ($7.95) and *The Baltimore One-Day Trip Book,* by Elois Paananen, EMP Publications ($8.95).

For help in finding your way around Maryland, write to the Office of Tourist Development (address below) and ask for *Maryland Travel Guide.*

Some Special Events: NASA Goddard Flight Center Model Rocket Launching in Greenbelt (first and third Sunday of every month); Winterfest in

McHenry and Maryland Day Celebration in St. Mays City (March); Children's Festival in Annapolis and Main Street Festival in Laurel (May); Barbara Fritchie Motorcycle Race in Frederick (July); Jonathan Hager Frontier Crafts Day in Hagerstown and Crab Feast in Gaithersburg (August); Prince George's County Fair in Upper Marlboro (September); and Harvest Weekend in Ellicott City (October).

Hitching: Hitchhiking is illegal on Maryland's highways. The only exception is when an occupant of a disabled vehicle is allowed to seek assistance. As the Maryland State Police told us: "Last year nearly 7,000 pedestrians were killed on America's high-speed roads. Considering these staggering figures, I hope you can fully understand the concern for the safety of the pedestrians and why the Maryland legislature enacted a law against hitchhiking."

Tourist Information: Office of Tourist Development, 45 Calvert St., Annapolis, MD 21401. Telephone: 301/269-3517.

Baltimore

This is famous for its Harbor Place, which includes plenty of food markets, boutiques, and an aquarium. The Marble Bar is a rock-and-roll club within walking distance of the Harbor, and it gets its name from the genuine marble bar that Gene Kelly danced on once upon a time. Fells Point is another popular spot with its neighborhood bars and Bertha's Mussels, a popular spot specializing in mussels and other seafood treats as well. Another recommended Baltimore sight is the city's Museum of Art, at 10 Museum Dr. off North Charles St., where the collection of impressionist paintings is certainly worth a visit.

If you are going to spend a while in Baltimore, you may want a copy of *Day Trips from Baltimore*, by Gwyn Willis ($7.95), published by East Woods Press, 429 East Blvd., Charlotte, NC 28203.

Tourist Information: Baltimore Office of Promotion and Tourism, 34 Market Place, Suite 310, 21204. Telephone: 301/752-8632.

Help: Travelers Aid, 601 North Howard St., 21201. On mezzanine of Greyhound Terminal. Telephone: 301/685-3569.

Accommodations: Abbey Hotel, 723 St. Paul St., corner of Madison St., 21202. Telephone: 301/332-0405. $33 single; $36 double; $45 triple. "European-style" hotel.

● Baltimore International Hostel (AYH), 17 West Mulberry St., 21201. Telephone: 301/576-8880. $7 summer, $8 winter for AYH members.

"Make sure you stop at the Lexington Market on Lexington and Eutaw Sts. for the freshest seafood around. Another place I really enjoyed was the Peabody Book Store on Charles St. It was an old, comfortable, dusty bar which looks like a library and has a wonderful fireplace."

Berlin

Camping: Assateague Island National Seashore, Rte. 2, Box 294, 21811. Telephone: 301/641-1441. Three campgrounds on the island about ten miles south of Ocean City. Two primitive facilities open year-round ($5 per campsite), one modern facility open April through October ($8 per campsite).

Betterton

Accommodation: Ye Lantern Inn (AYH), P.O. Box 310, Ericsson Ave., 21610. Telephone: 301/348-5809. Closed October 23 to December 23. $7 summer, $8 winter for AYH members. Advance reservations necessary.

Cambridge

Accommodation: Cambridge Home Hostel (AYH), c/o Albert B. & Annette R. Atkinson, 1311 Race St., 21613. Telephone: 301/228-7455. $5.25 for AYH members. Advance reservations necessary.

Capital Centre

Accommodation: Motel 6, I-95 & Central Ave., 20743. $17.95 for one; $21.95 for two; $2 for each additional person.

Cumberland

Accommodation: YMCA, 205 Baltimore Ave., 21502. Telephone: 301/724-5445. One block from bus station; two blocks from train station. Men only. $12.88. Weekly rate: $34.40 plus $5 key deposit. Meals available across the street at Lynn's Restaurant.

Elkridge

Accommodation: Econo Lodge, V, 5895 Bonnie View Lane, 21227. Telephone: 301/796-1020. $29.95 for one; $32.95 for two in one bed; $35.95 for two in two beds.

Fort Meade

Accommodation: Econo Lodge, V, 1630 Annapolis Rd., 21113. Telephone: 301/674-8900. $29.95 for one; $31.95 for two in one bed; $35.95 for two in two beds.

Gaithersburg

Accommodation: Red Roof Inn, ♿, 497 Quince Orchard Rd., 20878. Telephone: 301/977-3311. $29.95 for one; $34.95 for two in one bed; $36.95 for two in two beds; $38.95 for three or four in two beds.

Greenbelt

Camping: Greenbelt Park, 6565 Greenbelt Rd., 20770. Telephone: 301/344-3948. Twelve miles from Washington, D.C. 174 sites open all year. $4 per campsite per night.

Hagerstown

Accommodations: YMCA, 149 North Potomac St., 21740. Telephone: 301/739-3990. Four blocks from the bus station. Men only. $10 single. Weekly rate: $35.
● Friendship Mid-Town Motel, 16 North Prospect St., 21740. Telephone: 301/790-0800. $26 to $28 for one; $29 to $32 for two.

Hanover

Accommodation: Red Roof Inn, ♿, 7306 Parkway Dr., 21076. See Gaithersburg listing for rates.

Havre-de-Grace

Accommodation: Best Value Midtown Motel, √, 912 Pulaski Hwy. (U.S. 40), 21078. Telephone: 301/939-4567. $29 for one; $29.40 for two in one bed; $31.50 for two in two beds.

Jessup

Accommodation: Parkway Inn, Rte. 175 & Baltimore–Washington Pkwy., P.O. Box 367, 20794. Telephone: 301/799-0300 or 776-5510. $25.95 for one; $28.95 for two in one bed; $31.95 for two in two beds.

Joppa

Accommodation: Friendship Lakeside Motel, 1015 Pulaski Hwy., 20185. Telephone: 301/676-2700. Limited airport service available. $30 to $32 for one; $32 to $34 for two in one bed; $34 to $36 for two in two beds.

Knoxville

Accommodation: Kiwanis Hostel (AYH), Rte. 2, P.O. Box 248E, 21758. Telephone: 301/834-7652. Open April 1 to November 1. $6 summer, $7 winter for AYH members. Call information on shuttle service.

Laurel

Accommodations: Budget Host—Valencia Motel, ♿, 10131 Washington Blvd., 20707. Telephone: 301/725-4200. $27 to $37 single; $32 to $37 double or efficiency.
● Red Carpet Inn, √ ♿, 9920 U.S. Rte. 1, 20708. $29.99 for one; $33.99 for two in one bed; $36.99 for two in two beds.

Millersville

Accommodation: Friendship Inn Motel, 8204 Rte. 3 S., 21108. Telephone: 301/969-3010. Limited airport service available. $28 to $32 single; $30 to $33 for two in one bed; $32 to $36 for two in two beds.

Princess Anne

Accommodation: Hospitality House, ⑤ ★ √ ⬥, Univ. of Maryland Eastern Shore, 21853. Telephone: 301/651-2078. $12 single; $18 double; $24 triple; $28 quad.

Salisbury

Accommodation: Lord Salisbury Motel, √, Rte. 13 N., 21801. Telephone: 301/742-3251. $25 to $28 for one; $31 for two in one bed; $34 for two in two beds.

Sharpsburg

Camping: Chesapeake and Ohio Canal National Historical Park, P.O. Box 4, 21782. Telephone: 301/739-4200. Free camping along the Canal year-round. Also hiker-biker units, accessible by trail, boat, bike, and horseback, are located at intervals along the towpath. Primitive facilities. No fee.

Thurmont

Camping: Catoctin Mountain Park, 21788. Telephone: 301/663-9330. Owens Creek campground open from mid-April to November 20. $4 per campsite per night.

Waldorf

Accommodation: Waldorf Motel, Rte. 301, 20601. Telephone: 301/645-5555. $31.50 for one; $33.60 for two in one bed; $36.75 for two in two beds; $3.15 for each additional person.

Williamsport

Accommodation: Days Inn, √, I-81 & U.S. 11, 310 East Potomac, 21795. Telephone: 301/582-3500. $29 for one; $33 for two; $4 for each additional person.

Massachusetts

At first look the Commonwealth of Massachusetts seems typically New England, but it has lots about it that's unique. Massachusetts's beauty, although somewhat showy in the fall, is more hidden and unexpected in the other seasons. Winter is a difficult time to travel in this state since the weather, at best, is unpredictable. Summer and fall, although unbearably hot or disappointingly short, are the most sensible times to travel and sightsee.

If you travel through Massachusetts, try to include the Berkshires and the musical events at Tanglewood, the Amherst region with its rich cultural life that is rooted in the area's many colleges and universities, lovely but sometimes overcrowded Cape Cod, and of course the cities of Boston and Cambridge. Massachusetts can show you rocky shores, sandy beaches, salt marshes, cranberry bogs, gentle hills, valleys, woods, meadows, and fields. Nearly every town has a river, a lake, or a pond to be proud of.

Because so much of the important early history of the U.S. took place in Massachusetts, there are many historic sights to visit—Lexington and Concord, Boston Harbor, Salem. But there's more than the reminders of the past to see. There are lots of offbeat, less well known sights that will amuse; a medieval castle in Gloucester, a church built like an upturned ship in Hingham, the "Littlest House," also in Hingham, and on and on. According to one native, every town has its oddity—just ask.

You'll have no trouble at all gathering information about Massachusetts. Not only is there information from a vast number of public sources, but most of the people you'll meet will be happy to pass information on, to tell the legends and scandals of their town, and of course, to throw in a few complaints about their government.

Three books about Massachusetts that are recommended for the city-weary are the *AMC Massachusetts and Rhode Island Trail Guide* ($12.95), the *AMC Guide to More Country Walks Near Boston*, by Alan Fisher ($6.95), both available from the Appalachian Mountain Club, 5 Joy St., Boston, MA 12108, and *Short Walks on Cape Cod and the Vineyard,* by Heather Sadlier, Globe Pequot Press, Chester, CT 06412 ($5.95).

Some Special Events: The 26-Mile Patriot's Day Marathon Race in Boston (April); Flea Market in Brimfield (May); and Blessing of the Fleet in Gloucester and Provincetown (June); Tanglewood Music Festival in Lenox (June and July); Heritage Days in Salem, Boston's Harbor Festival (July); New England Renaissance Festival in South Carver, Colonial Fair and Fife Drum Master in Sudbury, and Cranberry Festival in South Carver (September); Haunted Happenings in Salem (Halloween weekend); and First Night in Boston (December).

Hitching: The Massachusetts State Police told us that it is illegal to hitchhike in Massachusetts.

Tourist Information: Division of Tourism, Massachusetts Department of Commerce and Development, 100 Cambridge St., Boston, MA 02202. Telephone: 617/727-3203. Call for a free Spirit of Massachusetts Vacation Planner.

Amesbury

Accommodation: Susse Chalet Motor Lodge, I-95 at Rte. 110, 10913. Telephone: 617/388-3400. $27.70 for one; $31.70 for two; $34.70 for three; $37.70 for four.

Amherst

Help: Direct Information Service, Jones Library. Telephone: 413/256-0121.
● Council Travel Services, 79 South Pleasant St., 2nd Floor. Telephone: 413/256-1261.

On Campus: This is a lovely New England college town—just what you'd expect—with Amherst College, the University of Massachusetts, and Hampshire College. There's a free bus that connects these schools and two others nearby—Smith in Northampton and Mount Holyoke in South Hadley. The place to meet students is the Blue Wall in the University of Massachusetts Campus Center or the Pub on East Pleasant St. For what's going on in town, check the Five College Calendar at the Campus Center's Information Desk. If you're looking for an inexpensive place to stay, and have a car, consider the Motel 6 in South Deerfield—it's not far from Amherst. During the summer, check with Summer Conference Housing at U. Mass for possibilities.

Beverly

Help: Project Rap, 617/922-0000.
Accommodation: YMCA, 245 Cabot St., 01930. Telephone: 617/922-0990. Men only. $15. Weekly rate: $30 to $50 for members only.

Boston/Cambridge

The Boston/Cambridge area is an absolute haven for students. Harvard, Radcliffe, MIT, Boston University, Northeastern, and Boston College are the largest schools in town and there are lots of smaller ones. You'll see students everywhere, but probably nowhere in greater concentration than in Harvard Square in Cambridge. Boston is a well-loved city that's easy to walk around and easy to get to know in a fairly short time. A city of neighborhoods, Boston has Beacon Hill; Back Bay, with the Boston Common and the Public Gardens; and the North and South Ends. Adjacent to the North End are Haymarket Square, the Faneuil Hall Marketplace, which attracts tourists by the droves, Waterfront Park, and Boston's historic wharves. Boston's Chinatown is the third-largest in the U.S. and a nice place for wandering.

To know what's going on in the area while you're there, check the section of the *Boston Globe* that comes out on Thursday and is called "Calendar." *Boston Magazine* is a monthly guide to what's happening, and an alternative paper, *The Phoenix,* can be counted on to provide a good rundown on what to do, what movies and plays are around, etc.

Most bookstores have a good selection of books on the city. Three that are worth looking at are:

I Love Boston Guide, by Marilyn J. Appleberg (Collier Books, $6.95). Brief and to the point, with over 1800 entries.

Car-Free in Boston: A User Guide to Public Transportation in Greater Boston and New England (Association for Public Transportation, Inc., P.O. Box 192, Cambridge, MA 02238. $2.95 plus $1 shipping and handling). Explains how to use the transit system with routes and schedules.

Arthur Frommer's Guide to Boston, by Faye Hammel (Frommer/Pasmantier, $4.95). The familiar guidebook to points of interest, hotels, shopping, and nightlife.

Foreign visitors who plan to spend more than just a few days in Boston may want a copy of *Hello Boston,* a publication of the World Affairs Council of Boston, 22 Batterymarch St., 02109 (tel. 617/482-1740).

The Globe Pequot Press publishes a very handsome book about Boston: *AIA Guide to Boston,* by Susan and Michael Southworthy ($14.95); *Historic Walks in Old Boston,* by John Harris ($9.95), *Greater Boston Park and Recreation Guide,* by Mark Primack ($9.95); *In and Out of Boston With or Without Children* ($10.95), and *Boston's Freedom Trail* ($6.95). These should all be available in bookstores but if not, they can be ordered from the press in Chester, CT 06412.

Getting There: From the Airport: Logan Airport is only about two miles from the city. To get to town from Logan, simply take the free shuttle bus that stops at each major airline terminal and takes passengers to the Airport station on the Blue Line of the MBTA (subway). Take the Blue Line to Government Center (the fourth stop), change to the Green Line, and go one stop to the Park St. station, the heart of the city, or ask for directions on getting where you want to go. The MBTA fare is 60¢.

● From the Bus Station: The Greyhound station is at 10 St. James Ave. near the Arlington St. subway station (tel. 542-4304). The Trailways station is at 555 Atlantic Ave., across from South Station (tel. 482-6620). Both are close to the center of town.

● From the Train Stations: Trains may stop at North Station or South Station. Both North and South Stations are stops on the subway system.

Getting Around: Taxi: There are taxi stands at major intersections. You can either hail a cab or call one. The fare is 90¢ for the first one-sixth of a mile and 20¢ for each additional one-sixth.

● Subway: The fare is 60¢ for rides underground; 20¢ or more if you go above ground. All MBTA stations are color coded according to line (orange, red, blue, and green) and are marked with a large "T."

- Bus: The bus fare is 50¢. A special double-decker bus runs along the major shopping streets.
- Car Rentals: Just check the Yellow Pages for the rates. Expect to be quoted about $30 per day for a compact car.

Tourist Information: There are information booths on Tremont St. next to the Park St. subway station or in the National Park Building at 15 State St. next to the Old State House.

- Greater Boston Convention and Tourist Bureau, Prudential Plaza, P.O. Box 490, 02199. Telephone: 617/536-4100. Call 267-6446 for events of the day.
- MBTA Information: 617/722-5657 or 722-5700.
- Bostix, in Quincy Hall Marketplace. For further information and tickets to concerts, plays, and other special events. Some tickets are discounted.
- Council Travel Services, 729 Boylston St., Suite 201, Boston, 02110. Telephone: 617/266-1926.

Help: Travelers Aid, 711 Atlantic Ave. at East St. Telephone: 617/542-7286 or 542-7296.

- Project Place, 32 Rutland Pl. Telephone: 617/267-9150. Drop in from 9 a.m. to 10 p.m. or call 24 hours a day, seven days a week. "From stubbed toes to suicide calls."
- Bridge Over Troubled Waters, Inc., 147 Tremont at West St. Telephone: 617/423-9575. Counseling and free medical service.
- For information about Cambridge and just about anywhere else you're going, contact Harvard Student Agencies, Thayer Hall-B, Cambridge, 02139. Telephone: 617/495-5230.

On Campus: At Northeastern University, check the bulletin board at the Student Lounge in the ELL Center for apartments and rides. Some of the recommended places to eat nearby are the Mandalay Restaurant, 329 Huntington Ave., for Burmese food; Thai Cuisine on Westland Ave. for Thai food, and Kyoto Restaurant on Huntington Ave. for Japanese food. NU students can usually be found at Our House East at 55 Gainesborough St. or at the very inexpensive Husky Rest, 280 Huntington Ave.

Accommodations: (See also listings for Charlestown and Newton, which are nearby suburbs and convenient to the city.)

- Berkeley Residence Club, 40 Berkeley St., 02116. Between Copley Square and Arlington St. MBTA stations. Telephone: 617/482-8850. Women only. $23 single; $28 double; $2 extra for first night if guest is not a YMCA member. Advance reservations of one week necessary. There's a cafeteria in the building, "a lovely walled garden," and a swimming pool.
- International Fellowship House, 386 Marlborough St., 02115. Telephone: 617/247-7248, and ask for manager. June 1 to August 15 for transients. Male foreign students only. $15 per person. Breakfast and dinner available. "The International Fellowship House is sponsored by several Christian businessmen who desire to provide a family-like atmosphere for international students far from their own homes."
- Boston YMCA, 316 Huntington Ave., 02115. Telephone: 617/536-7800. Men and women. Near Northeastern University and the Museum of Fine Arts. On MBTA's Arborway/Huntington Ave. line. $22 single; $35 double; $5 key deposit.
- Garden Hall Dormitories, 164 Marlborough St., 02116. Telephone: 617/

267-0079 or 266-5232. Men, women, and children. July 20 to August 20. $12 per night with a three-night minimum. Weekly rate: $72. Reservations and advance payment required. Bring a sleeping bag—there's no linen.

- Anthony's Town House, 1685 Beacon St., Brookline, 02146. Telephone: 617/566-3972. Near Boston University, 15 minutes by subway to downtown Boston. $30 to $35 single; $40 double; $50 triple. This brownstone has 14 rooms; "it's a very nice, friendly place."

- YMCA, 820 Massachusetts Ave., Cambridge, 02139. Telephone: 617/876-3860. Men only. $20 single. Near Harvard and MIT.

- YWCA-Tanner House, 7 Temple St., Cambridge, 02139. Telephone: 617/491-6050. Near Central Square. Women only. $25 single plus $5 key deposit. Advance reservations of 4 to 8 weeks necessary. Inexpensive restaurants nearby; swimming pool.

- Armed Services YMCA, Ⓢ, 32 City Square, 02129. Telephone: 617/242-2660. "YMCA front desk is open and available 24 hours and 365 days a year —will refer and offer help." $16 single.

- Susse Chalet Motor Lodge, off the Southeast Expwy., 800 Morrissey Blvd., 02122. Telephone: 617/287-9100. $26.70 for one; $30.70 for two; $33.70 for three; $36.70 for four.

- The Longwood Avenue Guest House, ★, 83 Longwood Ave., Brookline, 02146. Telephone: 617/277-1620. Only 1½ blocks from MBTA at Beacon St., which will transport you to the Boston area in 10 minutes. $20 to $30 single; $30 to $40 double; $34 to $45 triple; $40 to $50 quad. Advance reservations of one week necessary. "An old Victorian home converted to a ten-room guest house."

- Boston International Hostel (AYH), ♿, 12 Hemenway & Haviland Sts., 02115. Telephone: 617/536-9455. $7 summer, $10 winter for AYH members; $10 summer, $11 winter for nonmembers. Advance reservations suggested June 15 to September 30.

- Beacon Inn, ∨, 1087 & 1750 Beacon St., 02146. Telephone: 617/566-0088. $28 single; $38 (shared bath) to $43 (private bath) double. Non-refundable deposit of one night's rate to hold all rooms. Advance reservations of one week necessary in summer. "Four-floor traditional brownstone with ornate fireplaces and modern facilities."

Where to Eat: Note—we've included both Cambridge and Boston possibilities here.

- Legal Seafoods, in the Park Plaza Hotel, Arlington St. and Columbus Ave. Telephone: 426-4444. Fish is featured, but the meat and chicken are just as good. This is a very popular place so expect up to an hour's wait at dinnertime.

- Jacob Wirth, 31 Stuart St. Telephone: 338-8586. Open every day. The food is German and American and you can choose from a generous-size sandwich to a full dinner. This is an old, popular eating place with a saloon atmosphere that's best known for its specially brewed dark beer.

- Wursthaus, 4 Boylston St., Cambridge. Telephone: 491-7110. Another German/American place with good hot pastrami, a wide choice of beers, and a friendly Bavarian atmosphere.

- Joe Tecce's Restaurant, 55 North Washington St. Telephone: 742-6210. In the Italian North End, off Haymarket Square and right by Government Center. A meal of pasta, meat, and vegetables can cost $10, and according to one fan, "is worth every penny."

- Rubin's Kosher Deli, 500 Harvard St., Brookline. Telephone: 566-8761. A short MBTA ride out of the city but worth it when you crave real kosher deli. A full meal will cost almost $6, but a good and filling sandwich is under $3.

● No-Name Restaurant, 15½ Fish Pier (just past Anthony's Pier Four on the Wharf). Telephone: 338-7539. Fresh seafood at reasonable prices; well known for the chowder. Bring your own wine and expect a waiting line.

● Durgin Park, 340 Faneuil Hall Marketplace, North Market Building. Telephone: 227-2038. "Established before you were born." In the same spot since the late 1800s, this place is a definite part of the Boston tradition and a favorite with tourists.

● Brandy Pete's, 82 Broad St. Telephone: 482-4165. A little of everything—steak, spaghetti, seafood, sandwiches. A short walk from Quincy Market. Closed on weekends.

● Quadalaharry's, 20 Clinton St. Telephone: 720-1190. Next to Quincy Market. Great Mexican food and margaritas—an average meal is $7 at night.

● Pizzeria Uno, 731 Boylston St. in Boston and 22 JFK St. in Cambridge. A pizza for one and a salad or soup is $2.95 at lunchtime.

● Union Oyster House, 41 Union St. (near Quincy Market). Telephone: 227-2750. New England seafood favorites in Boston's oldest restaurant. The average cost of an entree at dinnertime is $8.95.

What to See and Do: Boston Common and Public Garden: The Common is the oldest park in the U.S. and provides a nice piece of green in the heart of downtown. The Public Garden, right across Charles St. from the Common, is where you'll find the swan boats in summer.

● Freedom Trail: There are two trails and you can walk along either or both. One is the Freedom Trail—Downtown, which includes the sites connected with the Revolution—Faneuil Hall, Old South Meeting House, Boston Tea Party Ship and Museum, and the Granary Burying Ground. The other is the Freedom Trail—North End, which includes the Old North Church, Paul Revere's House, and Copp's Hill Burying Ground.

● Hancock Tower Observatory: Go to the top of this Copley Square building for a view of the city. Open 9 a.m. to 10:15 p.m. $2.75 for adults; $2 for children ages 5 to 12; $2.25 for students.

● Prudential Center: For a different view of the city, go up to the Skywalk on the 50th floor of the "Pru." Open 9 a.m. to 11 p.m., until midnight on weekends. $2 for adults; $1 for children; $1.50 for students.

● Museum of Fine Arts, 465 Huntington Ave. Telephone: 267-9377. Egyptian, Classical, and Asiatic art; impressionist painting; and early American furniture. The Huntington Ave. streetcar stops right in front of the museum and there's a restaurant inside and a place for you to eat if you bring your own lunch. $4 for adults; children under 6 free. Free on Saturdays, 10 a.m. to noon.

● Museum of Science, Science Park. Telephone: 723-2500. Take the Green Line from Park St. to Science Park station. Exhibits about man's natural world and the things he has invented. Wonderful for all ages. Open every day. $5 for adults; $3 for children.

● Isabella Stewart Gardner Museum, 280 The Fenway. Telephone: 734-1359. Isabella Gardner was a fascinating, eccentric Bostonian whose fabulous art collection is housed in this reconstruction of a Florentine palace. Included is a Titian, some Vermeers, and paintings by Botticelli, Corot, etc.—all arranged by Mrs. Gardner with the stipulation that they must never be moved. There are free chamber music concerts at the museum; call for the schedule, which varies with the season.

● Faneuil Hall Marketplace: One of the major tourist attractions in the country, Fanueil Hall/Quincy Market is a conglomeration of small shops and restaurants. Be prepared to elbow through crowds wherever you go, but do go.

● Beacon Hill: Originally, the hill was twice as high and it had a beacon on top of it so that sailors could find the city. The New Statehouse (the old one stands on Washington St.) was designed by Charles Bulfinch and built in 1797, and is the prototype for many other capitols, including the one in Washington. Louisburg Square with its lovely town houses and Charles St. are the epitome of Boston charm.

● Haymarket: In the North End near Faneuil Hall, this open-air market attracts crowds, especially on Friday and Saturday.

● New England Aquarium, Central Wharf, near Quincy. Telephone: 742-8870. The world's largest fish tank and dolphin, whale, and scuba-diving shows. $5 for adults; $3 for children.

● John F. Kennedy Library, Columbia Point on Dorchester Bay. Telephone: 929-4567. $1.50 for adults; children under 16, free. The life and times of John F. Kennedy as shown through photos, memorabilia, and a 30-minute film.

● Harbor cruises go on the hour and whale-watching boats leave the wharf near Faneuil Hall every weekend during the summer. Call Boston Harbor Cruises, 227-4320; Bay State-Spray and Provincetown Steamship Company, 723-7800; or AC Cruise Line, 426-8419.

● For a sightseeing tour of Boston by bus, contact The Gray Line (tel. 481-3840), which is offering a 50% discount to ISIC holders on any tour on a space-available basis.

● Charles River Esplanade. At the bottom of Beacon Hill, this is a wonderful park along the Charles River, for running, hiking, or strolling.

● For a free walking tour of the Harvard campus, go to the Admissions Office in Byerly Hall, 8 Garden St., Cambridge. Telephone: 495-5000. Tours on weekdays and Saturdays. For a look at MIT's campus, go to the school's information office inside the main entrance at 77 Massachusetts Ave.

● All in the Harvard area of Cambridge are the Fogg Art Museum, 32 Quincy St. (tel. 495-4544) with medieval, Oriental, and impressionistic works; the Busch-Reisinger Museum (tel. 495-2338), a collection of the art of central and northern Europe; and the Peabody Museum, 11 Divinity Ave., a collection of archeological, botanical, and geological exhibits and home of the famous glass models of nearly every flower on earth.

At Night: Jack's, 952 Massachusetts Ave., Cambridge. The cover here is $1 to $3 and the style is casual. The music is blues, southern rock, rock and roll, and new wave. There's a small dance floor.

● Jonathan Swift's, 306 Boylston, Cambridge. Telephone: 661-9887. Live music every night from folk to blues to rock. Low cover charge unless someone well-known appears.

● Oxford Ale House, 36 Church St., Harvard Square, Cambridge. Open daily until 3 a.m. A casual place where young people like to dance. Night cover charge.

● Ryle's, 212 Hampshire St., Inmar Square, Cambridge. A good place to hear jazz. The music begins at 9:00. Take bus no. 69 to the Lechmere stop.

● Metro and Spit, 15/13 Landsdowne St. Popular with college students and local young people. "Metro's a disco, Spit's a little more punk." Both clubs are gay on Sundays.

● Passim's, 47 Palmer St., Harvard Square. This daytime café turns into folk music headquarters at night. It's small and nice.

● Symphony Hall, 301 Massachusetts Ave. Telephone: 266-1492. The home of the Boston Symphony. Call for performance schedule and prices—the season runs from September through April. "One of the most acoustically perfect concert halls in the world."

● Boston Ballet Company, the Metropolitan, 553 Tremont St. The season runs from November to March. Call 542-3945 for information.

● Resident theater groups like Boston Shakespeare, the Lyric Stage, the Next Move Theater, and the American Rep offer good theater at prices that are reasonable.

Shopping: Barnes and Noble, with several branches in the city, has popular books at discount prices.

● Brentano's, 91 D Plaza, Prudential Center. Just about everything you might want to read.

● Reading International, corner of Brattle and Church Sts., Cambridge (Harvard Square). Mostly paperbacks; large selection of periodicals and some foreign-language magazines, journals, and papers.

● Wordsworth, 30 Brattle St., Cambridge. Good selection, all books discounted—10% for paperbacks and 15% for hardcovers.

● Harvard Co-op, 1400 Massachusetts Ave., Cambridge. Books, records, clothing, and just about everything else.

● Strawberries, 709 Boylston St., Boston, and 30 Boylston St. in Harvard Square, Cambridge. Contemporary records and tapes.

● Filene's, 426 Washington St. A specialty store with a well-known bargain basement that's the oldest in the U.S. All the merchandise is dated and every 15 days the price drops 30%.

● Hilton Tent City, 272 Friend St. Discount store for camping and hiking gear.

Cambridge

(See Boston/Cambridge listing.)

Cedarville

Accommodation: Camp Massasoit (AYH-SA), Sand Pond Rd., 02360. Telephone: 617/888-2624. Open June 15 to Labor Day. $5.25 for AYH members. Advance reservations necessary. Arrival between 4:30 p.m. and 7 p.m.; hostel closed between 10 a.m. and 4:30 p.m. Flashlights necessary.

Charleton

Accommodation: YMCA, 32 City Square, 02129. Telephone: 617/242-2660. Men and women. $16 single; $20 double.

Dudley

Accommodation: Dudley Home Hostel (AYH). Telephone: 617/943-6520.

$6 for AYH members. Advance reservations necessary. "Active dairy farm—country setting."

East Bridgewater

Accommodation: Train Hostel (AYH), Ⓢ √ ♿ ★, 234 Central St., 02333. Telephone: 617/378-4046. $5.75 summer, $6.75 winter for AYH members. Advance reservations of three to seven days necessary.

Eastham

Accommodations: Starfish Youth Hostel (AYH), Ⓢ ★, RR1, Box 140, 02642. Telephone: 617/255-1441. Bus will stop in front of hostel at your request. Open April 15 to October 31. $5.25 summer, $6.25 winter for AYH members; $7.25 summer, $8.25 winter for nonmembers. Advance reservations necessary.
- Mid-Cape Hostel (AYH), RR 1, Box 167, 02642. Telephone: 617/255-2785. Open May 15 to September 15. $6 for AYH members.

Granville

Accommodation: Old Lilacs Home Hostel (AYH), c/o M/M William S. Pratt, RFD, 01034. Telephone: 413/357-6637 or 357-6446. Open May 15 to September 15. $2.25 for AYH members. Advance reservations necessary. No motor vehicles.

Haverhill

Accommodations: YMCA, 81 Winter St., 01830. Telephone: 617/374-0506. Men over 18 only. $50 per week.
- YWCA, 107 Winter St., 01830. Telephone: 617/374-6121. Women over 18 only. $32 to $37 per week.

Holyoke

Accommodation: Susse Chalet Inn, Rte. 5, I-91 (Exit 17, 17A), 01040. Telephone: 413/536-1980. $30.70 single; $34.70 double; $37.70 triple; $40.70 quad.

Hyannis

Accommodation: Hyland Youth Hostel, ♿, 465 Falmouth Rd., 02601. Telephone: 617/775-2970. $6. Advance reservations of four to five months necessary for July and August.

Lawrence

Accommodation: YMCA, 40 Lawrence St., 01841. Telephone: 617/686-

6191. Men over 18 only. $15. Weekly rate: $44. $5 refundable key deposit required.

Lenox

Accommodation: Susse Chalet Motor Lodge, Mass. Turnpike (Exit 2) on Rtes. 7 & 20, 01240. Telephone: 413/637-3560. November 1 to April 30: $27.70 single, $31.70 double weekdays; $39.70 single or double weekends. May 1 to October 31: $41.70 single or double weekdays; $95 single or double weekends.

Leominster

Accommodations: Susse Chalet Motor Lodge, Rte. 2 at Rte. 13 Exit near Searstown, 01453. Telephone: 617/537-8161. See Amesbury listing for rates.
● Leominster Motor Inn, 665 Central St., 01453. Telephone: 617/537-1741. $25 for one; $27 for two in one bed; $30 for two in two beds.

Littleton

Accommodation: Friendly Crossways Youth Hostel (AYH), ♿, Whitcomb Ave., 01460. Telephone: 617/456-3649 or 456-9386. $7 summer, $8 winter for AYH members; $15 for nonmembers. Advance reservations necessary with a 50% deposit and a stamped, self-addressed envelope. "A privately owned country conference center that prides itself on being homey."

Lunenburg

Accommodation: Coach House Inn, jct. of Rtes. 2A & 13, 01462. Telephone: 617/582-9921. $28 for one; $29 for two; $36 for two in two beds.

Martha's Vineyard

Accommodations: Titticut Follies Guest House, 43 Narragansett Ave., Oak Bluffs, 02557. Telephone: 617/693-4986. Two blocks from bus station. Open June 1 to September. $36 for a double. Reservations recommended. "An old house restored to its original gingerbread style in the tradition of the Victorian seaside resort."
● Manter Memorial International Youth Hostel (AYH), ♿, Edgartown Rd., West Tisbury, 02575. Telephone: 617/693-2665. Open April 1 to November 30. $7 for AYH members; $10 for nonmembers. Advance reservations necessary; send a stamped, self-addressed envelope for confirmation. Buy food before arrival at hostel. "Bikers and hikers only; no motorists."

Nantucket

Accommodation: Star of the Sea Youth Hostel (AYH), 02554. Telephone: 617/228-0433. Three miles from Nantucket town on south side of the island; take ferry from Hyannis. Open April 1 to October 31. $6 for AYH members; $9 for introductory members. The hostel, built in 1873, is an old Coast Guard Station. Advance reservations are necessary. Buy food before arrival at hostel.

Newburyport

Help: Turning Point, 5 Middle St. Telephone: 617/462-8251.

Accommodations: Civic Center YMCA (AYH-SA), 96 State St., 01950. Telephone: 617/462-6711. Open July 1 to Labor Day. $4.50 for AYH members. Advance reservations necessary.

● YWCA, ★, 13 Market St., 01950. Telephone: 617/465-0981. Women only. $15 single. Weekly rate: $35 to $45. Advance reservations of two months required. "A beautiful old sea captain's house located near the center of town and the water."

Northampton

On Campus: Not far from Amherst is Northampton, home of Smith College. One of the most popular spots in town is the Iron Horse Coffeehouse on Center St., where a light meal costs under $3.50 and there's live folk or jazz music every night. Another good place to eat is the North Star, on Green St. Not far from Northampton, on Main St. in Florence, is the Miss Florence Diner, which the *New York Times* rated as one of the ten best diners in New England.

Northfield

Accommodation: Monroe and Isabel Smith Hostel, Daly House (AYH), NMH, Highland & Pine Sts., 01360. Telephone: 413/498-5311, ext. 502. Open June 10 to August 20. $6 for AYH members. "Victorian house in a quiet, beautiful residential area."

Quincy

Accommodation: YMCA, 79 Coddington St., 02169. Telephone: 617/479-8500. Men only, 18 years and over. $16 single.

South Deerfield

Accommodation: Motel 6, Rte. 5-10, 01373. Telephone: 413/665-2681. $17.95 for one; $21.95 for two; $2 for each additional person. Heated enclosed pool. Located in the heart of the Berkshires and Pioneer Valley.

Springfield

Accommodations: YMCA, ⑤√★, 275 Chestnut St., 01104. Telephone: 413/739-6951. Men and women. Single $24 per night. Health facilities available to guests.
● Susse Chalet Motor Lodge, Mass. Turnpike (Exit 6). Telephone: 413/592-5141. See Amesbury listing for rates.

Truro

Accommodation: Little America Youth Hostel (AYH), P.O. Box 402, 02666. Telephone: 617/349-3889 or 349-3726. Open June 12 to September 4. Advance reservations necessary; contact AYH National Office, 1332 I St. NW, Washington, D.C. 20005. $6 for AYH members. "An old Coast Guard Station converted to dorm-like accommodations." Buy food before arrival at hostel.

Washington

Accommodation: Bucksteep Manor, Camp Karu, Washington Mountain Rd., 01223. Telephone: 413/623-5535. Ten miles east of Pittsfield, in the Berkshires. "We offer you a mellow blend of the rural life, mixed as you like it with sports, entertainment, and cultural attractions." Cabins, $10 per person. They also have rooms in the Manor Inn which cost $55 double.

Worcester

Help: Crisis Center, 617/791-6562.
Accommodation: YWCA, 1 Salem Square, 01608. Telephone: 617/791-3181. Women only. Weekly rate: $42.

Wrentham

Accommodation: Stardust Motor Inn, 900 Washington St., 02093. Telephone: 617/384-3176. $30 for one or two in one bed; $39 for two in two beds.

Michigan

Your first thoughts when you hear "Michigan" are probably Detroit and cars. Michigan is, after all, America's leading producer of automobiles and the headquarters of the United Auto Workers, the second-largest union in the country.

But there's much of Michigan beyond Detroit—much that's beautiful, rustic, and serene. The state motto, "If You Seek a Pleasant Peninsula, Look Around You," can quite accurately describe the Upper Peninsula of Michigan, where the streams to fish, forests to camp and hike, mines to explore, and where in winter there's skiing, snowmobiling, tobogganing, and skating. You'll enjoy taking a ferry from Mackinaw City to Mackinac Island during the summer; there are no cars on the island, but hundreds of bicycles are available to rent for exploring this popular summer resort.

The Henry Ford Museum and Greenfield Village, not far from Detroit in Dearborn, is a popular tourist attraction where Americana is king: Ford had famous homes, laboratories, stores, and other buildings gathered from all over the U.S. and deposited in his park.

Ann Arbor, the home of the University of Michigan, is a lively town, certainly worth a visit, especially if you're a student.

Some Special Events: Blossomtime Festival in Benton Harbor, and Tulip Festival in Holland (May); Rose Festival in Jackson, and Seaway Festival in Muskegon (June); National Cherry Festival in Traverse City, and Bass Festival in Crystal Falls (July); Country Festival in Canton, and Indian Pow Wow in Cross Village (August); Peach Festival in Romeo, and Riverfest in Lansing (September).

Hitching: The issue of hitchhiking in Michigan is a controversial one. Some of our friends said that it is accepted among the students, but they recommend caution for both the driver and the hitchhiker. Others wrote to us that they would definitely not recommend hitchhiking, warning that the crime rate in the Detroit area is particularly high. Officially, hitching is legal except on limited-access highways. Some cities may prohibit hitchhiking within their corporate limits, but the cities that do this vary from year to year.

Tourist Information: Travel Bureau, Michigan Department of Commerce, P.O. Box 30226, Lansing, MI 48909.

Alpena

Accommodation: Budget Inn—Thunderbird Bay Motel, 2717 South U.S. 23, 49707. Telephone: 517/354-8001 or 365-4111. $26 to $31 for one; $31 to $36 for two in one bed; $34 to $39 for two in two beds.

Ann Arbor

"A unique blend of cosmopolitan opportunities and small-town charm."

Help: Ann Arbor Conference and Visitor Hotline, 313/995-7281.
● Washtenaw Crisis Center, 313/996-4747 or 994-1616.
On Campus: The University of Michigan is in Ann Arbor, and according to one Ann Arborite "the university is the whole town." A good source of help there, especially for foreign visitors, is the University of Michigan International Center, 603 East Madison St., 48109 (tel. 313/764-9310).

Be forewarned: Finding low-cost accommodations in Ann Arbor is difficult, according to one person who's tried it and another who lives there, and on football weekends it's next to impossible. It may be possible for students to stay at the residence halls of the University of Michigan during the summer—call the International Center for information.

For an inexpensive Mexican meal, try the Central Cafe, 332 South Main St. or the Pan Tree on Liberty St. between 5th and Division. There you will find homemade soups, salads, omelettes, etc.

Accommodations: Ann Arbor Y, ⅍, 350 South Fifth Ave., 48104. Telephone: 313/663-0536. Men and women. Near bus and train station. $15.56. Weekly rate: $58.12.
● Red Roof Inn, ⅍, 3621 Plymouth Rd., 48105. Telephone: 313/996-5800. $24.95 for one; $29.95 for two in one bed; $31.95 for two in two beds; $33.95 for three or four in two beds.

Battle Creek

Accommodations: Michigan Motel, 20475 M66 N., 49017. Telephone: 616/963-1565. $24 for one; $28 for two in one bed; $30 for two in two beds.
● Regal 8 Inn, 4775 Beckley Rd. (Capital Ave. at I-94), 49017. Telephone: 616/979-1141. $22.88 for one; $27.88 for two in one bed; $32.88 for two in two beds.

- TraveLodge, ✓ ♿, 90 North Division St., 49017. Telephone: 616/965-7761. $25 for one; $30 for two in one bed; $34 for two in two beds.
- Comfort Inn, ✓, 165 Capital SW, 49015. Telephone: 616/965-3976. $28.95 to $31.95 for one; $34.95 to $35.95 for two.

Bay City

Accommodations: Budget Hotel—Empire House Motel, ✓, (10%), 1305 Washington Ave., 48708, Telephone: 517/894-2711. $23 for one; $26 for two in one bed; $28 for two in two beds.
- Friendship Betrands Inn, 910 South Euclid, 48706. Telephone: 517/684-4100. $22 to $24 for one; $26 to $28 for two in one bed; $30 to $32 for two in two beds.

Benton Harbor

Accommodation: Red Roof Inn, ♿, 1630 Mall Dr., 49022. Telephone: 616/927-2484. $22.95 for one; $27.95 for two in one bed; $29.95 for two in two beds; $31.95 for three or four in two beds.

Brevport

Accommodation: Gustafson's Resort, U.S. 2, 49760. Telephone: 906/292-5541. $18 for one; $24 for two in one bed; $28 for two in two beds; $36 to $38 quad.

Center Line

Accommodation: Gatewood Home Hostel (AYH), c/o Harold and Gloria Gatewood, 8585 Harding Ave., 48015. Telephone: 313/756-2676. Ten miles from Detroit. $5 for AYH members. "A unique home filled with odds and ends from all over the world and assorted pets."

Charlevoix

Accommodation: Durance Home Hostel (AYH), ✓, c/o Frances Durance, 541 North Mercer, 49720. Telephone: 616/547-2937. $3.75 for AYH members.

Cheboygan

Accommodation: Cheboygan Motor Lodge, 1355 Mackinaw Ave., 49721. Telephone: 616/627-3129. $30 for one; $34 for two in one bed; $38 for two in two beds; $46 for four in two beds. Winter rates are $5 lower.

Coloma

Accommodation: Camp Warren (AYH-SA), 2456 Maple Ave., 49038. Telephone: 616/849-1433. $5.25 summer, $6.25 winter for AYH members. Advance reservations necessary. Free pick-up and return to bus station.

Delton

Accommodation: Circle Pines Center (AYH-SA), 8650 Mullen Rd., 49046. Telephone: 616/623-5555. $15 adults; $7.50 children ages 3 to 13; under age 3, free. $8.25 summer, $10.25 winter for AYH members. Rooms sleep four to six. Twenty-five miles from bus or train stations; guests may call for a ride at a special fee. Chores required. Bring sleeping bags. Meals are served daily in the summer. When meals are not available, kitchen use is $2 per day. "We are an educational cooperative established in 1938. We own 284 acres of woods and meadows, with one-third mile of lakefront with a sandy beach. There are 40 buildings; a lodge, a farmhouse, and many cabins."

Detroit

Tourist Information: Visitors Information Center, 2 East Jefferson. Telephone: 313/567-1170.

Help: Travelers Aid, 1553 Woodward, Room 406, 48226. Telephone: 313/962-6740.

● Travelers Aid, 130 East Congress (Greyhound Bus Station), 48226. Telephone: 313/961-1532.

● Hotline: 313/298-6262. What's happening in Detroit.

"Detroiters do not wear mechanics' coveralls to the symphony!"

Except possibly when it plays under the stars at Meadowbrook at Oakland University on summer nights (call 377-2100 for information). Also look into the free jazz and blues concerts sponsored by the Jefferson-Chalmen Citizens' District Council in summer (call 822-0006). Check with the housing office of Oakland University in suburban Rochester, or the University of Detroit—they might have a room available for a night or two.

Accommodations: YMCA, 2020 Witherell, 48226. Telephone: 313/962-6126. Men only; must be at least 18 years old. $13 per person in dormitory-style rooms. Fully equipped health facilities.

● YMCA, 1601 Clark Ave., 48209. Telephone: 313/554-2136. Men only. $15.60 per night plus $6 key deposit.

● Manning Hall, Mercy College, 8200 West Outer Dr., 48219. Telephone: 313/592-6170. Ask for Director of Housing. Men, women, and children. Open May to August. $18.50 single; $13.50 per person double; $9.50 per person triple. Advance reservations of one month necessary.

● Red Roof Inn, 🦽, 24300 Sinacola Ct., Farmington Hills, 48018. Telephone: 313/478-8640. $25.95 for one; $30.95 for two in one bed; $32.95 for two in two beds; $34.95 for three or four in two beds.

● Red Roof Inn, 🦽, 32511 Concord, Madison Heights, 48071. Telephone: 313/583-4700. See listing above for rates.

- Red Roof Inn, 39700 Ann Arbor Rd., Plymouth, 48170. Telephone: 313/459-3300. See listing above for rates.
- Red Roof Inn, 31800 Little Mack Ave., Roseville, 48066. Telephone: 313/296-0310. See listing above for rates.
- Red Roof Inn, ♿, 2350 Rochester Rd., Troy, 48083. Telephone: 313/689-4391. See above listing for rates.
- Red Roof Inn, ♿, 26300 Dequindre Rd., Warren, 48091. Telephone: 313/573-4300. See above listing for rates.
- Quantrill's Retreat (AYH), 18964 Pinehurst, 48221. Telephone: 313/864-1141. $4.25 for AYH members. Advance reservations necessary.
- American Fort Wayne Hotel (AYH-SA), 400 Temple, 48201. Telephone: 313/831-7150. Near bus and train. Telephone: 313/831-7150. $10.75 single for AYH members.
- Old Redford Home Hostel (AYH), 16901 Burgess, 48219. Telephone: 313/533-9597. $5 for AYH members. Advance reservations required; send a self-addressed stamped envelope.
- The Malvern (AYH-SA), 93 Seward, 48202. Telephone: 313/875-9660. $10 for AYH members. Advance reservations suggested.

East Lansing

Help: Listening Ear, 547½ East Grand River Ave., 48823. Telephone: 517/337-1717. Phone or drop in, seven days a week.

On Campus: Michigan State University is here, and according to a member of the Union Activities Board, the attitude toward people on the road in the area is "liberal because of the college atmosphere." Nearly all of the local meeting places are just across the street from campus on Grand River Ave. When hunger strikes, you can find an inexpensive meal at Beggar's Banquet, 218 Abbott; Al Azteco, 203 M.A.C.; or Olga's Kitchen, 131 East Grand River.

Elk Rapids

Accommodation: Honey House Home Hostel (AYH), 613 South Bayshore Dr., 49629. Telephone: 616/264-9768. Open May 1 to November 1. $4.25 for AYH members. Advance reservations necessary. Hikers, bicyclists, sailors, or foreign travelers only.

Empire

Camping: Sleeping Bear Dunes National Lakeshore, 49630. Telephone: 616/352-9611. Camping all year at D.H. Day and Platte River for $6 per campsite per night. Wilderness camping available April to November at North and South Manitou Island; permit required.

Flint

Tourist Information: Flint Area Convention and Visitors Bureau, 400 North Saginaw St., Suite 101, 48502. Telephone: 303/232-8900, or toll free within Michigan 800/482-6708.

Help: Voluntary Action Center, 202 East Boulevard Dr., Room 330, 48503. Telephone: 313/767-0500. For information and referral.

Accommodations: Mott Lake Hostel (AYH), 6511 North Genesee Rd., 48506. Telephone: 313/736-5760. Bring a sleeping bag or your own linens. Their backyard is a 4000-acre park that includes a 600-acre lake. Under age 18: $3.75 summer, $4.75 winter. Over age 18: $5.25 summer, $6.25 winter for AYH members. Anyone who reserves with full payment receives $1 discount first night. Bike, canoe, sailboat, and sled rentals available. Kitchen facilities provided; bring your own food. Twelve miles from Autoworld Entertainment Park.

- Red Roof Inn, G-3219, Miller Rd., 48507. Telephone: 313/733-1660. See Ann Arbor listing for rates.
- Econo Lodge, √ (10%), 2002 South Dort Hwy., 48503. Telephone: 313/235-6621.

Frankfort

Accommodation: Brookwood Home Hostel (AYH), c/o Marjorie Pearsall-Green, 538 Thomas Rd., 49635. Telephone: 616/352-4296 (summer) or 312/292-5820 (winter). Open June 15 to September 5. $4.75 for AYH members. Advance reservations necessary.

Fruitport

Accommodation: Steury Home Hostel (AYH), 353 2nd St., 49415. Telephone: 616/865-3555. $5 for AYH members. Advance reservations necessary.

Gaylord

Accommodation: Budget Host—Royal Crest Motel, √ &, 803 South Ostego Ave., 49735. Telephone: 517/732-6451. $28 to $31 for one or two in one bed; $32 to $38 for two in two beds.

Grand Marais

Accommodation: Budget Host—Welker's Lodge, end of Mich. 77 on Lake Superior Coast Guard Point, Canal St. (Box 277), 49839. Telephone: 906/494-2361 or 494-2562. $23 to $26 for one; $26 to $27 for two in one bed; $29 to $34 for two in two beds. Indoor pool, sauna, Jacuzzi, mini health spa.

Grand Rapids

Help: Switchboard Crisis Center, 616/774-3535. Open 24 hours.

Accommodations: Home Hostel (AYH), c/o Charles and Elizabeth French, 1117 Paradise Lake SE, 49506. Telephone: 616/676-9247 or 459-3421. AYH membership required. Advance reservations of seven days necessary. Breakfast and dinner provided at no charge.

● Red Roof Inn, 5131 East 28th St., 49508. Telephone: 616/942-0800. $23.95 for one; $28.95 for two in one bed; $30.95 for two in two beds; $32.95 for three or four in two beds.

● Best Value Beltline Motel, 171 28th St. SE, 49508. Telephone: 616/241-0151. $23 for one; $25 for two in one bed; $30 for two in two beds.

● Exel Inn, 4855 28th St. SE, 49508. Telephone: 616/957-3000. $24.95 for one; $29.95 for two in one bed; $31.95 for two in two beds.

● Motel 6, 3524 28th St. SE, 49508. Telephone: 616/949-8112. $17.95 for one; $21.95 for two; $2 for each additional person.

● Motel 6, 777 Three Mile Rd., 49504. Telephone: 616/784-1616. See above listing for rates.

● Cascade Inn, 🔣, 2865 Broadmoor SE, 49508. Telephone: 616/949-0850. $22 to $23 for one; $30 for two; $3 for each additional person. Cash payment required for accommodations Thursday through Sunday.

Greenville

Accommodation: Wabasis Lake North Country Hostel (AYH), 🔣, 11277 Springhill Dr., 48838. Telephone: 616/691-7260. Open mid-May to mid-September. $3.50 for AYH members.

Hart

Accommodation: Hart Home Hostel (AYH), c/o William and Leola Hanna, 19 Courtland, 49420. Telephone: 616/873-4565. $3.25 summer, $4 winter for AYH members. Advance reservations necessary.

Holland

Help: Crisis Intervention, 616/396-4357.
Accommodation: Budget Host—Wooden Shoe Motel, U.S. 31 Bypass & 16th St., 49423. Telephone: 616/392-8521. $25 for one; $30 to $38 for two. Heated pool.

Houghton

Camping: Rock Harbor Lodge & Cabins, Isle Royale National Park, 87 North Ripley St., 49931. Telephone: 906/337-4993. Thirty-one campgrounds, some accessible only by trail, some only by boat. Open mid-June to Labor Day. The park is a large island on Lake Superior and 50 miles from Houghton. There is ferry service from Houghton to Isle Royale.

Houghton Lake

Accommodation: Sands Resort Motel, 9192 Old U.S. 27, 48629. Telephone: 517/422-5295. Summer: $38 for one; $43 for two. Winter: $28 for one; $33 for two.

Inkster

Accommodation: Friendship Dearborn Motel, 25925 Michigan Ave., 48141. Telephone: 313/565-7200. $24 to $27 for one; $26 to $30 for two in one bed; $30 to $36 for two in two beds.

Ironwood

Accommodation: Crystal Dairy Home Hostel (AYH), c/o Irene and Don Mildren, P.O. Box 203, N10408 Lake Rd., 49938. Telephone: 906/932-2222. $4.25 summer, $5.25 winter for AYH members. Advance reservations necessary.

Iron Mountain

Accommodation: Cooney's Mountaineer Motel, Jct. 141, 49801. Telephone: 906/774-2918. $20 for one; $30 for two in one bed; $35 for two in two beds.

Iron River

Accommodation: Iron Inn, 225 West Cayuga, 49935. Telephone: 906/265-5111. $25.50 single; $30.50 double.

Kalamazoo

Help: Helpline, 616/381-4357.
● Lodging Assistance Hotline, 616/385-8199.
On Campus: Kalamazoo College and Western Michigan University are in Kalamazoo. A friend of ours who is a student there describes his town as having a "strong academic and cultural flavor" and a friendly attitude toward young people on the road. Knollwood Tavern is a popular student spot, and you can find a low-priced meal in the college dining rooms. One of the best spots for an inexpensive breakfast, lunch, or dinner is Theo's right in the center of town at 234 West Michigan.
Accommodations: Red Roof Inn, 3701 East Cork St., 49001. Telephone: 616/382-6350. See Grand Rapids listing for rates.
● Red Roof Inn, 🚹, 5425 West Michigan Ave., 49009. Telephone: 616/375-7400. See Grand Rapids listing for rates.
● TraveLodge, √, 1211 South Westnedge Ave., 49008. Telephone: 616/381-5000. $27 for one; $30 for two in one bed; $34 for two in two beds.

Lakeview

Accommodation: Painter Home Hostel (AYH), c/o Robert and Phyllis Painter, 10350 Orchard Lane, 48850. Telephone: 517/352-6351. $2.50 for AYH members. Hikers and bikers only. Advance reservations necessary.

Lansing

Help: Emotional Crisis, 517/372-8460.

Accommodations: YMCA, 301 West Lenawee, 48933. Telephone: 517/484-4000. Men only. $10.45 plus $5 key deposit. Three blocks from bus station.

● Red Roof Inn, [&], 3615 Dunckle, 48910. Telephone: 517/332-2575. See Grand Rapids listing for rates.

● Red Roof Inn, [&], 7412 West Saginaw Hwy., 48917. Telephone: 517/321-7246. See Grand Rapids listing for rates.

● Motel 6, 112 East Main St., 48933. Telephone: 517/372-2666. See Grand Rapids listing for rates.

● Regal 8 Inn, 6501 South Cedar St., 48910. Telephone: 517/393-2030. $21.88 for one; $26.88 for two in one bed; $31.88 for two in two beds.

Ludington

Accommodation: Home Hostel (AYH), c/o Ron and Joan Wilson, Sherman St., 49431. Telephone: 616/843-4245. $4.25 for AYH members. Advance reservations necessary. Hikers or bikers only.

Mancelona

Accommodation: Northwoods Lodge (AYH-SA), Schuss Mt. Rd., 49659. Telephone: 313/545-7305. $5.50 weekdays, $6.25 weekends summer; $7 weekdays, $8 weekends winter. Advance reservations necessary.

Marquette

Accommodations: Friendship Birchmont Motel, 2090 South U.S. 41, 49855. Telephone: 906/228-7538. $20 to $32 for one; $24 to $34 for two in one bed; $28 to $38 for two in two beds.

● Wahlstrom's Parkway Motel and Restaurant, 5057 U.S. 41 S., 49855. Telephone: 906/249-1404. $22 for one; $26 for two in one bed; $30 for two in two beds.

Midland

Accommodation: Northwood Institute, NADA Center, 3225 Cook Rd., 48640. Telephone: 517/835-7755. Open year round. $20.80 single; $27.04 double. College cafeteria available to guests.

Milford

Accommodations: Milford Foote Hostel (AYH-SA), [&], 1845 Dawson Rd., 48042. Telephone: 313/684-1434. Under age 18: $4.25 summer, $5.25 winter. Over age 18: $5.75 summer, $6.75 winter for AYH members.

● Heavner Home Hostel and Ski Center (AYH), c/o Alan Heavner, 2775 Garden Rd., 48042. Telephone: 313/685-2379. $4 summer, $5 winter for AYH members. Canoe rentals, cross-country skiing, bicycling, horseback riding, hiking, and skating nearby. Bring your own linens. "Cozy tri-level home in the country." Advance reservations necessary.

Munising

Camping: Pictured Rocks National Seashore, P.O. Box 40, 49862. Telephone: 906/387-2607. Camping at three drive-in campgrounds: Little Beaver Lake, Twelvemile Beach, and Hurricane River; register upon arrival at campground. Thirteen backcountry campsites available to backpackers and hikers. Permits required for camping. Open year-round; no fee.

Accommodation: Terrace Motel, 420 Prospect St., 49862. Telephone: 906/387-2735. $28 for one or two in one bed; $32 for two in two beds.

Muskegon

Accommodation: Days Inn, &, 150 Seaway Dr., 49444. Telephone: 616/739-9429. June 1 to September 15: $31 to $37 for one; $36 to $42 for two. September 16 to November 30: $29 to $35 for one; $34 to $40 for two. Indoor pool and whirlpool.

Newberry

Accommodations: The New Falls Hotel, Ⓢ √ ★, 301 South Newberry Ave., 49868. Telephone: 906/293-5111. $18 to $22 for one; $26 to $30 for two in one bed; $28 to $32 for two in two beds. Price includes continental breakfast.

● Friendship Manor Motel, 123 South Newberry Ave., 49868. Telephone: 906/293-5000. $28 to $34 for one or two in one bed; $32 to $40 for two in two beds.

Petoskey

Accommodation: Friendship Golf View Motel, 1011 U.S. 31 N., 49770. Telephone: 616/347-8281. $18 to $30 for one; $23 to $32 for two in one bed; $30 to $40 for two in two beds.

Portland

Accommodation: Pontzerosa Home Hostel, c/o Terry and Vicki Pontz. Telephone: 517/647-2550. Advance reservations necessary.

Saginaw

Accommodations: University Center, Saginaw Valley (AYH-SA), Department of Residential Life, Saginaw Valley College, 2250 Pierce Rd., 48710. Telephone: 517/790-4255. Open May through August 31. $4 for AYH members. Advance reservations necessary.

- Red Roof Inn, 966 South Outer Dr., 48601. Telephone: 517/754-8414. See Grand Rapids listing for rates.
- Comfort Inn, √ &, 3425 Holland Ave., 48601. Telephone: 517/753-2461. $27.95 for one; $33.95 for two.

St. Ignace

Accommodation: Budget Host—Chalet North Motel, √, 1140 North State St., 49781. Telephone: 906/643-9141. Open May 15 to October 14. $25 for one; $32 for two. Heated pool.

Sault Ste. Marie

Accommodation: Bavarian Motor Lodge, √, 2006 Ashmun St., 49783. Telephone: 906/632-6864. Summer: $27 for one; $30 for two in one bed; $38 for three in two beds; $40 for four in two beds; $45 family unit. Winter: $23 for one; $25 for two in one bed; $28 to $30 for three in two beds; $35 for four in two beds.

Sturgis

Accommodation: Green Briar Motor Inn, 71381 South Centerville Rd., 49091. Telephone: 616/651-2361. $28 to $30 for one or two in one bed; $32 to $35 for two in two beds.

Tawas City

Accommodation: Tawas Motel, √, P.O. Box 248, 1124 U.S. 23 S., 48764. Telephone: 517/362-3822. $29 to $31 for one; $32 to $35 for two in one bed; $36 to $39 for two in two beds.

Three Rivers

Accommodations: Friendship Greystone, Rte. 131 Bypass, 49093. Telephone: 616/278-1695. Limited airport service available. $22 to $26 for one; $28 for two in one bed; $34 for two in two beds.

- Budget Host—Redwood Motel, √ (10%), 59389 U.S. 131, 49093. Telephone: 616/278-1945. $23 for one; $26 for two in one bed; $33 for two in two beds.

Twin Lake

Accommodation: Home Hostel (AYH), c/o Mary Payne, 3175 First St., 49457. Telephone: 616/828-6675. Canoeing on the lake in summer; cross-country skiing in winter. Advance reservations necessary.

White Cloud

Accommodation: North Country Trail Association Schoolhouse Hostel (AYH), 3962 North Felch, 49349. Telephone: 616/689-6876. $3 summer, $3.50 winter for AYH members. Bring sleeping bag.

Williamston

Accommodation: Home Hostel (AYH), c/o Ed and Lynnae Ruttledge, 115 East Riverside, P.O. Box 24, 48895. Telephone: 517/655-2830. Advance reservations necessary.

Yale

Accommodation: Kurtz Home Hostel (AYH), c/o Frank and Barbara Kurtz, 8220 Logana Rd., 48097. Telephone: 313/327-6885. $4 for AYH members.

Ypsilanti

On Campus: If you're at Eastern Michigan University, call for information on possible accommodations at Hoyt Conference Center (tel. 313/487-4109).

Minnesota

Summer activities in Minnesota revolve mainly around the water, since there are 12,000 lakes and 3000 miles of canoeing rivers. The Boundary Waters Canoe Area is the only federally designated wilderness canoe area in the country. In the winter many hardy Minnesotans even go camping with their snowshoes and cross-country skis. There is more camping, fishing, and boating available up near the northern border of the state in International Falls at Voyageurs National Park, a water-based park of 30 lakes. French-Canadian voyagers transported their furs through this forested lake country in the 1700s and 1800s—hence the name.

Fishing, waterskiing, and swimming are also very popular and can be done easily in or near the Twin Cities—the metropolitan area of Minneapolis/St. Paul has over 100 lakes within its limits.

One of the most beautiful canoe trips in the country is down the St. Croix River, which divides Minnesota and Wisconsin. It is possible to rent canoes at several points along the river and to canoe from four hours to several days, camping along the shores as you go. At the end you can leave your canoe and get transportation back at a moderate price.

Another interesting camping area is Rainy Lake, at the Canada-Minnesota border. A number of islands in the lake have tidy campsites on them, owned and kept in shape for the general public by an area lumber company. The lake is rock bottomed, very deep, and has many underwater rock mountains. The cold water is excellent for fishing, scuba diving, and snorkeling.

For those who like the bigger cities, Minnesota's twin cities of Minneapolis and St. Paul have lots to offer. Cultural activities include the nationally renowned Guthrie Theater, Minneapolis Children's Theater, the Minneapolis Institute of Arts, St. Paul Chamber Orchestra concerts at the new Ordway Music Theatre, the Science Museum of St. Paul and its Omnitheater, and Walker Art Center. The University of Minnesota has a number of concert, dance, and opera series throughout the year. Minnesota Orchestra concerts, held year-round, are exceptional and shouldn't be missed on any trip to the area.

In Minnesota, the Scandinavian and German influence is quite noticeable. Other groups exist, but not in any great numbers, comparatively. In fact, it's been said that there are as many Lutheran churches in Minnesota as there are lakes.

Some recommended guidebooks on the state are *Minnesota Travel Companion,* by Richard Olsenius, Bluestem Productions, Box 334, Wayzata, MN 55391 ($9.95); *Minnesota Walk Books* (there are six in the series, one for each area), by James Buchanan, Nodin Press, 525 North 3rd St., Minneapolis, MN 55401 ($4.50); and *Minnesota Guide,* Dorn Publications, 7831 Bush Lake Rd., Edina, MN 55435 ($8.95).

Some Special Events: Smelt Fry in Garrison (April); Festival of Nations in St. Paul, and Syttende Mai Fest in Spring Grove featuring Norwegian food, crafts, and dances (May); Good Times Days in Boyd, Noble County Dairy Days in Ellsworth, Swedish Festival in Cambridge, and International Polka Festival and Tug of War in Pine City (all in June); Taste of Minnesota in St. Paul (July), Aquatennial in Minneapolis (July), St. Paul Winter Carnival (January), Minnesota Renaissance Festival in Shakopee (August, September), Whiz Bang Days in Robbinsdale, Lake of the Woods County Fair in Baudette, Lumberjack Days in Cloquet, and Song of Hiawatha Pageant in Pipestone (all in July); Strawhat and Sunbonnet Days in Verndale, Victorian Crafts Festival in St. Paul, and Sweet Corn Festival in Ortonville (August); Cherry Area Fair and Rodeo in Iron and Lac Qui Parle County Fair in Madison (September).

Hitching: A friend says that hitchhiking across the state is fair to good but that "highway patrolmen on Interstate 94 may escort a hitchhiker to an entrance ramp." Forget hitching in winter, though—it's miserable in the cold. Officially, no one may solicit a ride from the roadways and pedestrians are prohibited on controlled-access highways.

Tourist Information: Minnesota Office of Tourism, 240 Bremer Building, 419 North Robert St., St. Paul, MN 55101. Telephone: 612/296-5029, or toll free 800/652-9747 within Minnesota, 800/328-1461 outside Minnesota. The center is open Monday through Friday from 8 a.m. to 5 p.m.

Albert Lea

Accommodation: Friendship Countryside Inn, 2102 East Main St., 56007. Telephone: 507/373-2446. $22 to $24 for one; $25 to $28 for two in one bed; $32 to $35 for two in two beds.

Alexandria

Accommodation: Thrifty Scot Motel, 4810 Hwy. 29 S., 56308. Telephone: 612/762-1171. $24.80 to $27.80 for one; $28.90 to $33.90 for two.

Barnum

Accommodation: Camp Wanakiwin (AYH-SA), c/o Joan Wimme, 55707. Telephone: 218/722-7425 or 389-6981. Open May 1 to October 31. $2.50 for AYH members. Advance reservations necessary.

Bemidji

Accommodations: Paul Bunyan Motel, 915 Paul Bunyan Dr. NE, 56601. Telephone: 218/751-1314. $24 to $28 for one; $28 to $32 for two.
● Thrifty Scot Motel, 2420 Paul Bunyan Dr. NW, 56601. Telephone: 218/751-0390. $21.90 to $26.90 for one; $26.90 to $31.90 for two.

Bloomington

Accommodation: Oakmere Home Hostel (AYH). Telephone: 612/944-1210. Call for reservation.

Brainerd

Accommodations: Thrifty Scot Motel, Jct. 210 & 371 W., 56401. Telephone: 218/829-0391. $22.90 to $25.90 for one; $27.90 to $30.90 for two.
● Econo Lodge, ∨, Hwy. 371 S., 56449. $24.90 for one; $28.90 for two.

Burnsville

Accommodation: Red Roof Inn, I-35 at Burnsville Pkwy., 55337. Telephone: 612/890-1420. $23.95 for one; $28.95 for two in one bed; $25.95 to $32.95 for two to four in two beds. Children 18 and under stay for free.

Caledonia

Accommodation: Hazel's Hostel Haven (AYH), 305 North Pine, 55921. Telephone: 507/724-3447. $6 for AYH members. Advance reservations of one week necessary.

Cambridge

Accommodation: Imperial Hotel, Hwy. 65 N., 55008. Telephone: 612/689-2200. $28.50 for one; $38.50 for two.

Cloquet

Accommodation: Driftwood Motel, 1413 Hwy. 33 S., 55720. Telephone: 218/879-4638. $19 for one; $25 for two in one bed; $29 for two in two beds.

Collegeville

Accommodation: St. John's University Summer Programs, 56321. Telephone: 612/363-3487. Greyhound bus stops on campus. Open June 1 to August 15. $15 single; $20 double. Reservations requested. Tennis courts, indoor pool, lake swimming, and boating nearby. "We are a Benedictine monastic community also—respect our quiet."

Duluth

Help: Information and Referral, 218/727-8538.
Accommodations: College of St. Scholastica, ♿, 1200 Kenwood Ave., 55811. Ask for Director of Housing. Telephone: 218/723-6000. Men, women, and children. Near local bus. Open June 13 to August 24. $15 single; $30 double. Weekly rate available. Advance reservations of one day necessary.
● YWCA (AYH-SA), 202 West 2nd St., 55802. Telephone: 218/722-7425. Open May to September. $3.75 for AYH members.
● Thrifty Scot Motel, 909 Cottonwood St., 55801. Telephone: 218/727-3110. $25.90 to $30.90 for one; $30.90 to $35.90 for two.

Fairmont

Accommodation: Best Value Lakeside Inn, 101 Albion Ave., 56031. Telephone: 507/238-4406. $15.90 for one; $24.38 for two.

Faribault

Accommodation: Friendship Inn Faribault Motor Lodge, 841 Faribault Rd., 55021. Telephone: 507/334-1841. $18.80 to $21 for one; $23 to $26 for two in one bed; $23.90 to $27 for two in two beds.

Grand Marais

Accommodations: Friendship Lamplighter, southwest on U.S. 61, P.O. Box 667, 55604. Telephone: 218/387-1369. Open June to October. $26 to $30 for one; $30 to $40 for two.
● East Bay Hotel, Box 246, 55604. Telephone: 218/387-2800. Near bus station. $11 single with shared bath, $18 with private bath; $17 double with shared bath, $26 with private bath; $19 triple with shared bath, $28 with private bath. Advance reservations of two or three days required in July and August. "An historic hotel located on Lake Superior—clean and comfortable with a fabulous view."

Hibbing

Accommodation: Thrifty Scot Motel, 1520 Hwy. 37 E., 55746. Telephone: 218/263-8306. $23.90 to $26.90 for one; $28.90 to $31.90 for two.

International Falls

Camping: Voyageurs National Park, P.O. Box 50, 56649. Telephone: 218/283-9821. Campgrounds accessible only by boat. Open year-round. No fee.

Accommodation: Thrifty Scot Motel, P.O. Box 182, Hwy. 53, 56679. Telephone: 218/283-9441. $21.90 to $24.90 for one; $26.90 to $29.90 for two.

Lake City

Accommodation: Frontenac United Methodist Camp, (AYH), Ⓢ √ ★, Rte. 2, Box 197, 55041. Telephone: 612/345-3146. Two miles from bus station. $7.75 for AYH members, plus $2 linen charge. $16 single; $16.50 double; $24 triple; $27.50 quad. Advance reservations of two days necessary except in winter.

Lakeville

Accommodations: Friendship Inn Lakeville, 17296 I-35, 55044. Telephone: 612/435-7191. $21 to $29 for one; $25 to $33 for two in one bed; $28 to $36 for two in two beds.

● Thrifty Scot Motel, 11274 210th St., 55044. Telephone: 612/469-1900. $24.90 to $29.90 for one; $29.90 to $34.90 for two.

Minneapolis

Note: See St. Paul too, since Minneapolis and St. Paul are "twin cities" divided only by the Mississippi River.

Minneapolis is a well-kept secret, according to a friend there. It has a rich cultural life, it is an easy place to get around (the transit service is generally reliable and easy to use) and hiking in the lakes area is a special pleasure.

Tourist Information: City of Minneapolis Information. Telephone: 612/222-5561.

● Parks and Recreation Information, 310 4th Ave. S. Telephone: 612/348-2226.

● Luxton, Cultural Activities Information. Telephone: 612/348-3541.

Help: First Call For Help (Travelers Aid), 404 South 8th St., 55404. Telephone: 612/340-7431.

● Contact-Twin Cities, 612/341-2896.

On Campus: The University of Minnesota is in Minneapolis. A good place to go on campus for travel information (primarily international travel) is the International Study and Travel Center, 40 Coffman Memorial Union, 300 Washington Ave. SE. Telephone: 612/373-0180.

Accommodations: For information on temporary housing near the University of Minnesota, contact the Housing Office, Comstock Hall East, University of Minnesota, 210 Delaware St. SE, Minneapolis, MN 55455. Telephone: 612/373-7542.

● Downtown YMCA, (AYH-SA), 30 South 9th St., 55402. Telephone: 612/371-8750. Open June 15 to September 15. Near public transportation and bus station. Men and women. $7 for AYH members. Advance reservations necessary.

● Snelling Motor Inn, √ ($2), 5346 Minnehaha Ave. S., 55417. Telephone: 612/721-4841. $26 to $35 for one; $30 to $35 for two in one bed; $33 to $38 for two in two beds.

● Budget Host—Gopher Campus Motor Lodge, 925 S.E. 4th St., 55414. Telephone: 612/331-3740. $30 to $36 for one; $33 to $36 for two in one bed; $36 for two in two beds.

● Sunnyside Home Hostel (AYH), c/o Rebecca Jackson. Telephone: 612/729-8871 or 373-9900 (call first). Open September 16 to June 15. $5 summer, $6 winter for AYH members. Advance reservations necessary.

● Exel Inn, 2701 East 78th St., Bloomington, 55420. Telephone: 612/854-7200. $29.95 for one; $34.95 for two in one bed; $36.95 for two in two beds.

● Friendship Palm Plaza, 1225 East 78th St., 55420. Telephone: 612/854-3322. $23 to $30 for one; $26 to $33 for two in one bed; $30 to $35 for two in two beds.

● Red Roof Inn, ⓕ, 12920 Aldrich Ave. S., Burnsville, 55337. Telephone: 612/890-1420. $23.95 for one; $28.95 for two in one bed; $30.95 for two in two beds; $32.95 for three or four in two beds.

● Imperial 400 Motor Inn, 2500 University St. SE, 55414. Telephone: 612/331-6000. $26 to $30 for one; $28 to $33 for two in one bed; $30 to $36 for two in two beds.

● Thrifty Scot Motel, 6445 James Circle, 55430. Telephone: 612/566-9810. $25.90 to $30.90 for one; $30.95 to $35.90 for two.

Where to Eat: Al's Breakfast, 413 14th Ave. SE (tel. 331-9991); LaVerne's Diner, 717 West Lake St. (tel. 823-0151); and La Peep, 89 South 10th St. (tel. 333-1855); are all recommended for breakfast.

● For lunch, choose from the Miles of Ailes Café, 1810 Riverside Ave. (tel. 375-0108); Lavender Kitchen, 430 Oak Grove St. (tel. 874-6502); or Tuthill's General Store and Ice Cream Parlor, 2455 Hennepin Ave., (tel. 377-4011).

At dinnertime, four possibilities are:

● Ping's, 1401 Nicollet Mall (tel. 874-9404). Great atmosphere and reasonably priced food.

● New Riverside Café, 329 Cedar Ave. S. (tel. 333-4814). The food is good in this university favorite for relaxing and just hanging out. It's a vegetarian restaurant with live entertainment Tuesday through Thursday.

● St. Anthony Main, 219 S.E. Main St. (tel. 379-4528). This is a complex of shops where you can sample a large variety of foods.

● Seward Community Café, 2129 Franklin Ave. E. (tel. 332-1011). This café is co-op owned and operated. The kitchen is run by members of a collective but out front they're all volunteers who work in return for a free meal. "This is a great place to meet locals in a rather funky vegetarian environment."

What to See and Do: Omni Theater/Science Museum of Minnesota, corner of Wabasha and Exchange, St. Paul. Telephone: 221-9400 or 221-9456. Shows every hour on the hour. $4.50 adults, $3.50 children and seniors.

● At the Foot of the Mountain, 2000 S. 5th St. (tel. 375-9487). A feminist theater with a sliding fee scale.

● Guthrie Theater, 725 Vineland Pl. (tel. 377-2225). One of America's finest repertory companies. For student rush tickets, go to the box office one hour before showtime—the best seats in the house will be $7.50.

● Theatre de la Jeune Lune/Southern Theater, 1420 Washington Ave. (tel.

333-6200). A half-French, half-American company that performs in both countries. The company prides itself on doing original work and has received some great reviews from critics.

● Toon the Grain Exchange!, 400 South 4th St. Telephone: 338-6212. Free tours at 8:45 a.m. and 10 a.m. No small children allowed.

● Minneapolis Institute of Art, 2400 3rd Ave. S. Telephone: 870-4046. An excellent collection. Open every day except Monday. $2 adults; $1 students; free for children under 12 and seniors.

● Minneapolis American Indian Art Gallery, 1530 East Franklin. Telephone: 871-9421. Open Monday to Friday only. Reserved exclusively for the arts and crafts of the American Indian.

● Mixed Blood Theater Company, 1501 South 4th St. Telephone: 338-6131. "A marvelous theater featuring the work of Black artists."

● **At Night:** The New French Bar/Café, 128 North 4th St. Telephone: 338-3790. An interesting Minneapolis environment and great café au lait. The bar is a good place to meet locals. "A nice mix of art deco, uptowners, good times, and lively conversation. Nice place to spend an evening."

Moorhead

On Campus: Moorhead State University is in this town. For information while you're there, call Campus Information (tel. 218/236-2011), or the Exchange in the Comstock Union (tel. 218/236-2261). At night, try Mick's Office, the Trader and Trapper, or East Gate Lounge to meet people.

Northfield

On Campus: St. Olaf College and Carleton College are both here in Northfield, the town that is famed for "its defeat of Jesse James." A student there describes it as "a typical small Midwestern town with a college emphasis."

For a full meal at lunchtime for $2.25, the Cage on the St. Olaf campus is the place to go. You can meet St. Olaf students at the Rueb-n-Stein in Northfield, and the A & M Bar in Dundas, a small community three miles away.

Owatonna

Accommodation: Thrifty Scot Motel, I-35 & Hwy. 14 W., P.O. Box 655, 55060. Telephone: 507/451-0380. $20.90 to $26.90 for one; $26.90 to $31.90 for two.

Rochester

Accommodations: Colony Inn Motel, Hwy. 52 & 2nd St. SW, 55902. Telephone: 507/282-2733. $22.99 for one to four people in one room.

● Friendship Centre Towne Travel Inn, 116 S.W. 5th St., 55901. Telephone: 507/289-1628. $22 to $29 for one; $26 to $34 for two in one bed; $26 to $36 for two in two beds.

● Motel 6, 2107 West Frontage Rd., 55901. Telephone: 507/282-8947. $17.95 for one; $21.95 for two; $2 for each additional person.

● Econo Lodge, V, 519 Third Ave. SW, 55901. Telephone: 507/288-1855. $28 for one; $30 for two in one bed; $34 for two in two beds.
● Comfort Inn, V &, 111 S.E. 28th St., 55904. Telephone: 507/286-1001. $25 to $26 for one; $33 to $34 for two.

Roseau

Accommodation: Guest House Motor Inn, 216 North Main Ave., 56751. Telephone: 218/463-2542. $17 to $27 for one; $4 for each additional person.

Roseville

Accommodations: Northwestern College, & (limited), 3003 North Snelling Ave., 55113. Telephone: 612/636-4840, extension 217. $22 single; $34 double; $40.50 triple. If you stay longer than one night the rates become lower. "Spectacular—new—similar to a fine hotel room."
● Cricket Inn of Roseville, Ⓢ&, 2550 Cleveland Ave. N., 55113. Telephone: 612/636-6730. $30.95 for one; $35.95 for two in one bed. Price includes continental breakfast.

St. Charles

Accommodation: Friendship White Valley Motel, Rte. 3, 55972. Telephone: 507/932-3142. $20 for one; $24 for two in one bed; $27 for two in two beds.

St. Cloud

On Campus: A student at St. Cloud University says the people there are "friendly and interested in conversing and finding things that they have in common." You can meet this talkative group at the Pub, the Red Carpet, the Loose Tie, D. B. Searle's, or the Persian Club. For inexpensive food, there's Alvie's, the Swan Café, Taco John's, McRudy's Pub, and the Cantina.
Accommodations: Thrifty Scot Motel, 130 14th Ave. NE, 56301. Telephone: 612/253-6320. $22.90 to $25.90 for one; $27.90 to $30.90 for two.
● Thrifty Scot Motel, 40 South 10th Ave., Waite Park, 56387. Telephone: 612/253-7070. $20.90 to $25.90 for one; $25.90 to $30.90 for two.
● Friendship Gateway Motel, 310 Lincoln Ave., 56301. Telephone: 612/252-4050. $20 to $24 for one; $22 to $26 for two in one bed; $26 to $30 for two in two beds.

St. Paul

Tourist Information: St. Paul Convention Bureau, Landmark Center, B-100, 55102. Telephone: 612/292-4360.
On Campus: The people at Hamline University in St. Paul recommended the food at Al's Breakfast at 413 14th Ave., SE in Minneapolis. Al obviously thinks that breakfast is not only the most important meal of the day, but also the only meal of the day, since his restaurant is open only for breakfast. Not far from

the St. Paul campus of the University of Minnesota you'll find the Muffuletta, 2260 Como Ave., a friendly neighborhood restaurant. For a good meal in St. Paul, you can go to the Caravan Serai, an Afghani restaurant, at 2046 Pinehurst Ave.

Students at the St. Paul campus of the University of Minnesota congregate at the student center, Valli Pizza, and Sammy D's. They also recommended contacting the Hennepin City and Ramsey City Historical Societies for information on the wonderful architecture in St. Paul, which includes art deco and late Victorian. The Ramsey number is 222-0701; Hennepin's is 870-1329.

Accommodations: Red Roof Inn, ⑤, 1806 Woodland Dr., Woodbury, 55125. Telephone: 612/738-7160. $22.95 for one; $27.95 for two in one bed; $29.95 for two in two beds; $31.95 for three or four in two beds.

● Exel Inn, 1739 Old Hudson Rd., 55106. Telephone: 612/771-5566. $27.95 for one; $32.95 for two in one bed; $34.95 for two in two beds.

● Hall Home Hostel (AYH), c/o John Teisbury. Telephone: 612/647-0611. $5 for AYH members. Advance reservations necessary.

Sauk Centre

Accommodation: Palmer House Hotel and Restaurant, 500 Sinclair Lewis Ave., 56378. Telephone: 612/352-3431. Near bus station. $13 single; $10 for each additional person. Advance reservations of two weeks necessary in summer. A restored 1901 hotel which is the model for Sinclair Lewis's "Minniemashie House" in his novel *Main Street.* There's a restaurant on the premises which will on occasion prepare a nine-course gourmet meal at a very reasonable price.

Stillwater

Accommodation: Driscoll Home Hostel (AYH), c/o Mina Driscoll, 1103 South 3rd St., 55082. Telephone: 612/439-7486. $5 for AYH members; $45 double for bed and breakfast accommodations.

Winona

Help: Winona Volunteer Services, 507/452-5591.

Accommodations: Prentice-Lucas Hall, ⑤, Winona State University, 265 West King St., 55987. Telephone: 507/457-5321. Seven blocks from bus; five blocks from train. Open June 4 to August 15. $10 single; $7 per person double.

"It is kept sparkling clean, and very, very quiet. I was treated like a member of the family."

● Sterling Motel, √, jct. 14-61 & Gilmore Ave., 55987. Telephone: 507/454-1120. $21 for one; $26 for two in one bed; $29 to $32 for two in two beds.

● Thrifty Scot Motel, 420 Cottonwood Dr., 55987. Telephone: 507/454-6930. $22.90 for one; $27.90 to $30.90 for two.

Worthington

Accommodations: Oxford Motel, Inc., 1801 Oxford St., 56187. Telephone: 507/376-6126. $16.96 for one; $20.14 for two in one bed; $23.32 for two in two beds.

- Sunset Motel, 207 Oxford St., 56187. Telephone: 507/376-6155. $22 single; $25 double; $28 triple; $30 quad.

Mississippi

Mississippi has made rich contributions to the literature of the U.S. with such native authors as William Faulkner, Eudora Welty, and Richard Wright. Rural and quite poor by national standards, Mississippi has much beauty to be seen, especially in some of its state parks. For a free guide to these parks, write to the Department of Natural Resources, Bureau of Recreation and Parks, P.O. Box 10600, Jackson, MS 39209.

Must-see sights in Mississippi would have to include the Natchez antebellum homes, the largest and—some say—most beautiful collection of preserved homes from the era before the Civil War. Cotton was king in Natchez, a Mississippi River port, and wealth was everywhere in the beginning of the 1800s. Natchez Trace Parkway is administered by the National Park Service, and on the portion between Tupelo and Natchez, drivers can stop at well-marked sites of historic or natural interest. Probably the most unsettling sight near the parkway is the view of the ruins of Windsor—40 columns are all that's left of a once-fabulous mansion.

And for those who are interested in the history of the Civil War, there's a national military park at Vicksburg, site of the 47-day Union siege after which the field was surrendered to General Grant. At the Visitors Center, the story of the battle is told through film and a variety of exhibits.

Some Special Events: Gum Tree Festival in Tupelo (May); Blessing of the Fleet in Biloxi (June); Deep-Sea Fishing Rodeo in Gulfport, and Choctaw Indian Fair in Philadelphia (July); Neshoba Country Fair in Philadelphia (August); and the Delta Blue Festival in Greenville, and Gumbo Festival of the Universe in Necaise Crossing (September).

Hitching: Although hitchhiking is not illegal in Mississippi as long as it's not done from the roadway, we've been told that the attitude toward young people on the road is generally unfriendly and suspicious. If you want to hitchhike concentrate your efforts on Interstates 55, 59, 10, and 20.

Tourist Information: Division of Tourism, Mississippi Department of Economic Development, Box 849, Room 1301, Walter Sillers Building, Jackson, MS 39205. Telephone: 601/359-3414. Ask for their vacation guide, *All the Things You're Missing. . . .*

Biloxi

Accommodation: Scottish Inn, 4660 West Beach Blvd., 39531. Telephone: 601/388-2610. July 1 to September 10: $25 to $35 for one; $30 to $40 for two in one bed; $35 to $55 for two in two beds. September 11 to December 31: $20 to $25 for one; $22 to $28 for two in one bed; $24 to $30 for two in two beds.

Corinth

Accommodation: Econo Lodge, √ &, Hwy. 72 & 45, P.O. Box 510, 38834. Telephone: 601/287-4421. $25.95 for one; $28.95 for two in one bed; $31.95 for two in two beds.

Dennis

Camping and Accommodation: Tishomingo State Park, Rte. 1, Box 310, 38838. Telephone: 601/438-6914. Family cabins equipped for light housekeeping. $34 for a one-bedroom cabin; $38 for a two-bedroom cabin which sleeps up to six. Advance reservations necessary. 13 miles of nature trails, canoeing, and lodge built by CCC.

Durant

Camping: Holmes County State Park, Rte. 1, Box 153, 39063. Telephone: 601/653-3351. Well equipped rustic cabins in great condition, with a view of the lake, for $32 to $34 per night; modern duplex cabins for $42 to $44 per night. Room for four to six people in cabins. Advance reservations necessary.

Grenada

Accommodation: Comfort Inn, I-55 & Miss. 8, Exit 54, Rte. 3, Box 300, 38901. Telephone: 601/226-6222. $28 for one; $32 for two.

Gulfport

Accommodation: Red Carpet Inn, 3314 West Beach Blvd., 39502. Telephone: 601/864-1381. $25 to $27 for one; $30 to $45 for two.

Hattiesburg

Camping and Accommodation: Paul B. Johnson State Park, 39401. Telephone: 601/582-7721. Besides camping at $5 to $9.50 per campsite, there are cabins that hold up to six people and rent for $39 to $42 per night. Bed linens and cooking utensils are furnished and some cabins have a fireplace.

Accommodations: Days Inn, 🏚, 3320 Hwy. 49 N., 39401. Telephone: 601/268-2251. $25.88 for one; $29.88 for two; $2 for each additional person.

● Motel 6, 3109 Hwy. 49 North, 39401. Telephone: 601/544-5016. $17.95 for one; $21.95 for two; $2 for each additional person.

● Econo Lodge, ✓, 3501 Hwy. 49 N., 39401. Telephone: 601/544-3475. $21.95 to $24.95 for one; $24.95 to $27.95 for two in one bed; $27.95 to $30.95 for two in two beds. Higher rates apply during special events.

Holly Springs

Camping and Accommodation: Wall Doxey State Park, Hwy. 7 S., 38635. Telephone: 601/252-4231. Modern vacation cabins with kitchen. $33 to $44 per night per cabin. Four to seven people per cabin. Camping: $5 to $8.50 per night. Advance reservations suggested. "A family-oriented park."

Iuka

Camping and Accommodation: J.P. Coleman State Park, Rte. 5, 38852. Telephone: 601/423-6515. Vacation cabins with bedroom, bath, kitchen, and some with living rooms. $37 to $45 per night per cabin. Motel rooms at park for $30.

Jackson

Help: Travelers Aid, 2906 North State St., Suite 105, 39202. Telephone: 601/366-3891.

Accommodations: Motel 6, 970 I-20 W., North Frontage Rd., 39201. Telephone: 601/948-3692. See Hattiesburg listing for rates.

● Days Inn, 🏚, 616 Briarwood Dr., 39211. Telephone: 601/957-1741. $29 for one; $34 for two.

● Days Inn, 🏚, Jackson I-20, U.S. 49 & U.S. 80 E., P.O. Box 6034, 39208. Telephone: 601/939-8200. $28 for one; $33 for two.

● Red Roof Inn, 🏚, 700 Larson St., I-55 & High St., 39202. $24.95 for one; $29.95 for two in one bed; $31.95 for two in two beds; $33.95 for three or four in two beds.

● Red Roof Inn, 🏚, 828 Hwy. 51 N., 39157. See above listing for rates.

● Scottish Inn, ✓, 2263 U.S. 80 W., 39204. Telephone: 601/969-1144. $19.95 for one; $21.95 for two in one bed; $24.95 for two in two beds.

● Red Carpet Inn, 2275 Hwy. 80 W., 39204. Telephone: 601/948-5561. $19.88 for one; $21.88 for two in one bed; $24.88 for two in two beds.

McComb

Camping and Accommodation: Percy Quin State Park, Rte. 3, 39648. Telephone: 601/684-3931. Men and women over 21. Besides rustic camping there are cabins furnished with linens and a kitchen. $38 to $55 per night. Some of the cabins can hold up to 12 people. Reservations necessary well in advance for cabins. Camping area is first come, first served for most sites.

Meridian

Accommodation: Motel 6, 2305 South Frontage Rd., 39300. See Hattiesburg listing for rates.

Morton

Camping and Accommodation: Roosevelt State Park, Star Route, 39117. Telephone: 601/732-6316. One-bedroom cabin with double beds, $29 to $36 per night; two-bedroom cabin with four double beds, $39 per night; three-bedroom cabin with six double beds, $43 per night. Three-night minimum in summer; two nights at other times. Advance reservations suggested.

Natchez

Accommodation: Scottish Inn, √, 40 Sargent Prentiss Dr., 39120. Telephone: 601/442-9141. $24 to $30 for one or two in one bed; $30 to $34 for two in two beds.

Oakland

Camping and Accommodation: George Payne Cossar State Park, Rte. 1, Box 64, 38648. Telephone: 601/623-7356. $42 per cabin which accommodates four people. Advance reservations suggested. "Eight duplex cabins with central air conditioning and heat, kitchens, screened porch, and fireplace—very modern." Designed to accommodate four people but roll-away beds are available for $3 each. Limit of three-night stay during summer months.

Oxford

On Campus: A friend at the University of Mississippi told us you can go to the Grill at the Student Union and find someone there who will be glad to help you find a place to stay. According to this same friend, the people at the university are very helpful and friendly. Foreign student visitors who need help may call the foreign student advisor's office. Telephone: 232-7404.

Since the legal age for beer drinking was lowered to 18 a few years ago, several bars have sprung up in Oxford. One friend's favorites are the Gin, in the old cotton gin, because it's "cheap, informal, and has good sandwiches and loud music," and the Warehouse, "because it has a lovely patio and a nice atmosphere, especially when the weather's nice."

To find a ride to wherever you're going, check the Ole Miss Union Ride Board.

Oxford was the home of William Faulkner and one Oxfordian wants you to be sure to visit the Faulkner home there. At the end of July there's a week-long Faulkner festival in the town which attracts writers from all over the world.

There are rooms available at the Residence Halls. The charge is $5 per person in a double room; you must provide your own linens. For information, call the Miller Housing Office at 601/232-7328.

Accommodation: Ole Miss Motel, 1517 East University Ave., 38655. Telephone: 601/234-2424. About four blocks from the campus of U. Miss. $19.44 to $21.50 single; $24.61 and up double.

Sardis

Camping and Accommodation: John W. Kyle State Park, Rte. 1, P.O. Box 115, 38666. Telephone: 601/487-1345. Twenty cabins that rent for $35 to $36 per night. 200 campsites available (electricity, water, and bath houses). Advance reservations of two months suggested. Three-night minimum May 1 to September 15; two-night minimum at other times.

Tupelo

Camping: Natchez Trace Parkway, RR 1, NT-143, 38801. Campgrounds at Jeff Busby, Meriwether Lewis, and Rocky Springs. Open year-round. No fee.

Camping and Accommodation: Tombigbee State Park, Rte. 2, Box 336E, 38801. Telephone: 601/842-7669. Open year round. Cabins large enough for four to six people that rent for $26 to $46 per night; campsites at $8.50 per night.

Vicksburg

Accommodation: Scottish Inn, 3955 Hwy. 80 E., 39180. Telephone: 601/638-5511. $21.88 for one; $24.88 for two in one bed; $24.88 to $28.88 for two in two beds.

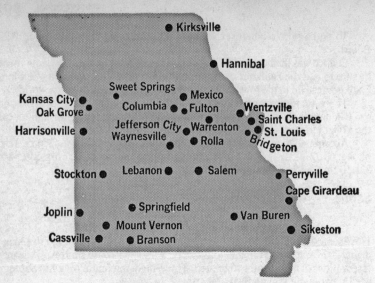

Missouri

Missouri is partly southern and partly western in philosophy and has produced such diverse personalities as Jesse James, Mark Twain, T. S. Eliot, and Harry S. Truman.

The northwestern part of the state is called the Pony Express Region, since it was from St. Joseph, in 1860, that the first Pony Express rider galloped on his way. Camping, picnicking, and water sports abound—and some people like to take a look at the home where the outlaw Jesse James was shot and killed. In the Mark Twain Region in the northeast, the town of Hannibal has preserved the author's boyhood home and has a Twain museum and the restored Becky Thatcher home.

In the center of the state, the huge Lake of the Ozarks attracts water lovers. And the there are the cities—Kansas City and St. Louis. Going south, the Ozark Playground Region has two of the area's best-known attractions: Silver Dollar City, a recreated 1870s town and entertainment park, and the outdoor pageant at Shepherd of the Hills Farm, which depicts the story of Ozarks frontier life.

Some Special Events: Women's Jazz Festival in Kansas City (March); Dogwood Festival in Camdenton (April); Valley of Flowers Festival in Florissant, and Family Bluegrass Music Weekend in Hermitage's Pomme de Terre State Park (May); International Festival in St. Louis, and Hillbilly Days in Bennett Spring State Park, Lebanon (June); National Tom Sawyer Fence Painting Contest in Hannibal (July 4); Bootheel Rodeo in Sikeston (August); Cotton Carnival in Sikeston (September); and Crafts Festival in Arrow Rock (October).

Hitching: Missouri is one of the states mentioned in the introduction that does not have laws against hitchhiking—except on Interstates. The State Highway Patrol put it this way: "Hitchhiking is legal in Missouri with no statutory limitations. Any road should suffice, so long as it takes you where you want to go. However, some municipalities have local ordinances which prohibit hitchhiking in the St. Louis, Columbia, and Kansas City areas on their way across country. One state police lieutenant warns hikers: "Be careful, especially at night when hitching at ramps that enter the interstate systems—this is where most of our accidents happen."

Tourist Information: Missouri Division of Tourism, P.O. Box 1055, Jefferson City, MO 65102. Telephone: 314/751-4133.

Branson

Accommodations: Friendship Paramount Inn, North Hwy. Bus. 65, 65616. Telephone: 417/334-2111. $28 to $30 for one; $30 to $32 for two in one bed; $32 to $36 for two in two beds.
- Friendship Inn Lampliter, 502 North 2nd, 65616. Telephone: 417/334-3431. $24 for one; $32 for two.
- Econo Lodge, √ ⑤, West Hwy. 76, 65616. Telephone: 417/334-3946. $28.95 for one; $32.95 for two in one bed; $36.95 for two in two beds.

Cape Girardeau

Accommodation: Sands Motel, √, I-55 Bus. Loop, Rte. 34, 63701. Telephone: 314/334-2828. $25 for one; $30 for two in one bed; $34 for two in two beds.

Cassville

Accommodation: Holiday Motel, 85 South Main St., 65625. Telephone: 417/847-3163. $22 for one; $24 for two in one bed; $28 for two in two beds.

Columbia

Accommodations: Red Roof Inn, 201 East Texas Ave., 65202. Telephone: 314/442-0145. $23.95 for one; $28.95 for two in one bed; $30.95 for two in two beds; $32.95 for three or four in two beds.
- Budget Host—Midway Budget Inn, I-70 & Hwy. 40, 65201. Telephone: 314/445-9565. $19.88 for one; $24.88 for two in one bed; $27.88 for two in two beds.
- Motel 6, 1718 North Providence Rd., 65201. Telephone: 314/442-3155. $17.95 for one; $21.95 for two; $2 for each additional person.
- Regal 8 Inn, 1800 I-70 Dr. SW, 65201. Telephone: 314/445-8433. $21.88 for one; $26.88 for two in one bed; $31.88 for two in two beds.

Fulton

Accommodation: Budget Host—Westwoods Motel, √, 422 Gaylord Dr.,

65251. Telephone: 314/642-5991. Airport transportation available. $21 for one; $24 for two in one bed; $28 for two in two beds.

Hannibal

Accommodation: Friendship Town House, 502 Mark Twain Ave. N. on Hwy. 36, 63401. Telephone: 314/221-4100. Limited airport service available. $22 to $28 for one; $26 to $32 for two in one bed; $28 to $34 for two in two beds.

Harrisonville

Accommodations: Budget Host—Cortez Motel, √ ($1), 1302 North Commercial (Box 58), 64701. Telephone: 816/884-3208. $20 for one; $26 for two in one bed; $28 for two in two beds.
● Friendship Caravan Motel, √ ($2), 39 miles southeast of Kansas City on U.S. 71 and three blocks north on Hwy. 291, 64701. Telephone: 816/884-4100. $23.65 for one; $28.38 for two in one bed; $31.21 for two in two beds.

Jefferson City

Accommodation: Regal 8 Inn, 808 Stadium Dr., 65101. Telephone: 314/634-2848. See Columbia listing for rates.

Joplin

Accommodations: Motel 6, 3031 South Range Line Rd., 64801. Telephone: 417/781-9115. See Columbia listing for rates.
● Budget Inn—Tropicana Motel, √ (10%), 2417 Rangeline Rd., 64801. Telephone: 417/624-8200. $24.50 for one; $26.50 for two in one bed; $28.50 for two in two beds. Extra large Olympic-size pool.

Kansas City

Tourist Information: Convention and Visitors Bureau of Greater Kansas City, Visitor Information Office, City Center Square, 1100 Main St., Suite 2550, 64105. Telephone: 816/221-5242.

On Campus: Once you're in Kansas City, stop by the Student Life Office, 131 University Center at 50th and Holmes, on the University of Missouri campus. The office can give you information on upcoming lectures, concerts, films, off-campus housing, and tuition-free classes through Kansas City's free university.

Accommodations: Red Roof Inn, 🚻, 3636 Northeast Randolph Rd., 64117. Telephone: 816/452-8585. September 3 to May 23: $24.95 for one; $29.95 for two in one bed; $31.95 for two in two beds; $33.95 for three or four in two beds. May 24 to September 2: $27.95 for one; $32.95 for two in one bed; $34.95 for two in two beds; $36.95 for three or four in two beds.

- Red Roof Inn, 13712 East 42nd Terrace, Independence, 64055. Telephone: 816/373-2800. $24.95 for one; $29.95 for two in one bed; $31.95 for two in two beds; $33.95 for three or four in two beds.
- Motel 6, 901 West Jefferson St., Blue Springs, 64015. Telephone: 816/229-7430. See Columbia listing for rates.
- Motel 6, 8230 N.W. Prairie View Rd., 64152. Telephone: 816/587-0287. See Columbia listing for rates.
- TraveLodge, ✓ ⓱, 921 Cherry St., 64106. Telephone: 816/471-1266. $27 for one; $30 for two in one bed; $32 for two in two beds.
- Regal 8 Inn, 6400 East 87th St., 64138. Telephone: 816/333-4468. $23.88 for one; $28.88 for two in one; $33.88 for two in two beds. Indoor pool.
- Budget Host—Royale Inn, ✓, 600 Paseo, 64106. Telephone: 816/471-5544. $21 to $25 for one; $27 to $32 for two in one bed; $34 to $40 for two in two beds. Heated pool and sundeck.
- Budget Host—Canaan Motel, 10301 East 40 Hwy., Independence, 64055. Telephone: 816/353-1413. $24 to $35 for one or two in one bed; $32 to $42 for two in two beds.
- Schuyler Hotel (AYH-SA), 1017 Locust, 64106. Telephone: 816/842-6550. $10 for AYH members.
- Thrifty Scot Motel, 2232 Taney St., 64116. Telephone: 816/421-6000. $25.90 to $30.90 for one; $30.90 to $35.90 for two.

Kirksville

On Campus: Northeast Missouri State University is in this town, which is described by a friend there as "All American." We're told that the general attitude toward young people "on the road" is good, but that hitchhiking is not recommended.

An inexpensive place to stay in town is the Village Inn Motel, at 1304 South Baltimore, 63501. For moderate-priced meals, try Manhattan Restaurant, 108 South Elson St.; Golden Corral, 1707 South Baltimore; Country Kitchen, 2700 South Baltimore; or any of the fast-food chains in the area. A favorite gathering place for young people is The Oz. For information on apartments, rides, etc., check the bulletin board in the Student Union Building or the campus newspaper, *The Index.*

Lebanon

Accommodations: Friendship Holiday Motel, Exit 130 off I-44, City Rte. 66 E., 65536. Telephone: 417/532-7176. Limited airport service available. $15.95 to $21.60 for one; $19.95 to $29.60 for two in one bed; $29.60 to $36.85 for two in two beds.

- Econo Lodge, ✓ ⓱, Bus. Loop I-44 W., 65536. Telephone: 417/588-3226. $28.95 for one; $32.95 for two in one bed; $36.95 for two in two beds.

Mexico

Accommodation: Air Park Motel, √ (10%), Hwy. 54 E., 65265. Telephone: 314/581-2795. $25 for one; $27 for two in one bed; $29 for two in two beds. There is a 3% cash discount.

Mount Vernon

Accommodation: Budget Host—Ranch Motel, jct. I-44 & Hwy. 39 (Box 6B), 65712. Telephone: 417/466-2125. $20 to $22 single; $24 to $27 for two in one bed; $26 to $30 for two in two beds.

Oak Grove

Accommodation: Econo Lodge, √, 300 South Outer Belt Rd., 64075. Telephone: 816/625-3681. $25.95 for one; $28.95 for two in one bed; $31.95 for two in two beds.

Perryville

Accommodations: Park-Et Motel, Hwy. 61, Rte. 2, 63775. Telephone: 314/547-4516. $20 for one; $24 for two; $28 for three; $32 for four.
● Town House Motel, √ (10% with cash only), 1207 Kings Hwy., 65401. Telephone: 314/341-3700. $19.95 for one; $22.95 for two in one bed; $24.95 for two in two beds.
● Budget Host-Interstate Motel, √ (5%), 1631 Martin Spring Dr., 65401. Telephone: 314/341-2158. $16.90 to $19.90 single; $20.95 to $23.95 for two in one bed; $23.95 to $29.95 for two in two beds.

Rolla

Accommodation: Econo Lodge, √ Ⓑ, I-44 W. & Martin Spring Dr., 65401. $19.95 for one; $22.95 for two in one bed; $24.95 for two in two beds.

St. Charles

Accommodation: Budget Host—Budget Motel, 3717 I-70, 63301. Telephone: 314/724-3717. $29 to $30 for one or two in one bed; $34 to $45 for two to four in two beds.

St. Louis

Lewis and Clark launched their two-year expedition from St. Louis, at the confluence of the Mississippi and Missouri Rivers. The Gateway Arch is the symbol of modern St. Louis, but not far from it are reminders of St. Louis's past: the Old Courthouse and the Basilica of St. Louis King of France, the oldest cathedral west of the Mississippi River, where Mass is celebrated daily. Not far, too, is Laclede's Landing, the last remaining historic area of the city's waterfront where buildings dating from 1830 have been restored and converted into restaurants, shops, and offices. A long time ago, in 1904, St. Louis hosted a World's Fair in a 1400-acre Forest Park, which has since become a well-loved tourist attraction with its Zoo, Planetarium, Municipal Opera, Art Museum, and Historical Society.

Good sources of information on what's happening in St. Louis are *St. Louis Magazine* and the magazine's annual, *Inside St. Louis* ($3.95), Thursday's edition of the *Post Dispatch,* radio station KSHE-AM, or Fun Phone (tel. 421-2100). You'll also want to have a copy of the Convention and Visitors Bureau's *St. Louis Visitor's Guide;* it's free. The Convention and Visitors Bureau is at 10 South Broadway, 63102 (tel. 421-1023 or 421-2100) for a special-events recording. If you're driving into the city you may want to stop at the Missouri Tourism-St. Louis office on the I-270 at the Riverview exit in North St. Louis. Telephone: 869-7100.

St. Louis loves holidays and likes to celebrate in grand style. The Veiled Prophet Fair, held over the 4th of July weekend, is the largest 4th of July celebration in the U.S. The National Ragtime and Jazz Festival is held in the early part of June. Check the Calendar of events in the *Post Dispatch* for current information.

Getting There: The airport is about ten miles from town and a limousine connection costs $5.90 one way. The limousine will also take you to St. Louis and Washington Universities. A taxi costs about $18. It's possible, too, to take the public bus from the airport to downtown—the Natural Bridge Bus—for only 75¢. The Greyhound Terminal is at 801 North Broadway; Trailways is just a few steps away at 706. The train station is at 550 South 16th St. Transportation from both stations is available by bus or taxi.

Getting Around: The bus fare is 75¢; 85¢ if you want a transfer. Bus stop (in St. Louis they call them bus starts, for a more positive image) signs are posted on lampposts, at just about every corner. Taxis can be flagged or called ahead. They charge 90¢ a mile. Express buses are $1.

Accommodations: Bed & Breakfast St. Louis is a reservation service which lists accommodations in private homes in the St. Louis area for $30 single and $35 to $50 for a double. For details, write to them at 4418 West Pine St., St. Louis, MO 63108.

● Washington University Guest Housing, 6515 Wydown Blvd., P.O. Box 1075, 63015. Telephone: 314/889-5073. Ask for Tootie Williams, Guest Housing Director. Men, women, and children. Open June 1 to August 15. $14 single; $12 per person double. Meals available during weekdays. Advance reservations preferred.

● YWCA, 2709 Locust St., 63103. Telephone: 314/533-9400. Women only, 18 and over. $14 single; $13 per person double. $1 off rates for AYH members.

● Huckleberry Finn Youth Hostel (AYH), 1904–1906 South 12th St., 63104. Telephone: 314/241-0076. Closed January 1 to 31. $6.25 summer, $7.25 winter for AYH members. Advance reservations necessary April to September.

● Ivy Motel, 10143 Old Olive St., 63141. Telephone: 314/993-9785. A small hotel. $22 single; $25 to $30 double.

● Westward Motel, 1580 South Kirkwood Rd., 63127. Telephone: 314/822-7171. $28 single; $30 for two in one bed; $34 for two in two beds. Advance reservations necessary during summer.

- Air-Way Motel, √ (10%), 4125 North Lindbergh Blvd., Bridgeton, 63044. Telephone: 314/291-3414. $27.19 to $35.42 for one or two in one bed; $32.68 for two in two beds. Price includes continental breakfast.
- Scottish Inn, 4607 Airflight Dr., 63134. Telephone: 314/428-9310. Courtesy car to airport. $24.95 to $34.95 for one; $38.95 to $44.95 for two.
- Regal 8 Inn, 3655 Pennridge, Bridgeton, 63044. Telephone: 314/291-6100. See Columbia listing for rates.
- Motel 6, 4576 Woodson Rd. (at airport), 63134. Telephone: 314/427-6100. See Columbia listing for rates.
- Motel 6, I-270 & Bellefontaine Rd., 63138. See Columbia listing for rates.
- Red Roof Inn, ⓖ, 3470 Hollenberg, Bridgeton, 63044. Telephone: 314/291-3350. See Kansas City listing for rates.
- Red Roof Inn, 307 Dunn Rd., Florissant, 63031. Telephone: 314/831-7900. See Kansas City listing for rates.
- Red Roof Inn, ⓖ, 5823 Wilson Ave., 63110. See Kansas City listing for rates.
- Red Roof Inn, ⓖ, 11837 Lackland Rd., 63146. $26.95 for one; $31.95 for two in one bed; $33.95 for two in two beds; $35.95 for three or four in two beds.
- Econo Lodge, √, 4575 North Lindbergh Blvd., Bridgeton, 63044. Telephone: 314/731-3000. $26.95 for one; $28.95 for two in one bed; $32.95 for two in two beds. Higher rates apply during special events.
- Curtis Home Hostel (AYH), c/o Ted Curtis, 355 Marion Ave., Webster Grove, 63119. Telephone: 314/962-0853. $4 for AYH members. Advance reservations necessary by phone.
- Forest Park Hotel, 4910 West Pine, 63108. Telephone: 314/361-3500. Regular rates are $42 for a single and $46 for a double but there's a student rate of $36 single, $40 double. In suites for three or more, the per-person rate goes down. "This hotel is in one of the most interesting sections of town—the Central West End—and is within walking distance of just about whatever you'd want to do in St. Louis."

Where to Eat: One of the best areas of town to find good food at reasonable prices is the Loop in University City on the 6200 to 6500 blocks of Delmar Blvd. This area has the highest concentration of ethnic restaurants in the city. Some possibilities:

- Zorba the Greek, 6346 Delmar Blvd. Telephone: 721-5638. Serves appetizers—tzantziki ($1.25), spanakopita ($1.95), gyros ($2.75), and full dinners of moussaka, rice, salad, and pita for $4.95. Combine dinner at Zorba's with a film at the Tivoli next door.
- Cicero's. A typical Italian restaurant with an all-you-can-eat special on weekdays.
- Koh-I-Noor, 6271 Delmar. Simple and basic decor but the Pakistani food is delicious.
- Saleems, 6501 Delmar. Telephone: 721-7947. A beautiful atmosphere and excellent Lebanese food. There are dinners but the sandwiches like shish-taouk, (marinated broiled chicken in pita bread with vegetables and tahini sauce for $3.95) are filling enough for a meal.
- La Patisserie, 6269 Delmar. Telephone: 725-4902. A perfect breakfast place for the pastry lover.
- Blueberry Hill, 6504 Delmar. This rock 'n' roll memorabilia haven has

darts, pinball machines, poetry readings and other unexpected treats along with food.

The Central West End is a wonderful area for the visitor to St. Louis to explore. Many of the restaurants in the area have tables outside in fair weather. It's fun to stroll along Euclid Street or to sit and watch the passing parade. Some possibilities.

● Cellini's, 331 North Euclid, is a good vantage point. You can have a salad, sandwiches, dessert, or a pasta special.

● West End Café, 2 North Euclid. For nighthawks; open until 3 a.m. and offers a fairly extensive menu with most dishes under $5. Chicken wings are a St. Louis specialty, and at the West End Café they're about half the price than they are down the street at Culpepper's.

● Magic Wok, Maryland Plaza. Telephone: 367-2626 or 2657. Good for a Chinese lunch.

● Dressels, 419 N. Euclid and Llewellyn's, 4747 McPherson, are two Welsh-style pubs. "I like Llewellyn's best—the homemade potato chips are great and the beer selection is extensive."

What to See and Do: Gateway Arch, 111 North 4th St. Designed by Eero Saarinen, the 630-foot arch is the nation's tallest memorial. Each leg of the arch has a passenger train to carry visitors to the top for a 30-mile-wide view. The ride costs $1 for adults, 50¢ for children.

● Museum of Westward Expansion, in the underground area beneath the arch, which tells the story of the pioneers and the people who made St. Louis.

● Huck Finn, Samuel Clemens and Tom Sawyer Riverboat, foot of Washington Ave. Telephone: 621-4040. Cruises from Memorial Day to Labor Day. $5. Dinner-dance cruises are $19.75 and include dinner and cocktails.

● Soulard Market, 7th and Lafayette. An interesting public market in South St. Louis.

● Laclede's Landing. Near the Gateway Arch and Mississippi River. Neighborhood of stores, bars, and restaurants—the "original" St. Louis. Park at the riverfront, go to the Arch, and walk around. In the evening, enjoy jazz at the Lt. Robert E. Lee Riverboat.

● Grant's Farm, 10501 Gravois. Telephone: 843-1700. Land once farmed by Ulysses S. Grant. A train without tracks takes you through a game preserve.

● Jewel Box, Forest Park. Telephone: 535-4111. A floral conservatory that's open all year.

● Six Flags Over Mid-America, in Eureka. A big theme park with rides, games, shops, etc. Admission for the day, $10.99.

● St. Louis Art Museum, Forest Park. Telephone: 721-0067. Over 70 galleries displaying representative pieces of art of the last 3000 years. Free admission. Tours on Wednesday, Friday, Saturday, and Sunday.

● Municipal Opera, in Forest Park. Telephone: 361-1900. World's largest outdoor summer musical theater—seats 12,000. In summer, features a ten-week repertory of light operas, musicals, and dance performances.

● Central West End, with Euclid St. at its heart, is only a few blocks away from Forest Park. Most of the fun here is walking around, looking at the stately mansions, the outdoor cafés and the lively street life. Two blocks from Euclid, at the corner of Lindell and Newstead, is the New St. Louis Cathedral, built in 1907, which combines Byzantine and Romanesque architecture and has a fine collection of mosaics.

- Laumeier Sculpture Garden, Geyer and Rotts Rd. Telephone: 821-1209. A 97.8-acre park with art, nature trails, picnic facilities, and an amphitheater for summer plays and concerts.
- Missouri Botanical Gardens, 4344 Shaw. Telephone: 577-5100. A national historic landmark; home of the Climation, the world's largest geodesic-dome greenhouse, a traditional Japanese garden, and more. $1 admission.
- McDonnell Planetarium, 5100 Claydon Rd., Forest Park. Telephone: 781-0900. More than 2500 animals in a naturalistic setting. A children's zoo and a zoo line railroad. Admission is free.

Shopping: The 6200-6500 blocks of Delmar are as good for shopping as they are for ethnic eating. Try Paul's Books (there really is a Paul); Streetside Records, 6314 Delmar for classical, rock, and soul; Vintage Vinyl, 6354 Delmar for used records. With the St. Louis conservatory of music a few blocks away, this is a good place for sheet music and musical instruments too.

Salem

Accommodation: Steelman Lodge, ♿, in Montauk State Park, Rte. 5, RFD Box 278, 65560. Telephone: 314/548-2434. Accommodations include a modern motel with a restaurant, 14 housekeeping cabins, and 10 individual nonhousekeeping cabins. Facilities are open March 1 to October 31 and cost from $25 to $50. Specialties of the area are trout fishing and floating on Current River.

Sikeston

Accommodation: Econo Lodge, ∨, I-55 & Hwy. 62, P.O. Box 701, 63801. Telephone: 314/471-7400. $23.95 for one; $26.95 for two in one bed; $30.95 for two in two beds.

Springfield

Accommodations: Regal 8 Inn, 3114 North Kentwood, 65803. Telephone: 417/833-0880. See Columbus listing for rates.
- Motel 6, 2455 North Glenstone Ave., 65803. Telephone: 417/865-1151. See Columbus listing for rates.
- TraveLodge, ∨, 505 St. Louis St., 65806. Telephone: 417/866-0801. $21 for one; $23 for two in one bed; $27 for two in two beds.
- Friendship Inn Springfield, 2555 North Glenstone Ave., 65803. Telephone: 417/864-8459. $20 to $24 for one; $22 to $28 for two in one bed; $24 to $30 for two in two beds.
- Scottish Inn, 2601 North Glenstone, 65803. Telephone: 417/865-6565. $22 to $25 for one; $24 to $27 for two in one bed; $28 to $32 for two in two beds.

Stockton

Accommodation: Lake Stockton Motel, 506 East Hwy. 32 (Box 538), 65785. Telephone: 417/276-5151. $18 for one; $20 for two in one bed; $23 for two in two beds.

Sweet Springs

Accommodation: Budget Host—The Marmaduke Inn, √ 🚳 ($2), 1001 North Locust, 65351. Telephone: 816/335-6315. $20 to $25 for one; $24 to $28 for two in one bed; $26 to $31 for two in two beds.

Van Buren

Camping: Ozark National Scenic Riverway, P.O. Box 490, 63965. Eleven campgrounds open year round. Canoe rentals available at three of them. $5 per campsite per night.

Accommodation: Smalley's Budget Host Motel, √ ($1), Hwy. 60 (Box 358), 63965. Telephone: 314/323-4263 or 4264. Besides the motel, there are two cabins available. $20 for one; $25 for two in one bed; $30 to $35 for two in two beds; $45 for cabins with 3 beds; $70 for a cabin with four beds and kitchen.

Warrenton

Accommodation: Budget Host—Raja Inn, √, 220 Arlington Way, 63383. Telephone: 314/456-4301. $22 for one or two in one bed; $27 for two in two beds.

Waynesville

Accommodation: Friendship Deville Motor Inn, Box A, Bus. Rte. I-44 E., 65583. Telephone: 314/336-3113. Limited airport service available. $24 to $28 for one or two in one bed; $28 to $36 for two in two beds.

Wentzville

Accommodation: Budget Host—Budget Motel, I-70 at Hwy. 61, 63385. Telephone: 314/327-5212. $24.50 for one or two in one bed; $29.21 for two to four in two beds.

Montana

Montana, especially the western part with its mountains and mountain valleys, is camping, hiking, and horseback-riding country. The scenery is spectacular and there's enough space for everyone. Montana is home to the Awesome Glacier National Park, miles of hiking trails, incredible wildlife, and seven North American tribes. If you visit any of the reservations you'll discover some very small museums, filled with samples of some absolutely exquisite Indian crafts. Three of the entrances to Yellowstone National Park are in Montana, but since most of the park is in Wyoming, see the section on that state for the Yellowstone listing.

Falcon Crest, P.O. Box 279 M, Billings, MT 59103, publishes five guides to the state—*The Angler's Guide to Montana,* by Mike Sample ($7.95); *The Hiker's Guide to Montana,* by Bill Schneider ($7.95); *The Nordic Skier's Guide to Montana,* by Elaine Sedlach ($6.95); *The Rockhound's Guide to Montana,* by Bob Feldman; and *The Traveller's Guide to Montana,* by Gary Turlach ($7.95).

Some Special Events: Community College Rodeo in Miles City (April); Memorial Day Pow-wow in Lame Deer (May); Centennial Celebration in Glendive (July); Dawson County Fair and Rodeo in Glendive, Eastern Montana Fair in Miles City, Northern Cheyenne Labor Day Rodeo in Busby, and White River Cheyenne Pow-wow in Busby (all in September).

Hitching: The law states that no one "shall stand in a roadway for the purpose of soliciting a ride." When we asked the State Police whether they had any special advice for hitchhikers in Montana, they answered: "Don't thumb from the traveled portion of any roadway. Stay in the southern and western part of the state."

A friend in Great Falls advises hitchhikers to stay away from that city and use a more southerly route through Montana—people just aren't interested in helping hitchhikers in that area of the state.

Tourist Information: Travel Montana, Department of Commerce, Helena, MT 59620.

Billings

Accommodations: Motel 6, 5400 Midland Rd., RR 9, 59102. Telephone: 406/248-7759. $17.95 for one; $21.95 for two; $2 for each additional person.

● Regal 8 Inn, I-90 & Midland Rd., 59102. Telephone: 406/248-7551. $21.88 for one; $26.88 for two in one bed; $31.88 for two in two beds. Indoor pool.

● Kings Rest Motel, 1206 East Main St., 59105. Telephone: 406/252-8451. $24 for one; $26 for two in one bed; $28 for two in two beds.

● Lewis & Clark Inn, 1709 First Ave. N., 59101. Telephone: 406/252-4691. $22 for one; $27 for two in one bed; $29 for two in two beds.

● Juniper Motel, 1315 North 27th St., 59101. Telephone: 406/245-4128. $26 to $28 for one; $30 to $32 for two in one bed; $32 to $34 for two in two beds.

● Esquire Inn, 3314 First Ave. N., 59101. Telephone: 406/259-4551. $32 for one or two in one bed; $38 for two in two beds.

● Thrifty Scot Motel, 1345 Mulberry Lane, 59101. Telephone: 406/252-2584. $33.90 for one; $30.90 to $37.90 for two.

● Imperial 400 Motor Inn, √ (10%), 2601 Fourth Ave. N., 59101. Telephone: 406/245-6646. $27 to $31 for one; $31 to $34 for two in one bed; $34 to $39 for two in two beds.

● Picture Court Motel, √, 5146 Laurel Rd., 59101. Telephone: 406/252-8478. $21 for one; $25 for two in one bed; $30 for two in two beds.

Bozeman

Accommodations: Rainbow Motel, 510 North Seventh Ave., 59715. Telephone: 406/587-4201. $18 to $22 for one; $20 for two in one bed; $24 for two in two beds; $30 for three in three beds. Rates are $2 lower in winter months.

● Imperial 400 Motor Inn, √ (10%), 122 West Main St., 59715. Telephone: 406/587-4481. $22 to $30 for two in one bed; $28 to $32 for two in two beds.

● Thrifty Scot Motel, 1321 North Seventh Ave., 59715. Telephone: 406/587-5251. $22.90 to $28.90 for one; $27.90 to $33.90.

Butte

Accommodation: Mile Hi Hotel, √ ★, 3499 Harrison Ave., 59701. Telephone: 406/494-2250. $22 to $32 single; $30 to $40 double; $38 to $45 triple. Advance reservations suggested. Heated pool.

Columbia Falls

Accommodation: Mountain Shadows Motel, Box O, jct. U.S. 2 & 206, 59912. Telephone: 406/892-4333. $21 for one; $24 for two in one bed; $29 for two in two beds.

Cooke City

Accommodations: Friendship Paulsens High Country Inn, west on Hwy. 212, west of Cooke City General Store, 59020. Telephone: 406/838-2272. $22 to $26 for one; $26 to $30 for two in one bed; $28 to $30 for two in two beds.

● All Seasons Inn, √, U.S. 212, Box 1130, 59020. Telephone: 406/838-2251. $24 for one; $28 to $45 for two in one bed; $32 for two in two beds.

Darby

Accommodation: Tipi Hostel, Box 16, 59829. Telephone: 406/821-3792, c/o Jenny Sweet. Open in late spring to late October. $3 per night in a tipi. "An informal place to stay with spacious lawn for tents and a shower and cooking facilities." Bikers preferred.

Fort Smith

Camping: Bighorn Canyon National Recreation Area, P.O. Box 458, 59035. Camping May 1 to November 1 at Black Canyon Boat Camp, (access by boat only) and all year at Horseshoe Bend, Barry's Landing, and Black Canyon Boat Camp (access by boat only). $3 per campsite per night at Horseshoe Bend.

Glendive

Accommodation: Thrifty Scot Motel, 2000 North Merrill Ave., 59330. Telephone: 406/365-6011. $21.90 to $26.90 for one; $26.90 to $31.90 for two.

Great Falls

Help: Crisis Center, 406/453-6511
Accommodations: Wright Nite Wagon Wheel Motel, √ (10%), 2620 Tenth Ave. S., 59405. Telephone: 406/761-1300. $22.50 to $26.50 for one; $32 to $34 for two in one bed; $38.50 to $40.50 for two in two beds.
● Imperial 400 Motor Inn, √ (10%), 601 Second Ave. N., 59401. Telephone: 406/452-9581. $24 to $28 for one: $27 to $30 for two in one bed; $30 to $34 for two in two beds.

Helena

Accommodations: Motel 6, 800 North Oregon, 59601. Telephone: 406/442-1311. See Billings listing for rates.
● Imperial 400 Motor Inn, √ (10%), 524 North Last Chance Gulch, 59601. Telephone: 406/442-0600. $26 to $30 for one; $30 to $34 for two in one bed; $34 to $38 for two in two beds.
● Thrifty Scot Motel, 2001 Prospect Ave., 59601. Telephone: 406/442-3280. $23.90 to $28.90 for one; $28.90 to $33.90 for two.

Kalispell

Accommodations: Motel 6, 1540 Hwy. 93 S., 59901. Telephone: 406/755-6669. See Billings listing for rates.

● Thrifty Scot Motel, 1830 Hwy. 93 S., 59901. Telephone: 406/755-3798. $25.90 to $32.90 for one; $29.90 to $36.90 for two.

Miles City

Accommodation: Motel 6, 1314 Haynes Ave., Rte. 2, Box 3396, 59301. Telephone: 406/232-6662. See Billings listing for rates.

Missoula

Help: Crisis Center, 406/543-8277.

Accommodations: University of Montana Residence Halls, c/o Room 101 Turner Hall, 59812. Telephone: 406/243-2611 or 243-2612. Ask for Ron Brunell. For men and women who are affiliated with the university in some capacity, e.g., visiting faculty, students, those attending workshops on campus, prospective students, etc. Open June 10 to August 10. $9 single; $7 per person double (rates subject to change). Advance reservations necessary.

● The Birchwood Youth Hostel, 600 South Orange St., 59801. Telephone: 406/728-9799. Closed December 15 to December 30. $4.25 to $4.75. Priority given to members of AYH/IYHF, bicycle tourists, backpackers, and foreign visitors; others welcome as space permits. Reservations recommended during the summer. Fully equipped kitchen. Bicycle storage and laundromat.

Polebridge

Accommodation: North Fork Hostel (AYH), Ⓢ∨ ★, end of Beaver Dr. (mailing address: P.O. Box 1, 59928). Telephone: 406/888-5518. Open year-round, except December 14 to 31. Large rustic log cabin adjacent to Glacier National Park. No electricity. $6 for AYH members; $7 for other. Shower and complete kitchen. Bring sleeping bag. Advance reservations of two weeks suggested.

Red Lodge

Accommodations: Best Value Valli Hi Motor Lodge, 320 South Broadway, P.O. Box 849, 59068. Telephone: 406/446-1414. $22 to $29 for one; $25 to $31 for two in one bed; $28 to $32 for two in two beds.

● Friendship Yodeler Motel, 601 South Broadway, Rte. 212. Telephone: 406/446-1435. $22.50 to $30 for one; $28 to $35 for two in one bed; $30 to $40 for two in two beds.

Shelby

Accommodation: O'Haire Manor Motel, 204 2nd St. S., 59474. Telephone: 406/434-5555. $24 for one; $30 for two in one bed; $36 for two in two beds.

West Glacier

Camping: Glacier National Park, 59936. Fifteen campgrounds open June to September (except for Apgar, which is open May to October). Horseback riding nearby at four: Sprague Creek, Many Glacier Corral, Lake McDonald Corral, and Apgar Corral. $4 to $6 per campsite per night; Bowman Creek and River (North Fork) are free.

West Yellowstone

Help: Social Services Center, 236 Yellowstone Ave. Telephone: 406/646-7311.

Accommodations: Alpine Motel, 120 Madison, 59758. Telephone: 406/646-7544. Across from bus station. Open May 1 to October 15. $23 single; $32 double; $48 triple. Recommended by a reader from West Germany.

• Best Value Traveler's Lodge, ∨, 225 Yellowstone Ave. (P.O. Box C), 59715. Telephone: 406/646-7773. $25 to $30 for one; $25 to $38 for two in one bed; $28 to $44 for two in two beds.

• Friendship Three Bear Lodge, 2½ blocks west of park entrance, 217 Yellowstone Ave., 59758. Telephone: 406/646-7353. $26 to $36 for one; $20 to $38 for two in one bed; $32 to $42 for two in two beds.

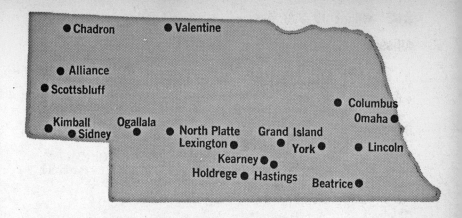

Nebraska

Not surprisingly, the people at the Division of Travel and Tourism in Nebraska want you to save time for what they call "the Good Life of Nebraska." Nebraska's "good life" is available both indoors and out. Canoeists should write for *Canoeing Nebraska* and bikers should ask for *Backpacking: Trails to Nebraska's Great Outdoors*, both available free from the address below.

For those who prefer museums, Nebraska has three that may interest you: the Joslyn Art Museum in Omaha, which has a well received collection of art from ancient to modern times and a group of paintings and artifacts from the Maximillian expedition to the upper Missouri in the mid-1800s; the Museum of the Fur Trade, near Chadron, which tells the story of that lively enterprise from the point of view of the traders, trappers, and Indians; and the University of Nebraska State Museum in Lincoln, a museum of natural history which features, among other things, "Ceres the Transparent Woman."

Since the sport of rodeo began in Nebraska in 1882, it would seem appropriate to attend at least one while you're in that state. North Platte, Burwell, and Omaha host three of the biggest rodeos.

Some Special Events: Brownville Spring Festival, and Gold Old Days Jubilee in Crete (May); Buffalo Bill Rodeo in North Platte (June); Republican River Canoe Race in Franklin (July); Frontier County Fair in Stockville, and Nebraska State fair, Lincoln (September).

Hitching: A friend at Nebraska Free University in Lincoln says that hitching in Lincoln is acceptable, but in Omaha it's more difficult. He suggests sticking to main roads and standing on the curb. "If you're planning to go into Colorado from Nebraska, make sure you can get a ride through to your destination because Colorado police are tough on hitchhikers." Officially, hitchhiking is legal in Nebraska on all roads except the Interstate system.

Tourist Information: Division of Travel and Tourism, Nebraska Department of Economic Development, P.O. Box 94666, 301 Centennial Mall South, Lincoln, NE 68509. Telephone: 402/471-3796 or 800/228-4307 out of state, 800/742-7595 in Nebraska.

Alliance

Accommodation: Budget Host—McCarroll's Motel, 1028 East 3rd, 69301. Telephone: 308/762-3680. $24.50 to $26.50 for one or two in one bed; $28.50 to $30.50 for two in two beds.

Beatrice

Accommodation: Budget Host—Holiday Villa, 1820 North 6th (Box 708), 68310. Telephone: 402/223-4036. $22 to $26 for one; $24.50 to $28 for two in one bed; $29 to $33 for two in two beds.

Chadron

Accommodation: Friendship Grand Motel, 1050 West Hwy. 20 (two blocks east of 385 Jct.), 69337. Limited airport service available. Telephone: 308/432-5595. $18 to $24 for one; $20 to $28 for two in one bed; $24 to $32 for two in two beds.

Columbus

Accommodation: Friendship Gembol's Inn, 3220 8th St., 68601. Limited airport service available. Telephone: 402/564-2729. $18 to $24 for one; $20 to $26 for two in one bed; $24 to $30 for two in two beds.

Grand Island

Tourist Information: Visitor Information, Hall County Convention and Visitors Bureau, P.O. Box 1486, 309 West 2nd St., 68802. Telephone: 308/382-9210.
Accommodations: Friendship Lazy V Motel, 2703 East Hwy. 30, 68801. Telephone: 308/384-0700. $18 for one; $22 for two in one bed; $25 for two in two beds.
● TraveLodge, √, 507 West 2nd St., 68801. Telephone: 308/384-1000. $25 for one; $30 for two in one bed; $34 for two in two beds.

Hastings

Accommodations: Friendship Inn X-L Motel, jct. of U.S. Hwy. 6, 34 & 281 W., 68901. Telephone: 402/463-3148. $20 to $22 for one; $25 to $27 for two in one bed; $27 to $30 for two in two beds.
● Budget Host—Rainbow Motel, √, 1000 West J St., 68901. Telephone: 402/463-2989. $22 for one; $27 to $31 for two in one bed; $28 to $33 for two in two beds.

Holdrege

Accommodation: Friendship Plains Motel, six blocks west of jct. U.S. 183

& 6-34, 68949. Telephone: 308/995-8646. $18 to $28 for one; $26 to $30 for two in one bed; $28 to $36 for two in two beds.

Kearney

Accommodations: Friendship Inn Western, 824 East 25th St., 68847. Telephone: 308/234-2408. $16 to $20 for one; $20 to $24 for two in one bed; $22 to $28 for two in two beds.
● Budget Host—Hammer Budget Inn, ✓ 🛆, West Hwy. 30, 68847. Telephone: 308/237-2123. $18.50 to $22.50 for one; $20.50 to $24.50 for two; $24.50 to $28.50 for two in two beds.

Kimball

Accommodation: Friendship Inn Kimball Motel, east on Hwy. 30, 69145. Telephone: 308/235-4606. $19 to $21 for one; $23 to $25 for two in one bed; $25 to $35 for two in two beds.

Lexington

Accommodations: Friendship Toddle Inn, South Hwy. 283, 68850. Telephone: 308/324-5595. $20 to $26 for one; $25 to $29 for two in one bed; $28 to $34 for two in two beds.
● Hollingsworth Motel, ★, 500 East Hwy. 30, 68850. Telephone: 308/324-2388. $21.50 to $24.50 for one; $24.50 to $28.50 for two; $5 for each additional person. Lower rates apply in winter.

Lincoln

On Campus: There are three universities in Lincoln. The University of Nebraska is the largest—25,000 students. There are also Nebraska Wesleyan University and Union College. For travel information and advice on accommodations, stop at the Overseas Opportunities Center, Suite 345 in the Nebraska Union, and for counterculture-type information go to Dirt Cheap, 217 North 11th St.

The people from the University of Nebraska were anxious to recommend places to eat in the city-center area, where the food is good, and inexpensive too. Here's their list: Greenwich Café, 1917 O St., great fish and chips; Duffy's Bar, 1412 O St., a college tradition, with beef stew; Kuhl's, 1038 O St., home-cooked chicken dinners; Arturo's Taco Hut, 249 North 11th, the best Mexican food in eastern Nebraska; Valentino's, 232 North 13th, pizza and salad; and for late-night eaters there are Stoney's Kitchen and the Zoo Bar.

"Football Saturdays are a great time for strangers to see what football mania can do to a town."

Accommodations: Cornerstone Youth Hostel (AYH-SA), 640 North 16th St., 68508. On University of Nebraska Campus. Telephone: 402/476-0355. Open year round. $3.50 for AYH members.

- Thrifty Scot Motel, 2920 NW 12th St., 68521. Telephone: 402/475-3616. $23.90 to $29.90 for one; $27.90 to $33.90 for two in one bed.
- Motel 6, 3001 NW 12th St., 68521. Telephone: 402/475-9502. $17.95 for one; $21.95 for two; $2 for each additional person.
- Friendship Senate Inn, 2801 West "O" Hwy. 2 & 6, 68528. Telephone: 402/475-4921. Limited airport service available. $18 to $22 for one or two in one bed; $26 to $28 for two in two beds.
- Budget Host—Great Plains Hotel, √ (10%), 2732 O St., 68510. Telephone: 402/476-3253. $24 to $26 for one; $28 to $30 for two in one bed; $31.50 to $33.50 for two in two beds.

North Platte

Accommodations: Friendship Rambler Court, 1420 Rodeo Rd., 69101. Telephone: 308/532-9290. $16 to $21 for one; $20 to $26 for two in one bed; $22 to $28 for two in two beds.
- Friendship Inn Stanford Lodge, 1400 East 4th St. on East Hwy. 30, 69101. Telephone: 308/532-9380. $22.75 to $24.75 for one; $24.75 to $26.75 for two in one bed; $26.75 to $28.75 for two in two beds.
- Motel 6, 1520 South Jeffers St., 69101. Telephone: 308/534-3510. See Lincoln listing for rates.
- Budget Inn—Park Motel, 1302 North Jeffers St., 69101. Telephone: 308/532-6834. $19.50 for one; $22.50 for two in one bed; $25.50 for two in two beds.
- TraveLodge, √, 602 East 4th St., 69101. Telephone: 308/534-4020. Airport transportation available. $26 for one; $30 for two in one bed; $36 for two in two beds.

Ogallala

Accommodations: Friendship Western Paradise Inn, 221 East 1st, 69153. Telephone: 308/284-3684. $16.50 to $25 for one; $21 to $25 for two in one bed; $24 to $30 for two in two beds.
- Budget Host—Lakeway Lodge Motel, 918 North Spruce, 69153. Telephone: 308/284-4004. $22 to $26 for one; $26 to $28 for two in one bed; $32 to $34 to two in two beds.

Omaha

Tourist Information: Omaha Convention and Visitors Bureau, Suite 1200 —Civic Center, 1819 Farnam St., 68183. Telephone: 402/444-4660.

Help: Personal Crisis Service, 5078 South 108th St., Box 129, 68137. Telephone: 402/444-7442 or 444-7443. They recommend Together, Inc., an organization that helps stranded travelers, should you find yourself in that position.

On Campus: The University of Nebraska has a campus in Omaha that goes from 60th to 66th St. When you get hungry, try the Bohemian Café, 1406 South 13th St. (Czech food and atmosphere—the duck is good); Joe Tess's Fish Place, 5460 South 24th St., for delicious fish sandwiches and dinners at good prices; and Chicago, 3259 Farnham (two blocks from Dodge St.), for great hamburgers and reasonable prices. One more place recently recommended to us is Caniglia's at 7th and Pierce, where for $5 to $6 you can get a steak, salad, soup, potato, spaghetti, fried ravioli, pizza bread . . . and drink.

The drinking age is 21 in Omaha. Howard Street Tavern, a bar in the Old Market area of Omaha, at 1112 Howard, is a popular place with young people. In fact, on weekends the entire Old Market area (where the once-upon-a-time market space has been rejuvenated) is a good place to meet people. There are a number of restaurants in the area.

A friend from Omaha wrote to say that "besides claiming the world's largest stockyard, Omaha is Gerald Ford's birthplace."

Accommodations: Imperial 400 Motor Inn, √ (10%), 2211 Douglas St., 68102. Telephone: 402/345-9565. $23 to $26 for one; $25 to $30 for two in one bed; $28 to $32 for two in two beds.

● Friendship Ben Franklin Motel, I-80 & Hwy. 50, 68046. Telephone: 402/895-2200. $24.95 to $27.95 for one; $29.95 to $34.95 for two in one bed; $31.95 to $37.95 for two in two beds.

● Budget Host—Hiway House Motor Inn, I-80 & Hwy. 370, 68138. Telephone: 402/332-3900. $26.95 to $29.95 for one; $31.95 to $39.95 for two.

● TraveLodge, √ ♿, 3902 Dodge St., 68131. Telephone: 402/558-4000. $29 for one; $32 for two in one bed; $36 for two in two beds.

● Motel 6, 10708 M St., 68127. Telephone: 402/331-2331. See Lincoln listing for rates.

Scottsbluff

Accommodation: Friendship Inn Sands Motel, 814 West 27th St., 69361. Telephone: 308/632-6191. $18.75 to $21 for one; $23 to $25 for two in one bed; $26 for two in two beds.

Sidney

Accommodation: Friendship Inn El Palomino, 2220 Illinois St., 69162. Telephone: 308/254-5566. Limited airport service available. $22 to $32 for one; $26 to $36 for two in one bed; $28 to $42 for two in two beds.

Valentine

Accommodation: Friendship Inn Raine Motel, west on U.S. 20, 69201. Telephone: 402/376-2030. Limited airport service available. $23 to $30 for one; $26 to $35 for two in one bed; $33 to $40 for two in two beds.

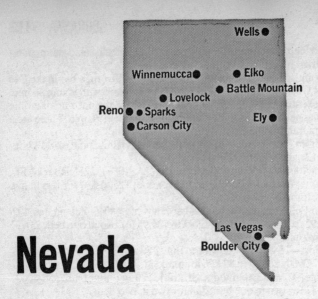

Nevada

Nevada has more neon lights than people, and Las Vegas wins the plastic city award hands down.

In case you hadn't heard, gambling is legal in Nevada, and practically all of the population depends on the industry for its livelihood. One good thing about Las Vegas and Reno: any poor traveler over 21 years old can get a good, cheap meal in the casinos and hotels. The idea behind the "bargain" is that once you're there you'll gamble, so if you just eat and run you can save quite a bit.

"You hit the secret of Vegas on the nose—if you stay away from gambling, you can really get off cheap. Pick up some of the tourist newspapers in every hotel lobby. They feature free coupons for nickels to play the slots and free meals at some casinos and other giveaways like a three-minute phone call to anywhere in the U.S."

Try desert camping in Nevada; the stars are fantastic, the air is cold and clean, and the sand makes a good mattress.

For a guidebook to Nevada that's a combination of history and travel information, look for *The Compleat Nevada Traveler*, by David W. Toll, available in bookstores for $6.95; or from the Gold Hill Publishing Co., P.O. Drawer F, Virginia City, NV 89440, for $8.

Some Special Events: Winter Carnival in South Lake Tahoe (January); All-Breed Bull Sale in Fallon and Winterskol, a week of ski events in Incline Village (February); Fireman's Ball in Gardnerville (March); World Series Poker in Las Vegas—where else? (April); Mexican Fiesta in Moapa Valley and Jim Butler Days, National and State Mucking and Drilling Championships in Tonopah (May); Carson Valley Days in Gardnerville, Rodeo in Reno, and Helldorado Days, a rodeo and parade in Las Vegas (June); National Basque Festival in Elko (July); Arts Alliance Festival in Carson City (August); Nevada State Fair in Reno, Great Reno Balloon Race, and the National Championship Air Races in Reno (September).

Hitching: It is illegal to hitchhike in most places in Nevada, although a friend there told us that police surveillance is not very tight, and that the general attitude toward hitchhikers is "mostly indifferent." The trooper we contacted had this to say: "There is a large amount of desert area with great distances between towns and lots of rattlesnakes."

Tourist Information: Nevada Commission on Tourism, Capitol Complex, Carson City, NV 89710.

Battle Mountain

Accommodation: Friendship Colt Motor Inn, 650 West Front St., 89820. Telephone: 702/635-5424. $30 to $33 for one; $32 to $35 for two in one bed; $38 for two in two beds.

Boulder City

Camping: Lake Mead National Recreational Area, 601 Nevada Hwy., 89005. Telephone: 702/293-4041. Ten campgrounds with 1148 sites open year round. Be prepared to share most of the campgrounds with trailers. $5 per campsite per night.

Carson City

Accommodations: Friendship Desert Hills Motel, 1010 South Carson St., 89701. Telephone: 702/882-1932. $22 to $35 for one; $25 to $40 for two in one bed; $28 to $45 for two in two beds. Jacuzzis in some rooms.
● Motel 6, 2749 South Carson St., 89701. Telephone: 702/883-1150. $17.95 for one; $21.95 for two; $2 for each additional person.

Elko

Accommodations: Motel 6, 3021 Idaho St., 89801. Telephone: 702/738-9768. See Carson City listing for rates.
● Friendship Towne House, 500 West Oak, 89801. Telephone: 702/738-7269. Limited airport service available. $22 to $32 for one; $24 to $36 for two in one bed; $28 to $40 for two in two beds.

Ely

Accommodation: Motel 6, 7th & Ave. O, 89301. Telephone: 702/289-3566. See Carson City listing for rates.

Las Vegas

"Eating out in Las Vegas is cheaper than cooking at home. Most of the casinos have smörgasbords with all of the extras for less than you can buy groceries. Every casino has what are called 'fun books,' and if you utilize them you can have a lot of fun for very little money. I have a free pancake, egg, and coffee breakfast

every morning, and where it's not free, breakfast can be found in many hotels for $1.99. As a rule, prices are cheaper downtown than in the luxurious Strip hotels. If you are a gambler, you'll find the odds more in your favor downtown."

Tourist Information: Las Vegas Convention and Visitors Authority, Las Vegas Convention Center, 3150 Paradise Rd., 89109. Telephone: 702/733-2323.

Accommodations: Motel 6, 195 East Tropicana Blvd., 89109. Telephone: 702/736-4904. See Carson City listing for rates.

● Allstar Inn, 4125 Boulder Hwy., 89121. Telephone: 702/457-8051. $23.95 to $25.95 for one; $3 for each additional person.

● Allstar Inn, 5085 South Industrial Rd., 89118. Telephone: 702/739-6747. See above listing for rates.

● Budget Host—Koala Motel, V, 520 South Casino Centre Blvd., 89101. Telephone: 702/384-8211. $23 to $25 for one; $25 to $30 for two in one bed; $30 to $35 for two in two beds.

● Las Vegas International Hostel (AYH), 1208 South Las Vegas Blvd., 89104. Telephone: 702/382-8119. $7 for AYH members.

● E-Z 8 Motel, 5201 South Industrial Rd., 89118. Telephone: 702/739-9513. $18.88 for one or two in one bed; $26.88 for three or four in two beds.

● Imperial 400 Motor Inn, ★ (10%), 3265 Las Vegas Blvd., 89109. Telephone: 702/735-5102. Airport courtesy car. $32 to $40 for one; $35 to $45 for two in one bed; $38 to $45 for two in two beds. Heated Olympic-size pool.

● Friendship King Albert, 185 Albert Ave., 89109. Telephone: 702/734-1687. $22.50 to $34.50 for one or two in one bed; $28.50 to $38.50 for two in two beds.

● Friendship Tam O'Shanter Inn, 3317 Las Vegas Blvd., 89109. Telephone: 702/735-7331. $32 for one; $32 to $45 for two in one bed; $34 to $50 for two in two beds.

Lovelock

Accommodation: Friendship Lafons Motel, Bus. 80, 515 Cornell Ave., 89419. Telephone: 702/273-2924. $20.95 to $25.95 for one; $22.95 to $27.95 for two in one bed; $25.95 to $31.95 for two in two beds.

Reno

Help: Crisis Call Center, 702/323-6111 or toll free 800/992-5757. For 24-hour telephone crisis counseling, information, and referral.

On Campus: A friend at the University of Nevada-Reno wants you to know that "although Reno is basically known for its gambling aura, you shouldn't forget that it's an all-around tourist area with summer sports, winter skiing, hiking, etc."

One friend wrote to tell us about her stay in Reno. She described the Reno campus as "the most beautiful in the country and the center of all the cultural life of Reno."

Accommodations: Senator Hotel, 136 West 2nd St., 89501. Telephone: 702/322-2125. Older hotel that's centrally located. $22 single; $24 double.

● Motel 6, 1901 South Virginia, 89502. Telephone: 702/825-8401. See Carson listing for rates.

- Motel 6, 866 North Wells, 89512. Telephone: 702/786-0180. See Carson City listing for rates.
- Motel 6, 1400 Stardust St., 89503. Telephone: 702/747-2676. See Carson City listing for rates.
- Allstar Inn, I-80 at 666 North Wells Ave., 89512. Telephone: 702/329-8681. See Las Vegas listing for rates.
- Friendship Mirador Inn, 1150 West 2nd St., off I-80 on Keystone Exit— south to West 2nd St., 89503. Telephone: 702/323-0331. $24 to $34 for one; $30 to $40 for two in one bed; $35 to $45 for two in two beds.
- Friendship Coach Inn, 500 North Center St., 89501. Telephone: 702/323-3222. $22 to $30 for one; $30 to $36 for two in one bed; $32 to $40 for two in two beds.

Sparks

Accommodation: Blue Fountain Inn, Ⓢ∨★, 1590 "R" St., 89431. Telephone: 702/359-0359. $19 to $32 single; $24 to $36 double; $36 to $45 twin; $40 quad. Higher rates given apply on weekends.

Wells

Accommodation: Motel 6, I-80/U.S. 40 & U.S. 93, 89835. Telephone: 702/752-3696. See Carson City listing for rates.

Winnemucca

Accommodation: Motel 6, 1600 Winnemucca Blvd., 89445. Telephone: 702/623-5775. See Carson City listing for rates.

New Hampshire

New Hampshire is one place to go when you've had enough of cities. Its mountains, lakes, and wilderness are delicious to anyone who has been cramped up for any time and needs some space to move around in. Since New Hampshire has the highest mountains in the Northeast, the state is especially popular with people who like mountain hiking and skiing.

Some Special Events: Spring Fair in Hampton, and National Historic Preservation Week in Concord (May); Old Timers Fair in Hanover (June); Merchants Street Fair in Keene (July); Old Time Farm Day in Milton, and Blue Grass Festival in West Ossipee (August); Fireman's Parade and Muster in Keene (October).

Hitching: As of 1974, hitchhiking became lawful in New Hampshire—as long as the hitchhiker stays off the paved portion of the road. The Department of Safety says that it is "opposed to hitchhiking per se; however, inasmuch as the legislature saw fit to make it permissible, we will adhere to the spirit of the law." A representative of the State Police advised hitchhikers to "Be alert and wear clothing that can be easily seen by motorists."

Tourist Information: New Hampshire Vacations, P.O. Box 856, Concord, NH 03301.

Alton

Accommodation: Green Tops Youth Hostel (AYH), &, R.D. 1, from Rte. 28, Robert's Cove Rd., 03809. 400 yards from Lake Winnipesaukee. Telephone: 603/569-9878. Open May 20 to September 7. $6 for AYH members, $7 for nonmembers in dorm-style accommodations. Cabins: $25 for one or two people; $40 for three or more. Advance reservations necessary.

Waterskiing, sailing available, lake and pool swimming nearby, "with an island, yet!"

Boscawen

Accommodation: Daniel Webster Motor Lodge, ⑤∨ ★, U.S. Rtes. 3 & 4, RFD 7, Box 246, 03303. Telephone: 603/796-2136. $28 single; $36 to $42 for two. Lower rates apply in winter.

Franconia

Accommodation: Pinestead Farm Lodge, Easton Rd., Rte. 116, 03580. Telephone: 603/823-8121. Lodge will pick up guests from bus station, by prior arrangement only. $14 per night. "An old farmhouse located in the White Mountains offering simple rooms for guests seeking country pleasure."

Gorham

Accommodation: Appalachian Mountain Club, Pinkham Notch Camp, Box 298, 03581. Telephone: 603/466-2727. Men, women, and children. $21.75 for one adult including one meal, $11 for children; $28.75 including two meals, $14.50 for children (at least one meal must be purchased). $3 discount for AMC members. Advance reservations strongly advised for weekends and holiday periods. "Modern, rustic lodge with small bunk rooms with two, three, or four beds per room."

Grantham

Accommodation: Ledges Farm (AYH-SA), 03755. Telephone: 603/863-1002. $7 for AYH members.

Hanover

On Campus: Here in this quaint New England town you'll find Dartmouth College. The heart of the college activities seems to be at Hopkins Center—the Hop and Collis Center, College Hall. The Hop bulletin board and *The Dartmouth,* the daily newspaper, should keep you informed of what's going on in and around town. While you're in the area consider going tubing on the White River, cross-country skiing, golfing, or swimming at the Ledges. For inexpensive meals try Rick's Cafe or Lou's Restaurant.

Tourist Information: Hanover Chamber of Commerce, telephone: 643-3115.

Keene

Accommodation: Doyle House (AYH-SA), Keene State College, Main St., 03431. Telephone: 603/352-9602 (between 4 and 8 p.m., August 2 to May

31: Monday to Friday 9 a.m. to 4:30 p.m., 603/352-1909, ext. 230). Open June 1 to August 1. $5 for AYH members.

Lyme

Accommodations: Loch Lyme Lodge and Cottages, Ⓢ, Rte. 10, 03768. Telephone: 603/795-2141. The Lodge will provide transportation from bus and train stations. Twenty-five cabins open from late May to September; the main lodge, a farmhouse built in 1784, is open year-round. Advance reservations of up to one year are strongly suggested. $20 to $27.50 for one; lower rates for children. Price includes breakfast. Various meal plans are available in the dining room. All types of summer and winter recreational facilities are available, from swimming to skiing and ice fishing.

● Red Roof Inn, 🏷, 77 Spitbrook Rd., 03063. Telephone: 603/888-1893. $29.95 for one; $34.95 for two in one bed; $36.95 for two in two beds; $38.95 for three or four in two beds.

North Haverhill

Accommodation: The Lime Kilns Youth Hostel (AYH), Ⓢ, Lime Kiln Rd., 03774. Telephone: 603/989-5656. Open Memorial Day through Labor Day. Call hostel for a ride. $4.75 for AYH members; $6.50 for nonmembers. Swimming at hostel. Campsites available as well.

Peterborough

Accommodation: Sharon Studio Barn Hostel (AYH), Sharon Cross Rd., Sharon, 03458. Telephone: 603/924-6928. $6 summer, $7 winter for AYH members. New England barn set in the woods.

Randolph

Accommodation: Bowman Base Camp (AYH), U.S. Rte. 2, 03570. Telephone: 603/466-5130. Open May 30 to October 12. $6.25 for AYH members. Advance reservations suggested.

Raymond

Accommodation: Walnut Hill Seminar House (AYH-SA). Rte. 102, 03077. Telephone: 603/895-2437. Open Memorial Day to Labor Day. Group reservations accepted year round. $7 summer, $8 winter for AYH members. Advance reservations of two weeks necessary during winter months.

West Ossipee

Accommodation: Chocorua Camping Village (AYH), P.O. Box 1180, 03890. Telephone: 603/323-8536 (summer); 659-2790 (winter). Open May 30 to

October 12. $5.25 for AYH members. $10 to $28 single or double; $8 to $12 per person triple or quad. Advance reservations necessary July 1 to September.

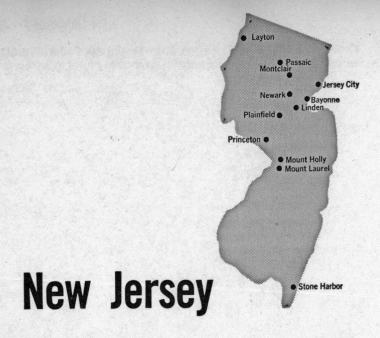

New Jersey

New Jersey is a much maligned member of the Middle Atlantic States. It's true that the northeastern part of New Jersey represents the worst of what can happen when industrialization hits an area. But trust us: the state really does deserve to be called the Garden State. Once you're off the New Jersey Turnpike, you'll enter a New Jersey that's unknown to most of the rest of the country.

The New Jersey coast—Cape May, Long Beach Island, and Barnegat Light —is an area of exceptional beauty. The farther south you go, the more beautiful it seems to become. Its 127 miles of wide beaches are quiet on the mild days of fall and spring and busy with vacationers in summer.

On the western border of New Jersey is the Delaware River and in the far northwest, along the river, there are rolling hills, streams, and ponds. The Appalachian Trail passes through the area at the Delaware Water Gap, which has been made a national recreation area. Along this part of the river there are a number of places to rent canoes. If you do so, you'll experience rapids and calm stretches, passing high banks, cliffs, and rolling fields.

The Pine Barrens, in southeastern New Jersey, are more than 100 miles of scraggly pine and cedar trees that live in a series of swamps and on the banks of freshwater streams. This region is ideal for spring and fall camping and canoeing. The Bass River State Forest in New Gretna is the center of activity for the area.

New Jersey boasts more than 800 lakes and ponds, more than 100 rivers and creeks, more than 1400 miles of freshly stocked trout streams, 40 state parks, and 11 state forests.

There's no lack of historic sites to visit in New Jersey. Over 100 Revolutionary War battles were fought on New Jersey soil, including the important Battle of Trenton. Some of the names from New Jersey's proud past are Von Steuben, Livingston and Molly Pitcher, Edison, Whitman, and Wilson. For those who want to visit New Jersey's history preserved, we recommend the New Jersey

Division of Travel and Tourism's booklet *A Guide to New Jersey's Unique Heritage* and their "Vacation Kit".

Some Special Events: New Jersey Folk Festival at Rutgers University in New Brunswick (April); Spring Festival of the Arts in Atlantic City (May); Italian, Ukrainian, Polish, and Irish Heritage Festivals at Garden State Arts Center in Holmdel (June); Cape May County 4-H Fair in Cape May (July); and the New Jersey State Fair, which is held in a different location each year (September).

Hitching: New Jersey is one of those states that uses "highway" in its law (see pages 13 and 14). It is illegal here. When we asked local people about hitching, we got generally negative responses. Students hitching around the area of their schools usually manage to get rides.

Tourist Information: Division of Travel and Tourism, CN 826, Trenton, NJ 08625. Telephone: 609/292-2470.

Bayonne

Accommodation: YWCA, 44 West 32nd St., 07002. Telephone: 201/339-7676. Women only. $10 to $12. Weekly rate: $40 to $50. Advance reservations of four weeks necessary. Very little room available for transients.

Jersey City

Help: CONTACT Hudson County, 201/831-1870 (covers Bayonne, Jersey City, North Bergen, Weehawken, Guttenberg, West New York, and Union City).

Accommodation: YMCA, 654 Bergen Ave., 07304. Telephone: 201/434-3211. Men and women. $22.50. Weekly rate: $65 first week; $50 and up second week. Reservations necessary. Twenty minutes from New York City.

Layton

Accommodation: Old Mine Road Youth Hostel (AYH), two miles north of Dingman's Ferry Bridge on Old Mine Rd. 521, 07860. Telephone: 201/948-6750. $6 for AYH members; $9 for nonmembers. In the Delaware Water Gap National Recreation Area. River swimming one-quarter mile away. Advance reservations suggested.

Linden

Accommodation: Friendship Benedict Inn, 136 Garden St., 07036. Telephone: 201/862-7700. Limited airport service available. $30 to $45 for one or two in one bed; $34 to $48 for two in two beds.

Montclair

Help: Help Line, 201/744-1954.
Accommodation: YMCA, 25 Park St., 07042. Telephone: 201/744-3400. The bus from New York City stops at the Y. Men only. $13. Weekly rate: $40.

Mount Holly

Accommodation: Friendship Mount Holly Concord Inn, Rte. 38, 08060. Telephone: 609/267-7900. $25 to $30 for one; $27 to $32 for two in one bed; $30 for two in two beds.

Mount Laurel

Accommodations: Red Roof Inn, ♿, 603 Fellowship Rd., I-295 at Hwy. 73 (Exit 36A), 08054. Telephone: 609/234-5589. $27.95 for one; $32.95 for two in one bed; $34.95 for two in two beds; $36.95 for three or four in two beds.
   ● McIntosh Inn, Rte. 73 & Church Rd., 08054. Telephone: 609/234-7194. $26.95 for one; $31.95 for two.

Newark

Help: North Jersey Community Union, 201/642-0280.
   Accommodation: YM/WCA, ♿, 600 Broad St., 07102. Telephone: 201/624-8900. Men and women. $21. Weekly rate: $62 to $68.

Passaic

Accommodation: YWCA, 114 Prospect St., 07055. Telephone: 201/779-1770. Women only. $15 single. Weekly rate: $50 to $60. Reservations requested two weeks in advance.

Plainfield

Accommodation: YMCA, 518 Watchung Ave., 07060. Telephone: 201/756-6060. Men only. $15 single; $10 key deposit required. Transient rooms are scarce. Advance reservations necessary.

Princeton

Help: Council for Community Services in Princeton, 609/924-5865.
   On Campus: The well-known Princeton University is here as well as the Institute for Advanced Studies. It's a good place to see "well preserved, lived-in American architecture of the 18th and 19th centuries." While you're there you can visit the university's excellent art museum or take the "Orange Key" tour of the campus.
   A popular student hangout which also happens to have very good, inexpensive meals is the Annex, 128½ Nassau St. For Greek food and pizza, try the Athenian, 25 Witherspoon St. For excellent homemade ice cream in a variety of flavors, try Thomas Sweet, 179 Nassau St. And for fine dining, try Nassau Inn, Palmer Square.
   Accommodations: Red Roof Inn, ♿, 3203 Brunswick Pike, I-295 & U.S.

1, Lawrenceville, 08648. Telephone: 609/896-3388. See Mt. Laurel listing for rates.

● McIntosh Inn, 🚹, U.S. 1 & QuakerBridge Mall, Lawrenceville, 08648. Telephone: 609/896-3700. $28.95 for one ($33.95 for one on Fridays & Saturdays); $33.95 for two.

Stone Harbor

Accommodation: Fairview Guest House, 8700 Pennsylvania Ave., 08247. Telephone: 609/368-9872 or 368-2065 in season, 609/848-4371 off-season. Open mid-May to late September. $23 to $39 double in season; $16 to $28 double off-season.

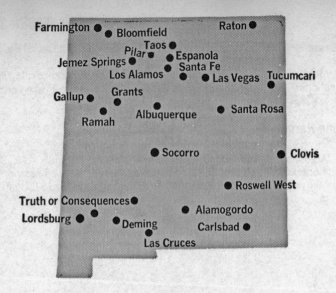

Farmington ● ● Bloomfield Raton ●
Taos ●
Pilar ● Espanola ●
Jemez Springs ● ● Santa Fe
Los Alamos ● ● Las Vegas Tucumcari ●
Grants ●
Gallup ● ● Santa Rosa
Ramah ● Albuquerque ●
Socorro ● Clovis ●
Roswell West ●
Truth or Consequences ●
Lordsburg ● ● ● Alamogordo
Deming ● Carlsbad ●
Las Cruces

New Mexico

Certain states attract dreamers and New Mexico is one. In the late '60s and early
'70s, young Americans considered New Mexico their Utopia. Communes
formed, young people arrived, and all seemed well. By now lots of those communes have dissolved and the people have moved on. But the reality of New
Mexico is almost as beautiful as their dream, so do try to spend some time there.

What shall you see while you're there? Carlsbad Caverns National Park,
with more than 50 caves; White Sands National Monument; Taos Pueblo, 2½
miles north of Taos, where you can wander and watch some of the 1400 Indians
who make their home in this terraced pueblo. New Mexico is a state to explore
and a state where there is much to be learned about the Spanish and Indian
cultures of the American Southwest.

Some Special Events: Santa Fe Film Festival (April); Four Corners Balloon
Rally in Farmington Lake (May); Summer Festival in Ruidoso (June); Indian
Pueblo Arts and Crafts Fair in Albuquerque, and Fiesta de Taos (July); Indian
Market in Santa Fe, and Inter Tribal Indian Ceremonial in Gallup (August);
State Fair in Albuquerque, Chile Festival in Hatch, and Santa Fe Fiesta (Sep-
tember); and Albuquerque International Balloon Fiesta (October).

Hitching: Hitchhiking is not legal on any Interstate highway in New Mexico. Otherwise, hitchhiking is officially legal from the road shoulder, but may be
prohibited in some municipalities. The State Police advise: carry photo identification if possible, and if you're under 18, be able to provide a phone contact to
verify that you are allowed to be on your own. The State Police stand prepared
to assist any traveler in any way possible during his or her stay in New Mexico.
Visitors are always welcome in the "Land of Enchantment"!

Tourist Information: New Mexico Travel Division, Economic Development and Tourism Department, Bataan Memorial Building, Santa Fe, NM 87503. Telephone: 505/827-6230 or toll free 800/545-2040.

Alamogordo

Accommodations: Motel 6, 251 Panorama Blvd., 88310. Telephone: 505/437-9358. $17.95 for one; $21.95 for two; $2 for each additional person.

● Friendship Satellite Inn, 2224 North White Sands Blvd. at 23rd St., 88310. Telephone: 505/437-8454. $24 to $28 for one; $28 to $34 for two in one bed; $34 to $40 for two in two beds; $40 to $44 for family units.

● TraveLodge, √ ♿, 508 South White Sands Blvd., 88310. Telephone: 505/437-1850. $29 for one; $34 for two in one bed; $38 for two in two beds.

Albuquerque

Tourist Information: Albuquerque Convention and Visitors Bureau, P.O. Box 26866, 87125. Telephone: 505/243-3696.

Accommodations: Canterbury Youth Hostel (AYH-SA), 1721 Sigma Chi NE, 87106. Telephone: 505/247-4204, 5 p.m. to 9 a.m. $6.25 summer, $7.75 winter for AYH members. Advance reservations necessary in summer. No showers.

● Friendship Inn Crossroads, 1001 Central Ave. NE, 87106. Telephone: 505/242-2757. $22 to $24 for one; $24 to $28 for two in one bed; $26 to $28 for two in two beds.

● Budget Host—Capri Motor Hotel, √ (10%), 1213 Central Ave. NW, 87102. Telephone: 505/247-1061. $22 for one; $25 for two in one bed; $28 for two in two beds. Heated pool.

● Allstar Inn, ♿, 3400 Prospect Ave. NE, 87107. Telephone: 505/883-8813. $25.95 for one; $28.95 for two; $31.95 for three; $34.95 for four.

● Allstar Inn, ♿, 1000 Stadium Blvd. SE, 87102. Telephone: 505/243-8017. See above listing for rates.

● Motel 6, 13141 Central Ave. NE, 87123. Telephone: 505/296-4891. See Alamogordo listing for rates.

● Motel 6, 1701 University Blvd. NE, 87102. Telephone: 505/843-6100. See Alamogordo listing for rates.

● Regal 8 Inn, 5701 Iliff NW at Coors, 87105. Telephone: 505/831-8888. $21.88 for one; $26.88 for two in one bed; $31.88 for two in two beds.

● TraveLodge, √ ♿, 3711 Central Ave. NE, 87108. Telephone: 505/265-6961. $30 for one; $34 for two in one bed; $38 for two in two beds.

● Red Carpet Inn, √, 12901 Central Ave. NE, 87123. Telephone: 505/298-6861. $23 to $45 for one; $26.50 to $45 for two in one bed; $28.50 to $45 for two in two beds.

Bloomfield

Camping: Chaco Culture National Historical Park, Star Rte. 4, P.O. Box 6500, 87413. Telephone: 505/786-5384. Campground with 46 sites at Gallo Wash, one mile east of Visitors Center. Open year-round. No fee.

Carlsbad

Camping: Guadalupe Mountains National Park, 3225 National Parks Hwy., 88220. Campgrounds at Pine Springs TX, 55 miles southwest of Carlsbad, with 24 tent sites and 17 RV sites. Open year-round. $4 per night.

Accommodations: Budget Host—Driftwood Motel, $\sqrt{}$, 844 Canal South St., 88220. Telephone: 505/887-6522. $18 to $20 for one; $21 to $24 for two in one bed; $24 to $29 for two in two beds.

● Friendship Stagecoach Inn, 1819 South Canal, 88220. Telephone: 505/887-1148. $20 to $24 for one; $22 to $28 for two in one bed; $26 to $32 for two in two beds.

● Motel 6, 3824 National Parks Hwy., 88220. Telephone: 505/885-8807. See Alamogordo listing for rates.

● Econo Lodge, $\sqrt{}$, 3814 National Parks Hwy., 88220. Telephone: 505/887-0341. $29.95 for one; $34.95 for two in one bed; $39.95 for two in two beds.

● TraveLodge, $\sqrt{}$, 401 East Greene St., 88220. Telephone: 505/885-3117. $28 for one; $33 for two in one bed; $38 for two in two beds.

Clovis

Accommodation: Motel 6, 2620 Mabry Dr., 88101. Telephone: 505/762-3186. See Alamogordo listing for rates.

Deming

Accommodation: Motel 6, I-10 & Motel Dr., P.O. Box 970, 88031. Telephone: 505/546-9663. See Alamogordo listing for rates.

Espanola

Accommodation: Friendship Western Holiday Motel, one mile south on U.S. 64/68/285, Rte. 1, Box 249, 87532. Telephone: 505/753-2491. $28 to $32 for one; $34 to $38 for two in one bed; $38 to $42 for two in two beds.

Farmington

Accommodations: Regal 8 Inn, 510 Scott Ave., 87401. Telephone: 505/327-0242. See Albuquerque listing for rates.

● Motel 6, 1600 Bloomfield Hwy., 87401. Telephone: 505/327-7600. See Alamogordo listing for rates.

Gallup

Accommodations: Motel 6, 3306 West Hwy. 66, SR 2, Box 18, 87301. Telephone: 505/722-4084. See Alamogordo listing for rates.

● Budget Host—Colonial Motel, $\sqrt{}$ (10%), 1007 West Coal Ave., 87301.

Telephone: 505/863-6821. $16 to $20 for one; $18 to $22 for two in one bed; $22 to $28 for two in two beds.

- Econo Lodge, √ &, 3101 West Hwy. 66, 87301. Telephone: 505/722-6677. $22.95 to $26.95 for one; $27.95 to $29.95 for two in one bed; $27.95 to $34.95 for two in two beds.
- Friendship Road Runner Inn, 3012 East Hwy. 66, 87301. Telephone: 505/863-3804. $22 to $26 for one; $24 to $28 for two in one bed; $28 to $32 for two in two beds.

Grants

Accommodations: Friendship Desert Sun Motel, Hwy. 66, 1121 East Santa Fe Ave., 87020. Telephone: 505/287-7925. Limited airport service available. $19 to $23 for one; $22 to $36 for two in one bed; $28 to $42 for two in two beds.
- TraveLodge, √, 1204 East Santa Fe Ave., 87020. Telephone: 505/287-2991. $28 for one; $35 for two in one bed; $39 for two in two beds.
- Allstar Inn, Grants Spur Hwy., 87020. Telephone: 505/287-2952. See Albuquerque listing for rates.
- Motel 6, East Santa Fe Ave. (I-40 Interchange), P.O. Box 1478, 87020. Telephone: 505/287-7566. See Alamogordo listing for rates.
- Motel 6, 509 North Marland Blvd., 88240. Telephone: 505/397-2879. See Alamogordo listing for rates.
- Budget Host, √, 1300 East Broadway, 88240. Telephone: 505/393-5101. $24.50 for one; $26 for two in one bed; $28 for two in two beds.

Jemez Springs

Accommodation: Canyon Quarters Hostel (AYH), Canyon Quarters, 87025. Telephone: 505/829-3005. Open April 15 to October 15. $5.25 for AYH members. Advance reservations suggested.

Las Cruces

Accommodations: Motel 6, 235 La Posada Lane, 88001. Telephone: 505/526-3276. See Alamogordo listing for rates.
- Friendship Town House Inn, Exit 70 from I-10 or I-25 or Motel Blvd., 88005. Telephone: 505/524-7733. $13 to $14 for one; $15 to $16 for two in one bed; $18 to $20 for two in two beds.
- Allstar Inn, 3091 South Main St., 88001. Telephone: 505/525-0994. See Albuquerque listing for rates.

Las Vegas

Accommodation: Friendship Palomino Inn, 1330 Grand Ave., 87701. Telephone: 505/425-3548. $20 to $23 for one; $23 to $25 for two in one bed; $25 to $27 for two in two beds.

Lordsburg

Accommodation: Friendship Aloha Motel, 816 East Motel Dr., 88045. Telephone: 505/542-3567. $16.50 to $17.95 for one; $19.95 to $23 for two in one bed; $24.95 to $27 for two in two beds.

Los Alamos

Camping: Bandelier National Monument, 87544. Telephone: 505/672-3861. Campground at Juniper (one-tenth mile inside entrance). Open March 1 to November 30. $5 per campsite per night.

Pilar

Accommodation: The Plum Tree Café and Hostel (AYH), Ⓢ★, Hwy. 68, Box 1-A, 87571. Telephone: 505/758-4696. Domes: $15 single, $17.50 breakfast included. Hostel: $8.50, $11 breakfast included. Honeymoon suite: $24.50 for two, $29.50 breakfast included. Bus stops in front of hostel. The Plum Tree is also a restaurant which has a delicious, reasonably priced, creative menu. Discount applies to rooms only. Hot tub, sauna, and raft trips.

Ramah

Camping: El Morro National Monument Campground, 87321. Telephone: 505/783-4226. Campground one-half mile from headquarters with nine free sites. Open year round. No fee.

Raton

Accommodations: Melody Lane Motel, Restaurant and Lounge, ✓ ♿, 136 Canyon Dr., 87740. Telephone: 505/445-3655. $29 to $49 single; $33 to $49 double. Higher rates apply on weekends and in summer.
● Friendship Capri Motel, 304 Canyon Dr., 87740. Telephone: 505/445-3641. $16 to $27 for one; $24 to $34 for two in one bed; $28 to $38 for two in two beds.
● Motel 6, 1600 Cedar St., 87740. Telephone: 505/445-9666. See Alamogordo listing for rates.

Roswell West

Accommodation: TraveLodge, ✓, 2200 West 2nd St., 88201. Telephone: 505/623-3811. $25 for one; $28 for two in one bed; $30 for two in two beds.

Santa Fe

"The very old Indian and Spanish heritage and culture of the majority of people here is almost sacred."

Accommodations: Private homes of members of Council on International

Relations, P.O. Box 1223, 100 East San Francisco St. (La Fonda Hotel, Suite #3, Mezzanine), 87501. Telephone: 505/982-4931 (mornings only, except mid-July to early September, which is 2 to 5 p.m. weekday afternoons). Foreign visitors only. Donation of $9 per night requested for a stay of no more than three to four days, breakfast included. Advance reservations preferred.

"The Council is really fantastic. The members are very friendly and helpful."

- Santa Fe International Hostel, 1412 Cerrillos Rd., 87501. Telephone: 505/988-1153 or 983-9896. Limousine service from Lamay bus station. $8 for dorm; $20 single; $24 triple; $28 quad.
- Motel 6, 3007 Cerrillos Rd., 87501. Telephone: 505/471-2442. See Alamogordo listing for rates.
- Allstar Inn, ♿, 3383 Cerrillos Rd., 87501. Telephone: 505/471-4140. See Albuquerque listing for rates. Advance reservations necessary for summer weekends.

"It is always worth checking at both the College of Santa Fe and St. John's College for dormitory space."

"Don't miss the Opera Under the Stars in the summer for $3. Standing room is usually available."

Santa Rosa

Accommodation: Motel 6, 3400 Will Rogers Dr., 88435. Telephone: 505/472-3266. See Alamogordo listing for rates.

Socorro

Accommodation: Motel 6, 807 South U.S. 85, 87801. Telephone: 505/835-1492. See Alamogordo listing for rates.

Taos

Accommodation: The Abominable Snowmansion (AYH-SA), Ⓢ★, P.O. Box 3271. Telephone: 505/776-8298. Shuttle bus to hostel. $12.50 summer: $15 for bed and breakfast winter. $7.75 summer for AYH members. Camping sites available. Meals available at hostel.

Truth or Consequences

Accommodation: Friendship Ace Lodge, 1014 Date St., 87901. Telephone: 505/894-2151. $22 to $24 for one; $23 to $25 for two in one bed; $25 to $30 for two in two beds.

Tucumcari

Accommodations: Motel 6, 2900 East Tucumcari Blvd., Rte. 4, Box 196, 88401. Telephone: 505/461-4316. See Alamogordo listing for rates.
- TraveLodge, ∨, 1214 East Tucumcari Blvd., 88401. Telephone: 505/461-1401. $29 for one; $34 for two in one bed; $38 for two in two beds.

New York

What can you say about New York that hasn't already been said? Like California, New York is a place that people want to see. But most people think of New York as New York City. It's especially hard for New York City residents to remember that all those other people in the state are New Yorkers, too. If you visit New York, don't leave without immersing yourself in New York City for at least a few days, but leave yourself enough time to see some of the beautiful rural areas of the the state, too.

With a little exploring, you'll find that much of New York State is rural with miles of farmland, small towns, and abundant wildlife. Outdoor recreational opportunities are endless. The southwestern part of the state offers beautiful countryside, especially during early to mid-October, unbounded recreation in the Finger Lakes region, and some very special tourist possibilities like Genesee Gorge in Litchmouthe State Park; Watkins Glen for racing; and Timespeels, a laser light-and-sound spectacular; Corning Glass Works and Museum; and the many wineries that dot the area from Watkins Glen to Hammondsport. For hikers or campers, what could be more inviting than the Adirondacks or the Catskills? Anyone with a car should try to do some exploring, too, along the Hudson where there are so many restored homes, museums, and pretty little towns just a few hours' ride from the New York City area. And don't forget the ocean beaches of Long Island, easily reached on the Long Island Railroad.

And without going too far from the city, you can also enjoy some lovely hikes and walks—just consult the *New York Walk Book,* Doubleday ($7.95).

Another publication is *A Kid's New York,* by Peter Lawrence, Avon Books ($6.95). The city from a kid's perspective.

Some Special Events: Peach Blossom Square Dance Festival in Canajoharie, and Civil War Encampment in Youngstown (May); Art Show and Tuna Tournament in Bay Shore, St. Lawrence County Dairy Princess Parade and Festival in Canton, and Northeast Craft Fair in Rhinebeck (June); Old Catskill Days in Catskill, Newport Jazz Festival in Saratoga, and Bluegrass Festival in Upper Jay (July); Shaker Museum Festival in Old Chatham, and Annual Summer Bazaar and Crafts Fair in Sackets Harbor (August); Chowder Society Celebration in Old Bethpage, and New York State Fiddler's Contest in Osceola (September); Fall Festival in Lake Luzerne, and Harvest and Arts Festival Salute to the Farmers of America in Elmira (October).

Hitching: To quote the New York State Police: "Soliciting a ride is prohibited at the entrances and exits and any space within the limits of a State Expressway or Interstate Route Highway or where signs are posted prohibiting hitchhiking." On all other state highways, outside of cities and villages, "no person shall stand in a roadway for the purpose of soliciting a ride." The term "roadway" is defined as the improved or paved portion of the highway. "Therefore, hitching is permitted if the person is standing on the shoulder of the highway. Each town, village, and city has the authority to enact laws regarding hitchhiking . . ."

Most of the people we talked to from upstate (northern New York) consider hitchhiking common and acceptable, except on the New York State Thruway. Although they recognize that it's a common means of travel, they hesitate to recommend it because of "occasional tragedies." A golden rule for hitchhiking out of New York City (and any major city, for that matter), is to get out of the city limits first. Hitching within New York City is virtually impossible, and, frankly, you'd have to be a little crazy to even consider it.

Tourist Information: Division of Tourism, New York State, One Commerce Plaza, Albany, NY 12260.

Albany

Tourist Information: Albany County Convention and Visitors Bureau, 60 Broadway, 12207. Telephone: 518/463-2124.

Accommodations: Red Roof Inn, 🛇, 188 Wolf Rd., I-87 at Albany Shaker Rd. (Exit 4), 12205. Telephone: 518/459-1971. $27.95 for one; $32.95 for two in one bed; $34.95 for two in two beds; $36.95 for three or four in two beds.

● Susse Chalet Inn, I-87 (Northway Exit 2E), on Wolf Rd. Telephone: 518/459-5670. $30.70 for one; $34.70 for two; $37.70 for three; $40.70 for four.

● Econo Lodge, √ 🛇, 1632 Central Ave., 12205. Telephone: 518/456-8811. $28.95 to $35.95 for one; $32.95 to $39.95 for two in one bed; $35.95 to $39.95 for two in two beds.

Auburn

Accommodation: Sleepy Hollow Motel, Rte. 20, 13021. Telephone: 315/253-3281. $26 for one; $32 for two in one bed; $34 to $36 for two in two beds.

Big Indian

Accommodation: Cold Spring Lodge, Ⓢ √ ★ 🛇 (mid-October thru June, except holidays), Oliverea Rd., 12410. Telephone: 914/254-5711. Modern efficiency cabins with fireplaces which accommodate up to eight people. $25 per cabin per night. Firewood supplied. They also have boardinghouse-style rooms for $20 single. Restaurant on premises; cabins have kitchens. "We own 40 acres of land situated in a beautiful valley in the Catskill Mountains."

Buffalo

On Campus: There are five colleges and universities in Buffalo—the State University of New York at Buffalo, Buffalo State College, Daemen College, Canisius College, and D'Youville College. All of them will have a great deal of helpful information on their bulletin boards. Many students congregate on the Elmwood Strip, where you'll find Cole's, Mr. Goodbar, Bullfeathers, Pano's, and Casey's. For a good meal in a warm, comfortable atmosphere, try Sign of the Steer on Main St. near the SUNY Buffalo campus. They have burgers, Mexican food, fried potato skins, and fantastic drinks. For "great tasting wings," try Buffalo's Famous Chicken. If you can make it to Fort Erie, Canada, which is ten minutes from Buffalo, go to George's Good Food Restaurant for an inexpensive Chinese meal. It's a real establishment.

Accommodations: YWCA Residence (AYH-SA), 245 North St., 14201. Telephone: 716/884-4761. Women only. $5 for AYH members; mothers can bring small children age 6 and under. $10 single; $12 double. Advance reservations requested with advance deposit of $2. Cafeteria in building. Bring sleeping bag.

• Red Roof Inn, 🚹, 42 Flint Rd., I-290 & Millersport Hwy. N., Amherst, 14226. Telephone: 716/689-7474. $25.95 for one; $30.95 for two in one bed; $32.95 for two in two beds; $34.95 for three or four in two beds.

• Red Roof Inn, 🚹, 5370 Camp Rd., Hamburg, 14075. Telephone: 716/648-7222. See listing above for rates.

• Hotel Lenox, Ⓢ √ 🚹 ★, 140 North St., 14201. Telephone: 716/884-1700. $24 and up single; $8 for each additional person. Advance reservations suggested in summer.

Canandaigua

Accommodation: Econo Lodge, √ 🚹, 170 Eastern Blvd., 14424. Telephone: 716/394-9000. $28.95 to $32.95 for one; $32.95 to $36.95 for two.

Cape Vincent

Accommodation: Tibbetts Point Lighthouse Hostel (AYH), 13618. Telephone: 315/654-3450. Open May 15 to September 15. $5.25 for AYH members.

Clyde

Accommodation: Honey Farm Home Hostel (AYH), RD 1, Kelsey Rd. E, 14433. Telephone: 315/923-7102. $3.50 for AYH members. Advance reservations necessary by phone.

Cooperstown

Accommodation: Cooperstown Hostel (AYH), Box 704, 13326. Telephone: 607/293-7324. Open May 15 to October 15. $5 for AYH members. Advance reservations suggested.

Cortland

Accommodation: Budget Host—Riverside Motel, √ ($2), 4408 North Homer Ave., 13045. Telephone: 607/753-3388. $22.43 to $26.17 for one; $25.23 to $28.04 for two in one bed; $27.57 to $30.14 for two in two beds. Breakfast included. Free transportation available to anywhere in Cortland.

Geneseo

On Campus: For travel information, contact the Travel Center at SUNY/College at Geneseo, located in Room 326 of the College Union (tel. 716/245-5864 or 245-5851). For overnight accommodations, there's Wayne Hall for $11 per person per night in double-occupancy rooms, corridor style, shared bath. Sleeping-bag space is also available in lounge areas at $3 per person. You must provide your own linen. For arrangements, contact the Residence Life Office, Erwin Administration Bldg., SUNY/College of Geneseo, 14454 (tel. 716/245-5726).

On campus, The Hub in Blake A and the College Union Snackbar provide meals. In the area, students recommend the Normal Café, T & J Restaurant, Club 41, and several fast-food spots, all on Main St. Park St. (adjacent to campus,) offers cuisine at K-Gardens Restaurant. Route 20A just east of the village is dotted with McDonald's, Burger King, and Pizza Hut. Nearby Conesus Lake features the Tee and Gee, Bojangles, and P.J. Remington's. For drinks and new friends, the Idle Hour on Center St. offers "happy hour" daily; The Vital Spot, Gentleman Jim's (GJ's) and the In Between ("in between" GJ's and the Vital Spot, more like the "video" spot) are both within an area adjacent to the east side of campus.

Gilbertsville

Accommodation: The Major's Inn Ice House (AYH-SA), on Commercial St. opposite the Post Office, 13776. Telephone: 607/783-2412. $2.50 for AYH members. Advance reservations suggested October 1 to May 14. "Somewhat primitive but interesting."

Glens Falls

Accommodations: Susse Chalet Motor Lodge, I-87 (Northway Exit 18), 12801. Telephone: 518/793-8891. $27.70 for one; $31.70 for two; $34.70 for three; $37.70 for four.

● Friendship Inn Landmark Motor Lodge, P.O. Box 376, 12801. Telephone: 518/793-3441. $28 to $55 for one; $32 to $60 for two in one bed; $38 to $65 for two in two beds.

Ithaca

On Campus: There are thousands of students in Ithaca—at Cornell or Ithaca College—and either campus will welcome you. To find out what's happening on the two campuses, pick up copies of the *Ithaca Journal,* the *Cornell Daily Sun,* the *Grapevine,* or the *Ithaca New Times.* For a bulletin board with rides and apartments listed, go to Willard Straight Hall at Cornell and to the third floor of the Student Union building at Ithaca.

Our friend at Ithaca College tells us that "the city is on a lake, and during the warm months, there are boating trips and sailing facilities. There's also a wide selection of summer stock theaters in the area. . . ."

Accommodation: International Living Center, North Campus 8, Cornell University, 14853. Telephone: 607/256-5299. Men and women (children with difficulty). Accommodation only for those with official business at Cornell. Preference is given to foreign students. June 1 to August 16. $7.50 single; $6 per person double. $1 charge for linen, which can be waived if you bring a sleeping bag. Advance reservations suggested. Cooking facilities available. During the academic year, dorm-style accommodations are available for $6 per person; advance reservations necessary.

Jack's Reef

Accommodation: Whitmore Home Hostel (AYH), 7213 Kingdom Rd., Memphis, 13112. Telephone: 315/689-9064. $4 summer, $5 winter for AYH members. Advance reservations necessary. Located on a working farm.

Jamestown

Accommodations: YMCA (AYH-SA), 101 East 4th St., 14701. Telephone: 716/664-2802. Men only, age 18 or over. $7 summer, $8 winter for AYH members. $14 single for nonmembers. Sleeping bags required.

● YWCA, 401 North Main St., 14701. Telephone: 716/485-1137. Three blocks from bus station. Women only over age 18. $7 to $10 single. Weekly rate: $28 to $39.

Kingston

Accommodation: YMCA, 507 Broadway, 12401. Telephone: 914/338-3810. Men only. $15. Weekly rate: $30 to $36.50.

Lake George

Accommodation: Lake George Youth Hostel (AYH), 🦽 (partial), Upper Bay Rd., P.O. Box 176, 12845. Telephone: 518/668-2634 (May 1 to September 31); 518/668-2001 (rest of year, for information only). Open May 27 to September 5. $4.75 for AYH members. Advance reservations necessary July to August. No check-in after 8 p.m. without deposit.

Lake Placid

Accommodation: Lake Placid Youth Hostel (AYH-SA), 54 Main St., P.O. Box 311, 12946. Telephone: 518/523-3490. $6.25 summer, $7.75 winter for AYH members. Advance reservations necessary.

Little Falls

Accommodation: YMCA, 15 Jackson St., 13365. Ten miles from Adirondack Mountains. Telephone: 315/823-1740. Men only. $10. Weekly rate: $30.

Malone

Accommodation: Nord Veld Guest House, Ⓢ √ (20%), 65 Park St., 12953. Telephone: 518/483-0454. Walking distance to bus station. $25 for one; $35 for two; $45 for three; $55 for four. Advance reservations of one day necessary. "A comfortable, fully equipped second-floor apartment."

Marathon

Accommodation: Friendship Three Bear Inn & Restaurant, 3 Broome St., 13803. Telephone: 607/849-3258. $23.90 for one; $25.90 for two in one bed; $29.90 for two in two beds.

New Baltimore

Accommodation: New Baltimore Home Hostel (AYH), c/o Robert Gaesser, P.O. Box 205, South Main St. at Pichler Rd., 12124. Telephone: 518/756-9097. $4.25 summer, $5.75 winter for AYH members. Advance reservations necessary. "A small private home on the banks of the Hudson River near Albany, NY."

New York City

"I agree with Comden and Green, 'a wonderful town.'"

It doesn't matter how you get to New York just as long as you make sure to get there. New York is an incredible city. There's no place quite like it anywhere and everyone should see it for themselves at least once. In fact, most people aren't satisfied with just one visit—they keep coming back again and again. Since New York is so big and so fast-paced, you can use a little help getting acquainted with this small and crowded island. Here are some books that will help:

Arthur Frommer's Guide to New York, by Faye Hammel, Frommer/Pasmantier Publishers ($4.95). A good, general guide to what there is to see and do. Particularly helpful to orient you to where you are and what you can do there.

New York on $45 a Day, by Joan Hamburg and Norma Ketay. Frommer/Pasmantier ($9.95). Another Frommer Guide, this one with emphasis on the bargain spots.

The Hip Pocket Guide to New York City, compiled and edited by Tim Page. Harper/Colophon Books ($5.95). Thirty-one people give their opinions on restaurants, the performing arts, discos, clubs, record shops, and just about everything else that's New York. It is well-written and comprehensive—we recommend it.

Michelin Guide to New York City, Michelin ($7.95). (Available in bookstores.) New York done the classic Michelin way, i.e., thoroughly researched and fascinating.

I Love New York Guide, by Marilyn J. Appleberg, Collier Macmillan ($4.95). Dedicated to helping you find it in New York—whatever "it" may be. This is a terrific pocket guide to everything and everywhere in New York.

Another easily carried guide to the city is *New York in Your Pocket*. Very brief—a bit like a mini-Yellow Pages for visitors. Published by Barron's ($2.95).

The City Observed: A Guide to Architecture, by Paul Goldberger, Vintage Press ($7.95). A thorough and thoughtful guide to our buildings when you have enough time to do some exploring.

For anyone who needs to get away from it all for a day or so, we recommend *Natural New York*, by Phyllis and Bill Thomas, published by Holt, Rinehart and Winston ($17.95). The book leads you to the parks, wildlife sanctuaries, recreation areas, and other open spaces within 50 miles of New York City.

Also, to know what's going on when you're in town, refer to the *Village Voice*, *New York* magazine, the *New Yorker*, or the *New York Times* (especially the Sunday "Arts and Leisure" section and the Friday "Weekend" section).

"This is a city that's culturally diverse, intellectually alive, and vigorous."

A first stop in New York, especially for student visitors, should be CIEE's New York Student Center, which offers up-to-the-minute information on what's happening in the city, and discount tickets for a variety of activities in town. A Council Travel Office there provides help in planning travel throughout the United States and the world. What's more, the Student Center is an ideal place to stay (see listing on page 341), as well as a great spot to meet other travelers. You can book a room by sending a cashier's check or money order made payable to CIEE. Send reservations to the Student Center, located in the William Sloane House, 356 West 34th St., New York, NY 10001 (tel. 212/695-0291). Confirmation vouchers will be sent to you.

N.B. A little while ago, two major changes were made in telephone service in New York. Pay phone calls went from 10¢ to 25¢ and the folks who live in Brooklyn, Queens, and Staten Island were given a new area code. Now it's necessary to dial 1-718 before any number in these three boroughs. This doesn't affect the cost of the call, though, it's still considered "local."

Getting There: From the Airports: You'll land in the borough of Queens at either JFK or La Guardia, or in New York's somewhat less glamorous neighbor, New Jersey, at Newark Airport. Banish thoughts of a taxi—the fare is $25 or more from JFK. Fortunately, there are several alternatives. A few years ago, a new subway route called the JFK Express was inaugurated with much hoopla and attendant publicity. The "Express," which is really a combination bus and train ride, takes about one and a half hours and costs $5.10 plus a 90¢ token. From JFK, the bus takes passengers to the Howard Beach-JFK Airport station where they board the train for stops at Jay St. in Brooklyn, and seven stops in Manhattan: Broadway-Nassau, Chambers Street (World Trade Center), West 4th St. (Washington Square), 34th St. (Sixth Ave.), 42nd St. (Sixth Ave.), 47th-50th Sts. (Rockefeller Center), and 57th St. (Sixth Ave.).

A somewhat slower but less expensive ($1.80) bus/train combination has been around a lot longer than the JFK Express: From JFK take a Q10 bus to the Union Turnpike-Kew Gardens station, the Lefferts Blvd.-Liberty Ave. station of the IND subway, or the 121st St. and Jamaica Ave. station. From the first station you can take an E or F train; from the second, board an A train right into the heart of Manhattan; and from the third, you can catch a J train. Allow 2 hours for this method.

From LaGuardia, take the Q33 bus to 74th St./Broadway in Jackson Heights and then switch to the no. 7 train which goes to Times Square. From there you can get just about anywhere in the city.

If you have lots of luggage or are unwilling to spend your first hour in New York on the subway, take a Carey bus from either JFK or La Guardia to Grand Central Station or Port Authority. From JFK the ride costs $8 and takes about one hour; from La Guardia it's $6 and takes one-half hour. Carey buses run approximately every 20 minutes from JFK between 5:35 a.m. and 11:45 p.m., and from La Guardia between 6:50 a.m. and midnight. The Carey number is 718/632-0500.

A bus will also take you from Newark Airport to the Port Authority Bus Terminal on the West Side of Manhattan at Eighth Ave. and 40th St. The 45-minute trip costs $5.

● By Train: If you come by train, you'll arrive at either Grand Central Station on the East Side at 42nd St. and Vanderbilt Ave. or at Pennsylvania Station at 32nd St. and Seventh Ave. Both stations have information booths where you can find out how to get where you're going by public transportation. There are subway stations in both terminals and bus stops right outside.

● By Bus: Anyone coming by bus will arrive at the recently renovated Port Authority Bus Terminal, 40th St. and Eighth Ave. There's a subway station entrance in the terminal and buses outside.

Getting Around: The best way to get around Manhattan is on foot. Just remember that most streets and avenues are laid out on a grid, that streets are numbered consecutively north of 4th St., and that the avenues (with some exceptions) are numbered from the East to the West Side. Fifth Avenue divides East and West; uptown is north of where you are, downtown is south, and crosstown is east or west toward either the East River or the Hudson River. The New York Convention and Visitors Bureau has a free map, but it's not very detailed, so we recommend either buying the paperback *New York in Flash Maps,* by Toy Lasker, or a Hagstrom map.

For bus and subway travel information between any two points in the five boroughs, call 718/330-1234.

● By Bus: For visitors who don't want to walk, the bus is best. Buses go up and down the avenues and across the major streets, and on most routes they run frequently during the day and with limited service at night. The bus fare is 90¢ (exact change or a subway token), and free transfers are available on some routes: e.g., when you go crosstown on a bus, you can get a free transfer to take you uptown or downtown on any of the avenues that have bus routes.

● Subway: Since 1904, New Yorkers have been riding on and complaining about the subway. It's noisy, it's dirty, and it's graffiti-scarred—but it's usually fast and costs only 90¢ to go anywhere on the system. You need to buy a token before you can enter the platform. Token booths are supposed to have a supply of subway maps.

● Taxis: You'll be able to tell whether or not a taxi's free by the light on top—if it's lit up, it's vacant. A taxi ride costs $1.10 for the first one-seventh mile and 10¢ for each additional one-ninth mile. At night and on weekends you must pay a 50¢ surcharge. The tip should be 20% of the fare. Try to avoid taking a taxi because they're expensive and slow—especially when you're making a cross-town trip in rush hour. Most taxis are yellow—these are the ones licensed by the City of New York. Taxis by any other colors are called gypsy cabs and their drivers boast: "We're not yellow—we'll go anywhere."

Tourist Information: New York Convention and Visitors Bureau, 2 Columbus Circle, 10019. Telephone: 212/397-8222. Everything here is free—from maps to calendars of events to tickets for television shows.

● Jazz-Line. Dial 718/465-7500 to find out what's going on jazz-wise all over town.

● New York Magazine Information Service. Call 880-0755 to find out what tickets are still available on the day you call. They can also provide hotel and restaurant information. Hours: Monday, 12:30 to 6 p.m., Tuesday to Friday, 10:30 a.m. to 4:30 p.m.

Help: Travelers Aid Society of New York, 1465 Broadway, 10036. Telephone: 212/944-0013.

Accommodations: Urban Ventures, Inc., P.O. Box 426, 10024. Telephone: 212/594-5650. A bed-and-breakfast service run by Mary McAulay. "We inspect every room we list, and interview every host." Here's one sample listing: "A twin-bedded room on East 80th St. and York Ave. in the home of a vivacious teacher. The bus to Bloomingdale's stops right in front of the door." Prices range from about $26 to $65 for a single; $38 to $80 for a double. Write for more details.

● Hotel Chelsea, 222 West 23rd St., 10011. Telephone: 212/243-3700, $55 double with one bed; $65 with two beds; $75 for an efficiency; $85 and up for a quad. Advance reservations of one week necessary. "The Chelsea has been and is an artistic and creative haven for many of New York's and the world's famous characters, including Thomas Wolfe, Arthur Miller, Jane Fonda, Dylan Thomas, and Lenny Bruce."

● New York Student Center, Ⓢ, William Sloane House, 356 West 34th St., 10001. Telephone: 212/695-0291. Six blocks from Port Authority Bus Station; two blocks from Penn Station. Huge 1485-room facility. Rates: $22 single; $15 per person for a twin-bedded room. Rates are for rooms without baths, although a few rooms with bath are available at a higher price. Weekly rates and meal plans are also available for resident students. Facilities available to guests include a newly renovated cafeteria, lounges, reading rooms, game room, television room, gymnasium, and laundry. CIEE and YMCA cooperate in offering the services at the Student Center. The Council Travel Office at Sloane House issues airline and bus tickets, and arranges low-cost transportation and tours while helping students plan their travels in the U.S. and abroad. ISIC holders receive 10% discount on New York City bus and boat tours. The Hospitality Center offers information on activities in New York, including walking tours and discount tickets to plays and other events.

The Student Center is also a good meeting place, especially in summer. Other pluses are the ride board and multilingual staff at the center.

● International Student Center, 38 West 88th St., 10024. Telephone: 212/787-7706. Open year round. $8. Foreign students under age 30 only.

● West Side YMCA, Ⓢ, 5 West 63rd St., 10023. Telephone: 212/787-4400. Male and female students. $25 and up single; $34 and up double. Reservations preferred three weeks in advance with first night's deposit. Cafeteria in the building.

● Vanderbilt YMCA, Ⓢ, 224 West 47th St., 10017. Telephone: 212/755-2410. Men and women. $24 to $27 single; $32 to $35 double; $45 to $48 triple; $56 to $59 quad. Excellent cafeteria.

● YMCA, 99 Meserole Ave., Greenpoint, Brooklyn, 11222. Telephone: 718/389-3700. Men only. $18. One block from Nassau Ave. subway stop. Newly renovated. Health facilities available. One-half hour by subway from midtown Manhattan.

● YWCA, 30 Third Ave., Brooklyn, 11217. By subway, take the "A" train to Hoyt-Schermerhorn. Telephone: 718/875-1190. Women only. $15 single. Weekly rate: $50. Advance reservations of one to two weeks necessary.

● Parkside Evangeline Residence, 18 Gramercy Park S., 10003. Telephone: 212/677-6200. Women only. "This is a businesswomen's residence for permanent residency for 300 women, serving predominantly young business women." When there is room in the summer, a transient can stay for $20 a night. Weekly rate: $102 including two meals a day. Advance reservations of one to two months necessary.

● McBurney YMCA, 206 West 24th St., 10011. Telephone: 212/741-9226. Men only. $20 to $22 single.

Where to Eat: There are two kinds of eating to be done in New York. First is the grab-it-while-you-can-get-it type and second are the more peaceful, more leisurely meals that are best when shared with someone else. For the first kind you can depend on some of the chains like Blimpies, Nathan's Famous, or Arby's. And don't forget the "street pizza" that's usually $1 a slice and often filling and delicious. Another good "picnic" possibility are the salad bars in so many of the produce markets around town. Usually for $2.60 or $2.80 a pound, you can enjoy a salad that you can create from 20 or 30 choices of ingredients. You'll never be far from one of these wherever you are in the city.

If you're interested in saving money at dinnertime, why not take advantage of the "happy hour" that many midtown restaurants observe. Usually the happy hour lasts from 5 to 7 p.m., and during these two hours it's possible to have a drink and all the hors d'oeuvres you can eat for the cost of the drink alone. Some places serve quite substantial hors d'oeuvres—like fried chicken, pepper steak, meatballs, etc. Some places you might consider in midtown are the Old Stand, 914 Third Ave.; Molly Mog's, 65 West 55th St., and for happy hour Indian style, Tandoor, 40 East 49th St.; and RJ's, 770 Second Ave. (at 41st St.).

For the second type of eating, here are some possibilities. We've chosen these because we feel that they offer, above all, good value. (Remember that to save money it's always best to have your big restaurant meal at lunchtime since the prices on the dinner menu are much higher.) The following suggestions are some of our favorites, places where you can feel comfortable and won't have to spend a fortune. Call ahead for hours and don't be too shy to ask about prices.

● Front Porch, 253 West 11th St. (in the West Village, tel. 675-8083); 2272 Broadway at 82nd St. (Upper West Side, tel. 877-5220); and 119 East 18th St.

(Gramercy Park, tel. 473-7940). The specialty here is thick soups that are accompanied by homemade breads, sandwiches, salads, casseroles, and rich desserts.

● Chumley's, 86 Bedford St. (the West Village). Telephone: 675-4449. The quintessential Village bar and restaurant that was once a speakeasy. Hearty food, surprisingly low prices, and plenty of beer. For a remembrance of things past.

● Spring Street Natural Restaurant and Bar, 149 Spring St. (in Soho). Telephone: 466-0290. The food is good—soups, vegetable tempura, etc.—and the staff, at least when we've been there, is anxious to please.

● Spring Street Restaurant, 162 Spring/401 West Broadway (in Soho). Telephone: 219-0157. One of the first restaurant/bars in Soho and still one of the most popular. The management doesn't mind if you sit and talk a while over your drink or your meal.

● Leshko's, 111 Ave. A (near East 7th St.). Telephone: 470-9208. An order of meat-filled pirogi (a pocket of dough with meat inside) is filling and inexpensive. Other Polish and Ukrainian specialties, too.

● Kiev, 117 Second Ave. (at 7th St.). A good bargain—fabulous *challah* French toast, homestyle soups, apple pancakes, and kasha. Colorful crowd, right by NYU's film school.

● Yaffa Café, 97 St. Marks Place. Telephone: 674-9302. Vegetarian food (like broccoli over brown rice with melted cheese) and "regular" dishes, too. You can bring your own wine and enjoy it all on the back patio in nice weather. Three people can eat here for under $20.

● Odessa Coffee Shop, 117 Ave. A (at East 7th St.). Telephone: 473-8916. Foods of the Ukraine that are reasonably priced and served by amiable waitresses. We recommend the potato pirogies, fried and served with sour cream, the stuffed cabbage, or lamb stew.

● Mitali, 334 East 6th St. (between First and Second Aves.). Telephone: 533-2508. An Indian restaurant on a block that's lined with Indian restaurants. Explore the block; there are lots of good possibilities. Entrees here are $4 or $5. Bring your own wine.

● Another 6th St. favorite is Romna, for delicious curries. Bring your own wine or beer.

● King Crab, 871 Eighth Ave. (at 52nd St.). Telephone: 765-4393. A good seafood meal here is inexpensive and the restaurant is convenient to the theater district.

● Bangkok Cuisine, 885 Eighth Ave. (at 52nd St.). Telephone: 581-6370. For wonderful Thai food within an easy walk of the theater district. Most fun with a large group of people.

● Nom Wah Tea Parlor, 13 Doyers St. Telephone: 962-6047. Featured in this Chinatown restaurant is the dim sum lunch consisting of an assortment of dumpling-like creations that are stuffed with pork, seafood, bean curd, and vegetables.

● Hee Seung Fung Restaurant and Teahouse, 46 Bowery. Telephone: 374-1319. Another very popular Chinatown restaurant. At lunchtime waiters carry around trays of dim sum specialties and you pick what looks good. At the end of the meal you pay according to the number of empty plates left on your table.

● Silver Palace Restaurant, 50 Bowery. Telephone: 964-1204. What fun this place is on a Sunday morning. Dim sum and lots of people enjoying it all in this enormous (particularly for Chinatown) space.

- Hunan Garden, 1 Mott St. Telephone: 732-7270. A popular Chinatown restaurant with enclosed sidewalk café. Varied menu with Hunan specialties—hot and spicy dishes printed in red on the menu.
- Hwa Hsing Yuan Szechuan Inn, 40 East Broadway. Telephone: 674-1700. Yet another Chinatown favorite (there's nearly always a line in the evening). Superb Szechuan cuisine.
- Luna's, 112 Mulberry St. Telephone: 226-8657. In the very heart of Little Italy, Luna's serves southern-Italian-style food. Usually crowded, always noisy, and rude help but still fun.
- Akasaka, 715 Second Ave. Telephone: 867-6410. The sushi, the tempura, and all else is delicious. The restaurant is Japanese; the owners from Japan via France.
- Manganaro's Hero-Boy Restaurant, 492 Ninth Ave. Telephone: 947-7325. In the middle of the Italian market section; serves all kinds of hero sandwiches.
- Molfeta's, 307 West 47th St. Telephone: 840-9537. Greek food that's good and reasonably priced. Only steps from most of the Broadway theaters.
- Symposium, 544 West 113th St. Telephone: 865-1011. (Near Columbia University). Friendly popular Greek restaurant with a pleasant summertime garden.
- Souen, 2444 Broadway at 90th St. (Upper West Side). Telephone: 787-1110. In case you thought that macrobiotic food was just good for you, Souen will show you that it can be delicious, too. If you're in the Village, try the Souen at 210 Sixth Ave. Telephone: 807-7421.
- Gargantua, 110th St. and Broadway (near Columbia). Good food like onion soup, salads, burgers, and pasta at reasonable prices.
- Z, 117 East 15th St. (near Irving Place). Telephone: 254-0960. A nice place for a not-too-expensive Greek meal. Try the avgolemono soup, the poikilia (a mixed Greek antipasto), and the lamb dishes.
- Second Avenue Deli, 156 Second Ave. at 10th St. Telephone: 677-0606. Everything you've always wanted from a kosher deli—pastrami, borscht, chicken soup, chopped liver—in an atmosphere that's noisy, crowded, and fun.
- West End Café, Broadway between 113th and 114th Sts. (near Columbia). Telephone: 666-8750. You can eat here—good omelettes, sandwiches, hamburgers, etc.—but it's the music that we recommend. Starting at about 9 every night, in a side room that's all dark and smoky, you can hear terrific swing jazz played by the people who worked with Ellington and others as famous.
- Delphi Restaurant, 109 West Broadway, corner of Reade St. (A short walk from the World Trade Center). Telephone: 267-5463. Greek food in a pleasant atmosphere. "Everything I tasted was so good and I was amazed at the low prices."
- Rathbones, 1702 Second Ave. at 88th St. Telephone: 369-7361. Relaxed, comfortable setting but can get noisy at times. The bar is buzzing at night.
- Jackson Hole, 232 East 64th St. Telephone: 371-7187. Other locations too, but this is the best. "Great burgers with exotic toppings and low prices. Very trendy and always, always crowded. Expect to wait."
- Smokey's, 230 Ninth Ave. at 24th St. Telephone: 924-8181; and 685 Amsterdam Ave. at 93rd St., telephone: 865-2900. (On the Upper West Side.) This brother-sister operation caught on fast. People swarm to Smokey's for the ribs with sauce—hot, mild, or mixed, you take your choice—the fried potato skins, the chili, and the chicken.
- Chirping Chicken, 350 Amsterdam Ave. at 77th St., 1260 Lexington Ave.

at 85th St., and 2755 Broadway at 106th St. One friend whom we consider an expert on such matters gives Chirping Chicken a four-star rating—the chicken is charcoal-broiled with a tasty marinade and sauce. It's inexpensive too—only $3.39 for a half chicken, $5.89 for a whole. Eat in or take out—how about a picnic starring a chirping chicken?

● Squid Row, 1468 Second Ave. at 77th St., telephone: 249-4666; The Cock-Eyed Clams, 1678 Third Ave. at 94th St., telephone: 831-4121; and Hobeau's, 963 First Ave. at 53rd St., telephone: 421-2888, are all owned by the same people, and all serve quite good seafood and are all amazingly inexpensive.

● All up and down Columbus Ave.: The Upper West Side's a revitalized and very trendy strip—you'll find restaurants and cafés. For the price of a drink you can usually sit out at a sidewalk table and watch the passing parade. (One friend is sure it won't be long before the laundromats on Columbus will put tables and chairs out front, too.) And now, Amsterdam Avenue, one block west, is going the way of Columbus—new boutiques, restaurants, and bars open almost daily.

● And then there's Brooklyn: A short subway ride from Manhattan (the no. 2 or no. 3 train to Court St. or the no. 4 or no. 5 train to Borough Hall) are the glories of Atlantic Ave. and its Middle Eastern restaurants. One we can recommend is the Tripoli, on Atlantic Ave. at Clinton St. After you've eaten there or at any other Atlantic Ave. spot, walk over to the Brooklyn Heights Promenade for a beautiful view of the Lower Manhattan skyline.

What to See and Do: We can only scratch the surface here—there's so much to do—but here are a few suggestions if your time is limited.

● Free in the Parks: The New York Philharmonic, the Metropolitan Opera, and the Shakespeare Festival Company all perform in the parks of New York every summer for free. Take a picnic along and enjoy some of the world's most creative people in a superb setting. Call 472-1003 or 755-4100 for a recorded message about what's going on in the parks.

"I'd encourage visitors to check the papers for any street fairs that might be on during their stay; they strike me as New York at its very best."

● Museums: There are 75 museums in New York, each with something special to offer. With a limited time to spend in the city you will probably want to choose from some of the better known: the American Museum of Natural History, 79th St. and Central Park West; the Metropolitan Museum of Art, Fifth Ave. between 80th and 84th Sts.; the Museum of Modern Art, 11 West 53rd St. (newly expanded and beautified); the Guggenheim Museum, Fifth Ave. at 89th St.; the Cooper-Hewitt Museum (the Smithsonian Institution's National Museum of Design) at 2 East 91st St.; and the Frick Collection, 1 East 70th St.

To find out what exhibits are where, the hours of the museums, and admission policies (most have fees), check a copy of *New York* magazine, *The New Yorker,* or the free calendar of events distributed by the New York Convention and Visitors Bureau.

● One museum with a difference is the South Street Seaport Museum, along the East River in Lower Manhattan. "This is not a building or a ship; it is what remains of New York's great 19th-century port." The Seaport is a group of historic properties, restored or to be restored, to the area's 19th-century glory, as well as chic restaurants, boutiques, malls, and public terraces.

● The Museum of Holography, 11 Mercer St., near Canal, features a form of 3-D photography which involves the use of lasers. This is the place for a unique, interesting, "wave of the future" experience in Soho. Call 925-0526. Open noon to 6 p.m., Wednesday to Sunday.

● The United Nations. Hour-long tours of the U.N. are available every 15 minutes from 9 a.m. to 4:45 p.m., every day of the week. Tickets are $1.75 for students, $3 for others. A "walk-through" exhibit explains it all. Children under 5 are not allowed on the tour. Free tickets to open sessions of the General Assembly are also available on a first-come, first-served basis; they are distributed at the information booth at the 45th St. entrance. Call 754-7713 for information.

● Central Park: The park—840 miraculous acres of it—is one of New York's greatest attractions. It's bigger than Monaco, has almost 25,000 trees (who do you suppose counted them?), and lately has been having its various parts restored and renovated. In the recent past the Dairy, Belvedere Castle, and the Conservatory Garden at 105th St. and Fifth Ave. have been restored, and improvements are being made constantly to other sections. "Central Park is our jewel; try to enjoy some of it while you're here."

● The Buildings: For a view from the top that you won't forget, go to the 107th floor of the World Trade Center, Tower 2, on the Lower West Side. It costs $2.95 for adults ($1.50 for children 6 to 12; children under 6 are free), to go to the observation deck and from there you can go to an open walkway on the roof. Hours are from 9:30 a.m. to 9:30 p.m. Call 466-7377. The Empire State Building, 34th St. and Fifth Ave., has another view of Manhattan to offer from its 102nd floor. Costs $3 for adults; $1.75 for children under 12. Open 9:30 a.m. to midnight every day. Call 736-3100. To combine a beautiful view of New York on one side and New Jersey on the other with a drink, go to the Top of the Park Restaurant, 60th St. and Broadway (no sneakers, please).

● Staten Island Ferry. For 25¢ round trip you can take this poor-man's cruise across New York harbor. You'll pass the Statue of Liberty en route but if you want to actually visit the statue, walk around her, and climb into her crown, you can reach her by ferry from South Ferry and Battery Park. The round trip costs $2 for adults ($1 for children) and includes admission to the American Museum of Immigration in the statue's base. Call 269-5755 for ferry information. (Note: The statue itself may be closed for repairs.)

● Circle Line. One of the nicest ways to see the island of Manhattan is from a boat which cruises around all of it in three hours. The boat ride is a good way to begin a trip to New York, helping you to orient yourself to what's where on the island. The first boat leaves at 9:30 a.m., and there's a sailing every 45 minutes. The ride costs $5 for children under 12, $12 for adults, and it begins at Pier 83 on the Hudson River at the foot of 43rd St. It runs from the last day of March through November. Call 563-3200 for information. (ISIC holders are entitled to a 10% discount on Circle Line tickets purchased at the NY Student Center, 356 W. 34th St.).

● Tour of Harlem. Since most visitors are curious about Harlem, a black-operated tour company called Penny Sightseeing has tours of the area on Tuesdays, Thursdays, and Saturdays. On Thursday the tour is called Harlem Gospel Tour and it includes a stop at a church to hear gospel music; the Saturday tour is called Harlem As It Is. Thursday's tour costs $17, the other is $15; both last three hours. Call 246-4220; reservations are required.

● Neighborhoods. A walk in and around the neighborhoods of New York is the most fun of all. You can choose from the Financial District, Chinatown, Little Italy, the Lower East Side, Soho, Greenwich Village, the Garment Center, Midtown, the Upper East Side, and the Upper West Side. Leave yourself lots of time to stroll, go in and out of shops, and explore any place that attracts you. One of the guides listed on pages 338 and 339 will help you find your way.

● The Prospect Park Environmental Center sponsors interesting walks, workshops, bus and boat trips, all focusing on Brooklyn. Call 718/788-8500 for information.

● Theater. See at least one play while you're in New York. For up-to-the-minute listings of what is playing either on Broadway, off-Broadway, or off-off-Broadway, check the *New York Times* (the Sunday "Arts and Leisure" section especially) or *New York* magazine. Take advantage, too, of the bargains offered at the TKTS booths at 47th St. and Broadway in Duffy Square and on the mezzanine of no. 2 World Trade Center in Lower Manhattan. At 3 p.m. on the day of the performance, leftover tickets go on sale for half their original price at the 47th St. booth and tickets for matinees are available at noon; the World Trade Center booth opens at 11:30 a.m. and closes at 5:30 p.m.—it has tickets for evening performances only. The line can be long and you may not get your first choice, but after all, a bargain is a bargain.

● Lincoln Center. Whether it's dance, opera, symphony, or theater that excites you, you'll find some or all of them going on at once in the Lincoln Center complex. The Metropolitan Opera, Avery Fisher Hall, the New York State Theater, the Vivian Beaumont Theater, Alice Tully Hall are all there. At times, student rush tickets are available to performances in the Lincoln Center halls—call the individual box offices for details.

● Performing Arts. Not long ago a Music and Dance Booth was opened in Bryant Park, just behind the 42nd St. library between Fifth and Sixth Aves. Tickets to performing arts presentations in all five boroughs are available at half price on the day of performance. The booth is open seven days a week from noon to 7 p.m. Call 382-2323 for information. A gem of a hall where so many of New York's performing artists appear is up on the Upper West Side. It's called Symphony Space and at just about any time you're in town, you'll find something interesting on the schedule. Call 864-5400 for information.

● Brooklyn Bridge: The bridge remained stately and serene amid all the hoopla of its centennial celebration and now, even with the centennial over, it's an enormously popular tourist spot. Walking tours of the bridge are given once a season by the Prospect Park Environment Center, 718/788-8500.

● *Intrepid* Sea, Air and Space Museum. One of New York's newest sights, this museum on an aircraft carrier that was built in 1943 and decommissioned in 1974 is docked at Pier 86, 46th St. and Twelfth Ave. It's open from 10 a.m. to 5 p.m. every day, except Monday and Tuesday. Admission is $4.75 for adults; $2.50 for children under 12. Call 245-0072 for information.

● Swimming. When New York gets steamy, take a break and head for the John Jay Park Pool at York Ave. and 77th St. Telephone: 397-3159. It's a big, luxurious public pool.

● Film. If you want to see a commercial release, it's easy enough to find out what's playing where in the listings in the daily newspapers. But for those who are attracted to the lesser known films—films by "undiscovered" directors, independent films, or early or overlooked films by known directors—there are several possibilities. The Museum of Modern Art, the Whitney Museum, and the Little Theater in Joseph Papp's Public Theater are the most obvious; a bit less well-known are Film Forum, 57 Watts St.; Millennium, 66 East 4th St.; and Collective for Living Cinema, 52 White St.

● Clubs. We've got lots of them. Some, where you'll hear the newest in rock 'n' roll, are in the Village—Kenny's Castaways, 157 Bleecker St.; Doctor B's, 77 Greene St.; and R.T. Firefly's, 75 Bleecker St. Call for cover and minimum information—it changes from day to day. Danceteria, 30 West 21st St. between 5th and 6th Aves., features punk and new wave music, Sunday to Tuesday; the cover is $3.

Shopping: Does anyone pay full price for anything in New York? We sometimes wonder.

Some specific suggestions for the shoppers among us:

For Books: Barnes and Noble Sale Annex, two main locations, at 600 Fifth Ave., and at 18th St. and Fifth Ave., and branches all over town. A bookstore offering such good reductions on all bestsellers and others that it's worth a trip from wherever you are.

● The Complete Traveller, 199 Madison Ave. (at 35th St.). Telephone: 679-4339. The only bookstore in New York City that specializes in travel. Books, guides, and maps—old and new. Has a large selection on New York City.

For Records: Sam Goody's, Third Ave. and 43rd St., 235 West 49th St.; and 1290 Ave. of the Americas. Check Goody's ads in the Sunday *New York Times* for special bargains on all kinds of records and tapes.

● The Record Hunter, 507 Fifth Ave. One reader insists it's "better than Sam Goody's."

● Disco-Mat, branches all over Manhattan. Cheap, cheap records and tapes.

● Tower Records, 692 Broadway (at East 4th). The place to see and be seen and find just about any record you can imagine while you're at it. Open 9 a.m. to midnight every day. There's a video department here too, and an entire store devoted to video up at 1975 Broadway at 67th St.

Gifts: Bloomingdale's, 59th St. and Lexington Ave. Even *Time* magazine was inspired to superlatives by this extraordinary department store. Stop at Fiorucci's—just up the block at 125 East 59th—it's a "must-see" store for the 80s.

● Hudson's, Third Ave. and 13th St. For camping equipment, jeans, outdoor clothing, etc., head downtown to one of New York's best-loved stores.

● The Pottery Barn, 24th St. and Tenth Ave. There are other branches of this chain in other parts of the city but this is the biggest. It's filled with cooking accessories, ceramic ware, and gift-type things to bring home with you.

● United Nations Gift Shop, at the United Nations, 46th St. and First Ave. Usually forgotten by New Yorkers, this is an excellent place to buy gifts for everyone. Merchandise is selected from all over the world and whoever does the choosing has excellent taste.

● 47th Street Photo, 67 West 47th St. What a place! Hectic and wild no matter when you go, but what bargains on everything electronic—video equipment, watches, typewriters, computers, cameras, and on and on. Others at 115 West 45th St. and 38 East 19th. Closed Saturdays.

● The Lower East Side. Bargains galore along Orchard St. especially—stylish clothing for men, women, and children. Durable underwear, pretty lingerie, fashionable shoes—all at least 20% below "uptown" prices. Remember that most of the stores here are closed Saturdays but open on Sundays.

Niagara Falls

Help: Travelers Aid, Family and Children's Service of Niagara Falls, Inc., 826 Chilton Ave., 14301. Telephone: 716/285-6984.

Accommodations: YMCA, 1317 Portage Rd., 14301. Telephone: 716/285-8491. Men only. $11 single.

● Niagara Falls Frontier Youth Hostel (AYH), 1101 Ferry Ave., 14301. Telephone: 716/282-3700 or 282-8429. Closed December 15 to February 1. $7 summer, $8 winter for AYH members. Bring sleeping bag. Advance reservations necessary in July and August.

Oneonta

Help: Project, 85 Chestnut St. Telephone: 607/432-2111.

On Campus: A branch of the State University of New York is here, and a student mentioned that Market St. has several bars where students meet. Perkins Pancake and Steak House on Rte. 7, East End, is a good place to get a reasonable meal.

You'll find the most informative bulletin boards in the basement of Schumacher Hall and in the Administration Building across from the Housing Office.

Palmyra

Accommodation: Canaltown Home Hostel (AYH), c/o Robert Liesten, 119 Canandaigua St., 14522. Telephone: 315/597-5553. $6.25 for AYH members; $9.25 for nonmembers. Advance reservations necessary in July.

Patchogue

Camping: Fire Island National Seashore, 120 Laurel St., 11772. Telephone: 516/289-4810. Twenty-nine campsites at Watch Hill on Fire Island. Ferry terminal across the street from Long Island Railroad on West Ave. in Patchogue. Open year-round, but ferry operates from May to October only, requiring a private boat otherwise. No fee for camping; ferry charge of $3.75 one way. Advance reservations required.

Pawling

Accommodation: Holiday Hills YMCA, Charles Colman Blvd., 12564. Telephone: 914/855-1550. $24 single; $34 double. "New York YMCA's finest vacation and conference center." Advance reservations of one to four weeks necessary.

Pine Hill

Accommodation: Belleayre Youth Hostel (AYH), P.O. Box 665, Bonnieview Ave., 12465. Telephone: 914/254-4200. $6 summer, $8 winter for AYH members. Ski hostel located on Belleayre Ski Mountain. Advance reservations advised during ski-season weekends.

Plattsburgh

Accommodation: Econo Lodge, √ &, 610 Upper Cornelia St., 12901. Telephone: 518/561-1500. $26.95 to $31.95 for one; $29.95 to $35.95 for two in one bed; $34.95 to $39.95 for two in two beds.

Rochester

Accommodation: Red Roof Inn, &, 4820 West Henrietta Rd., I-390 (Exit 46), Henrietta, 14467. Telephone: 716/359-1100. See Albany listing for rates.

Schenectady

Accommodations: YMCA, 13 State St., 12305. Telephone: 518/374-9136. Bus station across the street. Men only. $16.50 to $18.50 single. Weekly rate: $51 to $55. Advance reservations of one month necessary. Cafeteria in lobby.
● YWCA, 44 Washington Ave., 12305. Telephone: 518/374-3394. Two blocks from bus station. Women only. $15 single for members; $20 for nonmembers.

Skaneateles

Accommodation: Budget Host—Bel-Aire Motel, 797 West Genesee St., 13152. Telephone: 315/685-6720. $18 to $20 for one; $21 to $23 for two in one bed; $23 to $25 for two in two beds.

Staatsburg

Accommodation: Avalor, ⑤ √ ★, Fiddlers Bridge Rd., 12580. Telephone: 914/266-4120. Open April to November. $49 for one to four people. Bring your own linen. Advance reservations of one week necessary.

Star Lake

Accommodation: Star Lake Campus (AYH-SA), State University College of Arts and Science at Potsdam, 13690. Telephone: 315/848-3486 or 848-2480 (ask for Doc Catana). Open year round. Men, women, and children. Near beach. $6.25 summer, $7.75 winter for AYH members.

Syracuse

Help: Volunteer Center, 315/474-7011.
On Campus: Some suggestions for anyone who gets hungry around the campus of Syracuse University: Danzer's on Park St. for "dynamite corned beef

and roast beef sandwiches"; Faegan's Pub, 734 South Crouse Ave., a pub with a garden; Hungry Charley's, 727 South Crouse Ave., a good place for sangria, sandwiches, and meeting friends; and King David's on Marshall St. for Middle Eastern cuisine. The bulletin boards listing rides, apartments, etc., can be found in the basement of the Bird Library, in H. B. Crouse Hall, and in the basement of the Hall of Languages and Hendrick's Chapel. For film buffs, inexpensive films are shown at the H. B. Crouse Building on campus; most are open to the public.

Accommodations: Downing International Hostel, 459 Westcott St., 13210. Telephone: 315/472-5788. Open year round. $5 for AYH or IYHF members only.

● Downtown Branch YMCA, 340 Montgomery St., 13202. Telephone: 315/474-6851. Men only. $22 single, plus $3 key deposit. Weekly rates: $55 to $70. Advance reservations of two weeks necessary.

● TraveLodge, √ ⓰, 940 James St., 13203. Telephone: 315/472-6281. Airport transportation available. $30 for one; $34 for two in one bed; $38 for two in two beds.

Troy

Accommodation: YWCA, ⓰, 21 1st St., 12180. Telephone: 518/274-7100. Women only. $18 for members; $20 for nonmembers. Advance reservations of one to two weeks necessary.

Trumansburg

Accommodation: Podunk International Hostel (AYH-SA), Podunk Rd., 14886. Telephone: 607/387-6716. $5 summer, $7 winter for AYH members. Advance reservations of one day suggested, especially in summer.

Vernon

Accommodation: Conland Home Hostel (AYH), c/o Robert and Katrina Conland, Rte. 1, Box 61-G, 13476. Telephone: 315/829-2315. Closed July 1 to 15. $4 for AYH members. Bicyclists only. Advance reservations of one day necessary.

Yonkers

Accommodation: YWCA, ⓰, 87 South Broadway, 10701. Telephone: 914/963-0640. Women only. $30. Advance reservations of one week necessary.

North Carolina

North Carolina shares the Blue Ridge Parkway with Virginia and the Great Smoky Mountains National Park with Tennessee. Both are spectacular to see. For those who like the seashore best, North Carolina has some of that too: the well-known Outer Banks project a jagged coastline where currents can sometimes be treacherous, marine life is prolific, and there are some of the loveliest beaches on the entire Atlantic Coast. In this same area you'll find Kitty Hawk, the stretch of land where the Wright Brothers made their first flight in 1903. Campers love North Carolina and hikers can enjoy any or all of the 68 miles of the Appalachian Trail that run through the state.

The cities of North Carolina include Asheville in the mountainous west, where you can tour the Vanderbilts' Biltmore House and Gardens; Winston-Salem, "cigaretteville," a combination of the Moravian-founded town of Salem and the contemporary industrial town of Winston-Salem, Raleigh, the old state capital; Chapel Hill, the home of the University of North Carolina (Thomas Wolfe's alma mater), the Ackland Memorial Art Center, the Coker Arboretum, and the Morehead Planetarium; and Durham, the home of Duke University and the place where the tobacco industry got started. For a guide to the historical landmarks of the state listed by county, see Marguerite Schumann's *Tar Heel Sights: Guide to North Carolina's Heritage* ($8.95), published by the East Woods Press, 429 East Boulevard, Charlotte, NC 28203.

Some Special Events: Fiddler's Convention in Denver, and Folk Music and Dance Festival in Louisburg (March); Shad Festival in Grifton, and Azalea Festival in Wilmington (April); Strawberry Festival in Chadbourn (May); Bluegrass and Old Time Fiddlers Convention in Mount Airy, and National Hollerin' Contest in Spivey's Corner (June); Lumber River Raft and Canoe Regatta in Wagram, and Highland Games at Linville (July); Festival of Outer Banks Folk Music at Cape Lookout National Seashore, and the Strange Seafood Exhibition (tasting marinated octopus, fried squid, and charcoaled shark) in Beaufort (August); Mule Days Festival in Benson, and Masters of Hang Gliding Championship in Linville (September).

Hitching: Hitchhiking is legal, except on the Interstate system, as long as you stay off the traveled portion of the road. The Highway Patrol doesn't recommend it but most friends at North Carolina colleges seem to think that hitching in the area of the school is okay; with all the student traffic, the wait for a ride shouldn't be too long.

Tourist Information: North Carolina Travel and Tourism, Department of Commerce, 430 North Salisbury St., Raleigh, NC 27611. Telephone: 919/733-4171.

Asheboro

Accommodation: Econo Lodge, √, U.S. 220 Bypass & N.C. 49 on Albemarle Rd., Rte. 3, 27203. Telephone: 919/625-1880. $25.95 for one; $29.95 for two in one bed; $31.95 for two in two beds. Higher rates apply during special events.

Asheville

Accommodations: Econo Lodge, √ ⓹, 190 Tunnel Rd., 28805. Telephone: 704/254-9521. $24.95 to $29.95 for one; $26.95 to $33.95 for two in one bed; $29.95 to $37.95 for two in two beds.
● Days Inn, ⓹, I-40 & 70 E. (Exit 55), Box 9708, 28815. Telephone: 704/298-5140. $27 to $40 for one; $32 to $45 for two. Higher rates apply during special events.
● Days Inn, ⓹, I-40 & E. Canton Exit 37, Rte. 5, P.O. Box 95, Candler, 28715. Telephone: 704/667-9321. See above listing for rates.
● Days Inn, ⓹, 183 Underwood Rd., Fletcher, 28732. Telephone: 704/684-2281. See above listing for rates.
● Budget Host—Four Seasons Motor Inn, 820 Merrimon Ave., 28804. Telephone: 704/254-5324. November to April: $19 to $21 for one; $23 for two. May to October: $23 to $30 for one; $28 to $35 for two.

Bakersville

Accommodation: Trailridge Mountain Camp (AYH), Rte. 2, Hughes Gap Rd., 28705. Telephone: 704/688-3879. Open May 1 to August 31. $5 for AYH members. Advance reservations suggested.

Benson

Accommodation: Econo Lodge, √ ⓹, I-95 & N.C. 50 (Exit 79), 27504. Telephone: 919/894-2031. $22.88 to $24.88 for one; $26.88 to $28.88 for two.

Blowing Rock

Accommodation: Blowing Rock Assembly Grounds (AYH-SA), ⓹, Goforth Rd., 28605. $5 summer, $8 winter for AYH members. $16 to $26 single; $26 to $32 double; $24 to $33 triple; $28 to $36 quad. Higher rates apply in winter.

Boone

Accommodation: Scottish Inn, 905 East King St., 28607. Telephone: 704/264-9002. December 16 to March 14 and May 16 to November 14: $32 to $38 for one or two in one bed; $38 to $42 for two in two beds. November 15 to December 15: $17 for one; $19 for two in one bed; $25 for two in two beds.

Chapel Hill

"Chapel Hill has had a reputation for being progressive, diverse, and activist since the '60s. It's a great town. I grew up here, left for college, and chose to move back. Please come!"

On Campus: Some 23,000 students inhabit Chapel Hill, many of them studying at the University of North Carolina. One of them recommends that you check with the Department of University Housing, Carr Building, UNC Campus 103A, about possible dorm space for a night or two. You might check the bulletin board or information desk in Frank Porter Graham Union for details on special events, rides, etc., or the *Village Advocate,* campus newspaper. Students meet at Four Corners, East Franklin St., and He's Not Here, 112½ West Franklin. You can find an inexpensive home-style meal at the Porthole on Old Fraternity Row, or Dip's Country Kitchen, 405 West Rosemary.

The Student Consumers Action Union (located in the Student Union) researches and rates all restaurants in Chapel Hill and then publishes the results in the *Franklin Street Gourmet.* "It's the best source of up-to-date quality and prices."

Charlotte

Accommodations: Motel 6, 3430 St. Vardell Lane, 28210. Telephone: 704/527-0230. $17.95 for one; $21.95 for two; $2 for each additional person.

● Motel 6, 3433 Mulberry Church Rd., 28208. Telephone: 704/394-0189. See above listing for rates.

● Days Inn, 4419 Tuckaseegee Rd., 28208. Telephone: 704/394-5181. $28 to $35 for one; $33 to $40 for two.

● Days Inn, I-85 & Sugar Creek Rd., 1408 Sugar Creek Rd., 28213. Telephone: 704/597-8110. See above listing for rates.

● Econo Lodge, V, 1415 Tom Hunter Rd., P.O. Box 26623, 28213. Telephone: 704/597-0470. $25.95 for one; $29.95 for two in one bed; $33.95 for two in two beds. Higher rates apply during special events.

● Econo Lodge, V, I-85 & Little Rock Rd., P.O. Box 668203, 28266. Telephone: 704/394-0172. See above listing for rates.

● Red Roof Inn, ♿, 5116 I-85 N., I-85 & Sugar Creek Rd., 28213. Telephone: 704/596-8222. $26.95 for one; $31.95 for two in one bed; $33.95 for two in two beds; $35.95 for three or four in two beds.

● Red Roof Inn, ♿, 3300 I-85 S., I-85 at Billy Graham Pkwy., 28208. Telephone: 704/392-2316. See above listing for rates.

● Red Roof Inn, ♿, 131 Greenwood Dr., I-77 at Nations Ford Rd., 28201.

$24.95 for one; $29.95 for two in one bed; $31.95 for two in two beds; $33.95 for three or four in two beds.

Concord

Accommodation: Days Inn, I-85 & N.C. 73, P.O. Box 3322, 28025. Telephone: 704/786-9121. $25 for one; $30 for two.

Creedmoor

Accommodation: Econo Lodge, √ 🔖, I-85 & S.R. 56, Rte. 2, Box 179-B, 27522. Telephone: 919/575-6451. $23.95 for one; $27.95 for two in one bed; $29.95 for two in two beds.

Dillsboro

Accommodation: Smokeseege Lodge (AYH), P.O. Box 179, 28725. Telephone: 704/586-8658. Closed November to December. $6 summer, $7 winter for AYH members. Advance reservations necessary.

Dunn

Accommodation: Comfort Inn, I-95 & East Broad St., 28334. Telephone: 919/892-1293. $27 to $31 for one; $31 to $35 for two.

Durham

Accommodations: Days Inn, I-85 & Redwood Rd., 27704. Telephone: 919/688-4338. $27 to $32 for one; $32 to $37 for two.
- Econo Lodge, 2337 Guess Rd., 27705. Telephone: 919/286-7746. $26 for one; $32 for two in one bed; $34.95 for two in two beds. Higher rates apply during special events.
- Motel 6, 2101 Holloway St., 27703. Telephone: 919/682-8043. See Charlotte listing for rates.
- Imperial 400 Motor Inn, √ (10%), 605 West Chapel Hill St., 27701. Telephone: 919/682-5411. $26 to $30 for one; $28 to $32 for two in one bed; $30 to $34 for two in two beds.

Fayetteville

Accommodations: Days Inn, I-95 & U.S. 13 (Exit 58), Rte. 1, Box 216BB, Wade, 28395. Telephone: 919/323-1255. $26 to $33 for one; $30 to $37 for two.
- Motel 6, 525 South Eastern Blvd., 28301. Telephone: 919/323-1957. See Charlotte listing for rates.
- Quality Inn Americana, 2507 Gillespie St., 28306. Telephone: 919/485-5161. $28 to $30 for one; $33 to $35 for two.
- Econo Lodge, √, 442 Eastern Blvd., 28301. Telephone: 919/483-0332.

$23.95 to $24.95 for one; $27.95 to $28.95 for two in one bed; $31.95 for two in two beds. Higher rates apply during special events.

Gastonia

Accommodation: Days Inn, I-85 & Edgewood Rd., P.O. Box 338, Bessemer City, 28016. Telephone: 704/867-0231. $25 for one; $30 for two.

Gold Rock

Accommodation: Imperial 400 Motor Inn, √ (10%), Rte. 1, Box 877, 27809. Telephone: 919/977-3505. $28 to $32 for one; $32 to $36 for two.

Goldsboro

Accommodations: Days Inn, &, U.S. 70 Bypass & 2000 Wayne Memorial Dr., 27530. Telephone: 919/734-9471. $27 for one; $31 for two.
● Motel 6, 701 Hwy. 701 Bypass E., 27530. Telephone: 919/736-7140. See Charlotte listing for rates.
● Econo Lodge, √, 704 Hwy. 70 Bypass E., 27530. Telephone: 919/736-4510. $23.95 for one; $25.95 for two in one bed; $28.95 for two in two beds.

Graham

Accommodation: Econo Lodge, √ &, P.O. Box 852, 27253. Telephone: 919/228-0231. $26.95 for one; $30.95 for two in one bed; $32.95 for two in two beds.

Greensboro

Accommodations: Econo Lodge, √ &, I-85 at Lee St. Exit, P.O. Box 16163, 27416. $23.88 for one; $26.88 for two in one bed; $29.88 for two in two beds. Higher rates apply during special events.
● Econo Lodge, √ &, 135 Summit Ave., 27401. Telephone: 919/370-0135. $29.95 for one; $33.95 for two in one bed; $35.95 for two in two beds.
● Motel 6, 831 Greenhaven Dr., 27406. Telephone: 919/294-1305. See Charlotte listing for rates.
● Days Inn, &, 501 Regional Rd. S., 27409. Telephone: 919/668-0476. $25.88 to $45 for one; $30 to $45 for two.
● Red Roof Inn, 2101 West Meadowview Rd., I-40 at High Point Rd., 27403. Telephone: 919/852-6560. $24.95 for one; $29.95 for two in one bed; $31.95 for two in two beds; $33.95 for three or four in two beds.

Greenville

Accommodation: Econo Lodge, √, 810 Memorial Dr., 27834. Telephone: 919/752-0214. $23.95 for one; $27.95 for two in one bed; $29.95 for two in two beds.

Henderson

Accommodation: Econo Lodge, I-85 & Ruin Creek Rd., P.O. Box 808, 27536. Telephone: 919/492-4041. $23.95 for one; $25.95 for two in one bed; $29.95 for two in two beds.

Hendersonville

Accommodation: Briarwood Motel, 1510 Greenville Hwy., 28739. Telephone: 704/692-8284. $28 to $33 for one double bed; $30 to $39 for two double beds.

High Point

Accommodations: Motel 6, 200 Ardale Dr., 27260. Telephone: 919/886-5041. See Charlotte listing for rates.
● TraveLodge, √, 425 South Main St., 27260. Telephone: 919/882-0147. Airport transportation available. $27 for one; $30 for two in one bed; $36 for two in two beds.

Jacksonville

Accommodation: Econo Lodge, 🚻, 497 Western Blvd., 28540. Telephone: 919/347-3311. $28.95 to $30.95 for one; $32.95 to $34.95 for two in one bed; $36.95 to $38.95 for two in two beds. Higher rates apply during special events and weekends.

Kinston

Accommodation: Econo Lodge, √, 212 East New Bern Rd., 28501. Telephone: 919/523-8146. $26.95 for one; $28.95 for two in one bed; $31.95 for two in two beds.
● Econo Lodge, √🚻, 206 Blowing Rock Blvd., 28645. Telephone: 704/754-0731. $26.95 to $29.95 for one; $29.95 to $33.95 for two in one bed; $33.95 to $37.95 for two in two beds.

Lumberton

Accommodations: Days Inn, I-95 & N.C. 211 Exit, P.O. Box 937, 28358. Telephone: 919/738-6401. $26 to $32 for one; $30 to $36 for two.
● Motel 6, I-95 Service Rd., Rte. 3, 28358. Telephone: 919/738-8930. See Charlotte listing for rates.
● Susse Chalet Motor Lodge, I-95 (Exit 14), at jct. of U.S. 74, 28358. Telephone: 919/738-1444. $27.70 for one; $31.70 for two; $34.70 for three; $37.70 for four.
● Scottish Inn, I-95 & Carthage Rd., 28358. Telephone: 919/738-2441. $20.95 for one; $25.95 for two in one bed; $28.95 for two in two beds.

● Econo Lodge, √, P.O. Box 693, 28358. Telephone: 919/738-7121. $21.95 for one; $25.95 for two in one bed; $28.95 for two in two beds.

Maggie Valley

Accommodation: Scottish Inn, 35 Soco Rd., 28751. Telephone: 704/926-1251. July 1 to October 31: $35 to $40 for one or two people. November 1 to December 31: $25 for one or two people.

Manteo—Cape Hatteras

Camping: Cape Hatteras National Seashore, Rte. 1, P.O. Box 675, 27954. Five campgrounds at Cape Point, Frisco, Ocracoke, Oregon Inlet, and Salvo. $8 per campsite per night.

Morganton

Accommodations: Days Inn, I-40 & Hwy. 18 S., 28655. Telephone: 704/433-0011. $28 for one; $32 for two.
● Econo Lodge, √, 2217 South Sterling St., 28655. Telephone: 704/437-6980. $22.95 for one; $25.95 for two in one bed; $29.95 for two in two beds.

New Bern

Accommodation: Friendship Curtis Motel, 113 B St., 28519. Telephone: 919/638-3011. Limited airport service available. $20 to $22 for one; $22 to $24 for two in one bed; $26 to $28 for two in two beds.

Pembroke

Accommodation: The House (AYH-SA), c/o Winston Hardman, P.O. Box 25, Red Springs Rd., 28372. Telephone: 919/521-8777. $5 for AYH members. Advance reservations necessary.

Raleigh

Help: Family Services of Wake County, 3803 Computer Dr., Suite 101, 27609. Telephone: 919/781-9317.
Accommodations: Econo Lodge, √, 5110 Holly Ridge Dr., 27612. Telephone: 919/782-3201. $25.95 for one; $28.95 for two in one bed; $31.95 for two in two beds. Higher rates apply during special events.
● Econo Lodge, √ &, 3500 Wake Forest Rd., 27609. Telephone: 919/872-9300. $26.95 for one; $29.95 for two in one bed; $32.95 for two in two beds. Higher rates apply during special events.
● Econo Lodge, √, 309 Hillsborough St., 27603. Telephone: 919/833-5771. $25.95 for one; $28.95 for two in one bed; $31.95 for two in two beds.

Rocky Mount

Accommodations: Days Inn, I-95 & N.C. 48, Goldrock Exit 145, Rte. 1, Box 155, Battleboro, 27809. Telephone: 919/446-0621. $27 to $35 for one; $31 to $39 for two.

● Econo Lodge, Rte. 1, Box 161B, Battleboro, 27809. Telephone: 919/446-2411. $25.95 for one; $29.95 for two in one bed; $35.95 for two in two beds. Higher rates apply during special events.

Rowland

Accommodation: Days Inn, &, I-95 & U.S. 301 (South of the Border exit), Rte. 2, 28383. Telephone: 919/422-3366. $21.88 to $27.88 for one; $25.88 to $31.88 for two.

Salisbury

Accommodation: Econo Lodge, V, 1011 East Innes St., 28144. Telephone: 704/633-8850. $23.95 for one; $27.95 for two in one bed; $34.95 for two in two beds. Higher rates apply during special events.

Sanford

Accommodation: Econo Lodge, V, 404 Carthage St., 27330. Telephone: 919/775-2328. $23.95 for one; $28.95 for two in one bed; $30.95 for two in two beds. Higher rates apply during special events.

Selma

Accommodations: Econo Lodge, P.O. Box 786, 27576. Telephone: 919/965-5756. $23.95 for one; $27.95 for two in one bed; $31.95 for two in two beds. Higher rates apply during special events.

● Days Inn, I-95 & U.S. 70A (Exit 97), Rte. 3, Box 22, 27576. Telephone: 919/965-3762. $22 to $28 for one; $26 to $32 for two.

Southern Pines

Accommodation: Econo Lodge, V &, Hwy. 1 & 15-501, P.O. Box 150, 28387. Telephone: 919/944-2324. $23.95 for one; $25.95 for two in one bed; $33.95 for two in two beds.

Statesville

Accommodations: Scottish Inn, P.O. Box 1748, 28677. Telephone: 704/872-9891. $24 for one; $28 for two in one bed; $30 for two in two beds; $32 for three or four in two beds.

● Red Roof Inn, &, 1508 East Broad St., 28677. Telephone: 704/878-2051. See Greensboro listing for rates.

● Days Inn, I-40 W. & U.S. 21 N., 28677. Telephone: 704/873-5252. $27 to $31 for one; $32 to $36 for two.
● Econo Lodge, 725 Sullivan Rd., 28677. Telephone: 704/873-5236. $24.95 for one; $29.95 for two.

Washington

Accommodation: Econo Lodge, √, 1220 West 15th St., 27889. Telephone: 919/946-7781. $24.95 for one; $26.95 for two in one bed; $29.95 for two in two beds.

Weldon

Accommodation: Econo Lodge, √, 1615 Roanoke Rapids Rd., 27890. Telephone: 919/536-2131. $28.95 for one; $32.95 for two in one bed; $36.95 for two in two beds.

Wesser

Accommodation: Nantahala Outdoor Center (AYH-SA), &, U.S. 19 W., Box 41, Bryson City, 28713. Telephone: 704/488-2175. $5 for AYH members. Advance reservations suggested.

Wilmington

Accommodations: Days Inn, &, U.S. 17 & U.S. 74, 5040 Market St., 28405. Telephone: 919/799-6300. $25.88 to $38.88 for one; $29.88 to $35.88 for two.
● Econo Lodge, &, 4118 North Market St., 28403. Telephone: 919/762-4426. $25.95 to $28.95 for one; $28.95 to $31.95 for two in one bed; $31.95 to $34.95 for two in two beds. Higher rates apply during special events.
● Motel 6, 2828 Market St., 28403. Telephone: 919/762-4496. See Charlotte listing for rates.

Winston-Salem

Accommodation: Motel 6, 3810 Patterson Ave., 27105. Telephone: 919/724-7240. See Charlotte listing for rates.

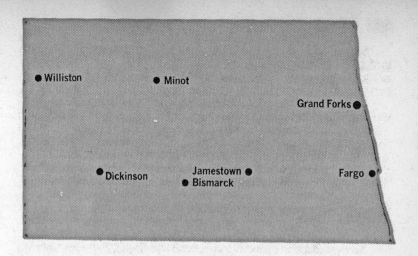

North Dakota

The sunsets, the thunderstorms, the cloud formations, and the northern lights of August are bound to dazzle anyone who has never before experienced "the plains" of North Dakota. The summers there are hot and dry, and the winters are cold and snowy. No matter what the time of year, the wide-open spaces are breathtaking.

North Dakota is primarily an agricultural state, with flatlands and wheat fields in the east and the rugged Badlands in the west. Most of the people who live there are of Scandinavian or German descent or they represent several tribes of native Americans including the Mandan and the Sioux.

Ten percent of the state's population lives in Fargo, the home of North Dakota State University. Not surprisingly, Fargo boasts a very active arts community—a symphony orchestra, opera company, community theater, and dance troupe. It's also the location of Bonanzaville, a restored western pioneer village, and Trollwood, a park devoted to the arts. During fair weather there are free outdoor concerts and arts-and-crafts exhibits, and during the winter there's cross-country skiing and ice skating. Fargo is near the border of Minnesota and its "sister city" of Moorhead, Minnesota. Moorhead State University and Concordia College, both liberal arts schools, are in Moorhead. The university has an excellent theater department with a good performing arts series and a summer theater workshop.

Other places to visit in North Dakota include the capital city of Bismarck, located on the Missouri River and the site of the reconstructed Slant Indian Village; Fort Totten Indian Reservation; the International Peace Gardens, on the border between the U.S. and Canada; and most certainly, the Badlands at and around Medora, where you'll find the Theodore Roosevelt National Park. The park, definitely worth a visit, features restorations, museums, and on summer nights, outdoor performances commemorating the history of the area through drama and music.

Some Special Events: Winterfest in Minot (February); Jaycee Rodeo Days in Mandan, and Riverboat Days in Grand Forks (July); Pioneer Days at Bonanzaville, West Fargo (August); United Tribes Powwow in Bismarck (September).

Hitching: A North Dakota law prohibits soliciting a ride from the roadway, which is defined as the main traveled portion of the highway. A friend from North Dakota State University says that although hitchhiking is not very well accepted, and hitchhikers are often considered to be nuisances by many people, hitching is probably safer in North Dakota than in many other states.

Tourist Information: North Dakota Tourism and Promotion Division, State Capitol Grounds, Bismarck, ND 58505. Telephone: 701/224-2525.

Bismarck

Accommodations: Friendship Bismarck Motor Hotel, 2301 East Main St., 58501. Telephone: 701/233-2474. $20 to $22 for one; $22 to $25 for two in one bed; $25 to $28 for two in two beds.

● Thrifty Scot Motel, 1300 Capitol Ave. E., 58501. Telephone: 701/223-9151. $22.90 to $27.90 for one; $27.90 to $32.90 for two.

● Motel 6, 2433 State St., 58513. Telephone: 701/255-1851. $17.95 for one; $21.95 for two; $2 for each additional person.

● Select Inn, ∨, 1505 Interchange Ave., 58501. Telephone: 701/223-8060. $24 to $32 single; $33 double; $36 triple; $38 quad.

● Comfort Inn, ∨ &, 1030 Interstate Ave., 58501. Telephone: 701/223-1911. $25 to $30 for one; $32 to $39 for two.

Dickinson

Accommodations: Friendship Nodak Inn, East I-94 Business Loop, Hwy. 10 on 600 East Villard St., 58601. Telephone: 701/225-5119. $17 to $22 for one; $20 to $22 for two in one bed; $24 to $26 for two in two beds.

● Comfort Inn, ∨ &, 6th Ave. W. & 21st St. W., 58601. Telephone: 701/225-3399. $25 to $27 for one; $30 to $32 for two.

● Select Inn, ∨ &, 642 12 St. W., 58601. Telephone: 701/227-1894. $22 to $29 single; $29 double; $32 triple; $34 quad.

● Econo Lodge, ∨ &, 529 12th St. W., Exit 13, 58601. Telephone: 701/225-9123. $28 for one; $32 for two in one bed; $34 for two in two beds.

Fargo

On Campus: The Student Affairs Office at North Dakota State University is the best place to go for help in getting your bearings. At the Trader and Trapper in Moorhead and the Old Broadway in Fargo you'll run into lots of students.

Accommodations: YWCA, 411 Broadway, 58102. Telephone: 701/232-2547. Women only. $10 single; $12 twin. Weekly rate: $60 to $72. Open 24 hours.

● Motel 6, 2202 South University Dr., 58102. Telephone: 701/235-4411. See Bismarck listing for rates.

- Thrifty Scot Motel, 901 38th St. SW, 58103. Telephone: 701/282-9100. $22.90 to $27.90 for one; $28.90 to $33.90 for two.
- Select Inn, √ &, 1025 38th St. S., 58103. Telephone: 701/282-6300. $23 to $30 single; $29 double; $32 triple; $35 quad.
- Regal 8 Inn, 1202 36th St. S., 58103. Telephone: 701/232-9251. $21.88 for one; $26.88 for two in one bed; $31.88 for two in two beds. Indoor pool.
- Econo Lodge, √ &, 1401 35th St. S., 58103. Telephone: 701/232-3412. $21.95 for one; $25.95 for two in one bed; $27.95 for two in two beds.

Grand Forks

Accommodation: Regal 8 Inn, 1211 47th St. N., 58201. Telephone: 701/775-0511. See Fargo listing for rates.

Jamestown

Accommodation: Friendship Inn Tumbleweed Motor Hotel, 824 S.W. 20th St., 58401. Telephone: 701/252-5222. $18.96 to $26.93 for one; $20.94 to $28.96 for two in one bed; $24.95 to $32.92 for two in two beds.

Minot

Accommodations: Select Inn, √, U.S. 83 at 22nd Ave. NW, 58702. Telephone: 701/852-3411. $23 to $30 single; $31 double; $34 triple; $37 quad.
- Thrifty Scot Motel, 2100 4th St. SW, 58701. Telephone: 701/852-3646. $23.90 to $28.90 for one; $28.90 to $33.90 for two.

Williston

Accommodation: Select Inn, √ &, 213 35th St. W., 58801. Telephone: 701/572-4242. $20 to $26 single; $26 double; $28 triple; $30 quad.

Ohio

Ohio, the Iroquois word for "beautiful river," became a state in 1803. But its history dates back to the early Mound Builders, whose large earthworks can still be seen at places like Great Serpent Mound near Hillsboro and Fort Ancient near Lebanon.

There is rich farmland in the northwestern part of the state, while the southeastern lands abound with recreational areas, including the caves of the Hocking Hills. There's a famous Pumpkin Festival each fall at Circleville, the gateway to the Hocking Hills.

Ohio played an important role in the story of the underground railroad. Many runaway slaves came up the Scioto and Olentangy Rivers after crossing the Ohio River through Columbus and Worthington. In the Worthington Historical Society's annual tours of old homes, you can see some of the slave hiding places.

The first organized settlement in the Northwest Territory was founded in 1788 at Marietta on the Ohio River. Marietta College, the Lafayette Hotel (named for its most famous guest), and an old riverboat and museum are among the attractions there.

In northern Ohio, Blossom Music Center, an outdoor amphitheater near Akron, is the summer home of the Cleveland Symphony.

Springfield, home of Wittenberg University, is located just off I-70 between Columbus and Dayton. The old National Road ended here at one time and the Pennsylvania House was the inn at the "end of the trail." A town of 80,000, Springfield has a symphony, a theater group, an art center, and a long-established photographic society. The Summer Arts Festival offers performing arts throughout July, free to the public, in Cliff and Snyder Parks near the campus. And just nine miles south of Springfield is Yellow Springs, an interesting village of small shops and the home of Antioch University.

Ohio has 71 state parks, 59 of which have lakes. One of them, Hueston Woods, is located near Oxford, the home of Miami University and the place where McGuffey wrote his *Eclectic Readers*.

Ohio has produced eight presidents of the United States and a variety of other famous people from Thomas Edison (whose birthplace can be visited in Milan) to the Wright Brothers. The famous Air Force Museum near Dayton depicts the history of aviation and the Neil Armstrong Museum at Wapakoneta is named for the first man to walk on the moon.

Some Ohioans think of themselves as Easterners, some as Midwesterners. You'll have to decide for yourself whose side you're on. Ohio has many, many college towns where you'll be welcome.

For a guide to some of the lesser-known sights in Ohio, see *Ohio Off the Beaten Path*, by George Zimmerman, published by East Woods Press, 429 East Blvd., Charlotte, NC 28203 ($5.95). All about the more undiscovered pleasures of the state.

Some Special Events: Maple Syrup Festival in Chardon (April); Delta Queen Homecoming in Cincinnati (May); Holy Toledo! It's Spring in Toledo (June); Budweiser Cleveland Grand Prix in Cleveland (July); Ohio State Fair in Columbus (August); Air Show in Cleveland, and Oktoberfest in Cincinnati (September); Pumpkin Show in Circleville (October); and Winterfest in Kings Island, Cincinnati (December).

Hitching: It's legal if you stay off the traveled portion of the road, except on freeways or Interstates. The State Highway Patrol says that, in general, hitching is discouraged in Ohio. From what we could figure out from information sent to us by several campuses, hitching is okay in the area around campus but not very good in more rural sections.

Tourist Information: Ohio Office of Travel and Tourism, P.O. Box 1001, Columbus, OH 43216. In Ohio call toll free 800-BUCKEYE; out-of-state, call 614/466-8844. The office is an excellent source of information, and on request will provide free maps and brochures.

Akron

On Campus: At the University of Akron, check the Off-Campus Housing Office at Spanton Hall for apartments, rides, etc. To meet Akron's young people, try the Townhouse, Splash, Mugs, the Campus Lounge, Mike's Gold Bar, and the Sun. For inexpensive meals, there's Parasson's (Italian food), Brown Derby Steak House, Trecaso's, Sarah's Delicatessen, and the Ground Round, along with many of the usual fast-food chains.

Accommodation: Red Roof Inn, 🛆, 99 Rothrock Rd., I-77 at Ohio 18, 44321. Telephone: 216/666-0566. $23.95 for one; $28.95 for two in one bed; $30.95 for two in two beds; $32.95 for three or four in two beds.

Ashland

Accommodation: Scottish Inn, 1120 U.S. Rte. 250, 44805. Telephone: 419/289-8911. $15 for one; $17 for two in one bed; $22 for two in two beds.

Athens

On Campus: The Ohio University is in this small, lively university town. Traveling young people will find the people receptive. For sources of information on rides, apartments, odd jobs, etc., check the *Athens News* or the *Ohio University Post*. For good, inexpensive meals, there's C.J.'s, Bojangles, Casa Que Pasa, Dexters, Krazy Kat Kafe, and Towne House—all in the center of town.

Beavercreek

Accommodation: Beavercreek Home Hostel (AYH), c/o John & Beth Anne Gordon, 3425 Napanee Dr., 45430. Telephone: 513/426-9537. $5.25 for AYH members. Advance reservations necessary.

Bowling Green

On Campus: Bowling Green State University is described by a student as "quite dull, really," but she does concede that you can call the Fact Line (tel. 419/372-2445) for information on the good variety of concerts and movies in Bowling Green. There are several bars where students congregate, including Uptown, Buttons, Howard's Club, and Mr. Bojangles. The Union Hotel at the university has reasonably priced rooms. If all else fails, "there is a good, unobstructed view of tomato, wheat and soybean fields."

Accommodation: Wintergarden Youth Hostel (AYH), Wintergarden Rd., mail: c/o 244 Biddle St., 43402. Telephone: 419/352-9349 or 352-9806. $3.25 summer, $3.75 winter for AYH members. Advance reservations necessary.

Canton

Accommodation: Red Roof Inn, 5353 Inn Circle St. NW, I-77 at Everhard Rd. (Exit 109), 44720. Telephone: 216/499-1970. See Akron listing for rates.

Chillicothe

Accommodation: Home Hostel (AYH). Telephone: 614/775-3632 or 773-3989. $3.25 for AYH members. Advance reservations necessary.

Cincinnati

"The downtown area of Cincinnati is thriving, unlike lots of other cities."

Accommodations: Home Hostel (AYH). Telephone: 513/541-1972. $3.25 summer, $4.25 winter for AYH members. Advance reservations necessary.
● Koenig Home Hostel (AYH), c/o Phillip Koenig, 972 Ludlow Ave., 45220. Telephone: 513/961-7541. $5 for AYH members. Advance reservations necessary.
● Red Roof Inn, 🔣, 5300 Kennedy Rd., Norwood, 45213. Telephone:

513/531-6589. $29.45 for one; $30.95 for two in one bed; $32.95 for two in two beds; $34.95 for three or four in two beds.

- Red Roof Inn, 11345 Chester Rd., Sharonville, 45246. Telephone: 513/771-5141. See above listing for rates.
- Red Roof Inn, 🚻, 4035 Mt. Carmel-Tobascco Rd., Beechmont, 45230. Telephone: 513/528-2741. See above listing for rates.
- Red Roof Inn, 🚻, 5900 Pfeiffer Rd., 45242. Telephone: 513/793-8811. See above listing for rates.
- Days Inn, 150 Garver Rd., Monroe, 45050. Telephone: 513/539-9221. $27.88 to $30.88 for one; $32.88 to $39.88 for two.
- Days Inn, I-275 & U.S. 42, 45241. Telephone: 513/554-1400. $27.88 to $37.88 for one; $33.88 to $45 for two.
- Econo Lodge, √, 8367 Cincinnati-Dayton Rd., West Chester, 45069. Telephone: 513/777-5121. $25 to $40 for one; $30 to $46 for two.

Cleveland

Tourist Information: Cleveland Convention and Visitors Bureau, 1301 East 6th St., 44114. Telephone: 216/621-4110.

Help: Travelers Aid Center for Human Services, 1001 Huron Rd., 44115. Telephone: 216/241-6400. Also at Greyhound Bus Terminal, 1465 Chester Ave., and Cleveland Hopkins International Airport.

Accommodations: Red Roof Inn, 6020 Quarry Lane, Independence, 44131. Telephone: 216/447-0030. See Cincinnati listing for rates.

- Red Roof Inn, 🚻, 17555 Bagley Rd., Middleburg Heights, 44130. Telephone: 216/243-2441. See Akron listing for rates.
- Red Roof Inn, 15385 Royalton Rd., 44136. Telephone: 216-238-0170. $21.95 for one; $26.95 for two in one bed; $28.95 for two in two beds; $30.95 for three or four in two beds.
- Red Roof Inn, 🚻, 29595 Clemens Rd., 44145. Telephone: 216/892-7920. See Akron listing for rates.
- Red Roof Inn, 4166 S.R. 306, Willoughby, 44094. Telephone: 216/946-9872. See Akron listing for rates.
- Scottish Inn, √, 9029 Pearl Rd., 44136. Telephone: 216/234-3575. $17.95 to $21.95 for one; $21.95 to $25.95 for two in one bed; $24.95 to $28.95 for two in two beds.
- Red Carpet Inn, 4353 Northfield Rd., North Randall, 44128. Telephone: 216/475-4070. $19 for one or two in one bed; $30 for two to four beds.
- Airport Budget Motor Inn, Ⓢ √ ★, 16789 Brookpark Rd., Rte. 17, 44142. Telephone: 216/267-0100. $22.95 to $25.95 single; $25.96 to $32.98 double; $32.97 to $35.97 triple; $36.92 to $39.96 quad. "A full-service motel, clean, comfortable, and a good value for budget-conscious travelers."

Columbus

"The city America is discovering for its vitality and growth."

Tourist Information: Columbus Convention Bureau, 50 West Broad St., Suite 1600, 43215. Telephone: toll free 800/821-5785 or 614/221-6623.

On Campus: Ohio State is in Columbus. The Union is at 1739 North High St. Off-Campus Student Center is at 1712 Neil Ave. To meet students, go to any bar or restaurant along High St.; Nangees Café, 21 East 15th Ave.; Bernie's Bagels and Deli, 67 East Gay St. and 1896 North High St.; or the Blue Danube, 2439 North High St.

Accommodations: YWCA, 65 South 4th St., 43215. Telephone: 614/224-9121. Women only. $19.50 to $35.50 per week.

● Central Branch, YMCA, 40 West Long St., 43125. Telephone: 614/224-1131. Men only. $16 single. Weekly rate: $45.

● Imperial 400 Motor Inn, $\sqrt{}$ (10%), 655 West Broad St., 43215. Telephone: 614/224-5151. $25 to $29 for one; $30 to $34 for two.

● Red Roof Inn, ⑤, 441 Ackerman Rd., 43202. Telephone: 614/267-9941. See Akron listing for rates.

● TraveLodge, $\sqrt{}$, 1070 Dublin Rd., 43215. Telephone: 614/486-0651. $24 for one; $28 for two in one bed; $32 for two in two beds.

● Heart of Ohio Hostel (AYH), 95 East 12th Ave., 43201. Telephone: 614/294-7157. $6 summer, $7 winter for AYH members. Closed Christmas Day. Advance reservations suggested. Sleeping bag required.

● Days Inn, 5930 Scarborough Rd., 43227. Telephone: 614/868-9290. $26 to $28 for one; $32 to $34 for two.

● Days Inn, 3131 Broadway, Grove City, 43213. Telephone: 614/871-0065. See above listing for rates.

● Red Roof Inn, 2449 Brice Rd., Reynoldsburg, 43068. Telephone: 614/864-3683. See Akron listing for rates.

● Red Roof Inn, 750 Morse Rd., 43229. Telephone: 614/846-8520. See Akron listing for rates.

● Red Roof Inn, 1900 Stringtown Rd., 43123. Telephone: 614/875-8543. $21.95 for one; $26.95 for two in one bed; $28.95 for two in two beds; $30.95 for three or four in two beds.

● Red Roof Inn, 5001 Renner Rd., 43228. Telephone: 614/878-9245. See Canton listing for rates.

● Red Roof Inn, ⑤, 5125 Post Rd., Dublin, 43017. Telephone: 614/764-3993. See Akron listing for rates.

● Red Roof Inn, ⑤, 7474 North High St., Worthington, 43085. Telephone: 614/846-3001. $24.95 for one; $29.95 for two in one bed; $31.95 for two in two beds; $33.95 for three or four in two beds.

Dayton

Help: Travelers Aid, 184 Salem Ave., 45406. Telephone: 513/222-9481.

On Campus: For advice and general help during office hours you can call International Students Office at the University of Dayton (tel. 513/229-2638). There's a bulletin board in the lower level of the Kennedy Union and you can meet University of Dayton students in the snackbar of the Union or in one of several bars in the Brown Street area adjacent to campus. Some of the nearby restaurants for good, inexpensive meals are Milano's, Orient Occident Restaurant, The Shed, Skyline Chili, Submarine House, and Westward Ho Cafeteria —all on Brown St.

Accommodations: Central YMCA, $\sqrt{}$, 117 West Monument Ave., 45402.

Telephone: 513/223-5201. Men only. $16. Weekly rate: $39. Cafeteria in building.

- YWCA, 141 West 3rd St., 45402. Telephone: 513/461-5550. YWCA membership required. $9 to $12 single; $14 to $18 double. Advance reservations of one day necessary.
- Red Roof Inn, 222 Byers Rd. Miamisburg, 45342. Telephone: 513/866-0705. See Akron listing for rates.
- Red Roof Inn, 7370 Miller Lane, 45414. Telephone: 513/898-1054. See Akron listing for rates.
- Days Inn, 7470 Miller Lane, 45414. Telephone: 513-898-4946. $25 to $27 for one: $31 to $33 for two.
- Days Inn, 2455 Dryden Rd., Moraine, 45439. Telephone: 513/298-0380. See above listing for rates.

Findlay

Accommodation: Econo Lodge, ∨, 316 Emma St., 45840. Telephone: 419/422-0154. $27.95 for one; $31.95 for two in one bed; $33.95 for two in two beds. Higher rates apply during special events.

Franklin

Accommodation: Econo Lodge, ∨, 4385 East 2nd St., 45005. Telephone: 513/746-3627. $23.95 to $24.95 for one; $25.95 to $26.95 for two in one bed; $27.95 to $28.95 for two in two beds. Higher rates apply during special events and weekends.

Gallipolis

Accommodation: Econo Lodge, ∨, 389 Jackson Pike, 45631. Telephone: 614/446-7071. $26.95 for one; $29.95 for two in one bed; $31.95 for two in two beds. Higher rates apply during special events.

Kent

Help: Town Hall II Help Line, 223 East College Ave., 44240. Telephone: 216/678-4357 or 800/533-4357 (24 hours a day). The people here are willing to help: "We will do our best to help those who call or come to our door." They cannot, however, provide shelter.

On Campus: You can get from the Kent campus to other parts of the city cheaply on the KSU bus—it's available to nonstudents, too. A good place to meet other students is at one of the cafeterias on the Kent State campus, or one of about 15 bars in the area—Filthy McNasty's, J.B.'s, Ray's Place, Loft, Genesis, Robin Hood, or Townhouse. "This town is oriented toward young people." You may be able to stay at Korb Guest Hall on campus; call 672-7000 for information.

Accommodation: Friendship Eastwood Inn, 2296 Main St., Rte. 59, 44240. Telephone: 216/678-1111. $23.50 to $28 for one; $26 to $28 for two in one bed; $28 to $45 for two in two beds.

Lima

Accommodation: Lima Home Hostel (AYH). Telephone: 419/222-7301 or 226-3169. $2.75 for AYH members. Advance reservations necessary.

Lorain

Accommodation: Beachcomber Inn, $\vee$, 2800 West Erie Ave., 44053. Telephone: 216/244-5251. $24 for one or two people.

Lucas

Accommodation: Malabar Farm Youth Hostel (AYH), Rte. 1, Bromfield Rd., 44843. Telephone: 419/892-2784. $3.25 summer, $4.25 winter for AYH members. Advance reservations and deposit for one night's stay necessary September to May.

Mansfield

Accommodation: Friendship Inn 42 Motel, 2444 Lexington Ave., 44907. Telephone: 419/884-1315. $24 to $26 for one; $28 to $29 for two in one bed; $33 to $36 for two in two beds. Higher rates apply during special-events weekends in May through September.

Marietta

Accommodation: Econo Lodge, $\vee$, 702 Pike St., 45750. Telephone: 614/374-8481. $23.95 for one; $29.95 to $31.95 for two.

Medina

Accommodations: Budget Host—Suburbanite Motel, Ⓢ🚹 (10%), 2909 Medina Rd., 44256. Telephone: 216/725-4971. $19.95 (plus $4 during summer) for one; $21.95 for two in one bed; $23.95 for two in two beds.
● Scottish Inn, 841 Lafayette Rd., 44256. Telephone: 216/725-9814. $15 for one; $17 for two in one bed; $20 for two in two beds.
● TraveLodge, $\vee$, 2860 Medina Rd., 44256. Telephone: 216/725-0561. $30 for one; $35 for two.

Middletown

Accommodation: Regal 8 Inn, 2425 North Verity Pkwy., 45052. Telephone: 513/423-9403. $21.88 for one; $26.88 for two in one bed; $31.88 for two in two beds.

Montpelier

Accommodation: Friendship Exit 2 Motel, RR 3, (600 feet from I-80), I-90 at Exit 2, 43543. Telephone: 419/485-3139. $25 to $27 for one; $27 to $30 for two in one bed; $32 to $34 for two in two beds.

New Philadelphia

Accommodation: Motel 6, 181 Bluebell Dr. SW, 44663. Telephone: 216/339-6530. $17.95 for one; $21.95 for two; $2 for each additional person.

North Ridgeville

Accommodation: Travelers Inn, √ 🕭 ★ (5%), 5003 Cleveland Rd. E., 44039. Telephone: 216/327-6311 or 777-7456; toll free: 800/421-5146. $28 single or double; $33 triple; $38 quad. Advance reservations of three days necessary.

Oxford

On Campus: Miami University is in Oxford, a small college town which is very receptive to young travelers. There are three inexpensive motels in the area, and you might be able to stay on campus in the summer if you speak with someone in the housing office. Oxford is known for its Apple Butter Festival and there are many campus events throughout the year. You can meet students at Lottie Moon's, CJ's, Ozzies, Dipaolo's, and Attractions.

"Oxford is definitely off any main path for travelers but provides a friendly student atmosphere and plenty of places to meet people, both on campus and in town."

Portsmouth

Accommodation: Days Inn, 🕭, 8402 Ohio River Rd., Wheelersburg, 45694. Telephone: 614/574-8431. $28.88 for one; $32.88 for two.

St. Clairsville

Accommodations: Friendship Inn Twin Pines, National Rd. W., one-quarter mile east of I-70, Exit 213 on Rte. 40, 43950. Telephone: 614/695-3720. $20 to $24 for one; $25 to $28 for two in one bed; $28 to $32 for two in two beds.
 • Red Roof Inn, 🕭, 68301 Red Roof Lane, 43950. Telephone: 614/695-4057. $24.95 for one; $29.95 for two in one bed; $31.95 for two in two beds; $33.95 for three or four in two beds.

Sidney

Accommodations: Days Inn, I-75 & Ohio 47, Exit 92, Folkreth Ave., 45365. Telephone: 513/492-1104. $26 for one; $30 for two.
● Quality Inn, √, 2009 West Michigan St., 45365. Telephone: 513/492-9164. $25 to $28 for one; $28 to $37 for two.

Springfield

Accommodation: TraveLodge, √ 🕭, 325 West Columbia St., 45504. Telephone: 513/324-5601. $28 for one; $30 for two in one bed; $32 for two in two beds.

Strongsville

Accommodations: Friendship Inn Pike View Motel, 10590 Pearl Rd., 44136. Telephone: 216/238-2888. $20 for one; $22 for two in one bed; $25 for two in two beds.
● Budget Host—La Siesta Motel, 8300 Pearl Rd., 44136. Telephone: 216/234-4488. $19 for one; $20 for two in one bed; $23 for two in two beds.

Toledo

Help: Travelers Aid, First Call for Help, One Stranahan Square, Suite 260, 43604. Telephone: 419/244-3728.
Accommodations: Days Inn, I-75 & Ohio 20 at Exit 193 on I-75, Ohio Turnpike Exit 5, 43551. Telephone: 419/874-8771. $24 to $26 for one; $28 to $30 for two.
● Red Roof Inn, 1570 Reynolds Rd., Maumee, 43537. Telephone: 419/893-0292. See Akron listing for rates.
● Red Roof Inn, 🕭, 1214 Corporate Dr., Holland, 43528. Telephone: 419/866-5512. See Akron listing for rates.
● Toledo Home Hostel (AYH), 4027 McGregor Lane, 43623. Telephone: 419/474-1993. Open in summer. $4.25 for AYH members. Advance reservations necessary.

Warren

"This is the most overcast section of the country; we never see the sun. The fall is usually very short, winters are cold and damp. . . ."

Accommodation: Scottish Inn, √, 4258 Youngstown Rd. SE, 44484. Telephone: 216/369-4100. $25 for one; $27 to $30 for two.

Wilmington

Accommodation: Caesar Creek Youth Hostel (AYH), 8823 Center Rd.,

45177. Telephone: 513/488-3755. $3.25 summer, $4.25 winter for AYH members. Advance reservations necessary October to May.

Wooster

Accommodation: Econo Lodge, √⬛, 2137 Lincolnway E., 44691. Telephone: 216/264-8883. $26.95 for one; $30.95 for two in one bed; $33.95 for two in two beds.

Youngstown

Help: Hotline, 216/747-2696.

Accommodations: YWCA, Ⓢ√⬛ ★, 25 West Rayen Ave., 44503. Telephone: 216/746-6361. Women only. $10 plus $7 key deposit. Weekly rate: $50. Advance reservations suggested.

● Days Inn, ⬛, 1610 Motor Inn Dr., Girard, 44420. Telephone: 216/759-3410. $26 to $36 for one; $31 to $41 for two.

● Motel 6, 1600 Motor Inn Dr., Girard, 44420. Telephone: 216/759-2183. See New Philadelphia listing for rates.

● Econo Lodge, √, 1615 East Liberty St., Girard, 44420. Telephone: 216/759-9820. $29.95 for one; $33.95 for two in one bed; $36.95 for two in two beds. Higher rates apply during special events.

● Econo Lodge, √⬛, 1300 Youngstown-Warren Rd., 44446. Telephone: 216/544-1301. $24.95 for one; $26.95 for two in one bed; $31.95 for two in two beds.

● Red Carpet Inn, √, 9694 Mahoning Ave., 44451. Telephone: 216/538-2221. $22 to $35 for one; $28 to $45 for two in one bed; $31 to $48 for two in two beds.

● Quality Inn, √⬛, 8392 Market St., 44512. Telephone: 216/758-2371. $25 to $30 for one; $38 to $47 for two.

● Comfort Inn, √, 10076 Market St., North Lima, 44452. Telephone: 216/549-2187. $23.95 to $30.95 for one; $25.90 to $30.95 for two.

Zanesville

Help: Crisis Center Hotline: 614/454-9766.

Accommodations: Buck Home Hostel (AYH), 1024 Culbertson Ave., 43701. Telephone: 614/454-2637. Near bus station. $2 for AYH members. Advance reservations necessary.

● YWCA, ⬛ ★, 49 North 6th St., 43701. Telephone: 614/452-2717. Women only. Limit of three-night stay. $7.50 per person. Weekly rate: $22 to $32. Bring sleeping bag.

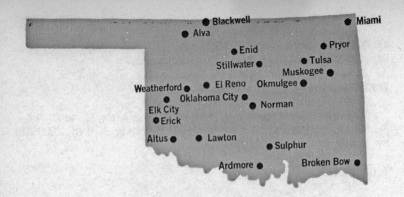

Oklahoma

Oklahoma has the second-largest Indian population in the United States and has lots of Indian attractions within its borders. Oklahomans, according to one we know, are generally open, friendly, and hospitable in the western style. Spring and fall are the best times to visit—the summer is very, very hot.

As you plan your stay in Oklahoma, consider visiting Anadarko, a town with several Indian museums and Indian City USA, an outdoor museum that depicts the life of the various tribes. Also try to include in your itinerary the Cowboy Hall of Fame and Western Heritage Center in Oklahoma City; the Stouall Museum of Science and History at the University of Oklahoma in Norman; the Woolaroc Museum in Bartlesville, the creation of the founder of Phillips Oil Company; the Thomas Gilcrease Institute of American History and Art in Tulsa, which has a fine collection of western paintings, Aztec manuscripts, and manuscripts of the early Spanish explorers; and the Cherokee Heritage Center in Tahlequah, which has both a museum and a pageant called the Trail of Tears that runs from early June through August.

There's tent camping in all 36 Oklahoma state parks and 24 recreation areas. The Tourism and Recreation Department tells you to "just pitch your tent by a beautiful lake, enjoy the Sooner State's clean air and pure water and have a ball." There are also five state resorts located near lakes that are reasonably priced.

Some Special Events: International Finals Rodeo in Tulsa (January); Rattlesnake Hunt in Waurika (March); Azalea Festival in Muskogee (April); Strawberry Festival in Stilwell, and Rooster Day Celebration in Broken Arrow (May); Kiamichi Owa Chito Festival of the Forest (Choctaw for "Happy Hunting Party") in Broken Bow (June); Huckleberry Festival in Jay, and Pow Wow in Tulsa (July); All-Night Gospel Sing in Konowa, and Watermelon Festival in Rush Springs (August); and Will Rogers Birthday Celebration in Claremore (November).

Hitching: Officially, hitchhiking is allowed except from roadways and turnpikes. The attitude in Oklahoma toward hitching doesn't seem to be enthusiastic. But a teacher friend at the University of Oklahoma in Norman polled his classes, and about one-half said they'd pick up a hitchhiker. Nearly all said they did not recommend hitchhiking though, and that "in this area nearly all interstate travel is on limited-access Interstate Highways."

Tourist Information: Oklahoma Tourism and Recreation Department, 500 Will Rogers Memorial Bldg., Oklahoma City, OK 73105. Telephone: 405/521-2406. To order any brochures about the state, call 405/521-2409.

Altus

Accommodation: Econo Lodge, √ &, 3202 North Main St., 73521. $25.95 for one; $29.95 for two in one bed; $33.95 for two in two beds.

Alva

Accommodation: Friendship Vista Inn, 1400 Oklahoma Blvd., 73717. Telephone: 405/327-3232. $22 to $27 for one; $25 to $30 for two in one bed; $28 to $32 for two in two beds.

Ardmore

Accommodation: Motel 6, 120 Holiday Dr., 73401. Telephone: 405/226-6212. $17.95 for one; $21.95 for two; $2 for each additional person.

Blackwell

Accommodation: Friendship Plainsman Inn, two miles west at jct. of I-35 & Hwy. 11, 74631. Telephone: 405/363-2911. $22 to $24 for one; $26 to $28 for two in one bed; $30 to $32 for two in two beds.

Broken Bow

Accommodation: Econo Lodge, √, 1912 South Park Dr., 74728. Telephone: 405/584-9103. $24.95 for one; $26.95 for two in one bed; $30.95 for two in two beds.

El Reno

Accommodation: Friendship Inn Western Sands Motel, Rte. 1, Box 108B, 73036. Telephone: 405/262-6000. $24.96 and up for one; $28.08 and up for two in one bed; $31.20 and up for two in two beds.

Elk City

Accommodation: Motel 6, 2500 East Hwy. 66, 73644. Telephone: 405/225-0961. See Ardmore listing for rates.

Enid

Accommodation: Earl Butts Residence Halls and Clay Hall, 125 Lakeview, 73702. Telephone: 405/237-4433. Prefer no small children. Open May 15 to August 1. $10 single; $8 to $10 per person, double. Advance reservations of two weeks necessary. Bring your own linen.

Erick

Accommodation: Econo Lodge, √ 🦽, 73645. Telephone: 405/526-3315. $23.95 for one; $27.95 for two in one bed; $30.95 for two in two beds.

Lawton

Accommodation: Friendship Inn Corral Motel, 1709 Cache Rd. NW on Hwy. 62, 73501. Telephone: 405/353-2772. $16 to $20 for one or two in one bed; $22 to $35 for two in two beds.

Miami

Accommodations: Friendship Thunderbird Inn, 1307 Steve Owens Blvd., I-44 Will Rogers Turnpike, Miami Exit, 74354. Telephone: 918/542-4435. $19 to $21 for one; $22 to $24 for two in one bed; $25 to $27 for two in two beds.
 ● Townsman—Budget Host, 900 Steve Owens Blvd., 74354. Telephone: 918/542-6631. $22 to $24 for one; $25 to $26 for two in one bed; $28 to $31 for two in two beds.

Muskogee

Accommodations: Friendship Sooner Motel, 335 North 32nd St., 74401. Telephone: 918/687-4477. $18 to $22 for one; $20 to $22 for two in one bed; $25 to $30 for two in two beds.
 ● Motel 6, 903 South 32nd St., 74411. Telephone: 918/687-5280. See Ardmore listing for rates.

Norman

Help: Number NYNE, Oklahoma University Crisis Hotline, 650 Parrington Oval, 73019. Telephone: 405/325-6963.

On Campus: For inexpensive lodging on campus, call 405/325-1011 and you might be able to stay in Walker Tower for $20 a night. To meet OU students, head for Mr. Bill's, Town Tavern, Service Station, Interurban, or Monte. For a meal, try Town Tavern, corner of Boyd and Asp, or Love Light on Jenkins St. The Union at 900 Asp seems to be the center of the OU universe—go there to meet students and check the ride board, too.

Accommodations: Budget Host—O.U. Motel, √, 2420 Classen Blvd., 73069. Telephone: 405/321-4670. $20 for one; $22 for two in one bed; $24 for two in two beds.

- Econo Lodge, √ &, 1430 24th Ave. SW, 73069. Telephone: 405/329-6990. $28.95 for one; $32.95 for two in one bed; $34.95 for two in two beds.

Oklahoma City

Help: Travelers Aid, 601 N.W. 5th St., 73102. Telephone: 405/232-5507.

Accommodations: Motel 6, 820 South Meridian Ave., 73108. Telephone: 405/946-6703. See Ardmore listing for rates.
- Motel 6, I-40 & Hudiburg Dr., 73110. Telephone: 405/733-5817. See Ardmore listing for rates.
- Motel 6, 1417 North Moore Ave., Moore, 73160. Telephone: 405/799-9190. See Ardmore listing for rates.
- Motel 6, 11900 N.E. Expressway, 73131. Telephone: 405/478-3776. See Ardmore listing for rates.
- Regal 8 Inn, 5801 Tinker Diagonal, Midwest City, 73110. Telephone: 405/737-8851. $21.88 for one; $26.88 for two in one bed; $31.88 for two in two beds.
- Regal 8 Inn, 12121 N.E. Expressway, 73131. Telephone: 405/478-4030. $22.88 for one; $27.88 for two in one bed; $32.88 for two in two beds.
- Days Inn, &, I-40 & MacArthur, 720 South MacArthur, 73128. Telephone: 405/947-0681. Five minutes from airport. $26 for one; $33 for two.
- Red Carpet Inn, √, 11901 N.E. Expressway, 73111. Telephone: 405/478-0243. $23 to $29 for one; $27 to $31 for two in one bed; $29 to $33 for two in two beds.
- Red Carpet Inn, √, 2616 South I-35, 73129. Telephone: 405/677-0521. $29.95 for one; $39.95 for two. Full breakfast included.
- Friendship Inn Carlyle, 3600 N.W. 39th St., 73112. Telephone: 405/946-3355. $28 for one or two in one bed; $34 to $40 for two in two beds.
- TraveLodge, √ &, 501 N.W. 5th St., 73102. Telephone: 405/235-7455. $28 for one; $31 for two in one bed; $34 for two in two beds.
- Econo Lodge, √ &, 8200 West I-40, 73127. Telephone: 405/787-7051. $20.95 for one; $24.95 for two in one bed; $26.95 for two in two beds.

Okmulgee

Accommodation: Friendship Carriage Inn, 1800 South Wood Dr. on Hwy 75, 74447. Telephone: 918/756-6614. Limited airport service available. $20 for one; $22 for two in one bed; $28 for two in two beds.

Pryor

Accommodation: Budget Host—Holiday Motel, 701 South Mill, 74362. Telephone: 918/825-1204. $22 to $27 for one; $26 for two in one bed; $31 for two in two beds.

Stillwater

Accommodation: Motel 6, 5122 West 6th Ave., 74074. Telephone: 405/377-7339. See Ardmore listing for rates.

Sulphur

Camping: Chickasaw National Recreation Area, P.O. Box 201, 73086. Camping all year at Buckhorn, The Point, and Rock Creek, and from April to October at Cold Springs and Guy Sandy. $5 per campsite per night; $10 for groups or $1 per person with a minimum charge of $10.

Tulsa

Tourist Information: Convention and Visitors Division, Metropolitan Tulsa Chamber of Commerce, 616 South Boston Ave., 74119. Telephone: 918/585-1201.

Accommodations: YMCA, √ ♿ ★, 515 South Denver, 74103. Telephone: 918/583-6201. $10.45 to $12.05 single. After four nights, $41.80 to $49.30 per week. Men and women.

● Days Inn, I-44 & 11th St., 11910 East 11th St., 74128. Telephone: 918/437-8980. $24.88 to $28.88 for one; $29.88 to $33.88 for two.

● Motel 6, 5828 Skelly Dr., 74107. Telephone: 918/446-6661. See Ardmore listing for rates.

● Motel 6, 1011 South Garnett Rd., 74128. Telephone: 918/438-2208. See Ardmore listing for rates.

● TraveLodge, √ ♿, 5311 West Skelly Dr., 74107. Telephone: 918/446-3371. $28 for one; $33 for two in one bed; $36 for two in two beds.

Weatherford

Accommodations: Scottish Inn, √, 616 East Main St., 73096. Telephone: 405/772-3349. $18.95 to $22.95 for one; $20.95 to $24.95 for two in one bed; $24.95 to $28.95 for two in two beds.

● Econo Lodge, √, Hwy. 54 & I-40, Exit 80, 73096. Telephone: 405/772-7711. $20.95 for one; $23.95 for two in one bed; $27.95 for two in two beds.

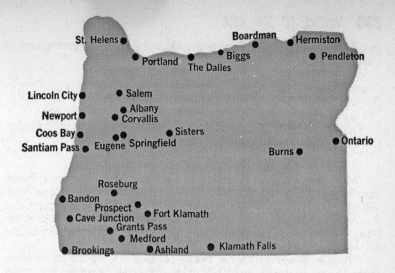

Oregon

The population of Oregon is a little over two million, so for those of you coming from a highly populated area, Oregon will give you a chance to breathe. Oregon has mountains, deserts, fields, and the ocean. From Eugene, for example, one can travel an hour west and be at the coast, or an hour east and be in the mountains.

Green is the color of Oregon. There's a lot of rain in winter (it's snow in the mountains); in color and scenery, late spring is the most beautiful season. In summer and fall, the weather is perfect for swimming in mountain lakes and hiking in the wilderness. Winter in Oregon is usually gray, but ski resorts like Mt. Bachelor near Bend, Mt. Hood (approximately 50 miles east of Portland), and Mt. Ashland near Ashland are worth a winter visit.

Most of Oregon's history is centered on Indian history, early settlers, explorers, and trappers. One of the small towns that has been restored to look as it did in the early days is Applegate, in southern Oregon near Ashland.

The major sightseeing attractions include Cannon Beach, Newport, and Gold Beach along the coast. Eastern Oregon is very different geographically from the west. There is a lot of cattle raising in eastern Oregon, and the terrain is extremely dry. The area around Pendleton, the Steens mountains, and the Alvord desert are particularly attractive sections of the state.

Portland is an interesting city to visit. It's built into the trees so that it never seems as large as it is. It may not be spectacular as far as cities go (it could not really be compared to Seattle, San Francisco, Chicago, or New York, for example), but it is clean, quiet, and appealing. Eugene is somewhat more lively for a city of its size. The home of the University of Oregon, it has lots of ethnic restaurants, an extensive bike-path system, a public market, a Saturday market, some nice parks, and the cultural productions and sports activities that are part of the university. The Shakespeare Festival in Ashland in the summertime is quite well known and worth a stop.

"I guess the best thing I could say about Oregon is that it has lots more to offer than just large urban centers and that Oregon is there to explore. I think many people would find out a lot about Oregon if they were left on their own just to hike through the mountains or spend a day at the coast, drive through the back roads or swim in a mountain lake." (This quote is from a homesick Oregonian, in exile in Ohio.)

Some Special Events: Pear Blossom Festival in Medford (April); Pacific Northwest Championship All-Indian Rodeo in Tygh Valley (May); Rose Festival in Portland (June); World Championship Timber Carnival in Albany, and Crooked River Round-Up in Prineville (July); Threshing Bee and Draft Horse Show in Dufur (August); Alpenfest in Wallowa Lake (September); Kraut and Sausage Feed and Bazaar in Verboot (November).

Hitching: Hitching is legal in Oregon, as long as you stand off the pavement. The official wording is: "It is illegal to solicit rides from drivers of private vehicles while standing in a road or on the paved or graveled shoulder designed for vehicle use." Friends from Oregon have been more enthusiastic than any others about hitchhiking in their state. Oregon is used to hitchhikers who are on their way from California to Canada on U.S. 101. Oregonians have tried to make things comfortable for travelers by setting up hostels along the route, and, in Eugene, a system of signs marking the best and safest places for hitchhikers to stand. The signs say "ride stop" and are blue with a yellow hand (thumb extended) on them. A New Yorker who hitched his way along the western coast of Oregon says that it is spectacular. He took 101 all the way from California to Washington: "Wild blueberries grow everywhere in August. Delicious, sweet, and very distracting from hitching."

Tourist Information: Oregon Tourism Division, 595 Cottage St. NE, Salem, OR, 97310. Telephone: 503/378-3451 or 800/547-7842.

Albany

Accommodation: Friendship Inn Al-Ray Motel, exit 234 North Bound on I-5, exit 234 from South Bound on I-5, 97321. Telephone: 503/926-4246. $22 to $32 for one; $25 to $35 for two in one bed; $28 to $35 for two in two beds.

Ashland

On Campus: According to someone from Southern Oregon State College, Ashland is a young, artistic, and cosmopolitan town with a relaxed atmosphere and a well-known summer Shakespeare festival.

Some recommended restaurants in Ashland are Dave's Mexican, 2425 Siskiyou, good meals for $3 or $4; Good Times, 1951 Hwy. 66, with frequent two-for-one specials; and Breadboard, 744 West Main, home-cooked meals for under $3.

Accommodation: The Ashland Hostel (AYH), 150 North Main St., 97520. Telephone: 503/482-9217. Two blocks from bus station. $6 for AYH members; $8 for nonmembers. Kitchen facilities on premises.

Bandon

Accommodation: Sea Star Hotel (AYH), 375 2nd St., 97411. Telephone: 503/347-9533. Near bus station, river, and beach. Open year round. $5 for AYH and IYHF members; $7 for nonmembers.

"The hostel building was a condemned structure which was brought back to life by completely renovating it with walls of natural cedar, big skylights, and many personal touches—one would never know the state it came from nor the work that went in. The town itself is a unique coastal town with a beautiful ocean beach. Many artists live in the town of 2500 which has two artist cooperatives and many shops."

Biggs Junction

Accommodation: Friendship Inn Nu Vu Motel, Star St., 97065. Telephone: 503/739-2525. $20 to $25 for one; $24 to $30 for two in one bed; $27 to $35 for two in two beds.

Boardman

Accommodation: Friendship Riverview Motel, Front & 1st Sts. on I-84, 97818. Telephone: 503/481-2775. $24 to $28 for one; $28 to $32 for two in one bed; $28 to $35 for two in two beds.

Brookings

Accommodation: Econo Lodge, √ 🦽, 1144 Chetco Ave., 97415. Telephone: 503/469-2141. $22.95 to $30.95 for one; $26.95 to $34.95 for two in one bed; $30.95 to $38.95 for two in two beds.

Burns

Accommodation: Motel 6, 997 Oregon Ave., 97720. Telephone: 503/573-6663. $17.95 for one; $21.95 for two; $2 for each additional person.

Cave Junction

Accommodation: Fordson Home Hostel (AYH), c/o Jack and Mary Ann Heald, 250 Robinson Rd., 97523. Telephone: 503/592-3203. $4 summer, $5 winter for AYH members. Advance reservations necessary by phone or mail May to November.

Coos Bay

Accommodation: The Sea Gull Youth Hostel (AYH-SA), P.O. Box 847, 438 Elrod, 97420. Telephone: 503/267-6114. Open May 27 to September 3. $6.75 for AYH members. Price includes dinner and breakfast.

"The rate at the Coos Bay Hostel includes two superb home-cooked meals provided by a group of local ladies—other towns would do well to copy!"

Corvallis

On Campus: Oregon State University is in this small city, and in Corvallis people love to bicycle. There are bike paths throughout the city and into the neighboring towns. Each year the university presents hundreds of public events such as lectures, concerts, theater productions, films, and art exhibits. Many are free. Information on daily events is available on television monitors in the Memorial Union building.

Corvallis has a variety of good and inexpensive restaurants. Try the Valley Restaurant to meet some of the locals on 3rd St. for sandwiches, soups, salads, and vegetarian main dishes. Mazzi's on 9th St. is noted for Sicilian food, and Woodstock's Pizza on King's Blvd. is one of the most popular pizza parlors. Toa Yuen or China Blue, both on 9th St., are popular Chinese restaurants and Papagayos on N.W. Harrison Blvd. has been noted as "one of Oregon's best" for Mexican food. If you are looking for seafood, try the Tower of London at 3rd and Harrison, which is an informal seafood restaurant and English pub, or the more formal Class Reunion on 9th St. or Michael's Landing near the Willamette River waterfront on 2nd St. Allan Brother's coffee house, the OSU Memorial Union Commons in the Memorial Union Building, and a bar called Mother's Mattress Factory are good places to meet students.

Eugene

Help: Eugene Switchboard, 503/686-8453. They'll help you find a place to stay in Eugene—stop at their office at 566 Pearl St. Check with them, too, for rides, odd jobs, and general information on the area.

On Campus: The University of Oregon in Eugene is a popular stop for young people on their way from California to Canada. Erb Memorial Student Union Bldg., in the center of the campus at 13th and University Sts., is a good first stop. Pick up a copy of the *Daily Emerald*, the university's daily paper, which lists rides, jobs, housing, etc. For food, try Old Taylor's, which has a large variety of burgers and imaginative sandwiches on health breads, and Rennies Landing, which has a similar menu. They are also popular nightspots, along with DeFrisco's, Duffey's, and Max's.

We hear that the switchboard on KZEL 96 FM has a ride-assistance service. There are many excellent bicycle paths in Eugene, keep an eye out for plays on the mall during summer, and stop by at the wonderful public market at 5th St. on Saturday and Sunday.

Accommodations: Motel 6, 3690 Glenwood Dr., 97403. Telephone: 503/342-6177. See Burns listing for rates.

● Motel 6, 3752 International Ct., Springfield, 97477. Telephone: 503/741-0666. See Burns listing for rates.

● TraveLodge, √, 540 East Broadway, 97401. Telephone: 503/342-1109. $29 for one; $34 for two in one bed; $38 for two in two beds.

● Continental Motel, Ⓢ √ ⓖ ★, 390 East Broadway, 97401. Telephone: 503/343-3376. $19 to $20 single; $22 to $26 double; $25 to $28 triple; $28 to $32 quad.

Fort Klamath

Accommodation: Fort Klamath Lodge (AYH-SA), Hwy. 62, 97626. Telephone: 503/381-2234. $6.25 for AYH members in dorms; $19 single; $22 double. Advance reservations of two weeks suggested in summer.

Grants Pass

Accommodations: Motel 6, 1800 N.E. Seventh, 97526. Telephone: 503/476-9096. See Burns listing for rates.
● TraveLodge, √, 748 S.E. 7th St., 97526. Telephone: 503/476-7793. $29 for one; $32 for two in one bed; $38 for two in two beds.
● Allstar Inn, 1835 N.E. 7th St., 97526. Telephone: 503/479-7173. $23.95 to $25.95 for one; $3 for each additional person.

Hermiston

Accommodation: Budget Host—Dunes Motel, √, 635 South Hwy. 395, 97838. Telephone: 503/567-5561. $20 for one; $24 for two in one bed; $26 for two in two beds. Courtesy car available. Heated pool.

Klamath Falls

Accommodations: Motel 6, 5136 South 6th St., 97601. Telephone: 503/884-6273. See Burns listing for rates.
● Friendship Inn North Entrance Motel. Hwy. 97 N., 97601. Telephone: 503/884-8104. $15 to $18 for one; $20 to $24 for two in one bed; $22 to $26 for two in two beds.
● TraveLodge, √ 🖦, 124 North 2nd at Main, 97601. Telephone: 503/882-7741. Bus transportation available. $30 for one; $34 for two in one bed; $38 for two in two beds.

Lincoln City

Accommodation: Econo Lodge, √, 1713 N.W. 21st, 97367. Telephone: 503/994-5281. $21.95 to $27.95 for one; $25.95 to $31.95 for two in one bed; $29.95 to $35.95 for two in two beds.

Medford

Accommodation: Motel 6, 950 Alba Dr., 97504. Telephone: 503/779-6470. See Burns listing for rates.

Newport

Accommodation: Newport Hostel, 212 N.W. Brook St., P.O. Box 1641, 97365. Telephone: 503/265-9816. $5.50 for AYH members.

Ontario

Accommodation: Motel 6, 275 Butler St., 97914. Telephone: 503/889-6604. See Burns listing for rates.

Pendleton

Accommodations: Motel 6, 325 S.E. Nye Ave., 97801. Telephone: 503/276-6665. See Burns listing for rates.
● Imperial 400 Motor Inn, √ (10%), 201 S.W. Court Ave., 97801. Telephone: 503/276-5252. $28 to $30 for one; $30 to $32 for two in one bed; $34 to $36 for two in two beds.

Portland

Tourist Information: Portland Convention Bureau, 26 S.W. Salmon Ave., 97204. Telephone: 503/222-2223.
Help: Portland Metro Hotline, 503/223-6161.
On Campus: The University of Portland, Portland State University, and Lewis and Clark College are here. The city attracts many young people, especially from the East, who like its recreational opportunities, its reputation for being politically independent, and its friendly, liberal people.
There's no lack of places to eat in Portland: Hamburger Mary's, 840 S.W. Park; and Dave's Delicatessen, 1110 S.W. 3rd, a downtown kosher deli. The meeting place on the University of Portland's campus is the Pilot House; off campus it's the Twilight Room, 5242 North Lombard, which has earned a solid reputation for its hamburgers. The Metro is supposed to be a good place to meet people downtown. It's on Broadway, right across from the Hilton.
Portland has an art museum and the Oregon Museum of Science and Industry. The downtown area is being restored and lots of interesting shops are opening all the time. The Saturday Market gives local artists and merchants a chance to show their wares under the Burnside Bridge.
Accommodations: YWCA, ⑤, 1111 S.W. 10th Ave., 97205. Telephone: 503/223-6281. Women only. $13.25 single, $16.95 double without bath; $16.95 single, $19.08 double with bath. Hostel rooms that sleep three or four: $6.36 per person; $5.30 if you bring your own sleeping bag. Advance reservations of one to three days necessary. "Exceptional value, very clean, with a friendly staff. A great supermarket next door."
● Budget Host—Viking Motel, ⑤ √ (10%), 6701 North Interstate Ave., 97217. Telephone: 503/285-6687. $24 to $26 for one; $28 to $30 for two in one bed; $30 to $32 for two in two beds. Heated pool.
● Friendship Inn Sands Motel, 3800 North Interstate Ave., 97227. Telephone: 503/287-2601. $20 to $23 for one; $24 to $27 for two in one bed; $28 to $31 for two in two beds.
● Imperial 400 Motor Inn, √ (10%), 518 N.E. Holladay St., 97232. Telephone: 503/234-4391. $30 to $34 for one; $34 to $38 for two in one bed; $36 to $40 for two in two beds.
● Motel 6, 3104-06 S.E. Powell Blvd., 97202. Telephone: 503/233-8811. See Burns listing for rates.

- Portland Hawthorne Blvd. Hostel (AYH), 3031 S.E. Hawthorne Blvd., 97214. Telephone: 503/236-3380. $6 summer, $7 winter for AYH members. Doors opened at 5 p.m. and locked at 11 p.m.
- Motel 6, 17950 S.W. McEwan Rd., Tigard, 97224. Telephone: 503/639-0631. See Burns listing for rates.
- Motel 6, 1610 N.W. Frontage Rd., 97060. Telephone: 503/661-5450. See Burns listing for rates.
- Econo Lodge, √, 4810 N.E. Sandy Blvd., 97213. Telephone: 503/282-7711. $21.95 to $25.95 for one; $28.95 to $29.95 for two in one bed; $32.95 to $33.95 for two in two beds.
- Allstar Inn, 17959 S.W. McEwan Rd., 97062. Telephone: 503/684-0760. $23.95 to $25.95 for one; $3 for each additional person.

Prospect

Accommodation: Prospect Hostel (AYH-SA), 480 Mill Creek Dr., Box 246, 97536. Telephone: 503/560-3795. $6.25 summer, $8.25 winter for AYH members.

Roseburg

Accommodation: Friendship Inn Holiday, 44 S.E. Oak Ave., 97470. Telephone: 503/672-4457. $22 to $28 for one; $24 to $34 for two in one bed; $28 to $36 for two in two beds.

St. Helens

Accommodation: Orcadia Hotel (AYH), 30 Cowlitz St., 97051. Telephone: 503/397-0014. $6 summer, $7 winter for AYH members.

Salem

Accommodations: YMCA, 685 Court St. NE, 97301. Telephone: 503/581-9622. Men over 18 only. $8 single. "The Y is within walking distance of six or seven cafés and restaurants. Many of our residents walk to nearby Salem Memorial Hospital at Winter and Oak Sts., where the cafeteria has good meals and welcomes public patronage.

- YWCA, 768 State St., 97301. Behind State Capitol Bldg., next door to Willamette University and near train and bus stations. Telephone: 503/581-9922. Women only. $9.50 single; $5.50 if you have a sleeping bag. $44 weekly. Advance reservations of one week suggested.
- Friendship City Center Motel, 510 Liberty St. SE, 97301. Telephone: 503/364-0121. Limited airport service available. $23 for one; $25 for two in one bed; $28 for two in two beds.
- Friendship Holiday Lodge, 1400 Hawthorne NE, 97303. Telephone: 503/585-2323. $18 to $23 for one; $22 to $32 for two.
- Motel 6, 2250 Mission St. SE, 97302. Telephone: 503/588-0220. See Burns listing for rates.

● TraveLodge, $\sqrt{}$ &, 1555 State St., 97301. Telephone: 503/581-2466. $29 for one; $34 for two in one bed; $38 for two in two beds.

● Allstar Inns, 1401 Hawthorne Ave. NE, 97301. Telephone: 503/371-8024. See Portland listing for rates.

Santiam Pass

Accommodation: Santiam Lodge (AYH), Star Route Sisters, 97759. Open May 1 to November 1. $6 summer, $7 winter for AYH members. A Presbyterian camp.

Springfield

Accommodations: Motel 6, 3752 International Court, 97477. Telephone: 503/741-0666. See Burns listing for rates.

● Mill Street Hostel (AYH), 542 Mill St., 97477. Telephone: 503/726-5012. $5 for AYH members; $7 for nonmembers. Closed December 20 to January 4. During winter months, a call before arrival would be appreciated.

The Dalles

Accommodation: Econo Lodge, $\sqrt{}$ &, 2500 West 6th, 97058. Telephone: 503/296-1191. $23.95 to $25.95 for one; $27.95 to $29.95 for two in one bed; $31.95 to $33.95 for two in two beds.

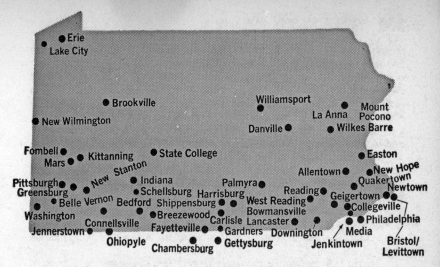

Pennsylvania

Pennsylvania is rich in history. Philadelphia was the patriots' capital through most of the Revolutionary War period. In this state one can visit the site of the country's greatest agonies as well as some of its greatest joys.

In Philadelphia you can visit Independence Hall, which still looks as it did 200 years ago when the Second Continental Congress gathered there to choose George Washington as the commander-in-chief of the Continental Army, where it heard the Declaration of Independence read, and where it convened throughout the war.

Valley Forge National Historical Park, not far from Philadelphia, where Washington led over 10,000 ragged and starving men into an agonizing winter encampment in December 1777, has been called the most famous military camp in the world. More places to visit on the trail of the Revolutionary War are Washington Crossing State Park, the Betsy Ross House, and the Liberty Bell. And for those who are interested in the Civil War, Pennsylvania is the site of the Gettysburg National Military Park, where 51,000 men fell in the bloodiest battle of the entire war.

Besides an abundance of historic sites, Pennsylvania has some very beautiful country, particularly in the Poconos and the often-visited Pennsylvania Dutch country. Urban types will gravitate toward Philadelphia and Pittsburgh; country types will want to explore Lancaster County and the Pocono Mountain area instead. Anyone planning to spend time in the Philadelphia area should look at a copy of *Philadelphia Resource Guide,* an access catalog put together by the Synapse Communications Collective and subtitled "Resources for Living Effectively in Philadelphia." For a copy of the third edition, write to Synapse, Inc., 3420 Sansom St., Philadelphia, PA 19104.

If the idea of a farm vacation strikes you, write to the Pennsylvania Department of Agriculture, Bureau of Rural Affairs, 2310 North Cameron St., Harrisburg, PA 17110, for their *Farm Vacation Directory,* which lists 25 Pennsylvania farms that offer accommodations and activities. Most are within our price range and are generally family oriented.

Some Special Events: Mummers Parade in Philadelphia (January); Cherry Blossom Festival in Wilkes-Barre (April); Northern Appalachian Festival in Bedford (May); Delco Scottish Games and Country Fair in Devon, and Annual Snake Hunt (prize for the longest snake, the snake with the most rattles) in Cross Fork (June); Woodsmen's Festival in Cherry Springs State Park (August); and Mountain Craft Days in Somerset (September).

Hitching: Hitchhiking is not legal in Pennsylvania, although many police departments do not enforce the law unless complaints are received about hitchhikers standing on the roadway. It seems to be an accepted means of travel but is not particularly encouraged. One friend from Pittsburgh said, "it is considered acceptable for males but is less acceptable for women. I myself use it for getting around and have as yet had no problems." The State Police think differently: "It is our contention that the hazards well outweigh the advantages of this method of travel."

Tourist Information: Pennsylvania Department of Commerce, Bureau of Travel Development, 416 Forum Bldg., Harrisburg, PA 17120. Telephone: toll free 800/VISIT-PA, or 717/787-5453 locally. Write to Department SXA for a free copy of *Best of Friends,* the state's travel guide. The Bureau also publishes two other useful booklets, *Bed & Breakfast in Pennsylvania* and *Pennsylvania Country Inns.*

N.B. To locate a bed-and-breakfast accommodation in the Philadelphia area, contact Bed and Breakfast of Philadelphia, P.O. Box 680, Devon, PA 19333. Telephone: 215/688-1633. Rates in 1985 ranged from $20 to $55 for a single; $35 to $80 for a double.

Allentown

Accommodations: Days Inn, I-78 & 15th St. Exit, Rte. 22 & 15th St., 18104. Telephone: 215/435-7880. $26.99 for one; $31.99 for two.
● Red Roof Inn, [♿], 1846 Catasauqua Rd., U.S. 22 & Airport Rd. S., 18103. Telephone: 215/264-5404. $25.95 for one; $30.95 for two in one bed; $32.95 for two in two beds; $34.95 for three or four in two beds.
● McIntosh Inn, [♿], Rte. 22 & Airport Rd. S., 18103. Telephone: 215/264-7531. $23.95 for one; $28.95 for two.

Bedford

Accommodation: Econo Lodge, √, Bus. Rte. 220 N., at Pa. Turnpike Exit 11, 15522. Telephone: 814/623-5108. $22.95 to $23.95 for one; $25.95 to $26.95 for two in one bed; $28.95 to $29.95 for two in two beds. Higher rates apply during special events.

Belle Vernon

Accommodation: Scottish Inn, √, Rte. 51 & I-70, 15012. Telephone: 412/929-4501. $25.95 for one; $29.95 for two in one bed; $31.95 for two in two beds.

Bowmansville

Accommodation: Bowmansville Youth Hostel (AYH), Rte. 625, 17507. Telephone: 215/445-4831. Closed December 20 to January 6. Send stamped, self-addressed envelope with reservation request. $5 for AYH members. The houseparent at the hostel told us about a local Mennonite farmer who serves meals to travelers: Phares Hurst, RR1, Narvon, PA 17555. Telephone: 215/445-6186. Reservations for meals should be made a few days in advance.

Breezewood

Accommodations: Penn Aire Motel—Superior, ✓⑤, Rte. 30 W. at I-70, 15533. Telephone: 814/735-4351. $27 to $28 single; $28 to $30 double; $31 to $33 triple; $33 to $38 quad. Advance reservations necessary.
● Econo Lodge, ✓, Box 101A, RD 1, 15533. Telephone: 814/735-4341. $24.95 to $28.95 for one; $28.95 to $32.95 for two in one bed; $32.95 to $36.95 for two in two beds. Higher rates apply during special events.

Bristol/Levittown

Accommodation: Friendship Inn Del-Val, Rte. 13 & Beaver Dam Rd., 19007. Telephone: 215/788-9272. $22 to $26 for one; $28 to $32 for two in one bed; $30 to $36 for two in two beds.

Brookville

Accommodation: Gold Eagle Inn, RD 3, Rtes. 322/28/36, 15825. Telephone: 814/849-7344. $25 for one; $27 for two in one bed; $28 for two in two beds.

Carlisle

Accommodation: Budget Host—Coast-to-Coast Motel, ✓, 1252 Harrisburg Pike, 17013. Telephone: 717/243-8585. $22 to $26 for one; $25 to $29 for two in one bed; $29 to $33 for two in two beds. Higher rates apply during special events and weekends.

Chambersburg

Accommodation: Econo Lodge, ✓⑤, 1110 Sheller Dr., 17201. Telephone: 717/264-8005. $27.95 for one; $29.95 for two in one bed; $32.95 for two in two beds.

Collegeville

Accommodation: Evansburg State Park Youth Hostel (AYH), 837 Mayhall Rd., 19426. Telephone: 215/489-4326. Near bus station. $6 for AYH members. "Home-like atmosphere; located in 3,400-acre state park."

Connellsville

Accommodation: Friendship Melody Motor Lodge, U.S. 119 S., Box 822, 15425. Telephone: 412/628-9600. Limited airport service available. $26 to $27 for one; $28 to $29 for two in one bed; $30 to $32 for two in two beds.

Danville

Accommodation: Red Roof Inn, RD 2, I-80 at Pa. 54 (Exit 33), 17821. Telephone: 717/275-7600. See Allentown listing for rates.

Downington

Accommodation: Marsh Creek State Park Hostel (AYH), East Reeds Rd., P.O. Box 376, Lyndell, 19354. Telephone: 215/458-5881. $6 for AYH members; $9 for nonmembers. Advance reservations suggested. "A beautiful old house surrounded by woods, fields, and farms in the Brandywine Valley."

Easton

Accommodation: YWCA, 41 North 3rd St., 18042. Telephone: 215/258-6271. $10 single (rarely available). Weekly rate: $40.

Erie

Accommodations: Red Roof Inn, ♿, 7865 Perry Hwy., I-90 at Pa. 97 (Exit 7), 16509. Telephone: 814/868-5246. $24.95 for one; $29.95 for two in one bed; $31.95 for two in two beds; $33.95 for three or four in two beds.
● TraveLodge, √, 826 Sassafras St., 16501. Telephone: 814/453-6614. Airport transportation available. $28 for one; $31 for two in one bed; $34 for two in two beds.

Fayetteville

Accommodation: Budget Host—Rite Spot Motel, √, ($2), 5651 Lincoln Way E., 17222. Telephone: 717/352-2144. $25 for one or two in one bed; $29 for two in two beds. Near Caledonia State Park with pool-picnic area.

Fombell

Accommodation: Camp Silver Lake Hostel (AYH), Box 810, RD 2, 16123. Telephone: 412/452-6720. Open April 16 to October 14. $4.25 for AYH members. Advance reservations necessary.

Gardners

Accommodation: Ironmaster's Mansion Youth Hostel (AYH), ♿, RD 2,

Box 397B, Pine Grove Furnace State Park, 17324. Telephone: 717/486-7575. $6 summer, $7 winter for AYH members.

Geigertown

Accommodation: Shirey's Hostel (AYH), P.O. Box 49, 19523. Telephone: 215/286-9537. Open March 1 to December 1. $5.25 summer, $6.25 winter for AYH members. Advance reservations necessary.

Gettysburg

Accommodation: Friendship Penn Eagle Motel, 1031 York Rd. Telephone: 717/334-1804. $19 to $39 for one; $19 to $43 for two in one bed; $21 to $49 for two in two beds.

Greensburg

Accommodation: Friendship Greensburg Inn, Rte. 30 E. Bypass, 15601. Telephone: 412/836-1648. $26 for one; $29 to $32 for two in one bed; $32 for two in two beds.

Harrisburg

Accommodations: Days Inn, ⬚, I-83 Exit 18 & Pa. Turnpike Exit 18, 353 Lewisberry Rd., New Cumberland, 17070. Telephone: 717/774-4156. $29 to $31 for one; $35 to $37 for two.
● Red Roof Inn, 400 Corporate Circle, I-81 at North Progress Ave. (Exit 24) 17110. Telephone: 717/657-1445. See Allentown listing for rates.
● Red Roof Inn, 950 Eisenhower Blvd., I-283 at Pa. 441 (Exit 1), 17111. Telephone: 717/939-1331. See Allentown listing for rates.
● YWCA, 215 Market St., 17101. Telephone: 717/234-7931. Weekly rate: $34.50 to $57.50 single; $28.75 per person double.

Indiana

Accommodation: Budget Host—College Motel, √, Rear 886 Wayne Ave., 15701. Telephone: 412/463-8726. $24 for one; $28 for two.

Jennerstown

Accommodation: Camp Sequanota (AYH), P.O. Box 245, 15547. Telephone: 814/629-6627. $6 summer, $7 winter for AYH members. Advance reservations necessary June 7 to September 1.

Kittanning

Accommodation: Friendship Plaza Inn, √ (10%), RD 6, 422 East, 16201.

Telephone: 412/543-1100. $26 for one; $31 for two in one bed; $34 for two in two beds.

LaAnna

Accommodations: LaAnna Youth Hostel (AYH), Rte. 2, P.O. Box 1026, Cresco, 18326. Telephone: 717/676-9076. $6 summer, $5 winter for AYH members. $9 summer, $8 winter for nonmembers. Advance reservations with full deposit and stamped, self-addressed envelope necessary November 1 to April 1.

● LaAnna Guest House, Rte. 191, 18326. Telephone: 717/676-4225. $12 per person. Rooms have one to four beds. "Victorian-style home, spacious rooms, furnished with Victorian and Empire antiques, situated on 25 acres in a quiet mountain village."

Lake City

Accommodation: YMCA Camp Sherwin Outdoor & Conference Center (AYH), 8600 West Lake Rd., 16425. $5.25 for AYH members.

Lancaster

Tourist Information: Pennsylvania Dutch Visitors Bureau, 1799 Hempstead Rd., 17601. Telephone: 717/299-8901.

Help: Crisis Intervention, 717/394-2631.

Accommodation: YWCA, Ⓢ ♿ √ ★ (10% for all), 110 North Lime St., 17602. Telephone: 717/393-1735. Women only. $14.84 single. Weekly rate: $74.80. Advance reservations suggested.

Mars

Accommodation: Planet Stop Home Hostel (AYH), c/o Mr. and Mrs. Norton, Box 326, 16046. Telephone: 412/625-1180. $3 for AYH members. Advance reservations necessary. Bicyclists only.

Media

Accommodation: McIntosh Inn, Rte. 1 & 352, 19063. Telephone: 215/565-5800. $26.95 for one; $31.95 for two.

New Hope

Accommodation: Wedgewood Bed and Breakfast Inn, 111 West Bridge St., 18938. Telephone: 215/862-2570. $35 single; $50 double; $54 triple; $60 quad. Price includes breakfast. Advance reservations necessary on weekends. "Hardwood floors, lofty windows, and antique furnishings re-create a warm, comfortable 17th-century feeling. Filled with Wedgwood pottery, original art, handmade quilts, and fresh flowers."

New Stanton

Accommodation: New Stanton Motel, Ⓢ √ ★, 110 West Penna Ave., 15672. Telephone: 412/925-7606. $26 to $32 for one; $32 to $36 double or triple; $34 to $42 quad. Advance reservations preferred; call before 9 p.m. day of arrival.

New Wilmington

On Campus: Westminster College is located in this "pleasant, slow-paced rural community in an area of 'Old Order Amish'—more conservative than what you saw in the film *Witness*." To meet the local young people, stop at Shelter from the Storm. The hub of campus life is at the Walton Manye Memorial Union Bldg. on campus. For a meal, try Rachel's Roadhouse on Rte. 19, 2-3 miles south of I-80, or Ryder's Restaurant at the intersection of Rtes. 208 and 18.

Newtown

Accommodation: Tyler State Park Hostel (AYH), P.O. Box 94, 18940. Telephone: 215/968-0927. $6 for AYH members. Ten miles from Washington Crossing State Park. Park gate locked at sunset.

Ohiopyle

Accommodation: Ohiopyle State Park Youth Hostel (AYH), Box 99, Ohiopyle State Park, 15470. Telephone: 412/329-4476. $4 summer, $5 winter for AYH members. Whitewater rafting on Youghiogheny River.

Palmyra

Accommodation: Camp Seltzer Youth Hostel (AYH-SA), 697 South Franklin St., 17078. Telephone: 717/838-4957. Bunkhouse accommodations in a rustic retreat lodge. $6.75 for AYH members. Advance reservations necessary with deposit and stamped, self-addressed envelope.

Philadelphia

"Backpacking and hitchhiking types should try to get to the South Street area between 3rd and 6th—for all information and goings-on."

Tourist Information: Philadelphia Convention and Visitors Bureau, 1525 John F. Kennedy Blvd., 19102. Telephone: 215/636-3300. Open 9 a.m. to 5 p.m. every day except Christmas. The bureau offers personalized itineraries, information for the handicapped including braille maps and free guidebooks for wheelchair users, and tickets to various events including the New Year's Day Mummers Parade and the Mann Music Center.

Help: Traveler's Aid, 311 South Juniper St., 19107. Telephone: 215/546-0571 (days); 386-0845 (evenings).

"I would definitely recommend Philadelphia as a town to visit. I have been to many towns and have found Philadelphia to be the most exciting yet."

On Campus: Temple University and the University of Pennsylvania are in Philadelphia. At Temple there's a bulletin board at the Student Assistance Center, Student Activities Center, 13th and Montgomery, where apartments, rides, etc., are listed. For similar information, you can also listen to WRTI, the Temple radio station, or WXPN, the Penn Station; or you can get a copy of the city paper *Electricity*. For good, inexpensive meals near the Temple campus, there are lots of gourmet-type cafeterias with an international menu (where most good meals are under $5) plus an open-air market. To meet students on the Penn campus, go to one of the many college bars, such as P.T.'s/Dobbs or City Lights, where there's a mixed crowd for dancing.

Accommodations: International House of Philadelphia, &, 3701 Chestnut St., 19104. Telephone: 215/387-5125. "For academically oriented Americans and foreign visitors." $30 single; $35 double (limited number); $40 apartments (limited number). Reservations requested; room is sometimes scarce. "Beautiful, modern, award-winning building." Someone at International House told us that the residence facilities at the University of Pennsylvania are available to their residents who stay a month or more.

● YWCA, Ⓢ √ ★, 2027 Chestnut St., 19103. Telephone: 215/564-3430. Women only. $23 single, $45 double for Y members. Advance reservations of one to two weeks necessary.

● Chamounix Mansion International Youth Hostel (AYH), West Fairmount Park, 19131. Telephone: 215/878-3676 (Monday through Thursday, 4:30 to 8 p.m.). Three-quarters of a mile from no. 38 bus stop. In a house built in 1802. Open year-round except December 15 to January 15. $6.25 for AYH members; $8.75 for nonmembers. "A gracious summerhouse mansion located in a quiet area of Fairmount Park."

● Red Roof Inn, &, 49 Industrial Hwy., I-95 & U.S. 420, Essington, 19029. $29.95 for one; $34.95 for two in one bed; $36.95 for two in two beds; $38.95 for three or four in two beds.

Pittsburgh

Tourist Information: Pittsburgh Convention and Visitors Bureau, Inc., 4 Gateway Center, 15222. Telephone: 412/281-7711.

Help: Travelers Aid, Greyhound Bus Station, 11th St. & Liberty Ave., 15222. Telephone: 412/281-5474 or 281-5466.

On Campus: Duquesne University, Carnegie-Mellon University, the University of Pittsburgh, and Point Park College are in this city. To meet students from Duquesne, go to Frank and Wally's on Forbes Ave. or Van Braams Café on Van Braam off Forbes. Since the University of Pittsburgh is a commuter campus, it's harder to find students in any one place. The Student Union might be a good place, though—worth a try. In the Point College Park area, try Bahama Mama on Wood St. for a large, tasty meal for about $6.

Other places to meet people in a comfortable atmosphere are CJ Barneys and the Wooden Keg, a bar in Oakland on the Pitt campus; Squirrel Hill Café, for cheap beer, or at the downtown YMCA's Tuesday night folk dancing.

For information on rides, apartments, odd jobs, etc., try the University of Pittsburgh Student Union's bulletin boards. Specifically for rides, mail the details of where you are going and where you can be reached to radio station WYEP/Rides America, 4 Cable Pl., 15213.

"Ethnic food abounds. Try Middle Eastern food restaurants in the Oakland area and for Italian food go to the Bloomfield section."

Accommodations: YMCA, 304 Wood St., 15222. Telephone: 412/227-6420. Men only. $19.02 single. Weekly rate: $54 first four weeks, $44 after that. $10 key deposit required. Reservations requested three or four days in advance. Cafeteria in the building.

● YMCA, 600 West North Ave., 15212. Telephone: 412/321-8594. Men only. $21.12 single (includes $3 key deposit). Weekly rate: $47.87. "We are directly across the street from a park which is six blocks long and has everything you would want to do."

● Point Park College (AYH), 201 Wood St., 15222. Telephone: 412/392-3824. $7.25 for AYH members. AYH or IYH membership required. Advance reservations suggested September to May.

● Red Roof Inn, 20009 Rte. 16, Pa. 19 & I-76 (Pennsylvania Turnpike), Warrendale, 16046. Telephone: 412/776-5670. See Allentown listing for rates.

● Red Roof Inn, 6404 Steubenville Park, Old U.S. 22/30 at Pa. 60, 15205. Telephone: 412/787-7870. See Allentown listing for rates.

● Motel 6, Rte. 19, RD #7, Box 1316, 16046. Telephone: 412/776-9010. $17.95 for one; $21.95 for two; $2 for each additional person.

Pocono Mountain

Accommodation: Econo Lodge, √ 🚹, I-80 & Pa. Rte. 715 (Exit 45), 18372. Telephone: 717/629-4100. $28.95 to $31.95 for one; $32.95 to $35.95 for two in one bed; $34.95 to $36.95 for two in two beds.

Quakertown

Accommodation: Weisel Youth Hostel (AYH), RD 3, 18951. Telephone: 215/536-8749. $5 for AYH members; introductory passes available for nonmembers. Advance reservations for weekends are strongly recommended. "Lovely rustic manor house in a state park."

Reading

Accommodation: Econo Lodge, √, 2310 Fraver Dr., 19605. Telephone: 215/378-1145. $28.95 for one; $32.95 for two in one bed; $36.95 for two in two beds.

Schellsburg

Accommodation: Living Waters Hostel (AYH), RD 1, One Mile West, 15559. Telephone: 814/733-4607. $5.25 summer, $7 winter for AYH members.

Shippensburg

Accommodation: Budget Host—Shippensburg Inn, √, I-81 (Exit 10), Box 349, 17257. Telephone: 717/530-1234. $25 to $32 for one; $32 to $39 for two in one bed; $34 to $41 for two in two beds.

State College

Accommodation: Imperial 400 Motor Inn, 118-120 South Atherton St., 16801. Telephone: 814/237-7686. $30 to $35 for one; $35 to $42 for two in one bed; $38 to $45 for two in two beds.

Washington

Accommodation: Red Roof Inn, 1399 West Chestnut St., 15301. Telephone: 412/228-5750. See Erie listing for rates.

West Reading

Accommodation: Friendship Penn-View Inn, 250 Penn Ave., 19602. Telephone: 215/376-8011. $24 to $30 for one; $28 to $35 for two in one bed; $30 to $40 for two in two beds.

Wilkes-Barre

Accommodation: Friendship Imperial Motor Inn, 400 Kidder St., Pa. 115 N., 18702. Telephone: 717/823-2171. $20 for one; $24 for two in one bed; $26 for two in two beds.

Williamsport

Accommodation: Econo Lodge, √, 2401 East Third St., 17701. Telephone: 717/326-1501. $29.95 for one; $34.95 for two.

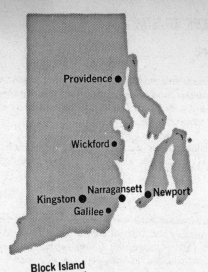

Providence ●

Wickford ●

Kingston ●   Narragansett ● Newport
Galilee ●

Block Island

Rhode Island

We received lots of information about Rhode Island from the staff of the Council Travel Office in Providence. They rave about their state. They recommend the beaches, particularly Moonstone Beach off Rte. 1 in South Kingston—"a particularly fun beach where all stages of dress or undress are acceptable; Narragansett Town Beach has rolling surf and is immaculately maintained; Misquamicut State Beach, Westerly has a waterslide, wonderfully greasy clamcakes, and plenty of parking."

You can go to Newport on the coast and absorb the splendor of the Newport mansions. Once upon a time, before there was an income tax, the richest of the rich anchored their yachts at Newport and built themselves summer cottages along the shore. No one wants to rough it, after all, even in a resort home, so they included Tiffany windows, French ballrooms, Italian dining rooms, and animal topiary gardens in their plans. Extraordinary to see.

You can write to the Tourist Division, Rhode Island Department of Economic Development (address below) and ask for their *Rhode Island Tourist Guide.*

The Appalachian Mountain Club publishes the *AMC Massachusetts and Rhode Island Trail Guide,* which is available for $12.95 from the publisher at 5 Joy St., Boston, MA 02108.

Some Special Events: Twelfth Night Celebration in Westerly (January); Mardi Gras in Newport (February); International Fair in Providence (April); Arts Festival in Pawtucket (June); Blessing of the Fleet in Galilee (July); Jazz Festival in Newport (August); and Harvest Festival in Cranston (September).

Hitching: Hitchhiking is illegal in Rhode Island, says the law. It's done, but not to any great extent.

Tourist Information: Rhode Island Department of Economic Development, 7 Jackson Walkway, Providence, RI 02903. Telephone: 401/277-2601.

Block Island

"This gorgeous island, just off the coast of Rhode Island, is a vacationer's dream. Beautiful beaches, good biking, eating, and relaxing. It's easy to reach any ferry from several points in Rhode Island including Galilee, Newport, and Providence. From Galilee the round-trip ferry fare is $8."

Block Island has more guest houses than hotels. One good one is The Driftwinds, High St. Telephone: 401/466-5548. $25 single; $35 double.

Galilee

"Another picturesque harbor community with hundreds of working vessels to watch. It's probably best to stay at a guest house in Narragansett if you're going to visit Galilee. (See Narragansett listing further on.) While in Galilee, eat at George's—wear your bathing suit, everyone else does."

Kingston

Accommodation: University of Rhode Island Youth Hostel (AYH), ⑤★, Rte. 138, Memorial Union, 02881. Telephone: 401/789-3929. Closed December 20. Men, women, and sometimes children. $5.25 for AYH members. Two-story farmhouse built around 1860; one mile west of the University of Rhode Island entrance.

Narragansett

"This is a beautiful seaside community with superb beaches, surfing, guest houses, and restaurants."

Accommodations: Seagull Guest House, 50 Narragansett Ave., 02882. Telephone: 401/783-4636. $20 single, $25 double weekdays; $30 single, $35 double weekends. Shared baths. A 50% non-refundable deposit must accompany a reservation. One block from beach.
● Regina Cottages, Kingston Rd. Telephone: 401/783-1875. $35 double.

Newport

Tourist Information: Newport County Chamber of Commerce, P.O. Box 237, 02840. Telephone: 401/847-1600.
● Newport Council for International Visitors, 40 Dearborn St., 02840. Telephone: 401/846-0222. A member of the council has provided us with some good tips about the area; Salve Regina College is here and you might be able to find ride and apartment information on their bulletin board. Also check the bulletin board at O'Hare Academic Center and Miley Hall. You can meet students at Newport Creamers, Spindrift Restaurant, and "many, many waterfront bars and grills." Basically, "Newport is wall-to-wall people in the summer, accommodations are hard to find, and everything is expensive."
Accommodation: Armed Services YMCA (AYH-SA), 50 Washington

Square, 02840. Telephone: 401/846-3120. $6.50 for AYH members. $15 to $20 single; $20 to $25 double. Advance reservations suggested in summer.

Providence

"Providence is a great little city—restaurants are wonderful. One of America's leading repertory companies (Trinity Square, tel. 351-4242) is here. Art galleries are easy to find. There are lots of films, antique shops, boutiques, and two superb shopping galleries. It's an easy city to get around; the public transportation system is efficient and the train station is right downtown. For information on what's happening, pick up a copy of The New Paper.*"*

Tourist Information: Greater Providence Convention and Visitors Bureau, 10 Dorrance St., 02903. Telephone: 401/274-1636.

Help: Travelers Aid, 46 Aborn St., 02903. Telephone: 401/521-2255. They can provide you with listings of shelter accommodations.

On Campus: Brown University and the Rhode Island School of Design are in Providence, a town one citizen calls "the East Coast's best-kept secret." For food in Providence, try Rue de l'Espoir, 99 Hope St.; Taj Mahal, 230 Wickenden St.; and LaSerre on Angell St.

Accommodations: International House, 8 Stimson Ave., 02906. Telephone: 401/421-7181. $20 per night; two-day minimum stay.

● YMCA, 160 Broad St., 02903. Telephone: 401/456-0100. Men and women. $16 single.

● Susse Chalet Inn, U.S. 6 & 114A off I-195, Seekonk, MA 02771. Telephone: 617/336-7900. $30.70 for one; $34.70 for two; $37.70 for three; $40.70 for four.

Where to Eat: Café Plaza, 99 Kennedy Plaza. Telephone: 351-1350. Very inexpensive spot. Try the eggs Benedict.

● Meeting Street Café, 220 Meeting St. Telephone: 273-1066. A great lunch spot—enormous sandwiches.

● Montana, 272 Thayer St. Telephone: 272-7573. Tex-Mex food and great ribs too.

● Little Chop Sticks, 488 Smith St. (behind the State House). Telephone: 351-4290. Excellent Chinese cooking; low prices.

● Andreas, 268 Thayer St. Telephone: 331-7879. Reasonably priced Greek food right on College Hill.

● Amara's, 231 Wichendon St. Telephone: 621-8919. Low prices, eclectic, all-natural cooking.

Wickford

"This is a lovely little harbor town that offers an annual art festival on the weekend after July 4th, and offers an international Quahog Festival the last Sunday in the month of August."

Accommodation: 1798 House, 49 Main St., P.O. Box 552, 02852. A bed-and-breakfast spot. $45 double.

South Carolina

Most of South Carolina has been left the way it was in the beginning—and that's good. You'll find beaches, subtropical islands, mountains, streams, and lakes. The city of Charleston is as aristocratic a city as the U.S. can claim. If your time in South Carolina is limited, you'll probably want to spend most of it in Charleston and the area around it.

Historic Charleston, founded in 1670, is a lovely place to explore on foot. Start your stroll at Battery Park and then walk slowly by the beautiful 18th-century homes. Save time for a visit to the Heyward-Washington House; the second-oldest synagogue in the U.S.; the Charleston Museum; the Dock Street Theater (dating from 1736); and Cabbage Row, the inspiration for *Porgy and Bess*. And only ten miles from this wonderful city, you'll enjoy the 25-acre Magnolia Gardens, where the camellias, oaks, and cypresses draped with moss and wisteria are breathtaking. You may walk the trails, ride a bicycle through, rent a canoe, or take a guided boat tour of the area.

Two areas that are enormously popular with young people, because of the beaches and the nightlife, are the Grand Strand and one of the beaches on it, Myrtle Beach. The Grand Strand is 55 miles of uninterrupted beach that stretches from Little River at the state line south of Pawley's Island.

Some Special Events: Spoleto Festival, one of the world's most comprehensive arts festivals, in Charleston (May and June); Hampton County Watermelon Festival in Hampton (June); Water Festival in Beaufort, and Tobacco Festival in Lake City (July); Governor's Frog Jump and Egg Striking Contest in Springfield (April); South Carolina State Fair in Columbia (October); and Chitlin' Strut (a day of country music, dancing, a Pig Calling Contest, parade, and chicken barbecue) in Salley (November).

Hitching: A friend at the University of South Carolina says that hitchhiking around the university area—Columbia—is commonplace. Since the school is not on a major road, not many people hitch through. If they do, though, they'll find university people "nice and helpful." Although the tourist office doesn't recommend hitchhiking anywhere, the Department of Highways and Public Transportation says it's legal except on the "roadway, the traveled portion of a street or highway."

Tourist Information: Division of Tourism, South Carolina Department of Parks, Recreation and Tourism, Suite 113, Edgar A. Brown Bldg., Columbia, SC 29201. Although it is possible to rent cabins in South Carolina's state parks, reservation requests for one year must be received by November 1 of the year before. All requests, whether by mail or telephone, should be made to the specific park. Write to the tourist office (address above) for information and the brochures *South Carolina* and *South Carolina State Parks: Facilities, Activities and Fees*.

Beaufort

Accommodation: Budget Host—The Pines Motel, U.S. Hwy. 21 (Box 4236), 29902. Telephone: 803/524-3322. $20 to $22 for one; $21 to $24 for two in one bed; $27 to $30 for two in two beds.

Charleston

Tourist Information: Charleston Trident Chamber of Commerce, 85 Calhoun St., 29401.

Accommodations: Econo Lodge, √, 4750 Arco Lane, 29405. Telephone: 803/747-3672. $22.95 for one; $26.95 for two in one bed; $30.95 for two in two beds.

• Econo Lodge, √, 2237 Savannah Hwy., 29407. Telephone: 803/571-1880. $29.95 for one; $33.95 for two in one bed; $35.95 for two in two beds. Higher rates apply during special events.

• Days Inn, 🔣, I-26 & West Montague Ave., 2998 West Montague Ave., 29405. Telephone: 803/747-4101. $31 to $39 for one; $36 to $44 for two.

• Motel 6, 2058 Savannah Hwy. (intersection of Hwy. 17 & Rte. 7), 29407. Telephone: 803/571-0560. $17.95 for one; $21.95 for two; $2 for each additional person.

Clemson

Help: Clemson University/Campus Hotline, 803/654-1040. "They will try to help most anyone." Hours 8 p.m. to 7 a.m. daily.

On Campus: Although the housing situation is tough around the campus area, stop by the University Union Travel Center (tel. 803/656-5833) for help in finding a place to stay. According to our friend at the Travel Center, Clemson isn't a bad place at all, "just a little behind the times." Another friend says it's not behind at all, only marching to the beat of a different drummer. There is one place you are sure to meet people in Clemson; Edgar's Night Club in the University Union complex. There are also lots of nightclubs downtown, within walking distance from the campus.

Accommodations: Days Inn, I-85 & SC 187, Exit 14, 29621. Telephone:

803/287-3550. $28.88 for one; $33.88 for two; $29.88 for an efficiency; $38.88 for a lodge.

● Clemson Motel, SC 93 & 123, P.O. Box 249, 29631. Telephone: 803/654-2744. $22 single; $25 double; $5 for each additional person.

● Thunderbird Motor Inn, SC 123, P.O. Box 311, 29631. Telephone: 803/654-4605. $26.75 for one; $32.10 for two; $37.45 for three; $42.80 for four.

Columbia

Help: Family Service Center (Travelers Aid), 1800 Main St., P.O. Box 7876, 29201. Telephone: 803/733-5450.

On Campus: Here in the largest city in the state, you'll find the state university. To eat well in Columbia, try Lizard's Thicket (southern cooking) at 4545 Broad Rd. and four other locations; The Elite Epicurean (good and filling food, Greek specialties), 1736 Main St.; or The Basil Pot (natural foods), 2721 Rosewood.

For campus news, listen to WVSC 90.5 FM, the university-owned and student-operated radio station and check the *Gane Coch*, the university newspaper. To meet young people, go to the Five Points area at the intersection of Harden and Blossom Sts. For rides, apartments to rent, etc., check the bulletin board on the first floor of the Russell House Student Union.

Accommodations: Days Inn, 7128 Parklane Rd., 29223. Telephone: 803/736-0000. $29.88 for one; $34.88 for two.

● Red Roof Inn, &, 7580 Two-Notch Rd., 29204. Telephone: 803/736-0850. $24.95 for one; $29.95 for two in one bed; $31.95 for two in two beds; $33.95 for three or four in two beds.

● Red Roof Inn, &, 10 Berryhill Rd., 29210. Telephone: 803/798-9220. See above listing for rates.

● Red Carpet Inn, V, 505 Knox Abbott Dr., Hwy. 321 & 176, 29033. Telephone: 803/796-6550. $26 to $30 for one; $28 to $33 for two in one bed; $32 to $37 for two in two beds.

● Econo Lodge, V, 127 Morninghill Dr., 29210. Telephone: 803/772-5833. $26.95 for one; $30.95 for two in one bed; $32.95 for two in two beds. Higher rates apply during special events.

● Econo Lodge, V, 1617 Charleston Hwy., 29169. Telephone: 803/796-3714. $26.95 for one; $30.95 for two in one bed; $32.95 for two in two beds. Higher rates apply during special events.

● Comfort Inn, V &, 827 Bush River Rd., 29210. Telephone: 803/772-9672. $25.95 to $30.95 for one; $27.95 to $30.95 for two.

Dillon

Accommodations: Days Inn, I-95 & SC 9 (Exit 193), Rte. 1, 29536. Telephone: 803/774-6041. $22 to $29 for one; $26 to $33 for two.

● Econo Lodge, V, I-95 & SC 9 (Exit 193), P.O. Box 76, 29536. Telephone: 803/774-4181. $21.95 for one; $25.95 for two in one bed; $28.95 for two in two beds. Higher rates apply during special events.

● Comfort Inn, V &, I-95 at Exit 193, 29536. Telephone: 803/774-7047. $27 to $29 for one; $31 to $33 for two.

Fair Play

Accommodation: Comfort Inn, Lake Hartwell, I-85 & SR 59, 29643. Telephone: 803/972-9001. $27 to $29 for one; $34 to $38 for two.

Florence

Accommodations: Econo Lodge, √, I-95 & U.S. 52, 29502. Telephone: 803/665-8558. $25.95 for one; $29.95 for two in one bed; $31.95 for two in two beds.
- Days Inn, I-95 & U.S. 76 (Exit 157), P.O. Box 3806, 29502. Telephone: 803/665-8550. $25 for one; $27 to $29 for two.
- Quality Inn, √ &, P.O. Box 1512, 29503. Telephone: 803/669-1715. $28 to $30 for one; $32 to $34 for two.

Goose Creek

Accommodation: Econo Lodge, √ &, 198 Central Ave., 29445. Telephone: 803/797-8200. $27.95 for one; $29.95 for two in one bed; $33.95 for two in two beds.

Greenville

Help: Family Counseling Service/Travelers Aid for Greenville County, "300" Bldg., Suite 108, University Ridge, P.O. Box 10306, Federal Station, 29603. Telephone: 803/232-2434.

Accommodations: Econo Lodge, √, 536 Wade Hampton Blvd., 29609. Telephone: 803/232-6416. $26.95 for one; $30.95 for two in one bed; $32.95 for two in two beds. Higher rates apply during special events.
- Econo Lodge, √, U.S. 276, P.O. Box 643, Mauldin, 29662. Telephone: 803/288-1770. $19.95 for one; $22.95 for two in one bed; $24.95 for two in two beds. Higher rates apply during special events.
- Econo Lodge, √, 107 Duval Dr., 29606. Telephone: 803/288-6600. $22.95 for one; $26.95 for two. Higher rates apply during special events.
- Red Roof Inn, &, 2801 Laurens Rd., I-85 & U.S. 276, 29607. Telephone: 803/297-4458. $22.95 for one; $27.95 for two in one bed; $29.95 for two in two beds; $31.95 for three or four in two beds.
- TraveLodge, √, 10 Mills Ave., 29605. Telephone: 803/233-3951. $28 for one; $30 for two in one bed; $34 for two in two beds.
- Scottish Inn, √, 601 Pendleton St., 29601. Telephone: 803/235-8591. $20 for one; $21 for two in one bed; $24 for two in two beds. Higher rates apply in March, June, July, August, and October.
- Quality Inn, √ &, 755 Wade Hampton Blvd., 29602. Telephone: 803/233-5393. $28 to $30 for one; $33 to $35 for two.
- Comfort Inn, √ &, I-85 at U.S. Hwy. 25 (Bus.) Exit Frontage Rd., Exit 45A, 29605. Telephone: 803/277-8630. $22.95 to $25.95 for one; $26.95 to $30.95 for two.

Hardeeville

Accommodation: Econo Lodge, √, I-95 & U.S. 17, 29927. Telephone: 803/784-2201. $23.95 for one; $27.95 for two in one bed; $31.95 for two in two beds.

Manning

Accommodations: Days Inn, I-95 & U.S. 301 (Exit 115), Rte. 4, 29102. Telephone: 803/473-2596. $25 to $29 for one; $29 to $33 for two.
● Econo Lodge, √, I-95 & U.S. 301, P.O. Box 268, 29102. Telephone: 803/473-2525. $19 for one; $22 to $23 for two in one bed; $22 to $25 for two in two beds. Higher rates apply during special events.
● Red Carpet Inn, √ &, Rte. 5, Box 448, 29102. Telephone: 803/473-2541. $22 to $24 for one; $22 to $25 for two in one bed; $26 to $34 for two in two beds.

Mt. Pleasant

Accommodation: Econo Lodge, √, 301 U.S. 17 Bypass, 29464. Telephone: 803/884-1411. $30 for one; $34 for two in one bed; $38 for two in two beds.

Rock Hill

Accommodation: Econo Lodge, √ &, 962 River View Rd., 29730. Telephone: 803/329-3232. $25.95 for one; $30.95 for two in one bed; $32.95 for two in two beds. Higher rates apply during special events.

Saint George

Accommodation: Scottish Inn, √ &, I-95 & Rte. 78, Exit 77, 29477. Telephone: 803/563-4195. $24 for one; $27 for two in one bed; $29 for two in two beds.

Santee

Accommodations: Days Inn, I-95 & SC 6 (Exit 98), P.O. Box 9, 29142. Telephone: 803/854-2175. $24 to $32 for one; $28 to $36 for two.
● Econo Lodge, √, P.O. Box 505, 29142. Telephone: 803/478-2366. $21.95 for one; $25.95 to $27.95 for two in one bed; $27.95 to $29.95 for two in two beds.

Spartanburg

Accommodations: Days Inn, I-85 & SC 9 (Exit 75), 1355 Boiling Springs Rd., 29303. Telephone: 803/585-2413. $30 for one; $34 for two.
● Red Carpet Inn, √, Rte. 9, Box 553, I-85 & Sigsbee Rd., 29301. Telephone: 803/576-7270. $25 for one or two in one bed; $30 for two in two beds.

- Econo Lodge, √, I-85 & Boiling Springs Rd., 29303. Telephone: 803/578-9450. $24.95 for one; $28.95 for two in one bed; $32.95 for two in two beds.
- Quality Inn, √, 578 North Church St., 29305. Telephone: 803/585-4311: $27 to $30 for one; $33 to $36 for two.
- TraveLodge, √, 416 East Main St., 29302. Telephone: 803/585-6451. $27 for one; $29 for two in one bed; $33 for two in two beds.

Summerton

Accommodation: Friendship Inn Lake Marion, Hwy. 301 & 15, Exit 108 I-95, 29148. Telephone: 803/485-2325. $18 to $21 for one; $21 to $23 for two in one bed; $23 to $25 for two in two beds.

Summerville

Accommodation: Econo Lodge, √ &, 110 Holiday Inn Dr., 29483. Telephone: 803/875-3022. $28 for one; $32 for two in one bed; $34 for two in two beds.

Sumter

Accommodation: Econo Lodge, √ &, U.S. Rte. 521 & U.S. Rte. 376-378 (Broad St.), 29150. Telephone: 803/469-9210. $25.95 for one; $31.95 for two in one bed; $35.95 for two in two beds.

Walterboro

Accommodation: Econo Lodge, √ &, 1057 Sniders Hwy., P.O. Box 618, 29488. Telephone: 803/538-3830. $20.95 for one; $26.95 for two in one bed; $29.95 for two in two beds.

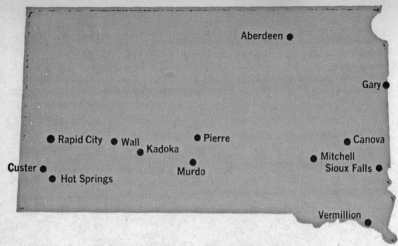

South Dakota

As you plan your days in South Dakota, you'll concentrate on the natural wonders of the state because they are quite spectacular. The most interesting geological formations are the Black Hills and the Badlands. The Black Hills are the highest mountains east of the Rockies. The Badlands, caused by centuries of erosion, are beautifully colored cliffs, rides, and spires.

Once a prehistoric swamp, the Badlands National Monument is one of the richest fossil beds in the world. Along the Fossil Walk you can examine pieces of the past, like a dog-size camel, a three-toed horse, and a sabre-toothed cat. For children, there's a special "Feelie Room" at the Park Visitor Center.

And no one would want to leave the state before getting a look at sculptor Gutzon Borglum's Mount Rushmore National Memorial. This granite monument to Washington, Jefferson, Lincoln, and Theodore Roosevelt is bound to astound you. Every night during the summer there's a lighting ceremony at the monument.

And for those who like the romance of the Old West, there should certainly be a visit to Deadwood, a town that once had wide-open gambling and bawdy houses and the Number 10 Saloon, where Wild Bill Hickok never did hear Jack McCall's six-gun go off.

Some Special Events: Old Time South Dakota Fiddlers Jamboree in Lake Norden (April); Jackrabbit Stampede (includes a rodeo) in Brookings (May); Czech Days in Tabor, and Expeditionary Volksmarch in Custer (June); Sitting Bull Stampede Rodeo in Mobridge, Black Hills Roundup in Belle Fourche, and Gold Discovery Days in Custer (July); Days of '76 in Deadwood, and Sioux Empire Fair in Sioux Falls (August); State Fair in Huron, and KGFX Suicide Ride in Pierre (September).

Hitching: Hitching, at least in the area of South Dakota State University, is good, and rides are not difficult to get. Forget about hitchhiking in winter, though. South Dakotans are accepting of people on the road as long as they are open and friendly in return. The South Dakota Highway Patrol sent us a list of the best roads for hitchhikers: I-90, I-29, U.S. 12, U.S. 212, U.S. 14, U.S. 18, U.S. 81, U.S. 281, U.S. 83, U.S. 385, and S.D. 79, but they don't recommend hitchhiking. It is prohibited on the roadway; hitchhike on ramps only.

Tourist Information: South Dakota Tourism, Box 6000, Pierre, SD 57501. Telephone: 605/773-3301. Statewide, toll-free information and referral service: 800/843-1930. Open 8 a.m. to 5 p.m. Monday through Friday. For a complete listing of facilities and things to see across the state, request the *South Dakota Vacation Guide.*

Aberdeen

Accommodation: Budget Host—Sands Motel, 1111 Sixth Ave. S.E., 57401. Telephone: 605/225-6000. $17.89 for one; $19.89 for two in one bed; $22.89 for two in two beds.

Canova

Accommodation: Skoglund Farm Bed & Breakfast, Rte. 1, Box 45, 57321. Telephone: 605/247-3445. $20 for adults, $15 for teenagers, $10 for children, free for children under age 5.

Custer

Accommodation: Friendship Custer Motel, 109 Mt. Rushmore Rd., 57730. Telephone: 605/673-2876. Limited airport service available. $18 to $30 for one; $18 to $34 for two in one bed; $20 to $38 for two in two beds.

Gary

Accommodation: Pleasant Valley Lodge (AYH), Rte. 1, Box 256, 57237. Telephone: 605/272-5614. Open April to November. $6 summer, $7 winter for AYH members. Advance reservations suggested.

Hot Springs

Camping: Wind Cave National Park, 57747. Telephone: 605/745-4600. Camping at Elk Mountain (one-half mile north of headquarters) from May 15 to September 15. $6 per campsite per night.

Accommodation: Friendship Inn Battle Mountain Court, 402 Battle Mountain Ave., north on Hwy. 385, 57745. Telephone: 605/745-3182. $24 to $40 for one; $28 to $40 for two in one bed; $28 to $42 for two in two beds.

Kadoka

Accommodation: Friendship Inn Sundowner, SD 73 & I-90, Exit 150, 57543. Telephone: 605/837-2296. $28 to $36 for one or two in one bed; $32 to $46 for two in two beds.

Mitchell

Accommodation: Motel 6, 1309 South Ohlman St., 57301. Telephone: 605/996-9696. $17.95 for one; $21.95 for two; $2 for each additional person.

Murdo

Accommodation: Friendship Zoart Inn, I-90 Bus. Loop downtown, 57559. Telephone: 605/669-2322. June 1 to September 1: $26 to $33 for one or two in one bed; $28 to $35 for two in two beds. Lower rates apply during off-peak season.

Pierre

Accommodations: Motel 6, 815 Wells Ave., 57501. Telephone: 605/224-6387. See Mitchell listing for rates.
- Thrifty Scot Motel, 520 West Sioux Ave., 57501. Telephone: 605/224-0411. $20.90 to $27.90 for one; $24.90 to $31.90 for two.

Rapid City

Accommodations: Marion's Guest House, 830 Quincy, 57701. Six blocks from bus station. Telephone: 605/342-1790. $15 to $18 single; $15 double; $20 triple; $25 quad. Advance reservations suggested. "A comfortable, homey atmosphere."
- YMCA (AYH-SA), 815 Kansas City St., 57701. Telephone: 605/342-8538. Men and women. Open June 1 to August 30. $3.50 for AYH members. Must bring own bedding. Complimentary health facilities.
- Home on the Range, 2422 Canyon Lake Dr., 57702. Telephone: 605/343-1368. $10 to $15 single. Many recreational facilities nearby. "There are 16 eating places less than 10 blocks away."
- Colonial Motel, ★ (5%), 511 East North St., 57701. Telephone: 605/342-1417. $18 to $38 for one; $22 to $45 for two. Higher rates apply during summer season. Heated outdoor pool.
- Motel 6, 620 East Latrobe St., 57701. Telephone: 605/343-1220. See Mitchell listing for rates.
- Friendship Town House, 210 St. Joseph St., 57701. Telephone: 605/342-8143. $25 to $30 for one; $27 to $32 for two in one bed; $31 to $36 for two in two beds.

Sioux Falls

Accommodations: YWCA, 300 West 11th St., 57102. Telephone: 605/336-3660. Women only. $8.50 single; $15 double. Weekly rate: $45. Advance reservations necessary.
- Motel 6, 3009 West Russell St., 57104. Telephone: 605/336-0071. See Mitchell listing for rates.
- Budget Host—Plaza Inn Motel, 2620 East 10th St., 57103. Telephone: 605/

336-1550. $16.95 to $19.95 for one; $21.95 to $24.95 for two in one bed; $24.95 to $29.95 for two in two beds. Heated pool. Courtesy car.

- TraveLodge, √ ⓑ, 809 West Ave. N., 57104. Telephone: 605/336-0230. Airport transportation available. $25 for one; $32 for two in one bed; $35 for two in two beds.

- Thrifty Scot Motel, 5001 North Cliff Ave., 57104. Telephone: 605/331-5959. $19.90 to $28.90 for one; $28.90 to $32.90 for two.

- Thrifty Scot Motel, 3401 Gateway Blvd., 57106. Telephone: 605/361-9240. $19.90 to $28.90 for one; $23.90 to $32.90 for two.

- Exel Inn, 1300 West Russell St., 57104. Telephone: 605/331-5800. $21.95 for one; $26.95 for two in one bed; $28.95 for two in two beds.

- Friendship Pine Crest, S.R. 42, U.S. 16 (old) & I-29, Exit 79, 57106. Telephone: 605/336-3530. $20.50 to $30 for one; $22.50 to $34.50 for two in one bed; $24.50 to $38.50 for two in two beds.

- Select Inn, √ ⓑ, 3500 South Gateway Blvd., 57106. Telephone: 605/361-1864. $20 to $27 single; $28 double; $30 triple; $32 quad.

Vermillion

Accommodation: Friendship Tomahawk Motor Inn, jct. Hwy. 19 & Bus. 50, 57069. Telephone: 605/624-2601. $18 to $21 for one; $21 to $25 for two in one bed; $25 to $30 for two in two beds.

Wall

Accommodation: Friendship Elk Motel, P.O. Box 384, Jct. Hwys. 14, 16 & 240, 57790. $14.50 to $28.50 for one; $18.50 to $32.50 for two in one bed; $22.50 to $34.50 for two in two beds.

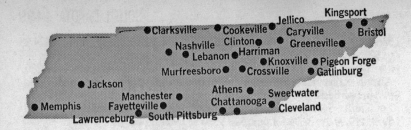

Tennessee

Tennessee is rich in natural and man-made attractions. So much of what people come to Tennessee for has to do with music. Is there anyone who hasn't heard of the Grand Ole Opry, of Elvis Presley's home, called Graceland, of Beale Street Blues, or of the folk ballads of the Appalachians? There's more than music, though, in Tennessee. The state boasts the Mud Island Mississippi River Museum in Memphis, which explains the history of the river and its importance in the life of the state; the Hermitage, Andrew Jackson's home in Nashville; in Greeneville, the home and shop owned by Andrew Jackson, the 17th president of the U.S.; the Casey Jones railroad museum in Jackson; the resort city of Gatlinburg, at the northern edge of the Smokies; Rock City Gardens, on the bluffs overlooking Chattanooga Valley; and the Jack Daniel Distillery in Lynchburg, now a National Historic Site.

Someone who lives in Tennessee put it this way: "The main things I like around here are the mountains and tiny towns where people live set apart from a lot of the world—like the tiny area about 90 miles from Knoxville where the Melungeons live. Stories vary about who the Melungeons are—some say they're descendants of Spaniards and some escaped slaves. Whatever the truth is, they remain aloof and apart and have kept alive some old crafts like making buckets of wood with no nails. There are dulcimer makers here too, and I suppose I should mention Gatlinburg—the tourist center of Tennessee. Lots of people like it, but it's too touristy for me—too many Ye Olde Shoppes, etc. But on the way to Gatlinburg there's a grist mill dating back to 1850 where corn and wheat are still ground by water power. It's a pretty place."

Some Special Events: Dogwood Arts Festival in Knoxville (17-day salute to spring and the beauty of the dogwood trees), Mule Day in Columbia, and the World's Largest Fish Fry in Paris (all in April); Appalachian Music Days in Bristol, and Spring Music and Crafts Festival in Rugby (May); Dulcimer Convention in Cosby, Country Music Days in Elizabethton, and Rhododendron Festival in Roan Mountain (all in June); Old-Time Fiddler's Jamboree in Smithville, and Gatlinburg Craftsmen's Fair in Gatlinburg (July); Memphis Music Festival: A Tribute to Elvis in Memphis (August); and the Tennessee State Fair in Nashville (September).

Hitching: It can be tricky to hitchhike in Tennessee. Legally you must stay off the "roadway." Police tend to be hard on hitchhikers. Some discouraging words from a student at the University of Tennessee: "Very few hitchhikers are able to get a lift, even around the university area. People are leery of hitchers lately." Perhaps it would be best to do what many students do instead of hitchhiking—they hike or ride their bikes.

Tourist Information: Department of Tourist Development, P.O. Box 23170, Nashville, TN 37202. Telephone: 615/741-2158.

Athens

Accommodation: Scottish Inn, I-75 & Hwy. 30, 37303. Telephone: 615/745-5800. $18.88 for one; $21.88 for two in one bed; $23.88 for two in two beds.

Bristol

Accommodation: Comfort Inn, √, 536 Volunteer Pkwy., 37620. Telephone: 615/968-2171. $30 for one; $40 for two.

Caryville

Accommodation: Budget Host—Tennessee Motel, 101 Tennessee Dr., Box 16, 37714. Telephone: 615/562-9595. $17.94 to $24 single; $21 to $26 double; $24 to $29 triple. "Facing beautiful Cove Lake in State Park; mountainous, scenic view."

Chattanooga

Tourist Information: Chattanooga Area Convention and Visitors Bureau, 1001 Market St., 37402. Telephone: 615/756-2121.

Accommodations: Days Inn, I-75 & U.S. 41 (Eastridge Exit 1), 1401 Mack Smith Rd., 37412. Telephone: 615/894-7480. $27 to $34 for one; $32 to $37 for two; $34 to $38 for single lodge; $39 to $43 for double lodge.

● Days Inn, 101 East 20th, 37408. Telephone: 615/267-9761. $26 to $32 for one; $29 to $36 for two.

● Scottish Inn, √, 6510 Ringgold Rd., 37412. Telephone: 615/894-0911. $22.95 for one; $25.95 for two in one bed; $28.95 for two in two beds.

● Scottish Inn, √ 🚻, 7707 Lee Hwy., 37421. Telephone: 615/889-1301. $22.95 for one; $25.95 for two in one bed; $28.95 for two in two beds.

● Scottish Inn, √, 3210 South Broad St., 37408. Telephone: 615/267-0414. $23.95 to $25.95 for one; $27.95 to $28.95 for two in one bed; $29.95 to $36.95 for two in two beds.

Clarksville

Accommodations: Motel 6, 881 Kraft St., 37040. Telephone: 615/552-3315. $17.95 for one; $21.95 for two; $2 for each additional person.

● Comfort Inn, 1112 S.R. 76 & I-24, Exit 11, 37043. Telephone: 615/358-2020. $26.88 for one; $30.88 for two.

Cleveland

Accommodation: Scottish Inn, ∨, 2650 Westside Dr. NW, 37311. Telephone: 615/472-3281. $20.95 for one; $25.95 to $27.95 for two in one bed; $29.95 to $31.95 for two in two beds.

Clinton

Accommodation: Budget Host—Riverview Motel, South Main St. & Hwy. 25 W., 37716. Telephone: 615/457-3333. $21.95 for one; $23.95 for two in one bed; $26.95 for two in two beds.

Cookeville

Accommodations: Days Inn, I-40 & Tenn. 111 (Exit 288), Rte. 8, 38501. Telephone: 615/528-5411. $22 to $26 for one; $29 to $31 for two.
  ● Scottish Inn, ∨, 1330 Bunkerhill Rd., 38501. Telephone: 615/528-2020. $25 for one; $30 for two.

Crossville

Accommodation: Heritage Inn, ⑤∨ 🖵 ★, P.O. Box 581, 38555. Telephone: 615/484-9505. $25 single; $27.50 to $35 double; $30 to $40 triple; $30 to $45 quad. Advance reservations suggested.

Fayetteville

Accommodation: Budget Host—Bonanza Motel and Steak House, 1651 Huntzville Hwy., 37334. Telephone: 615/433-6121. $22 for one; $25 for two in one bed; $27 for two in two beds.

Gatlinburg

Camping: Great Smoky Mountains National Park, 37738. There are several campgrounds in this immensely popular park. Some are open all year, some during the summer season only. There are also trail shelters along the Appalachian Trail—one day's journey apart. Permits required for backcountry use. Reservations can be made through Ticketron, May through October.
  Accommodation: Wa-Floy Retreat Hostel (AYH), ⑤∨, P.O. Box 611, Rte. 3, 37738. Telephone: 615/436-7700 or 436-5575. $6 summer, $7 winter for AYH members. "We have 22 buildings total. A two-story lodge, a motel, and cottages and apartments of various sizes."

Greeneville

Accommodation: Star Motel, ⑤★, 1633 Tusculum Blvd., 37743. Telephone: 615/638-8124. $20 single; $22 double; $24 triple; $28 quad.

Harriman

Accommodation: Scottish Inn, √, Rte. 8, Box 55, 37748. Telephone: 615/882-6600. $18.95 to $22.50 for one; $19.95 to $23 for two in one bed; $23 to $28 for two in two beds.

Jackson

Accommodation: Friendship Thunderbird Inn, three miles south on U.S. 45, 38301. Telephone: 901/422-5536. $24.98 for one or two in one bed; $29.42 for two in two beds.

Jellico

Accommodations: Days Inn, I-75 & U.S. 25 W., Exit 160, P.O. Box 299, 37762. Telephone: 615/784-7281. $25 to $30 for one; $30 to $35 for two.
● Quality Inn, √, I-75 & U.S. 25 W., 37762. Telephone: 800/251-9498. $25.50 for one; $30.50 for two.

Kingsport

Accommodation: Econo Lodge, 1704 East Stone Dr., 37660. Telephone: 615/245-0286. $25.95 for one; $29.95 for two in one bed; $32.95 for two in two beds. Higher rates apply during special events.

Knoxville

Tourist Information: Knoxville Area Council for Conventions and Visitors —Knoxville Convention and Visitors Bureau, P.O. Box 15012, 37901. Telephone: 615/523-2316.

On Campus: According to someone at the University of Tennessee, Knoxville is "a great place to live, a fair place to visit, and a great place to travel through." If you are passing through, you can count on meeting students in the Student Center or at any of the bars and restaurants that appear and disappear on Cumberland Ave. between the 1500 and 2000 blocks.

To find out what's going on on campus, get a copy of the *Daily Beacon,* the university paper. Everyone reads it, so if you want to put a notice somewhere about a ride, apartment, etc., put it in the *Beacon.* The various bulletin boards in the Student Center are also a good source of information.

Just off Cumberland Avenue, there's an area known as "The Strip." Fast-food spots, eating and drinking places, and small restaurants galore. Some possibilities: Old College Inn, sandwich platters for $2.50 to $3.50; Arnolds's, deli-style sandwiches for $1.80 to $2.65; Varsity Inn, breakfast anytime; Campus Inn; Mom & Pop's Restaurant; Cumberland; and Ruby's, Cumberland & 21st Sts., a place that's popular with the drinking crowd at night at the UT Student Center. Try Smokey's Cafeteria, where plate lunches are under $3. Anyone can eat here—"institution food but surprisingly good—build your own sandwiches, a salad bar and a wide variety of desserts."

Accommodations: Days Inn, 200 Lovell Rd. NW, 37922. Telephone: 615/966-5801. $27 to $34 for one; $32 to $39 for two.

● Red Roof Inn, ⓚ, 5640 Merchants Center Blvd., 37912. Telephone: 615/689-7100. $21.95 for one; $26.95 for two in one bed; $28.95 for two in two beds; $30.85 for three or four in two beds.

● Department of Residence Halls, University of Tennessee, Suite 405, Student Services Bldg., 37996. Telephone: 615/974-2571. Open in June and August. Men, women, and children. $12 single; $20 double. Guests must be involved in educationally-related activities. Advance reservations suggested.

● Scottish Inn, 104 Bridgewater Rd., 37923. Telephone: 615/693-5331. $18.95 for one; $22.95 for two in one bed; $24.95 for two in two beds.

● Red Carpet Inn, √ ⓚ, 503 Merchants Rd., 37912. Telephone: 615/689-7666. $17.88 for one; $21.88 for two in one bed; $23.88 for two in two beds.

● Motel 6, 10115 Watkins Blvd., 37922. Telephone: 615/966-7528. See Clarksville listing for rates.

● Econo Lodge, √ ⓚ, 6712 Central Ave. Pike, 37912. Telephone: 615/689-6600. $19.88 for one; $22.88 for two in one bed; $25.88 for two in two beds.

● Comfort Inn, √, 5334 Central Ave. Pike, 37912. Telephone: 615/688-1010. $22 to $27 for one; $26 to $34 for two.

Lawrenceburg

Accommodation: Budget Host—David Crockett Motel, √ (10% with cash payment), 503 East Gaines St., 38464. Telephone: 615/762-7191. $25 for one; $28 for two in one bed; $30 for two in two beds.

Lebanon

Accommodations: Days Inn, I-40 & U.S. 231 S., 37087. Telephone: 615/449-2900. $23 to $36 for one; $27 to $41 for two.

Manchester

Accommodation: Days Inn, I-24 & U.S. 41 (Exit 114), 37355. Telephone: 615/728-9530. $21 to $28 for one; $4 to $6 for each additional person.

Memphis

Tourist Information: Convention and Visitors Bureau of Memphis, 203 Beale St., 38103. Telephone: 901/526-1919.

Help: Travelers Aid, 46 North 3rd St., 38103. Telephone: 901/525-5466.

Accommodations: Regal 8 Inn, 1360 Springbrook Rd., 38116. Telephone: 901/396-3620. $22.88 for one; $27.88 for two in one bed; $32.88 for two in two beds.

● Red Roof Inn, ⓚ, 6055 Shelby Oaks Dr., 38134. Telephone: 901/388-6111. $26.95 for one; $31.95 for two in one bed; $33.95 for two in two beds; $35.95 for three or four in two beds.

- Red Roof Inn, ♿, 3875 American Way, I-240 & Getwell Rd. at American Way, 38118. Telephone: 901/363-2335. See above listing for rates.
- Days Inn, ♿, I-240 & 5301 Summer Ave., 38122. Telephone: 901/761-1600. $26 to $37 for one; $4 to $6 for each additional person.
- Days Inn, ♿, I-55 & Brooks Rd., 38116. Telephone: 901/345-2470. Five minutes from airport. $29 to $31 for one; $34 to $36 for two.
- Days Inn, ♿, I-55 & East Shelby Dr. Exit, 1970 East Shelby Dr., 38116. Telephone: 901/332-0222. $25 to $35 for one; $4 to $6 for each additional person.
- Red Carpet Inn, 1831 Getwell Rd., 38111. Telephone: 901/744-4650. $23.95 for one or two in one bed; $26.95 for two in two beds.
- Motel 6, 1321 Sycamore View Rd., 38134. Telephone: 901/377-0493. See Clarksville listing for rates.

Murfreesboro

Accommodations: Days Inn, ♿, I-24 & U.S. 231 (Exit 8), 2036 South Church St., 37130. Telephone: 615/893-1090. June 1 to August 28 and September 8 to November 30: $20 to $33 for one. August 29 to September 7: $50 for one.
- Motel 6, 114 Chaffin Pl., 37130. Telephone: 615/890-1910. See Clarksville listing for rates.
- Quality Inn, √, I-24 & U.S. 231 S., 37130. Telephone: 615/896-5450. $24.50 to $30.50 for one; $29.50 to $39.50 for two.

Nashville

Tourist Information: Convention and Visitors Division, Nashville Area Chamber of Commerce, 161 Fourth Ave. N., 37219. Telephone: 615/259-3900.

Help: Travelers Aid, 105 Eighth Ave. N., 37203. Telephone: 615/256-3168 or 256-3169.

On Campus: Vanderbilt University is in Nashville. Rand Hall on campus is the hub of student activity and *The Hustler* is the campus newspaper. There are lots of small restaurants around Vanderbilt but one that was recommended in particular is the International Market, 2010 Belmont Blvd., where a Thai-Chinese dinner will cost only about $5. One campus correspondent recommends that when you're in Nashville, be sure "to visit our catfish restaurants and country music halls and bars like The Station Inn."

Accommodations: Scottish Inn, 1501 Dickinson Rd., 37207. Telephone: 615/226-6940. November 1 to May 31: $20 for one; $25 for two in one bed; $30 for two in two beds. June 1 to October 31: $38 for one; $43 for two in one bed; $48 for two in two beds.
- Motel 6, 95 Wallace Rd., 37211. Telephone: 615/834-1231. See Clarksville listing for rates.
- Motel 6, 311 West Trinity Lane, 37207. Telephone: 615/227-6878. See Clarksville listing for rates.
- Red Roof Inn, ♿, 110 Northgate Dr., I-65 at Long Hollow Pike (Exit 97), 37072. $24.95 for one; $29.95 for two in one bed; $31.95 for two in two beds; $33.95 for three or four in two beds.
- Days Inn, I-65 & West Trinity Lane, Exit 87B, 37207. Telephone: 615/226-

4500. August 25 to November 30: $26 to $38 for one; $32 to $44 for two. June 1 to August 24: $39 to $49 for one; $45 to $55 for two.

● Days Inn, 🦽, I-24 & Murfreesboro Rd. (Exit 52), 321 Plus Park Blvd., 37217. Telephone: 615/367-9180. June 1 to September 2: $39 for one; $45 for two. September 3 to November 30: $24 for one; $35 for two.

● Econo Lodge, ✓🦽, I-24 E. & Old Hickory Blvd., Exit 62, 37211. Telephone: 615/793-7721. $30 to $38 for one; $35 to $44 for two.

● Econo Lodge, ✓🦽, 2460 Music Valley Dr., 37214. Telephone: 615/889-0090. April 1 to May 31 and September 1 to 30: $29.95 for one; $41.95 for two. June 1 to August 31: $38.95 for one; $52.95 for two. Higher rates apply during Opryland weekends.

Pigeon Forge

Accommodation: Wier Farm Home Hostel (AYH), Rte. 15, Box 32, Wier Farm Rd., 37863. Telephone: 615/453-2033. Open April to November. $4.25 for AYH members. Advance reservations necessary.

South Pittsburg

Accommodation: Scottish Inn, ✓, I-24 jct. at Kimball, 37347. Telephone: 615/837-7933. $20 for one; $25 for two in one bed; $28 to $30 for two in two beds.

Sweetwater

Accommodations: Red Carpet Inn, South Main St., 37874. Telephone: 615/337-3585. $19.95 for one; $22.95 for two in one bed; $27.95 for two in two beds.

● Econo Lodge, ✓, I-75 & Hwy. 68 (Exit 60), 37874. Telephone: 615/337-9357. $21.95 for one; $24.95 for two in one bed; $26.95 for two in two beds.

● Quality Inn Mar-Vel, ✓🦽, I-75 & SR 68, Exit 60, 37874. Telephone: 615/337-3541. $29.50 for one; $34.65 to $38.50 for two.

● Comfort Inn, ✓🦽, U.S. 11 & SR 68, South Main St., 37874. Telephone: 615/337-6646. $20 for one; $24.50 to $27 for two.

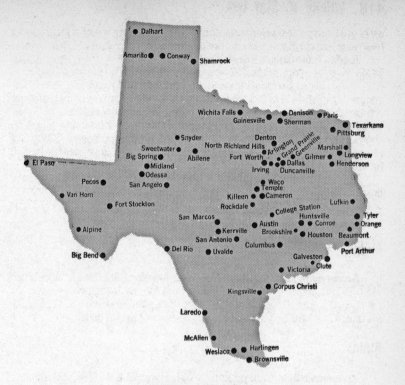

Texas

Texas is big—maybe not as big as Alaska but still very, very big (7½% of the total U.S. land area). Texans love the bigness and don't seem to mind being teased about it. Texas cities are some of the fastest-growing and most prosperous urban areas in the U.S. at a time when most cities are on the decline. North, central, and east are the most developed; western Texas is still a land of vast deserts, mountains, and prairies, with all the huge ranches that you've seen in John Wayne movies. There are tropical areas in the south, along the Mexican border and Gulf of Mexico.

Because of the general prosperity in much of Texas, there are part-time unskilled jobs to be had in most of the cities—Houston and Dallas especially.

Some Special Events: Cotton Bowl Parade and Football Game in Dallas on New Year's Day, Livestock Show and Rodeo in El Paso, and Charro Days in Brownsville (February); Dogwood Trails Festival in Palestine (March); Neches River Festival in Beaumont, Buccaneer Days in Corpus Christi (April); Magnolia Homes Tour in Columbus (May); Watermelon Thump in Laking (June); Black-Eyed Pea Jamboree in Athens (July); and Texas Folklore Festival in San Antonio (August).

Hitching: It is illegal to hitchhike on a public roadway. Most of the people we heard from on Texas campuses don't think hitchhiking is such a great idea in their state and seem to agree that drivers tend to be suspicious of hitchhikers.

Tourist Information: Texas, Dept. DHT, P.O. Box 5064, Austin, TX 78763. Ask for a copy of their 224-page booklet *Texas! Travel Handbook.*

N.B. Bed and Breakfast Texas Style, 4224 West Red Bird Lane, 75237. Telephone: 214/298-5433 or 298-8586. Arranges lodgings in private homes, offering comfortable rooms, shared and private baths, and either continental or Texas-style breakfasts. Locations are offered in each city's most desirable neighborhoods. Also available are lovely suburban and ranch-style homes. $20 to $29 (budget) and $20 to $40 (comfort) for singles; $30 to $40 (budget) and $40 to $60 (comfort) for doubles. Write for details.

The Sand Dollar Hospitality/Bed and Breakfast has a listing of residential homes, several of which are near the water, for $20 to $25 single; $25 to $30 double. For details, contact them at 3605 Mendenhall, 78415 or phone: 512/853-1222.

Abilene

Accommodations: Motel 6, 4951 West Stamford St., 79603. Telephone: 915/673-2561. $17.95 for one; $21.95 for two; $2 for each additional person.
● Econo Lodge, √ &, Box 47, 79601. Telephone: 915/673-5251. $22.95 for one; $24.95 for two in one bed; $27.95 for two in two beds.

Alpine

Accommodation: Comfort Inn, √ &, Hwy. 90 E., 79830. Telephone: 915/837-3417. $25 to $29 for one; $29 to $33 for two.

Amarillo

Accommodations: Friendship Inn Farrell Manor, 100 Amarillo Blvd. E., 79107. Telephone: 806/372-1261. $24 for one; $27 for two in one bed; $29 for two in two beds.
● Quality Inn, √, 601 Amarillo Blvd. W., 79107. Telephone: 806/376-4211. $26 to $33 for one; $32 to $39 for two.
● Friendship Inn Bronco Lodge, 6005 Amarillo Blvd. W., 79106. Telephone: 806/335-3321. $23 to $26 for one; $26 for two in one bed; $30 for two in two beds.
● Motel 6, 2032 Paramount Blvd., 79109. Telephone: 806/355-9861. See Abilene listing for rates.
● Motel 6, 3930 I-40 E., 79103. Telephone: 806/372-6318. See Abiline listing for rates.
● Regal 8 Inn, 6030 I-40 W., 79106. Telephone: 806/359-7651. $21.88 for one; $26.88 for two in one bed; $31.88 for two in two beds.
● Allstar Inn, &, 4301 I-40 E., 79104. Telephone: 806/373-3045. $23.95 to $25.95 for one; $2 for each additional person.

Arlington

On Campus: One friend at the University of Texas in Arlington says "You should feel at home at UTA—one out of every 12 students is an 'international.'"

Accommodations: Motel 6, 2626 Randol Mill Rd. E., 76011. Telephone: 817/649-1101. See Abilene listing for rates.
● Budget Host—Arlington Motor Inn, √, 818 East Division, 76012. Telephone: 817/277-1395. Rates begin at $27.

Austin

Tourist Information: Tourist and Convention Information, Austin Chamber of Commerce, P.O. Box 1967, 78767. Telephone: 512/478-9383.

On Campus: The largest campus of the University of Texas is in Austin. Students can be found all over Austin, with an especially high concentration in the Student Union. International students traveling in the area may contact the International Office at 512/471-1211 for general help and advice.

When you're hungry, go where the Austin Texans go—Mad Dog & Beans for hamburgers and trimmings, 512 West 24th St.; Mr. Gatti's Pizza, 503 West Martin Luther King Jr. Blvd.; Matt's El Rancho at 303 East 1st or Fonda San Miguel at 2330 West North Loop, both for Mexican food.

Taos Dormitory, 2612 Guadalupe, has single rooms for $22 and double rooms for $32.

Accommodations: Motel 6, 2707 Interregional Hwy. S., 78741. Telephone: 512/444-4842. See Abilene listing for rates.
● Allstar Inn, 8010 North I-35, 78753. Telephone: 512/837-9890. See Amarillo listing for rates.
● Imperial 400 Motor Inn, √ (10%), 901 South Congress Ave., 78704. Telephone: 512/444-3651. $24 to $28 for one; $28 to $32 for two in one bed; $30 to $34 for two in two beds.

Beaumont

Accommodations: Motel 6, 2640 I-10 E., 77703. Telephone: 713/898-2770. See Abilene listing for rates.
● Allstar Inn, 2052 I-10 S., 77701. Telephone: 409/842-0041. See Amarillo listing for rates.
● Comfort Inn, √, 30 North I-10, 77702. Telephone: 409/838-0581. $19.95 to $24.30 for one or two people.

Big Bend

Camping: Big Bend National Park, 79834. There's camping year-round at Cottonwood, Chisos, Basin, and Rio Grande Village. $2 to $4 per campsite per night.

Big Spring

Accommodation: Motel 6, 600 West I-20, 79720. Telephone: 915/263-6243. See Abilene listing for rates.

Brookshire

Accommodation: Comfort Inn, √, I-10 at FM 1489. Telephone: 713/934-8511. $25 to $32 for one; $25 to $36 for two.

Brownsville

Accommodation: Motel 6, 2255 North Expressway, 78521. Telephone: 512/546-6699. See Abilene listing for rates.

Cameron

Accommodation: Friendship Varsity Motel, Hwys. 190-77 & 36 S., 76520. Telephone: 817/697-6446. Limited airport service available. $23 to $26 for one; $26 to $29 for two in one bed; $30 to $33 for two in two beds.

Clute

Accommodation: Motel 6, 1000 Hwy. 332, 77531. Telephone: 409/265-6766. See Abilene listing for rates.

College Station

Accommodation: Motel 6, 2327 Texas Ave., 77840. Telephone: 409/696-1631. See Abilene listing for rates.

Columbus

Accommodation: Friendship Inn Baker Motel, 1136 Walnut St., 78934. Telephone: 409/732-2315. Limited airport service available. $28 to $32 for one; $32 to $35 for two in one bed; $33 and up for two in two beds.

Conroe

Accommodation: Motel 6, 820 I-45 S., 77304. Telephone: 409/756-6868. See Abilene listing for rates.

Conway

Accommodation: Friendship Inn L.A. Motel and Restaurant, Jct. I-40 & Hwy. 207, Rte. 2, Box 52A, 79068. Telephone: 806/537-5127 or 537-9927. $19 for one; $21 for two in one bed; $26 for two in two beds.

Corpus Christi

Camping: Padre Island National Seashore, 9405 South Padre Island Dr.,

78418. Telephone: 512/949-8173. Located 35 miles from downtown Corpus Christi. There are campgrounds at Malaquite Beach for $4 and primitive camping on other beaches.

Accommodations: Motel 6, 845 Lantana St., 78408. Telephone: 512/289-2041. See Abilene listing for rates.

● Motel 6, 8302 South Padre Island Dr., 78412. Telephone: 512/993-5811. See Abilene listing for rates.

● Econo Lodge, √, 6033 Leopard St., 78409. Telephone: 512/289-1116. $28.95 for one; $29.95 for two in one bed; $32.95 for two in two beds. Higher rates apply during special events.

● Dixie Shore Motel, Ⓢ√ ★, 4349 Ocean Dr., 78412. Telephone: 512/853-7339. $22.50 single; $27.50 double; $29.95 triple; $32.50 quad.

● Ranch Motel, ♿, 4206 Leopard St., 78408. Telephone: 512/884-3271. $17 to $21 single or double; $20 to $24 triple.

● Gulf Beach II, Ⓢ√ ★, 3500 Surfside, 78402. Telephone: 512/882-3500. $29.95 single; $34.95 double; $49.95 triple.

● TraveLodge, √, 1401 North Shoreline Blvd., 78401. Telephone: 512/882-6181. $30 for one; $36 for two.

Dalhart

Accommodation: Friendship Inn, 209 Liberal St., 79022. Telephone: 806/249-4589. $18 to $23 for one; $23 to $28 for two in one bed; $25 to $34 for two in two beds.

Dallas

Tourist Information: Dallas Convention and Visitors Bureau, Dallas Chamber of Commerce, 400 South Houston (in person) or 1507 Pacific (mailing address), 75201. Telephone: 214/954-1428.

Accommodations: Allstar Inn, 4220 Independence Dr., 75237. Telephone: 214/296-3331. See Amarillo listing for rates.

● Motel 6, 3629 Hwy. 80, 75150. Telephone: 214/279-7249. See Abilene listing for rates.

● Motel 6, 4610 South R.L. Thornton Freeway, 75224. Telephone: 214/372-1456. See Abilene listing for rates.

● Motel 6, 9626 C.F. Hawn Freeway, 75217. Telephone: 214/286-5206. See Abilene listing for rates.

● Red Roof Inn, ♿, 8150 Esters Blvd., Hwy. 114 & Esters Rd., Irving, 75063. $26.95 for one; $31.95 for two in one bed; $33.95 for two in two beds; $35.95 for three or four in two beds.

● Days Inn, U.S. 80 at Town East Blvd., 3817 Hwy. 80 E., 75150. Telephone: 214/270-7551. $29.88 for one; $33.88 for two.

Del Rio

Accommodations: Friendship Desert Hills Motel, 1912 Ave. F, 78840. Telephone: 512/775-3548. $20 for one; $22 to $24 for two in one bed; $24 to $26 for two in two beds.

- Motel 6, 2115 Ave. F, 78840. Telephone: 512/775-6635. See Abilene listing for rates.

Camping: Amistad National Recreation Area, P.O. Box 420367, 78842. Telephone: 512/775-7491. Camping all year at primitive campsites. No charge.

Denison

Accommodation: Friendship LaVilla Motel, Hwys. 69 & 75, 75020. Telephone: 214/465-8811. $22 to $24 for one; $25.50 to $26.50 for two in one bed; $28 to $36 for two in two beds.

Denton

Accommodations: Motel 6, 4125 I-35 N., 76201. Telephone: 817/387-0571. See Abilene listing for rates.

- Exel Inn, 42111-35E N., 76201. Telephone: 817/383-1471. $26.95 for one; $31.95 for two in one bed; $33.95 for two in two beds.

Duncanville

Accommodation: Allstar Inn, 4220 Independence Dr., 75237. Telephone: 214/296-3331. See Amarillo listing for rates.

El Paso

Help: El Paso Crisis Services, 915/779-1800.

Accommodations: Armed Services YMCA, Ⓢ √ ★ ($1), 315 East Franklin St., 79901. Telephone: 915/532-4957. $13 single; $19 double; $24 triple.

"After visiting the Armed Services YMCA on two occasions, I thought I must write to tell you of their excellence. The rooms are large, spotlessly clean, and all the staff very helpful."

- El Paso International Youth Hostel/Gardner Hotel (AYH-SA), 311 East Franklin Ave., 79901. Telephone: 915/532-3661. Five blocks from bus; eight blocks from train. $13 to $17 single; $16 to $20 double; $23 triple. $7.50 for AYH members, $9.50 for nonmembers in dorm beds. Listed on El Paso Historic Register and recently renovated. "It's a safe, clean, and friendly place to stay."
- Friendship Beverly Crest Motor Inn, 8709 Dyer St., 79904. Telephone: 915/755-7631. $22 to $24 for one; $22 to $25 for two in one bed; $25 to $28 for two in two beds.

- Motel 6, 11049 Gateway Blvd. W., 79935. Telephone: 915/591-6600. See Abilene listing for rates.
- Motel 6, 7840 North Mesa St., 79932. Telephone: 915/584-3485. See Abilene listing for rates.
- Imperial 400 Motor Inn, √ (10%), 6363 Montana Ave., 79925. Telephone: 915/778-3311. $28 to $34 for one; $30 to $36 for two in one bed; $32 to $38 for two in two beds.
- Warren Inn Hotel, √ 🖾, 4748 North Mesa St., 79912. Telephone: 915/544-4494. $25 for one; $33 for two in one bed; $38 for three in two beds; $43 for four in two beds. Free continental breakfast. Advance reservations of one week suggested.
- Allstar Inn, 1324 Lombaland Dr., 79935. Telephone: 915/592-6386. See Amarillo listing for rates.

Fort Stockton

Accommodation: Motel 6, 3001 West Dickinson Blvd., 79735. Telephone: 915/336-6631. See Abilene listing for rates.

Fort Worth

Tourist Information: Convention and Visitors Bureau, 700 Throckmorton St., 76102. Telephone: 817/336-8791.

Help: Catholic Social Service (Travelers Aid), 1404 Hemphill, 76104. Telephone: 817/921-9072.

Accommodations: Motel 6, 6401 Airport Freeway, Haltom City, 76117. Telephone: 817/834-3851. See Abilene listing for rates.
- Motel 6, 6600 South Freeway, 76134. Telephone: 817/551-5266. See Abilene listing for rates.
- Motel 6, 8701 I-20 W., 76116. Telephone: 817/244-6060. See Abilene listing for rates.
- Motel 6, 3271 I-35 W., 76106. Telephone: 817/624-8476. See Abilene listing for rates.
- Days Inn, I-35 W. & Felix St., 812 East Felix St., 76115. Telephone: 817/926-9211. $30 for one; $35 for two.
- Allstar Inn, 1236 Oakland Blvd., 76103. Telephone: 817/834-7361. See Amarillo listing for rates.
- Allstar Inn, 3275 I-35 W., 76106. Telephone: 817/625-8941. See Amarillo listing for rates.
- Budget Host—Caravan Motor Hotel, 2601 Jacksboro Hwy., 76114. Telephone: 817/626-1951. $28 for one; $32 for two in one bed; $38 for two in two beds.

Gainesville

Accommodation: Budget Host—Caravan Motor Hotel, Jct. I-35 & U.S. 82, P.O. Box 856, 76240. Telephone: 817/665-5555. $28 for one; $32 for two in one bed; $38 for two in two beds.

Galveston

Accommodation: Motel 6, 7404 Ave. J, RR 2, 77551. Telephone: 409/744-6666. See Abilene listing for rates.

Gilmer

Accommodation: Friendship Gilmer Inn, 1005 South Wood St., 75644. Telephone: 214/843-3033. $26 to $29 for one; $30 to $33 for two in one bed; $33 to $36 for two in two beds.

Grand Prairie

Accommodation: Motel 6, 406 East Safari Blvd., 75050. Telephone: 214/642-3497. See Abilene listing for rates.

Greenville

Accommodation: Motel 6, 5109 I-30, 75401. Telephone: 214/454-0972. See Abilene listing for rates.

Harlingen

Accommodation: Motel 6, 224 South U.S. Expressway 77, 78550. Telephone: 512/425-3731. See Abilene listing for rates.

Henderson

Accommodation: Friendship Woodlawn Hills Motel, 1204 North Hwy. 79, 75652. Telephone: 214/657-2511. $22 to $28 for one; $23 to $28 for two in one bed; $26 to $31 for two in two beds.

Houston

Houston is the fastest-growing city in the U.S. and seems to have escaped the economic problems that other U.S. cities face. Twenty-four of the 25 largest U.S. oil companies are active in Houston, along with 400 other not-so-large companies. Houston is, indeed, a modern-day boom town that seems to be bursting at the seams. An excellent guide to this big, rich, and aggressively modern city is *Texas Monthly's Guide to Houston*, by Felicia Coates and Harriet Howle ($3.95). *Texas Monthly* itself is a good guide to places to eat and things to do; look, too, at *Houston City Magazine* for the same kind of information. For free maps and information about tours and sightseeing, stop at the Greater Houston Convention and Visitors Council, 3300 Main St., 77002 (tel. 715/523-5050). Their monthly "Houston Day and Night" brochure and "Houston Area Maps and Attractions" are quite useful. They also have two toll-free numbers: 800/392-7722, inside Texas; and 800/231-7799, outside Texas. And be warned: Houston can be incredibly hot and steamy. Hot enough, in fact, to have made it necessary to build air-conditioned tunnels connecting the downtown buildings. Mid to late March is the time for the Houston Festival—a period when Houston applauds itself with a mélange of food, arts, music, crafts, and dance. If you're going to be on or around the campus of the University of Houston, you should probably stop at the offices of ACCESS, Room N-13, University Center. For up-to-the-minute information on Houston, contact Showtix, 400 Rush at Smith in Tranquility Park (tel. 227-9292).

Getting There: There's an airport limousine bus service from Intercontinental Airport to the Downtown Air Terminal in the Hyatt Regency Hotel. The 25-mile ride costs $6; the same trip by taxi would be $21.

● The Greyhound station is at 1410 Texas Ave. (tel. 222-1161); Trailways is at 2121 Main St. (tel. 759-6500); and Amtrak's terminal is at 902 Washington St. (tel. 224-1577).

Getting Around: *"This is a very difficult city to get around in if you don't have a car."*

● For 10¢ you can ride any bus within the boundaries of a Shoppers Special Route, on Main St. from Franklin on the north to Pierre on the south. The regular fare on the Metro bus is 55¢; transfers are free. Buses run every 15 to 30 minutes. For information on public transportation, you can visit the Metro Ride Store on the corner of Capital and Franklin, downtown, or call 635-4000. But the best way, by far, to see Houston is by car. If you don't have your own, you can get a good rental deal at Budget Rent-a-Car, with offices located all over town. A Toyota or Datsun costs $35 a day with unlimited mileage. Because Houston is such a car-orientated town, there are loads of other car-rental places too.

Help: Travelers Aid, 2601 Main St., Suite A, 77002. Telephone: 713/654-8072.

● Crisis Hotline of Houston, 713/228-1505.

● Crisis Help Line, 713/488-7222.

On Campus: The University of Houston—University Park has temporary housing in campus dorms available during the summer for $25 single and $18.50 per person double. Telephone: 713/749-2185.

On campus, the *Daily Cougar* newspaper is a good source of information on odd jobs, discount stores, rides, and what's going on—in addition to the board on campus in the University Center Underground. Through ACCESS (information/referral/off-campus housing), one can obtain discounted Astroworld passes, September to May discounted metro passes, and discounted cinema passes. Contact the University of Houston—University Center, ACCESS, N-13, Houston, 77004. Telephone: 713/749-3327.

Accommodations: YMCA, Ⓢ (10%), 1600 Louisiana St., 77002. Telephone: 713/659-8501. Men only. $14.50 per night; $62 to $68 per week. Air-conditioned; color television in every room; telephone included. "We have a complete referral service here . . . any traveler coming here will find that he will get assistance when needed."

● Houston Hostel, Ⓢ($1), 5530 Hillman, 77023. Telephone: 713/926-3444. $7 for AYH and ISIC members in dorm beds.

● The Grant Motel, Ⓢ√🚹, 8200 South Main St., 77025. Telephone: 713/668-8000. Near Rice University-Texas Medical Center area. $30 single; $38 double; $42 triple; $46 quad. "Quiet, clean rooms with extra-long beds."

● Regal 8 Inn, 4045 North Freeway, 77022. Telephone: 713/691-6671. $21.88 for one; $26.88 for two in one bed; $33.88 for two in two beds.

- Regal 8 Inn, 9535 Katy Freeway, 77024. Telephone: 713/467-4411. $23.88 for one; $28.88 for two in one bed; $35.88 for two in two beds.
- Regal 8 Inn, 8500 South Main St., 77025. Telephone: 713/666-4971. $21.88 for one; $25.88 for two in one bed; $30.88 for two in two beds.
- Days Inn, I-10 & F-M Rd. 1489, 77423. Telephone: 713/934-8511. $27 to $32 for one; $32 to $37 for two.
- Days Inn, I-45 & Cavalcade, 100 West Cavalcade, 77009. Telephone: 713/868-7121. $33.88 for one; $37.88 for two.
- Days Inn, I-45 at Wayside, 🚫, 2200 South Wayside, 77023. Telephone: 713/928-2800. See above listing for rates.
- Alamo Plaza Motel, 4343 Old Spanish Trail, 77021. Telephone: 713/747-6900. $20 to $21 for one or two in one bed; $25 for two in two beds.
- Motel 6, 9638 Plainfield Rd., 77036. Telephone: 713/778-9606. See Abilene listing for rates.

Where to Eat: The Original Ninfa's (there are three others), 2704 Navigation Rd. In the Port of Houston area near the bayou. Call 228-1175 for their hours. "Just about the best Mexican food in Houston." The atmosphere is pure fiesta. Tacos al carbon, the specialty of the house, costs about $6 at dinnertime.

- Goode Company, 5107 Kirby Dr., in the Rice University area. Telephone: 522-2530. Texas-style barbecue that you've got to try at least once while you're in Houston.
- The Old Spaghetti Warehouse, 901 Commerce St. at Travis (downtown). Telephone: 229-0009. Antiques, plants, and of course, spaghetti. A special spaghetti dinner with soup, salad, and a beverage costs $3.25.
- James Coney Island, 1142 Travis. Telephone: 652-3819. Chili, sandwiches, salads, and hot dogs. Conveniently located and usually open from 7 a.m. to 10 p.m. every day of the week. Two Coney Islands (hot dogs) and a beer are $3.25.
- Leo's Coffee Shop, 1203 Fannin (downtown). Telephone: 652-5955. Open 24 hours. American food, with nothing over $6. "The atmosphere is interesting —especially in the wee hours."
- Pancho's Mexican Buffet, 5311 Bissonnet. Telephone: 666-3531. Bellaire area. On the buffet you have your choice of enchiladas, tacos, guacamole, soup, chili rellenos, tamales, chalupas, rice, and beans—all for $3.99.
- Frenchy's Po Boy, 3919 Scott. Telephone: 748-2233. Fast food in the Creole style. Three pieces of chicken, fries, and "dirty" rice is $2.85 on the campus special—no wonder it's so popular with the students.
- Lyby's Cafeteria, 2730 Fondren Rd., and others all over Houston. In the heart of Bellaire. Nothing fancy, just clean and reliable.

What to See and Do: From May to October, the arts go outdoors to Miller Theater in Hermann Park near the Medical Center. Ballet, symphony, opera, plays—almost every night there's something to see and it's all free. Call 222-3576 for information.

- The Alley Theatre, 615 Texas, is reputed to be one of the best regional theaters in the U.S. Call 228-8421 for ticket information. There are student discounts of up to 25%—ask about them.
- NASA's Lyndon B. Johnson Space Center, 20 miles south of Houston. Here you can see Mission Control, where space flights from Gemini to the Space Shuttle *Columbia* have been monitored. Free walking tours are available Monday through Friday. Call 483-4321 for reservations.
- The Astrodome Sports Stadium claims to be the largest single attraction in the state of Texas. There are tours every day. Call 749-9500 for details.

- Rothko Chapel, 1411 Sul Ross. Fourteen of Mark Rothko's paintings hang in this ecumenical chapel in an interesting neighborhood southwest of downtown. For information, call 524-9839.
- Museums: The Museum of Fine Arts, 1001 Bissonnet (tel. 526-1361). Open Tuesday through Sunday, and the Contemporary Arts Museum (tel. 526-3129) at 5216 Montrose Blvd. follows the same schedule. Admission is free to both.
- Astro World, 9001 Kirby Dr. Telephone: 779-1234. An amusement park with rides like the Sky Screamer and LR8, Water World—a recreation park with lots of water games for anyone who wants to cool off, and the Southern Star Amphitheater (for ticket info, call 795-0395).
- If you're lucky enough to be in Houston at the end of March you'll be able to enjoy the Houston Festival, a celebration of the city that goes on all around town.

At Night: Paradise Island Club, 4705 Main St. Open until 2 a.m. Tuesday through Sunday. This is a smoky and usually loud spot where you can hear progressive jazz and rock 'n' roll, but probably not each other.

- Comedy Workshop, San Felipe at South Shepherd. Every night, for a $3 cover, you can see a comedy revue. Next door, at the Comic's Club Annex, you can hear stand-up comics. Call 524-7333.
- Todd's, 5050 Richmond. Nice dance-floor bar with free buffet from 6 p.m. to 9:30 p.m.
- Gilley's Club, 4500 Spencer Hwy. "A real honky-tonk immortalized by the film *Urban Cowboy.*"
- Corky's, 623 Hawthorne. A converted old wood-frame house where you can hear jazz from 6 p.m. to 2 a.m.
- Rockefeller's, 3620 Washington Ave. The place to see the stars of the jazz world, like Ramsey Lewis and Dave Brubeck. In a beautifully restored building about five minutes from downtown.
- Cooter's, 5164 Richmond. The crowd comes to dance, eat, drink, and meet others. Reputed to have the longest happy hour in Houston—from 3 to 9 p.m. every Monday through Friday. "A vibrant, warm club for eating, dancing, and socializing."
- Vagabond Club, 4815 North Freeway. Nonstop music that's mostly country and western.
- Jones Hall, 615 Louisiana. Telephone: 224-4240. Where the Houston Symphony performs and the Society for the Performing Arts presents ballet.
- Paraden Bar & Grill, 401 McGowen. A casual place to hear jazz and relax.

Shopping: Anything you could possibly desire should be somewhere in the Galleria Shopping Center, 5015 Westheimer Rd., which is becoming a tourist attraction in itself. The complex is covered, so you'll never know what the weather is like outside, and inside you can eat a Big Mac, go to a movie, or look at Gucci's latest.

- Books: B. Dalton Booksellers. All over Houston (and just about every other American city as well). Huge selections of popular books.
- Records: Sound Warehouse, 6520 Westheimer Rd., and Soundwaves, 9150 South Main.
- Camping equipment: Academy, 2030 Westheimer Rd.
- Gifts: Trading Fair II, 5515 South Loop E., and the Market Place, 10900 Old Katy Rd. Both markets with all kinds of merchandise to tempt you.

Huntsville

Accommodation: Motel 6, 1607 I-45, 77340. Telephone: 409/295-6666. See Abilene listing for rates.

Irving

Accommodation: Allstar Inn, 510 South Loop 12, 75060. Telephone: 214/445-1151. See Amarillo listing for rates.

Kerrville

Accommodation: Friendship Inn Del Norte, I-10 to Hwy. 27 W., 78028. Telephone: 512/257-6112. $25 to $32 for one; $28 to $40 for two in one bed; $30 to $45 for two in two beds.

Killeen

Accommodation: Red Carpet Inn, √, P.O. Box 149, 605 North Gray St., 76540. Telephone: 817/634-3151. $24 for one; $30 for two.

Kingsville

Accommodation: Motel 6, 101 North U.S. 77 Bypass, 78363. Telephone: 512/592-6897. See Abilene listing for rates.

Laredo

Accommodation: Motel 6, 5310 San Bernardo Ave., 78041. Telephone: 512/722-4666. See Abilene listing for rates.

Longview

Accommodations: YMCA, 1230 South High St., 75602. Telephone: 214/758-7323. Men only. $9 single. Weekly rate: $50. Monthly: $165. There are several restaurants nearby offering inexpensive meals. "This is a modern, $2½-million, air-conditioned building." One mile from bus and train stations.

● TraveLodge, √, 1507 East Marshall Ave., 75601. Telephone: 214/758-3303. $25 for one; $28 for two in one bed; $30 for two in two beds.

● Motel 6, 110 West Access Rd., 75603. Telephone: 214/753-1631. See Abilene listing for rates.

● Imperial 400 Motor Inn, √, 1019 East Marshall St., 75601. Telephone: 214/753-0276. $20 to $24 for one; $22 to $26 for two in one bed; $24 to $28 for two in two beds.

Lubbock

On Campus: People from Texas Tech University congregate at Fat Dawg's, 2408 4th St., or J. Patrick O'Malley's, 1211 University. When they're hungry they go to Gardski's Loft, 2009 Broadway, for great hamburgers, or Mesquite's, 2409 Broadway.

Accommodation: Motel 6, 909 66th St., 79413. Telephone: 806/745-6666. See Abilene listing for rates.

Lufkin

Accommodation: Motel 6, 1110 South Timberland, 75901. Telephone: 409/637-6585. See Abilene listing for rates.

Marshall

Accommodation: Motel 6, Rte. 1, I-20 & U.S. 59, 75670. Telephone: 214/935-2692. See Abilene listing for rates.

McAllen

Accommodations: Motel 6, 700 U.S. 83 Expressway, 78501. Telephone: 512/682-1071. See Abilene listing for rates.
- Friendship Inn Pen-Ann Motor Hotel, 1007 West Bus. 83, Pharr, 78577. Telephone: 512/787-3267. Limited airport service available. $22 to $24 for one; $26 to $28 for two in one bed; $30 to $35 for two in two beds.
- Allstar Inn, 200 East Expressway 83, 78501. Telephone: 512/783-1123. See Amarillo listing for rates.
- Red Carpet Inn, √, Expressway 83 & Jackson Rd., 78501. Telephone: 512/787-5921. $21 to $26 for one; $24 to $30 for two in one bed; $24 to $32 for two in two beds.

Midland

Accommodation: Motel 6, 1000 South Midkiff, 79701. Telephone: 915/694-1655. See Abilene listing for rates.

North Richland Hills

Accommodation: Allstar Inn, 7804 Bedford Euless Rd., 76118. Telephone: 817/485-3000. See Amarillo listing for rates.

Odessa

Accommodations: Motel 6, 2925 East Hwy. 80, 79761. Telephone: 915/333-6666. See Abilene listing for rates.

- Motel 6, 200 East I-20 Service Rd., 79766. Telephone: 915/337-7250. See Abilene listing for rates.
- Scottish Inn, √, 2405 East 2nd St., 79761. $21 for one; $23 for two in one bed; $29 for two in two beds.

Orange

Accommodation: Motel 6, 4407 27th St., 77630. Telephone: 409/886-3111. See Abilene listing for rates.

Paris

Accommodations: Quality Inn, √, 2501 North Main St., 75460. Telephone: 214/784-2526. $23 to $26 for one; $27 to $30 for two.
- Comfort Inn, √ ♿, 3505 NE. Loop, 75460. Telephone: 214/784-7481. $27.95 for one; $29.95 for two.

Pecos

Accommodation: Motel 6, 3002 South Cedar, 79772. Telephone: 915/445-3666. See Abilene listing for rates.

Pittsburg

Accommodation: Scottish Inn, 611 Greer Blvd., 75686. Telephone: 214/856-6574. $20 for one; $25 for two.

Port Arthur

Accommodations: Imperial 400 Motor Inn, √ (10%), 2811 Memorial Blvd., 77640. Telephone: 409/985-9316. $26 to $30 for one; $29 to $33 for two in one bed; $31 to $35 for two in two beds.
- Master Host Inn/Driftwood Motor Hotel, 3700 Memorial Blvd., 77640. Telephone: 409/983-1633. $26.95 to $32 for one; $30.95 to $36 for two. Airport limo. Heated pool, outdoor Jacuzzi, and waterfalls.
- Motel 6, 5201 East Parkway, 77619. Telephone: 409/963-2028. See Abilene listing for rates.

Rockdale

Accommodation: Friendship Rockdale Inn, Hwys. 77 & 79, P.O. Box 507, 76567. Telephone: 512/446-6163. $28 to $32 for one; $32 to $36 for two in one bed; $36 to $40 for two in two beds.

San Angelo

Accommodation: Motel 6, 311 North Bryant, 76901. Telephone: 915/655-6666. See Abilene listing for rates.

San Antonio

"This is a beautiful and charming city."

Tourist Information: San Antonio Convention and Visitors Bureau, P.O. Box 2277, 121 Alamo Plaza, 78298. Telephone: 512/299-8123 (outside Texas, telephone toll free 800/531-5700).

Help: Help Line, 512/227-4357.

Accommodations: Friendship Siesta Inn, 4441 Fredericksburg Rd., 78201. Telephone: 512/733-7154. $27 to $29 for one; $31 to $33 for two in one bed; $32 to $34 for two in two beds.

● San Antonio International Hostel & Guest House (AYH), Ⓢ √ ★, 621 Pierce St., 78208. Telephone: 512/223-9426. $7 for AYH members, $9 for nonmembers in dorm-style accommodations. Rooms: $19 to $24 single, $19 to $28 double for AYH members; $21 to $27 single, $21 to $32 double for nonmembers; $7 for each additional person.

● Motel 6, 9503 I-35 N., 78233. Telephone: 512/653-7320. See Abilene listing for rates.

● Motel 6, 138 North W.W. White Rd., 78219. Telephone: 512/333-2330. See Abilene listing for rates.

● Allstar Inn, 5522 North Panam, 78218. Telephone: 512/661-8791. See Amarillo listing for rates.

● Regal 8 Inn, 4621 East Rittiman Rd., 78218. Telephone: 512/653-8088. $22.88 for one; $27.88 for two in one bed; $32.88 for two in two beds.

San Marcos

Accommodation: Motel 6, 1321 I-35 N., 78666. Telephone: 512/353-7787. See Abilene listing for rates.

Shamrock

Accommodation: Friendship Inn Western, 104 East 12th, 79079. Telephone: 806/256-3244. $22 to $26 for one or two in one bed; $28 to $35 for two in two beds.

Sherman

On Campus: Austin College is in Sherman. Sherman is a "dry" town but Denison nearby is "wet." You can meet students at the "Pouch Club"—it requires membership, although two guests are allowed and you could be one of them. "The Chefette" on West Houston has good, home-style cooking to satisfy your hunger pangs.

Snyder

Accommodations: Friendship Purple Sage Inn, East Hwy. 180 (Bus. 84), Rte. 2, Box 201, 79549. Telephone: 915/573-5491. $24 to $32 for one; $27 to $35 for two in one bed; $29 to $37 for two in two beds.

● TraveLodge, √, 1006 25th St., 79549. Telephone: 915/573-9395. Airport transportation available. $28 for one; $32 for two in one bed; $37 for two in two beds.

Sweetwater

Accommodation: Motel 6, 510 NW. Georgia, 79556. Telephone: 915/235-3278. See Abilene listing for rates.

Temple

Accommodations: Motel 6, 1100 North General Bruce Dr., 76501. Telephone: 817/773-1766. See Abilene listing for rates.

● Econo Lodge, √, 1001 North General Bruce Dr., 76501. Telephone: 817/771-2234. $24 for one; $27 for two in one bed; $30 for two in two beds.

Texarkana

Accommodation: Motel 6, 1924 Hampton Rd., 75503. Telephone: 214/792-7666. See Abilene listing for rates.

Tyler

Accommodation: Motel 6, 3236 Brady Gentry Pkwy., 75702. Telephone: 214/595-2222. See Abilene listing for rates.

Victoria

Accommodation: Motel 6, 3716 Houston Hwy., 77901. Telephone: 512/578-6351. See Abilene listing for rates.

Van Horn

Accommodations: Regal 8 Inn, Broadway St., P.O. Box 867, 79855. Telephone: 915/283-2992. $25 to $29 for one or two in one bed; $28 to $34 for two in two beds.

● Friendship Regal Inn, Broadway St., 79855. Telephone: 915/283-2992. $25 to $29 for one; $28 to $34 for two.

● Quality Inn, √ ♿, I-10 & 80 East Hwy., 79855. $25 to $28 for one; $32 to $35 for two.

Waco

Accommodation: Motel 6, 1509 Hogan Lane, Bellmead, 76705. Telephone: 817/799-8552. See Abilene listing for rates.

Weslaco

Accommodation: Vali-Ho Motel, 2100 East Bus. 83, 78596. Telephone: 512/968-2173. $26 to $28 for one or two in one bed; $28 to $35 for two in two beds; $30 to $42 triple; $37 to $42 quad.

Wichita Falls

Accommodation: Motel 6, 1812 Maurine St., 76305. Telephone: 817/723-6666. See Abilene listing for rates.

Wildorado

Accommodation: Budget Host—Texan Motel, ∨, Main St., 79098. Telephone: 806/426-3315. $19 for one; $21 for two in one bed; $24 for two in two beds.

Utah

Brigham Young and his Mormon followers are the ones to thank for Utah. Brigham Young took one look, said "This is the place," and founded Salt Lake City in 1847. The Mormons have been behind just about everything that goes on in Salt Lake City, and therefore the rest of Utah, ever since.

What to see in Utah? In Salt Lake City: Mormon Temple Square, Beehive House (where Brigham Young lived with several of his wives), Trolley Square, Kennecott Copper Mine, Pioneer Trail State Park, Hogle Zoo, and Capitol Hill. Not to be missed, too, are the natural wonders of the state: Arches National Park, Bryce Canyon National Park ("a helluva place to lose a cow" is what one of the first settlers is reputed to have said of these beautiful badlands), Canyonlands National Park, Capitol Reef National Park, and Zion National Park. Flaming Gorge and Glen Canyon National Recreation Area offer boating, fishing, and camping facilities. The Great Salt Lake, 70 miles long and 30 miles wide, is what is left of a lake that was once ten times that size. If you take a dip, you'll bob like a cork.

Some Special Events: Re-enactment of the driving of the Golden Spike at Promontory Point (May); Utah Arts Festival in Salt Lake City (June); Utah Shakespearean Festival in Cedar City (July to mid-August); Festival of the American West in Logan (August); Swiss Days in Midway, Tomato Days in Hooper, and Melon Days in Green River (September); Oktoberfest at Snowbird (October); and the Annual Lighting of Temple Square in Salt Lake City (November).

Hitching: When we asked someone at Brigham Young about the general attitude toward people on the road in his area, he said they thought of it as a "very good learning experience if with good supervision." It seems that their idea of "on the road" is a bit different from ours. Legally, hitching is prohibited from the roadway or the shoulder of the highway. A trooper in the Utah Highway Patrol said simply, "Please do not hitchhike."

Tourist Information: Utah Travel Council, Council Hall, Capitol Hill, Salt Lake City, UT 84114.

Beaver

Accommodation: TraveLodge, √ ⑤, 6 North Main St., 84713. Telephone: 801/438-2409. $29 for one; $34 for two in one bed; $38 for two in two beds.

Bryce Canyon

Camping: Bryce Canyon National Park, 84717. Telephone: 801/834-5322. Two campgrounds. North open year-round; Sunset open June 1 to Labor Day. The exact season depends on the weather. Horseback riding. $5 per campsite per night.

Cedar City

Accommodations: Friendship Cedar City Inn, 2555 North Hwy. 91, 84720. Telephone: 801/586-7435. $29.50 for one; $34 for two in one bed; $36 for two in two beds.
- Imperial 400 Motor Inn, √ (10%), 344 South Main St., 84720. Telephone: 801/586-9416. $29 to $34 for one; $32 to $38 for two in one bed; $34 to $42 for two in two beds. Heated pool.

Fillmore

Accommodation: Friendship Inn Fillmore, 61 North Main St., 84631. Telephone: 801/743-5454. $19 for one; $21 for two in one bed; $28 for two in two beds.

Green River

Accommodations: Friendship Green River Motel, West City Limits on U.S. 6-50 & I-70, 84525. Telephone: 801/564-3234. $20 to $26 for one; $24 to $30 for two in one bed; $30 to $38 for two in two beds.
- Motel 6, 946 East Main, 84525. Telephone: 801/564-3266. $17.95 for one; $21.95 for two; $2 for each additional person.

Heber

Accommodations: Friendship Inn Hy-Lander Motel and Restaurant, 425 South Main St., 84032. Telephone: 801/654-2150. Limited airport service available. $20 to $26 for one; $28 to $32 for two in one bed; $30 to $34 for two in two beds.
- Budget Host—Green Acres Lodge, √, 989 South Main St., 84032. Telephone: 801/654-2202. Limited airport service available. $20 to $38 for one; $22 to $38 for two in one bed; $24 to $44 for two in two beds. Heated pool and Jacuzzi.

Kanab

Accommodation: Budget Host—K Motel, 330 South 100 East, P.O. Box 1306, 84741. Telephone: 801/644-2611. $22 for one; $24 to $26 for two in one bed; $26 to $30 for two in two beds. Courtesy car.

Logan

Accommodation: Friendship Sand Piper Inn, 364 South Main, 84321. Telephone: 801/753-5623. $23 to $27 for one; $26 to $28 for two in one bed; $30 to $34 for two in two beds.

Mexican Hat

Accommodation: Friendship San Juan Inn, U.S. 163 & the San Juan River, 84531. Telephone: 801/683-2220. Limited airport service available. $25 to $28 for one; $28 to $31 for two in one bed; $31 to $33 for two in two beds.

Moab

Camping: Canyonlands National Park, 84532. Campground at Squaw Flat and Willow Flat. Open all year. No water at Willow Flat.
● Arches National Monument, c/o Canyonlands National Park, 84532. Campground at Devil's Garden (18 miles north of Visitor Center). Open March to October. $4 per campsite per night. Free during the rest of the year, but there is no water. No wood or wood collecting.
● Natural Bridges National Monument, c/o Canyonlands National Park, 84532. Campground with 14 sites (four miles off Utah 95). No water. Entrance fee of $1.
Accommodations: Friendship Inn Apache Motel, 166 South 400 E., 84532. Telephone: 801/259-5727. $23 to $29 for one; $26 to $33 for two in one bed; $28 to $35 for two in two beds.
● Friendship Landmark Inn, 168 North Main, Hwy. 163, center of town, 84532. Telephone: 801/259-6147. $28 to $44 for one; $32 to $48 for two in one bed; $36 to $52 for two in two beds.

Monticello

Accommodation: Friendship Inn Canyonlands Motor Lodge, 389 North Main St., Hwy. 63 on 197 North Main, 84535. Telephone: 801/587-2266. Limited airport service available. $22 to $28 for one; $25 to $30 for two in one bed; $32 to $45 for two in two beds.

Nephi

Accommodation: Friendship Inn Safari, 413 South Main St. on Hwys. 15 & 89, 84638. Telephone: 801/623-1071. $16 to $28 for one; $20 to $32 for two in one bed; $26 to $34 for two in two beds.

Ogden

Accommodations: Budget Host—Millstream Motel, √ ♿, 1450 Washington Blvd., 84404. Telephone: 801/394-9425. Limited courtesy car transportation available. $24 for one; $26 for two in one bed; $28 to $32 for two in two beds.

● Motel 6, 1455 Washington Blvd., 84404. Telephone: 801/399-9261. See Green River listing for rates.

● TraveLodge, √, 2110 Washington Blvd., 84401. Telephone: 801/394-4563. $30 for one; $34 for two in one bed; $38 for two in two beds.

Panguitch

Accommodation: Friendship Inn Sands Motel, 390 North Main St., 84759. Telephone: 801/676-8874. May 1 to September 30: $26 for one; $30 to $32 for two in one bed; $34 to $40 for two in two beds. October 1 to April 30: $20 for one; $22 to $24 for two in one bed; $26 to $28 for two in two beds.

Price

Accommodation: Friendship Inn Crest, 625 East Main St., 84501. Telephone: 801/637-1532. Limited airport service available. October 1 to May 31: $21 to $30 for one; $25 to $34 for two in one bed; $30 to $38 for two in two beds. June 1 to September 30: $25 to $33 for one; $29 to $37 for two in one bed; $33 to $41 for two in two beds.

Provo

On Campus: According to one student at Brigham Young University here, "This is a beautiful, clean college community close to the mountains, lakes, and big cities." While in the area, consider breakfast at Annie's Pantry, 150 South University (famous for scones); or lunch or dinner at the Brick Oven, 150 East 800 N.; The Underground (steak and sea food), North University Ave.; Grand View Café (Chinese food), 66 North 500 W.; Jimba's (burgers), 278 West Center; The Sensuous Sandwiche, 300 West Center; Los Hermanos (Mexican), 10 West Center; La France (French, of course), 463 North University Ave.; Bamboo Hut (Hawaiian), right next to Provo High on University.

The *Daily Universe* is the campus newspaper; ASBYU hotline is 378-3283. In the Wilkinson Center at the University, you'll find a ride/apartment board.

Accommodations: Motel 6, 1600 South University Dr., 84601. Telephone: 801/377-4666. See Green River listing for rates.

● Friendship City Center Motor Inn, 150 West 300 South St., 84601. Telephone: 801/373-8489. $24 to $26 for one; $26 to $28.90 for two in one bed; $29 to $32 for two in two beds.

● Friendship Inn Uptown Motel, 469 West Center St., 84601. Telephone: 801/373-8248. $19 to $22 for one; $20 to $26 for two in one bed; $24 to $30 for two in two beds.

● Budget Host—University Western Inn, √ (10%), 40 West 300 S., 84601. Telephone: 801/373-0660. $23 to $25 for one; $25 to $29 for two in one bed; $27 to $32 for two in two beds. Heated pool.

● TraveLodge, √ 🅖, 124 South University Ave., 84601. Telephone: 801/ 373-1974. May 15 to June 15: $28 for one; $31 for two in one bed; $34 for two in two beds. June 16 to September 10: $28 for one; $33 for two in one bed; $35 for two in two beds.

Richfield

Accommodation: Friendship Inn Topsfield Lodge, 1200 South Main, P.O. Box 556, 84701. Telephone: 801/896-5437. Limited airport service available. $23.50 for one or two in one bed; $25 to $30.50 for two in two beds.

St. George

Accommodations: Motel 6, 205 North 1000 East St., 84770. Telephone: 801/673-6666. See Green River listing for rates.

● Friendship Sands Motel, 581 East St. George Blvd., 84770. Telephone: 801/673-3501. $22 for one; $24 for two in one bed; $26 for two in two beds.

● TraveLodge, √, 175 North 1000 East St., 84770. Telephone: 801/673-4621. Airport transportation available. $28 for one; $33 for two in one bed; $37 for two in two beds.

● TraveLodge, √ 🅖, 60 West St. George Blvd., 84770. Telephone: 801/ 673-4666. Airport service available. $29 for one; $34 for two in one bed; $39 for two in two beds. Therapy pool and sauna.

Salt Lake City

Tourist Information: Salt Lake Valley Convention and Visitors Bureau, 180 South West Temple, 84101. Telephone: 801/521-2822. According to someone at the tourist office: "Salt Lake is a friendly, clean city."

On Campus: Year-round, you might be able to stay for $10 a night at the University of Utah campus. Contact Residential Living at Van Cott, Room S114D (tel. 801/581-5348). While you're there, you can have a reasonable meal at the Union Cafeteria in the student union, where there is also a ride board. Off-campus housing listings are available at the same address.

Accommodations: Avenues Residential Center (AYH-SA), 107 F St., 84103. Telephone: 801/363-8137. $8.25 for AYH members. Advance reservations suggested December 1 to May 1 and 1st week of October.

● Carlton Hotel, Ⓢ √ 🅖 ★, 140 East South Temple St., 84111. Telephone: 801/355-3418. Just 1½ blocks from bus station; 2½ blocks from train station. $27 single; $32 twin; $36 triple; $40 quad. "Older hotel, completely renovated, very clean and personable."

● Imperial 400 Motor Inn, √ (10%), 476 South State St., 84111. Telephone: 801/533-9300. $31 to $35 for one; $37 to $41 for two in one bed; $38 to $44 for two in two beds.

● Motel 6, 176 West 6th South St., 84101. Telephone: 801/521-3280. See Green River listing for rates.

- Motel 6, 1990 West North Temple St., 84116. Telephone: 801/322-3061. See Green River listing for rates.
- Motel 6, 496 North Catalpa, 84047. Telephone: 801/255-2204. See Green River listing for rates.
- Thrifty Scot Motel, 1900 West North Temple, 84116. Telephone: 801/539-8538. $26.90 to $31.90 for one; $31.90 to $36.90 for two.

Springdale

Camping: Zion National Park, one mile north of Springdale on S.R. 9, 84767. Telephone: 801/772-3256. Three campgrounds: Watchman, open year-round; South, open April 15 to September 15. $5 per campsite per night for up to seven people. Lava Point is an undeveloped campground located 37 miles from the Park Visitor Center with six campsites available at no charge.

Vernal

Accommodation: Econo Lodge, ∨, 311 East Main St., 84078. Telephone: 801/789-2000. $24.95 to $29.95 for one; $28.95 to $34.95 for two in one bed; $32.95 to $39.95 for two in two beds.

Wendover

Accommodation: Motel 6, 545 State Hwy., P.O. Box 190, 84083. Telephone: 801/665-2848. See Green River listing for rates.

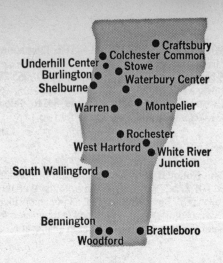

Vermont

Known as the "Green Mountain State," Vermont has tried zealously and successfully to protect its natural beauty. Some would say it's the most attractive state east of the Mississippi.

Vermont is a state of small, picturesque villages. Its largest city, Burlington, has fewer than 50,000 inhabitants. Its geography is characterized by a pleasant mix of mountain and valley, unmarked by intrusive billboards and commercial advertising. Its Long Trail is a mountain footpath extending the length of the state with free shelters every 10 to 20 kilometers.

As the state in which the United States' first ski tow was installed (in 1934), it has long been a leader in the field of winter sports. It has more than 20 major downhill ski areas and more than 50 cross-country ski touring centers. Ski-country accommodations range from austere dormitories to luxurious condominiums.

In summer, many of the ski areas are available for hiking, swimming, and mountain climbing, and there are numerous opportunities for water sports on the many lakes that dot the state. Besides physical beauty, the state offers a great deal in the way of cultural attractions: summer theaters, music festivals (the one at Marlboro is the best known), outstanding language schools at Middlebury College and the School for International Training, and a host of arts and crafts fairs.

The most popular time of the year for tourists to visit Vermont is in late September and early October, when fall weather turns the green of the mountains into an unbelievably colorful splash of red, orange, and yellow. But if you were to consult with the residents, you'd be told that late spring is equally colorful, when the apple blossoms turn the hillsides pink.

Because of its rather rugged winter climate, Vermont's people tend to be independent individualists. It is one of the few states that was once a republic; the founding fathers refused to join the original 13 colonies until it was proven that the experiment in federal government wasn't designed to concentrate too much power in one person. Life in Vermont today is an echo of those early days —the state is warmly hospitable to new ideas, to experimentalists, to people seeking freedom from urban pressures.

Chris Tree's book, *Vermont: An Explorer's Guide,* published by Country-man Press, is highly recommended for newcomers.

Some Special Events: Winter Carnival in Stowe, and Ice Harvest in Brook-field (January); Sled Dog Races in the Mad River Valley in Waitsfield (February); March Madness in Warren (March); Maple Festival in St. Allars, and Maple Sugar Festival in St. Johnsbury (April); Balloon Festival in Quechee, and Strawberry Festival in East Montpelier (June); State Championship Old Time Paddlers' Contest in Bellows Falls, and Aquafest in Newport (July); Antique and Classic Car Rally in Stowe (August); and Arts Festival in Stratton (September).

Hitching: The law prohibits hitchhiking from the "roadway" and on the Interstate system, and the Department of Public Safety suggests you "confine hitchhiking to the daylight hours. Many sections of Vermont's roads are remote and uninhabited; therefore, they may be dangerous from the standpoint of traffic safety and personal security." Young people hitchhike quite often; many who are at colleges in Vermont have no other choice since extensive public transportation isn't available, and unless they have their own wheels they have to hitch rides with others.

Tourist Information: Vermont Travel Division, 134 State St., Montpelier, VT 05602.

Bennington

On Campus: Bennington College is in this historic town in southwestern Vermont with its famous battlefield and monument. We're told that the attitude toward young people on the road is "generally helpful, although there is a New England reserve." There are numerous family-run restaurants in the area where travelers can get an inexpensive meal—two possibilities are Northside Diner and Geannelis Restaurant. A good place to meet young people is the Villager in North Bennington.

Brattleboro

Help: Hotline for Help, 17 Elliot St., 05301. Telephone: 802/257-7989. General counseling and referrals. They suggested the Latchis Hotel on South Main St., which is run-down but inexpensive, or the Holly Motel. Call them and they'll be happy to provide you with any information they can. Some places to go to meet local people are Common Ground Restaurant, Mole's Eye, Via Condotti, and the Tavern.

Accommodation: Susse Chalet Motor Lodge, I-91 (Exit 3) on Rte. 5 N., 05301. Telephone: 802/254-6007. $27.70 for one; $31.70 for two; $34.70 for three; $37.70 for four.

Burlington

On Campus: During the school year you'll find a high concentration of students at the Billings Student Center at the University of Vermont. While you're there you can pick up a copy of the student newspaper, the *Vermont Cynic,* to find out what's going on on campus and around town. Some of the favorite student haunts downtown include B. T. McGuire's on Church St., Minerva's, and Finbar's on Main St. For a reasonably priced meal try Carbur's for a sandwich (they have a 25-page sandwich menu so be sure to have plenty of time for reading), 119 St. Paul St., or Déjà Vu on Pearl St., a popular student hangout at night. For good, inexpensive Italian food, there's Filomenas Pizza on Riverside Rd. For great ice cream, it's Ben and Jerry's Homemade at 107 St. Paul St. If you'd rather be outdoors, take a ferry ride across Lake Champlain at sunset or hike on the Long Trail of the Green Mountains.

Colchester

Accommodation: Mrs. Farrell's Youth Hostel (AYH), Williams Rd., RD 4, 05446. Telephone: 802/878-8222. $4.50 for AYH members. Advance reservations necessary.

Craftsbury Common

Accommodation: The Craftsbury Center Hostel (AYH-SA), ⑤ (10% for nonmembers), P.O. Box 31, 05827. Telephone: 802/586-2514. $7 summer, $8 winter for AYH members. $14 for nonmembers with sleeping bags. Meals available at extra cost. Cross-country ski-touring center in the winter. "Longest snow season in New England."

Montpelier

Accommodation: Capitol Home Hostel (AYH), Box 2750, 05602. Telephone: 802/223-2104. $6 for AYH members. Advance reservations necessary.

Rochester

Accommodations: Schoolhouse Youth Hostel (AYH), ★ ($1), South Main St., 05767. Telephone: 802/767-9384. Open year-round except April 15 to May 15. $5 summer, $7 winter for AYH members, plus $1 linen charge. The hostel was built in 1827 as a church, was converted to a gym and school in 1940, and became a hostel in 1963. Near Killington and Sugarbush ski areas and adjacent to the Glen Mt. National Forest.
● The New Homestead, South Main St., 05767. Telephone: 802/767-4751. Open year round—as a ski lodge only during winter. $16 per person, double. Price includes breakfast and linens. Advance reservations necessary.

Shelburne

Accommodation: Econo Lodge, Rte. 7, Shelburne Rd., 05482. Telephone: 802/985-3334. April 1 to June 27: $22.95 to $29.95 for one; $24.95 to $32.95 for two in one bed; $26.95 to $35.95 for two in two beds. September 13 to 30: $39.95 for one; $42.95 for two in one bed; $45.95 for two in two beds. Higher rates apply during special events.

South Wallingford

Accommodation: Green Mountain Tea Room and Guest House, Rte. 7, 05773. Telephone: 802/446-2611. Vermont Transit and Greyhound buses stop in front of Tea Room. $12 to $16 single; $18 to $22 double. Breakfast and luncheon served at reasonable prices, "and afternoon tea is most definitely served. We have 15 varieties." An old colonial house dating from 1797.

Stowe

Accommodation: Vermont State Ski Dorm (AYH), RD 1, Box 2030, 05672. Telephone: 802/253-4010 or 253-4014. Open November 15 to April 30 and June 15 to September 30. Operates as a ski lodge only during winter. $5.30 summer, $21 winter (winter rate includes two meals) for AYH members.

Underhill Center

Accommodation: Underhill Center Youth Hostel (AYH), Box 148, West Bolton Rd., 05490. Telephone: 802/899-2375. Open May 1 to October 1. $6 for AYH members. No cars or buses allowed at hostel; parking one-half mile away.

Warren

Accommodation: Old Homestead, Ⓢ √ ★, P.O. Box 118, 05674. Telephone: 802/496-3744. Open year-round. $20 single; $30 double; $45 triple; $60 quad. Advance reservations preferred.

Waterbury Center

Accommodation: Ski Hostel Lodge Youth Hostel (AYH), P.O. Box 58, 05677. Open April 15 to November 15. Skiing at Mt. Mansfield six miles away. $6.25 for AYH members. Advance reservations suggested.

West Hartford

Accommodation: Clifford's Guest Home, Pomfret Rd., 05084. Telephone: 802/295-3554. $12.72 per person, including breakfast. "A very lovely old farmhouse—pleasant rooms, comfortable, and clean."

White River Junction

Accommodation: Susse Chalet Motor Lodge, jct. of I-91, I-89 on Rte. 5. Telephone: 802/295-3051, or toll free 800/259-3051. $29.70 for one; $32.70 for two; $36.70 for three; $39.70 for four.

Woodford

Accommodation and Camping: Greenwood Lodge (AYH), Rte. 9, 05201 (mailing address in July and August: P.O. Box 246, Bennington, 05201; off-season: Ed and Ann Shea, 197 Lyons Rd., Scarsdale, NY 10583; tel. 914/472-2575). Telephone: 802/442-2547. Open July through Labor Day and fall foliage weekends. $9 per person in dorms; $19 double plus $5 for each additional person; $13 per person on fall foliage weekends. Tent sites summer and fall foliage weekends: $6 per person; $8 for two; $1.50 for each additional person to six per site. Recreational facilities on premises. Eight miles from Bennington; three miles from Appalachian and Long Trail hiking. Advance reservations necessary.

Virginia

Northern Virginia is physically and philosophically the gateway to the South. The state is rich with the echoes of history; Jamestown was the site of the first English settlement in North America, in 1607; a Virginian, Richard Henry Lee, introduced the motion to separate the 13 colonies from England in 1776; Thomas Jefferson was the guiding hand behind the Declaration of Independence; and no one has to be reminded that George Washington was from this state as well. Much of the agony of the Civil War took place in Virginia: it was at Appomattox that Robert E. Lee surrendered in 1865. To get a sense of Virginia's history—and the history of the entire U.S., in fact—you should plan a visit to Williamsburg, the beautifully reconstructed capital of 18th-century Virginia, George Washington's residence in Mount Vernon, Jefferson's Monticello in Charlottesville, and Yorktown, where the American Revolution ended with the British soldiers marching out to the tune of "The World Turned Upside Down." Somewhat less well known but still worth a visit are the Art Museum in Richmond, with its fine collection of Fabergé jewelry made for Russia's last czar, and the Mariners' Museum in Newport News.

For the people who like the out-of-doors, Virginia has lots of excellent camping. Shenandoah National Park and the Blue Ridge Parkway (see listing under Asheville, NC) stretch from western Virginia through to North Carolina and present campers with some exquisite spots to spend a night or two. The Skyline Drive, which winds through Shenandoah National Park, is a spectacular 105 miles of overlooks and trails that are a treat for city-worn tourists.

Virginia Beach, 28 miles of shoreline from Cape Henry to Virginia's Outer Banks, is a popular fair-weather retreat. And for the curious, there's Tangier Island in Chesapeake Bay, an unspoiled spot where some of the natives still speak "old English" and work as fishermen; there's a boat that connects the mainland with the island from Reedville, Virginia, at certain times of the year and from Crisfield, Maryland, all year.

Three books we recommend are *The Insider's Guide: Williamsburg, Virginia Beach, Norfolk, Hampton, and Yorklawn*, published by Insider's Publishing Group; *A Complete Traveler's Touring Guide: Virginia*, by George Scheer III, published by Burt Franklin and Co.; and *The Great Weekend Escape Book: From Williamsburg to Catly Hunk Island*, by Michael Spring, published by E.P. Dutton.

Some Special Events: Colonial Weekends in Williamsburg (January and February); Dogwood Festival in Charlottesville (April); Salt Water Fishing Tournament at Virginia Beach (May); Potomac River Festival at Colonial Beach (June); Wild Pony Round-up in Chincoteague (July); Old Fiddler's Contest in Galax, and East Coast Surfing Championships at Virginia Beach (August); State Fair in Richmond (September); and Oyster Festival in Chincoteague (October).

Hitching: Virginia is one of those states that does have laws prohibiting hitchhiking except on the Interstate System or controlled-access highways. Our campus friends from all over Virginia and the State Police don't recommend hitchhiking, though.

Tourist Information: Virginia State Travel Service, 9th St. Office Bldg., Richmond, VA 23219.

Alexandria

Accommodation: YMCA, 420 East Monroe Ave., 22301. Telephone: 703/549-0850. Six blocks from train station. Men, women, and children. $18 single; $20 double; $24 twin; $28 quad. Weekly rate: $108. Advance reservations of two months necessary.

Ashland

Accommodation: Econo Lodge, √ ⑤, I-95 & Rte. 54 jct., P.O. Box 308, 23005. Telephone: 804/798-9221. $23.95 to $30.95 for one; $27.95 to $35.95 for two in one bed; $31.95 to $40.95 for two in two beds. Higher rates apply during special events.

Blacksburg

On Campus: Virginia Polytechnic Institute is in Blacksburg—"a university town on a plateau between the Blue Ridge and the Appalachian Mountains." To eat inexpensively, go to Squires Student Center and have their buffet lunch for $3. At the University Mall, try the Chinese food at Hunan and don't leave without trying Gillie's Ice Cream. When you're in Blacksburg consider a tube ride down the New River, a hike to Cascades, a swim in Clayton Lake, or a car trip to Mabry Hill on the Blue Ridge Parkway.

Accommodation: Econo Lodge, √, 3333 South Main St., 24060. Telephone: 703/951-4242. $27.95 for one; $30.95 for two in one bed; $33.95 for two in two beds. Higher rates apply during special events.

Bluemont

Accommodation: Bears Den (AYH), Rte. 1, Box 288, 22012. Telephone: 703/554-8708. $6 summer, $7 winter for AYH members.

Bristol

Accommodations: Econo Lodge, √, 912 Commonwealth Ave., 24201. Telephone:: 703/466-2112. $21.95 to $23.95 for one; $25.95 to $27.95 for two in one bed; $29.95 to $31.95 for two in two beds. Higher rates apply during special events.
● Scottish Inn, √, 4795 Lee Hwy., 24201. Telephone: 703/669-4148. $20 to $24 for one; $24 to $26 for two in one bed; $28 to $32 for two in two beds.

Buchanan

Accommodation: Historic Hotel Botetourt on the James (AYH-SA), Lowe St. at Washington, 24066. Telephone: 703/254-1492. $8 summer, $7 winter for AYH members. Advance reservations necessary.

Carmel Church

Accommodation: Days Inn, I-95 & Va. 207, Carmel Church Rd., P.O. Box 70, Ruther Glen, 22546. Telephone: 804/448-2011. $28 to $36 for one; $32 to $40 for two.

Charlottesville

Accommodations: Econo Lodge, √, 2014 Holiday Dr., 22901. Telephone: 804/295-3185. $28.95 for one; $33.95 for two in one bed; $37.95 for two in two beds.
● Econo Lodge, √, 400 Emmet St., 22903. Telephone: 804/296-2104. $29.50 for one; $34.95 for two in one bed; $38.95 for two in two beds.

Chesapeake

Accommodations: Econo Lodge, √, 3244 Western Branch Blvd. (Rte. 17), 23321. Telephone: 804/484-6143. $29.95 for one; $32.95 for two in one bed; $35.95 for two in two beds.
● Econo Lodge, √, 4725 West Military Hwy., 23321. Telephone: 804/488-4963. $24.95 for one; $28.95 for two in one bed; $30.95 for two in two beds.

Chester

Accommodation: Days Inn, I-95 & Va. 10 (Exit 6 W.), P.O. Box AN, 23831. Telephone: 804/748-5871. $28 to $36 for one; $33 to $41 for two; $34 to $40 for single lodge; $39 to $45 for double lodge.

Christiansburg

Accommodations: Econo Lodge, ✓, 2430 Roanoke St. SE, 24073. Telephone: 703/382-6161. $23.95 for one; $27.95 for two in one bed; $31.95 for two in two beds. Higher rates apply during special events.

● Days Inn, [&], I-81 & U.S. 11 (Exit 37), P.O. Box 768, 24073. Telephone: 703/382-0261. $30 for one; $34 for two.

Culpeper

Accommodation: Econo Lodge, ✓, U.S. 15 & U.S. 29 Bypass, P.O. Box 407, 22701. Telephone: 703/825-5097. $29.95 for one; $33.95 for two in one bed; $35.95 for two in two beds. Higher rates apply during special events.

Emporia

Accommodations: Days Inn, I-95 & U.S. 58, Exit 58 W., 23847. Telephone: 804/634-9481. $29 to $35 for one; $33 to $39 for two.

● Quality Inn, ✓ [&], I-95 & U.S. 301, Exit 6, Rte. 2, 23847. Telephone: 804/535-8535. $24 to $28 for one; $26 to $31 for two.

Fredericksburg

Accommodations: Econo Lodge, ✓ [&], I-95 & Rte. 3, P.O. Box 36, 22404. Telephone: 703/786-8374. $24.95 for one; $28.95 for two in one bed; $32.95 for two in two beds.

● Econo Lodge, ✓ [&], 5321 Jefferson Davis Hwy., 22401. Telephone: 703/898-5440. $25.95 to $29.95 for one; $28.95 to $32.95 for two in one bed; $30.95 to $34.95 for two in two beds.

● Scottish Inn, ✓, P.O. Box 3645, College Station, 22401. Telephone: 703/898-1000. $26.95 and up for one; $29.95 and up for two in one bed; $31.95 and up for two in two beds.

● Days Inn, Falmouth & Warrenton Exit, I-95 & U.S. 17 N., Rte. 12, Box 36, 22401. $29 to $33 for one; $34 to $38 for two.

Front Royal

Accommodations: Budget Host—Cool Harbor Motel, 15th & Shenandoah Ave., 22630. Telephone: 703/635-2191. $28 to $30 for one; $32 to $34 for two in one bed; $36 to $40 for two in two beds.

● Friendship Skyline Motel, 622 South Royal, 22630. Telephone: 703/636-6739. $18 to $22 for one; $24 to $28 for two in one bed; $28 to $32 for two in two beds.

Gloucester Point

Accommodation: Friendship Inn, George Washington Hwy. at York River

Bridge, 23061. Telephone: 804/642-3337. $22 to $30 for one; $24 to $32 for two in one bed; $26 to $36 for two in two beds.

Hampton

Accommodations: Red Roof Inn, 🦽, 1925 Coliseum Dr., 23666. Telephone: 804/838-1870. $25.95 for one; $30.95 for two in one bed; $32.95 for two in two beds; $34.95 for three or four in two beds.
● Econo Lodge, √, 1781 North King St., 23669. Telephone: 804/723-0741. $25.50 for one; $28.50 for two in one bed; $32.50 for two in two beds.
● Econo Lodge, √, 2708 Mercury Blvd., 23666. Telephone: 804/821-8976. $25.95 to $28.95 for one; $28.95 to $32.95 for two in one bed; $31.95 to $35.95 for two in two beds.

Harrisonburg

Accommodations: Econo Lodge, √, Rte. 33 & I-81, 22801. Telephone: 703/433-2576. $30.95 for one; $39.95 for two.
● Eastern Mennonite College Residence Hall, College Ave., 22801. Telephone: 703/433-2771, ext. 135. Open May 1 to August 17. $10 single; $16 double. Weekly rate: $70 single; $56 double. Advance reservations of two days necessary.
● Red Carpet Inn, Rte. 11 S., P.O. Box 631, 22801. Telephone: 703/434-6704. $28 to $32 for one; $32 to $42 for two.

Leesburg

Accommodation: Caldwell Home Hostel (AYH), Caldwell, 314 Shenandoah St., 22075. Telephone: 703/777-1234. $6 for AYH members. Advance reservations necessary. Call before coming.

Lexington

"This is a rural area, most of the people are farming or working in factories. There is a strong work ethic—Scottish-Irish Presbyterian roots; people don't relate too well to folks who don't settle down to work, raise crops and kids."

Accommodations: Econo Lodge, √, I-64 & U.S. 11, P.O. Box 1088, 24450. Telephone: 703/463-7371. $30.95 for one; $34.95 for two in one bed; $36.95 for two in two beds. Higher rates apply during special events.
● Days Inn, I-81 & U.S. 11 (Exit 53), Rte. 5, P.O. Box 1329, 24450. Telephone: 703/463-9131. $29 for one; $33 for two.

Luray

Camping: Shenandoah National Park, Rte. 4, Box 292, 22835. Telephone: 703/999-2243. There are four major campgrounds with a total of over 600 sites, plus backcountry camping. $7 per campsite per night. Big Meadows open March to December; others open from April or May to October. You can make reservations through Ticketron for Big Meadows. Luray Caverns are nearby.

Lynchburg

Accommodations: YWCA, 626 Church St., 24504. Telephone: 804/847-7751. Women only. $8.50 single; $7.50 per person, double. Advance reservations suggested.
● Econo Lodge, √, 2400 Stadium Rd., P.O. Box 2028, 24501. Telephone: 804/847-1045. $25.95 for one; $28.95 for two in one bed; $32.95 for two in two beds.

Martinsville

Accommodation: Econo Lodge, √, 800 South Virginia Ave., 24078. Telephone: 703/647-3941. $21.95 for one; $25.95 for two in one bed; $27.95 for two in two beds. Higher rates apply during special events.

Mt. Sidney

Accommodation: Augusta Motel, Rte. 11, 24467. Telephone: 703/248-8040. $22 for one; $25 to $27 for two; $3 for each additional person.

Newport News

Accommodations: Econo Lodge, √ 🔄, 11845 Jefferson Ave., 23606. Telephone: 804/599-3237. $26.95 for one; $30.95 for two in one bed; $32.95 for two in two beds.
● Friendship Inn Warwick Hotel and Restaurant, 12304 Warwick Blvd., 23606. Telephone: 804/599-4444. $22 to $30 for one; $24 to $34 for two in one bed; $26 to $36 for two in two beds.
● Friendship Fort Eustis, 16923 Warwick Blvd., 23606. Telephone: 804/887-9122. $22 to $30 for one; $24 to $34 for two in one bed; $26 to $36 for two in two beds.
● Econo Lodge, √, 12340 Warwick Blvd., 23606. Telephone: 804/599-6035. $27.95 to $31.95 for one; $30.95 to $34.95 for two in one bed; $32.95 to $37.95 for two in two beds. Higher rates apply during special events.

Norfolk

Tourist Information: Norfolk Convention and Visitors Bureau, Monticello Arcade, 23510. Telephone: 804/441-5266.
Help: Family Service/Travelers Aid, Inc., 222 19th St. W., 23517. Telephone: 804/622-7017.
Accommodations: YMCA, ★, 312 West Bute St., 23518. Telephone: 804/622-6328. Men and women. $19. Fitness center available.

● Econo Lodge, √, 5819 Northhampton Blvd., 23452. Telephone: 804/464-9306. $29.95 to $34.95 for one; $35.95 to $38.95 for two in one bed; $38.95 to $42.95 for two in two beds.

Petersburg

Accommodations: Econo Lodge, √, 25 South Crater Rd., 23803. Telephone: 804/861-4680. $24.95 for one; $28.95 for two in one bed; $31.95 for two in two beds.

● Econo Lodge, √, 16905 Parkdale Rd., 23805. Telephone: 804/862-2717. $26.95 for one; $30.95 for two in one bed; $33.95 for two in two beds.

● Days Inn, 2310 Indian Hill Rd., Colonial Heights, 23834. Telephone: 804/520-1010. $27 to $33 for one; $27.88 to $29.88 for two.

Richmond

"A beautiful city representing four centuries of legend, history, and tradition."

Help: Travelers Aid, 515 East Main St., 23219. Telephone: 804/648-1767 or 643-0270.

Accommodations: Massad's House Hotel, Ⓢ★, 11 North 4th St., 23219. Telephone: 804/648-2893. Near bus station. $25 single; $32 double; $35 triple; $40 quad.

● Days Inn, 5500 Williamsburg Rd., Sandston, 23150. Telephone: 804/222-2041. $30 to $36 for one; $34 to $40 for two.

● Econo Lodge, √, 5408 Williamsburg Rd., Sandston, 23150. Telephone: 804/222-1020. $26.95 to $28.95 for one; $30.95 to $32.95 for two in one bed; $32.95 to $35.95 for two in two beds.

● Econo Lodge, √, 6523 Midlothian Turnpike, 23225. Telephone: 804/276-8241. $25.95 to $28.95 for one; $29.95 to $32.95 for two in one bed; $32.95 to $35.95 for two in two beds.

● Econo Lodge, √, 2125 Willis Rd., 23237. Telephone: 804/271-6031. $27.95 for one; $31.95 for two in one bed; $33.95 for two in two beds. Higher rates apply during special events.

● Econo Lodge, √ ♿, 1501 Robin Hood Rd., 23220. Telephone: 804/359-4011. $28.95 for one; $32.95 for two in one bed; $36.95 for two in two beds.

● Red Roof Inn, ♿, 4350 Commerce Rd., 23234. Telephone: 804/271-7240. See Hampton listing for rates.

● Red Roof Inn, ♿, 100 Grashamwood Place, Chippenham Pkwy. & Midlothian Turnpike, 23225. Telephone: 804/745-0600. See Hampton listing for rates.

● Motel 6, 5704 Williamsburg Rd., 23150. Telephone: 804/222-7318. $17.95 for one; $21.95 for two; $2 for each additional person.

Roanoke

Help: Salvation Army Traveler's Assistance, 724 Dale Ave. SE, 24013. Telephone: 703/343-5335.

Accommodations: TRUST, 3515 Williamson Rd. NW, 24012. About 1½ miles from I-81. Telephone: 703/563-0311. Provides emergency overnight housing and facilities for 24 hours. Men and women. No charge for services. Cooking facilities available. The people at TRUST invite you to stop by for information on Roanoke.

- Days Inn, I-581 & U.S. 460, P.O. Box 12325, 24024. Telephone: 703/342-4551. $26 for one; $30 for two.
- Econo Lodge, 6621 Thirlane Rd. NW, 24019. Telephone: 703/563-0853. $23.95 for one; $28.95 for two in one bed; $30.95 for two in two beds.
- Econo Lodge, 3816 Franklin Rd., 24014. Telephone: 703/774-1621. See above listing for rates.
- Econo Lodge, 308 Orange Ave. NW, 24016. Telephone: 703/343-2413. See above listing for rates.

Salem

Accommodation: Econo Lodge, 1535 East Main St., 24153. Telephone: 703/986-1000. $23.95 for one; $28.95 for two in one bed; $30.95 for two in two beds.

Skippers

Accommodation: Econo Lodge, ✓ ♿, I-95 S. & Hwy. 629 (Exit 1), 23879. Telephone: 804/634-6124. $24.95 for one; $28.95 for two in one bed; $31.95 for two in two beds.

South Hill

Accommodation: Econo Lodge, ✓, 623 East Atlantic St., 23970. Telephone: 804/447-7116. $25 for one; $29 for two in one bed; $33 for two in two beds.

Staunton

Accommodations: Econo Lodge, ✓ ♿, Rte. 4, Box 105A, 24401. Telephone: 703/885-5158. $25.95 for one; $29.95 for two in one bed; $33.95 for two in two beds. Higher rates apply during special events.

- Days Inn, I-81 & Va. 654 (Exit 55A), P.O. Box 2307, Mint Springs, 24401. Telephone: 703/337-3031. $28 for one; $32 for two.
- Master Host Inn, P.O. Box 149, 24401. Telephone: 703/248-0888. $24 to $32 single; $32 to $42 double.

Suffolk

Accommodation: Econo Lodge, ✓, 1017 North Main St., 23434. Telephone: 804/539-3451. $26.95 for one; $30.95 for two in one bed; $32.95 for two in two beds.

Triangle

Camping: Prince William Forest Park, 619 W., one-fourth mile from I-95, P.O. Box 209, 22172. Telephone: 703/221-7181. Group and individual tent camping and trailers year-round. Backcountry permit camping available mid-May to late September. $4 per family campsite per night; $10 per group campsite per night.

Urbanna

Accommodation: Sangraal-by-the-Sea (AYH-SA), ⓈV 🦽 ★, P.O. Box 187, 23175. Telephone: 804/776-6500. Call the hostel for a pickup from bus or train station in Williamsburg or Saluda (call ahead). $7 summer, $8 winter for AYH members. Nonmembers: $14 single; $11.25 per person double; $9.25 per person triple; $8.25 per person quad. Meals provided at extra cost. "Sangraal is a Swiss-style chateau lodge on the waterfront with canoeing, sailing, and hiking trails and is near the historical areas of Williamsburg and Yorktown."

Verona

Accommodation: Scottish Inn, ⓈV 🦽 ★, I-81 & Va. 612, P.O. Box 586, 24482. Telephone: 703/248-8981. $25 for one; $28 for two in one bed; $31 for two in two beds.

Virginia Beach

Accommodations: Red Roof Inn, 🦽, 196 Ballard Ct., 23462. Telephone: 804/490-0225. See Hampton listing for rates.

● Budget Host—The Boardwalk Inn, V, 2604 Atlantic Ave., 23451. Telephone: 804/425-5971. September to June: $22.50 and up. June 16 to September 8: $58.50 to $62.50 single or double.

● Angie's Guest Cottage (AYH-SA), 302 24th St., 23451. Telephone: 804/428-4690. Open April to November 1. $9.75 summer, $6.75 winter for AYH members.

Waynesboro

Accommodation: Budget Host—West Lawn Motel, V, 2240 West Main St., 22980. Telephone: 703/942-9551. $22 to $32 single; $28 to $38 double.

Williamsburg

On Campus: According to our correspondent at the College of William and Mary, the college itself does not have many activities that would be of interest to travelers, but Williamsburg is "a re-creation of an 18th-century colonial city—beautiful, fascinating, and definitely worth some time and effort." Busch Gardens, a beer and amusement park, also merits a stop.

Word has it the Greenleaf Café on Scotland St. serves excellent, cheap meals; another good place to eat is George's Campus Restaurant on Prince George St. Also recommended are Milton's Pizza, Sal's Italian Restaurant, Blue Rose Café on Jamestown Rd., and Hsing Ling Chinese Restaurant—all at Williamsburg Shopping Center. If you're up for a ferry ride, take the Jamestown ferry to (guess where?) Jamestown, and four or five miles down the only road is the Surrey House, which serves excellent Southern cooking for $3 to $10.

Late fall and very early spring are good times to visit, when there are a minimum of tourists.

Accommodations: Motel 6, 3030 Richmond Rd., 23185. Telephone: 804/565-2710. See Richmond listing for rates.

● Budget Host—Governor Spottswood Motel, ⬧, 1508 Richmond Rd., 23185. Telephone: 804/229-6444. $30 for one; $38 for two in one bed; $42 to $46 for two in two beds. Large secluded pool.

Winchester

Accommodations: Winchester Budget Hotel, ∨, Sunnyside Station, Rte. 522, 22601. Telephone: 703/667-1033. $19 for one; $23 for two in one bed; $26 for two in two beds.

● Econo Lodge, ∨ ⬧, 1507 Martinsburg Pike, 22601. Telephone: 703/662-4700. $29.95 for one; $34.95 for two.

Wytheville

Accommodation: Econo Lodge, ∨ ⬧, 1190 East Main St., 24382. Telephone: 703/228-5517. $26.95 for one; $30.95 for two in one bed; $33.95 for two in two beds.

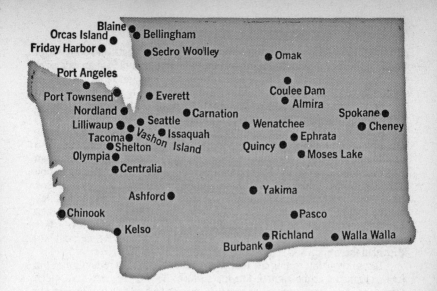

Washington

Let's start with the Olympic Peninsula, with its 8000-foot mountains, permanent glaciers, and hot springs. Much of the peninsula is un- or underinhabited and occupied by the Olympic National Park; its principal sight is the world's only nontropical rain forest, in the Hoh River Valley. This is great country for *experienced* hikers and backpackers, but mountain treks should be done in groups with someone who knows the terrain and how to survive when lost.

The ocean beach at Kalaloch is part of the national park and has highway access; there is a lodge on the beach, but it is always booked, summer and winter, far in advance and there is nowhere else to stay for miles. To get around the peninsula by road on Hwy. 101 takes a full day at top speeds without stopping. To see anything and to enjoy the country at all requires a minimum of three days. For those going on to Canada there is a ferry service several times daily from Port Angeles to Victoria, B.C. The peninsula is exceptionally rainy and the water off the beaches is much too cold for swimming. There's a summer arts and music festival in Port Townsend.

Southwest Washington is bordered by the Cascade Range on the east, the Pacific on the west, the Columbia River on the south, and the Olympic Peninsula on the north. Most of the area is densely forested and heavily logged. There's very little population here except in pulp-mill towns, the deep-sea fishing port of Ocean Shores, the dunes and beach area near Long Beach, the industrial town of Aberdeen, and the dull strip along Interstate 5 running from the state capital at Olympia to the Portland suburb of Vancouver, Washington.

The Puget Sound area extends from the Canadian border south to the state capital at Olympia along an inland sea over 100 miles in length and dotted with wooded islands and peninsulas, many of which are reachable via an extensive state ferry system. The Sound is noted for its delicious (and ever-dwindling) salmon, oysters, clams, mussels, octopus, and other marine life. Although this area contains the bulk of the population of the state of Washington, one is never far from mountain and coastal scenery.

Not all of the cities and towns of Puget Sound are notable, but the following rate a mention: Bellingham, with its Western Washington University, superb local museum in the 19th-century former city hall, interesting restored urban area with good restaurants, and rose gardens; Everett, a horror of air pollution and uncontrolled urban sprawl, but with redeeming features nearby including the harbor, lighthouse, and seafood restaurants at the ferry port of Mukilteo and the views of the Cascades as one travels up toward Stevens Pass. And then there's Puyallup (anyone able to pronounce the name of this place correctly is recognized as a Northwest native) with its fine views of Mount Rainier, daffodil festival in the spring, and state fair in September.

Tacoma is an interesting city that tries hard to live up to its reputation as the area's organized crime capital. On the surface, Tacoma doesn't have much going for it. One Seattle wit says Tacoma is the place where you find Velveeta in the gourmet cheese shop. And yet the north end of the city has some of the prettiest shoreline in the area, the bridge over the Narrows is an attractive replacement for the famous Galloping Gerties of the 1940s, and the city center is an attractive mix of new urbanism, pedestrian malls, and a few sensationally grotesque Victorian public buildings. Many of the inhabitants are descendants of Yugoslav fishermen who came to the Northwest in the early part of the century.

Olympia features tours of the Olympia Brewery in Tumwater with a nice little waterfall tumbling into the south end of Puget Sound and a beautiful view of the Capitol building overlooking the Sound. Once you leave the public buildings on Capitol Hill, you descend into the midst of what looks like an unkempt Norwegian fishing village—no beauty, but great character.

For something about Seattle, see page 461.

Some Special Events: International Plowing Match in Lynden (April); Apple Blossom Festival in Wenatchee, and Washington State Garden Show in Tacoma (May); Folk Life Festival in Seattle (June); Pioneer Rodeo in Roy, Festival of People in Montesano, and Indian Celebration in Nespelem (all in July); Threshing Bee in Lynden, and Grant County Fair and Rodeo in Moses Lake (August); Harbor Days Festival, and Tug Boat Races in Olympia (September); and Scandinavian Festival in Tacoma (October).

Hitching: Until recently, hitchhiking was illegal everywhere in Washington. Now that has been changed, and it's legal on all roads except limited-access facilities or freeways. Hitching, according to a friend, is good to excellent except in Olympia, which he says you should most definitely avoid if you're hitching. A friend at Central Washington State College in Ellensburg says that hitching from there to the coast is excellent, but getting rides to the eastern part of the state is not as easy. A friend in Bellingham says: "Both inside and outside of town, there is lots of thumb riding. In fact, it's the major means of transportation for a big piece of the population."

Tourist Information: Travel Development Division, Department of Commerce and Economic Development, General Administration Bldg., Olympia, WA 98504.

Almira

Accommodation: Almira Home Hostel (AYH), c/o Rick & Molly Brunner, Rte. 1, Box 14, 99103. Telephone: 509/639-2332. $4 for AYH members. Advance reservations of two days necessary. Closed last week in July and 1st and 2nd weeks of August.

Ashford

Accommodation: The Lodge Youth Hostel (AYH), P.O. Box 86, 98304. Telephone: 206/569-2312. $7 summer, $8 winter for AYH members.

Bellingham

"Bellingham is a fine town and has a lot of alternative-lifestyle people living in it. The south side of town is a traveler's dream, with restored buildings, easy-living people, and lots of color. People here are always helping each other and keeping up on the most recent information concerning politics, energy use, pollution, etc. There are a few places that house people for free, but the problem is that these houses are privately owned and do not advertise as places of refuge. Most people just stumble across them. If you come to Bellingham, walk our coastline. Although we haven't escaped pollution, there are some very fine places along the shore. Just follow the railroad tracks south of town."

Accommodations: Motel 6, 3701 Byron Ave., 98225. Telephone: 206/671-6006. $17.95 for one; $21.95 for two; $2 for each additional person.
● TraveLodge, √ 🚹, 202 East Holly St., 98225. Telephone: 206/734-1900. $30 for one; $34 for two in one bed; $38 for two in two beds.

Blaine

Accommodations: Camaray Motel, Ⓢ√ 🚹 ★, 288 D St. Telephone: 206/332-5603. $24.73 for one; $26.34 for two in one bed; $28.45 for two in two beds. Summer rates are 10% higher. Advance reservations of two days necessary.
● Birch Bay Hostel (AYH), former Blaine Air Force Base, Alderson Rd., 98230. Telephone: 206/371-2180. Open June 1 to September 30 and October 1 to May 31. $5 summer, $6.50 winter for AYH members. Advance reservations necessary.

Burbank

Accommodation: Burbank Home Hostel (AYH), 509 Maple St., Box 01, 99323. Telephone: 509/547-3420. $5.75 for AYH members. Advance reservations necessary.

Carnation

Accommodation: Carnation Hostel (AYH), 6602 Tolt Rd. NE, 98014. Telephone: 206/333-6175. Call the houseparents from the bus station (three miles) and they will pick you up. $4 for AYH members. The hostel is a 100-year old log cabin located on a 20-acre farm. "There are gardens, farm animals, and the Tolt River." They prefer that you bring your own sleeping bag. There is also room for camping.

Centralia

Accommodations: Motel 6, 1310 Belmont Ave, 98531. Telephone: 206/736-0750. See Bellingham listing for rates.
● Econo Lodge, √, 702 Harrison Ave., 98531. Telephone: 206/736-2875. $24.95 to $26.95 for one; $28.95 to $30.95 for two in one bed; $32.95 to $34.95 for two in two beds.

Cheney

Help: Rap-In, Eastern Washington University. Telephone: 509/359-7979. Closed during university vacations.
Accommodation: Eastern Washington State College Dormitories, ⑤ ⑥ ★, Louise Anderson Hall, 99004. Telephone: 509/359-7022. Open year-round but space is limited during fall, winter, and spring. $11 single, $9.50 per person, double. Student rate: $9 per person, double.

Chinook

Accommodation: Fort Columbia Youth Hostel (AYH), P.O. Box 224, 98614. Telephone: 206/777-8755. Open June 1 to September 15 (5 p.m. to 9 a.m.) $4.50 for AYH members.

Coulee Dam

Accommodation: Friendship Inn Ponderosa Motel, 10 Lincoln St., 99116. Telephone: 509/633-2100. $27 for one; $32 for two in one bed; $36 for two in two beds.

Ephrata

Accommodation: TraveLodge, √ ⑥, 31 South Basin St. SW, 98823. $30 for one; $36 for two in one bed; $41 for two in two beds.

Everett

Accommodations: Allstar Inn, 224 128th St. SW, 98204. Telephone: 206/353-8120. $23.95 to $25.95 for one; $3 for each additional person.
● Motel 6, 10006 Evergreen Way, 98204. Telephone: 206/355-1811. See Bellingham listing for rates.

● Imperial 400 Motor Inn, √ (10%), 952 U.S. Hwy. 99 N., 98201. Telephone: 206/259-5177. $22 to $27 for one; $25 to $31 for two in one bed; $28 to $34 for two in two beds.

Friday Harbor

Accommodation: Elite Hotel (AYH-SA), P.O. Box 555, 98250. Telephone: 206/378-5555. Friday Harbor is on San Juan Island, and the Elite is 1½ blocks from the ferry landing. $6.50 for AYH members. $21 for a single or double. Bring a sleeping bag, or linens available at extra cost. The hotel has a café, sauna, and hot tubs. Advance reservations of three weeks necessary in summer.

Issaquah

Accommodation: Motel 6, 1885 15th Pl. NW, 38027. Telephone: 206/392-9666. See Bellingham listing for rates.

Kelso

Accommodation: Motel 6, 1505 Allen St., 98626. Telephone: 206/636-3660. See Bellingham listing for rates.

Lilliwaup

Accommodation: Mike's Beach Hostel and Resort, Rte. 1, Box 95, 98555. Telephone: 206/877-5324. Open May 15 to October 15. $5 for AYH members.

Moses Lake

Accommodations: Motel 6, 2822 Wapato Dr., 98837. Telephone: 509/765-6676. See Bellingham listing for rates.
● Imperial 400 Motor Inn, √ (10%), 905 West Broadway, 98837. Telephone: 509/767-8626. $26 to $30 for one; $29 to $33 for two in one bed; $30 to $34 for two in two beds.
● TraveLodge, √ &, 316 South Pioneer Way, 98837. Telephone: 509/765-8631. Airport transportation available. $29 for one; $33 for two in one bed; $37 for two in two beds.

Nordland

Accommodation: Fort Flagler State Park Hostel (AYH), √, 98358. Telephone: 206/385-1288. Men, women, and children. $4.50 for AYH members; $6.50 for nonmembers. Advance reservations of one week necessary.

Olympia

Accommodation: Motel 6, 400 West Lee St., Tumwater, 98501. Telephone: 206/943-5000. See Bellingham listing for rates.

Omak

Accommodation: TraveLodge, √, 121 North Main St., 98841. Telephone: 509/826-0400. Airport transportation available. $28 for one; $32 for two in one bed; $36 for two in two beds.

Orcas Island

Accommodation: Doe Bay Village (AYH-SA), Star Route, Box 86, Olga, 98279. Telephone: 206/376-2291 or 376-4755. $7.50 for AYH members. Advance reservations necessary July 2 to September 8.

Pasco

Accommodations: Motel 6, 1520 North Oregon St., 99301. Telephone: 509/547-6666. See Bellingham listing for rates.
● Econo Lodge, √, 720 West Lewis St., 99301. Telephone: 509/547-7766. $23.95 to $25.95 for one; $27.95 to $29.95 for two in one bed; $31.95 to $33.95 for two in two beds.
● TraveLodge, √, 725 West Lewis St., 99301. Telephone: 509/547-7791. Airport transportation available. $24 for one; $28 for two in one bed; $32 for two in two beds.

Port Angeles

Accommodation: Friendship Aggie's Inn & Restaurant, 602 East Front St., 98362. Telephone: 206/457-0471. $28 to $35 for one; $34 to $45 for two in one bed; $36 to $50 for two in two beds.

Port Townsend

Accommodation: Fort Worden Youth Hostel (AYH), 98368. Telephone: 206/385-0655. Open year-round, except December 15 to January 3 and Thanksgiving Day. $5 for AYH members; $7 for nonmembers. Buy food on Water St. before coming to hostel.

"Hostels like the one in Port Townsend were fantastic—that place is a home away from home."

Quincy

Accommodation: Friendship Villager Inn, 711 Second Ave. SW, 98848.

Telephone: 509/787-3515. $18 for one; $24 for two in one bed; $26 for two in two beds.

Richland

Accommodation: Imperial 400 Motor Inn, √ (10%), 515 George Washington Way, 99352. Telephone: 509/946-6117. $25 to $29 for one; $28 to $32 for two in one bed; $30 to $34 for two in two beds.

Seattle

Built on seven hills (remind you of another famous city?), settled in between the Olympic and Cascade Mountain ranges, and right alongside the shores of Puget Sound and several freshwater lakes, Seattle is an appealing town. From the Observation Deck of the Space Needle, in Seattle Center (the park that was the site of the 1962 World's Fair), you can get a good look at it all: downtown, the Pike Place Market, the Waterfront, Pioneer Square, Fisherman's Terminal, Woodland Park and Zoo, Capitol Hill (Seattle's equivalent of Greenwich Village), Seattle University, the University of Washington, and 14,000-foot-high Mount Rainier. Anyone who's going to spend more than just a day or two in the Emerald City should probably take a look at some of these guidebooks:

Seattle Best Places, edited by David Brewster, Sasquatch Publishing, Seattle ($8.95).

The Poor Man's Guide to Seattle Area Restaurants, by Mary and Marvin Braunstein, West Seattle Associates, Inc. ($2.95).

1983 People's Yellow Pages, The Eyes, Ears, and Knows of Greater Seattle, Grange Printing, Inc. ($4.25).

Seattle Rainy Day Guide, by Cliffort Burke, Solstice Press, Chronicle Books, San Francisco.

Seattle, Past to Present, by Roger Sale, University of Washington Press, Seattle ($9.95).

Footsore: Walks and Hikes Around Puget Sound, by Harvey Manning, Mountaineers Press, Seattle. Four volumes at $8.95 each.

First Seattle Catalogue, second edition, by Colin Dobson and Kathleen Cain, Ensemble Publications ($8.95).

To find out what's happening and when, check any of the following newspapers: *The Weekly, The Rocket* (for music news), *Northwest Passage,* the *Seattle Times* and *Post Intelligencer Daily,* and/or the *Clinton Street Quarterly.* For maps and answers to tourist questions of any kind, stop at the Convention and Visitors Bureau at 1815 Seventh Ave. or at Sea-Tac International Airport. Both are open seven days a week. At the University of Washington, there's an information center at 4014 University Way NE (tel. 543-9198).

Getting There: The airport, Sea-Tac International (the Tac is for neighboring Tacoma), is about 15 miles from downtown Seattle. By taxi, the trip costs $25. For a more reasonable price, try the Greyline Downtown Airporter bus, which costs $4.75 (tel. 448-2070), or the Everett Airporter (a van, not a bus), which costs $7 one way or $12 round trip (tel. 743-3344). The biggest bargain of all is the Metro bus 174 that costs 85¢.

● The bus station is at 8th and Stewart Sts., and the train station at 3rd and Jackson Sts.; both are served by Metro bus. There are Metro information booths at each station, where you can pick up maps and bus schedules and directions to where you're heading.

Getting Around: To get into a taxi costs about $1 and it's $1 for every mile you ride, although fares vary. You can flag a taxi but that's tricky; it's best to call ahead one of the following: Farwest (tel. 622-1717); Yellow Cab, the cheapest (tel. 622-6500); or Grey Top (tel. 622-4949).

● To rent a car in Seattle you can, of course, seek out the standard brands— Avis, Hertz, etc.—but for something less expensive, try Yesterday's Rent a Car (tel. 789-5305 in Ballard), where it costs $13.95 for a big, damaged Chevy Impala or $2 more for something in somewhat better shape.

● The monorail links downtown Seattle and Seattle Center; a ride costs 35¢. The buses run often and cost 65¢ for a one-zone ride and $1 for one that covers two zones (55¢ and 85¢ off-peak and on weekends). Zone 1 covers the entire city; Zone 2, the periphery and surrounding King County. For bus information, dial 447-4800. If you have a bike and you want to take it on the bus with you, call the Bicycle Hot Line (tel. 522-BIKE) and find out how. Another rather unique feature of Seattle Metro Transit, called Magic Carpet, lets you ride for free in the downtown core area. The driver will explain how far you can travel without paying a fare. This certainly simplifies visits to the Pioneer Square and Pike Place Market areas, theaters, movies, shopping, and sports events at the Kingdome.

Tourist Information: Seattle-King County Convention and Visitors Bureau, 1815 Seventh Ave., 98101. Telephone: 206/447-7273.

Help: Travelers Aid, 909 Fourth Ave., 98104. Telephone: 206/447-3888.

● Crisis Clinic (for emotional crises), 1530 Eastlake Ave. East. Telephone: 206/447-3222.

Accommodations: Occasionally there's space in the University of Washington dormitories; telephone Campus Housing at 206/543-6222 to check.

● YMCA, Downtown Branch, 909 Fourth Ave., 98104. Telephone: 206/382-5000. $9.99 for AYH members. Sleeping bag required.

● YWCA, 1118 Fifth Ave., 98101. Telephone: 206/447-4888. Women only. $14.50 and up single; $25 double; $35 triple. Exercise equipment, and a pool in the building; a deli and coffeeshop for postexercise hunger. Advance reservations of two weeks suggested.

● College Inn Guest House, 4000 University Way NE, 98105. Telephone: 206/633-4441. A restored old inn with rooms without bath, as they were in the 1900s, but with period furnishings. Young and friendly management. College Inn Café and Pub downstairs are both student hangouts with moderately priced food and drink. $30 to $32 single; $37 to $44 double; $48 triple. Price includes a continental breakfast.

● Allstar Inn, 16500 Pacific Hwy. S., at Sea-Tac Airport, 98188. Telephone: 206/246-4101. See Everett listing for rates.

● Commodore Hotel, 2013 2nd Ave., 98121. Telephone: 206/448-8868. $18 to $24 single; $21 to $27 double.

● Motel 6, 18900 47th Ave. S., 98188. Telephone: 206/246-5520. See Bellingham listing for rates.

● Imperial 400 Motor Inn, √ (10%), 17108 Pacific Hwy. S., 98188. Telephone: 206/244-1230. $27 to $32 for one; $32 to $36 for two in one bed; $34 to $40 for two in two beds.

Where to Eat: Pike Place Market has a number of eateries, ranging from what many people consider Seattle's best restaurant—Labuznik, 1924 First Ave. (tel. 682-1624), with Central European food that's expensive—to ethnic places serving moderately priced French food (Le Bistro, 93A Pike St.; tel. 682-3049); inexpensive Greek food (Athenian Inn, Pike Pl.; tel. 624-7166); and not very expensive Bolivian food, Copacabana, Pike Pl. (tel. 622-6359). We've been told that the saltenas, deep-fried meat pastries, are especially good in this small but cozy restaurant, and one friend urges that you "try the shrimp soup."

- Pier 59 Seafood Bar and Deli, Pier 59, Alaskan Way. Telephone: 624-0312. On the waterfront right by the Seattle Aquarium.
- Ivar's Salmon House, 401 N.E. Northlake Way, in the university district. Telephone: 632-0767. You can get a classic meal of alder-smoked salmon, Indian style, with coleslaw and cornbread for $5.25 at lunch; expect to pay approximately $8 to $9 for dinner. There is also a takeout stand on Northlake Way near the restaurant entrance, and you can take your salmon ($4.25) or fish and chips ($2.09) down to the floating pier in front of the restaurant.
- Last Exit on Brooklyn, 3930 Brooklyn Ave. NE. Telephone: 545-9873. Good coffee, sandwiches, chess, and conversation.
- Woerne's European Café, 4108 University Way NE. Telephone: 632-7893. German food and pastries.
- Cause Célèbre Café, 524 15th Ave. East. Telephone: 322-1057. Near the Seattle Art Museum. Vegetarian food and homemade desserts. A hangout for "alternative" types—most nights, a musician entertains and there's always art on display.
- Sunlight Café, 6403 Roosevelt Way NE. Telephone: 522-9060. University district. Vegetarian dinners, weekend brunches, and an expresso bar in the morning. Soup, salad, and an entree for only $5.95. "This is a good place in the morning—people travel from all over for sesame waffles with all kinds of toppings, fresh orange juice, and good coffee with free refills. Laid back and very friendly."
- Rama House, 2228 Second Ave. Telephone: 624-2931. Thai food downtown. Inexpensive and excellent quality. Like things hot? Try the items on the menu with the four stars.
- Market Café, 1523 1st Ave. Telephone: 624-2598. Near Pike Place Market, on the waterfront. Simple food that's filling. The best blueberry pancakes around. It's a crowded, cheerful kind of place where the clientele ranges from local business types to the down and out.
- Taqueria Mexico, 4226 University Way, NE. Telephone: 633-5256. Inexpensive, authentic Mexican food in the university district. The tortillas are made right on the spot.
- Across the Street Café, 3423 Fremont North. Telephone: 632-2119. American-style food, three egg omelettes, hash browns, homemade muffin, and coffee is $3.95. A homey, neighborhood favorite with the best cinnamon rolls in town.
- Musashi's, 1400 North 45th. Telephone: 633-0212. A neighborhood secret with a devoted following. Only eight tables and what one friend considers "the best sushi in town."

What to See and Do: You'll have to visit the Seattle Center, the site of the World's Fair almost 20 years ago, which has been transformed into a park that offers performing arts, museums, the Pacific Science Center, shops, an amusement park, and the Space Needle.

- The Waterfront along Alaskan Way is another must-see. Here you'll find shops, restaurants, harbor tours, an aquarium, and a fine park.
- Pioneer Square, Seattle's birthplace, has been restored to the splendor of 1889, the year that the Seattle fire struck. Leaded windows, wrought iron, restored brick and stone storefronts, and two cobblestoned plazas are all wonderful reminders of Seattle's Klondike Gold Rush Days. After the fire of 1889, the streets of Pioneer Square were raised. The original sidewalk level remained beneath, leaving shop fronts in large caverns that were forgotten over the years. Now it's possible to take an underground tour of the area. Telephone: 682-4646 for information.
- Ballard Locks. Take bus 17 or 43 from downtown. Watch everyone indulge in Seattle's favorite pastime—boating. Locks open and close and water levels rise and fall. Quite a parade of yachts line up, but better even than watching boats is watching the migrating salmon as they leap up the fish ladders on their long trip home. There are underwater observation points as well as above-water viewing. Different species travel in different seasons, so your chances of seeing salmon when you're there are pretty good.
- Discovery Park. Take bus 33 from 4th and Union for nature walks and splendid views of Puget Sound.
- Seattle Art Museum, in Volunteer Park. Telephone: 447-4710. In a beautiful setting overlooking Puget Sound. Special exhibits and permanent collections.
- At Night: If you like theater, Seattle is a gold mine of small and large companies that often perform material which has never, or not yet, been to Broadway. Try particularly the Seattle Rep, A.C.T., the Intiman Theater, the Empty Space, the Bathhouse Theater, and the many small theaters around Pioneer Square. Many of these theaters offer student discounts or reduced-price last-minute tickets.
- The Seattle Symphony performs at the Opera House in Seattle Center. There are also many chamber music, vocal recitals, and University of Washington musical events all through the year. Check the newspapers.
- People who like rhythm and blues and rock congregate at the Central Tavern and Café, 207 1st St. South near Pioneer Square. Telephone: 622-0209. The crowd stands around the bar or sits, but either way they obviously enjoy themselves.
- There is lots of dance in Seattle, both from touring companies and resident troupes. The Pacific Northwest Ballet (tel. 447-4655) is functioning as of this writing, but some of the smaller, innovative companies may very well fall victim to "Reaganomics." Check newspapers for current dance events.
- Be sure to check the University of Washington *Daily* for university events: concerts, plays, film series, lectures, visiting celebrities, etc.
- Pier 70 Restaurant and Chowder House, Alaskan Way and Broad. There's a big terrace dance floor right on the waterfront, which attracts a large singles crowd because of its live music and the chance to dance. Expect a cover charge.
- Tug's Belltown Tavern, 2207 1st Ave. Telephone: 623-2813. No cover before 11 p.m., $1.50 to $2.50 after that. Funky danceteria with new wave, rock, reggae, and beyond. For serious dancing.
- Murphy's, 2110 N. 45th St. Telephone: 634-2110. A neighborhood favorite Irish pub complete with dart board. Traditional Irish music every night and lots of varieties of beer.
- Films: Seattle is a great movie town—maybe because of the notoriously wet

weather. There are many wonderful renovated theaters with a wide selection of mainstream to avant-garde films. The city has its own international film festival every May where many foreign films debut.

● Jazz Alley, 4135 University Way NE. Telephone: 632-7414 or 622-0007. The food's expensive but there's no cover charge. Excellent jazz by famous names.

Shopping: Pike Place Market, 1st and Pike, downtown. A series of roofed-over and open-air stalls where truck farmers and hawkers sell their wares—produce, flowers, antiques, crafts, art, etc. Open Monday to Saturday, 9 a.m. to 6 p.m.

● People in the Northwest love the out-of-doors. They hike, they ski, and they climb mountains with a vengeance. If you'd like to do the same, you might want to stop at Recreational Equipment, Inc., 1525 11th Ave., to take a look at the tents, packs, boots, etc. If you don't want to buy, you can rent here instead.

● University Book Store, 4326 University Way NE. Over 60,000 books to choose from.

● The Elliott Bay Book Company, 1st South and South Main (Pioneer Square). Lots more books.

● A Different Drummer, 420 Broadway East (Capitol Hill). New and used books, a wide selection.

● Shorey's, 110 Union and 119 South Jackson. Books in Pioneer Square.

● Peaches, 811 N.E. 45th St. All kinds of records in the university district.

● Wide World of Music, 215 Pike. Records downtown.

● Filippi's, 1351 East Olive, A great stock of used records and books.

● Northwest Native, 4214 University Way NE. A good place for one-of-a-kind souvenir T-shirts.

Sedro Woolley

Camping: North Cascades National Park, 98284. Hike-in campgrounds open from May to October 15. No vehicle access.

● Ross Lake National Recreation Area, c/o North Cascades National Park, 98284. Four campgrounds accessible by car; two closed Labor Day to June; two are open all year. Fifteen campgrounds are accessible by boat only or by boat and trail, and are open from June to November.

● Lake Chelan National Recreation Area, c/o North Cascades National Park, 98284. Twenty campgrounds are accessible by boat and trail. Boat launching at Chelan. Open April to November. No fee.

Shelton

Accommodation: Econo Lodge, √, 628 Railroad Ave., 98584. Telephone: 206/426-4468. $24.95 for one; $28.95 for two in one bed; $32.95 for two in two beds.

Spokane

Tourist Information: Spokane Convention and Visitors Bureau, West 301 Main, 99201. Telephone: 509/624-1341.

On Campus: On the Gonzaga University campus, near Crosby Library, you'll find a bulletin board with rides and apartments listed. For inexpensive food, try the Chef Restaurant, North 1329 Hamilton. Two places to go to meet students are Bulldog, 1300 block on Hamilton, and the Forum, 1400 block on Hamilton.

Accommodations: Friendship Inn Tiki Lodge, West 1420 Second Ave., 99204. Telephone: 509/838-2026. $26 to $28 for one; $28 to $30 for two in one bed; $28 to $32 for two in two beds.

● Motel 6, 1508 South Rustle St., 99204. Telephone: 509/838-6401. See Bellingham listing for rates.

● Thrifty Scot Motel, 1919 North Hutchinson Rd., 99212. Telephone: 509/926-5399. $24.90 to $29.90 for one; $29.90 to $34.90 for two.

Tacoma

Accommodations: Motel 6, 5201 20th St. E., Fife, 98424. Telephone: 206/922-6612. See Bellingham listing for rates.

● TraveLodge, √ &, 2512 Pacific Ave., 98402. Telephone: 206/383-3557. $28 for one; $32 for two in one bed; $35 for two in two beds.

● TraveLodge, √, 9915 South Tacoma Way, 98499. Telephone: 206/588-6615. $29 for one; $31 for two in one bed; $33 for two in two beds.

● Allstar Inn, 5817 20th St. E., Fife, 98424. Telephone: 206/992-1680. See Everett listing for rates.

Vashon Island

Accommodation: Vashon Home Hostel (AYH), c/o Judy Mulhair, Rte. 5, Box 349, 98070. Telephone: 206/463-2592. Open May 1 to October 31. $4.75 for AYH members; $7.75 for nonmembers. Advance reservations necessary.

Walla Walla

Accommodation: Imperial 400 Motor Inn, √ (10%), 305 North Second Ave., 99362. Telephone: 509/529-4410. $27 to $31 for one; $32 to $36 for two in one bed; $36 to $40 for two in two beds.

Wenatchee

Accommodations: Imperial 400 Motor Inn, √ (10%), 700 North Wenatchee Ave., 98801. Telephone: 509/663-8133. $26 to $28 for one; $34 to $36 for two in one bed; $36 to $38 for two in two beds.

● Friendship Inn Holiday, 610 North Wenatchee Ave., 98801. Telephone: 509/663-8167. $30 for one; $38 for two in one bed; $42 for two in two beds.

Yakima

Accommodations: Motel 6, 1104 North 1st St., 98901. Telephone: 509/452-0407. See Bellingham listing for rates.

● Imperial 400 Motor Inn, $\sqrt{}$ (10%), 510 North 1st St., 98901. Telephone: 509/457-6155. $28 to $30 for one; $32 to $34 for two in one bed; $36 to $38 for two in two beds.

● YWCA, 15 North Naches Ave., 98901. Telephone: 509/248-7796. Women only (18 and older). $5 single. Weekly rate: $30. Advance reservations of two weeks necessary.

West Virginia

West Virginia offers a great deal of natural beauty. The eastern part of the state has the highest mountains, several caverns, and glades. The western part, although more urbanized, has its share of rural scenery. West Virginia has 36 state parks and forests, many with camping facilities.

One of the most popular of the state's tourist attractions is Harpers Ferry National Historic Park, where the Shenandoah and Potomac Rivers meet. In the mid-19th century, this thriving town fell victim to the Civil War. Remains of the arsenal, some restored buildings, and special exhibits are on view in summer.

Some Special Events: Jazz Festival in Charleston, and Heritage Days in Parkersburg (April); Antique Steam and Gas Engine Show in Point Pleasant, and Vandalia Gathering in Charleston (May); Mountain Heritage Arts and Crafts Festival in Harpers Ferry, Regatta Festival in Sutton, and Mountain State Art and Crafts Fair in Ripley (June); Pioneer Days in Marlington, Augusta Festival in Elkins, and Marshall County Fair in Moundsville (July); Water Festival in Hinton, and Appalachian Arts and Crafts Festival in Beckley (August); Italian Heritage Festival in Clarksburg, and Harvest Moon Festival in Parkersburg (September).

Hitching: Hitchhiking is prohibited on Interstate routes and limited-access highways. Otherwise it is legal and, according to the Department of Public Safety, best on U.S. routes and state routes; however, they don't approve of hitching in general.

Tourist Information: Travel Development Division, Department of Commerce, Capitol Complex, 1900 Washington St., Charleston, WV 25305, toll free 800/624-9110 out of state.

For brochures on West Virginia bed-and-breakfast inns, write to Travel West Virginia, at the above address.

Beckley

Accommodation: Days Inn, &, 102 Harper Park Dr., 25801. Telephone: 304/255-5291. $26.88 to $29.88 for one; $31.88 to $34.88 for two.

Bluefield

Accommodation: Econo Lodge, √, 3400 Cumberland Rd., 24701. Telephone: 304/327-8171. $27.95 for one; $30.95 for two in one bed; $32.95 for two in two beds.

Charleston

Accommodations: Red Roof Inn, &, 6305 MacCorkle Ave., Kanawha City, 25304. Telephone: 304/925-6953. $24.95 for one; $29.95 for two in one bed; $31.95 for two in two beds; $33.95 for three or four in two beds.
● Red Roof Inn, &, 4006 MacCorkle Ave. SW, South Charleston, 25309. Telephone: 304/744-1500. See above listing for rates.
● Red Roof Inn, P.O. Box 468, Putnam Village Shopping Center, Hurricane, 25526. Telephone: 304/757-6392. $22.95 for one; $27.95 for two in one bed; $29.95 for two in two beds; $31.95 for three or four in two beds.

Fairmont

Accommodation: Red Roof Inn, &, Rte. 1, I-79 at U.S. 250 (Exit 132), 26554. Telephone: 304/366-6800. $24.95 for one; $29.95 for two in one bed; $31.95 for two in two beds; $33.95 for three or four in two beds.

Huntington

Accommodation: Red Roof Inn, &, 5190 U.S. Rte. 60 E., 25705. Telephone: 304/733-3737. See Fairmont listing for rates.

Lewisburg

Accommodation: Friendship Sunset Terrace Inn, Box 267, U.S. 60 W., 24901. Telephone: 304/645-2363. $18 to $26 for one; $26 for two in one bed; $26 to $32 for two in two beds.

Morgantown

On Campus: You're bound to meet students of West Virginia University at the Mountainlair Blue Tic Tavern on campus, or nearby at the Chestnut Pub on

Chestnut St., where people gather to play backgammon. Morgantown is known for its glass factories; if you're interested, you can arrange a tour of one.

Accommodations: Chestnut Ridge Camp (AYH), Rte. 1, Box 267, Bruceton Mills, 26525. Telephone: 304/594-1773. $1.50 for AYH members. Hostel is 15 miles east of Morgantown. There is no public transportation from town to the hostel. In the surrounding area are 13,000 acres of state forest with numerous hiking trails, and swimming, fishing, and skiing.

● Econo Lodge, √, 15 Commerce St., 26505. Telephone: 304/296-8774. $28 for one; $32 for two.

Parkersburg

Accommodations: Red Roof Inn, ⑤, 3714 East 7th St., 26101. Telephone: 304/485-1741. $20.95 for one; $25.95 for two in one bed; $27.95 for two in two beds; $29.95 for three or four in two beds.

● Days Inn, ⑤, I-77 & W. Va. 31 (Exit 185), 26187. Telephone: 304/375-3730. $19.88 to $21.88 for one; $24.88 to $26.88 for two.

● Econo Lodge, √, 6333 Emerson Ave., 26101. Telephone: 304/485-1851. $22.90 for one; $25.90 for two in one bed; $27.90 for two in two beds.

Princeton

Accommodation: Econo Lodge, √ ⑤, 901 Oakvale Rd., 24740. Telephone: 304/487-6161. $30 for one; $34 for two in one bed; $36 for two in two beds.

Wheeling

Accommodation: YWCA, ⑤, 1100 Chapline St., 26003. Telephone: 304/232-0511. Women only. $11.50. Weekly rate: $49.10. Advance reservations of one week necessary.

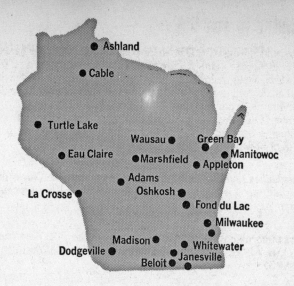

Wisconsin

Wisconsin is an Indian word meaning "gathering of the waters." The state has over 14,000 lakes offering visitors exciting water recreation, fishing, and relaxation year-round. Lakes Superior and Michigan bound the state to the northwest and east, with the Mississippi River punctuating bluffs and lowlands to the west. The northern half of the state hosts lush forests and dramatic waterfalls contrasting with the gently rolling hills and valleys to the south. Wisconsin summers are moderate, followed by brilliantly colorful falls, crisp white winters, and lush springs that bring out thousands of acres of cherry and apple blossoms.

The rich prairieland in the southern part of the state attracted the first settlers in droves in the mid-1800s and eventually larger numbers of immigrants—Germans, Poles, and Scandinavians—came to join them.

Some of the things to see in Wisconsin include Apostle Islands National Lakeshore, where Longfellow's Hiawatha lived by the "Shining Big Sea Water" of Lake Superior; Wisconsin Dells, a stretch of the Wisconsin River that has many man-made attractions, including a water show and an amusement park.

Since much of Wisconsin's economy depends on pulp and paper products, it would be interesting to pay a visit to the U.S. Forest Products Laboratory in Madison. Operated by the U.S. Forest Service and the University of Wisconsin, the laboratory is always experimenting with ways to use wood and wood products and to conserve the state's resources. Madison is also the home of the University of Wisconsin system, which has campuses in several other cities.

Two other products closely associated with Wisconsin are cheese and beer, so if you have enough time, consider a tour of a cheese plant or a brewery.

Some Special Events: Maifest in Jacksonport (May); International Picnic in

Green Bay, and Sawdust City Days in Eau Claire (June); King Richards Renaissance Faire in Kenosha (July); State Fair in Milwaukee's suburb of West Allis (August); U.S. Watermelon Seed-Spitting Championship in Pardeeville (September); Fall Festival in Sister Bay, and Harvest Festival and Grape Stomping Contest in Prairie du Sac (October).

Hitching: Officially, there's no hitchhiking on the roadway. To quote the State Protective Service: "It has been done on the curb or grassy part of the highway right-of-way."

"I have hitchhiked 12,000 miles in many states and countries and have found Wisconsin the best state. I would recommend it, but hitching on the Interstates will get you a ticket. Stay on the ramps."

Tourist Information: Wisconsin Division of Tourism, 123 West Washington Ave., P.O. Box 7970, Madison, WI 53707. Telephone: 608/266-1018; toll free 800/ESCAPES.

Adams

Accommodation: Oakcrest Motel, 324 North Main St., Box 146, 53910. Telephone: 608/339-3369. $18 for one; $21 for two in one bed; $30 for two in two beds. Advance reservations of one week necessary during summer.

Appleton

Accommodations: Quality Assured Inn, √, 2000 Holly Rd., P.O. Box 206, 54912. Telephone: 414/734-9872. $22 to $31 single; $27 to $34.50 double; $32 to $36 triple; $37 to $41 quad. Extra charge for linen. Good recreational facilities; outdoor pool.
● Exel Inn, 210 North Kools St., 54914. Telephone: 414/733-5551. $24.95 for one; $29.95 for two in one bed; $31.95 for two in two beds.

Ashland

Accommodation: Friendship Ashland Inn, 2300 West Lake Shore Dr., 54806. Telephone: 715/682-5503. $22 to $34 for one; $26 to $36 for two in one bed; $30 to $42 for two in two beds.

Beloit

On Campus: You'll meet students and find out about rides and apartments in the Campus Center of Beloit College. If you're hungry while you're in the neighborhood of the campus, try DK's snackbar in the Campus Center, Domenico's for pizza, on the main downtown street (534 East Grand Ave.); Lucille's for good diner food; and Quinn's 615, 615 Broad, for sandwiches and full dinners. At night you'll find good company by going to Goody's Bar.

Cable

Accommodation: Ches Perry Youth Hostel (AYH), Box 164, 54821. Telephone: 715/798-3367. Open ski season, from Thanksgiving to the end of March. $4.50 for AYH members. Advance reservations necessary April to November. Write to AYH, 3712 North Clark St., Chicago, IL 60613.

Dodgeville

Accommodations: Spring Valley Trails (AYH-SA), 🦽 ★, RR 2, Box 170, 53533. Telephone: 608/935-5725. Open year-round. $5. Recreational facilities available.
● Folklore Village Farm (AYH), Rte. 3, 53533. Telephone: 608/924-3725. $3.50 summer, $4.50 winter for AYH members. Closed December 25. Advance reservations necessary.

Eau Claire

On Campus: If you need anything while you're in Eau Claire, put a notice up in one of the local bars or at the university union, Davies Center. To meet students, go to any of the places on Water St. like the Old Home Tavern, the Joynt, Shenannigan's. At Old County Buffet, you can have an all-you-can-eat feast for $5. To find a place to stay, stop at the Lobby Shoppe information desk, one of the dorms, the housing office, or a bar near campus—"some of the local customers usually have a line on places where people can be accommodated temporarily."

For information on campus accommodations, contact the Housing Office (tel. 715/836-3674).

For a tour of the campus, go to the Admissions Office at 11 a.m. or 2 p.m. weekdays, 11 a.m. on Saturday. Chippewa Valley Museum is outstanding for a regional museum. Water St. is an interesting old business section near campus with lots of bars, and Putnam Park is a good place for a hike.

Accommodation: Exel Inn, 2305 Craig Rd., 54701. Telephone: 715/834-3193. $24.50 for one; $29.50 for two in one bed; $31.50 for two in two beds.

Fond du Lac

Accommodations: Motel 6, 738 West Johnson St., 54935. Telephone: 414/923-1990. $17.95 for one; $21.95 for two; $2 for each additional person.
● Thrifty Scot Motel, 107 North Pioneer Rd., 54935. Telephone: 414/923-6790. $22.90 to $27.90 for one; $27.90 to $32.90 for two.

Green Bay

"Green Bay is a provincial town, big on bowling and football."

Help: Green Bay Area New Community Clinic, 414/437-9773.
● Crisis Line, 414/432-8832.
Accommodations: YMCA, 🦽, 235 North Jefferson St., 54301. Tele-

phone: 414/435-5361. Men only. $11 single. Weekly rate: $41 first week. Six blocks from bus station.
- Motel 6, 1614 Shawano Ave., 54303. Telephone: 414/499-1407. See Fond du Lac listing for rates.
- Exel Inn, 2870 Ramada Way, 54304. Telephone: 414/499-3599. $26.95 for one; $31.95 for two in one bed; $33.95 for two in two beds.
- Imperial 400 Motor Inn, $\sqrt{}$ (10%), 119 North Monroe, 54301. Telephone: 414/437-0525. $22 to $28 for one; $26 to $32 for two in one bed; $30 to $36 for two in two beds.

Janesville

Accommodation: Motel 6, 2422 Fulton St., 53545. Telephone: 608/756-4541. See Fond du Lac listing for rates.

La Crosse

Help: First Call for Help, 608/782-8010.

On Campus: Here is the home of the University of Wisconsin at La Crosse. The town is located on the banks of the Mississippi River and is surrounded by rolling bluffs. Travelers can call the Student Information Desk on campus, 608/785-8877 or the La Crosse Area Convention and Visitors Bureau, 608/782-2366.

Accommodations: Exel Inn, 2150 Rose St., 54603. Telephone: 608/781-0400. See Appleton listing for rates.
- Bluff View Inn, 3715 Mormon Coulee Rd., 54601. Telephone: 608/788-0600. $24 for one; $32 for two in one bed; $36 for two in two beds.
- Night Saver Inn, 1906 Rose St., 54601. Telephone: 608/781-0200. $25.50 for one; $31.75 for two in one bed; $35 for two in two beds.

Madison

"A big small town with lovely scenery and lakes; lots of activities both in and out of doors for all ages."

Help: Dane County Mental Health/Crisis Intervention, 608/251-2341 or 251-2345.
- Madison Community Health Center, 1133 Williamson St., 53703. Telephone: 608/255-0704. Provides low-cost health care.
- Women's Transit Authority, 608/263-1700. Evening transport service.

On Campus: A friend at the University of Wisconsin in Madison gave us five telephone numbers for travelers to use if they need advice or help: Wisconsin Union Main Desk, 608/262-1331; Campus Assistance Center, 608/263-2400; Counseling Center, 608/262-1744; Visitors Information Booth, 608/262-3318; and the Union Travel Center, second floor, Memorial Building, 608/262-6200. To meet students, have an inexpensive meal, check the ride boards, stop at the Memorial Union to taste Babock's ice cream, 800 Langdon St., or Union South, corner of Randall Ave. and Johnson St. According to one Madisonian, his city is "a great place to visit or go to school. It welcomes young people and student travelers."

Three good places in Madison for an inexpensive, filling meal are Shanghai

Minnie's, 608 University Ave.; Husnu's, 547 State; Amy's Café, 414 West Gilman, for veggie sandwiches; and Lakefront Cafeteria, 800 Langdon St., for good cafeteria fare.

What to do in Madison? Visit the State Capitol, visit the university, bike or hike through the arboretum, walk down State St. and see the State St. Mall. In spring, summer, and fall, visit the Saturday Farmer's Market on Capitol Square.

For up-to-date information on many entertainment events, pick up an *Isthmus* newspaper at any State St. store. It comes out every Thursday.

Accommodations: YWCA, ⓰, 101 East Mifflin St., 53703. Telephone: 608/257-7722. Women, couples, or small families (no men alone). $15 to $17.50 single; $23 double; $27 family suite.

● University YMCA (AYH-SA), 306 North Brooks St., 53715. Telephone: 608/257-2534. AYH and weekly space available May 15 to August 15 only. Men and women; no small children. Near bus station and recreational facilities. $6 for AYH members. Located on the University of Wisconsin, Madison campus.

● Friendship Aloha Inn, 3177 East Washington Ave., 53704. Telephone: 608/249-7667. $22 to $25 for one; $26 to $29 for two in one bed; $29 to $32 for two in two beds.

● Red Roof Inn, ⓰, 4830 Hayes Rd., 53704. Telephone: 608/241-1787. $22.95 for one; $27.95 for two in one bed; $29.95 for two in two beds; $31.95 for three or four in two beds.

● Exel Inn, 4202 East Towne Blvd., 53704. Telephone: 608/241-3861. $23.95 for one; $28.95 for two in one bed; $30.95 for two in two beds.

● Motel 6, 6402 East Broadway, 53704. Telephone: 608/221-2291. See Fond du Lac listing for rates.

● Regal 8 Inn, 1754 Thierer Rd., 53704. Telephone: 608/241-8101. $22.88 for one; $27.88 for two in one bed; $32.88 for two in two beds. Indoor pool.

Manitowoc

Accommodation: Thrifty Scot Motel, 4004 Calumet Ave., 54220. Telephone: 414/684-7841. $23.90 to $28.90 for one; $28.90 to $33.90 for two.

Marshfield

Accommodation: Friendship Inn Downtown, 750 South Central Ave., 54449. Telephone: 715/387-1111. $18 to $22 for one; $21 to $25 for two in one bed; $23 to $28 for two in two beds.

Milwaukee

Tourist Information: Greater Milwaukee Convention and Visitors Bureau, Inc., 756 North Milwaukee St., 53202. Telephone: 414/273-3950.

Help: Advocates/Travelers Aid, 3517 West Burleigh St., 53210. Telephone: 414/873-1521.

On Campus: The University of Wisconsin has a campus in Milwaukee. The UWM Student Union on Kenwood Blvd. has a bulletin board where apartments, rides, etc., are listed. For a good and inexpensive meal in the area, you could try Kalt's on Oakland Ave. (restaurant and bar); or William Ho's, on North Oakland Ave. (for Chinese food). Some good places to meet students are the Union Snack Bar, Gasthaus, and Brubaker's.

Accommodations: Red Barn Youth Hostel (AYH), 6750 West Loomis Rd., Greendale, 53129. Telephone: 414/529-3299. Open May 1 to October 31. $5 (plus 50¢ day fee) for AYH members. Advance reservations suggested in summer; necessary October 1 to 31.

● Motel 6, 5037 South Howell Ave., 53207. Telephone: 414/481-7800. See Fond du Lac listing for rates.

● Exel Inn, 5485 North Port Washington Rd., 53217. Telephone: 414/961-7272. $29.95 for one; $34.95 for two in one bed; $36.95 for two in two beds.

● Exel Inn, 1201 West College Ave., 53221. Telephone: 414/764-1776. $24.95 for one; $29.95 for two in one bed; $31.95 for two in two beds.

● Exel Inn, 115 North Mayfair Rd., Wauwatosa, 53226. Telephone: 414/257-0140. $29.95 for one; $34.95 for two in one bed; $36.95 for two in two beds.

● Red Roof Inn, 🛆, 6360 South 13th St., Oak Creek, 53154. Telephone: 414/764-3500. $22.95 for one; $27.95 for two in one bed; $29.95 for two in two beds; $31.95 for three or four in two beds.

Oshkosh

Accommodations: Motel 6, 1015 South Washburn St., 54901. Telephone: 404/235-6720. See Fond du Lac listing for rates.

● Gruenhagen Conference Center, University of Wisconsin at Oshkosh, 54901. Telephone: 414/424-1121. Over one mile from bus station. $6.75 single; $11.50 single for adults. Open only to guests or individuals currently enrolled in an educational institution.

Turtle Lake

Accommodation: Timberlake Lodge (AYH), RR 2, 54889. Telephone: 715/986-2484. $6 summer, $7 winter for AYH members. Hostel is on a 900-acre recreational and educational center with hiking, canoeing, and skiing. "An excellent place for peace and quiet." Advance reservations necessary December 1 to March 15.

Wausau

Accommodation: Exel Inn, 116 South 17th Ave., 54401. Telephone: 715/842-0641. $24.95 for one; $29.95 for two in one bed; $31.95 for two in two beds.

Whitewater

Accommodation: The Dock (AYH-SA), Rte. 3, 53190. Telephone: 608/883-2856. Open June 1 to August 31. $6.50 for AYH members. Advance reservations suggested.

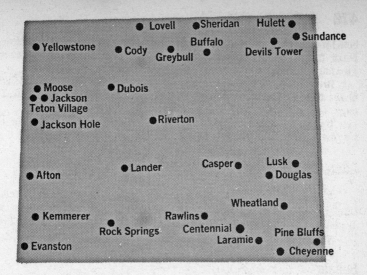

Wyoming

Wyoming is blessed with a great number of tourist attractions and just about all of them are natural. Yellowstone National Park, our oldest national park with over two million acres, was set aside in 1872 and is preserved to this day in all its beauty. The geyser Old Faithful still spouts. And now 300 miles of paved roads connect the park's various features and its campsites. And then there's Grand Teton National Park—another beautiful place to fish, hike, or camp. Wyoming can also claim two national monuments—Devil's Tower (the oldest, designated by Teddy Roosevelt) and Fossil Butte. There are seven national forests in Wyoming, including Shoshone—the nation's first. Two regions are designated national recreation areas—Big Horn Canyon and Flaming Gorge. And there are historic spots to visit all along the Oregon Trail, the first road west, which crosses Wyoming from Fort Laramie to Fort Bridger. It seems to be no exaggeration for Wyoming to claim the title of the "First State in Outdoor America." Rodeo is king in Wyoming during the summer and nearly every community has one of its own.

The Wyoming Travel Commission (address below) offers a variety of travel publications including *Self-Guided Tours,* a series of four brochures giving drive-yourself itineraries; *Vacation Guide, The Oregon Trail, Wyoming Travel Tips,* and *Family Water Sports.* All are free.

Some Special Events: Wyoming State Winter Fair in Lander (January); Winter Festival in Pinedale (February); Old Time Fiddle Contest in Shoshone (May); Woodchoppers Jamboree in Encampment, and Indian Tribal Pow Wows and Sun Dances in Fort Washakie (June); Jubilee Days Rodeo in Laramie, and Frontier Days in Cheyenne, the world's largest outdoor rodeo that lasts for nine days (July); Gift of the Waters Pageant (commemorating the deeding of the hot springs from the Shoshone Indians to the people of Wyoming) in Thermopolis (August).

Hitching: Wyoming has traditionally been hard on hitchhikers, and there's no reason to suspect that will change in the near future. It's one of the states (see pages 13 and 14) that used the world "highway" in its law.

Tourist Information: Wyoming Travel Commission, I-25 at College Dr., Cheyenne, WY 82002. Telephone: 307/777-7777; or toll free 800/443-2784.

Afton

Accommodation: Friendship Lazy B Inn, Hwy. 89 to Jackson St. & Yellowstone National Park, 83110. Telephone: 307/886-3187. Limited airport service available. $24 to $30 for one; $26 to $32 for two in one bed; $30 to $38 for two in two beds.

Buffalo

Accommodations: Budget Host—Wyoming Motel, Clearmont Rte. (Box 11), 82834. Telephone: 307/684-5505. $21 to $35 for one; $24 to $37 for two in one bed; $26 to $52 for two in two beds. Heated pool. Airport pick-up and return.

● Friendship Z-Bar Motel, 626 Fort St., 82834. Telephone: 307/684-5535. $27 for one; $31 for two in one bed; $33 for two in two beds; $34 for rooms with kitchen.

Casper

Accommodations: Friendship Inn Westridge, 955 Cy Ave., 82601. Telephone: 307/234-8911. $26 to $30 for one; $26 to $32 for two in one bed; $32 to $38 for two in two beds.

● Motel 6, 1150 Wilkins Circle, 82601. Telephone: 307/265-3062. $17.95 for one; $21.95 for two; $2 for each additional person.

● Thrifty Scot Motel, 821 North Poplar St., 82061. Telephone: 307/266-2400. $21.90 for one; $26.90 for two.

Centennial

Accommodation: Budget Host—The Old Corral Motor Hotel, &, Hwy. 130 (Box 217), 82055. Telephone: 307/745-5918. $24 for one; $30 for two. At foot of Snowy Range.

Cheyenne

Accommodations: Motel 6, 1735 Westland Rd., 82001. Telephone: 307/635-1676. See Casper listing for rates.

● Budget Host—Home Ranch Motel, 2414 East Lincolnway, 82001. Telephone: 307/634-3575. $28 to $34 for one or two in one bed; $32 to $38 for two in two beds.

- Friendship Inn Fleetwood, 3800 East Lincolnway, 82001. Telephone: 307/638-8908. $22 to $31 for one; $24 to $34 for two in one bed; $28 to $40 for two in two beds.

Cody

Accommodations: 7K's Motel and RV Park, 232 West Yellowstone Ave., 82414. Telephone: 307/587-2532 or 587-5890. Open May through October. $24 single; $28 double; $42 quad. Advance reservations of ten days necessary in July and August.

- Friendship Skyline Motel and Cafe, 1919 17th St., 82414. Telephone: 307/587-4201. Limited airport service available. $30 to $34 for one or two in one bed; $44 for two in two beds.

Devils Tower

Camping: Devils Tower National Monument, 82714. Telephone: 307/467-5370. Campground at Belle Fourche River open May through September. $6 per campsite.

Douglas

Accommodation: Friendship Vagabond Motel, 5th & Richards, Box 52, 82633. Telephone: 307/358-4311. Limited airport transportation available. $25 for one; $27 for two in one bed; $31 for two in two beds.

Dubois

Accommodations: Friendship Stagecoach Motor Inn, P.O. Box 216, 82513. Telephone: 307/455-2303. $24 to $28 for one; $28 to $34 for two in one bed; $28 to $36 for two in two beds.

- Branding Iron Motel, V, 401 West Ramshorn, 82513. Telephone: 307/455-2893 or 455-2446. $18 to $20 single; $20 to $26 double; $26 to $30 triple. Lower rates apply in winter.
- Budget Host—Sage Motel, 505 West Ramshorn, P.O. Box 595, 82513. Telephone: 307/455-2344 or 455-2626. $24 to $28 for one or two in one bed; $26 to $30 for two in two beds.

Evanston

Accommodation: Friendship Classic Lodge, 202 Hwy. 30 E., 82930. Telephone: 307/789-6830. $28 to $30 for one; $30 to $32 for two in one bed; $35 to $42 for two in two beds.

Greybull

Accommodation: Antler Motel, 1116 North 6th, 82426. Telephone: 307/765-4404. $20 to $25 for one or two in one bed; $28 to $35 for two in two beds.

Hulett

Accommodation: Hulett Motel and Café, √ 🚹 ★, 202 Main St., 82720. Telephone: 307/467-9909. $15 to $24 for one; $32 for up to four.

Jackson

Accommodations: Motel 6, 1370 West Broadway, 83001. Telephone: 307/733-9666. See Casper listing for rates.
● Friendship Western, Glenwood & Simpson Sts. Downtown, 88045. Telephone: 307/733-3291. $21 to $38 for one or two in one bed; $48 to $54 for two in two beds.

Jackson Hole

Accommodation: The Hostel (AYH-SA), Box 546, Teton Village, 83025. Telephone: 307/733-3415. $13.50 for one; $25 for two; $32 for three; $36 for four. All rooms have private baths. Advance reservations necessary in winter.

Kemmerer

Accommodation: Friendship Lazy U Motel, U.S. 189, 521 Coral, 83110. Telephone: 307/877-4428. $22 to $25 for one; $25 to $30 for two in one bed; $30 to $35 for two in two beds.

Lander

Accommodations: Silver Spur Motel, Ⓢ√, 340 North 10th, 82520. Telephone: 307/332-5189. $24 for one; $28 for two in one bed; $34 for two in two beds. Advance reservations suggested during summer months.
● Friendship Downtown, 569 Main, 82520. Telephone: 307/332-3164. $22 to $26 for one; $24 to $30 for two in one bed; $26 to $46 for two in two beds.

Laramie

"This is a small town with a friendly atmosphere; close to mountain ranges and good skiing."

On Campus: The University of Wyoming is in Laramie. In the Student

Union, you'll find a ride board and in the campus paper, *The Branding Iron,* you'll find out what's happening on campus.

Accommodations: Motel 6, 621 Plaza Lane, 82070. Telephone: 307/742-0542. See Casper listing for rates.

● Budget Host—Camelot Motel, 523 Adams, 82070. Telephone: 307/721-8860. $25 for one; $28 to $34 for two in one bed; $32 to $38 for two in two beds.

Lovell

Accommodation: Friendship Horseshoe Bend, 375 East Main, 82431. Telephone: 307/548-2221. Limited airport service available. $21 to $23 for one; $24 to $26 for two in one bed; $27 to $29 for two in two beds.

Lusk

Accommodation: Budget Host—Trail Motel, 8th & Linn, Box 1087, 82225. Telephone: 307/334-2530. $30 to $36 for one or two in one bed; $32 to $42 for two in two beds. Heated indoor pool. Courtesy car to and from airport.

Moose

Camping: Grand Teton National Park, P.O. Drawer 170, 83012. Telephone: 307/733-2880. Six campgrounds. Open May to September. $7 per campsite per night.

● John D. Rockefeller, Jr., Memorial Parkway, c/o Grand Teton National Park, P.O. Drawer 170, 83012. Telephone: 307/733-2880. Trailer village at Flagg Ranch. $7 and up per campsite. Camping June 1 to early September, depending on weather.

Pine Bluffs

Accommodation: Friendship Travelyn Motel, Pine Bluffs Exit Ramp I-80 at 7th St., 82082. Telephone: 307/245-3226. $20 to $26 for one; $24 to $32 for two in one bed; $26 to $36 for two in two beds.

Rawlins

Accommodations: Budget Host—Sunset Motel, 1302 West Spruce, 82301. Telephone: 307/324-3448. $22 to $26 for one; $24 to $28 for two in one bed; $32 to $35 for two in two beds.

● Friendship Jade Inn, 5th & Spruce, 82301. Telephone: 307/324-2791. $22 to $28 for one; $28 to $30 for two in one bed; $34 to $36 for two in two beds. Lower rates apply in winter.

● TraveLodge, √ &, 1507 West Spruce St., 82301. Telephone: 307/324-3451. Airport transportation available. $30 for one; $36 for two in one bed; $40 for two in two beds.

Riverton

Accommodation: Friendship Inn El Rancho, 221 South Federal, 82501. Telephone: 307/856-2268. $20 to $24 for one or two in one bed; $25 to $35 for two in two beds.

Rock Springs

Accommodations: Motel 6, 2615 Commercial Way, 82901. See Casper listing for rates.
● Budget Host—Springs Motel, 1525 9th St. (Box 1596), 82901. Telephone: 307/362-6683. $26 for one; $30 for two in one bed; $32 to $36 for two in two beds.
● Friendship Nomad Inn, Jct. I-80 & U.S. 191. Telephone: 307/362-5646. $24.95 to $34.95 for one; $28.95 to $38.95 for two in one bed; $31.95 to $41.95 for two in two beds.

Sheridan

Accommodation: Budget Host—Rancher Motel, ♿, 1552 Coffeen Ave., 82801. Telephone: 307/672-2428. November 1 to May 1: $20.80 for one; $22.88 for two in one bed; $25 for two in two beds. May 1 to November 1: $24.95 for one; $41.60 for two.

Sundance

Accommodation: Budget Host—Arrowhead Motel, Box 191, 82729. Telephone: 307/283-3307. $30 for one; $34 for two.

Wheatland

Accommodation: Friendship Inn Vimbos, Box 188, Hwy. 87 & I-26, 82201. Telephone: 307/322-3842. Limited airport service available. $28 to $30 for one; $32 to $34 for two in one bed; $34 to $36 for two in two beds.

Yellowstone

Accommodations: Yellowstone Park Division, TW Services, Inc., 82190. Telephone: 307/344-7311. There are cabins operated by the Yellowstone Park Division throughout the park that are reasonably priced.
● At Lake Yellowstone, open mid-June to late September. Family cabins: $41 to $55 with bath or $28 without bath for one or two; $5 for each additional person. Children under 11 are free.
● At Old Faithful Inn, open May 6 to October 14. See above listing for rates.
● At Old Faithful Snow Lodge and Cabins, open May to November and mid-December to mid-March. See Lake Yellowstone listing for rates. Hotel rooms without baths or cabins available.
● At Mammoth Hot Springs Hotel and Cabins, open late May to mid-

September. $51 deluxe cabin; $36 to $42 budget cabin. See Lake Yellowstone for family rates.

Note: Reservations at all of the above are highly recommended. Write to Yellowstone Park Division for a detailed brochure and instructions on how to go about reserving space or telephone the number above.

Camping: Yellowstone National Park, ♿, 82190. Telephone: 307/344-7381. Twelve campgrounds open May or June through September or October, except Mammoth Campgrounds, which is open year-round. Bridge Bay, three miles south of Lake Village, and Grant Village, two miles south of West Thumb Junction, are the largest with 438 sites each. $5 or $6 per campsite per night.